SEA VOYAGES AND BEYOND

EMORY STUDIES IN EARLY CHRISTIANITY

Editors
Vernon K. Robbins
David B. Gowler

Associate Editor
Robert H. von Thaden Jr.

Editorial Board
Richard S. Ascough
L. Gregory Bloomquist
Peder Borgen
J. J. Bernard Combrink
David A. deSilva
Anders Eriksson
Thomas H. Olbricht
Russell B. Sisson
Duane F. Watson

Number 14

SEA VOYAGES AND BEYOND

Emerging Strategies in Socio-Rhetorical Interpretation

Vernon K. Robbins

Atlanta

Copyright © 2018 by SBL Press
Originally published by Deo Publishing, 2010

Publication of this volume was made possible by the generous support of the Pierce Program in Religion of Oxford College of Emory University.

All rights reserved. No part of this work may be reproduced or transmitted in any form or by any means, electronic or mechanical, including photocopying and recording, or by means of any information storage or retrieval system, except as may be expressly permitted by the 1976 Copyright Act or in writing from the publisher. Requests for permission should be addressed in writing to the Rights and Permissions Office, SBL Press, 825 Houston Mill Road, Atlanta, GA 30329 USA.

The Odyssea Greek font used in the publication of this work is available from Linguist's Software, Inc., www.linguisticsoftware.com, P.O. Box 580, Edmonds, WA 98020-0580 USA, tel. (425) 775-1130.

Library of Congress Control Number: 2018952662

Cover design is an adaptation by Bernard Madden of Rick A. Robbins, Mixed Media (19" x 24" pen and ink on paper, 1981). Online: http://home.comcast.net/~rick1216/Archive/1981penink.htm. Cover design used by permission of Deo Publishing.

Printed on acid-free paper.

From David:

*In memory of
Bethany Leah Gowler
(1984–2002)*

From Vernon:

*With love to
Deanna
on our fiftieth anniversary*

Contents

Acknowledgments xi

Introduction by David B. Gowler
The End of the Beginning:
The Continuing Maturation of Socio-Rhetorical Analysis 1
Prolegomenon: Dynamics of Social Context 4
Essays focusing on Social and Cultural Interpretation 6
Emerging Strategies of Socio-Rhetorical Interpretation 17

Chapter 1
By Land and By Sea:
The We-Passages and Ancient Sea Voyages 47
Narrative Style in Ancient Sea Voyages 49
Third Person Narration in Greek Literature 56
Parallels to Voyages in Acts 59
The We-Passages as Sea Voyage Literature 63
The Function of the We-Passages in Luke-Acts 76
Conclusion 79

Chapter 2
Sailing with Paul on Ideological Waters:
The We-Voyages in Acts 82
My View during the 1970s of the Inner Texture of the We-Passages in Acts 84
Moving beyond Literary-Historical Interpretation to a Socio-Rhetorical Paradigm 87
Limiting the Rhetography of the We-Passage Sea Voyages to Literary-Historical
    "Documentation," "Eyewitness," or "Narrative Witness" 90
    Limiting the Rhetography to Causes that can be "Documented" 90
    Limiting the Rhetography to Lukan "Authorial" Cause 94
    Limiting the Rhetography to Untidy "Editorial" Causes 95
    Limiting the Rhetography to Writing in a Pauline School 96
    Limiting the Rhetography to Narrative Eyewitness that Replaces Barnabas 98
Rebuilding the Ship in the Midst of the Voyage: the Greek Text of the We-
    Passages 100
Seeing the Rhetography of the We-Voyages through a Socio-Rhetorical Under-
    standing of Acts as Prose Epic 104
    Dennis R. MacDonald's Voyage with Homer's Odyssey 105

Marianne Palmer Bonz's Journey with Virgil's Aeneid 106
Loveday Alexander's Journey with Cognitive Geography: Luke's Paul invades
    Greek Cultural Territory by Sea 109
Freeing the Rhetography of the We-Voyages for 21st Century Exploration
    of the Christian Journey of Acts throughout the Mediterranean World 111

Chapter 3
The Social Location of the Implied Author of Luke-Acts 114
Introduction: Social Location 114
    Defining Social Location 115
    Social Base of Knowledge 115
A Model of the Social Location of Narrative Discourse 118
    Social Science Model of Social Location 118
    Narrative Discourse Model 118
        Characters and Audiences 119
        Narrator 120
        Inscribed Author and Inscribed Reader 120
        Implied Author and Implied Reader 120
The Model Applied to Luke-Acts 121
    Previous Events 121
    Natural Environment and Resources 124
    Population Structure 125
    Technology 128
    Socialization and Personality 131
    Culture 133
    Foreign Affairs 137
    Belief Systems and Ideologies 138
    Political-Military-Legal System 140
Conclusion 142

Chapter 4
Rhetoric and Culture:
Mark 4–11 as a Test Case 145
Overcoming Dualistic Social and Cultural Approaches 149
Social and Cultural Analysis of Texts 150
    A. Religious Types of Social Rhetoric 151
    B. Types of Culture Rhetoric 153
Thaumaturgic Social Rhetoric in Markan Miracles 157
    A. Specific Social Topics in Markan Miracles 159
    B. Thaumaturgic Argumentation in Mark 160
    C. Subculture Thaumaturgic Rhetoric in Mark 162
    D. Conclusion 166
Gnostic-Manipulationist Social Rhetoric in Markan Parables 167
    A. Specific Social Topics in Markan Parables 167
    B. Gnostic-Manipulationist Argumentation in Mark 4 168
    C. Subculture Gnostic-Manipulationist Rhetoric in Mark 4 169
Miracle and Parable Rhetoric as Subcultural Rhetorics in Mark 172

Contraculture Rhetoric 174
Counterculture Rhetoric 176
Conclusion 181

Chapter 5
Social-Scientific Criticism and Literary Studies:
Prospects for Cooperation in Biblical Interpretation 182
Disciplinary, Interdisciplinary and Eclectic Methods of Interpretation 182
A Model for Interdisciplinary Investigation 186
The Beginning Point for the Literary and Social-Scientific Critic 189
The Things Literary and Social-Scientific Critics Personify 193
Unexamined Presuppositions of Literary and Social-Scientific Critics 196
Conclusion 199

Chapter 6
Picking up the Fragments:
From Crossan's Analysis to Rhetorical Analysis 201
How we begin influences where we go 203
What we look for influences what we see 216
How we relate an aphorism to other aphorisms influences how we understand
    the tradition 223
Conclusion 231

Chapter 7
Writing as a Rhetorical Act in Plutarch and the Gospels 233
Recitation Composition in Traditional Rhetorical Culture 237
Argumentation in Progymnastic Composition 245
Conclusion 256

Chapter 8
The Reversed Contextualization of Psalm 22 in the Markan Crucifixion:
A Socio-Rhetorical Analysis 258
Introduction 258
Repetitive and Progressive Form in the Crucifixion of Jesus in Mark 262
    1. Selection of Prisoner to be Humiliated and Crucified: Mark 15:1-15 263
    2. Mockery of Jesus as Royalty: Mark 15:16-24 264
    3. Ridicule of Jesus while He Hangs on the Cross: Mark 15:25-32 265
    4. Jesus' Crying Out and Death: Mark 15:33-39 267
    5. Permission for and Burial of Jesus' Corpse: Mark 15:40-46 268
    Conclusion 269
The Markan Crucifixion and a Persian Ritual at the Sacian Feast 270
Psalm 22 (LXX: 21) and the Markan Crucifixion 273
Conclusion 279

Chapter 9
Socio-Rhetorical Criticism:
Mary, Elizabeth, and the Magnificat as a Test Case 282
The Emergence of Socio-Rhetorical Criticism 282
Inner Texture: Every Reading has a Subtext...291
Intertexture: Every Comparison has Boundaries..299
Social and Cultural Texture: Every Meaning has a Context 305
Ideological Texture: Every Theology has a Politics 315
Conclusion..320

Chapter 10
The Present and Future of Rhetorical Analysis 323
Proemium: We are participants in an exciting time that calls for responsible action 323
Statement of the Case: Rhetorical interpreters should reinvent rhetorical method
   and theory into an interpretive analytics..324
Reconstructing the Texture of Discourse..330
Revaluing the Modes of Biblical Discourse...332
    a. Assertions and Rationales 333
    b. Social and Cultural Analysis of Assertions and Rationales 335
    c. Chreia Analysis of Assertions and Rationales 336
    d. Rhetorical Elaboration...338
    e. Jewish and Greco-Roman Modes of Argumentation 340
    f. Reinventing the Decades of First-Century Christianity.........................341
Reconfiguring the Discourse of Commentary...343

Chapter 11
From Enthymeme to Theology in Luke 11:1-13..349
Chreia and Enthymeme in Luke 11:1-4..351
Ideological Subversion of a Social Enthymeme in Luke 11:5-8 359
A Cultural Enthymeme as a Rationale for the Lord's Prayer in Luke 11:9-10.......364
A Social-Cultural Enthymeme as a Theological Conclusion in Luke 11:13............366
Conclusion..370

Chapter 12
The Socio-Rhetorical Role of Old Testament Scripture in Luke 4-19...........372
Luke 4:1-13: The Testing of Jesus 374
Luke 4:14-7:35: The Poor, the Blind, the Leprous, the Dead, and the Deaf 377
Luke 7:36-14:24: Eating with Pharisees 379
Luke 15: Seeking and Saving the Lost...381
Conclusion..384

The Major Writings of Vernon K. Robbins 385

Index of Names...393
Index of Biblical and Other References 398

Acknowledgments

It is my pleasure to thank David Gowler for writing the opening essay, overseeing the selection and organization of the essays, and securing funding for the publication of this volume. His ongoing encouragement, expertise, and commitment to teaching, learning, friendship, and integrity exhibit those prized characteristics that cause him to be treasured by a wide circle of friends among whom I am fortunate to be included. I am also deeply grateful to Robert von Thaden, who accepted the responsibility for bringing a semblance of uniformity to the footnotes and references throughout the essays in this volume. Beyond his labor of love with these particular essays, his skillful advancement of socio-rhetorical interpretation with conceptual integration theory is a contribution that is helping to bring this interpretive analytics dramatically into a twenty-first century mode of interpretation. In addition, my deepest appreciation to Kristen Peterson, who graciously found time during her final semester in Emory College to create the indices of authors and references.

The essays in this volume emerge from a wide range of academic settings for which I am deeply grateful. During the 1970s, members of the Chicago Society for Biblical Research and the SBL Seminar on Luke-Acts enthusiastically supported my initial work on the we-passages in Acts. During the 80s and early 90s, members of the Institute for Antiquity and Christianity at Claremont and the Westar Institute, and friends and colleagues in Norway, Sweden, Denmark, the Netherlands, England, Scotland, Germany, and Belgium helped me to develop socio-rhetorical strategies of analysis and interpretation. Also, special colleagues and friends in the Context Group helped me to deepen and broaden my understanding of social and cultural phenomena and to develop strategies for including them in a full-bodied mode of interpretation. During the 1990s, valued friends and colleagues in South Africa nurtured my life and career in extraordinary ways, during a time when periodic meetings of international rhetoric conferences nurtured by Thomas A. Olbricht also created contexts for the advancement of my particular approach to rhetorical interpretation. As the millennium turned, colleagues and friends opened doors for me in the Czech Republic, Iceland, and Finland. I hold in my heart a deep sense of gratitude to a long list of people in these contexts and settings who provided nurture and care for my body, soul, mind, and spirit in multiple ways.

Through some uncanny incident of providence, this volume is appearing during the fiftieth year of my extraordinarily blessed marriage to my dear wife Deanna. I dedicate this book to her with affectionate gratitude for her sweet friendship and love during this lifetime voyage together.

Vernon K. Robbins
June 2, 2010

Permissions

The following essays are reproduced by kind permission of Continuum International Publishing Group, London SE1 7NX UK. All rights reserved.
"Rhetoric and Culture: Exploring Types of Cultural Rhetoric in a Text," in *Rhetoric and the New Testament: Essays from the 1992 Heidelberg Conference*, ed. S.E. Porter and T.H. Olbricht. Sheffield: JSOT Press, 1993: 443-463.
"Socio-Rhetorical Criticism: Mary, Elizabeth, and the Magnificat as a Test Case," in *The New Literary Criticism and the New Testament*, ed. E.S. Malbon and E.V. McKnight. Sheffield: Sheffield Academic Press, 1994: 164-209.
"The Present and Future of Rhetorical Analysis," in *The Rhetorical Analysis of Scripture: Essays from the 1995 London Conference*, ed. S.E. Porter and T.H. Olbricht. Journal for the Study of the New Testament Supplement Series 146. Sheffield: Sheffield Academic Press, 1997: 24-52.
"Writing as a Rhetorical Act in Plutarch and the Gospels," in *Persuasive Artistry: Studies in New Testament Rhetoric in Honor of George A. Kennedy*, ed. D.F. Watson. Sheffield: JSOT Press, 1991: 157-186.

The following essay is reprinted by permission of Taylor & Francis, Hampshire SP10 5BE UK. All rights reserved:
"Social-Scientific Criticism and Literary Studies: Prospects for Cooperation in Biblical Interpretation," in *Modelling Early Christianity: Social-Scientific Studies of the New Testament in Its Context*, edited by P.F. Esler. London: Routledge, 1995: 274-289.

The following essays are reprinted by permission of Mercer University Press, Macon, GA 31210-3960 USA. All rights reserved:
"By Land and By Sea: The We-Passages and Ancient Sea Voyages," *Perspectives on Luke-Acts*, ed. C.H. Talbert, Perspectives in Religious Studies, Special

Studies Series, No. 5. Macon, GA: Mercer University Press and Edinburgh: T. & T. Clark, 1978: 215-242.

"From Enthymeme to Theology in Luke 11:1-13," in *Literary Studies in Luke-Acts: A Collection of Essays in Honor of Joseph B. Tyson*, ed. R.P. Thompson and T.E. Phillips. Macon, GA: Mercer University Press, 1998: 191-214.

The following essay is reprinted by permission of Hendrickson Publishers, Peabody, MA 01961-3473 USA. All rights reserved:
"The Social Location of the Implied Author of Luke-Acts," in *The Social World of Luke-Acts: Models for Interpretation*, ed. J.H. Neyrey. Peabody, MA: Hendrickson, 1991: 305-332.

The following essay is reprinted by permission of Uppsala Exegtiska Sällskap, 751 20 Uppsala, Sweden. All rights reserved:
"Interpreting Miracle Culture and Parable Culture in Mark 4-11," *Svensk Exegetisk Årsbok* 59 (1994): 59-81.

The following essay is reprinted by permission of Leuven University Press, B-3000 Leuven, Belgium. All rights reserved:
"The Reversed Contextualization of Psalm 22 in the Markan Crucifixion: A Socio-Rhetorical Analysis," in *The Four Gospels 1992. Festschrift Frans Neirynck*, ed. F. van Segbroeck, C.M. Tuckett, G. van Belle, J. Verheyden, volume 2, BETL 100. Leuven: Leuven University Press, 1992: 1161-1183.

The following essay is reprinted by permission of Polebridge Press, Salem, OR 97301 USA. All rights reserved:
"Picking Up the Fragments: From Crossan's Analysis to Rhetorical Analysis," *Forum* 1.2 (1985): 31-64.

The following essay previously appeared as follows. All rights reserved:
"The Socio-Rhetorical Role of Old Testament Scripture in Luke 4-19," in *Z Noveho Zakona /From the New Testament: Sbornik k narozeninam Prof. ThDr. Zdenka Sazavy*, ed. Hana Tonzarova and Petr Melmuk. Praha: Vydala Cirkev ceskoslovenska husitska, 2001: 81-93.

The End of the Beginning: The Continuing Maturation of Socio-Rhetorical Analysis

David B. Gowler
The Dr. Lovick Pierce and Bishop George F. Pierce Professor of Religion, Oxford College of Emory University and The Center for Ethics, Emory University

> I therefore leave the readers to examine the following chapters in order to determine for themselves the merits of the theoretical underpinnings of socio-rhetorical criticism, its congruence with these ancient texts, its functional, interpretive utility, and its ability to encourage constructive dialogue. In my final recommendation, I can merely echo the words of Sancho to Don Quixote: "Y, si no, al freir de los huevos lo verá."[1]

Over a decade has passed since I edited and wrote the introductory chapter for *New Boundaries in Old Territory: Forms and Social Rhetoric in Mark*, the first collection of essays of Vernon K. Robbins that appeared in 1994 in the *Emory Studies in Early Christianity* series. *New Boundaries in Old Territory* chronicled the scholarly journey of Vernon Robbins and socio-rhetorical interpretation from 1973 to 1990, specifically focusing on the Gospel of Mark. That volume contained essays from the "pre-textures" era of socio-rhetorical analysis, that is, the time period before the paperback edition of *Jesus the Teacher* and before the publica-

---

[1] "If you don't believe it, you will see when you go to fry the eggs." *Don Quixote*, part I, chapter XXXVII (Miguel de Cervantes, *El ingenioso hildalgo Don Quijote de la Mancha* [Barcelona: Ediciones Nauta, S.A., 1970], 369). Or as Motteux paraphrased in his English translation: "The proof of the pudding is in the eating." See Miguel de Cervantes, *Don Quixote de la Mancha* (trans. Peter Motteux; New York: Random House, 1941), 419. The entire paragraph comes from my "The Development of Socio-Rhetorical Criticism," in Vernon K. Robbins, *New Boundaries in New Territory: Form and Social Rhetoric in Mark* (ed. David B. Gowler; Emory Studies in Early Christianity 3; New York: Peter Lang, 1994), 36: http://userwww.service.emory.edu/~dgowler/chapter.htm.

tion of Robbins's seminal works, *The Tapestry of Early Christian Discourse* and *Exploring the Texture of Texts*.[2]

I am pleased to reprise my role for this second installment, *Sea Voyages and Beyond: Emerging Strategies in Socio-Rhetorical Interpretation*. This volume primarily focuses on the methodological progression in socio-rhetorical analysis that led to (1) the emergence, delineation, and exploration of the five (or four) textures and (2) the initial stages of the emergence and investigation of multiple rhetorolects within early Christian discourse. The current socio-rhetorical efforts, such as the breakthroughs in the arena of conceptual blending, are likely topics for future volumes. The current volume, though, fills in critical gaps between the "pre-textures era" and the "conceptual blending era." With the exception of three chapters in this volume, all of these essays were written during the 1990's – a critical and dynamic era in New Testament studies.[3]

The quote at the beginning of this chapter is from my concluding comments in the introduction to *New Boundaries*, and it creates the context and impetus for the current volume. The proof of the pudding is indeed in the eating, and many scholars have "gone to fry the eggs": More and more scholars are utilizing the insights, methodology, and advances that socio-rhetorical analysis has already provided and the additional insights that it continues to generate.[4]

Robbins himself, of course, not only created socio-rhetorical interpretation, but he also continues to be at the forefront of the continuing advances being made with socio-rhetorical analysis. As always, his work is in a dialogical relationship with scholars of various disciplines both within and outside the guild of New Testament studies. In fact, one of the critical achievements of socio-rhetorical analysis is that it provides a profoundly dialogic, interdisciplinary approach by which we

---

[2] Vernon K. Robbins, *Jesus the Teacher: A Socio-Rhetorical Interpretation of Mark* (paperback ed. with new introduction and additional indexes; Minneapolis: Fortress, 1992; repr. Fortress ex libris, 2009); idem, *The Tapestry of Early Christian Discourse: Rhetoric, Society and Ideology* (London: Routledge, 1996); idem, *Exploring the Texture of Texts: A Guide to Socio-Rhetorical Interpretation* (Valley Forge, Penn.: Trinity Press International, 1996).

[3] For an assessment of the development of socio-rhetorical analysis during the 1970's and 1980's, please see my "The Development of Socio-Rhetorical Criticism" in *New Boundaries*. For an overview of socio-rhetorical interpretation, as well as the advances during the "post-textures" phase, see Vernon K. Robbins, "Socio-Rhetorical Interpretation," *Blackwell Companion to the New Testament* (ed. David E. Aune; Oxford: Blackwell Publishing, 2009).

[4] Marked most dramatically, I suppose, by the publication of a *Festschrift* in Robbins's honor: *Fabrics of Discourse: Essays in Honor of Vernon K. Robbins* (ed. David B. Gowler, L. Gregory Bloomquist, and Duane F. Watson; Harrisburg, Penn.: Trinity Press International, 2003). For a display of socio-rhetorical interpretation, see the website: http://www.religion.emory.edu/faculty/robbins/SRI/defns/index.

can interpret numerous texts – not just biblical texts – as well as our own and others' interpretations of those texts.⁵ Robbins's socio-rhetorical interpretation provides a programmatic model to establish and facilitate an arena where differing approaches – such as the myriad of approaches currently found in New Testament studies – can be in dialogue with each other.

In my view, Robbins's socio-rhetorical interpretation can be situated within – or at least closely aligned with – the "Dialogic Criticism" initiated by the philosopher and classicist Mikhail Bakhtin. Robbins's dialogical principles recognize other scholars' positions not as obstacles to be overcome or as enemy lines to be breached. Robbins does very strongly critique positions held by other scholars, especially ones that make some pretense of monologic superiority or ideological neutrality.⁶ The works of other scholars, however, serve as catalysts for Robbins's own insights. Robbins realizes that his position is never independent of other scholars' endeavors, and that his own works would be incomplete without a dialogic response to those other positions. As Don Bialostosky puts it concerning Bakhtin's Dialogism: "As a self-conscious practice, dialogical criticism turns its inescapable involvement with some other voices into a program of articulation itself with all the other voices of the discipline, the culture, or of the world of cultures to which it makes itself responsible."⁷

So, in Robbins's view, any scholarly voice is inescapably involved with a myriad of other voices: We should "... develop approaches that celebrate dialogue, that show interplays of closure and openness, and that encourage us to announce our agendas in public forum and to listen as people show us the implications, limitations, and biases of

---

⁵ For a brief summary of the "five textures" and socio-rhetorical interpretation's relation to rhetorical criticism, see David B. Gowler, "Heteroglossic Trends in Biblical Studies: Polyphonic Dialogues or Clanging Cymbals?" *RevExp* 97:4 (2000): 443–66; "Socio-Rhetorical Criticism," in W. Randolph Tate, *Interpreting the Bible: A Handbook of Terms and Methods* (Peabody, Mass.: Hendrickson Publishers, 2006), 342–6.

⁶ Robbins calls such oppositional rhetoric a "rhetorical half turn." Instead, he calls for a "rhetorical full turn" and asserts that we should "nurture a transmodern environment where we keep our colleagues on an equal playing field." See my discussion of Chapter 10 below ("The Present and Future of Rhetorical Analysis"), as well as Robbins's "The Rhetorical Full-Turn in Biblical Interpretation and Its Relevance for Feminist Hermeneutics," in *Her Master's Tools?* (ed. C. Vander Stichele and T. Penner; Atlanta: Society of Biblical Literature, 2005), 109-27.

⁷ Don Bialostosky, "Dialogic Criticism," in *Contemporary Literary Theory* (ed. G. Douglas Atkins and Laura Morrow; Amherst: The University of Massachusetts Press, 1989), 223. This builds upon Bakhtin's arguments that the significance of any utterance must be understood in the context of other utterances on the same theme. See Mikhail Bakhtin, *The Dialogic Imagination* (ed. Michael Holquist; Austin: University of Texas Press, 1981), 254.

these agendas."[8] Therefore, the value of socio-rhetorical interpretation not only lies in its ability to facilitate our dialogue with these narratives, but in the fact that it also makes more possible productive dialogues among interpreters of these texts. In addition, as Robbins believes, we should continue to expand the boundaries of interpretation, to extend the dialogues, and to broaden the avenues of discussion. This diversity is indeed in the spirit of Robbins's work, because socio-rhetorical interpretation attempts to create a "dialogical environment for analytical strategies from widely different arenas of investigation."[9] In this essay – and in that dialogical spirit – I offer my own dialogic response to the significant contributions to scholarship that he has made in these essays.

Prolegomenon: Dynamics of Social Context

The volume begins with Robbins's 1978 essay, "By Land and By Sea: The We-Passages in Acts and Ancient Sea Voyages."[10] At first blush, this essay may appear to be an anachronistic essay to include in a second volume dedicated to the continuing development of social-rhetorical analysis. Yet, as Robbins notes in the Introduction to the paperback edition of *Jesus the Teacher*, his work during the mid-1970's on the "we-passages" in Acts was the seminal event for the development of socio-rhetorical analysis.[11] The import of this study was that a well-known social convention could greatly influence the rhetoric of a literary narrative. In the process of comparing the we-passages of Acts with accounts of sea voyages in Mediterranean antiquity, Robbins concluded that traveling in a boat on the sea with other people "created a social environment that made it natural for some authors in antiquity to use the first-person plural" for literary accounts of sea voyages. Therefore, it became clear to Robbins that social environ-

---

[8] Robbins, *Jesus the Teacher*. The quote is from the new introduction to the 1992 paperback edition, xxxviii; see idem, "Response – Using Bakhtin's *Lexicon Dialogicae* to Interpret Canon, Apocalyptic, New Testament, and Toni Morrison," in *Bakhtin and Genre Theory in Biblical Studies* (ed. R. Boer; Semeia Studies 63; Atlanta: SBL, 2007) 187-203.

[9] Robbins, *Tapestry*, 15.

[10] Vernon K. Robbins, "By Land and By Sea: The We-Passages in Acts and Ancient Sea Voyages," in *Perspectives in Luke-Acts* (ed. C.H. Talbert; Macon, Ga.: Mercer University Press, 1978), 215–42. This essay revises and combines two previous essays from Robbins: "The We-Passages in Acts and Ancient Sea Voyages," *Biblical Research* 20 (1975): 5–18 and "By Land and by Sea: A Study in Acts 13–28," *SBL Seminar Papers, 1976* (SBLSP 15; Missoula, Mont.: Scholars Press, 1976), 381–96.

[11] Robbins, *Jesus the Teacher*, xix-xx.

ments have a critical role to play in the creation and reading of narratives.[12]

Robbins's essay is almost as often misunderstood as it is cited. For that reason, we include in this volume a response from Robbins to the various critics of his analysis (see Chapter 2). Therefore, I will not give an extensive analysis of his original essay. It is clear to me, however, that the negative critiques of Robbins's analysis most often result from two major reasons. First, there appears to be an automatic reaction from scholars who attempt to buttress the historical veracity of the book of Acts. The we-passages serve, for these scholars, as a means to ensure that the events described are narrated by an eyewitness – whether personally by the author or from a "travel diary" utilized by the author. A second and sometimes inter-related perspective stems from those scholars who remain entrenched within a more traditional, theological, historical-critical paradigm and do not share Robbins's more progressive understanding of intertextuality.[13]

Robbins's "we-passages" essay, however, discusses much more than just whether sea voyage narratives in Greek and Roman literature had become a "distinct genre" (48), a genre that included the use of the first person plural as one of its features. Robbins first analyzes various sea voyage narratives in Greek and Roman literature in order to discern its "narrative style." He explores such narratives as Homer's *Odyssey*, Virgil's *Aeneid,* poems from Alcaeus, Aeschylus's *Seven Against Thebes* and *The Libation Bearers,* Varro's *Menippean Satires,* as well as works by Dio Chrysostom, Petronius, Josephus, Ovid, Lucian, Achilles Tatius, and Heliodorus. Robbins admits that such authors as Thucydides and Xenophon use third person narration for voyages – even for

---

[12] This study also led Robbins to realize that social environments have a beginning, middle, and end, which, in turn, led to the next major advance toward socio-rhetorical interpretation found in Robbins's "Mark 1:14–20: An Interpretation at the Intersection of Jewish and Greco-Roman Traditions," in *New Boundaries*, 137–54; repr. from *NTS* 28 (1982): 220–36. In this article on Mark 1:14–20, Robbins's intratextual study of the internal rhetoric of the passage includes an intertextual analysis of the Septuagint and Greco-Roman literature. The investigation of the phases of the teacher/disciple cycle found in Mark then pushed Robbins to examine the social environment presupposed by this portrayal of Jesus and the disciples. Robbins appropriately turns to cultural anthropology to understand these processes, since the Gospel of Mark is a "foreign" piece of literature written by and for people very different from Robbins and other twenty-first century interpreters.

[13] With few exceptions, most of the negative responses to Robbins's article – ones that more-or-less defend the historicity of Acts – are dependent on the work of Colin Hemer. See Colin J. Hemer, *The Book of Acts in the Setting of Hellenistic History* (ed. Conrad Gempf; WUNT 49; Tübingen: Mohr-Siebeck, 1989) and "First Person Narrative in Acts 27–28," *Tyndale Bulletin* 36 (1985): 79–109.

places where the author participated in the events narrated. Yet there are texts that alternate between third person and first person narration. Robbins concludes that apt comparisons can be drawn between the we-passages in Acts and such texts as *Voyage of Hanno the Carthaginian*, *Episodes from the Third Syrian War*, and *Antiochene Acts of the Martyrdom of Ignatius*. In addition, various features are common to sea voyage narratives, such as landing in unfamiliar places and hoping to establish an amiable relationship with the people in the area where the landing occurs. The major lesson to be drawn from these comparative texts is that the author of Luke-Acts is a "versatile Hellenistic writer who is an intelligent participant in the literary arena of Mediterranean culture" (49).

Robbins's attention to literary considerations is easily seen in this 1978 essay as well. He draws attention to the "position" of the we-passages in the book of Acts, carefully describes the various events in the four we-passages, and examines the dynamics of the we-passages within the structure of Luke-Acts. With respect to the last issue, Robbins makes appropriate use of the 1974 study by Charles Talbert of the architectonic structure and the correspondences between Luke and Acts.[14] Three sections in Acts correspond to three sections in the Lukan travel narrative. We can also see development in Paul's journeys in Acts, both in the increasing number of verses and the increasing amount of first-person narration, which is due, of course, to the increasing amount of sea travel narrated. All three of Paul's missions are inaugurated by we-sections, and the we-sections play a decisive role in the latter stages of Acts and the establishment of the gospel in Rome (79). They also play a significant role in orienting early Christianity from the "Lake" of Galilee and Jerusalem to the Mediterranean Sea and Rome.[15]

Essays focusing on Social and Cultural Interpretation

Chapter 3, "The Social Location of the Implied Author of Luke-Acts," is one of the earliest attempts in New Testament scholarship to merge

---

[14] Charles H. Talbert, *Literary Patterns, Theological Themes, and the Genre of Luke-Acts* (Missoula, Mont.: Scholars Press, 1974). Robbins also notes some of the differences between the two volumes, an issue that would be explored many years later in various ways by other scholars. See, for example, David B. Gowler, *Host, Guest, Enemy, and Friend: Portraits of the Pharisees in Luke and Acts*, Emory Studies in Early Christianity 1 (New York: Peter Lang, 1991), esp. 301–305 and Mikeal C. Parsons and Richard I. Pervo, *Rethinking the Unity of Luke and Acts* (Minneapolis: Fortress, 1993).

[15] For the rest of the discussion of this essay, the critiques of it, and Robbins's response, see Chapter 2.

the insights of literary criticism and social-scientific criticism.[16] Robbins's use of literary modes of analysis had become much more explicit in the late 1980's,[17] but this article is his first full-fledged attempt to merge insights from both perspectives.[18] Thus, in my view, this essay is a methodological advance that provocatively and creatively merges social and literary-critical forms of analysis.[19]

At this stage (1991), however, Robbins's "narrative discourse model" had not yet reached the sophistication of his approach in *Tapestry*.[20] Luke-Acts is *narrative* discourse, and Robbins utilizes Seymour Chatman's narrative communication model – as adapted by Jeff Staley – to analyze these inner textual elements.[21] This essay prepares us for Robbins's later critiques of certain literary critics who set limited "poetic" boundaries (121), who do not use a rhetorically comprehensive approach (117), and who allow themselves to be "seduced by the narrator"

---

[16] Originally published in *The Social World of Luke-Acts: Models for Interpretation* (ed. Jerome H. Neyrey; Peabody, Mass.: Hendrickson, 1991), 305–32.

[17] Note, for example, how Robbins's interest in "social reality" is juxtaposed with his recognition that a *narrator* is telling the story in his "The Woman who Touched Jesus' Garment: Socio-Rhetorical Analysis of the Synoptic Accounts," *NTS* 33 (1987): 502–15. This essay is also found in Robbins's *New Boundaries*, 185–200.

[18] All of Robbins's later "Five Textures" – as found in *Exploring* (1996) and *Tapestry* (1996) – are present either explicitly or implicitly in this article. See also Robbins's "Luke-Acts: A Mixed Population Seeks a Home in the Roman Empire," in *Images of Empire* (ed. Loveday Alexander, JSOT 122; Sheffield: JSOT Press, 1991), 202–21. To a certain extent, literary critics' fear of the so-called "referential fallacy" initially prevented them from acknowledging the social function and interaction of all discourse. Robbins asserts in this article, however, that Luke-Acts is a "narrative map grounded in an ideology that supported Christians who were building alliances with local leaders throughout the eastern Roman Empire." Its language thus "merges social and historical geography" (202). The methodologies in these essays therefore go beyond what New Testament literary critics to that point had suggested. Cf. Norman Petersen's discussion of the "referential fallacy" in his *Literary Criticism for New Testament Critics* (Philadelphia: Fortress, 1978), 38–40 with his "sociological" analysis of Paul's "narrative world" in *Rediscovering Paul: Philemon and the Sociology of Paul's Narrative World* (Philadelphia: Fortress, 1985).

[19] I will certainly admit to my own bias in this regard. When Robbins served as the external reviewer for my doctoral dissertation in 1989, which attempted a similar methodology, Robbins shared this article with me. In addition, he invited my manuscript to be published as the inaugural volume of this series, Emory Studies in Early Christianity: David B. Gowler, *Host, Guest, Enemy, and Friend*. Cf. my "Characterization in Luke: A Socio-Narratological Approach," *BTB* 19:2 (1989): 54–62; "Hospitality and Characterization in Luke 11:37–54: A Socio-Narratological Approach, *Semeia* 64 (1993): 213–51; "Text, Culture, and Ideology in Luke 7:1–10: A Dialogic Reading," in *Fabrics of Discourse: Culture, Ideology, and Religion* (Harrisburg, PA: Trinity Press International, 2003), 89–125; and "'At His Gate Lay a Poor Man': A Dialogic Reading of Luke 16:19–31," *Perspectives in Religious Studies* 32:3 (2005): 249–65.

[20] E.g., Robbins, *Tapestry*, 37.

[21] For a more mature example of Robbins's foundational theoretical literary assumptions, see *Tapestry*, 18–43.

and merely re-enact the rhetoric of the narrator rather than exhibit the nature of that rhetoric.[22]

This analysis of the social location of the implied author represents a beginning; as the title intimates, Robbins only integrates two major aspects of literary and social approaches: the "social location" of the "implied author." Robbins explores aspects of the "implied author," the "singular consciousness which the reader constructs from the words of the text ... the static overarching view of a text that a reader might develop from multiple readings" (120). As Robbins notes elsewhere, words in texts "imply" authors, and the "implied author" is the kind of author that a reader constructs on the basis of the words in a text.[23] Secondly, for Robbins, a "social location" is a position in a social system that reflects a worldview: "a perception of how things work, what is real, where things belong, and how they fit together" (115).[24] Since language signifies social functions, it is constitutive of social communication whose intratextual functions presuppose extratextual systems of social interaction. Thus Robbins believes that language is produced out of social interaction among people; the presence of a speaker/writer presupposes the real or assumed presence of a hearer/reader. From a Bakhtinian perspective, this means that the author/speaker's orientation toward the reader/hearer is an orientation toward a specific conceptual horizon. The author/speaker, to achieve a better hearing of her/his word, must be oriented toward the conceptual horizon of the reader/hearer and enter into a dialogical relationship with certain elements of the (real or assumed) readers/hearers.[25] In a similar dialogic fashion, Robbins's socio-rhetorical interpretation always includes an analysis of the interrelations among the author, the text, and the reader, including the historical, social, cultural, and ideological relations among people and the texts they read and write.[26]

From my own perspective, Robbins correctly insists that understanding is a present activity: "[A]ll knowledge is contemporary knowledge, even what we call knowledge of the past" (117). If the interpreter wants to situate Luke-Acts into its pre-industrial society in the first-century Mediterranean context, then it is essential to find appropriate frameworks and scenarios that are designed to bring our

---

[22] Note, for example, Robbins's numerous mentions of "restrained rhetoric" in the essays in this volume.

[23] Robbins, *Tapestry*, 21.

[24] Robbins is dependent here, of course, on the groundbreaking work by Peter Berger and Thomas Luckmann, *The Social Construction of Reality* (Garden City, N.Y.: Doubleday, 1966).

[25] Bakhtin, *Dialogic Imagination*, 282. See similar comments in my "Text, Culture, and Ideology in Luke 7:1–10," 91.

[26] Robbins, *Tapestry*, 39.

modern knowledge in dialogue with these ancient social contexts. This leads to Robbins's thesis:

> If we can identify the arenas of the social system presupposed by various phenomena in the text, and if we can delineate the location, role, and competencies certain phenomena exhibit within different arenas of the social system, then we can make some progress toward identifying the social location of thought within the entire document (117-118).

Robbins integrates four aspects of inner textual functions in Luke-Acts (characters/audiences; narrator/narratee; inscribed author/inscribed reader; implied author/implied reader) with nine arenas of the social system.[27] The primary goal is to identify the social location of the implied author as constituted in the language, ideology, and social relations in the text. Robbins focuses on the social location of the implied author because it involves "all of the competencies that signify certain kinds of relations to and activities within processes at work in various arenas of Mediterranean society" (121).

Robbins then explores aspects of the implied author's social location through brief examinations of each of the nine arenas. Luke-Acts, for example, uses *previous events* to create and maintain relationships among various Christians, Jews, and Romans. The presentation evokes a social location similar to Josephus (124). The arena of *population structure* is striking because of the ethnic variety of the "mixed population" who are members of the Christian movement in Acts. Aspects of the *technology* arena reflect the implied author's expertise as a "technical writer," a location that appreciates the artisan class—unlike the typical disdain of such artisans and their work by members of the elite (129). In the arena of *socialization and personality*, the implied author finds it advantageous to communicate with person(s) of some prestige in Roman society (e.g., "Most excellent Theophilus") and to adopt a (slightly lower) subordinate stance of respect in relation to those of some prestige (133). The implied author also places Jesus within the social sphere of (Jewish) reading culture (135; Luke 4:16–22), yet Jesus' stance is bicultural—not only grounded in Jewish culture but also competent in Greco-Roman culture. The implied author, in the arena of *Foreign Affairs*, wants the "foreign affairs" (of Christianity) to find an accepted place within the affairs of Rome. And the implied author's ideological posi-

---

[27] They are: (1) Previous Events; (2) Natural Environment and Resources; (3) Population Structure; (4) Technology; (5) Socialization and Personality; (6) Culture; (7) Foreign Affairs; (8) Belief Systems and Ideologies; (9) Political-Military-Legal System. Here Robbins is dependent on Thomas Carney, *The Shape of the Past: Models and Antiquity* (Lawrence, Kans.: Coronado, 1975). Much of the following is revised from my "Text, Culture, and Ideology in Luke 7:1–10," 92–94.

tion is that God ordained a certain place for the foreign affairs of Christianity within the affairs of the Roman Empire. In my view, one of Robbins's crucial insights is that Luke-Acts has a more aggressive ideological stance than most interpreters during this era realized: Instead of merely being an "apologia" for Christianity that seeks to demonstrate that Christians are not guilty of illegal activity, Luke-Acts attempts to support those Christians who are building alliances with Roman leaders throughout the eastern Roman Empire and seek their (rightful, in their view) home within that empire.

Thus the final social arena, the *Political-Military-Legal System*, contains a number of the upper-level representatives of the emperor – prefect, proconsul, or king – who, although they "exhibit some social distance from Christianity," take no legal action against individual Christians. Centurions in particular are portrayed as favorable to Jesus (in Luke) and the apostles (in Acts), so Robbins concludes that in the social location of the implied author of Luke-Acts a number of centurions are members of the Christian community (Luke 7:1–10; 23:47; Acts 10:1–11:18; Acts 27:3, 42–43).[28] Christianity thus has a "comfortable place" within the Roman political-military-legal system, albeit with a deep uneasiness over this "at homeness" (e.g., "imprisonment" in Acts reflects this ambivalent ideological stance; 141).

Robbins's "Luke-Acts: A Mixed Population seeks a Home in the Roman Empire" (also published in 1991) furthers these insights.[29] His underlying thesis is that Luke-Acts is a *narrative* map grounded in an aggressive *ideology* that merges *social and historical geography*.[30] As noted above, the narrative's strategy is to support alliances between Christians and local leaders in the eastern Roman Empire, because the narrator assumes that this area is an appropriate "workplace" for the emissaries of God. So Luke-Acts is far from being a "defensive" narrative; it in fact is an "aggressive" narrative concerned with power (and wealth) and working in an environment "teeming with opportunities" (203). From the perspective of Luke-Acts, the power structure of Christianity

---

[28] Joseph Tyson reaches similar conclusions in his study of the implied reader of Luke-Acts. For Tyson, the implied reader in many respects is similar to the "Godfearers" in Luke-Acts – devout Gentiles who are attracted to Jewish religious life (e.g., Luke 7:1–10; Acts 10–11). See Joseph B. Tyson, *Images of Judaism in Luke-Acts* (Columbia: University of South Carolina Press, 1992) and his "Jews and Judaism in Luke-Acts," *NTS* 41:1 (1995): 24–25. For a more nuanced view of the Pharisees in Luke-Acts, however, see my *Host, Guest, Enemy, and Friend*.

[29] As noted above, due to the limitations of space, "Luke-Acts: A Mixed Population" is not included in this volume.

[30] Emphasis mine, for the reason of highlighting the fact that Robbins implicitly was working through aspects of all "five textures" long before he explicitly formulated that socio-rhetorical taxonomy. Intertextual elements are also included in the article (e.g., 220), so it is an excellent example of that comprehensive approach.

works compatibly and symbiotically with the power structure of Rome (e.g., with Roman centurions), and the upper levels of Rome's military and legal structure are treated with special deference in the narrative.

Robbins correctly observes that the narrator's[31] rhetorical strategy implicitly connects Christianity to the success of Rome by showing – the inverse of Rome's expansion – the expansion of Christianity from Jerusalem to Rome (205). The key difference is that, for the narrator, the power that brings Paul to Rome is the God of Israel. Therefore one of the defining issues for Luke-Acts is the relation of the power of the emperor to the power of God (207).

I extend these insights in my essay contained in Robbins's *Festschrift*.[32] In that essay, I argue that Luke-Acts is actually even more aggressive and indeed subversive than it first appears. In Luke-Acts, God's activity presupposes, advances, inverts, and seeks to transform in a radical way the hierarchical structures within the greater imperial system and Greco-Roman society. Robbins comes closer to this view in Chapter 12 of this volume, "The Socio-Rhetorical Role of the Old Testament in Luke 4–19."

Chapter 4, "Rhetoric and Culture: Mark 4–11 as a Test Case," actually is a combination of two essays, one published in 1993 and the other in 1994.[33] Readers will certainly note numerous connections between this essay and other essays in this volume, as well as with Robbins's books *Exploring* and *Tapestry*.

A central element in almost all of Robbins's publications from at least 1973 until the present is an implicit or explicit plea to biblical interpreters to enlarge the boundaries of discussion. In other words, his approach is truly dialogic, whether it is to include Hellenistic-Roman texts and contexts as well as Jewish texts and contexts in our comparative data for New Testament interpretation, to incorporate the insights of other approaches and methodologies in our interpretations (a primary plea of the next chapter), or to encourage a more dialogic approach with each other in our work as biblical scholars.

---

[31] Robbins uses the term *implied author*. I prefer the term *narrator*, which denotes the "voice" of the implied author.

[32] David B. Gowler, "Text, Culture, and Ideology in Luke 7:1–10."

[33] Vernon K. Robbins, "Rhetoric and Culture: Exploring Types of Cultural Rhetoric in a Text," in *Rhetoric and the New Testament: Essays from the 1992 Heidelberg Conference* (ed. Stanley E. Porter and Thomas H. Olbricht; Sheffield: JSOT Press, 1993), 443–63; and "Interpreting Miracle Culture and Parable Culture in Mark 4–11," *SEÅ* 59 (1994): 59–81.

In this essay, Robbins's primary target is the practice of "restrained rhetoric," the limiting of one's interpretation of a text because of methodology and/or ideology. Robbins highlights essays by Wilhelm Wuellner that bring this issue of "restrained rhetoric" to the fore, and he agrees with Wuellner that rhetorical criticism must be "practical criticism": rhetoric "revalued" or "reinvented." This "new" rhetoric "approaches all literature, including inspired canonical biblical literature as *social* discourse."[34]

Robbins had long been working toward such a goal, and this particular essay focuses on the social and cultural texture of socio-rhetorical interpretation, exhibits the importance of ideological texture (since ideology limits one's vision of "acceptable" approaches), builds upon Wuellner's insights, and critiques the times that Wuellner lapses back into "restrained rhetoric."[35]

Robbins also correctly argues that interpreters must attempt to overcome the standard dualistic views of Christianity that "good" Christianity cannot "mix" with culture. Robbins asserts that Christianity inherently is cultural; indeed, in all of its variations, it as a "plethora of cultures." Robbins fully understands, as did Bakhtin, that discourse is a social phenomenon. No narrative, discourse, or utterance is created in a literary, cultural, social, or historical vacuum. New Testament narratives thus were created in conversations with their cultural environments, are active participants in that dialogical social discourse, and serve as rejoinders in the greater social dialogues. Thus the style and content of New Testament narratives are influenced – directly and indirectly – by their interrelationships with the other rejoinders in the greater social dialogues.[36]

So, in this essay, Robbins creates the basic frameworks for exploring the different modes of social and cultural rhetoric that he later deli-

---

[34] Wilhelm H. Wuellner, "Where is Rhetorical Criticism Taking Us?" *CBQ* 49 (1987): 462. I read Robbins's arguments that texts are read and reread, interpreted and reinterpreted as forms of and inseparable from social activity and social relations in the context not only of the new rhetoric and new historicism but also in the much older Bakhtinian Dialogism and its critique of Russian Formalism.

[35] For additional insights into ideological texture, ones that build upon Robbins's insights in *Exploring* and *Tapestry*, see the following chapters in *Fabrics of Discourse*: H. J. Bernard Combrink, "Shame on the Hypocritical Leaders in the Church: A Socio-Rhetorical Interpretation of the Reproaches in Matthew 23," 1–35; John Kloppenborg, "Ideological Texture in the Parable of the Tenants," 64–88; David B. Gowler, "Text, Culture, and Ideology in Luke 7:1–10," 89–125; L. Gregory Bloomquist, "Paul's inclusive language: The Ideological Texture of Romans 1," 165–93; Charles A. Wanamaker, "'By the Power of God': Rhetoric and Ideology in 2 Corinthians 10–13," 194–221; and Russell Sisson, "The Common Agon: Textual Structure and Ideology in Philippians," 242–63.

[36] Bakhtin, *Dialogic Imagination*, 291–92.

neates in *Exploring* and *Tapestry*.[37] Robbins begins by utilizing Bryan Wilson's typology of sects in order to categorize the "specific (or "material") social topics."[38] The second categorization of "common topics" consists of such common social and cultural topics as kinship, honor, limited good, hospitality, and so forth. The third type is exceedingly important because it involves those topics that most decisively present one's cultural location; Robbins categorizes them as "final topics."[39]

Why are this new terminology, this categorization, and analyses of such rhetoric important? At the very least, they should enable New Testament scholars to admit that New Testament texts are not merely "embedded in, and surrounded and protected by, Jewish culture" (156). Do these texts, for example, view Jewish culture as a dominant culture or as a subculture in a dominant Hellenistic-Roman culture? A more specific question would be whether Paul's language, thought, and action can be seen as thoroughly subcultural Jewish rhetoric. Robbins argues – correctly, in my view – that to answer that latter question in the affirmative is to practice at least one form of "restrained rhetoric."

The thaumaturgic language in Mark 4–11 suggests that some early Christians created, developed, and "lived in" a relatively autonomous, comprehensive thaumaturgic culture during the years 30–60 CE.[40] In relation to dominant "Jewish culture," Markan thaumaturgic rhetoric functions as Jewish subculture rhetoric and, at times, as contraculture rhetoric. With relation to Hellenistic-Roman culture, in which its own thaumaturgic rhetoric is subculture rhetoric, the rhetoric in Mark 4–11 has a subculture relation to this Hellenistic-Roman subculture rhetoric. In both instances, however, the goal of the rhetoric is to fulfill expressed thaumaturgic values in dominant Jewish culture and Hellenistic-Roman subculture in better ways than these other cultures do.

The rhetoric of the parables in Mark 4–11, however, functions in a significantly different way. The parables stand in relation to both Jewish culture and Hellenistic-Roman culture because they exhibit both subcultural Jewish rhetoric and subcultural Hellenistic-Roman rhetoric.[41]

---

[37] Robbins, *Exploring*, 71–94; *Tapestry*, 144–91.

[38] These specific social topics are conversionist, revolutionist, introversionist, gnostic-manipulationist, thaumaturgical, reformist, and utopian. The term and concept of "specific" (or "material") topics comes from Aristotle's *Rhetoric* 1.4–8. See Bryan Wilson, *Magic and the Millennium: A Sociological Study of Religious Movements of Protest among Tribal and Third-World Peoples* (New York: Harper & Row, 1973), 22–26.

[39] They include dominant culture rhetoric, subculture rhetoric, counterculture rhetoric, contraculture rhetoric, and liminal culture rhetoric.

[40] Compare Robbins, *Tapestry*, 240–43.

[41] Robbins takes as his starting point – but substantially modifies and extends – the work of Burton L. Mack who acknowledged that the images of field, sowing, seeds, and harvest used in Mark 4 are standard metaphors in Jewish apocalyptic, wisdom, and pro-

Robbins goes on to argue, however, that the ultimate goal of such parable rhetoric in Mark 4 was to ask — and, for some, to answer — the question: "How can a person receive the kingdom of God and become fruitful?" In social terms, this type of rhetoric is gnostic-manipulationist because it seeks a transformed set of relationships. The social rhetoric of Mark 4 interacts with both Jewish culture and Hellenistic-Roman culture by assuming many elements of those cultures; on the other hand, in this complex and variegated relationship, the parables in Mark also reject, subvert, or transform other features found in Jewish and in Hellenistic-Roman cultures.

In the Markan pronouncement stories, though, we find another significant difference: countercultural Jewish rhetoric rather than subcultural Jewish rhetoric. In addition, as Burton Mack, John Kloppenborg, and others had shown, it also stands in some kind of relation to Cynic rhetoric. What does this mean about the early sector of the Jesus movement that Mack and Kloppenborg describe? This early Christian contraculture rhetoric was deeply embedded in and dependent on Jewish culture, and the short-lived contraculture that Mack and Kloppenborg describe most likely (at its earliest stage) had a subcultural relation to Hellenistic-Cynic counterculture. As Robbins notes, this type of complexity is exactly what we should expect to find in the syncretistic, eclectic cultural environments of the first-century Mediterranean world.

Such advances in our understanding of the Jesus movement(s) and early Christianity are made possible by an ideological commitment to a rhetoric "revalued" or "reinvented."[42] Robbins in the past had called for an "open poetics" in a similar plea to interpreters not to close doors and set up false boundaries that close off essential comparative texts, methodologies, and resources for interpretation.[43] If we fail to establish

---

phetic traditions for God's dealings with Israel. Mack also demonstrated, however, that such agricultural images as "seeds" and "sowing" also were standard analogies for *paideia* during the first-century; such metaphors would have immediately recalled the "stock image" for instruction, especially that of inculcating Hellenistic culture. These stock analogies utilized the sower (teacher) who sowed (taught) his seed (words) upon various soils (students). See Burton L. Mack, *A Myth of Innocence: Mark and Christian Origins* (Philadelphia: Fortress, 1988), 160–5.

[42] For another example of a revised understanding of the formation of early Christianity, see Vernon K. Robbins, "Making Christian Culture in the Epistle of James," *Scriptura* 59 (1996): 341–51. In that article, Robbins replaces the "trajectories" of James M. Robinson and Helmut Koester with the socio-rhetorical approach of looking at the multiple traditions of discourse in earliest Christianity, a "model of making Christian culture," in other words.

[43] Robbins used the term *open poetics* in his "A Socio-Rhetorical Look at the Work of John Knox on Acts," in *Cadbury, Knox, and Talbert: American Contributions to the Study of Acts* (ed. Mikeal C. Parsons and Joseph B. Tyson; Atlanta: Scholars Press, 1992), 91–105.

those dialogues – whether because of an ideology/theology that unduly restricts our vision or because of other limitations – we leave the New Testament marooned on an island far from the contexts in which these texts were created. Socio-rhetorical interpretation attempts to bridge this gulf, as Robbins himself notes: "Socio-rhetorical criticism challenges the interpreter to widen the intertextual boundaries to include the Mediterranean world in which early Christians lived, to widen the social and cultural boundaries to include customs, behaviors, and attitudes of people in Mediterranean society, and to widen the ideological boundaries beyond a culture of the mind...."[44]

Chapter 5, "Social-Scientific Criticism and Literary Studies: Prospects for Cooperation in Biblical Interpretation,"[45] is a subject intimately intertwined with my own research interests since the 1980's.[46] My initial scholarly publications contained an integration of literary and cultural anthropological analyses that I called "socio-narratological criticism."[47] Thus I am one of those "other interpreters" mentioned in this essay who see "some kind of merger" between literary and social-scientific criticisms as "essential" (182; first page).

As he does in *Tapestry*, Robbins pulls back the ideological curtain on purely disciplinary approaches – they are hierarchical power structures with "purity systems" that judge whether certain approaches are acceptable ("pure") or unacceptable ("impure"). These purity systems place other approaches in a subordinate position.[48]

Robbins then offers a model for interdisciplinary investigation; not surprisingly he chooses rhetoric as a "bridge" between disciplines, since it is necessary "to have a mode of analysis that guides the interdisciplinary arbitration." Rhetoric, it appears, is "first among equals." The

[44] Vernon K. Robbins, "Using a Socio-Rhetorical Poetics to Develop a Unified Method: The Woman who Anointed Jesus as a Test Case," *SBL Seminar Papers, 1992* (SBLSP 31; Atlanta: Scholars Press, 1992), 302–13.

[45] Vernon K. Robbins, "Social-Scientific Criticism and Literary Studies: Prospects for Cooperation in Biblical Interpretation," in *Modelling Early Christianity: Social-Scientific Studies of the New Testament in Its Context* (ed. Philip F. Esler; London: Routledge, 1995), 274–89.

[46] Some examples may be found in Gowler, "Characterization in Luke"; idem, *Host, Guest, Enemy and Friend*; idem, "Socio-Rhetorical Criticism"; idem, "Hospitality and Characterization"; idem, "Heteroglossic Trends"; idem, "Text, Culture, and Ideology in Luke 7:1–10"; and idem, "'At His Gate Lay a Poor Man.'"

[47] The nomenclature was a nod toward Robbins's socio-rhetorical criticism of that era, as evidenced in his *Jesus the Teacher*, but my own scholarly interests were primarily literary criticism and social-scientific criticism.

[48] See Robbins's discussion of the ways in which historical-critical scholars "control people's interpretation of the Bible" in "Divine Dialogue and the Lord's Prayer: Socio-Rhetorical Interpretation of Sacred Texts," *Dialogue* 28:3 (1995): 127–29.

"socio-rhetorical model of textual communication" is graphically illustrated by the same diagram as will appear in *Tapestry*.[49]

Robbins argues, by using John Dominic Crossan and Richard Rohrbaugh as examples, that both literary critics and social-scientific critics begin with models "in their own world that function as a context for interpretation" for New Testament texts, that is, modern literary theory and modern social-scientific theory. This valuing of modern theory is the first hint that these scholars *could* have a productive dialogue: Both start with phenomena outside of New Testament texts and create models with which to interpret those texts. Similarities are also found in the ways that literary critics such as Crossan and social-scientific critics such as Rohrbaugh tend to personify things: for Crossan it is forms of literature such as the "story"; for Rohrbaugh it is the author "Luke" and the reader. Robbins further suggests that these approaches might actually be in continuum with each other. Crossan's literary approach may begin where Rohrbaugh's social-scientific approach ends.[50]

Robbins comments on the necessity of dialogue between literary and social-scientific critics, but – primarily because of the differing phenomena that they "personify" and because of the unexplored presuppositions of each – he is not sanguine about fruitful dialogue – at least until the presuppositions of each are adequately explored. The first step should consist of an interdisciplinary spirit that includes "an admission by both sides that the other side has data that is important for the act of interpretation."[51]

Robbins, however, goes farther that merely proposing an "overlap of interest" between these two disciplines. He argues that each "needs to have a much more comprehensive conception of the nature of text." This point, of course, is where rhetorical criticism (as the "first among equals") becomes involved for Robbins, and he returns to themes common in many of the essays in this volume: literary criticism as "restrained rhetoric" that pays significant attention only to four of the forty-eight rhetorical tropes (see chapters 9 and 10), the incorporation of Bryan Wilson's typology of sects (see chapters 4 and 9), chreia elaboration (see chapters 7, 10, and 11), and the analysis of the final topics of culture (chapters 4, 9, and 10).

---

[49] *Tapestry*, 37. This essay also contains the four textures of *Tapestry*, not the five textures of *Exploring*.

[50] See a similar plea in my "Socio-Rhetorical Criticism," 35; idem, "Hospitality and Characterization"; idem, *Host, Guest, Enemy, and Friend*; idem, "Heteroglossic Trends"; and idem, "Characterization in Luke."

[51] Jerome Neyrey, for example, is a social-scientific critic who has worked diligently to bridge this divide by utilizing rhetorical approaches in his work. See, for example, "The Social Location of Paul: Education as the Key," in *Fabrics of Discourse*, 126–64.

In many respects, this essay takes up the case earlier (in 1992) argued in "Using a Socio-Rhetorical Poetics to Develop a Unified Method." Although Robbins appropriately no longer uses the term "unified method," this early essay about the "four textures" lays out many of the problems and limitations inherent in solitary "disciplinary" approaches. It also makes a strong case for why socio-rhetorical interpretation is needed, such as the necessity of engaging a broader and more significant range of comparative data, expanding intertextual boundaries, and incorporating the insights of various disciplinary approaches. A key question of that 1992 essay still remains critically important today: "Will our turf battles be strategies to keep deeper issues out of sight?"[52] The answer then, as it is (sadly) today, is more often "yes" than "no." Socio-rhetorical interpretation, however, still offers a way to mediate these turf battles and to provide an arena for frank, open, and collegial discussions.[53]

Emerging Strategies of Socio-Rhetorical Interpretation

The chapter, "Picking Up the Fragments: From Crossan's Analysis to Rhetorical Analysis," was written for the inaugural meeting of the Jesus Seminar and is an extended review, critique, and extension of John Dominic Crossan's *In Fragments: The Aphorisms of Jesus*.[54] As such, the essay was written well before the recent onslaught of works in historical Jesus studies, including Crossan's later thrusts and parries in that onslaught.[55] Yet, as we look carefully at Robbins's analysis of

---

[52] Robbins, "Using a Socio-Rhetorical Poetics to Develop a Unified Method," 314.

[53] A personal note: In years past, I have served as a member of the SBL Rhetoric and the New Testament Steering Committee, attended many of their SBL Rhetoric and New Testament sessions, participated in some of the "pre-SBL" meetings of the socio-rhetorical (Rhetoric in Religious Antiquity) working group, and participated in other meetings of that group in Atlanta. Although I am not a socio-rhetorical critic, I must say that the interdisciplinary openness and collegiality of this group is stunning. Not only were the sessions of the SBL Rhetoric and New Testament Sections intentionally constructed in a way to incorporate a wide variety of voices, but the meetings of the Rhetoric in Religious Antiquity group were paradigms of how scholars could and should work together in a collaborative, collegial fashion.

[54] Originally published in *Forum* 1, no. 2 (1985): 31–64. See John Dominic Crossan, *In Fragments: The Aphorisms of Jesus* (San Francisco: Harper & Row, 1983).

[55] Crossan's later works include: *The Historical Jesus: The Life of a Mediterranean Peasant* (San Francisco: HarperSanFrancisco, 1991); idem, *Jesus: A Revolutionary Biography* (San Francisco: HarperSanFrancisco, 1994); idem, *The Essential Jesus: Original Sayings and Earliest Images* (San Francisco: HarperSanFrancisco, 1994); idem, *Who Killed Jesus? Exposing the Roots of Anti-Semitism in the Gospel Story of the Death of Jesus* (San Francisco: HarperSanFrancisco, 1995); idem, *The Birth of Christianity: Discovering What Happened in the Years Immediately after the Execution of Jesus* (San Francisco: HarperSanFrancisco, 1998);

Crossan's pioneering study, we see issues that resonate with Robbins's previous work,[56] as well as important aspects of the textures and rhetorolects that would later emerge in socio-rhetorical interpretation. These aspects can be discerned, with the benefit of hindsight, as pieces of an intricate socio-rhetorical latticework that more fully emerges in the late 1990's. A close reading therefore can also reveal many of Robbins's foundational philosophical beliefs and methodological approaches.

Robbins asserts that the purpose of a socio-rhetorical method is to probe the inner reasoning and modes of argumentation in the data – in this instance the action and speech attributed to Jesus. The reader produces "meaning," but only by participating in a complex of socially constructed practices.[57] As a beginning point then, it is essential to understand "the dynamics of communication and transmission in Mediterranean culture at the time of the beginning of Christianity" as a basic context for facilitating our understanding of the transmission of traditions about Jesus (202).

The clarity of Crossan's approach invites a much-needed conversation about the aphorisms of Jesus, and Robbins's socio-rhetorical analysis enters such a dialogue with Crossan's work within the three following analytic rubrics:

1. *How we begin influences where we go.* Crossan begins with a discussion of the nature of aphorisms, which establishes a framework for detailed analysis of approximately 40% of the synoptic "wisdom" sayings. Crossan correctly observes that a "proverb" presents collective wisdom, whereas an "aphorism" presents a personal vision through a personal voice. Robbins notes that, as such, a proverb is a γνώμη. It circulates without attribution to a specific person; it is general, not specific; it can be applied to various situations in daily life; it is a saying rather than an action, and it is concrete rather than abstract (204). Robbins goes on to argue, however, that Crossan's use of the term *aphorism* is essential to an ancient rhetorician's understanding of what is

---

John Dominic Crossan and Jonathan L. Reed, *Excavating Jesus: Beneath the Stones, Behind the Texts* (San Francisco: HarperSanFrancisco, 2001); Marcus Borg and John Dominic Crossan, *The Last Week: The Day-by-Day Account of Jesus' Final Week in Jerusalem* (San Francisco: HarperSanFrancisco, 2006); and idem, *The Last Week: What the Gospels Really Teach about Jesus's Birth* (New York: HarperOne, 2007).

[56] See, for example, the essays in and my introduction to *New Boundaries*.

[57] Thomas McLaughlin, "Introduction," in *Critical Terms for Literary Study* (ed. Frank Lentricchia and Thomas McLaughlin; Chicago: The University of Chicago Press, 1990), 6. Or as Robbins noted: "... any suggestion that a text can be read 'simply on its own terms' is illusory. Every text is read in terms of socio-ideological situations outside itself, because every reader is dependent on real or imagined social situations to give meaning to the patterned signs in the text." See "A Socio-Rhetorical Look at the Work of John Knox on Acts," 99–105.

called a χρεία: "every concise γνώμη, if it is attributed to a person, makes a χρεία" (205). A χρεία may be constituted by either a saying or an action – or a combination of both. As Theon notes, "A χρεία is a concise statement or action attributed with aptness to some specific person or something analogous to a person."[58] Thus a χρεία speaks from within the horizons of a specific person's thought and action. It is this failure of clarification that haunts the rest of Crossan's analysis (207). An aphorism must not be isolated from the person to whom it is attributed, and Crossan's analysis does not engage the inner workings (e.g., rhetorical aspects) of the aphorisms attributed to Jesus.

As Crossan later notes, "Put crudely but accurately: 'A stitch in time saves nine' is a γνώμη, but 'Jesus said: a stitch in time saves nine' is a χρεία." Once an aphorism is attributed, Robbins counters, the issue always becomes: "To what did that person apply the proverb?" Here, in my view, is an essential distinction between Crossan and Robbins, and it demonstrates some foundational presuppositions of each.[59] Crossan makes a distinction between the "aphoristic tradition" – where the setting is simply a frame – and the "dialectical tradition" – where the setting and saying are in interactive relationship so that the saying is "hermeneutically banal" or "grammatically incomplete" without the setting.[60] Although Crossan makes important points that relate to the authenticity of the "frames" in which the aphorisms are located, what Robbins argues is that *within the rhetoric of the aphorism itself* are significant clues to answering the question as to what Jesus applied the proverb. The aphoristic compound, Robbins asserts, is an argumentative package that reflects the aphoristic tradition of Jesus rather than general proverbial tradition, and an investigation of the rhetorical reasoning and argumentation will start interpreters on a program to establish the network of communication that exists within presuppositions and arguments in the aphoristic tradition (211-212).

Since this type of investigation will form the heart of some of the later articles in this volume (see chapters 10, 11, and 12), I will summarize Robbins's analysis of the aphoristic compound that Crossan labels "Patches and Wineskins."[61] The emphatic position of the personalized negative "no one" focuses attention on a person engaged in some inappropriate activity. Each aphorism contains a rationale clause

---

[58] Quoted by Robbins (206). Also quoted by Crossan (277, cf. 228-37).

[59] Robbins's work on the *chreia*, for example, helped to lead to his groundbreaking work with enthymemes. See chapters 7, 10, and 11 in this volume.

[60] Crossan, *In Fragments*, 278.

[61] *In Fragments*, 121-27. The title refers to the sayings found in Matt 9:16-17; Mark 2:21-22; Luke 5:36-37; Gos. Thom. 47b.

that gives argumentative support to the initial assertion; these rhetorical syllogisms are *enthymemes* (syllogisms with implicit premises). Robbins argues that an analysis of the rhetorical logic of the sayings is only the beginning point for investigating its internal and external means of communication. In this instance, the sayings present a personalized argument that arises out of a situation of conflict and is designed to censure or defend a particular form of action. This particular aphoristic compound supports actions that violate established conventions by utilizing images from conventional daily living. Any new attempt to reconstruct the teaching of Jesus must investigate the network of presuppositions inherent in the action and speech attributed to Jesus. In this specific instance, the implied general premise seems to be, "No one damages or destroys a thing useful for life." The next question to be asked, then, is: "Does this underlying premise cohere with premises presupposed by other aphorisms attributed to Jesus?" As Robbins asks, "Are the majority of these analogies based on conventional values in daily life? Aphorisms which communicate inductively through analogy should be gathered and their presuppositions and assertions should be analyzed systematically" (215).[62] Robbins concludes this section by noting that this approach should start interpreters on a program of establishing the "network of communication" that exists within the presuppositions and arguments in the aphoristic tradition.

2. *What we look for influences what we see.* As with the first rubric within which Robbins critiques Crossan's approach, this rubric also begins with inner texture but moves beyond it to discuss, for example, elements of social and cultural texture. Such moves are paradigmatic of Robbins's overall approach and emblematic of his philosophical orientation: All textures of these texts deserve a programmatic investigation. The specific delineation of the various textures of texts, of course, would not appear until later works,[63] but this article is well aware of aspects of the "warp and woof" of communication (227). This apt choice of words – warp and woof – foreshadows the titles of Robbins's later seminal works on socio-rhetorical interpretation, *Exploring* and *Tapestry*.

Robbins expresses appreciation for Crossan's significant contribution to our understanding of how aphorisms were transmitted in oral tradition (e.g., "performancial" and "hermeneutical" variations). Yet Crossan's argument that aphorisms exist in oral memory as *ipsissima structura* not *ipsissima verba* involves a crucial limitation: It "generalizes" aphor-

---

[62] See the creation of this type of analysis, although in a context not limited to historical Jesus research, in chapters 10, 11, and 12 of this volume.

[63] See, for example, Robbins's introduction to the paperback edition of *Jesus the Teacher*, xix–xliv.

isms into proverbial forms. Robbins counters by suggesting "postured meaning effects" that contain basic rhetorical effect in a tensive framework (217). The tensive pattern involves the inner texture, the semantic structure that has some aspect of specificity within the horizons of activity and thought associated with the tradition attributed to Jesus. The rhetorical effect (which involves intertexture, social and cultural texture, and ideological texture) involves an ordering of words and thoughts that positions the saying in relation to alternatives that may exist in the culture(s).

Hints of Robbins's indebtedness to form criticism appear occasionally in this article (218, 221),[64] but it is very clear that he is instead more dependent upon the works of theorists such as Kenneth Burke: Performances of aphorisms presuppose specific social situations – a crucial aspect that Crossan overlooks when he collapses them into a common structure. Since Robbins claims that early Christian tradition exhibits the process in which aphorisms were "generalized" or "proverbialized" as they circulated in Mediterranean society and culture, it is implicit in his critique that Crossan sometimes follows a similar path of domestication. In fact New Testament scholarship as a whole often gravitates toward the proverbialized forms, because those forms can be more easily applied to modern life than can aphoristic forms that transmit aspects of the specific situation in which they arose and in which they functioned (220).[65]

Proverbs circulate "freely," but aphorisms arise from specific situations and adapt when applied to other situations. At this point, Robbins makes a critical observation, one to which he would return several times in later works: New Testament scholars mistakenly contrast "oral" versus "scribal" culture. This dichotomy is a fundamental misunderstanding of communication in the first century Mediterranean. Robbins's important insights stem from his study of the ancient rhetorical treatises entitled *Progymnasmata*, an issue to which I will return in my discussion of Robbins's groundbreaking essay, "Writing as a Rhetorical Act in Plutarch and the Gospels."[66]

3. *How we relate an aphorism to settings and other aphorisms influences how we understand the Tradition.* Crossan gathered variations of aphor-

---

[64] See Robbins's "Form Criticism: New Testament," *The Anchor Bible Dictionary* (ed. by David Noel Freedman; vol. 2; New York: Doubleday, 1992), 841–44.

[65] The implicit connections to Robbins's much later arguments about "enthymematic networks" are quite clear. See, for example, "The Present and Future of Rhetorical Analysis" (Chapter 10) and "From Enthymeme to Theology" (Chapter 11).

[66] See also Robbins's article published just prior to this *Forum* article: "Pronouncement Stories and Jesus' Blessing of Children: A Rhetorical Approach," a 1991 essay reprinted in *New Boundaries*, 155–84.

isms; he did not attempt to uncover the relation of the argumentation in various aphorisms.[67] In addition, Robbins considers Crossan's rubric of "aphoristic tradition" (see above) to be the basic weakness of the book, a weakness of "isolation" inherited from form criticism and intensified by semiotic deconstruction. Instead of perpetuating Rudolph Bultmann's emphasis on "independently circulating sayings," interpreters should investigate the nature of the "dialectic" within the entire aphoristic tradition attributed to Jesus. As Robbins states, "Every saying emerges from a situation" – it is initially related to and dependent upon that situation. Therefore, Robbins argues, we should look at every saying from the perspective of its dialectic (or, as I would prefer, its "dialogic relations") with other aphorisms and with situations and actions in the tradition.

Robbins provides a more concrete illustration of this method in action in the next issue of *Forum*.[68] He proposes a method that attempts to "preserve and appreciate the fields of discourse which early Christians used to transmit the settings, action, and speech of Jesus" (35). His primary thesis is that we should work "to reform methods which were designed to establish the history of textual traditions, manuscript dependence, and the editing of traditions so they exhibit the tacit promises and presuppositions of actors in social situations where identities were formed through action and discourse" (36). Thus Robbins seeks to perform a synchronic analysis *prior* to a diachronic analysis; extant fields of discourse in these texts serve as an aid for understanding the development of fields of discourse in the tradition.[69]

---

[67] The six forms were aphoristic: saying, compound, cluster, conclusion, dialogue, and story. Crossan devotes a chapter to each of these forms and attempts to provide a detailed history of the transmission of traditions in each form.

[68] Vernon K. Robbins, "Pragmatic Relations as a Criterion for Authentic Sayings," *Forum* 1, no. 3 (1985): 35–63.

[69] An important example, and one that will bear much fruit in Robbins's later works, is his argument that if a text performs like a syllogism, it reveals pragmatically presupposed premises that remain hidden in ordinary discourse (38). Thus the relationship between stated and unstated premises becomes crucial to envisioning this set of pragmatic relations. Robbins builds his case with an examination of a reconstructed "Q version" of the beatitudes that was proposed by Eugene Boring: Eugene Boring, "Criteria of Authenticity: The Beatitudes as a Test Case," *Forum* 1, no. 4 (1985): 3–38. Robbins's use of this reconstructed Q version is interesting in light of his call to begin our analysis with a synchronic approach. The versions as they appear in both Matt and Luke therefore would seem to be a more appropriate starting point, although Robbins analyzes the Matthean and Lukan forms later in the article. One also wonders whether every reader would create the same "unstated" premise, or whether a limited range of options is possible, depending on the reader. As Robbins notes, "We omit one or more of the premises (the reasons), because we know, *or hope* (emphasis mine), that the other person presupposes it along with us" (40).

From the perspective of my Bakhtinian "dialogical criticism," Robbins's insistence on examining both the words and actions in their settings and contexts is exactly correct. In addition, his recognition that the only way a saying has "meaning" is to have meaning both within it and alongside it simultaneously, has a Bakhtinian ring.[70] Similarly, Robbins's foundational belief that value and meaning are the outcomes of an active reading process that always occurs within specific cultural contexts finds an ally in Bakhtin's "sociological poetics":

> At the basis of our analysis lies the conviction that every literary work is internally and immanently sociological. Within it living social forces intersect; each element of its form is permeated with living social evaluations. For this reason a purely formal analysis must take each element of the artistic structure as a point of refraction of living social forces, as a synthetic crystal whose facets are structured and ground in such a way that they refract specific rays of social evaluations, and refract them at a specific angle.[71]

At this point in his career Robbins had not yet read Bakhtin's works, but it is clear why Robbins later incorporated some of Bakhtin's ideas into socio-rhetorical analysis. Such a dialogic view of literature (and discourse) not only makes Robbins's rhetorical approach possible, but absolutely essential. In fact, Bakhtin extends the enthymematic nature of language even further than Robbins does at this stage.[72]

The action, therefore, is moved out of the horizon of the historical Jesus and placed within the horizon of the text's contemplator.[73] Every event, every phenomenon, every thing that is represented in literature, when it comes into contact with the present through the retelling/rehearing of the story, acquires a relationship – in one form or another and in one degree or another – to the ongoing event of our current life.[74] Even direct quotations can never be true repetitions of

---

[70] Bakhtin makes a strong case for even deeper dialogical (i.e., not binary or dialectic) simultaneity in such works as "Author and Hero in Aesthetic Activity," in *Art and Answerability* (ed. Michael Holquist and Vadim Liapunov; Austin: University of Texas Press, 1990), 4–256.

[71] This statement was included in the preface of the 1929 edition of Bakhtin's book on Dostoevsky. It may now be found in Appendix I of Mikhail Bakhtin, *Problems of Dostoevsky's Poetics* (ed. Caryl Emerson; Minneapolis: University of Minnesota Press, 1984), 276.

[72] See my quote of Bakhtin in the section on "The Present and Future of Rhetorical Analysis," in which Bakhtin claims that *every* "utterance" can be analogous to an "enthymeme."

[73] See Mikhail Bakhtin, "Author and Hero in Aesthetic Activity," 46.

[74] Mikhail Bakhtin, "Epic and Novel," in *Dialogic Imagination*, 30–31.

the "original"; the historical and cultural circumstances, as well as the time of the event itself, create a new situation and new connotations. The sophisticated rhetorical analysis within the various textures of texts thus enables socio-rhetorical interpretation to escape many of the philosophical limitations of reader-response theory and allows it to stress the specific relation between creator and contemplators – the complex correlation between texts and contexts, between the alleged "original" context and the contexts that are created as the texts are being read and reread.

Chapter 7, "Writing as a Rhetorical Act in Plutarch and the Gospels," demonstrates the type of advances that socio-rhetorical interpretation can make through its social and rhetorical readings of comparative texts, specifically, in this instance, the fundamental importance of the ancient rhetorical treatises entitled *progymnasmata* for the study of the synoptic gospels.[75]

It is fitting that this chapter originally appeared in a *Festschrift* for George Kennedy, because Kennedy had critiqued Robbins's *Jesus the Teacher* for its limited use of the "concepts and terminology of classical rhetoric as set out by Aristotle, Cicero, or Quintilian."[76] The book *Patterns of Persuasion*, as well as some of Robbins's other articles during this era, addressed this issue more directly, but it seems to me that more to the point are the extensive insights generated by Robbins's utilization of the chreia tradition and the progymnastic treatises. As this chapter makes abundantly clear, the stages of rhetorical composition in the gospels are closer to the progymnastic tradition than to any other rhetorical treatises. As Robbins notes, what he labels as *progymnastic composition* "bridges the gap" between the kind of rhetorical analysis performed by Kennedy and textual, source, form, and redaction criticisms (237).

The insights from this chapter, as well as Robbins's other early works utilizing the *progymnasmata*, shake the foundations of New Tes-

---

[75] "Writing as a Rhetorical Act in Plutarch and the Gospels," in *Persuasive Artistry: Studies in New Testament Rhetoric in Honor of George A. Kennedy* (ed. Duane F. Watson; JSNTSup 50; Sheffield: Sheffield Academic Press, 1991), 142–68. For a brief introduction to the chreia that highlights Robbins's work, see David B. Gowler, "The *Chreia*," in *The Historical Jesus in Context. Princeton Readings in Religions, Volume 12* (ed. John Dominic Crossan, Amy-Jill Levine, and Dale Allison, Jr.; Princeton: Princeton University Press, 2006), 132–148.

[76] Robbins had indeed made greater use of modern rhetoric, such as the works of Kenneth Burke. Kennedy admitted, however, that Robbins dealt "in his own way" with classical rhetoric's emphases on invention, arrangement, and style. See Kennedy's review of *Jesus the Teacher* in *Rhetorica* 4, no. 1 (1986): 67–72. Robbins will still insist, however, that we must utilize the "new rhetoric," which is "reinvented rhetoric."

tament scholarship.[77] This seismic shift is delineated in the very first section, where Robbins notes the significant developments in our understanding of these ancient texts as interpreted via the primary lens of textual criticism to source criticism to form criticism to redaction criticism to (finally) the issue of the relation of oral to written speech. Robbins insists that a correct understanding of this issue must incorporate the existence of a "rhetorical culture" in Mediterranean antiquity.

Utilizing Stanley F. Bonner's, *Education in Ancient Rome*,[78] Robbins observes the crucial differences between oral culture, scribal culture, rhetorical culture, and print culture. New Testament documents were produced in a culture characterized by interaction among the first three types of culture, and the term *rhetorical culture* designates an environment where oral and written speech interact closely with one another.[79]

Evidence for this rhetorical culture may be discovered, for example, in the preliminary rhetorical exercises found in *progymnasmata*. The exercises in these ancient rhetorical treatises represent widespread educational practices going back to early first century BCE. As I have noted elsewhere:

> The "rhetorical culture" which produced the New Testament was an environment where oral and written speech interact very closely with each other. Writing and rewriting brief literary units were preparatory

---

[77] I am, of course, thinking primarily of the form critical assumptions of such scholars as Dibelius, Bultmann, and Taylor, as well as later redaction critics such as Bornkamm, Conzelmann, and Marxsen. The seeds that are germinated in Robbins's insights in this chapter were initially planted during his stint with the Chreia Project at the Institute for Antiquity and Christianity at Claremont in the spring of 1982. For further reading, see Robbins's chapter, "Chreia and Pronouncement Story in Synoptic Studies," in Burton L. Mack and Vernon K. Robbins, *Patterns of Persuasion in the Gospels* (Sonoma, Calif.: Polebridge, 1989; Eugene, Ore.: Wipf & Stock, 2008), 1–29. See also his "The Chreia" in *Greco-Roman Literature and the New Testament* (ed. David E. Aune; Atlanta: Scholars Press, 1988), 1–23; as well as his "Pronouncement Stories and Jesus' Blessing of Children: A Rhetorical Approach," in *New Boundaries*, 155–84; and "Progymnastic Composition and Pre-Gospel Traditions: A New Approach," in *The Synoptic Gospels: Source Criticism and the New Literary Criticism* (ed. Camille Focant; Leuven: Leuven University Press, 1993), 111–47.

The last essay mentioned above, "Pronouncement Stories and Jesus Blessing of Children," is intimately connected to this "Writing as a Rhetorical Act" essay. Robbins argues that the transmission of speech attributed to Jesus could be analyzed as moderately expanded chreiai and correctly stresses the necessity for interpreters to scrutinize not only the internal rhetoric of individual pericopes, but also their rhetorical functions in the larger narrative.

[78] Stanley F. Bonner, *Education in Ancient Rome* (Berkeley: University of California Press, 1977).

[79] This culture exhibited a spectrum within five types of writing: (a) scribal reproduction; (b) progymnastic composition; (c) narrative composition; (d) discursive composition; and (e) poetic composition.

exercises for adapting a unit for a larger rhetorical/literary persuasive setting. Theon's exercises, for example, prepared students to use chreiai rhetorically within extended prose composition. These exercises also greatly influenced the oral skills of argumentation, since students were required to express them orally as well.[80]

Robbins builds a convincing case concerning "recitation composition" through his comparative study of Plutarch's three versions of Lysander's use of his sword in a discussion of territorial boundaries with Jesus' healing of Peter's mother-in-law in Matt 8:14–15, Mark 1:29–31, and Luke 4:38–39. The literary-historical paradigm, such as Crossan's distinctions between "performancial" and "hermeneutical" variations, needs to be corrected by an understanding of how the dynamics of rhetorical culture invade the act of writing itself. In addition, the search for "sources" becomes less relevant once we understand this process, as well as the fact that "whoever used whom as a source" has exercised (progymnastic) freedom in varying the wording.

Robbins then carefully examines the modes of argumentation in progymnastic composition. Plutarch's three renditions of Alexander's refusal to compete in a footrace at Olympia (*Moralia* 179D, *Alexander* 4.10, and *Moralia* 331B)[81] and the synoptic accounts of the woman who touched Jesus' garment (Matt 9:20–22; Mark 5:24b–34; Luke 8:43–48) serve as examples.[82] In both cases, each account shares

---

[80] Gowler, "The Development of Socio-Rhetorical Criticism," 25. See also Ronald F. Hock and Edward N. O'Neill, *Chreia and Ancient Rhetoric: Classroom Exercises* (Leiden: Brill, 2002). The work of Werner Kelber, *The Oral and Written Gospel* (Philadelphia: Fortress Press, 1983); Robert Fowler, *Let the Reader Understand: Reader-Response Criticism and the Gospel of Mark* (Minneapolis: Fortress, 1991); Whitney Shiner, *Proclaiming the Gospel: First-Century Performance of Mark* (Harrisburg, Penn.: Trinity Press International, 2003); and others should be critiqued in this regard. Cf. T. M. Lenz, *Orality and Literacy in Hellenic Culture* (Carbondale, Ill.: Southern Illinois University Press, 1989).

Robbins makes a further advance in his essay, "Oral, Rhetorical, and Literary Cultures: A Response," *Semeia* 65 (1994): 75–91. In that essay, Robbins refines his taxonomy to include: oral culture, scribal culture, rhetorical culture, *reading culture*, literary culture, print culture, and *hypertext culture* (the terms in italics are the categories added since his 1991 article).

Robbins will make use of these insights in other chapters of this volume. See, for example, Chapter 8, "The Reversed Contextualization of Psalm 22 in the Markan Crucifixion." Bonner's *Education in Ancient Rome* is also foundational in generating these insights in that essay.

[81] Plutarch, *Lysander* 22.1; *Moralia* 190E, and *Moralia* 229C. Another example would be Plutarch's versions of the encounter between Alexander and Diogenes in *Moralia* 782A and *Alexander* 14:1–5.

[82] Compare this essay with Robbins's 1987 article, "The Woman Who Touched Jesus' Garment." This brief essay succinctly demonstrates the potential dividends that socio-rhetorical interpretation in the pre-*Tapestry* era could offer. The emerging themes, emphases, perspective, and approach begin to come together in this article. The use of "comparative texts" and a "social base for communication" in the first century in the

enough verbatim language to suggest some sort of interdependence, but they are the results of compositional acts that produce significantly different versions – they are results of composition at the "progymnastic rhetoric level." At this rhetorical level, people are free to vary the stories to bring clarity and persuasiveness to the arguments at hand.

An interesting aside in Robbins's study of the Matthean version of the story is that the logic of the syllogism has been changed into a multivalent form of reasoning that perpetuates Jewish heritage, in connection to Jesus, but which also engages cultural beliefs in Asklepios's ability to heal (253). Thus Robbins returns, in this essay, to the same insight that appears ubiquitously throughout his works during the 1970's, 1980's, and 1990's: The Synoptics are intercultural documents that merge biblical patterns with Hellenistic patterns and conventions. As always, Robbins challenges us to widen intertextual, social, and cultural boundaries to include the Mediterranean world in which early Christians lived in order to include customs, behaviors, and attitudes of people in Mediterranean society.[83]

This obliterating of conventional, ideological boundaries of historical-critical New Testament scholarship is especially evident in Chapter 8, "The Reversed Contextualization of Psalm 22 in the Markan Crucifixion."[84] This essay not only contains important insights concerning the Markan passion narrative and various comparative texts, but it also displays several critical methodological moves that demonstrate the progression of socio-rhetorical analysis from *Jesus the Teacher* to *Exploring the Texture of Texts*. It expands the boundaries of intertextuality in significant ways, including the boundaries of comparative texts. And, in my view, key elements of these advances are achieved partially through Robbins's increasing awareness and utilization of the dialogical insights of Mikhail Bakhtin.

The major task in this essay is the intertextual study of the Markan account of Jesus' crucifixion. Robbins begins by noting that language is

---

"social environment of the Hellenistic-Roman world" are key elements. Robbins also, as he does in this "Writing as a Rhetorical Act" essay, only scratches the surface of the social and cultural dynamics that he explores in such essays as "Rhetoric and Culture" or in the books *Tapestry* and *Exploring*.

[83] Vernon K. Robbins, "Using a Socio-Rhetorical Poetics to Develop a Unified Method," 313. In this light, the title of the first collection of Robbins's essays, *New Boundaries in Old Territory*, is quite apt.

[84] Originally published in *The Four Gospels 1992. Festschrift Frans Neirynck* (ed. F. van Segbroeck, et al.; 2 vols.; BETL 100; Leuven: Leuven University Press, 1992), 2:1161–83.

a social possession.[85] Because of the nature of language, many voices actually speak, on some level, "through any individual person's use of language" (258).[86] In addition, all texts are "rewritings" of previous texts and a reaction to current texts, where *texts* may be seen as a literary text or as a general "text of culture." Therefore, intertextual study should not merely be limited to "parallels" – similar and different phenomena considered to be directly influenced by each other in a causal or diachronic way. Instead, intertextuality should be expanded to include "cultural discourse," because the Markan text is an excellent example of a text that lived, in Bakhtin's words, "a real life ... in an environment of social heteroglossia."[87]

Robbins's study concludes that Psalm 22 plays a "generative role" in the Markan formulation of the crucifixion account, but that Mark also dialogues with a "cultural discourse" of a ritual mocking and abuse of a prisoner at an annual festival (e.g., the Persian Ritual at the Sacian Feast). Some historical-critical scholars might still react to this use of comparative texts with cries of "parallelomania."[88] In contrast, perhaps the conclusion reached by Raymond Brown is an apt one to cite here.[89] He notes that "earlier scholars" who had unearthed such "parallels" operated with a simplistic "comparative-religion bias" and assumed that these similarities proved that early Christians invented the Roman mockery of Jesus. Brown concludes, though, that "the parallels establish verisimilitude.... Readers in the 1st cent. could have comprehended the scene as an effective capsulizing not only of the issue that

---

[85] Cf. Bakhtin, *The Dialogic Imagination*, 259: "Discourse is a social phenomenon – social throughout its range and in each and every one of its aspects. Texts inherently reflect the social life of discourse...."

[86] Cf. Bakhtin, *The Dialogic Imagination*, 293–95. As Robbins and I explain elsewhere, echoing Bakhtin: "Speakers do not utilize pristine words – 'untainted' and straight out of a dictionary – but rather these words have already existed in the mouths of others and thus already partially belong to others – each word 'tastes' therefore of the contexts in which it has lived its socially-charged life in previous speakers' personal, cultural, social, and ideological contexts." See Vernon K. Robbins and David B. Gowler, "Introduction," in *Recruitment, Conquest, and Conflict: Strategies in Judaism, Early Christianity, and the Greco-Roman World* (ed. Peder Borgen, Vernon K. Robbins, and David B. Gowler; Emory Studies in Early Christianity 6; Atlanta: Scholars Press, 1998), 10.

[87] Bakhtin, *Dialogic Imagination*, 292.

[88] The term points, of course, to the classic essay by Samuel Sandmel, "Parallelomania," *JBL* 81 (1962): 1–13. Sandmel correctly decried the misuse of various "parallels," especially uninformed uses of the rabbinic "parallels" collected in H. Strack and P. Billerbeck, *Kommentar zum Neuen Testament aus Talmud und Midrasch* (6 vols.; Munich: Beck, 1924–1928).

[89] I am summarizing the conclusions that he reaches about the "Roman Mockery and Abuse of Jesus" in Raymond E. Brown, *The Death of the Messiah* (2 vols.; New York: Doubleday, 1994), 1:870–87.

interested the Romans (kingship), but also of the Gentile attitude toward a crucified king...."[90]

Brown's comments are an interesting starting point; a Bakhtinian approach to these comparative texts, such as the sophisticated one that Robbins takes here, can lead us even further in our understanding of these texts and their dialogic interrelations. For example, Robbins also takes the issue of kingship a step farther than Brown does. He notes that interpreters of the Markan discourse should hear "the many voices in Mediterranean culture that are engaged in dialogue about the nature of kingship and sonship."

In another paper on the Markan crucifixion narrative, Robbins noted the "cultural and social affinity" of the Markan crucifixion with the death of Eleazer in 4 Maccabees.[91] Both accounts follow a general "conventional pattern and mode." Robbins also pointed to Josephus's account of Simon bar Giora's death, as well as Dio Chrysostom's discussion of true kingship (Discourses 3 and 4). There are variations on this conventional pattern, of course, because the authors have different rhetorical agendas. Psalm 22 is a direct *literary* connection, but the ideological, ironic perception of kingship should lead interpreters to explore other cultural discourses. Robbins does not claim that Mark, in generic literary-historical fashion, copied a literary text, but he does contend that Mark's structuring of the scenes is a "written performance of a cultural tradition."[92]

This essay on Mark and Psalm 22 builds upon Robbins's earlier work, such as the analysis of repetitive and progressive forms as found in *Jesus the Teacher* (e.g., duality, three-step progression).[93] The essay also evokes, however, his steadfast journey toward the recognition of the "textures" that he delineates in *Tapestry* (with four textures) and

---

[90] Raymond Brown, *Death of the Messiah*, 877.

[91] Vernon K. Robbins, "Rhetorical Analysis of the Crucifixion in Mark" (paper presented at the annual meeting of the SBL, Anaheim, California, 18 November 1994).

[92] Robbins, *Jesus the Teacher*, xxvi; cf. Robbins, "Picking up the Fragments." Robbins thus avoids "parallelomania," which in Sandmel's words is "that extravagance among scholars which first overdoes the supposed similarities in passages and then proceeds to describe source and derivation as if implying literary connection in an inevitable or predetermined direction" ("Parallelomania," 1).

[93] These issues, of course, will be clarified in both *Tapestry* and *Exploring*. Robbins also in this essay presages the concern with opening-middle-closing patterns that will be found in those two later books. Robbins's increasing literary sensitivities are also evident, such as in his treatment of the three groups who react to Jesus in Mark 15:25–32, his comments about how readers are directed to Jesus as he dies (Mark 15:33–39), and his concern to delineate the workings of the Markan narrator. Ideological emphases (part of Robbins's recognition of an ideological texture) are present in this essay as well.

Exploring (with five textures). In this study, though, Robbins concentrates on inner texture and intertexture.

The inner textual study concentrates on the five scenes that constitute the Markan version of Jesus' crucifixion. The section of Robbins's intertextual study that focuses on the *generative role* that Psalm 22 plays in the Markan formulation of the narrative operates, for the most part, within the "accepted" ideological boundaries of traditional New Testament scholarship – that is, investigating the direct influence that the Hebrew Bible plays in the creation of the Gospels.[94] Yet he also expands those boundaries by noting the use of "progymnastic composition" in this section of Mark, such as the "recitation" in 15:24, the "expansion" in 15:25–32, and the "recontextualization" in 15:33–39.[95] This analysis illustrates a fascinating aspect of the Markan rhetoric, one to which I still refer whenever I teach the Gospel of Mark, specifically the way in which Mark 15 inverts the sequence of Psalm 22, subverts the Psalm's rhetoric, and presents a completely abandoned Jesus who no longer has any hope of rescue from the agony of his death (278).

The section of the intertextual study, though, that focuses on Dio Chrysostom's account of the Persians mocking a condemned prisoner at the Sacian feast expands those boundaries much further. This comparative text does not function, as does Psalm 22, in a *generative* role for Mark 15, but it does give evidence of a broader cultural discourse. As Robbins has demonstrated for over thirty years now, the Gospel of Mark merges biblical patterns with Hellenistic patterns and conventions – it is profoundly intercultural.[96]

Robbins again productively uses Bakhtin's work, but it can be taken to another, even more provocative, level. Bakhtin's sense of *carnivalization* can give additional insight into the cultural discourses that interact dialogically with the passion narrative in Mark. According to Bakhtin, the carnivalesque – which reaches maturity in the work of Rabelais in the Late Renaissance – was foreshadowed by the Socratic dialogues

---

[94] As I have noted elsewhere ("Socio-Rhetorical Criticism," 33), many New Testament scholars are unwilling – for theological reasons or because of their unfamiliarity with the material – to admit that the Gospels contain appreciable amounts of Greco-Roman social and rhetorical patterns. As we should now realize, Hellenistic culture influenced all "Diaspora Judaism" and "Palestinian Judaism" to a certain albeit varying extent. For a somewhat ironic example of this tendency toward denial, see Martin Hengel, *The Son of God: The Origin of Christology and the History of Jewish-Hellenistic Religion* (Philadelphia: Fortress, 1976).

[95] For a more full discussion of these types of composition, see the "Intertexture" chapter in Robbins's *Exploring*, 40–70.

[96] A conclusion for which almost every chapter in *New Boundaries* gives evidence.

and the Menippean satire of the ancient world.[97] Bakhtin argues that the Menippean satire in particular exercised "a very great influence" on Christian literature "of the ancient period" and on Byzantine literature and had a "transforming power to penetrate other genres ... [including] ancient Christian literature."[98]

The primary carnivalistic act, according to Bakhtin, is the "mock crowning and subsequent decrowning of the carnival king," one that signifies, among other things, "death and renewal," and includes both ridicule and physical beatings.[99] Since, as Bakhtin notes, the one who is crowned is the "antipode of a real king," the "ironic dimensions" of the narrative that Robbins mentions – that Jesus is mocked as the King of the Jews but is indeed the Son of God – are heightened even further (271).

Therefore, I would argue that the next step in understanding this Markan passage better would be to incorporate the intertextual insights of Robbins in this chapter, the applicable aspects of Bakhtin's *carnivalesque*, and additional historical information, such as Raymond Brown gives in his *The Death of the Messiah* about (a) historical incidents, (b) games of mockery, (c) theatrical mimes, and (d) carnival festivals, such as the Sacian feast, the Saturnalia, and the Kronia.[100] Only then can we gain a more complete appreciation of the dialogic nature of this text, and socio-rhetorical interpretation provides the interdisciplinary modes of analysis that can best generate these additional insights.

Chapter 9, "Socio-Rhetorical Criticism: Mary, Elizabeth and the Magnificat as a Test Case," is one of the first places where the "textures" later delineated in *Exploring* and *Tapestry* are set forward in a programmatic way.[101] Robbins begins by setting forth part of the philo-

---

[97] *Socratic dialogues* include not only the ones written by Plato, but the ones also by Xenophon (the only other fully extant), Antisthenes, Aeschines, Phaedo, Euclid, Alexamenos, Glaucon, Simias, Crito, and others. See Bakhtin, *Problems of Dostoevsky's Poetics*.

[98] Bakhtin, *Problems of Dostoevsky's Poetics*, 113, 121. Bakhtin also notes, however, that "Christian narrative literature (independently of the influence of carnivalized menippea) was also subjected to direct carnivalization" (135). Here Bakhtin also notes the crowning and decrowning of the "King of the Jews" in the canonical Gospels (135). Robbins's insights about the role of the elite in such "decrownings" can be seen as a needed corrective to Bakhtin's sometimes overoptimistic, sometimes sentimental view of the *carnivalesque*.

[99] Bakhtin, *Problems of Dostoevsky's Poetics*, 124–25.

[100] Brown, *The Death of the Messiah*, 871–77.

[101] Originally published as "Socio-Rhetorical Criticism: Mary, Elizabeth and the Magnificat as a Test Case," in *The New Literary Criticism and the New Testament* (ed. E.S. Malbon and E.V. McKnight; Sheffield: Sheffield Academic Press, 1994), 164–209. Robbins notes that this essay was "his first programmatic multi-textural study" ("Beginnings and Developments in Socio-Rhetorical Interpretation"). The other two, earlier essays that

sophical approach and part of the context out of which socio-rhetorical criticism emerged.[102] The approach is appropriately dialogic, in that it invites social, cultural, historical, psychological, aesthetic, ideological, and theological information and approaches into a dialogue with "minute exegetical activity"; socio-rhetorical critics approach a text much like an anthropologist "reads" a village and its culture.[103]

Thus Robbins appropriately critiques the "restrained rhetoric" of – "most," in his view – literary critics, who reduce rhetoric to four master tropes – metaphor, metonymy, syndoche, and irony.[104] Robbins, as noted above, believes that rhetoric is the "first among equals" and must be the foundational means of approaching these texts. I would slightly demur, first noting that those rhetorical critics who only use the forms of classical rhetoric also have a "restrained rhetoric" (a proposition to which Robbins agrees; see "Rhetoric and Culture," for example), and then observing that there are forms of literary criticism (i.e., the Dialogism of certain Bakhtinians) that also offer more comprehensive approaches to these texts. The advantage of socio-rhetorical interpretation, however, is that it offers a programmatic and comprehensive interdisciplinary mode of interpretation.

The rest of the essay is not so much an exegesis of the Magnificat as it is a demonstration of the four textures[105] The section of the essay on "inner texture," for example, delineates many of the items later found in *Exploring*, such as repetitive, progressive, and narrational textures and

---

inaugurated the "four textures" were the "Introduction" to the paperback edition of *Jesus the Teacher* and "Using a Socio-Rhetorical Poetics to Develop a Unified Method," 302–19. For a graph of the entire textural mode of interpretation, see http://www.religion.emory.edu/faculty/robbins/SRI/defns/index.

Since 1999, Robbins has begun to distinguish between narrative descriptive ("rhetography") and argumentative-enthymematic elaboration ("rhetology"). See, for example, Vernon K. Robbins, "The Intertexture of Apocalyptic Discourse in the Gospel of Mark," in *The Intertexture of Apocalyptic Discourse in the New Testament* (ed. Duane F. Watson; Atlanta: Scholars Press/Leiden: Brill, 2002), 11–44; idem, "Rhetography: A New Way of Seeing the Familiar Text," in *Words Well Spoken: George Kennedy's Rhetoric of the New Testament* (ed. C.C. Black and D.F. Watson; Studies in Rhetoric and Religion 8; Waco: Baylor University Press, 2008) 81-106.

[102] This essay gives a helpful, concise summary of the works of scholars that helped to generate the "texture" stage of Robbins's socio-rhetorical criticism, such as Clifford Geertz, Amos Wilder, Wayne A. Meeks, Jonathan Z. Smith, Helmut Koester, James M. Robinson, Wilhelm Wuellner, Robert Tannehill, John Gager, John H. Elliott, Bruce J. Malina, Philip Esler, Kenneth Burke, Elisabeth Schüssler Fiorenza, and Burton L. Mack.

[103] Robbins is dependent here on the groundbreaking work of Clifford Geertz. For another introduction to these connections, see *New Boundaries*, 2–6.

[104] See Brian Vickers, *In Defence of Rhetoric* (Oxford: Clarendon, 1982).

[105] A fifth texture, "sacred texture," was added in *Exploring*, 120–31. It is my own view, however, that sacred texture is not a separate texture; it is a subset of ideological texture.

patterns.[106] The section on "intertexture" introduces readers to such intertextual comparisons as recitation, recontextualization, and reconfiguration.[107] Even here, though, Robbins's analysis is expanding boundaries and exploring new alternatives in dialogue with numerous other scholars and readings. Robbins appropriately includes in his intertextual repertoire not only the "long tradition of barren Israelite women" who finally conceive and bear a son – a topic well within the established boundaries of "scientific" (i.e., "acceptable") New Testament scholarship – but he also includes the various stories in the Septuagint about virgins being "humiliated" by men (e.g., Deut 22:23–24), as well as in the rest of the Mediterranean world about virgins who are overpowered and impregnated by gods. The "humiliation" of Mary must also be seen in light of these other, less "safe" comparative texts.

Robbins's analysis of the "social and cultural texture" also foreshadows the more comprehensive treatment in *Exploring*,[108] with the utilization of Bryan Wilson's investigation of the seven types of religious sects.[109] The other analysis in this section is what Robbins later calls "final cultural categories,"[110] the ones introduced in Chapter 4 above ("Rhetoric and Culture"): dominant culture, subculture, counterculture, contraculture, and liminal culture rhetorics. Mary's discourse, Robbins argues, is *reformist*; the emphasis is on changing the people in power. Yet this discourse shows no desire to eliminate the hierarchal power structures; the Magnificat instead puts forward the idea that those who hold positions of power should embody the thaumaturgical and conversionist powers of God.

This study of the social and cultural texture not only builds on the analyses of the inner texture and intertexture, but it also prepares the way for the powerful conclusions about the ideological texture that Robbins reaches.[111] This analysis also further develops the arguments that Robbins put forth in his "Social Location" essay and his "Mixed Population" essay (see above). As I have argued elsewhere, Luke-Acts is an amazing manifesto that is more subversive and aggressive than it

---

[106] See *Exploring*, 7–39.

[107] See *Exploring*, 40–70. Robbins, of course, makes numerous advances, additions, and refinements in *Exploring* that are not found in this essay.

[108] *Exploring*, 71–94.

[109] As noted above, they are: conversionist, revolutionist, introversionist, gnostic-manipulationist, thaumaturgical, reformist, and utopian. See Wilson, *Magic and the Millennium*, 22–26.

[110] *Exploring*, 86–88.

[111] An introduction to ideological texture may be found in *Exploring*, 95–119. Significant expansions and some corrections of Robbins's approach to ideological texture may be found in the various chapters of *Fabrics of Discourse* noted above (chapters by Combrink, Kloppenborg, Gowler, Bloomquist, Wanamaker, and Sisson).

may first appear.[112] In this essay, though, Robbins sets forth the case much more clearly than before. Mary's "shameful" position, pregnancy outside of marriage, actually will bring her honor, so she accepts it as an obedient client to a powerful patron. In this way, the narrator thus claims that Christians are specially favored as clients of God their patron. God's activity presupposes and advances these patriarchal, hierarchical structures but inverts (reforms) certain conditions within that structure. Christianity, as seen in Luke-Acts, is an ethnic subculture that actually fulfills the highest claims of dominant Roman government – (salvation and peace) – claims that, I would argue, the Lukan narrator contends the Roman imperial system cannot truly provide its people.[113]

Robbins then raises an even more pointed and specific ideological question: What about Mary's perspective? She claims that she has been afflicted and dishonored. Here is where Robbins gives a specific example of his attempts to hear the voices of the silenced, as he notes in one of my favorite quotes from him: "Should I pretend that I do not hear the voices and see the plights of the 'little people' who cry out in biblical texts... ? Just what are some of us white male Protestants supposed to do when we hear the voices, sight the boundaries and see both the plights of the people on the margins and the flaws of people at the center of the New Testament texts we read?"[114] In the past, male interpreters regularly celebrated Mary's speech as "liberating" for her and for others who are poor in social, political, or economic status. Yet Robbins, utilizing Victor Turner, notes that such rituals of reversal by those of lower status actually support and reaffirm the hierarchical system that is in place. People of higher status, then, if they are wise, permit and even encourage those persons of lower status to speak out, to enact their frustrations, and to announce such expectations of reversal. The enactment of reversal, contrary to first impressions, strengthens the ideology of hierarchy that is in place.

Here, as noted above, Robbins could have made use of, and indeed provided an important corrective to, Bakhtin's work on *carnival*. Robbins does, though, conclude with careful observations on the importance of *heteroglossia* (321). He also notes, although he doesn't use the Bakhtinian term "monologic," how the narrator's voice refigures the voice of Mary in the Gospel of Luke. Robbins concludes by saying, "[Mary] tries to speak, and it may be possible to recover a voice that

---

[112] See, for example, "Text, Culture, and Ideology in Luke 7:1-1-10," 119–25.

[113] For an introduction to the claims of "Roman imperial theology," see Warren Carter, *Matthew and Empire: Initial Explorations* (Harrisburg, Penn.: Trinity, 2001), 1–53, and idem, *The Roman Empire and the New Testament: An Essential Guide* (Nashville: Abingdon Press, 2006).

[114] Robbins, *Tapestry*, 25, 26.

has been trying desperately to speak but cannot because it is continually drowned out by men's voices, my own included" (322).

The essay found in Chapter 10, "The Present and Future of Rhetorical Analysis," strikes a number of themes echoed in *Exploring*, *Tapestry*, and other essays in this volume, but it also marks the place where Robbins introduces a new vision of the importance of enthymemes to socio-rhetorical analysis.[115] This focus on enthymemes became more prominent not only in this essay but also in Robbins's essays on wisdom discourse in the Gospel of Thomas and Q.[116]

This essay picks up where the previous essay left off: the critical importance of ethics in reading, interpreting, and responding to these texts. This concern with an ethical reading should not be surprising, because Robbins has made this case very clearly in a number of his writings, perhaps most notably in the personal and moving appeal in *Tapestry*.[117] For Robbins, "we are participants in an exciting time that calls for responsible action" (323). The (ab)use of rhetoric is critical in this regard, because people's use of words plays a central role in who benefits from their knowledge and abilities, as well as who is put at a disadvantage.[118]

The basic thesis of this essay is that an ethical and pragmatic response to the current situation in biblical studies and the world in which we live demands that rhetorical criticism move "beyond the traditional

---

[115] Vernon K. Robbins, "The Present and Future of Rhetorical Analysis," in *The Rhetorical Analysis of Scripture: Essays from the 1995 London Conference* (ed. Stanley E. Porter and Thomas H. Olbricht; Sheffield: Sheffield Academic Press, 1997), 24–52.

[116] Vernon K. Robbins, "Rhetorical Composition and Sources in the Gospel of Thomas," *SBL Seminar Papers, 1997* (SBLSP 36; Atlanta: Scholars, 1997), 86–114; idem, "Enthymematic Texture in the Gospel of Thomas," *SBL Seminar Papers, 1998* (SBLSP 37; Atlanta: Scholars, 1998), 343–66; idem, "Enthymeme and Picture in the Gospel of Thomas," in *Thomasine Traditions in Antiquity: The Social and Cultural World of the Gospel of Thomas* (ed. Jon Ma. Asgeirsson, April D. DeConick, and Risto Uro; Nag Hammadi and Manichaean Studies 59; Leiden: Brill, 2006) 175-207.

[117] Robbins, *Tapestry*, 24–27.

[118] I write this section of the essay as a truly Orwellian time in the United States finally comes to an end after eight long years of continual disinformation from the previous resident of the White House. As I said in a convocation address at Oxford College of Emory University on August 29, 2007: "No matter what we hear from some people, especially during the current presidential campaign, the real drain on our society are not undocumented workers, or flag burning, or the money we spend on the social safety nets of welfare, medicare, or social security. The real drain on society, the real danger to the fabric of our society, are those people who use their knowledge and their positions of power unethically, to abuse other human beings, wage preemptive wars, or manipulate the political system to enrich themselves or to gain more political power at the expense of others or our natural environment."

interplay of method and theory into the mode of a comprehensive interpretive analytics" (324). Rhetorical criticism as *method* had focused primarily on the speech-text rather than the speaker-author or the audience-reader. Robbins recognizes, as I argued above, that rhetorical critics who utilize this "traditional mode" of rhetorical analysis and interpretation also, in a way similar to some literary critics, operate in a mode of "restrained rhetoric." Here Robbins makes a significant move by declaring that rhetorical criticism must analyze and interpret the author, audience, and interpreter with "revalued and reinvented categories currently available to rhetorical criticism from modern communication theory, the social sciences, and postmodern theory and interpretation" (326). Robbins argues that only through this approach can we engage the past, present, and future of speaker-authors, speech-texts, and hearer-readers in order to reconstrue the political and ethical issues that lie in our own past, present, and future. From a Bakhtinian perspective, this approach is another way of recognizing *simultaneity*. Literary texts are *utterances*, words that cannot be divorced from particular subjects in specific situations. They depend not only on the speaker-author, but also on their "place," the social and historical forces at work when the text was produced and when it is heard-read. It is a dialogic exchange taking place on many different levels at the same time (i.e., simultaneity).[119] So this essay is Robbins's proposal to reinvent rhetorical criticism as an interpretive analytics, one that, to its credit, also includes the analysis and interpretation of "commentary discourse."[120]

Robbins begins by summarizing the (now) five textures before moving on to revaluing the modes of biblical discourse. He recommends several steps toward the "reinvention of rhetorical criticism as an interpretive analytics":

Assertions and Rationales: Once rhetorical critics know all the assertions that are supported by rationales – the components of the rhetorical enthymeme – they are on the "doorstep of serious cultural analysis of early Christianity" (as revealed by the extant Christian texts). Here, once again, Robbins makes a Bakhtinian move, although he does not cite Bakhtin as an inspiration here. Bakhtin had declared that any utterance could be compared to an "enthymeme," because "the situation

---

[119] See Michael Holquist, *Dialogism: Bakhtin and His World* (London: Routledge, 1990), 68.

[120] Robbins gives helpful examples of this analysis of commentary discourse towards the end of this essay, where he treats the works of Robert Tannehill, Hans Dieter Betz, Elisabeth Schüssler Fiorenza, Elizabeth Castelli, and David Jasper. In my view, commentary discourse is made even more complex by attempting to negotiate the centrifugal tendencies of historical analysis and the centripetal tendencies of theological interpretation.

enters into the utterance as a necessary constitutive element of its semantic structure. The quotidian utterance endowed with signification is therefore composed of two parts: (1) a realized or actualized verbal part, and (2) an implied part. That is why an utterance can be compared to an 'enthymeme.'"[121] Bakhtin, of course, critiqued Formalism, because Formalists incorrectly tried to isolate works of art from their social occurrences. The distinguishing feature in everyday discourse, Bakhtin argued, is its relative dependence on immediate context.[122] Bakhtin used the enthymeme as a rhetorical example of the same kind of simultaneity between what is expressed and what is unexpressed but at the same time necessary to the meaning of what is articulated.[123] Any utterance, in Bakhtin's view, is always a combination of what is actually verbalized and what is nonverbalized but assumed by both the speaker and addressee (another form of simultaneity).[124]

Social and Cultural Analysis of Assertions and Rationales: Here is where rhetorical critics need to reconstruct the unexpressed premises of the enthymemes. The social and cultural nature of the reasoning is a "gateway" into early Christianity as a social and cultural movement in the first century.

Chreia Analysis of Assertions and Rationales: The next step is to identify the "personage" to whom the enthymeme is attributed.[125] As Robbins notes elsewhere, the content of a chreia is a "well-aimed or apt statement or action attributed to a particular person." The emphasis on a particular person gave the chreia a "special place in the transmission of Hellenic-Roman heritage."[126] In this essay, Robbins asserts that the logic of the assertion can give the "logic of a particular cultural group."

Rhetorical Elaboration: The type of elaboration, Robbins claims, can give valuable evidence as to the "cultural discourse" of people and

---

[121] Voloshinov/Bakhtin, "Discourse in Life and Discourse in Poetry," as quoted by Tzvetan Todorov, *Mikhail Bakhtin: The Dialogical Principle*, 41.

[122] Bakhtin illustrated this with a Russian parable about two people sitting in a room. They are both silent until one of them says, "Well!" The other does not respond. As "outsiders" that utterance is incomprehensible to us. We lack the "extraverbal" context that made the word "well" meaningful to the people in the parable, their common spatial purview, knowledge and understanding of the situation, and their common evaluation of that situation. Noted by Katerina Clark and Michael Holquist, *Mikhail Bakhtin* (Cambridge, Mass.: The Belkap, 1984), 203.

[123] Clark and Holquist, *Mikhail Bakhtin*, 205. They go on to say that "We literally enact cultural values in our speech...."

[124] Clark and Holquist, *Mikhail Bakhtin*, 207.

[125] This insistence, as is clear above, is congruous with Robbins's critique of Crossan's *In Fragments*.

[126] Robbins, "The Chreia," 2–3.

groups.[127] For example, since a contracultural group presupposes the resources of a dominant culture, they give very few reasons for their own views and behaviors.

Jewish and Greco-Roman Modes of Argumentation: This step assumes that the New Testament merges Jewish and Hellenistic-Roman modes of understanding, action, and argumentation, all of which contributed to Christianity's growth in Mediterranean society and culture. This step also serves as an invitation to specialists in other areas – Hebrew Bible, apocrypha, and rabbinic literature[128] – for the purpose of "delineating and displaying the interplay of dominant, subcultural, countercultural, contracultural, and liminal Jewish and Greco-Roman argumentation in New Testament discourse."

Reinventing the Decades of First-Century Christianity: Robbins appropriately criticizes how most New Testament scholars have used the Acts of the Apostles – a "highly ideologically-driven narrative that appeared at the end of the first century" – to provide the basic framework for how scholars perceive the emergence of early Christianity. If scholars instead perform serious rhetorical analysis of these different cultures of discourse, they find significantly different *topoi* with significantly different modes of argumentation (which therefore imply more diversity and a different "story" of emergence). I should add that Robbins himself provides an extremely brief preview in *Tapestry* of how scholars can use rhetorical criticism as an "interpretive analytics" and use multiple modes of discourse to interpret New Testament texts.[129]

Reconfiguring the Discourse of Commentary: The final section of this essay focuses on the critical nature of how one's ideology influences, indeed limits, one's approach to and commentary on New Testament texts.[130] Robbins concludes that rhetorical critics need to analyze com-

---

[127] He delineates three types in this essay: expansion, Theonian elaboration, and Hermogenian elaboration.

[128] In light of Robbins's recent work, I'm sure that he would currently include the Qur'an in these dialogues. See, for example, Vernon K. Robbins and Gordon D. Newby, "A Prolegomenon to the Relation of the Qur'an and the Bible," *Bible and Qur'an: Essays in Scriptural Intertextuality* (ed. John C. Reeves; SBL Symposium Series; Atlanta: Society of Biblical Literature, 2003), 23-42; Vernon K. Robbins, "Lukan and Johannine Tradition in the Qur'an: A Story of *Auslegungsgeschichte* and *Wirkungsgeschichte*," in *Moving Beyond New Testament Theology? Essays in Conversation with Heikki Räisänen* (ed. T. Penner and C. van der Stichele; Publications of the Finnish Exegetical Society 88; Helsinki: Finnish Exegetical Society and Göttingen: Vandenhoeck & Ruprecht, 2005), 336-68.

[129] Robbins, *Tapestry*, 240–44. See also, "Making Christian Culture in the Epistle of James."

[130] Robbins appropriately critiques Elisabeth Schüssler Fiorenza's (and Elizabeth Castelli's) commentary on 1 Corinthians. He noted that in Fiorenza's criticism of Paul's authoritative, hierarchical rhetoric, she actually re-enacts the same type of authoritative, hierarchical rhetoric by adopting her own "powerful, authoritative rhetorical mode of discourse." This observation helped to lead to the dialogue between Fiorenza and Rob-

mentary discourse with the same range of methods and approaches with which they analyze and interpret New Testament texts themselves. He also makes a more significant decision, one in which he is joined by a number of other socio-rhetorical interpreters, that a new type of commentary is needed. That is why a number of scholars, under the leadership of Vernon Robbins and Duane Watson, are currently working to generate a series of socio-rhetorical commentaries, the "Rhetoric of Religious Antiquity" series.[131] This series of commentaries should serve to transform the way in which we write and read commentaries.

Chapter 11, "From Enthymeme to Theology in Luke 11:1–13," builds upon the insights of the previous essay, "The Present and Future of Rhetorical Analysis."[132] In this essay, Robbins provides a concrete, interdisciplinary answer to his call for enthymematic analyses of specific New Testament texts. He uses Luke 11:1–13 as a test case to demonstrate his arguments. This essay, in addition to making a significant step forward in rhetorical analysis and providing an example for what a socio-rhetorical commentary might look like,[133] also returns, in part, to

---

bins about the nature of socio-rhetorical analysis. See, for example, Vernon K. Robbins, "The Rhetorical Full-Turn in Biblical Interpretation: Reconfiguring Rhetorical-Political Power," in *Rhetorical Criticism and the Bible: Essays from the 1998 Florence Conference* (ed. Stanley E. Porter and Thomas H. Olbricht; Sheffield: Sheffield Academic Press, 2002), 48–60; and Elisabeth Schüssler Fiorenza, "Challenging the Rhetorical Half-Turn: Feminist and Rhetorical Biblical Criticism," in *Rhetoric, Scripture, and Theology: Essays from the 1994 Pretoria Conference* (ed. Stanley E. Porter and Thomas H. Olbricht; Sheffield: Sheffield Academic Press, 1996), 28–53. A history of this discussion may be found in Robbins's substantially reconfigured version of his original essay, "The Rhetorical Full-Turn in Biblical Interpretation and Its Relevance for Feminist Hermeneutics." In this revised essay, Robbins locates socio-rhetorical interpretation in "transmodernism." Robbins also discusses the six major rhetorolects that interweave in early Christian discourse in this context. This essay is critical for understanding some of the philosophical foundations of a socio-rhetorical approach to texts, to interpretation, and to the work of other scholars.

[131] See the website http://www.deopublishing.com/rhetoricofreligiousantiquity.htm for more details. For initial views of what form a socio-rhetorical commentary might take, see H.J. Combrink, "The Challenges and Opportunities of a Socio-Rhetorical Commentary," *Scriptura* 79 (2002): 106–21, and Duane F. Watson, "Why We Need Socio-Rhetorical Commentary and What Might It Look Like," in *Rhetorical Criticism and the Bible* (ed. S.E. Porter and D.L. Stamps; JSNTSup 195; Sheffield: Sheffield Academic Press, 2002), 129–57. The first volume of the series is Vernon K. Robbins, *The Invention of Christian Discourse. Volume 1* (Blandford Forum, UK: Deo Publishing, 2009).

[132] Vernon K. Robbins, "From Enthymeme to Theology in Luke 11:1–13," in *Literary Studies in Luke-Acts: A Collection of Essays in Honor of Joseph B. Tyson* (ed. Thomas E. Phillips and Richard Thompson; Macon, Ga.: Mercer University Press), 191–214.

[133] See also Combrink, "Socio-Rhetorical Commentary," and Watson, "Why We Need Socio-Rhetorical Commentary."

another tendril of Robbins's early roots: an interest in theology.[134] The integration of aspects of theology – albeit from a much different starting and therefore along new and exciting vantage points – are clearly seen in this article, as well as in such items as Robbins's addition of a fifth "texture": *sacred texture* in his *Exploring*.

Many of the arguments about the enthymeme that Robbins puts forth in this essay are once again reminiscent of a Bakhtinian approach, such as his observation that "[e]very text somehow enacts the social, cultural, and ideological context in which it was written. A reader who stands outside that context uses that enacted context as a medium for another context." Robbins then develops this understanding in a way similar to how literary critics had explored numerous literary patterns in Luke, such as through repetitions and developments in words, type-scenes, themes, characters, and so forth.[135] He argues that Luke creates an "enthymematic network" that evokes social, cultural, ideological, and theological enthymemes from outside Luke. This network is created by similar premises, both articulated and unarticulated, expressed in a number of places throughout Luke. Early Christians intertwined conventional premises and conclusions in an unconventional manner or with new insights in order to explain their way of life and to create new social, cultural, ideological, and theological patterns. Thus the rhetorical reasoning that creates these networks is not only critical to understanding the text more fully but also to understanding the distinctive identity of early Christians (as demonstrated by their commitment to this network of reasoning). Luke 11:1–4, for example, participates in a cultural and enthymematic network of reasoning about forgiving others and about petitioning God to forgive oneself and others.

Robbins incorporates his previous work on chreia elaboration with new insights into abductive reasoning – a reasoning that works with suggestion rather than formal logic. Here Robbins utilizes Richard Lanigan's groundbreaking insights on the rhetorical enthymeme. Lanigan demonstrates that enthymemes not only can be deductive (as is

---

[134] See, for example, the emphasis on theology and Christology in four of Robbins's early writings (from 1973 to 1980) that are now found in *New Boundaries*: "The Healing of Blind Bartimaeus in the Markan Theology" (37–57), "Δυνάμις and Σημεῖα in Mark" (59–72), "Last Meal: Preparation, Betrayal, and Absence (Mark 14:12–25)" (73–89), and "Mark as Genre" (81–117). In contrast, the last six chapters of that book (essays written by Robbins from 1982 to 1990) never – with four exceptions – mention either theology or christology. Robbins now, however, is beginning to recognize more and more the theological implications of socio-rhetorical interpretation.

[135] An early, somewhat Formalist approach can be found in Robert C. Tannehill, *The Narrative Unity of Luke-Acts: A Literary Interpretation* (vol. 1; Philadelphia: Fortress, 1986). A later, more developed approach, one that integrates social, cultural, and literary approaches, can be found in my *Host, Guest, Enemy, and Friend*.

commonly assumed) but also can use inductive and abductive reasoning.[136] Other scholars, who ignore Lanigan's work or approach these religious texts with the presuppositions of philosophical syllogistic analysis rather than religious rhetorical rhetoric, have erroneously critiqued Robbins's work in this regard. David Aune, for example, asserts that "Enthymemes, like syllogisms, are *always deductive*." Yet, on the very next page, Aune admits that abductive reasoning is "a formalized version of a common form of thought which reflects the way in which people make choices in daily living."[137] That is Robbins's point exactly, except Robbins (utilizing Lanigan) sees that both inductive and abductive reasoning can be enthymematic in religious rhetoric.[138] The enthymeme in Luke 11:5–7, for example, intertwines conventions of hospitality and friendship (including a similarity to the argument from analogy in Hermogenean elaboration)[139] but gives them a new twist: One's relation to God is implicated in one's relation to the needs of other people. This reasoning, Robbins argues, creates an enthymematic network that extends into other sections of the Gospel of Luke. The way that its enthymematic reasoning utilizes rhetorical elaboration and (re)configures social, cultural, and ideological topics moves this argumentation into topics that inhabit the sacred texture of Luke and which create a new theological and Christological world for its readers/hearers.[140]

---

[136] Richard L. Lanigan, "From Enthymeme to Abduction: The Classical Law of Logic and the Postmodern Rule of Rhetoric," in *Recovering Pragmatism's Voice: The Classical Tradition, Rorty, and the Philosophy of Communication* (ed. L. Langsdorf and A. R. Smith; Albany, N.Y.: SUNY Press, 1995), 49–70.

[137] David E. Aune, "Use and Abuse of the Enthymeme in New Testament Scholarship," NTS 49 (2003): 315–16. See a similar critique in Arthur Gibson, "Relations between Rhetoric and Philosophical Logic," in *Rhetorical Criticism and the Bible* (ed. S.E. Porter and D.L. Stamps; JSNTSup 195; Sheffield: Sheffield Academic Press, 2002), 97–128. See also Robbins's partial response in his "Beginnings and Developments in Socio-Rhetorical Interpretation."

[138] This rhetorical approach also can correct other misunderstandings of the text, such as Bernard Brandon Scott's misreading of *shamelessness* as an attribute of the sleeping friend in Luke 11:5–8. See Bernard Brandon Scott, *Hear Then the Parable: A Commentary on the Parables of Jesus* (Minneapolis: Fortress Press, 1989), 189.

[139] Robbins also discovers numerous similarities and intriguing differences from Hermogenes's elaboration of the chreia.

[140] As noted above, two additional essays, ones not found in this volume, are foundational to Robbins's construction of this approach to the inner relationship of enthymematic logia. First, Robbins's "Rhetorical Composition and Sources in the Gospel of Thomas" lays the foundation for the analysis of the configuration in the Gospel of Thomas. One year later, "Enthymematic Texture in the Gospel of Thomas" sets the stage for future studies by giving a concrete example of an analysis of enthymematic texture outside of the "canon." Robbins argues that the Gospel of Thomas contains an "inner network" of enthymematic logia that is built upon conventional Mediterranean wisdom,

42 Sea Voyages and Beyond

Chapter 12, "The Socio-Rhetorical Role of Old Testament Scripture in Luke 4–19," provides an apt conclusion to this volume of essays, because it gives a preview of how a socio-rhetorical commentary might envision the development of *topoi* in Luke.[141] One of the advances that resulted from the study of enthymemes in the previous two essays (see above) was the recognition that enthymemes work with – configure and reconfigure – social, cultural, ideological, and theological topics. What was also becoming clear during this time period was that the different ways of elaborating *topoi* held the key for what Robbins in a 1996 essay, "The Dialectical Nature of Early Christian Discourse," was now calling *rhetorolects*: a form of language variety or discourse identifiable on the basis of a distinct configuration of themes, topics, reasonings, and argumentation."[142]

---

although it also inverts and diverts conventional wisdom in ways that would seem mysterious, unusual, or even bizarre to ordinary readers (his arguments include "abductive reasoning" and "contrawisdom"). This type of rhetoric produces wonder and inducts people into a "special kingdom of knowledge that makes them royalty among other people of understanding."

[141] Vernon K. Robbins, "The Socio-Rhetorical Role of Old Testament Scripture in Luke 4–19," in *Z Noveho Zakona/From the New Testament: Sbornik k narozeninam Prof. ThDr. Zdenka Sazavy* (ed. Hana Tonzarova and Petr Melmuk; Prague: Vydala Cirkev ceskoslovenska husitska, 2001), 81–93. This essay, for example, provides necessary corrections to static works on the relationship of Luke and the Hebrew Bible such as David P. Moessner, *Lord of the Banquet* (Minneapolis: Fortress, 1989).

[142] See Vernon K. Robbins, "The Dialectical Nature of Early Christian Discourse," *Scriptura* 59 (1996): 356. In that essay Robbins argues that there are six modes of early Christian rhetorolects (which he elsewhere calls "discourse") that dialogue with each other to produce "early Christian discourse." This essay is a watershed essay in the development of socio-rhetorical interpretation, one that calls for a new analysis and interpretation of early Christian discourse and sets the agenda for much of the socio-rhetorical analysis that was done in the latter part of the 1990's. The names of the six rhetorolects have evolved from wisdom, miracle, apocalyptic, opposition, death-resurrection, and cosmic rhetorolects to wisdom, miracle, apocalyptic, prophetic, priestly, and pre-creation rhetorolects. See Robbins, "Beginnings and Developments in Socio-Rhetorical Interpretation." The agenda in 1996 can be summed up by a paraphrase of the Watergate-era dictum: "Follow the *topoi*!" This process, of course, is analogous to Robbins's analysis of the "enthymematic network" in the previous essay.

Although very different, these rhetorolects serve a similar function within Robbins's socio-rhetorical analysis as do the *chronotopes* of Bakhtin's Dialogism. Robbins's rhetorolects, though, can tell us much more about the inner workings of the text and give us much information about early Christianity. Another comparison between Robbins and Bakhtin is that Bakhtin's emphasis on centripetal and centrifugal aspects in language also can serve as a model for how Robbins envisions the interactions among rhetorolects. An excellent example of Robbins's vision is found in "Argumentative Textures in Socio-Rhetorical Interpretation," in *Rhetorical Argumentation in Biblical Texts: Essays from the Lund 2000 Conference* (ed. Anders Eriksson, Thomas H. Olbricht, and Walter Übelacker; Emory Studies in Early Christianity 8; Harrisburg: Trinity Press International, 2002), 27–65. In that essay Robbins discusses some of the catalysts for his discovery of the rhetorolects, such as the five kinds of discourse delineated by Paul Ricoeur. Showing his debt to

The essay begins with the thesis that Luke 4:1–13 introduces major topics about possessions and devotion to God that Luke reconfigures from Deuteronomy 6 and 8. Luke 4:14–30 reconfigures the same topics by utilizing passages from Isaiah and 1–2 Kings. Luke 7:11–35 summarizes the results of the attempts by both John the Baptist and Jesus to bring the "renewal" of Deuteronomy, 1–2 Kings, and Isaiah to the people of Israel. Major *topoi* from the same Hebrew Bible texts are then reconfigured in the three dinners in the homes of Pharisees (7:36–50; 11:36–54; 14:1–14); these dinners also serve as a beginning, middle, and end for Luke 7:36–14:35. The dynamics of these three stories prepare the way for a shift in Luke 15 to the *topos* of "seeking and saving the lost"[143] and include a reconfiguration of Ezekiel 34. Robbins concludes that in Luke, "social reform" is not only a matter of seeking justice for the poor and downtrodden, it is also a matter of reworking one's stereotypes so that sinners, outcasts, and unacceptable people of all kinds are "sought out" for the purpose of finding them, welcoming them, and bringing them into the "houses" where God offers healing, inclusion, and salvation."

As I have noted elsewhere,[144] Robbins's socio-rhetorical analysis could be strengthened and extended even further with additional insights from social-scientific approaches. As is quite obvious, his analyses implicitly and explicitly utilize such insights and cogently reveal various social and rhetorical interactions of early Christians with the other people who inhabited the first-century Mediterranean world. Note his use in this essay, for example, of the challenge-riposte dynamic, the importance of honor, and the fact that the illness of dropsy was a symbol of greed in the first century.[145] Robbins, however, could have utilized the context of hospitality in the first-century Mediterranean to buttress his arguments.[146]

Bakhtin, Robbins notes that a "major task for rhetorical interpretation is to describe the centripetal-centrifugal interaction" of the six rhetorolects in the New Testament texts. Robbins then goes on to give a brief analysis of how argumentation works in the six rhetorolects. For more recent advances, see his "Beginnings and Developments in Socio-Rhetorical Interpretation" and *The Invention of Christian Discourse*.

[143] For an extensive analysis of how the Pharisees fit within (and outside) this *topos*, see my *Host, Guest, Enemy, and Friend*, 1–27, 177–319.

[144] See my introduction to *New Boundaries*, 1–36.

[145] Here Robbins's uses the significant contributions to the understanding of Luke 14 made by Willi Braun, *Feasting and Social Rhetoric in Luke 14* (SNTSMS 85; Cambridge: Cambridge University Press, 1995).

[146] See Julian Pitt-Rivers, "The Stranger, the Guest and the Hostile Host: Introduction to the Study of the Laws of Hospitality," in *Contributions to Mediterranean Sociology* (ed. J.G. Peristiany; Paris: Mouton, 1968), 12–30. See also my *Host, Guest, Enemy, and Friend*, 223–25 and my "Hospitality and Characterization in Luke 11:37–54," 213–51.

Social-scientific criticism also would have brought clarity to Robbins's statement that it was not clear in Luke 4:18 who the "oppressed" were who are to be "set free." As Robbins notes, the encounter of Jesus and the devil sets the stage for the conflicts that Jesus will continue to endure, and Luke 4:16–30 (and Isaiah 61:1–2) performs a programmatic role. This inaugural statement of Jesus' mission and microcosm of the entire ministry of Jesus can be related to almost every later scene in Luke and Acts, especially the Galilean ministry (4:14–9:50). Jesus' proclamation of release (4:18–21) is a programmatic declaration of the narrator's claim that Jesus is doing what he was sent to do: bringing good news to the poor, proclaiming release to the captives, recovery of sight to the blind, liberty for the oppressed, and the acceptable year of the Lord. Elements of this mission during the Galilean ministry include: casting out an unclean demon (4:31–37); healing many people (4:38–41); cleansing a leper (5:12–16); healing a paralytic (5:17–26); healing a man with a withered hand (6:6–11); preaching to the poor and hungry (6:20–21); healing a centurion's servant (7:1–10); and other episodes (e.g., 7:11–17; 7:36–50; 8:26–33, 40–56; 9:37–43).[147]

Since an implicit cultural (enthymematic) assumption of Luke-Acts is that illnesses have social consequences, all of Jesus' healing activities fulfill this proclamation of release.[148] People possessed by unclean/evil spirits, for example, can be described as being oppressed or held prisoner by demons[149] (e.g., the spirit/demon in Luke 9:38–39 "seizes" the child, "convulses" him, "mauls" him, and will "scarcely leave" him). Thus I would argue that Robbins's insights are certainly correct and can be extended even further with additional insights from social-scientific criticism.

Conclusion

The quote from *New Boundaries* with which this essay began urged readers "to determine for themselves the merits of the theoretical underpinnings of socio-rhetorical criticism, its congruence with these ancient texts, its functional, interpretive utility, and its ability to encourage constructive dialogue." Needless to say, many scholars have "gone to fry the eggs" and have discovered the advantages of a socio-rhetorical approach however they choose to appropriate its insights.

---

[147] Gowler, "Text, Culture, and Ideology in Luke 7:1-1-10," 100.

[148] Noted by John J. Pilch, *The Cultural Dictionary of the Bible* (Collegeville, Minn.: Liturgical, 1999), 73.

[149] Pilch, *The Cultural Dictionary of the Bible*, 75.

As John Kloppenborg observed in his contribution to Robbins's *Festschrift*:

> It is rare in a discipline as seemingly conservative as the study of the New Testament to witness the rapid emergence of a methodological approach with such wide-ranging and revolutionary implications as socio-rhetorical criticism. Rarer still is the fact that this approach was effectively brought from its infancy to a degree of maturity by the efforts of a single scholar. It is not that Vernon Robbins created ex nihilo; of course, he drew on a variety of studies that arose from the ferment of the 1970's and 1980's – studies that focused on semiotics, on narrative criticism, on rhetorical features of biblical texts, on intertextuality, on the social world of biblical texts, and on the role of ideology in the production and use of literary texts. But Robbins had the clarity of mind to see how to integrate these diverse methods and approaches to the texts of antiquity into a multi-dimensional method which identifies various registers or "textures" in an effort to understand how a text works on the intellect, emotions and sensibilities of its readers and hearers and how the worlds of the readers or hearers variously affect the appropriation of the text.[150]

As Kloppenborg makes clear, socio-rhetorical interpretation has already made a significant impact on biblical scholarship through the insights generated during the process that led to the "textures" of *Exploring* and *Tapestry*. The essays in this volume therefore represent the "end of the beginning," because socio-rhetorical interpretation has already entered a new, exciting "post-textures" phase, one which, as have past phases, will evolve because socio-rhetorical interpretation is continually in transition, adapting and adopting constructive aspects from diverse methodologies, approaches, and perspectives – while using rhetoric as the "bridge" – seeking to pursue the interpretation of these texts with both precision and a manner of perceptive coherence.

So this volume represents just one important stage in the continuing evolution of socio-rhetorical interpretation, an approach which has developed over a period of thirty years during which Vernon Robbins and his fellow travelers have wrestled with these biblical texts, comparative texts, and increasingly intricate methodologies. The nuances and complexities of socio-rhetorical interpretation appropriately match the nuances and complexities of these texts and our interpretations of them. Socio-rhetorical interpretation thus not only gives us more discerning eyes and ears about these texts, but also about the processes of interpretation, and indeed ourselves as interpreters.

---

[150] Kloppenborg, "Ideological Texture in the Parable of the Tenants," 64.

1

By Land and By Sea:
The We-Passages and Ancient Sea Voyages

The accounts of Paul's travels throughout the Mediterranean world begin in Acts 13. Prior to this chapter Paul (Saul) was present at Stephen's death (8:1), temporarily blinded and permanently converted on the road to Damascus (9:1–9), blessed and baptized by Ananias (9:17–19), and transported by night out of Damascus so the Jewish residents could not kill him (9:20–30). After some time Barnabas took Paul to Antioch where they spent a year together with the Christian community (11:25–26). When Barnabas and Paul were selected to take relief offerings to Jerusalem (11:29–30), they brought John Mark with them on their return (12:25).

Throughout all of this, Paul travels on land. In fact, in all of Luke and Acts 1–12 no one travels on the sea. In contrast to Mark and Matthew where Jesus frequently travels on the Sea of Galilee, in Luke Jesus never even goes alongside the sea (παρὰ τὴν θάλασσαν).[1] On two occasions Jesus gets into a boat and goes onto or across "the lake" (ἡ λίμνη: 5:1, 2; 8:22, 23, 33). This "lake" is called Gennesaret in 5:1; never in Luke does Jesus go to or across "the Sea of Galilee." The author's choice of vocabulary indicates that he distinguishes between "the lake" and "the sea." "The lake" is a body of inland water on the eastern edge of Galilee. A person can sail across this lake (or "down" it, καταπλεύω: 8:26) to the land of the Gergesenes (or Gerasenes or Gadarenes) that lies opposite Galilee (ἀντιπέρα τῆς Γαλιλαίας: 8:26). In contrast, "the sea" is that expanse of water which can take you to Cyprus, Macedonia, Achaia, Crete, or Italy. Jesus sets a precedent for sea travel on the lake, but Jesus himself never travels or voyages on the sea. Even Peter and John never travel on the sea. Only Paul and his associates face the challenge, adventure, and destiny of voyaging across the sea.

---

[1] θάλασσα occurs 18 times in Mark, 17 times in Matthew, and 3 times in Luke. Each of the occurrences in Luke is in a saying rather than narration: Luke 17:2, 6; 21:25.

Sea travel appears for the first time in Acts 13. Paul and his company sail from Seleucia to the island of Cyprus, then from Cyprus to Pamphylia (13:4,13). This sea travel holds little adventure or danger. Only two short clauses relate the means of travel; all the narrated episodes occur on land. Two more short clauses recount sea transportation in this section of Acts. Paul and Barnabas are taken back to Syrian Antioch in a boat (14:26), and Barnabas and John Mark go to Cyprus in a boat after the disagreement with Paul (15:39). Still, however, no detailed sea voyage occurs. Only in chapter 15 do extended sea voyages begin, and when they occur, the narration moves into first person plural "we."

The coincidence of sea voyages and first person plural narration in Acts is striking. There are four we-sections in Acts: 16:10–17; 20:5–15; 21:1–18; 27:1–28:16. In each instance, a sea voyage begins as the first person plural narration emerges. While this observation can lead the interpreter in various directions, it points vividly to accounts of sea voyages in antiquity. Sea voyages are often couched in first person narration. Either the author narrates it as a participant (I sailed to Byblos ...) or the author stages a participant recounting the voyage (he then said, "As I was sailing to Byblos ..."). Sea voyage narratives in Greek and Roman literature, however, become a distinct genre. One of the features of this genre is the presence of first person plural narration. Undoubtedly the impetus for this is sociological: on a sea voyage a person has accepted a setting with other people, and cooperation among all the members is essential for a successful voyage. Therefore, at the point where the voyage begins, the narration moves to first person plural.

The author of Luke-Acts employs the sea voyage genre with great skill. His narrative builds toward a conclusion that is reached through a dramatic sea voyage. First plural narration emerges in the sections that present "mission by sea." There is evidence to suggest that Paul's voyages across the sea were in view during the composition of the first volume of the work. To explain the role of the we-passages in Acts, we will undertake six steps of analysis. (1) Since the we-passages in Acts present sea voyages, a survey is made of narrative style that accompanies sea voyages in Greek and Roman literature; (2) since third person narrative style surrounds the we-passages in Acts, an investigation follows concerning historiographical literature that is pervaded by third person narrative; (3) since there are other texts that alternate between third person and first person plural narration, Greek literature that reflects the same style of narration as Acts is presented; (4) on the basis of the survey, the primary features of the sea voyage genre are explored, and the we-passages are examined for the presence of these features; (5) the position of the we-passages in the structure of Acts is investigated; and (6) we posit a conclusion regarding the function of the we-passages in the purpose of Luke-Acts. These explorations are intended to suggest that the author of Luke-Acts is a versatile Hellenistic writer who is an intelligent participant in the literary arena of Mediterranean culture. The author has employed first person plural narration for the sea voyages, because it was conventional generic style within Hellenistic literature. This style contributes directly to the author's scheme of participation in history through narration of its dramatic episodes.

Narrative Style in Ancient Sea Voyages

There is a natural propensity for portraying sea voyages through the medium of first person narration. This style for narrating voyages extends as far back as the most ancient Mediterranean literature known to us. Two Egyptian tales, *The Story of Sinuhe* (1800 BCE) and *The Journey of Wen-Amon to Phoenicia* (11th cent. BCE), recount sea voyages through first person singular narration.[2] Also Utnapishtim, in the Akkadian *Epic of Gilgamesh*, recounts his voyage upon the waters in first person *singular*.[3] In the Egyptian and Mesopotamian accounts the narrator uses first person singular "I," even when others are present with him on the voyage.[4] Homer's *Odyssey*, in contrast, contains the earliest example among Mediterranean literature of a sea voyage that employs first person *plural* narration.

In books 9–12 of the *Odyssey*, the travels and adventures of Odysseus are recounted to the Phaeacians at a banquet. The reader therefore hears about the breath-taking episodes from the lips of Odysseus himself. This narrative technique allows the dynamics of traveling on the sea and encountering strange, new peoples to emerge directly through personal narration. When Alcinous, king of the Phaeacians, asks Odysseus to recount his adventures, he begins, after the initial formalities, with:

> From Ilios the wind bore me and brought me to the Cicones, to Ismarus. There I sacked the city and slew the men ... (9.39–41).[5]

---

[2] James B. Pritchard, ed., *Ancient Near Eastern Texts* (Princeton: Princeton University Press, 1955), 18–22, 25–29.

[3] Tablet XI, in ibid., 92–97.

[4] See *Wen-Amon* 10, where he refers to "a man of my ship," and *Gilgamesh* XI: 84, where he recounts that he made all his family and kin go aboard the ship.

[5] The quotations from the NT are taken from the Revised Standard Version; unless otherwise indicated, the quotations from Greek and Latin literature are from the Loeb Classical Library edition of the work.

Here, first person *singular* narration begins the account, and first person *singular* narration occurs frequently throughout these four books of the Odyssey. However, first person *plural* narration becomes a formulaic means for launching the ship, sailing for a number of days, and beaching the ship at the end of a voyage. Therefore, first person *plural* formulaic clauses unify the sailing accounts. Five times, voyages begin with all or part of the following first person *plural* formula:

> From there we sailed on, grieved at heart, glad to have escaped death, though we had lost our dear comrades ....[6]

Twice, the length of a voyage is recounted in another first person plural pattern:

> For nine (six) days we sailed, night and day alike ....[7] The voyage ending is captured in first person plural clauses that depict the beaching of the ship:

> Then, on coming thither, we beached our ship on the sands, and ourselves went forth upon the shore of the sea.[8]

In Homeric literature, therefore, first person narration transfers the excitement and anxiety of a sea voyage in the most vivid narrative technique available to the pen. Homeric couplets perpetuate the dynamics in poetic form, and first person plural narration becomes as familiar as the *Odyssey* itself:

> From there we sailed on, grieved at heart, glad to have escaped death, though we had lost our dear comrades ...[9]

The same technique is used by Virgil (70–19 BCE) in books 2–3 of the *Aeneid*. Since the structure of the *Aeneid* imitates the *Odyssey*, Virgil's use of first person narration results directly from Homeric influ-

---

[6] Ἔνθεν δὲ προτέρω πλέομεν ἀκαχήμενοι ἦτορ, ἄσμενοι ἐκ θανάτοιο, φίλους ὀλέσαντες ἑταίους. These two lines occur at 9.62–63; 9.565–566; 10.133–134. The first line occurs further at 9.105; 10.77. The variant ἔνθα κατεπλέομεν occurs at 9.142.

[7] 10.28; 10.80: Ἐννῆμαρ (ἑξῆμαρ) μὲν ὁμῶ πλέομεν νύκτας τε καὶ ἦμαρ.

[8] 9.546–547; 12.5–7: νῆα μὲν ἔνθ' ἐλθόντες ἐκέλσαμεν ἐν ψαμάθοισιν, ἐκ δὲ καὶ αὐτοὶ βῆμεν ἐπὶ ῥηγμῖνι θαλάσσης. Variations of this pattern occur at 9.149–151; 9.169. Cf. 9.85; 10.56; 11.20.

[9] Cf. Werner Suerbaum, "Die Ich-Erzählungen des Odysseus," *Poetica* 2 (1968): 176–77, n. 58. Also W.J. Woodhouse, *The Composition of Homer's Odyssey* (Oxford: Clarendon, 1930), 44: "The sea-stories proper constitute the content of a comparatively short portion of the life of the hero ... in the string of adventures supposed to be narrated by Odysseus himself at the court of king Alkinoos, Homer has raised these age-old stories to a power of illusive reality, to an artistic and ethical level, that together give this portion of the Odyssey its own special undying quality."

ence.[10] Aeneas himself recounts the destruction of Troy and the voyage that ends in a shipwreck offshore Carthage. In book 3, his first person account to Dido turns from the sack of Troy (book 2) to his subsequent travels that have brought him to Carthage. With the launching of the boat, first person *plural* narration becomes commonplace:

> With Asian power and Priam's tribe uprooted, though blameless, by heaven's decree; with Ilium's pride fallen, and Neptune's Troy all smoke and ash, God's oracles drove us on to exile, on to distant, lonely lands. We built a fleet down to Antander and Ida's Phrygian peaks, uncertain which way Fate led or where to stop. We marshaled our men. When summer first came on, Anchises bade us trust our sails to fate (3.1–9).[11]

These two examples come from the prestigious epic literature of Greek and Roman culture. Their influence was pervasive in the literature of the Mediterranean world. Sea voyages are not only adventurous but lead to the founding of new cities and the establishment of new leaders. Shipwrecks create the setting for man's display of strength and take the passengers, unplanned, to famous islands and cities of the Mediterranean world. Through these voyages, destiny unfolds and the ways of the gods with men are displayed.

From the seventh century BCE onwards, Greek poetry contained sea voyage imagery, and it is not unusual for the lines that contain this imagery to be formulated in first person plural style. Two poems by the lyric poet Alcaeus (b. ca. 620 BCE) reflect this style. Both poems were cited by Heraclitus (1st cent. CE) as allegories of political trouble in the state.[12] Alcaeus 6 maintains first person plural throughout the scene of sailing on dangerous waters:

> This wave again comes [like?] the one before: it will give us much labour to bale out, when it enters the vessel's [...] [...] let us fortify the [...] with all speed, and run into a secure harbour.
>
> And let not unmanly hesitance take hold of any one [of us]: a great [...] s clear before us. Remember our [toils] of yesterday: now let each prove himself a steadfast man. And let us not disgrace [by cowardice] our noble fathers lying under the earth ....[13]

---

[10] Cf. Brooks Otis, *Virgil: A Study in Civilized Poetry* (Oxford: Clarendon, 1963), 215–312.

[11] Virgil, The *Aeneid* (trans. Frank O. Copley; New York: Bobbs-Merril, 1965), 49.

[12] *Allegories of Homer* 5; available in Felix Buffiere, *Heraclite: Allegories d'Homere* (Paris: Societe d'edition 'Les Belles Lettres,' 1962), 4–5.

[13] Alcaeus 6 (Diehle)/A6 (Lobel and Page); this translation is from Denys L. Page, *Sappho and Alcaeus* (Oxford: Clarendon, 1955), 183.

Alcaeus 326 alternates between first person singular and plural as the poet captures the anxiety that attends the injury inflicted on a ship in a storm:

> I cannot tell where the wind lies; one wave rolls from this side, one from that, and we in their midst are borne along with our black vessel Toiling in a tempest passing great. The bilge is up over the masthold, all the sail lets the daylight through already, and there are great rents along it, And the woodings are slackening, the rudders ... both feet stay [entangled] In the sheets: that alone it is that [saves] me; the cargo ... is carried away above ....[14]

Theognis (fl. 544–541 BCE) continues this imagery and style of narration in the section of his lyric poetry that treats the city-state metaphorically as a ship on a turbulent sea:

> Now we are borne along with white sails, casting about on the open sea near Melos through the dark night; The crew does not want to bale; and the sea casts over us on both sides of the ship ... (671–674).[15]

The metaphor of the city-state as a ship on the sea also appears in tragic poetry. In *Seven Against Thebes*, Aeschylus (525/4–456 BCE) has a messenger announce the successful defense of the city against its aggressors in these words:

> Both in fair weather and in the many blows of the surging sea the city has not shipped water. The bastion is water-tight and we have bulwarked her ports with champions who in single-handed fight have redeemed their pledge (795–798).[16]

The attack on the city is like a storm that threatens to destroy a ship at sea. With disciplined effort and gradual abatement of the storm, the ship is successfully kept afloat. Aeschylus also uses sea voyage imagery in a speech by Electra in *The Libation-Bearers*:

> But the gods whom we invoke, know by what storms we are tossed like sailors. Yet, if it is our fate to win safety, from a little seed may spring a mighty stock (201–203).

---

[14] Alcaeus 326 (Diehle)/Z2 (Lobel and Page); translation from ibid., 186.

[15] Author's translation; for the text with commentary, see David A. Campbell, *Greek Lyric Poetry* (London: Macmillan, 1967), 85–86, 368–70. Pindar (518–438 BCE) used sea voyage imagery metaphorically to describe the process of writing an ode; see Gogo Lieberg, "Seefahrt und Werk," *Giornale Italiano di Fitologia* 21 (1969): 209–13. Nemea 4.36–8 is especially interesting for its use of first person plural; for analysis of this passage, see Jacques Peron, *Les Images maritimes de Pindare* (Paris: C. Klincksieck, 1974), 90–100. For a detailed study of first person in Pindar, see Mary R. Lefkowitz, "'ΤΩ ΚΑΙ ΕΓΩ' The First Person in Pindar," *HSCP* 67 (1963): 177–253.

[16] See the translation and commentary in Howard D. Cameron, *Studies on the Seven Against Thebes of Aeschylus* (Paris: Mouton, 1971), 63.

The difficult situation faced by Electra and her companions calls forth the danger of sailing on the sea. Mortals have little choice but to turn their petitions to heaven and hope for a successful outcome. First person plural narration attends this imagery in epic, lyric, and tragic poetry. During later centuries, this literature is copied, quoted, and read, and its influence is found in widespread sectors of Hellenistic and Roman civilization.

In his *Menippean Satires*, Varro (116–27 BCE) provides evidence that first person style persists in voyage imagery during the first century BCE.[17] Fragments 276 and 473, preserved by Nonius Marcellus (early 4th cent. CE), read respectively:

> 276: Here at the crossroads we boarded a swampboat, which the barge boys pulled along through the sedge with a rope.

> 473: Wherever we wanted to go, the wind blew against us.[18]

Nonius also recounts that Varro knew a two-book satire entitled *Periplous* (Voyage),[19] and fragment 418, from book 2, contains the first person plural narration.[20]

By the first century CE, sea voyages, interrupted by storms, were an established part of Mediterranean literature outside of epic. And first person narration of voyages appears to be not only fashionable but preferred. Dio Chrysostom (40–after 112 CE), from whom portions of 78 discourses are extant, most frequently recounts tales in third person narration. But in the seventh discourse, when a sea voyage, which ends in a shipwreck and a journey, is recounted, he uses first person narration:

> ... at the close of the summer season I was crossing from Chios with

---

[17] See Eduard Norden, *Agnostos Theos: Untersuchungen zur Formengeschichte Religiöser Rede* (Leipzig: Tuebner, 1913), 313. I have been informed at many places in this paper by his appendix, "*Zur Komposition der Acta Apostolorum*," 311–32.

[18] These fragments are most readily available in *Petronii Sarturae* (ed. F. Buecheler; Berlin: Weidmann, 1904), 193, 214:

> 276: *hic in ambivio navem conscendimus palustrem, quam nautici quisones per ulvam ducerent loro.*
> 473: *quocumque ire vellemus, obvius flare.*

I am indebted to my colleague, Professor David F. Bright, for the translations of the material from Buecheler.

[19] See M. Terenti Varronis, *Saturarum Menippearum* (ed. Alexander Riese; Leipzig: Tuebner, 1865), 197–8.

[20] Buecheler, *Petronii Sarturae*, 208: "... lest we wander, that there were many bypaths, and that the way was quite safe, but slow going" – *et ne erraremus, ectropas esse multas, omnio tutum, esse sed spissum iter.*

> some fisherman in a very small boat, when such a storm arose that we had great difficulty in reaching the Hollows of Euboea in safety (7.2).

After a short while on shore, a hunter invites him to travel with him. The narrative thus continues:

> As we proceeded on our way, he told me of his circumstances and how he lived with his wife and children ... (7.10).

Dio's use of first person narration for this tale of voyage and adventure suggests that he was responding to the genre itself. This style had established itself within the cultural milieu, and writers found it natural to respond to this convention.

Within sea voyage accounts, the shipwreck became an increasingly attractive feature. Petronius (1st cent. CE) exhibits this interest in shipwreck accounts and also shows the natural propensity for first person narration in them. It only seemed proper to recount the dangerous episode with first person plural:

> While we talked over this matter and others, the sea rose, clouds gathered from every quarter, and overwhelmed the day in darkness... . One moment the wind set towards Sicily, very often the north wind blew off the Italian coast, mastered the ship and twisted her in every direction; and what was more dangerous than any squall, such thick darkness had suddenly blotted out the light that the steersman could not even see the whole prow ... (ch. 114).

Even the Jewish historian Josephus mentions a sea voyage and a shipwreck in his biography. And little surprise it is that he shifts from first person singular to first person plural as he recounts it:

> I reached Rome after being in great jeopardy at sea. For our ship foundered in the midst of the sea of Adria, and our company of some six hundred souls had to swim all that night. About daybreak, through God's good providence, we sighted a ship of Cyrene, and I and certain others, about eighty in all, outstripped the others and were taken on board (3; sections 14–16).

By the first century CE the sea voyage, threatened by shipwreck, had established itself as a distinct genre. An essential feature of this genre was first person narration. The status of the genre provided the possibility for authors to employ the situation of a sea voyage to interpret many situations in life. Thus Ovid, in *Tristia* 1.2.31–34 (composed 8–9 CE), compares his life in exile to a sea voyage threatened by shipwreck:

> The helmsman is confused nor can he find what to avoid or what to seek; his very skill is numbed by the baffling perils. We are surely lost, there is no hope of safety ....

Being in exile is like being thrown on a ship that starts on a voyage. One is dependent upon the crew for the outcome, but even the crew cannot predict the fortune of the journey. Together they face the peril of the sea, and when the wind becomes a storm and the waves begin to threaten, every occupant of the ship faces the same jeopardy. Together they experience the confusion, the fear, and the hope that all is not lost. As Ovid uses this situation on the sea to explain his experience in exile, he expresses the anguish in first person plural: "We are surely lost, there is no hope of safety ...."

In the second century CE, Lucian (125–180 CE) wrote a sea voyage parody entitled *A True Story*. If Ovid's use of a sea voyage to interpret his exile leaves any doubt with regard to the status of this genre, Lucian's parody gives even firmer evidence. In his work Lucian recounts a fantastic voyage with tongue in cheek. His parody reveals the essential features of the sea voyage genre. He narrates the voyage as Odysseus, Aeneas, Dio Chrysostom, and Josephus narrate theirs. He begins in first person singular and shifts to first person plural at the embarkation.

> Once upon a time, setting out from the Pillars of Hercules and heading for the western ocean with a fair wind, I went a-voyaging.... For a day and a night we sailed before the wind making very little offing, as land was still dimly in sight; but at sunrise on the second day the wind freshened, the sea rose, darkness came on, and before we knew it we could no longer even get our canvas in.... On the eightieth day the sun came out suddenly and at no great distance we saw a high, wooded island.... Putting in and going ashore, we lay on the ground for some time in consequence of our long misery ... (1.5–6).

Even though Lucian made light of sea voyage accounts by presenting one of the most fantastic voyages imaginable, the sea voyage genre had a firm place within the literature of the culture. Thus Achilles Tatius (2nd cent. CE) includes a sea voyage in the *Adventures of Leucippe and Clitophon*, and the appeal of the account is strengthened by first person narration:

> ... as we arrived at the harbour of Berytus, we found a ship just sailing, on the very point of casting loose: so we asked no questions as to her destination, but embarked all our belongings aboard ... (2.31.6).

> On the third day of our voyage, the perfect calm we had hitherto experienced was suddenly overcast by dark clouds and the daylight disappeared, a wind blew upwards from the sea full in the ship's face, and the helmsman bade the sailyard be slewed around ... (3.1.1).

In 4.9.6. these adventures are summarized in first person plural:

> We escaped the terrors that awaited us at home, only to suffer shipwreck; we were saved from the sea, ... [lacuna]; we were rescued from the robbers, only to find madness waiting for us.

This style continues in the third century (220–250 CE) in Heliodorus' *Ethiopian Story* about Theagenes and Chariclea. The author has established third person style of narration up to this point, so he leads into the voyage with this style:

> When they got on board the Phoenician vessel, he said, in their flight from Delphi, the beginning of their voyage was quite agreeable, as they were borne along by a following wind of moderate strength ... (5.17).

But after only a few lines, Heliodorus turns the narrative over to Calasiris for a personal account of the voyage.

> Calasiris then pursued his narrative thus: "We made our way through the strait, he said, "and when we had lost sight of the Pointed Isles, we fancied that we could distinguish the headland of Zacynthus creeping into our view like a dark cloud ..." (5.17).[21]

Since first person narration emerged naturally in relation to sea voyage literature, there could be no complete reversal of the trend. The dynamic of voyaging on the sea brings with it the experience of working with others to achieve a safe voyage and of sharing with others the fear and desperation when storm threatens to end the voyage in shipwreck. The social setting that emerges through a voyage on the sea gave rise to the sea voyage genre recounted with the personal plural dynamic: "We thought we were lost, we did what we could, and we made it through."

Third Person Narration in Greek Literature

But now it is necessary to look at the genre where third person narration dominates. If the examples given thus far suggest a natural affinity between first person narration and sea voyages, they do not reveal the strong bias toward third person narration in Greek and Latin prose literature. At least as early as Thucydides (ca. 460–400 BCE) a standard had been set for narrative historiography that included third person narrative style. Thucydides carried this style through with remarkable candor, so that, beginning with book 4 of the *History of the Peloponnesian War*, he recounted his own activities in the army in third person narration. Thus he introduces himself into the narrative with these words:

> ... the opponents of the traitors ... acting in concert with Eucles the general ... sent to the other commander of the Thracian district, Thu-

---

[21] Heliodorus, *Ethiopian Story* (trans. Walter Lamb; New York: Dutton, 1961), 123–24.

cydides son of Olorus, the author of this history, who was at Thasos, a Parian colony, about a half-day's sail from Amphipolis, and urged him to come to their aid. And he, on hearing this, sailed in haste with seven ships which happened to be at hand ... (4.104.4ff).

Thucydides, the objective, truthful narrator features himself in the narrative for a number of pages, never using first person narration. By this means Thucydides hopes to persuade his readers that his account is based on the finest evidence and presented in the most accurate manner (1.1.1–2).

Xenophon (428/7–354 BCE) used this same style for the *Anabasis* and the *Hellenica*. Therefore he introduces himself into the narrative in book 3 of the *Anabasis* in the following way:

> There was a young man in the army named Xenophon, an Athenian, who was neither general nor captain nor private, but had accompanied the expedition because Proxenus, an old friend of his, had sent him at his home an invitation to go with him; Proxenus had also promised him that if he should go, he would make him a friend of Cyrus ... (3.1.4). Xenophon ... after offering the sacrifices to the gods that Apollo's oracle prescribed, set sail, overtook Proxenus and Cyrus at Sardis as they were on the point of beginning the upward march, and was introduced to Cyrus.... It was in this way, then, that Xenophon came to go on the expedition ... (3.1.8).

From this point on Xenophon becomes a participant in the action and the dialogue. Never, however, does the author use first person narration for his own participation.[22] Both Thucydides and Xenophon consider third person narration to be the proper historiographical style. They even recount sea voyages in this style.

From the same century as Xenophon's works, a sailing manual for mariners has been preserved.[23] This *Periplus of the Mediterranean Sea*, as it is entitled, is attributed to Scylax the Younger. The author starts the manual with first person singular: "I will begin [my description] from the Pillars of Hercules...." After this, the journalistic description of cities, people and distances is given in third person except for fourteen interjections where he says, "Now I will return to the coast, from

---

[22] Xenophon, in contrast with Thucydides, does not even claim authorship of the *Anabasis*, evidently because he was a participant in it. Instead, he claims, in *Hellenica* 3.1.2., that the *Anabasis* was written by Themistogenes of Syracuse.

[23] Walter W. Hyde, *Ancient Greek Mariners* (New York: Oxford University Press, 1947), 19, 116. Text in Karl Müller, *Geographi Graeci Minores* (2 vols.; Paris: Instituti Franciae, 1855–1861; repr., Hildesheim: Georg Olms Verlagsbuchhandlung, 1965), 1:15–96.

which I turned away [in my description]."[24] This document is too non-literary to be influenced by the historiographical tradition. Yet it does represent sea voyage information in a third person informational style.

A similar manual tradition emerges in the *Periplus of the Erythraean Sea* (50–95 CE).[25] This document is a third person description of the harbors, cities and peoples along the coastline of the Indian Ocean. Even in this account, however, the propensity for first person plural is exhibited. When the author is describing a dangerous section of the coastline, he automatically slips into first person plural style.

> Navigation is dangerous along this whole coast of Arabia, which is without harbors, with bad anchorages, foul, inaccessible because of breakers and rocks, and terrible in every way. Therefore we hold our course down the middle of the gulf and pass on as fast as possible by the country of Arabia until we come to the Burnt Island ... [26]

Thus, even in third person manual *periploi*, first person is likely to intrude.

A rather forthright perpetuation of third person historiographical style appears in the works of Arrian (96–ca. 180 CE) who imitated Xenophon in his *Anabasis of Alexander* and Herodotus in his *Indica*.[27] Therefore his account of Nearchus' sea voyage in *Indica* 8.20.1–8.36.9 is recounted in third person, though the reader is told that it is Nearchus' personal account.

> On this Nearchus writes thus: Alexander had a vehement desire to sail the sea which stretches from India to Persia; but he disliked the length of the voyage and feared lest, meeting with some country desert or without roadstands, or not properly provided with the fruits of the earth, his whole fleet might be destroyed (8.20.1f).... And Nearchus says that Alexander discussed with him whom he should select to be admiral of his fleet (8.20.4).... At length Alexander accepted Nearchus' willing spirit, and appointed him admiral of the entire fleet (8.20.7).... . Now when the trade winds had sunk to rest ... they put to sea ... (8.21.1).

---

[24] Ἐπάνειμι δὲ πάλιν ἐπὶ τὴν ἤπειρον, ὅθεν ἐξετραπόμην (with slight variation): 7, 13, 29, 34, 48, 53, 58, 67 (twice), 97, 98, 99 (twice), 103. In 21 he refers το νῆσοί ὧν ἔχω εἰπεῖν τὰ ὀνόματα and in 40 to ἡ ὁδὸς πρός τὴν ἐπὶ ἡμῶν θάλασσαν.

[25] Wilfred H. Schoff, *The Periplus of the Erythraean Sea* (New York: Longmans, Green, 1912), 8–9. Text in Müller, *Geographi*, 1:257–305.

[26] Schoff, *Periplus*, 30. Also in 57, first person emerges: κατὰ τὸν καιρὸν τῶν παρ' ἡμῖν, ἐτησίων ἐν τῷ Ἰνδικῷ πελάγει ὁ λιβόντος φαίνεται [Ἵππαλος] προσονομάζεσθαι [ἀπὸ τῆς προσηγορίας τοῦ πρώτως ἐξευρηκότος τὸν διάπλουν].

[27] See Lionel Pearson, *The Lost Histories of Alexander the Great* (London: American Philological Association, 1960), 112. A similar style is perpetuated by Apollonius of Rhodes in *Argonautica*.

Arrian, however, is credited with a *Periplus of the Euxine Sea*. Because the author formulated the account as a letter to Hadrian, he was able to recount the voyage in first person plural.[28]

While Arrian perpetuated the third person historiographical style as employed by Xenophon, Caesar (1st cent. BCE) allowed first person plural comments within a third person narrative style. Most frequently, in the *Gallic Wars*, first person plural emerges in accounts of battle. But in at least one voyage account the author allows first person plural to intrude.

> When the ships had been beached and the camp thoroughly well entrenched, Caesar left the same forces as before to guard the ships... . Here in mid-channel is an island called Man; ... some have written that in midwinter, night there lasts for thirty whole days. We could discover nothing about this by inquiries; but by exact measurements, we observed that the nights were shorter than on the continent (5.11).

In Caesar's account, therefore, an autobiographical feature is allowed within historiography, especially in battles and a voyage. Is it too much to suggest that this becomes a characteristic typology for historiography in the 1st century BCE and CE, and that the writer of Luke-Acts construes his narrative in relation to this typology?

This survey has been designed to show two things: (a) the genre of sea voyage narrative within Greek literature uses first person plural narration; (b) the standards of historiography brought in a necessity for third person narration, but, in spite of this, first person plural narration emerges in accounts of battles and voyages.

Parallels to the Voyages in Acts

But if the we-passages in Acts are to be understood in relation to these features in narrative literature, are there not more precise parallels? In Acts the narration shifts from third person to first person plural, and the narrator is not the main actor. A precise parallel exists in the *Voyage of Hanno the Carthaginian*.[29] This document exists in Greek and was written down between 350–125 BCE. It reflects the convergence of the historiographical tradition and sea voyage tradition as it appears in Acts.

---

[28] Text in Müller, *Geographi*, 370–401. On the letter form as a technique for presenting the account as a personal voyage, see Henry Chotard, *Le Périple de la Mer Noire par Arrien* (Paris: Remquet, 1860), 3–7.

[29] Text in Müller, *Geographi*, 1–14. At this point I must express my sincere gratitude to Professor Emeritus John L. Heller who called my attention to this document. His conversation with me about the shift from third person to first person plural in this voyage account inspired this entire investigation.

Some interpreters suggest it was translated from Punic into Greek under the influence of the historian Polybius; others suggest the influence of Herodotus.[30] This three page account begins with third person narration and shifts into first person narration in the following manner:

> It pleased the Carthaginians that Hanno should voyage outside the Pillars of Hercules, and found cities of the Libyphoenicians. And he set forth with sixty ships of fifty oars, and a multitude of men and women, to the number of thirty thousand, and with wheat and other provisions. After passing through the Pillars we went on and sailed for two days' journey beyond, where we founded the first city... . Having set up an altar to Neptune, we proceeded again, going toward the east for half the day ... (1–3).[31]

First person plural narration continues to the end of the document, where, on account of the lack of further supplies, they return to Carthage.

Another parallel to the style of narration in Acts is present in a four-column papyrus dated ca. 246 BCE, which is best entitled *Episodes from the Third Syrian War*.[32] I.1–II.11 contains third person narration. In II.12 the narration shifts to first person plural as a sea voyage is recounted:

> ... Arzibazos, the satrap in Cilicia, intended to send [the captured money] to Ephesus for Laodice's group, but when the people of Soli and the satraps immediately agreed among themselves, and the associates of Pythagoras and Aristocles vigorously helped, and all were good men, it happened that the money was kept and both the city and the citadel became ours. But when Arzibazos escaped and reached the passes of the Tauros and some of the inhabitants cut him off at the entrance, he went back to Antioch. Then we (made ready) the things on the ships, and, when the first watch began, we embarked in as many ships as the harbor of Seleucia (at Orontes) was likely to hold and sailed to a port called Poseidon and we anchored ourselves at the eighth hour. Then, getting away from there in the morning, we went to Seleucia. And the priest and rulers and other citizens and officers and soldiers, crowned with wreaths, met us ... (2.6–25).[33]

---

[30] W. Aly, "Die Entdeckung des Westens," *Hermes* 62 (1927): 317–39, suggests Polybian influence; G. Germain, "Qu'est-ce que le Périple d'Hannon? Document, amplification littéraire ou faux intégral?" *Hesperis* 44 (1957): 205–48, suggests that a later writer was influenced by Herodotus' style.

[31] Wilfred H. Schoff, *The Periplus of Hanno* (Philadelphia: Commercial Museum, 1913), 3.

[32] The first edition of the text is found in John P. Mahaffy, *The Flinders Petri Papyri* (3 vols.; Dublin: Academy House, 1891–1905), XLV (2:145–9), CXLIV (3:334–38). The re-edited text is available in L. Mitteis and U. Wilcken, *Grundzüge und Chrestomathie der Papyruskunde* (2 vols.; Leipzig: Teubner, 1912), vol. 1, pt. 2, 1–7.

[33] Translation by the author, consulting Mahaffy.

In second and third century Christianity, two documents of the Acts-genre contain first person plural in relation to sea voyages. Undoubtedly the first century Acts of the Apostles has influenced these documents. It is informative, however, to observe first person plural narration in the midst of sea voyage material. In the *Antiochene Acts of the Martyrdom of Ignatius*, third person narration shifts unannounced to first person plural as the author gives a summary of the voyage:

> ... passing through Philippi he [Ignatius] journeyed by land across Macedonia and the part of Epirus which lies by Epidamnus. And here on the sea coast he took ship and sailed across the Hadriatic sea, and thence entering the Tyrrhene and passing by islands and cities, the holy man when he came in view of Puteoli was eager himself to disembark, desiring to tread in the footsteps of the Apostle Paul; but forasmuch as a stiff breeze springing up prevented it, the ship being driven by a stern wind, he commended the love of the brethren in that place, and so sailed by. Thus in one single day and night, meeting with favourable winds, we ourselves were carried forward against our will, mourning over the separation which must soon come between ourselves and this righteous man....[34]

In these three texts and the book of Acts, third person narration is established as the style for recounting the events that occur. However, when a sea voyage begins the narration shifts, without explanation, to first person plural.

Yet another text holds interest for this study, although it does not represent an exact parallel to the narrative style of Acts. In *The Acts of Peter and the Twelve Apostles*, Nag Hammadi codex VI.1, the narrative alternates between first person and third person narration. Unfortunately, the first part of the text has been destroyed, so that it is impossible to know if the document began with first person or third person narrative style. The extant portion begins with a scene in which Peter and the apostles covenant with one another to take a special voyage on the sea. Immediately after this scene, they go down to the sea and begin their venture. First person plural narration governs the composition of these two episodes.

> [...] which [...] purpose [... after ...] us [...] apostles [...]. We sailed [...] of the body. [Others] were not anxious in [their hearts]. And in our hearts, we were united. We agreed to fulfill the ministry to which the Lord appointed us. And we made a covenant with each other.
>
> We went down to the sea at an opportune moment, which came to us

---

[34] J.B. Lightfoot, *The Apostolic Fathers* (5 vols.; London: Macmillian, 1885–1890), 2:577.

> from the Lord. We found a ship moored at the shore ready to embark, and we spoke with the sailors of the ship about our coming aboard with them. They showed great kindliness toward us as was ordained by the Lord. And after we had embarked, we sailed a day and a night. After that, a wind came up behind the ship and brought us to a small city in the midst of the sea (VI.1.1–29).[35]

The first person plural narrative style shifts to first person singular when the boat arrives at the dock.

> And I, Peter, inquired about the name of this city from residents who were standing on the dock. [A man] among [them] answered, [saying, "The name] of this [city is Habitation, that is], Foundation [...] endurance." And the leader [among them ... holding] the palm branch at the edge of [the dock]. And after we had gone ashore [with the] baggage, I [went] into [the] city, to seek [advice] about the lodging (VI.1.30–2.10).

At this point it appears that the narrative is recounted entirely in first person with Peter telling the story. A little further on, however, Peter is presented, without comment, through narration by the author in third person style.

> [The men asked Peter] about the hardships. Peter answered [that it was impossible to tell] those things that he had heard about the hardships of [the] way, because [interpreters were] difficult [...] in their ministry.

> He said to the man who sells this pearl, "I want to know your name and the hardships of the way to your city because we are strangers and servants of God. It is necessary for us to spread the word of God in every city harmoniously." He answered and said, "If you seek my name, Lithargoel is my name, the interpretation of which is, the light, gazelle-like stone" (VI.5.2–19)

As the story continues, the narrative style alternates, without explanation between first person and third person narration. Sometimes, in other words, Peter is telling the story, and at other times Peter is talked about in third person as a participant in the events. Finally, the document ends with a third person account of "the Lord" with the disciples (VI.10.14–12.22).

For the purposes of this study, it would be informative to know if *The Acts of Peter and the Twelve Apostles* began, as well as concluded, with third person narration. There is a possibility that it began with

---

[35] The quotations from *The Acts of Peter and the Twelve Apostles* are taken from *The Nag Hammadi Library in English* (ed. James M. Robinson; trans. Douglas M. Parrott and R. McL. Wilson; New York: Harper & Row, 1978), 454–59 and are used by permission of Harper and Row. I am grateful to Professor George W. MacRae, Harvard University, for calling these references to my attention.

third person narrative style adopted first person narrative style in the context of the sea voyage, then returned to third person style at the end of the account. Without further evidence, it is impossible to know. It does seem fair to conclude that this document probably written during the latter part of the second century[36] has been influenced both by the sea voyage material in the canonical book of Acts and by first person narrative style in romance literature.[37] Among the apocryphal Acts material, it attracts special interest because of the coincidence of first plural narration with a sea voyage. During the second and third centuries, however, first person narrative style influenced the apocryphal material beyond the context of sea voyages.[38]

In conclusion, there are three texts, in addition to the book of Acts, where third person narrative style shifts to first person plural when a sea voyage is initiated. In a fourth text, *The Acts of Peter and the Twelve Apostles*, the narration shifts freely among first person plural, first person singular, and third person narration.

It may be well to notice a feature of Luke-Acts that has not yet been mentioned. The author begins his narrative with a first person singular preface to Luke and another at the beginning of Acts. Therefore, the author uses first person narration in the prefaces, third person narration in the basic text, and first person plural narration in the accounts of sea voyages. Luke evidently adapts his style to the content that he presents. The we-passages fit the genre of sea voyage narratives. Such accounts would be expected to contain first person narration, whether or not the author was an actual participant in the voyage. Without first person narration the account would limp. By the first century CE, a sea voyage recounted in third person narration would be considered out of vogue, especially if a shipwreck or other amazing events were recounted. For this reason an alert writer like Luke would place himself on the journey by using first person plural.

The We-Passages as Sea Voyage Literature

The we-passages in Acts have captivated interpreters from Irenaeus[39] to the present.[40] And, for the most part, Irenaeus' shadow has fallen over

---

[36] Ibid., 265.

[37] For a discussion of first person narration in romance literature, see Ben E. Perry, "Appendix III: The Ego-Narrative in Comic Stories," in *The Ancient Romances* (Berkeley: University of California Press, 1967), 325–29.

[38] See, e.g., *Acts of John* and *Acts of Thomas* 1, in *The Apocryphal New Testament* (ed. and trans. M.R. James; Oxford: Clarendon, 1953), 228–70, 365.

[39] Irenaeus, *Against Heresies* 3.14.1.

the whole enterprise. For Irenaeus, the we-passages demonstrated that the author of Luke-Acts was a companion of Paul. Many interpreters since Irenaeus have left the impression that an author who used first person plural narration in his account must, by necessity, have been a participant in those events or must have used a diary of a participant.

Internally, however, the we-passages are not a unity. The variation from "we," which includes Paul, to "Paul and us" (16:17; 21:18) exhibits the use of first person plural as a stylistic device by the author himself. Also, the tension between "we" and "they" in Acts 27:1–44 reflects the author's employment of first person plural for sea voyaging even when it is difficult to sustain the personal narration in the context of the events that occur on the voyage.

Eduard Norden was aware that the we-passages in Acts represent the sea voyage genre.[41] Henry J. Cadbury read Norden's work and knew that these sections were a different genre from the other material in Acts.[42] He mentioned that it was a "regular custom for the *periplous*, as the account of a coasting voyage was called, to be written in first person"[43] but he did not take the next step. He concluded that the abrupt shift from third person narration to "we" was "peculiar and unexplained."[44]

The evidence within contemporary Mediterranean literature suggests that the author of Luke-Acts used "we" narration as a stylistic device. The influence for this lies in the Classical, Hellenistic, and Roman literary milieu.[45] This first plural technique is simply a feature of the sea voyage genre in Mediterranean antiquity. All of the features of this genre arise out of the dynamics of sailing on the sea, landing in unfamiliar places, and hoping to establish an amiable relationship with

---

[40] See Ernst Haenchen, *The Acts of the Apostles* (trans. R. McL. Wilson et al.; Philadelphia: Westminster, 1971) and Ward Gasque, *A History of Criticism of the Acts of the Apostles* (Tübingen: J.C.B. Mohr [Paul Siebeck], 1975).

[41] Norden, *Agnostos Theos*, 313–27.

[42] Henry J. Cadbury, *The Making of Luke-Acts* (New York: Macmillan, 1927), 60–61.

[43] Ibid., 144.

[44] Ibid., 358.

[45] During this time period, Semitic voyages do not use first person plural narrative style. Neither the biblical accounts of Noah nor Jonah use this technique. The voyage of Jonah raises the most interesting possibilities because of its widespread popularity. Beginning with the end of the third century CE, Jonah's voyage appears frequently in sarcophagi. For this information, see Cornelia C. Coulter, "The 'Great Fish' in Ancient and Medieval Story," *TAPA* 57 (1926): 32–50; Joseph Engemann, *Untersuchungen zur Sepulkralsymbolik der späteren römischen Kaizerzeit* (Münster: Aschendorff, 1973), 70–74. First person plural narration does appear in the Islamic account of Jonah's voyage: Quran Sura 37:139–141; see Richard Delbrueck, *Probleme der Lipsanothek in Brescia* (Bonn: P. Hanstein, 1952), 22–23. For a study of the Jonah traditions in the NT, see Richard A. Edwards, *The Sign of Jonah* (Naperville: Allenson, 1971).

the people in the area where the landing occurs.[46] During the short stay on land, before resuming the voyage, two kinds of episodes are especially frequent. First, an event often occurs in which some people of the area are friendly toward the voyagers. This event usually leads to an invitation to stay at someone's home.[47] The voyagers seldom remain neutral visitors in a locale where they land. Thus a second event will divide the people of the area over whether or not these voyagers are to be trusted. Usually the leader of the voyage will become involved in a major episode in which his extraordinary abilities are displayed. Often he will speak eloquently and perform some unusual feat.[48] If the voyagers are not driven forcibly from the place where they have landed, an emotional farewell scene occurs in which the people bring provisions and other gifts to the boat.[49]

A sea voyage account often opens with a statement regarding the purpose of the voyage, a comment about preparations for it, and a list of some of the participants in it.[50] When the voyage is under way, there is an account of the places by which the voyagers sail, and frequently short descriptive comments are given about the places. Also, the length of time it takes to sail from one place to another usually is indicated, and frequently the span of time is linked with the direction and force of the wind.[51] Gods are portrayed as determining the fate of the voyage. Visits of the gods, and signs and portents, frequently attend the voyage. In response, prayers are offered, altars are built, and sacred rituals are enacted.[52] At some point, almost every good sea voyage account portrays a storm that threatens or actually ends in a shipwreck.[53]

---

[46] For all kinds of information about ships and sea travel on and around the Mediterranean, including information about Paul's voyages, see the four works by Lionel Casson, *Travel in the Ancient World* (Garden City, N.Y.: Doubleday, 1964); idem, *Ships and Seamanship in the Ancient World* (Princeton: Princeton University Press, 1971); idem, *The Ancient Mariners* (New York: Macmillan, 1959); idem, *Illustrated History of Ships and Boats* (Garden City, N.Y.: Doubleday, 1964). For an account of the search for the remains of ancient ships and the estimates regarding the number of ships that traveled the Mediterranean and went down in the deep, see Willard Bascom, *Deep Water, Ancient Ships* (Garden City, N.Y.: Doubleday, 1976).

[47] Cf. *Voyage of Hanno* 6; Virgil, *Aeneid* 3.80–83, 306–55; Dio Chrysostom 7.3–5; Lucian, *A True Story* 1.33; 2.34; Achilles Tatius 2.33; Heliodorus, *Ethiopian Story* 5.18.

[48] Cf. *Odyssey* 9.43–61, 195–470.

[49] Cf. Virgil, *Aeneid* 3.463–505; Lucian, *A True Story* 2.27; Achilles Tatius 2.32.2.

[50] Cf. *Voyage of Hanno* 1; Lucian, *A True Story* 1.5.

[51] Cf. *Voyage of Hanno* 2–6, 8–17; Virgil *Aeneid* 3.124–27, 692–708.

[52] Cf. *Voyage of Hanno* 4; Virgil, *Aeneid* 3.4–5,19–21, 26–48, 84–120, 147–78, 358–460, 373–76, 528–29; Lucian, *A True Story* 2.47; Achilles Tatius 2.32.2; 3.5.1–4; 3.10.1–6.

[53] Cf. *Odyssey* 9.67–73; Virgil, *Aeneid* 3.192–208; Dio Chrysostom 7.2; Lucian, *A True Story* 2.40; 2.47; Achilles Tatius 3.1.1–3.5.6; Heliodorus, *Ethiopian Story* 5.27.

Virtually all of the features of ancient sea voyage literature are present in the we-passages in Acts. The first we-section, 16:10–17, begins in response to a vision which occurs during the night. In this vision a Macedonian says to Paul, "Come over to Macedonia and help us" (16:9). The narrator interprets this summons to mean that God is calling them to this area to preach the gospel (16:10). The success of this venture is assured by divine destiny no matter what obstacles threaten to undo it. Especially the sea voyages of Odysseus and Aeneas established visions, signs, and portents as a characteristic feature of this kind of literature. The first we-section emerges in the narrative of Acts with a dynamic that is well-known in Mediterranean sea voyage literature.

As first person plural narration begins and the boat is launched for Macedonia, the narrator recounts the places by which they sail and the time it takes to sail the distance (16:11–12). This is the first instance of a detailed account of a voyage in Acts, and it includes a comment about the prestige and role of Philippi--a typical feature in a sea voyage account. The narration of the voyage ends with the statement: "We remained in this city some days." This is a customary clause at the end of a paragraph in a voyage manual.[54]

Once they land at Philippi, a series of events occur that lead to the imprisonment and spectacular release of Paul and Silas. Only the first two events are narrated in first person plural. In the first event (16:13–15) the voyagers meet some women and begin to talk to them. A woman named Lydia "opens her heart" so that she invites them to come to her house and stay. This scene is a typical component of voyage narratives, and it contains first plural narrative style.

The second event (16:16–18) begins with first person plural narration but makes a transition to third person narration in 16:17. This event has a dynamic that is often present in sea voyage accounts. Paul performs an extraordinary act of power, and this act causes a disturbance among the local people. In this instance, Paul drives a spirit of divination out of a slave girl who brings money to her owners by soothsaying. As the episode develops into a detailed event in the city, first plural narration is left behind. With the re-emergence of third person narrative style, the events move from the sea to "the land." The next series of events does not conclude with a return to the boat; Paul and his company travel to Amphipolis, Apollonia, and Thessalonica on foot (17:1).

The transition from first plural to third person narration is achieved through the phrase "Paul and us" (16:10). This phrase is a signal to the reader that the events lead away from the boat to the land and its chal-

---

[54] Cf. *Voyage of Hanno* 6: παρ' οἷς ἐμείναμεν ἄχρι τινὸς, φίλοι γενόμενοι.

lenges. The same technique appears at the end of the third we-passage (21:18). At the end of the final we-passage, the transition is made by indicating that Paul was permitted to remain "by himself" with only the soldier guarding him (28:16). In all three instances the transition takes the event away from the sea; third person narration centers on Paul's influential activity on land.

The second we-section, 20:5–15, is the first half of a sea voyage to Jerusalem. First person plural narration emerges at the conclusion of a list of people who accompany Paul on the voyage (20:4). As in the first we-section, the voyage opens with a detailed account of the places to which they sailed and the duration of time. This introduction ends with the comment that they stayed in Troas for seven days (20:5–6). Again, first person plural narration begins as a boat is launched on the sea, and the opening verses are a typical beginning for a sea voyage account.

An event is recounted at Troas before the voyage continues, and it is narrated in first plural style (20:7–12). The episode begins as a farewell scene (20:7), but it ends as a spectacular event performed by Paul. When Paul's speech lasts far into the night, and a young man falls out of a third story window and is dead, Paul embraces him and revives him. This miraculous event is placed on the first day of the week, and Paul appears to "break bread" both before and after he brings the young man back to life. This setting for the event is not interpreted by the narrator, but it creates a context similar to the one created by the vision at the outset of the first voyage. This voyage is in the hands of God. Paul carefully follows the religious rites of the Christian community, and the power of God works through him. The reader knows (19:21) that Paul is headed for Jerusalem, and the reader also knows what happened to Jesus at Jerusalem. As the danger of taking this voyage to Jerusalem becomes prominent in the narrative, the will of God for Paul to go to Rome (19:21) becomes increasingly important. If Paul truly is an apostle through God's will, then he will fulfill the proper religious rites and receive the benefits of God's favor. For a person in the Hellenistic world, this feature is a natural part of a sea voyage account. It was the will of Zeus/Jupiter that both Odysseus and Aeneas complete their voyages without suffering death. All the delays, hardships, and apparent reversals of the decision are overcome by the rituals the voyagers perform and the destiny the supreme gods refuse to alter.

The final part of the second we-section (20:13–16) contains a typical detailed account of sailing from place to place and meeting people to take them on board. It ends by thematizing the purpose of the voyage:

Paul "was hastening to be at Jerusalem, if possible, on the day of Pentecost" (20:16). At this point there is an interlude in the voyage. They have sailed as far as Miletus, and Paul summons the elders of the church at Ephesus to come to him there. This event features Paul giving a speech, and third person narration is used to recount Paul's meeting with these church leaders (20:17–38).

The third we-section begins as soon as the Ephesian elders bring Paul back to the ship. The parting scene depicts them kneeling in prayer and bidding Paul farewell with weeping, embracing, and kissing. As the first person plural narration resumes, again there is a detailed account of the voyage that ends with a remark about the length of their stay in the city where they landed (21:1–4). This opening part reiterates the purpose of the voyage as the disciples tell Paul not to go on to Jerusalem.

The next two verses contain another typical parting scene. All the disciples, with their wives and children, accompany the voyagers to the beach, pray with them, and bid them farewell (21:5–6). After this, typical voyage narration occurs until they reach Caesarea (21:7–8). At Caesarea a prophet enacts a scene that foretells Paul's arrest and delivery to the Gentiles when he reached Jerusalem (21:8–14). In the sphere of literature in the Hellenistic world, this scene is like Odysseus' encounter with the prophet Teiresias in *Odyssey* 11.90–137. Both the reader and the protagonist in the story know the dangers that lie ahead and the outcome. For the moment, however, Paul forgets that "he must go to Rome" (19:21). He is ready "not only to be imprisoned but even to die at Jerusalem" (21:13). The destination at Jerusalem is the sole concern of the voyage, and scenes that are typical components of sea voyage literature are used to emphasize the danger that lurks at the end of the voyage.[55]

The final verses of the third we-section describe the trek from Caesarea to Jerusalem (21:15–18). Since the destination of the sea voyage is Jerusalem, first person plural narration continues until Paul goes in to James and the elders (21:18). At this point the events are committed to land, and the narration moves back to third person style. As the first we-section stopped once Paul and his company began the activity which brought them before the leaders of the city (16:17), so the second and third we-sections stop once Paul and his company begin the consultation with James and the elders at Jerusalem. The trials that ensue are Paul's mission on land once he has voyaged to this area.

The fourth we-section, 27:1–28:16, presents the final, climactic sea voyage of Paul and his company. There is a dramatic progression in the length and drama of the we-sections in Acts. The first we-section is

---

[55] Cf. the danger that awaits Odysseus when he returns to Ithaca.

brief (16:10–17), and it takes Paul and his associates on a straight sailing course from Troas to Philippi (16:11). The drama of the voyage arises from the vision at the outset, the invitation to stay at Lydia's house, and the encounter with the slave girl who has a spirit of divination. The second and third we-sections are longer (20:5–15; 21:1–18), and they take Paul and his company on an episodic, tearful voyage that systematically moves to Jerusalem. The drama of the voyage emerges through the farewell speech that develops into a miraculous event when Paul revives a young man (20:7–12), the farewell speech and scene with the Ephesian elders at Miletus (20:17–38), the farewell scene at Tyre (21:5–6), and the prophetic enactment at Caesarea of Paul's imprisonment and delivery to the Gentiles (21:8–14). The fourth we-section is longer yet, and more dramatic.

As Paul is taken to the boat to sail for Rome, first plural narrative again emerges in Acts (27:1). The opening part contains the typical information about sailing from port to port, and passing islands and other places (27:1–8). Beginning with 27:4, the narrator introduces the dynamic that furnishes the drama for this voyage. The wind is against them, and the sailing becomes more and more difficult. The second part of the section thematizes the danger that is increasing and features Paul in conversation with the people in charge about their plight (27:9–12). Paul's advice that the voyage temporarily be aborted is overruled by a majority of the people on the boat. The narration of the increasing danger impels the action to the next part with skill. The wind grows into the fury of a storm, and the detailed portrayal of the inability to control the ship, the necessity of throwing the cargo overboard, and the absence of sun and stars for many days takes the reader to the heart of the sea voyage narratives (21:13–20). Paul knows the divine destiny of the voyage that includes storm and shipwreck, just as Odysseus knows what will happen when the Sirens, Scylla and Charybdis threaten to kill every mortal on board including himself (*Odyssey* 12.35–126). Therefore, Paul tells them they should have listened to him, and he tells them what the outcome of this storm will be (27:21–26). As Paul predicts, the ship runs aground as the crew attempts to beach it, and everyone is forced to abandon ship and escape to the island of Malta (27:27–44). The detailed description of the maneuvering of the ship by the sailors, the sounding for fathoms, the casting of anchors, and the manning of ropes and sails ranks this account among the most exciting depictions of storms and shipwrecks in the sphere of Greek and Roman literature. In the midst of it Paul takes bread, gives thanks to God, breaks it in the presence of all, and begins to eat (27:35). As all the members of the ship eat, the sacred ritual for receiving God's favor is performed. Everyone escapes safely to land, in spite of plans by the crew to abandon the ship (27:30) and intentions by the soldiers to kill the prisoners (27:42). Divine destiny holds the controlling hand when storm and shipwreck dash ships and mortals back and forth upon the sea.

The storm and shipwreck take the voyagers to the island of Malta. The opening scene portrays the islanders as unusually friendly (28:1–6), and the islanders become even more kindly disposed before the voyagers depart. When a viper bites Paul and he does not fall down dead, the islanders perceive Paul as every bit as godlike as Odysseus or Aeneas (28:6). The warm relationship between the islanders and Paul grows even more when Paul heals the father of the chief man of the island. Not only does the chief man receive them and entertain them for three days, but the scene develops into a general healing episode after which the islanders bid them farewell by bringing gifts and provisions to the boat (28:7–10). These events on the island are narrated in typical sea voyage style. All detail is suppressed except the information that highlights the welcome to the island, the spectacular abilities of the protagonist on the voyage, and the farewell scene.

The final part of the voyage contains the customary sailing information as the boat proceeds from Malta to Rome (28:11–16). Details about putting in at ports and staying for a few days are included; the favorable winds and the warm receptions at the harbors also receive attention. As the boat lands, Paul offers the proper prayer to God and takes courage that the voyage has concluded with God's favor still upon him (28:15). The voyage is ended, and third person narration emerges once again as Paul turns toward his new mission on land (28:18).

The final we-section in Acts represents the sea voyage genre par excellence. Each time a we-section begins, the drama heightens; movement through space becomes a voyage across the sea. The final voyage takes the gospel to ports and islands far away, and the adventure, danger, and fear bring "Paul and us" to Rome with thanksgiving.

The We-Passages in the Structure of Luke-Acts

If the dynamic of sea voyaging is crucial for understanding the we-sections in Acts, the place of the passages in the arrangement of this two volume work is as important. There are two perspectives from which the arrangement is important for interpretation. First, the we-sections occur in the last half of Acts. Comparison of Luke with Acts indicates that both volumes contain a long travel narrative that leads into the concluding scenes. This feature suggests that the volumes contain some type of parallel structure. Second, the portion of Acts in which the we-sections occur represents the last fourth of this two volume narrative. In this final segment, Paul's travels spread the gospel "to the end of the earth" (1:8; 13:47). It will be important to discover the techniques by which the author has brought the entire narrative to its dramatic conclusion. The first aspect of the arrangement will be discussed here; the second aspect will be discussed in the next section.

The we-sections occur in a portion of Acts that shows significant points of relation with Luke. The journey narrative in Luke 9:51–19:28 is a distinctive feature of the Lukan narrative,[56] and the journeys of Paul in Acts 13:1–28:16 comprise the highpoint of the narrative of Acts. In general terms, Jesus' journey in Luke corresponds to Paul's journey in Acts. The journeys reflect the movement through time and space that is a central feature of Luke-Acts.

Closer observation reveals that specific architectonic parallels exist between the journeys in Luke and Acts.[57] There are three sections in Acts that correspond to three sections in the Lukan travel narrative. Paul's mission to the churches in Asia Minor, Macedonia, and Greece (Acts 13:1–19:20) corresponds to the mission of the seventy (Luke 10:1–24).[58] Paul's journey to Jerusalem (Acts 19:21–21:26) corresponds to Jesus' journey to Jerusalem (Luke 13:22–19:46). Agrippa's handing over of Paul to a centurion to be escorted to Rome (Acts 27:1–28:16) corresponds to Pilate's handing over of Jesus to the chief priests, rulers, and people to be crucified (Luke 23:26–49). Because of these correspondences, this study could include detailed analysis of Luke as well as Acts. Our immediate goal, however, is to interpret the role of the we-sections in the overall setting of Paul's journeys. Therefore, having noticed this parallel architectonic structure, we will proceed with analysis in Acts only. In the next section, more features of Luke will come into the discussion.

All three sections of Paul's journeys contain we-passages, and the length of the we-sections increases as the end of the narrative draws near. The first journey section (13:1–19:20) only contains eight verses of first plural narration. (16:10–17). The second journey section (19:21–21:26) contains twenty-nine verses of first plural narrative style, and the third journey section (27:1–28:16) is entirely a we-section (60 verses). Of course, the increasing amount of first plural narration is linked with the increasing amount of sea travel. The increasing length of sea voyage material affects the structure of Acts 13–28.

---

[56] Cf. Hans Conzelmann, *The Theology of St. Luke* (trans. G. Buswell; New York: Harpers, 1960), 60–73.

[57] For an explanation of architectonic structure and the correspondences between Luke and Acts, see Charles H. Talbert, *Literary Patterns, Theological Themes and the Genre of Luke-Acts* (Missoula, Mont.: Scholars Press, 1974), esp. 1–65.

[58] Ibid., 20.

Perhaps the most striking aspect of the structure in the journey sections is the chiastic arrangement that unifies the first and second sections. The second half of the first section (15:1–19:20) and the second section (19:21–21:26) represent a generally balanced chiastic structure.[59] The perimeters of the chiasmus are the Jerusalem council in 15:1–33 and Paul's return visit to Jerusalem in 21:15–26. The inside of the chiasmus is filled out by three balancing units and a series of episodes at the center. The travel and imprisonment in 15:36–17:15 is balanced by the travel and prophecy of arrest and imprisonment in 21:1–14. The speech at Athens in 17:16–24 is balanced by the speech at Ephesus in 20:17–38. The assembly at Corinth and subsequent travel in 18:1–23 is balanced by the assembly at Ephesus and subsequent travel in 19:21–20:16. The center of the chiastic structure is found in 18:24–19:20. This, therefore, is the chiastic outline:

A 15:1–34 Jerusalem council	A' 21:15–26 Report to Jerusalem Leaders
B 15:36–17:15 Travel and Imprisonment	B' 21:1–14 Travel and Scene of Binding
C 17:16–24 Speech at Athens	C' 20:17–38 Speech at Ephesus
D 18:1–23 Assembly at Corinth and Travel	D' 19:21–20:16 Assembly at Ephesus and Travel
E 18:24–19:20 Spreading the Gospel throughout Asia from Ephesus	

The center of a chiastic structure, in relation to the outside portions, reveals the essential dynamic of the literary arrangement.[60] Events at Ephesus where Paul corrects inadequate or improper understanding of the gospel stand at the center. Paul's encounters with the authoritative leaders at Jerusalem stand on the perimeters of the structure. The literary arrangement presents an interplay between Jerusalem and Ephesus as centers for spreading the gospel. Ephesus is the center for preaching the gospel to all residents of Asia, both Jews and Greeks (19:10). This assertion stands at the heart of the Ephesus events Jerusalem is the locale from which Paul's mission to Jews and Gentiles is authorized.

The relation of the we-passages to the chiastic arrangement introduces another dimension of this portion of Acts. There are no we-passages in the first half of the initial travel section (13:1–14:28), and

---

[59] Ibid., 56–58. Our analysis varies some from Talbert's, though agreement with regard to the extent of the chiasmus exists.

[60] For an excellent analysis of chiastic structure see Joanna Dewey, "The Literary Structure of Controversy Stories in Mark 2:1–3:6," *JBL* 92 (1973): 394–401.

this part of the first section is not a segment of the chiasmus. In other words, all of the we-sections except for the final dramatic voyage are included in the material that has been given a chiastic structure. This means that only with the chiasmus is mission "by land" and "by sea" emphasized.

With regard to structure, therefore, the initial travel section (13:1–19:20) has two halves. The Jerusalem council (Acts 15) stands between the first and second half. The first half portrays Paul establishing and nurturing churches in Galatia and Cyprus. This mission is inaugurated by the Holy Spirit who says, "Set apart for me Barnabas and Saul for the work to which I have called them."[61] After the prophets and teachers at Antioch fast and pray, they lay their hands on Barnabas and Saul and send them off (13:2–3). The Barnabas and Saul mission occurs in 13:1–14:28. This mission does not have the blessings of the Jerusalem leaders and it does not take Paul "to the other side of the sea." Travel by boat is included in this first half (13:4, 13; 14:26), and "Saul" becomes "Paul" after he has "sailed" to Cyprus (13:9). Paul and Barnabas travel by boat, but their mission occurs prior to the Jerusalem council and is limited to the easternmost portion of the Mediterranean Sea.

With the Jerusalem council (15:1–35) a new phase enters into Paul's mission activity. He no longer travels with Barnabas, and his mission is not limited to the environs of the eastern portion of the Mediterranean. Beginning with the Jerusalem council, the material is balanced chiastically, and after this council there is an interplay of mission "by land" and "by sea."

Paul's authoritative mission "by land" begins in Acts 15:36. Severing his relation with Barnabas, Paul chooses Silas and establishes a valid mission to the churches in Syria and Cilicia by delivering to them "the decisions which had been reached by the apostles and elders who were at Jerusalem" (16:4). But Paul does not stop with this; his mission by land is on the move in a way it could not be before the Jerusalem council. Paul and Silas travel through Phrygia and Galatia and would appear to have "a clear road ahead." But then the mission by land is temporarily hindered. The Holy Spirit will not allow Paul and Silas to speak the word in Asia, so they are forced to go down to Troas (16:6–7).

The apparent hindrance to Paul's mission by land inaugurates a new phase: mission "by sea." The first we-section introduces this phase (16:10–17). In contrast to the previous sea travel by Paul (13:4, 13; 14:26), now the destination lies "on the other side" of the sea. In a night vision a man of Macedonia says to Paul, "Come over to Mace-

---

[61] For the relation of statements by the Holy Spirit and prophets, see Haenchen, *Acts of the Apostles*, 395.

donia and help us" (16:9). In response, the first true sea voyage is launched, first plural narration emerges, and a new mission area opens to Paul and Silas.

Once Paul and Silas have reached Macedonia, their mission spreads "by land" (16:19–17:13). When Paul goes to another new area, Achaia,[62] again he goes "by sea" (17:14–15). The effort of the author to assert this mode of opening the mission at Athens has created an unusual grammatical construction in 17:14. The verse states that the brethren at Beroea sent Paul out "to go as far as upon the sea" (πορεύεσθαι ἕως ἐπὶ τὴν θάλασσαν). The peculiarity of ἕως and ἐπί in sequence caused copyists either to omit ἕως or replace it with ὡς.[63] The problem evidently arises because Beroea is not a coastal city, and the author wanted to indicate that Paul went to Athens "by sea." The meaning is clear, because the verse is constructed in parallel with 17:15a: οἱ δὲ καθιστάνοντες τὸν Παῦλον ἤγαγον ἕως ᾿Αθηνῶν ("those who conducted Paul brought him as far as Athens"). In like manner, the brethren at Beroea sent Paul out to go (by land) as far as "upon the sea." The narrator distinguishes between spreading the gospel "by land" and "by sea." The gospel spreads to new areas, e.g., Macedonia and Achaia, "by sea." Once Paul and his company arrive at a new area, the gospel spreads "by land." Later in the narrative, Paul travels "by land" between Achaia and Macedonia (20:2), but the initial mission is "by sea."

The irony of the chiastic structure is that mission "by sea" to Macedonia is balanced with mission "by sea" to Jerusalem. It would be wrong to think this is accidental. The voyage that takes Paul and Silas to Philippi where they are imprisoned and miraculously released (16:10–40) is balanced by the sea voyage that takes Paul to Caesarea where the prophet Agabus symbolically enacts the binding of Paul and his delivery to the Gentiles (21:1–14). Both voyages are we-sections, and Paul's voyage to Jerusalem is mission "by sea." Prior to this Paul has not had an opportunity to spread the gospel in Jerusalem. This area was closed to him. Now he goes to Jerusalem "ready not only to be imprisoned but even to die at Jerusalem for the name of the Lord Jesus" (21:13). His voyage to Jerusalem opens up an extensive mission "by land" from Jerusalem to Caesarea. Paul spreads the gospel not only to the people in Jerusalem (22:1–21) but also to the Sanhedrin in Jeru-

---

[62] During the first century, Achaia included the areas in which both Athens and Corinth were located, but it did not include the area in which Philippi and Thessalonica were located.

[63] Evidently the reading with ἕως would mean that they sent Paul away pretending that he would go by sea but actually going by land: "as though to go upon the sea" or "to go as it were upon the sea." See Bruce M. Metzger, *A Textual Commentary on the Greek New Testament* (New York: United Bible Societies, 1971), 455.

salem (23:1–10), the governor Felix in Caesarea (24:10–21), and to King Agrippa (26:1–29). Mission by sea has taken Paul not only to Macedonia and Achaia; it has taken Paul to Jerusalem itself and the political leaders who rule the area. Counterbalanced we-sections open both areas of mission to Paul "by sea."

As Paul's mission by sea to Macedonia provides the base for mission by sea to Jerusalem, so Paul's mission by sea to Jerusalem provides the base for mission by sea to Rome. All three missions are by sea, and all three missions are inaugurated by we-sections. The long, dramatic voyage to Rome (27:1–28:16) stands in notable contrast with the circumscribed beginnings of Paul's mission in the easternmost part of the Mediterranean Sea (13:1–14:28). On the way to Rome Paul even has a mission "upon the sea." When the voyage becomes dangerous, Paul begins conversation with the people in charge (27:10), and when a storm begins to hurl them mercilessly about on the sea, Paul has the opportunity to tell the people on the ship about the God to whom he belongs and whom he worships (27:21–26). The foreknowledge of events that he received from an angel of his God not only proves to be accurate, but it provides the opportunity for Paul to take bread, give thanks to God in the presence of all, and eat (27:35). And, says the narrator, "they all were encouraged and ate some food themselves" (27:36). This imagery will certainly not be missed by the reader; Paul has "broken bread" with the entire group on the ship. But this still is not enough. Paul's mission on the sea is made complete by miracles that attend his leadership.[64] When he sustains a viper bite, the natives on the island of Malta think he is a god (28:3–7); and when Paul heals the father of the chief man, Publius, all the diseased come to him and are cured (28:7–10). This mission "upon the sea" takes Paul to Rome. The remaining part of Acts presents Paul's mission by land in and around Rome.

The we-sections play a decisive role in the section in Acts that narrates the journeys of Paul. These sections add mission by sea to mission by land. By careful structuring throughout chapters 13–28, the author includes sections of sea voyage material that open new areas until the gospel spreads "to the end of the earth." By composing the journeys in three sections (13:1–19:20; 19:21–21:26; 27:1–28:16), the author develops a linear schema that portrays the spreading of the gospel from the land east of the Mediterranean to Italy. By a chiastic arrangement of the episodes from the Jerusalem council to Paul's return to Jerusalem (15:1–21:26), the author counterbalances the mission "to Macedonia and Achaia" with the mission "to Jerusalem and its environs." The first

---

[64] Cf. Acts 19:11–20.

person plural sea voyages furnish the dynamic for the movement through space, and the careful structuring of the episodes relates Paul's mission to Jerusalem and Rome.

The Function of the We-Passages in Luke-Acts

Analysis of the structure of Acts 13–28 indicates that the author uses the we-sections to create a special role for mission by sea. In this section of the paper the analysis moves a step further. Three aggregates of information suggest that the entire two volume work is designed to replace the Sea of Galilee, which dominates Mark, with the Mediterranean Sea. The we-passages systematically increase in length to focus all attention on the Great Sea that lies between Jerusalem and Rome. We recall that Paul's journeys in Acts 13:1–28:16 correspond to the long journey of Jesus in Luke 9:51–19:46. This suggests that the travel sections in Acts were designed to bring Lukan themes and actions to a dramatic conclusion. Our interest is to find any relationship between Luke and Acts that illumines the role of the we-passages.

The first items of importance are found in the vocabulary of Luke and Acts. The author never allows Jesus to go alongside or onto a "sea" (θάλασσα) in Luke. This stands in notable contrast to Matthew and Mark where Jesus does both many times.[65] This difference arises, because the Sea of Galilee is never mentioned in Luke; it does not seem to exist in Lukan geography. Instead, there is a place on the eastern edge of Galilee which the author calls "the lake" (ἡ λίμνη: Luke 5:1, 2; 8:22, 23, 33). Once this lake is called the Lake of Gennesaret (5:1).

The existence of "the lake" but not "the sea" in Luke appears to relate to the overall purpose of the author. It is designed to limit Jesus' activity in a particular way. Jesus is allowed to go to the lake only twice in Luke. All other occasions when Jesus went to the Sea of Galilee in Mark are omitted. On the first occasion, Jesus goes out in a boat with Simon, and James and John, the sons of Zebedee (5:1–11). The entire episode moves toward the conclusion in which the three fishermen become disciples of Jesus and turn to "catching men" (5:10–11). On the second occasion, Jesus gets in a boat and sails to the other side of the lake (8:22). This setting allows for the inclusion of the accounts of the calming of the storm and the healing of the demoniac in the country of the Gerasenes (8:22–39).

Each of the occasions when Jesus is linked with the lake in Luke has a twofold dimension in Luke-Acts. On the one hand, the occasions set a precedent for later action in the narrative. When Jesus goes onto the lake in 5:1–11, circles around, and comes back, he evokes the image of

---

[65] See n. 1.

the disciple as one who travels on water and fishes for men. It appears to be important that he does not go "across" the lake. This episode set a precedent that corresponds to the situation in Acts 13:1–14:28. We recall that this section in Acts presents the first instance of sea travel. The Holy Spirit calls Barnabas and Saul to "the work" to which they have been called (13:2), and they sail out from Antioch in a circle to Cyprus, then to Pamphylia, and back to Antioch (13:4, 13; 14:26). When Paul and Barnabas return, they are sent to Jerusalem where they are sanctioned as apostles to the Gentiles (15:23–29). Paul and Barnabas have traveled on the sea; therefore they "have risked their lives for the sake of our Lord Jesus Christ" (15:26). Paul has been called to his work as the disciples are called to their work in Luke 5:1–11. But Paul does not go "across" the sea until after the Jerusalem council.

In Luke 8:22–39 Jesus sets the precedent for "crossing over" the sea that occurs for the first time in the initial we-section (Acts 16:10–17). In the Lukan episode, Jesus gets into the boat and announces, "Let us go across to the other side of the lake" (8:22). This corresponds to the Macedonian's call to Paul, "Come over to Macedonia and help us" (Acts 16:9). With the voyage across the body of water, God's work is spread to a new region. The author of Luke revises Markan vocabulary in the account of the storm on the lake to orient the story toward the climactic voyage and storm in which Paul participates at the end of Acts. Jesus and the disciples "set out from shore" (ἀνήχθησαν: Luke 8:22), just as Paul and his company "set out" on a boat many times.[66] As they are "sailing along" (πλεόντων αὐτῶν: Luke 8:23), Jesus falls asleep. References to sailing are frequent in the voyages of Paul.[67] The revision of Markan vocabulary suggests that the author already has the sea voyages of Paul in view as he composes.

The other dimension of these two episodes in Luke has already been mentioned, but it must be recalled as we move to the next reference to "the sea" in episodes with Jesus and the disciples. Only Paul and his company voyage on the sea. In the first episode not only Jesus but Simon Peter is in the boat. But Peter never voyages on the sea in Luke-Acts; he was called to his work by sailing in a boat on "the lake" (Luke 5:1, 2). Likewise, the author suppresses any reference to "the sea" in the storm episode. Instead of saying the wind and sea obey Jesus (Mark 4:41), the disciples refer to the winds and "the water" (Luke 8:25).

---

[66] Cf. Acts 13:13; 16:11; 18:21; 20:3, 13; 21:1, 2; 27:2, 4, 12, 21; 28:10, 11.
[67] Cf. Acts 21:3; 27:2, 6, 24.

The selection of vocabulary in the first volume suggests that the author is setting precedents during the time of Jesus which become the major challenge during the time of the church. In order to do this, the author presents corresponding episodes in Luke and Acts, and he suppresses certain features in the account in Luke so these features can be more dramatically carried out during the time of the church.[68]

This vocabulary usage grows in importance when other information is added to it. Although the author never depicts Jesus on or alongside a "sea," he betrays special interest in "the sea" in sayings of Jesus. He does not refrain from including the saying about being cast into the sea with a millstone around one's neck (Luke 17:2) and the saying about the sycamine tree that can be rooted up and planted in the sea by faith (Luke 17:6). Luke is the only gospel that refers to the "distress of nations in perplexity at the roaring of the sea and the waves" in the apocalyptic discourse (Luke 21:25). The sea has a special place in his theology even in the gospel of Luke, but the author will not link Jesus directly with it. The sea is linked with Paul's mission to new regions around the Mediterranean. This conception is further indicated by the references to God "who made the heaven and the earth *and the sea*" in Acts 4:24 and 14:15. Also it is probably not accidental that Simon Peter is associated with "Simon a tanner, whose house is by the sea" in the dramatic sequence of episodes in which the Gentile Cornelius is converted and blessed by Simon Peter (10:6, 32). Mission on the sea presupposes mission to Gentiles as well as Jews, and the author systematically builds toward mission by sea in Luke and Acts 1–12.

Perhaps the most important piece of information which indicates that the author is composing toward a dramatic finish that is achieved through sea voyages is "the great omission" in Luke.[69] Luke shows dependence upon Mark as a source for most of the material in Mark 1–6:44. But beginning with Mark 6:45, and continuing through Mark 8:26, Markan material is not recounted in Luke. The proposal in this paper is that the manuscript of Mark that the author of Luke-Acts used contained Mark 6:45–8:26. He omitted this section of Mark because it took the ministry of Jesus too far into the type of mission that he wanted to portray for Paul.

---

[68] For a well known example of the technique in Luke-Acts, cf. Mark 14:62 with Luke 22:69 and Acts 7:56.

[69] For a summary of discussions of the great omission, see Walter E. Bundy, *Jesus and the First Three Gospels* (Cambridge: Harvard University Press, 1955), 265–67. He concludes that "there is no satisfactory explanation for this omission" (265).

As Luke used the material in Mark 1–6:44, he systematically omitted references to the sea.[70] As we have just previously noticed, Luke places the call of the disciples (Mark 1:16–20), the stilling of the storm (Mark 4:35–41), and the healing of the Gerasene demoniac (Mark 5:1–20) on "the lake." In this way he avoids reference to the sea. But when he gets to Mark 6:45, the mission of Jesus develops into a mission all around the Sea of Galilee and deep into Gentile territory. Precisely with the episode where Jesus walks on the sea (Mark 6:45–52), the author begins to omit all of the material. After this episode, Jesus and his disciples cross the sea again (Mark 6:53–56), a rationale for Gentile mission is established (Mark 7:1–23), then Jesus travels through Tyre and Sidon (7:24–37). Since the boat and the sea continue to play an important role through 8:21, the author of Luke omits all the episodes in the section from the walking on the sea (Mark 6:45–52) until the confession of Peter in 8:27–33. By omitting this material, the author narrates an uninterrupted ministry of Jesus in Galilee without excursions into Tyre and Sidon and other Gentile territory. Also, the author keeps Jesus out of a boat and off a body of water that may begin to play a major role in his ministry.

In sum, the vocabulary of Luke, the two episodes where Jesus goes onto the lake, and the great omission indicate that the two volume work of Luke-Acts has been designed to replace the Sea of Galilee with the Mediterranean Sea. The role of the we-passages is to orient early Christianity toward the sea that lies between Jerusalem and Rome. The author disapproves of the emphasis upon the Sea of Galilee in Mark. No inland body of water in Palestine should be called "the sea." The sea that explains the history of early Christianity is the Great Sea that extends to the end of the earth.

Conclusion

Why, then, does the author use first plural "we" as he narrates those voyages that move the Christian church "across the sea?" First, it appears that the natural tendency to employ first person plural style within the sea voyage genre was a major factor. The second reason appears in the preface to Luke. As the author, a member of the church, pens his narrative sitting in Rome, the question is how "we" got here when we started out in Jerusalem. This author feels a strong sense of union with the early Christian leaders about whom he writes. He says that all of the things about which he writes have been accomplished "among us" (Luke 1:1). This includes all of the events he recounts in the gospel

---

[70] Mark used θάλασσα 12 times in 1:1–6:44.

of Luke as well as the narrative of Acts. For him, the conception and birth of John the Baptist (Luke 1:5–80) is an example of an event that happened "among us." The author participates in these events even when they are transmitted to him by others (Luke 1:2). Therefore, he can say both that these things happened among us and that they were delivered to us. As he sits in Rome, he participates in the events of the Christian church, and explains to "Theophilus" how his community of believers got to be where they are (Luke 1:3–4). A Christian in Rome who knows the events well enough to pen them as this author does becomes a full participant in them. This is true even if he has experienced these events only through oral transmission and the written page. Thus he can say in his preface that the activities of Jesus, the disciples, and the apostles happened "among us." As Paul voyaged across the sea, "we" got here.

If we think it would be impossible for an author who did not participate in the events to compose in this style, we need to entertain one more piece of information. Xenophon, we recall, used third person narration throughout the Anabasis, even for scenes in which he depicts himself as a participant. A later copyist of the Anabasis, obviously not a participant in the events, wrote a concluding summary which he attached to the narrative. From his pen flowed these words:

> The governors of all the king's territories that we traversed were as follows: Artimas of Lydia, Artacamas of Phrygia, Mithradates of Lycaonia and Cappadocia, Syennesis of Cilicia.... The length of the entire journey, upward and downward, was two hundred and fifteen stages, one thousand, one hundred and fifty parasangs, or thirty-four thousand, two hundred and fifty-five stadia; and the length in time, upward and downward, a year and three months (7.8.25–26).[71]

This copyist, and many writers, entered into the narrative as a participant even though later analysts can see that the style of narration does not comply with the rest of the document. Perhaps we should suggest that Luke participated in the sea voyages precisely in this way.

If the author felt such a close relation to all of the events he wrote about, why did he not use first person plural all the way through? Why did he use it only in the we-sections? He did not use first person plural only in the we-sections. He used it in the two settings where it is emi-

---

[71] "Ἄρχοντες δὲ οἵδε τῆς βασιλέως χώρας ὅσην ἐπήλθομεν. Λυδίας Ἀρτίμας, Φρυγίας Ἀρτακάμας, Λυκαονίας καὶ Καππαδοκίας Μιθραδάτης, Κιλικίας Συέννεσί.... Ἀριθμὸς συμπάσης τῆς ὁδοῦ τῆς ἀναβάσεως καὶ καταβάσεως σταθμοὶ διακόσιοι δεκαπέντε, παρασάγγαι χίλιοι ἑκατὸν πεντήκοντα, στάδια τρισμύρια τετρακισχίλια διακόσια πεντήκοντα πέντε. χρόνου πλῆθος τῆς ἀναβάσεως καὶ καταβάσεως ἐνιαυτὸς καὶ τρεῖς μῆνες.

nently appropriate if the author construes his work in the genre of historical biography in the Hellenistic milieu toward the end of the first century CE. These two settings are prefaces and sea voyages.[72]

---

[72] I am grateful to the University of Illinois Research Board at the Urbana-Champaign campus for funds that facilitated the final production of this study. See my study of the prefaces to Luke and Acts: "Prefaces in Greco-Roman Biography and Luke-Acts," *PRSt* 6 (1979): 94–108.

2

Sailing with Paul on Ideological Waters: The We-Voyages in Acts

In 1975, I published an essay on the we-passages in Acts, presenting evidence to propose that the primary model for these first person plural accounts emerged from Mediterranean sea voyage literature rather than from journeys on land.[1] During the next few years, I expanded the study by analyzing the manner in which the focus on Ephesus in the account of Paul had claimed the center of the presentation and determined the overall literary structuring of the sea voyage accounts in Acts.[2] My study had emerged from a surprise that the we-passages did not recount extended journeys by Paul and others on land. It also emerged from my context in a Classics department. Prior to my analysis of the first person plural accounts, I had the impression that the we-passages featured extensive land travel through which Paul spread Christianity along the Roman roads that led from the Mediterranean east to Greece and Rome. I also had the impression that they were carrying forth a "conquest" of Asia Minor, Macedonia, Greece, and Rome, something like Israel's conquest of the land of Canaan. My close analysis of the we-passages revealed, in contrast, that the mode of travel in the we-passages was on water. It became clear that the times on land did not feature activities of journeying into new territories, but were simply times of going from a harbor city to a city of destination or times of staying in a harbor city one or more days before continuing on the voyage by sea.

When I wrote the essays, namely in the early stages of my career, I was naïve enough to think that all my colleagues in NT studies would

---

[1] V.K. Robbins, "The We-Passages in Acts and Ancient Sea Voyages," *Biblical Research* 20 (1975): 5–18.

[2] V.K. Robbins, "By Land and By Sea: The We-Passages and Ancient Sea Voyages," *Perspectives on Luke-Acts* (ed. C.H. Talbert; Perspectives in Religious Studies, Special Studies Series, 5; Macon, Ga: Mercer University Press and Edinburgh: T. & T. Clark, 1978): 215–42. Online: http://www.religion.emory.edu/faculty/robbins/Pdfs/WeSeaVoyages.pdf.

be as intrigued as I with the sea voyage nature of the we-passages. I imagined feminist critics exploring the role of Lydia in Acts 16:14–15; the slave-girl in 16:16; and Philip's four unmarried daughters with a gift of prophecy in 21:9 in the we-passages. I imagined interpreters interested in prophetic and miracle discourse in the we-passages, which include Paul's vision of "a man of Macedonia" in 16:9–10; Paul's raising of Eutychus from death in 20:9–12; the Judean prophet Agabus binding his feet and hands with Paul's belt in 21:10–11; people's assertion that Paul was a god when the bite of a viper did not kill him (28:1–6); and Paul's curing of the father of the leading man on the island of Malta, Publius, from fever and dysentery, which caused them to bestow honors and abundant provisions for the remaining part of the sea voyage (28:8–10). Moreover, I imagined social analysis and interpretation of the we-passage cities of Philippi as "a leading city of the district and a Roman colony" (16:12); Thyatira as a cite for producing purple cloth (16:14), Miletus as a city in relation to Ephesus (20:17); Tyre, Ptolemais, and Caesarea as harbor cities (21:7–8); and the role of the centurion on the sea voyage to Rome (27:1–44). I also imagined analysis of the Adramyttium and Alexandrian ships that took the "we" participants to the island of Malta and then from Malta to Rome (27:2; 28:6, 11).

Indeed, many of the things I imagined have occurred, and also some remarkable new information has emerged that I will discuss as this essay unfolds. The immediate response to my studies was highly favorable. A series of scholars referred positively to my studies,[3] and some key studies expanded the approach I took.[4] After a decade, however, some New Testament interpreters began to take issue with my approach. At present (December 2008), there is an essay on the Web oversimplifying the issues in a global claim that: "For those scholars who have actually taken the time to evaluate the basis of Robbin's (sic) theory, there appears to be a unanimous conclusion that it lacks merit."[5] The author of this global claim cites eight scholarly works to support the claim.[6]

---

[3] E.g., Schuyler Brown, *The Origins of Christianity: A Historical Introduction to the New Testament* (Oxford/New York: Oxford University Press, 1984), 27–28; Richard Pervo, *Profit with Delight: The Literary Genre of the Acts of the Apostles* (Philadelphia: Fortress Press, 1987), 57.

[4] Dennis R. MacDonald, "Luke's Eutychus and Homer's Elpenor: Acts 20:7–12 and Odyssey 10–12," *JHC* 1 (1994): 4–24; idem, "The Shipwrecks of Odysseus and Paul," *NTS* 45 (1999): 88–107.

[5] Christopher Price, "The "We Passages" of Acts as a Literary Device for Sea Travel? A Critique of Vernon Robbins": http://www.christiancadre.org/member_contrib/cp_wepassages.html, December 27, 2008.

[6] Colin Hemer, "First Person Narrative in Acts 27–28," *TB* 36 (1985): 70–109; Susan M. Praeder, "The Problem of First Person Narration in Acts," *NovT* 29 (1987): 193–218;

For various reasons, certain scholarly colleagues and others have considered my analysis and interpretation either to lack merit or to be "entirely" wrong. I have been fascinated not only by the resistance to my analysis but also by the intensity of some of the remarks about my conclusions. The intensity indicates that something significant has been occurring over the years both in and underneath the discussion. A major goal of this essay is to explore what lies beneath the intensity of the responses both among some in the scholarly community and among some in a broader community who are active on the Internet.

My View during the 1970s of the Inner Texture of the We-Passages in Acts

It is important at the outset to state clearly what I discovered about the we-passages in Acts during the 1970s. In five sections of Acts, third person narration shifts abruptly to first person "we" and "us" narration. At each abrupt shift, the narration recounts the beginning or continuation of a sea voyage.[7] The first shift occurs in Acts 16:10–12, where the narration says: "When he [Paul] had seen the vision [of the man of Macedonia], we immediately tried to cross over to Macedonia, being convinced that God had called us to proclaim the good news to them. We set sail from Troas to Samothrace, the following day to Neapolis, and from there to Philippi, which is a leading city of the district of Macedonia and a Roman colony. We remained in this city for some days." After recounting episodes with Lydia and a slave-girl with a spirit of divination in 16:13–18, "we" narration abruptly shifts to third person narration when it recounts the arrest and imprisonment of Paul and Silas. In other words, when the narration moves into events that occur beyond the response of Paul and "us" to "help" people in Philippi, the narration shifts back to third person narration.

After third person narration presents various travels on land and sea by Paul and others in Acts 17:1–20:4, the narration presents the second abrupt shift to "we" narration in 20:5–6, when "They went ahead and were waiting for us in Troas; but we sailed from Philippi after the days of Unleavened Bread, and in five days we joined them in Troas, where we stayed for seven days." Here it is important to state my position clearly. I have never tried to claim there was no voyaging on the sea in

---

C.K. Barrett, "Paul Shipwrecked," in B.P. Thompson (ed.), *Scripture: Meaning and Method* (Hull University Press, 1987), 53–55 [51–64]; Stanley Porter, *Paul in Acts* (Hendrickson Publishers, 2001), 12–24; Joseph Fitzmyer, *Luke the Theologian: Aspects of his Teaching* (Paulist Press, 1989), 16–23; John B. Polhill, *Acts* (The New American Commentary; Baptist Book Stores, 1992), 346; Ben Witherington, *The Acts of the Apostles* (Eerdmans, 1997), 483–84.

[7] Cf. MacDonald, "The Shipwrecks of Odysseus and Paul," 88–93.

Acts outside the we-passages. Rather, my observation is that we-passages always begin with travel on the sea to a particular destination. As a we-passage continues, the group either arrives at a harbor city where they stay for some days before continuing on the sea voyage, or the group arrives at the major city that is the destination of the sea voyage. As this essay unfolds, we will see that many interpreters suppress the fact that every we-passage in Acts begins at a point where a sea voyage begins. Since every sea voyage naturally has a destination on land, and because sea voyages regularly include times of staying in one or more harbor cities along the way, the we-passages recount periods of time on land as well as on the sea. Interpreters who wish to avoid the fact that the we-passages are sea voyages assert that the time on land is "travel" as well as the time on the sea. The only "travel" on land in the we-passages is travel inland from Caesarea to Jerusalem (21:16–17), which is the destination of the sea voyage from Troas, and travel from Puteoli to Rome (28:13–14). In both instances, the inland travel is simply part of the sea voyage to Jerusalem and to Rome, and not the result of land travel. Good examples of land travel, in contrast, can be found in the inland journies of Peter to Lydda, Joppa, Caesarea, and Jerusalem in Acts 9:32–11:18 or the inland travel of Jesus and his disciples from Tyre to Jerusalem in Mark 7:24–11:11 or Matthew 15:21–21:10.

The third shift to first person plural occurs in 20:13-15, which begins: "We went ahead to the ship and set sail for Assos, intending to take Paul on board there...." This we-passage recounts a sea voyage from Troas, "where we stayed for seven days" (20:5), along the harbor cities of Assos, Mitylene, Chios, and Samos to Miletus (20:13–15).

After Paul delivers his speech to the Ephesian elders at Miletus and the elders bring Paul to the ship (20:17–38), the fourth shift to first person plural occurs in 21:1–4 when "we parted from them and set sail." At this point, one notices a repetitive occurrence of the "we" group "staying seven days" at a point where they arrive: after sailing to Cos, Rhodes, Patara, Cyprus, and Tyre, "we looked up the disciples and stayed there seven days" (21:4; cf. 20:5; 28:14). Then, when "our days there [Tyre] were ended, we left and proceeded on our journey" (21:5). First plural continues as "they escorted us outside the city" to the beach, and "we went on board the ship, and they returned home" (21:7). There is no journeying from Tyre to somewhere else during the seven days in Tyre. Rather, the time in Tyre is simply a layover period at a harbor city on the route of the sea voyage from Troas to Jerusalem. Continuing on the sea from Tyre, first plural continues as the group sails to Ptolemais, and then to Caesarea (21:7–8). "We" narration continues as "we got ready and started up to Jerusalem" (21:15). There are no episodes of "land travel" as the group journeys inland to the city that is the destination of the sea voyage. Rather, "[w]hen we arrived in Jerusalem, the brothers welcomed us warmly. The next day Paul went with us to visit James; and all the elders were present" (21:18). With the arrival of Paul and "us" in the presence of James and the elders, the sea voyage travel from Troas to Jerusalem ends.

The fifth abrupt shift from third person narration to first plural narration begins with the sea voyage from Caesarea to Rome (27:1–28:16), after episodes that recount Paul's arrest in Jerusalem (21:33) and transfer to Caesarea (23:31–33). After Agrippa tells Festus, "This man could have been set free if he had not appealed to the emperor" (26:32), the narration shifts abruptly to: "When it was decided that we were to sail for Italy, they transferred Paul and some other prisoners to a centurion of the Augustan Cohort, named Julius. Embarking on a ship of Adramyttium that was about to sail to the ports along the coast of Asia, we put to sea, accompanied by Aristarchus, a Macedonian from Thessalonica" (27:1–2). "We" narration continues throughout chapter 27 until 28:16: "When we came into Rome, Paul was allowed to live by himself, with the soldier who was guarding him." The nature of coming to Rome on a sea voyage, however, is clear from their actual arrival at Puteoli, where "we found believers and were invited to stay with them for seven days. And so we came to Rome" (28:14). From the point of view of the "we" narration, the arrival on land at Puteoli is arrival by sea at "Rome"! They actually had to travel on land more than 100 miles from Puteoli to arrive in Rome. There is no account of this time on land, however, because the narrational point of view features voyaging by sea. From the perspective of this final we-passage, the travel from Puteoli to Rome is simply the end of the sea voyage from Jerusalem (by way of Caesarea) to Rome (28:13–14), just like the earlier travel from Caesarea to Jerusalem was simply the end of the sea voyage from Troas to Jerusalem (20:13–21:18). As a result of the emphasis on sea voyaging, there are no "episodes" on the road as they travel the "land" part of the sea voyage either from Caesarea to Jerusalem initially (21:15–17) or from Puteoli to Rome at the end of the final voyage (28:13:14).

As a result of the discovery that all of the we-passages launch sea voyages, I searched through Mediterranean literature for the presence of "we" narration in the context of sea voyages. Sea voyage literature was so well known in the Mediterranean world that the Greek word *periplus*, to "sail around," was used in the title of the famous sea voyages of Hanno the Carthaginian and sea voyages throughout the Erythraean Sea and the Black Sea. In addition, the famous sea voyages of Odysseus in Homer's *Odyssey* 9–12 and of Aeneas in Virgil's *Aeneas* were well known in antiquity, and of course the sea voyages recounted various periods of time on land as they proceeded gradually to their final destination. The abrupt shift from the third person opening of the *Periplus* of Hanno the Carthaginian to first person plural when they set sail, in addition to the first person plural Homeric couplets, indicated a natural relation between sea voyage literature and the we-passages in Acts, all of which begin when a ship is being launched on the sea.

Moving Beyond Literary-Historical Interpretation to a Socio-Rhetorical Paradigm

As David Gowler explains in the introductory essay in this book, the introduction to the 1992 paperback edition of *Jesus the Teacher* observed that the beginnings of sociorhetorical interpretation were clearly present in the we-passages essays in the 1970s.[8] In truth, the seeds for sociorhetorical interpretation of Luke-Acts were being planted during the 20th century in the investigations and interpretations of Eduard Norden, Henry J. Cadbury, Martin Dibelius, Ernst Haenchen, Hans Conzelmann, and Eckhard Plümacher, who explored dimensions of the creativity of the author of Luke-Acts within the boundaries of Mediterranean historiography.[9] The decisive shift toward sociorhetorical interpretation of Luke-Acts occurred, however, in the interplay between Charles H. Talbert's emphasis on the relation of Luke-Acts to Mediterranean biography[10] and Richard I. Pervo's insistence on the relation of Acts to ancient historical novels.[11]

A major difference between my approach to the we-passages and the approach of my critics is a difference in analytical-interpretive para-

---

[8] V.K. Robbins, *Jesus the Teacher: A Socio-Rhetorical Interpretation of Mark* (Minneapolis: Fortress Press, 1992, © 1984), xix.

[9] Joseph B. Tyson, "From History to Rhetoric and Back: Assessing New Trends in Acts Studies," in *Contextualizing Acts: Lukan Narrative and Greco-Roman Discourse* (ed. Todd Penner and Caroline Vander Stichele; SBL Symposium Series 20; Atlanta: SBL, 2003): 23–42; cf. Marianne Palmer Bonz, *The Past as Legacy: Luke-Acts and Ancient Epic* (Minneapolis: Fortress Press, 2000), 1–7.

[10] Charles H. Talbert, *Literary Patterns, Theological Themes and the Genre of Luke-Acts* (SBLMS 20; Missoula: Scholars Press, 1974); idem, *Perspectives on Luke-Acts* (Edinburgh: T. & T. Clark, 1978), in which Robbins, "By Land and By Sea" appeared (215–42); cf. Bonz, *The Past as Legacy*, 7–9.

[11] Richard I. Pervo, Profit with Delight: The Literary Genre of the Acts of the Apostles (Philadelphia: Fortress Press, 1987; cf. Bonz, The Past as Legacy, 10–14.

digm.[12] Either in the foreground or the background of the investigations of my critics lies a scientific approach that uses literary-historical analysis in a "scientific" manner designed to limit boundaries of interpretation. A characteristic of the approach, as my critics have used it, is to exclude broader social, cultural, and ideological views of the data as false. In contrast, my approach is guided by a multiple contextual approach properly called an interpretive analytics. An interpretive analytics "approaches texts as discourse and 'sees discourse as part of a larger field of power and practice whose relations are articulated in different ways by different paradigms' (Dreyfus and Rabinow 1983: 199). The rigorous establishment of the relations of power and practice is the analytic dimension. The courageous writing of a story of the emergence of these relations is the interpretive dimension."[13] Sociorhetorical interpretation moves through literary, historical, social, cultural, rhetorical, religious, and ideological contexts of interpretation to ascertain multiple functions of the discourse in the realm of human cognition, knowledge, and interaction among humans. Overall, the issue is a shift in paradigm from textual science characteristic of Enlightenment modernism, which presupposes that reasoning everywhere and at all times is "always the same," to an interpretive analytics characteristic of "transmodernism,"[14] which builds on the discovery of cultural anthropologists that there are differences in reasoning based on "the various ways that societies, cultures, and diverse individuals face the world."[15]

During the 19th and 20th centuries, literary-historical approaches dominated over all other approaches in New Testament study as an alliance was established between literary-historical analysis and theological interpretation. This paradigm opened new territories of investigation and produced remarkable advances in knowledge about the ancient Mediterranean world. Literary-historical investigations extended boundaries of interpretation to include Mesopotamia and Persia to the steppes of India in the east; Egypt to the upper regions of the

---

[12] See "V. The Priority of Paradigms," in Thomas S. Kuhn, *The Structure of Scientific Revolutions* (2d ed.; Chicago: University of Chicago Press, 1970): 43–52.

[13] V.K. Robbins, *The Tapestry of Discourse: Rhetoric, Society and Ideology* (London: Routledge), 11, quoting Hubert L. Dreyfus and Paul Rabinow, *Michel Foucault: Beyond Structuralism and Hermeneutics* (Chicago: University of Chicago Press, 1983), 199.

[14] V.K. Robbins, "The Rhetorical Full-Turn in Biblical Interpretation and Its Relevance for Feminist Hermeneutics," in *Her Master's Tools? Feminist and Postcolonial Engagements of Historical-Critical Discourse* (ed. Caroline Vander Stichele and Todd Penner; Global Perspectives on Biblical Scholarship Series 9; Atlanta: SBL and Leiden: Brill, 2005): 111–16 [109–27]. Online: http://www.religion.emory.edu/faculty/robbins/Pdfs/BerlinRhetFullFemPubPgs.pdf.

[15] Gianni Vattimo, "Toward a Nonreligious Christianity," in John D. Caputo and Gianni Vattimo, *After the Death of God* (ed. Jeffrey W. Robbins; New York: Columbia University Press, 2007), 30.

Nile in Africa in the south; and Asia Minor, Macedonia, Greece, and Rome to the West. During the last three decades of the 20th century, a noticeable division emerged among New Testament scholars who used the literary-historical paradigm to prevent new arenas of investigation from opening up and other New Testament scholars who explored new arenas of early Christian society, culture, and ideology with a combination of outward reaching literary, rhetorical, sociolinguistic, social scientific, cultural, and ideological forms of theory and criticism. Analysis and interpretation of the we-passages in Acts illustrates well the attempts during the last quarter of the 20th century of some literary-historical scholars to prevent new arenas of investigation from gaining an important place in New Testament interpretation. The major strategy of these practitioners of literary-historical interpretation has been to keep the issues focused on historical causality. These literary-historical interpreters insist that only analysis and investigation of forces that have the potential to "cause" the presence of something in a text are phenomena that deserve the attention of true scholarship.

A major issue at stake in the shift from a literary-historical paradigm to a sociorhetorical paradigm is the relation of the rhetology of a text, the "reasoning" in it, to the "rhetography" of the text, the rhetoric of the graphic images in it.[16] In sociorhetorical terms, the rhetography of a text invites interpreters and readers to picture a contextual environment for the discourse in their minds. This environment provides meanings that persuade a hearer or reader to think in particular ways about the world, about the people who live in it, and about specific ways to live responsibly in it. The literary-historical interpreters who are my critics limit the rhetography of the we-passages to "vividness" that exhibits some aspect of historical reality. In other words, they intercept, limit, and/or even bypass substantive aspects of the contextual rhetography of the text by introducing questions and conclusions that reduce the rhetography to a limited range of phenomena in the historical arena of the Mediterranean world. The phenomena these literary-historical interpreters see in the historical arena of the text regularly are fascinating and informative. The phenomena are interesting enough, indeed, to become the all-consuming interest of the interpreter. In contrast to a limiting literary-historical approach, a sociorhetorical approach uses literary and historical phenomena as a beginning point for envisioning the text as a social, cultural, ideological, and religious

---

[16] V.K. Robbins, "Rhetography: A New Way of Seeing the Familiar Text," in *Words Well Spoken: George Kennedy's Rhetoric of the New Testament* (ed. C.C. Black and D.F. Watson; Waco: Baylor University Press, 2008), 81–106.

product, possession, and tool that invites the hearers, readers, and interpreters into the contextual rhetography of the text.

Limiting the Rhetography of the We-Passage Sea Voyages to Literary-Historical "Documentation," "Eyewitness," or "Narrative Witness"

Limiting the Rhetography to Causes that can be "Documented"

The publications of Colin J. Hemer on the we-passages in Acts represent the most restrictive "modernist" use of the literary-historical paradigm of analysis and interpretation. He begins with argumentation about "authorial" and "personal" participation in the events of the we-passages that gives the impression that he might be interested in the actual experiences of the author and his companions.[17] This discussion, however, is only an introduction to argumentation that the visual texture of the text presents "historical" and "documentary" evidence, first, of a "general historical setting" and, second, of specific historical circumstances during the time of the travel of Paul's party on the Mediterranean Sea. To achieve his goal, he avoids the we-passages in 16:10–17; 20:5–15, and 21:1–18 and focuses only on the sea voyage from Caesarea to Rome in 27:1–28:16. His reasons for bypassing these other we-passages will come to light as we proceed.

The major section in Hemer's essay on the first person plural account of the sea voyage in Acts 27:1–28:16 is entitled "The Background and the Documents."[18] The general historical setting for the sea voyage, he argues, is the organization of the "Alexandrian Corn Fleet" by the early Roman empire that exercised "[t]he control of Egypt as an essential source of corn-supply" for Rome.[19] Discussion of the Alexandrian Corn Fleet (87–94), which provides the general historical setting of the voyaging from Myra (Acts 27:6) to Malta to Puteoli (28:11), occupies eight pages of the essay,[20] then a discussion of "Specific Documents" occupies nine pages[21] before the "Concluding Observations."[22] The strategy of the essay is to begin with the sea voyaging of Paul's party from Myra to Puteoli (27:6–28:11) as documentary evidence for the Alexandrian Corn Fleet and to use this evidence to argue that "there are so many progressive indications of the need to integrate the narrative with its ostensible historical situation and to link Luke

---

[17] Colin J. Hemer, "First Person Narrative in Acts 27—28," *TynB* 36 (1985): 79–86.
[18] Ibid., 87–102.
[19] Ibid., 87.
[20] Ibid., 87–94.
[21] Ibid., 94–102.
[22] Ibid., 103–109.

with Paul at the times and places of the events, it may be claimed that the onus lies rather on the doubter to establish his case for breaking this integration."[23] Then he argues: "Indeed, I should want to argue that Luke's history is an inseparable element within his theology, where his testimony to what actually happened is a necessary preliminary to his understanding of a gospel whose claim to truth is established thereby."[24]

The motivation to ground theology in verifiable history guided rationalist scholars during the nineteenth century, and the same motivation guided Hemer's analysis and interpretation of Acts until his untimely death thirteen years before the end of the 20th century.[25] The book containing Hemer's final writings explains clearly his location in Enlightenment analysis and interpretation. As he puts it: "Recent post-Enlightenment thought has been heavily influenced by a disposition to see faith in existential terms. But existential faith and the Biblical argument for faith are significantly different in substance."[26] In post-Enlightenment "existential" faith, he asserts, "faith as trust is stressed to the initial exclusion of faith as assent."[27] In contrast, "the New Testament argument is for trust which goes beyond (but includes) assent to a practical sufficiency of relevant evidence." Then he adds, "Indeed the factor of assent to what is believed true is an essential one, for trust apart from discrimination of the objective may be a commitment to the false or unreliable or harmful."[28] In the end, then, for Hemer the New Testament presents a 19th century view of faith grounded in historical rationalism. The problem lies, of course, in his phrase "what is believed true." I do not share Hemer's distrust of imagination, since I do not believe that any mode of thinking can or does bypass imagination. Perhaps he might have agreed that the issue is responsible use of imagination. For me, responsible use of imagination includes aesthetic, social, cultural, ideological, and religious patterns of cognition that extend so far beyond historical verifiability that it is essential to explore these other dimensions of discourse as energetically as one pursues historical verifiability.

Hemer's analysis leads the reader to fascinating information about the first century Mediterranean world. It does this, however, by removing or bypassing items from the broader discursive context of Acts

[23] Ibid., 107.
[24] Ibid., 108.
[25] Colin J. Hemer, *The Book of Acts in the Setting of Hellenistic History* (ed. C.H. Gempf; Tübingen: J.C.B. Mohr, 1989), vii.
[26] Ibid., 441.
[27] Ibid.
[28] Ibid.

so a specific set of items can be placed in a historical laboratory that seeks specific "documentary" information from ancient Mediterranean history. This has been a time-honored occupation for New Testament scholars since the beginning of the 19th century, and this activity has yielded remarkable information about the historical context of the emergence of early Christianity. The interesting part of Hemer's strategy is not so much his search for documentary evidence in ancient Mediterranean literature and archeology but his interest in disqualifying any approach that seeks to interpret the imaginative dimensions of the discourse in Acts. His search for documentary evidence is so skillful and detailed that one wishes he could have continued to search and record the results for many more years. His attempts to disqualify any approach that explores the imaginative dimensions of the discourse in Acts, however, must be resisted.

One of the key moves in Hemer's argumentative strategy is to argue that my approach is guided by "the notion that an exclusively defined *Gattung* can be isolated by simple or composite verbal or syntactical criteria across a wide variety of prose and poetry of different types and languages," which is "inherently suspect."[29] I have looked in vain through my essays to find a focus on "an exclusively defined *Gattung*." It never was my intention to argue that all sea-voyages had to contain first plural "we" narration. Rather, my observation was and still is that the we-passages in Acts are sea voyage narratives. Hemer himself admits that "Of course, nothing I have said disposes of the fact that voyage-narratives often are couched in the 'we'-form, but I contend that this is a natural tendency dictated by the natural situation, not an artificial literary device."[30] Here we see the dynamics of enlightenment historical analysis that guided his investigations and his criticisms of my essays. For Hemer, an interpreter must bypass or by some other means "overcome" the imaginative, subjective character of literature for the purpose of arriving at the "objective" historical truth to which the text points. This means that, for him, aspects of literature that are imaginative are "artificial." The reason, as indicated above, is theological. For him, faith based on something "existential," by which he means "imaginative," runs the risk of being false, unreliable, or harmful. "True" faith, he argues, must be based on historical truth. Therefore, from his perspective any dimension of imagination in the text must be resisted or bypassed for the purpose of identifying aspects of the text that are a window into the historical reality of the time.

Let us suppose that a large number of phenomena in the we-passages can function as "documents" for what "actually happened" with Luke

---

[29] Hemer, "First Person Narrative in Acts 27—28," 86.
[30] Ibid.

and Paul in multiple places. What would be gained for our understanding of the sociorhetorical function of the we-passages in Acts if we presupposed this? Suppose we believe that Luke and Paul actually were there and things happened much like Luke tells it. What has been gained? For Hemer, a person has gained a conclusion that Acts does not tell lies. From this, are we also to conclude that the author of Acts has not used his imagination? Here is the problem. For Hemer, "imagination" means "false images and idea." But what if all "truth" is embedded in "imagination"? From my perspective, humans have not created societies, cultures, ideologies, and political and religious traditions simply on the basis of "truth." Rather, what people perceive to be "truth" is grounded in the human ability to "imagine."

Hemer uses a rhetoric of documentation to provide a rationale for bypassing the rhetoric of the visual texture in Acts, namely its rhetography. It is noticeable that he never discusses Acts 16:10–17 in any detail. In a candid moment he admits that Acts 16 differs from the detail and vividness of Acts 20–21 and 27–28.[31] But he does not carefully analyze it. It is as though he wishes to avoid Acts 16, since he knows the Troad was identified with Troy during the time of the writing of Acts. In addition, he avoids the term *"periplus,"* which ancient writers used as a title for sea voyage literature. Hemer expresses exasperation in a long footnote about an abstractor of his essay who refers to him as "not accepting that the 'we' passages fit the dimensions of the sea voyage genre," since he does not grant that there is such a thing as a sea voyage genre.[32] His moment of candor, however, that "voyage-narratives often are couched in the 'we'-form" exhibits his inner struggle between what might be called a stylistic pattern of narration and an artificial literary device. The most revealing section of his writing occurs when he argues, indeed in a most generous fashion, that there must not be a convention of first person plural within sea voyages, because the we-passages represent the real basis for establishing a foundation for Luke's eyewitness participation in certain Pauline events in Acts.[33] When an interpreter like Hemer focuses his thinking so thoroughly within the logic of the literary-historical paradigm, it is natural that issues of participation and truthfulness can become so dominant that there will be almost complete resistance to any attention to the remarkable literary and rhetorical features of the we-voyages.

One must ask if the limitation of the rhetography of the we-passages to historical documentation is worth the price. Some readers may de-

---

[31] Hemer, *The Book of Acts*, 333.
[32] Ibid., 329–30, n. 59.
[33] Ibid., 316–21.

cide as this essay proceeds, while others will already have decided before reading through it. But I want to clarify once again, perhaps with slightly different words, that my goal is to broaden our understanding of the function of the we-passage sea voyage narratives in Acts. This means that I myself find the detailed information that someone like Hemer presents to be fascinating, interesting, and informative. I do not, however, consider it to limit the function of the we-passages. My point is that the we-passages in Acts feature sea voyaging, so the time on land in them is a time that focuses on the arrival at a city that was the destination of the sea voyage or was a time of staying on land one or more days before they continued on their sea voyage. This observation, for me, raises broad issues concerning the function of sea voyages in Mediterranean literature during the time when Acts was written. If sea voyages did somehow play an important role in the social, cultural, ideological, and religious conceptuality of people in the Mediterranean world, it will be important for us to understand this role as we seek to understand the function of the sea voyages in the earliest written account of the movement of Christians from Jerusalem to Rome during the decades following the crucifixion of Jesus of Nazareth in Jerusalem ca. 30 CE.

Limiting the Rhetography to Lukan "Authorial" Cause

In 1989, Joseph A. Fitzmyer published an essay with a much more carefully formulated argument than Hemer presented. In his essay, entitled "The Authorship of Luke-Acts Reconsidered," he clarified that he preferred a conclusion that the we-passages in Acts are a diary-like record of Luke's travels with Paul, rather than a sea voyage account.[34] His preference was the result of many years of searching through data in second, third, and fourth century CE Christian writings that discuss or refer to Luke as the author of Luke and Acts, as well as the conclusions of 19th and 20th century scholars.[35] While he raises keen issues about many of the examples I presented in my published work,[36] he says he would not want to deny the existence of a "conventional generic style" of first person plural in contemporary Greco-Roman literature,[37] and he accepts other examples as showing "that one can speak of a sea voyage genre (or possibly even of a shipwreck genre) in first century Greco-Roman literature."[38] He thinks these passages provide evidence that Luke was "a sometime companion of

---

[34] Joseph A. Fitzmyer, *Luke the Theologian: Aspects of His Teaching* (New York/Mahwah: Paulist Press, 1989), 1–26.
[35] Ibid., 1–16.
[36] Ibid., 16–22.
[37] Ibid., 17.
[38] Ibid., 21.

the Apostle," rather than "an inseparable companion, as Irenaeus would have us believe."[39] For Fitzmyer, then, the major issue is the relation of interpretation of Luke-Acts to interpretation by Christian writers during the second through fourth centuries CE. He is aware of a wide range of challenges and possibilities. In the context of these challenges and possibilities he simply states his preference, which is based heavily on the points of view of Christian writers during the second, third, and fourth centuries CE.

Limiting the Rhetography to Untidy "Editorial" Causes

Instead of working at the level of compositional style, Susan M. Praeder approached the issue of the we-passages from the perspective of the author's redaction of sources. In this context, her conclusion is that: "The first person passages are not the compositions of a careful author or redactor, if carefulness means identification of first person characters or source authorities and attention to the problems created by first person passages in an otherwise third person account and third person sections in the few first person passages."[40] Praeder, then, does not side with those who consider the we-passages to be a source, or with those who consider the we-passages to be the result of systematic redaction by the author. She also, however, excludes what she calls "comparative literary solutions,"[41] saying that: "If Luke thought that first person narration would prove that he was an ancient historian or was required by sea voyages in ancient literature, then it can only be concluded that he was poorly informed about the conventions of ancient literature."[42] In the end, however, Praeder argues for a "contextual solution," saying: "It is the interpretative contexts of Acts, not the text of Acts, that allow for solutions."[43] Here she exhibits the confusion of her argument. She wants "interpretative contexts," but she disallows "comparative solutions" as a way to search for those interpretative contexts. She seems not to realize that contextual analysis requires comparative analysis! There is no context without comparison of a text with other phenomena in the context. The interesting thing is the success of arguments like Praeder's that set up impossible standards to solve what she considers to be unsolvable "problems." Such arguments are especially successful in a context of competing paradigms of interpretation.

---

[39] Ibid., 22.
[40] Praeder, "The Problem of First Person Narration in Acts," 217.
[41] Ibid., 218.
[42] Ibid., 217.
[43] Ibid., 217.

To achieve her critical goal, Praeder changes my language from "Such accounts would be expected to contain first person narration,"[44] to "Robbins's solution rests on the claim that first person narration was one of the requirements of sea voyages in ancient literature."[45] Her change of language about expectation to language of requirement is very important. Once she has made this change, she reaches a conclusion that: "The untidiness of the first person and third person sections challenges the usual redaction critical and comparative literary view of Luke as a careful author or redactor whose choice of first person narration was dictated by his, another's, or others' participation in Paul's travels."[46] Her language of "was dictated by" exhibits a presupposition about ancient writers with which I do not agree. In my view, ancient writers wrote in contexts of "conventional expectations" rather than "dictated requirements." It appears here that Praeder is imposing on the author of Luke certain kinds of requirements that may have been imposed on certain scribes during the Middle Ages who were employed to make new copies of texts containing exactly the same wording as the text from which they were copying. For me, there is abundant evidence in Luke and Acts that the author did not write in the mode of a copy-scribe but in the mode of a writer who possessed the skills of people trained at a high level of progymnastic rhetorical writing.[47]

Limiting the Rhetography to Writing in a Pauline School

In a recent essay, A.J.M. Wedderburn has produced a very interesting alternative for understanding the we-passages within the realm of Luke-Acts as historiography.[48] With a focus on the importance of the we-passages for the authorship of Acts, for the trustworthiness of its information, and for its role in reconstructing the history of early

---

[44] Robbins, "By Land and By Sea," 216.
[45] Praeder, "The Problem of First Person Narration," 206.
[46] Ibid., 217.
[47] Vernon K. Robbins, "Progymnastic Rhetorical Composition and Pre-Gospel Traditions: A New Approach," in *The Synoptic Gospels: Source Criticism and the New Literary Criticism*, edited by Camille Focant. BETL 110. Leuven: Leuven University Press, 1993: 111–147. Online: http://www.religion.emory.edu/faculty/robbins/Pdfs/Progymnastic.pdf. For a level of rhetorical writing comparable to the author of Luke-Acts, see: V.K. Robbins, "Writing as a Rhetorical Act in Plutarch and the Gospels," in *Persuasive Artistry: Studies in New Testament Rhetoric in Honor of George A. Kennedy* (ed. D.F. Watson; Sheffield: JSOT Press, 1991): 157–86; cf. Mikael C. Parsons, "Luke and the *Progymnasmata*: A Preliminary Investigation into the Preliminary Exercises," in *Contextualizing Acts*, 43–64; idem, *Body and Character in Luke and Acts: The Subversion of Physiognomy in Early Christianity* (Grand Rapids: Baker Academic, 2006), 147–52.
[48] A.J.M. Wedderburn, "The 'We'-Passages in Acts: On the Horns of a Dilemma," *ZNW* 93 (2002): 78–98.

Christianity, Wedderburn presents two horns of the dilemma. On the one side, he proposes, the use of first person plural would seem to signal the presence of the author in the events narrated in this style. On the other side, however, is the difficulty of believing that the author of Acts had personal contact with the Paul who is known from his letters.

After careful deliberation on the phenomena in Acts in relation to accounts of journeys both on land and sea in Mediterranean literature, including very perceptive insights and comments on the function of "we" when people are "in the same boat" in contexts of the dangers of travel on the sea,[49] Wedderburn emphasizes the importance of Philip Vielhauer's conclusions about the distance of the Paul of Acts from the Paul of the letters.[50] After a discussion of the solutions offered by Jürgen Wehnert, Dietrich-Alex Koch, and Dennis MacDonald,[51] Wedderburn offers a solution in terms of a third Pauline "school." The first Pauline school is that which produced Ephesians and Colossians, and the second is that which produced the Pastoral Epistles. The third school, he proposes, is a "branch of the tradition" nearer to the Pastoral Epistles branch, "but still sufficiently distinct to be regarded as a discrete branch."[52] Perhaps it was originally connected with Luke, which helps to account for the name later attributed to the anonymous author of Luke and Acts. Wedderburn clarifies that he is not presupposing an institutional "school," like a Pauline academy in Ephesus or elsewhere, "but merely a variety of traditions of thought and writing claiming explicitly (through pseudonymity) or implicitly (through the role which the apostle plays in them) to be the heirs of this apostle and to continue his work and teaching."[53] The special reason for proposing the existence of a school is that "the author of Acts does not write in the name of Paul, indeed does not write in anyone's name, not even under his own name."[54] The author of Acts, in Wedderburn's view, received either oral or written tradition from "an otherwise relatively unimportant companion of Paul's,"[55] a companion who was present at only certain events. The author of Acts, whose name is not known and who admires Paul but only at a distance and second hand, uses first person plural when presenting tradition from this companion, whose name we cannot know. In other words, the absence of known names for both the companion of Paul and the author of Acts can best be

---

[49] Ibid., 79–85.
[50] Ibid., 85–88.
[51] Ibid., 88–93.
[52] Ibid., 94.
[53] Ibid., 94, n. 54.
[54] Ibid., 95.
[55] Ibid., 95.

explained by the existence of a school where people do not attribute their writing to their own, or anyone else's, name.

From Wedderburn's perspective, first person plural is not a conscious literary device to show the presence of the author or to create the impression of reliability. The writer used it not "to record that other person's witness to Paul for posterity," but because he was writing "in the service of that person." Also, because he is writing in the service of that other person he does not write in his own name. The effect of Wedderburn's proposal is to extend to the writing of Luke-Acts the issue of pseudonymity as it has been discussed in relation to Ephesians, Colossians, and the Pastoral Epistles. From our perspective, a weakness in Wedderburn's proposal again is a failure to observe that every we-passage begins a sea voyage. In other words, the writing style of the pupil of the pupil is imitation of voyaging on the sea. Wedderburn admits that there is an occasional allusion to the Odyssey in the we-passages.[56] His focus, however, is on the two horns of the dilemma he states at the beginning of his work concerning how the use of "we" appears to exhibit participation in the events, yet the information in the we-passages shows no direct knowledge of Paul's letters or the information in those letters.

Limiting the Rhetography to Narrative Eyewitness that Replaces Barnabas

William Sanger Campbell presents a fascinating theory, guided by narrative criticism, that the we-passages replace Barnabas as narrative eyewitness to Paul's reversal of the position of the Jesus movement by going to the Gentiles.[57] Campbell builds his theory on the observation that the we-passages begin in Acts 16:10, after the substantive partnership of Paul with Barnabas and the abrupt conclusion of that relationship (Acts 9:27–15:39).[58] Campbell uses in particular the theological insights of Ernst Haenchen, who argued that the we-passages connect readers to Paul's mission and God's plan to take the gospel to Gentiles, which is a central theological point of view in Luke and Acts.[59]

---

[56] Ibid., 93.

[57] William Sanger Campbell, *The "We" Passages in the Acts of the Apostles: The Narrator as Narrative Character* (Studies in Biblical Literature 14; Atlanta: SBL, 2007), 13.

[58] Ibid.

[59] Ernst Haenchen, "'We' in Acts and the Itinerary," *JTC* 1 (1965): 65–99; idem, *The Acts of the Apostles* (trans B. Noble and G. Shinn; Philadelphia: Westminster, 1970); idem, "The Book of Acts as Source Material for the History of Early Christianity," in *Studies in Luke-Acts* (ed. Leander E. Keck and J. Louis Martyn; Nashville: Abingdon, 1966), 258–78; idem, "Acta 27," in *Zeit und Geschichte* (ed. Erich Dinkler; Tübingen: Mohr Siebeck, 1964), 235–54; cf. Campbell, *The "We" Passages in the Acts of the Apostles*, 7, 11–12, 71–74, 89, 97.

Campbell's analysis and interpretation of the we-passages in Acts stands at a decisive transition point from a literary-historical paradigm to a sociorhetorical paradigm that focuses on language as discourse. There are so many aspects of Campbell's book that move toward sociorhetorical analysis and interpretation, in fact, that it is important to mention a few. First, Campbell prefixes his first chapter, "Stories, Storytellers, and Readers," with a quotation from Jacques Derrida that observes that a writer "writes in a language and in a logic whose proper system, laws, and life his discourse by definition cannot dominate absolutely.... And the reading must always aim at a certain relationship, unperceived by the writer, between what he commands and what he does not command of the patterns of the language that he uses."[60] One of the keys to this quotation is the reference to discourse, which has a logic that is unperceived even by the writer. Second, as Campbell continues he observes that "readers build readers," in other words they construct reading communities that "usually share to an extent reading conventions and dynamics that permit, at least tentatively, collective assertions."[61] Third, he observes that "No two readers are identical, so no two readers bring the same considerations to or get the same meaning from a literary work."[62] He argues fourth, however, that readers do "seek explicitly or intuitively to become competent readers, that is readers who possess what in their view is the requisite linguistic, generic, historical, verbal, and grammatical knowledge for understanding what they are reading."[63] His two examples for "improving reading competency" in relation to Dan Brown's *Angels and Demons* and a collection of poems are highly instructive for the goal of competently reading the sea voyaging activity in the we-passages. In this context, he appositely observes that "Such efforts at increasing reading competency are attempts by readers to shape themselves into readers that they imagine reflect the intended audience in order to correlate the cognitive and affective experience of reading from their current contexts in a way that is consonant with the contexts of the targeted readers."[64]

Unfortunately, in the context of Campbell's key observations about the nature of discourse in literary works, his approach remains amazingly unattentive to the sea voyaging nature of the we-passages. The horizons he establishes for reading competency of the we-passages are limited by a focus on a reader's participation in eyewitness experiences,

---

[60] Campbell, The "We" Passages in the Acts of the Apostles, 15.
[61] Ibid., 17–18.
[62] Ibid., 17.
[63] Ibid., 18.
[64] Ibid.

rather than voyaging on the sea! This means that instead of following the principles he introduces in the first chapter of his work, he limits the possibilities for reading competency of the we-passages to aspects of being a companion of Paul who witnesses to Paul's obedience to God's instructions to him to take the gospel to the Gentiles. This limitation is especially evident in chapter two and appendix B, where he limits his analysis to historical writings by Thucydides, Polybius, and Josephus.[65] In other words, while he makes superb observations both about the narrative function of characters in the discourse of the we-passages and about substantive theological ramifications for these functions, he completely loses sight of the fact that every we-passage begins a sea voyage!

The strength of Campbell's analysis and interpretation lies in a coherent exposition of his theory that the we-passages replace Barnabas at a crucial point in Acts where the mission of the gospel moves beyond Asia minor into the heavily Gentile areas of Macedonia and Greece, and then Rome. The weakness of his exposition lies in its failure to observe that every we-passage starts a sea voyage. By allowing this phenomenon to drop out of sight, Campbell limits his observations to data related to a literary-historical, rather than sociorhetorical, paradigm of interpretation. This means that he never seriously raises the question of the possible social, cultural, ideological, and religious significance of voyaging on the Mediterranean Sea to and from the cities and regions depicted in the we-passages. In the end, then, Campbell's interpretation is a reconfiguration of eyewitness modes of interpretation that is not able also to account for the sea voyaging discourse in the we-passages. A full sociorhetorical analysis and interpretation, we propose, must include both the phenomenon of participation and the phenomenon of traveling on the Mediterranean Sea in discourse contemporary with Acts.

Rebuilding the Ship in the Midst of the Voyage: the Greek Text of the We-Passages

In a way that is perhaps ironic because of his point of view toward Acts, Stanley E. Porter has established an excellent beginning place for exploring the sociorhetorical power of the we-voyages through careful analysis of the exact beginning and ending points of we-narration in Acts. Guided by literary-historical practices of textual science, he has isolated the we-voyages in a highly skillful manner and produced some excellent insights into the discourse in the mode of a historical-textual theology. He yielded to one "contextual" phenomenon in his interpretation of the we-voyages to produce his interpretation, namely the

---

[65] Ibid., 27–47, 99–115.

vision of the man of Macedonia to Paul in Acts 16:9, which stands immediately before the first we-voyage. As he states: "... the first 'we' passage does not actually depict the vision (found in Acts 16:9), but takes up the narrative that is in response to it."[66] Porter moves outside the text of the we-voyages to the vision of the man of Macedonia in the immediate context of Acts to make a keen observation about the beginning of the we-voyages. When he observes that the we-voyages in Acts begin in response to the vision of the man of Macedonia, and they abruptly interrupt third person narration with a first person plural account of a sea voyage in 16:10–17 that takes "us" from Troas to Philippi, a leading city and Roman colony in Macedonia with a place of prayer (16:12–13, 16),[67] he has made an observation that begins to free interpreters from "historical causality" and turn them to the rhetography of the we-voyages. In other words, at this point Porter moves beyond a textual analysis of the we-voyages that either limits the text to a mass of historical or literary artifacts, or even limits the mode of interpretation to a literary-historical paradigm. As he approaches the wording at the beginning of the we-voyages, he sees a contextual response to a vision that opens the door to the rhetography of the we-voyages in the Mediterranean social, cultural, religious, and ideological world of the first century Christian discourse of Acts. Unfortunately, after this first contextual observation, he allows almost no other contextual data to inform his theological interpretation. In other words, he consciously tries to exclude other contextual dimensions from his theological interpretation of the we-voyages, because his goal is to present their "textual" literary-historical theology.

One of the strengths of Porter's analysis is that he observes a significant list of phenomena that are "not" in the we-voyages. There is no emphasis on necessity or fulfillment; no emphasis on Jesus as Savior; nothing eschatological; nothing "apologetic," trying to show that Christians were not a threat to the Roman government; no overt defense of Paul and his teachings; no refutation of heresy or promotion of overt evangelism; and no emphasis on Paul's preaching or speechmaking.[68] Another wonderful contribution is the list of phenomena he identifies "in" the we-voyages. He accurately observes an understated depiction of divine guidance and a "Hellenist" orientation that shows little interest in Jews as a specific group distinct from any other group. In addition, he observes that the we-voyages include "virtually only

---

[66] Stanley E. Porter, *The Paul of Acts: Essays in Literary Criticism, Rhetoric, and Theology* (WUNT 115; Tübingen: Mohr Siebeck, 1999; Peabody, Mass.: Hendrickson, 2001), 51.

[67] Ibid., 56.

[68] Ibid., 63.

non-Jewish cities" in its itinerary. In this regard, he notices that the identification of Philippi as a Roman colony (16:12: *kolōnia*) in the we-voyages is the only occurrence of the word "colony" in the Greek NT.[69] Also, he observes that Caesarea, where the "we" group spends most of its time in the eastern Mediterranean, is "a center of Hellenistic and Roman culture in Palestine."[70] Moreover, he notices that the only two references to the major Hellenistic city of Alexandria in the NT occur in the we-voyages at 27:6 and 28:11 in relation to the centurion Julius.[71] In addition, he observes that the reference to a place of prayer (16:13, 16: *proseuchē*) "is probably Jewish terminology for a Diaspora place of gathering, rather than a formal synagogue."[72]

The overall emphasis of Porter is on the "understated" nature of the we-voyages, which produces "a credible portrait of Paul the apostle, without exaggeration or embellishment."[73] For example, the we-voyages do not depict Paul as a miracle worker, because it does not exploit the fullest rhetorical possibilities with the miracles Paul performs.[74] I agree with a number of Porter's observations about "understatement" in the we-voyages, but he does not balance these observations with an account of the many incredible phenomena in the passages. Is it really the case that raising a young man from death to life after he falls out of a window (20:7–12) is not the portrayal of Paul as a miracle worker? Is there really no special emphasis on miracle-working when people call Paul a god when a viper bite does not cause him to swell up and die? Many of Porter's observations about the lack of rhetorical embellishment and flourish are correct, but it becomes obvious that he overstates the case for the purpose of presenting Paul as "the practical man, one willing simply to place himself in God's hands."[75] Indeed, a major problem is that he does not identify the we-passages as sea voyages and correlate this insight with the rhetorical restraints and excesses in the accounts. It certainly is not the case that the fury of the winds, the storm, and the shipwreck in Acts 27 are understated! If Porter would properly identify the we-passages as sea voyages, he could appropriately account for the kinds of restraints and the kinds of ex-

---

[69] Ibid., 56.

[70] Ibid., 57.

[71] Ibid., 58; cf. "Alexandrian" in the description of Apollos in Acts 18:24.

[72] Ibid., 56, citing J. Gutman, "Synagogue Origins: Theories and Facts," in J. Gutman (ed.), *Ancient Synagogues: The State of Research* (BJS 22; Chico, Calif.: Scholars Press, 1981), 1–6; P. Pilhofer, *Philippi. I. Die erste christliche Gemeinde Europas* (WUNT 87; Tübingen: Mohr-Siebeck, 1995), 165–74; and esp. I. Levinskaya, *The Book of Acts in its First Century Setting. V. The Book of Acts in its Diaspora Setting* (Grand Rapids: Eerdmans, 1996), 207–25.

[73] Porter, *Paul in Acts*, 62.

[74] Ibid., 60–62.

[75] Ibid., 65.

cesses that exist in them. Instead, he makes "global" assertions about understatement in the we-voyages that reveal a suppression of sea voyage adventures, dangers, and happy endings for the purpose of arguing that the account is a credible portrait of Paul.

Beyond the excessive claims about "understatement," Porter emphasizes certain things in a manner that makes them inaccurate. He says, for example, that "there is no serious attention given to ecclesiology, with attendant issues such as baptism, wealth and possessions, and the like."[76] It is actually quite the contrary! There are quite remarkable moments of "group ritual" that look like emergent ecclesiology in these sea voyage accounts. The end result of Lydia's "listening to us" at the "place of prayer" is the baptism not only of Lydia but her entire household (16:14–15). In addition, there are some remarkable Eucharistic moments. In Troas, "we met to break bread" on the first day of the week (20:7), and Paul's speaking until midnight accompanied this breaking of bread. Later, when the first plural participants had sailed almost past Crete, Paul "took bread, and giving thanks to God in the presence of all, he broke it and began to eat. Then all of them were encouraged and took food for themselves" (27:35–36). It seems a bit overdrawn to assert that there is "no serious attention" to such things as baptism or Eucharistic gatherings in these sea voyage accounts. On the contrary, these scenes are quite remarkable in a narrational account of sea voyages. These are obviously voyages with significant ecclesiological overtones.

In the midst of both strong points and inaccurate statements in Porter's analysis and interpretation, there are also a significant number of weaknesses. On the one hand, there are certain things he does not emphasize enough. Perhaps most significant, he does not emphasize that the first person plural subjects of the narrative only travel on land from a harbor city to a major Hellenistic-Roman city inland from the harbor, and never travel on land from one region to another. He does not observe that there are no detailed accounts of travel on land, describing distances on land or objects along the way, in contrast to detailed accounts of the winds, the depth of the water, and the location of harbors in the we-voyages. He does not comment on this data, because it would bring into view that the we-passages are accounts of sea voyages. Indeed, his omission of this data causes him to suppress information about the exact nature of the sea voyages in the we-passages. In Porter's discussion of what the author of the we-voyages does and does not know, he asserts: "What he does know is that Paul traveled

---

[76] Ibid., 63.

from Philippi to Miletus to Palestine."[77] What he should have written was: What he does know is that the first person plural companions began their sea travel in Troas. After traveling from Troas to Philippi (16:11-12), they returned by sea to Troas (20:5-6) before continuing by way of Miletus (20:15) to Jerusalem via the harbor cities of Tyre, Ptolemais, and Caesarea (21:7-8). The first person plural companions appear again "When it was decided that we were to sail for Italy" (27:1). The sea voyage began from Caesarea (25:13) first on an Adramyttium ship (27:2) and then on an Alexandrian ship (27:6) that was destroyed by a storm alongside the island of Malta (28:1). Three months later they continued on to Rome in an Alexandrian ship that had wintered at Malta (28:11). "And so we came to Rome" (28:14). Porter suppresses these details by focusing on Paul rather than the "we" in the passages. With this focus, he is able to bypass the nature of the we-passages as sea voyages. Focusing on Paul rather than on the first person plural participants, he gives the false impression that the travel on land disqualifies the we-passages from being sea voyage accounts. In truth, the travel on land is simply a matter of traveling inland far enough from a harbor city to reach the major city that is the destination of the voyage.

Seeing the Rhetography of the We-Voyages through a Socio-Rhetorical Understanding of Acts as Prose Epic

As stated at the beginning of this essay, the sociorhetorical mode of analyzing and interpreting the we-voyages in Acts emerged in a context of interplay between the writings of Charles H. Talbert and Richard Pervo. After the appearance of my essays, Dennis MacDonald moved decisively into the arena of sociorhetorical interpretation of the we-voyages in the midst of his detailed studies on the relation of Acts to the writings of Homer. In effect, his studies have advanced a view of the sociorhetorical effect of the we-voyages by opening the door to the epic nature of travel on the sea in Acts. In the context of a transition from eyewitness issues to the epic nature of Acts, Marianne Palmer Bonz and Loveday Alexander have produced work that holds the potential for moving analysis of the we-voyages fully into a sociorhetorical mode. We will begin with some insights from the work of MacDonald to set the stage for a discussion of the work of Palmer Bonz and Alexander.

---

[77] Porter, *Paul in Acts*, 64.

Dennis R. MacDonald's Voyage with Homer's *Odyssey*

After writing a series of books and essays on the relation of Homer to early Christian writings,[78] Dennis MacDonald wrote an essay in 1999 that directly expanded on the insight that the we-passages in Acts are sea voyages.[79] His argument in the essay is that the we-voyages are less a matter of "sailing around" (*periplus*) than "returns" (*nostoi*) in a manner that imitates Homer's *Odyssey*.[80] One of the keys to this, he asserts, is the conventional identification of Troas, known as Alexandreia in the Troad, with the legacy of Troy/Ilium in late antiquity.[81] Julius Caesar had seriously considered moving the capital from Rome to Troas/Alexandreia, on account of its Trojan fame through Vergil's *Aeneid*.[82] Not only do the initial we-voyages begin from Troas and return to Troas (16:10–17; 20:5–15), but the second voyage features sailing from Troas to Jerusalem and the final we-voyage features a ship of Adramyttium (27:2) which is a port city in the Troad, "at the base of Mt Ida, famous in the *Iliad* as the gods' favourite lookout on Troy."[83] For this reason, MacDonald argues, "Luke seems to have intended his audience to contrast the shipwrecks of Odysseus and Paul."[84] In the remainder of the essay, then, he exhibits the close relation between the nautical and shipwreck terminology in Homer's *Odyssey* and Acts to show how the discourse in Acts imitates scenes in the *Odyssey*.[85] As MacDonald proceeds, he observes in addition how the accounts in Acts imitate Homer in a manner highly similar to Vir-

---

[78] Dennis R. MacDonald, "Intertextuality in Simon's 'Redemption' of Helen the Whore: Homer, Heresiologists, and *The Acts of Andrew*," in *SBL 1990 Seminar Papers* (ed. David J. Lull; Atlanta: Scholars Press, 1990), 336–43; idem, *Christianizing Homer: The Odyssey, Plato, and The Acts of Andrew* (New York/Oxford: Oxford University Press, 1994); idem, "Luke's Eutychus and Homer's Elpenor: Acts 20:7–12 and *Odyssey* 10–12," *Journal of Higher Criticism* 1 (1994): 5–24; idem, "The Soporific Angel in Acts 12:1–17 and Hermes' Visit to Priam in *Iliad* 24: Luke's Emulation of the Epic," *Forum*, n.s. 2.2 (1999): 179–87. Also see idem, "The Ending of Luke and the Ending of the *Odyssey*," in *For a Later Generation: The Transformation of Tradition in Israel, Early Judaism and Early Christianity* (ed. Randal A. Argall et al.; Harrisburg: Trinity Press International, 2000), 161–68; idem, *The Homeric Epics and the Gospel of Mark* (New Haven: Yale University Press, 2000); idem, "Tobit and the *Odyssey*," in *Mimesis and Intertextuality in Antiquity and Christianity* (ed. D.R. MacDonald; Studies in Antiquity and Christianity; Harrisburg: Trinity Press International, 2001), 11–40.
[79] MacDonald, "The Shipwrecks of Odysseus and Paul."
[80] Ibid., 89–91.
[81] Ibid., 91–93.
[82] Suetonius, *Lives of the Caesars* 1.79.
[83] MacDonald, "The Shipwrecks of Odysseus and Paul," 93.
[84] Ibid.
[85] Ibid., 93–107.

gil's *Aeneid*.[86] This is not, he argues, evidence that Luke used the *Aeneid* as a source. Rather, "Luke may well have wanted to write a prose epic to rival Vergil's *Aeneid*, but when he looked for literary models for particular tales, they often came from Homer.... Luke not only transformed the scriptural legacy of Judaism, he occasionally transformed the epic legacy of Hellenism much as Vergil had.... Luke is not Vergil's direct literary offspring but his younger, admiring, but independent sibling; both are sons of Homer."[87]

MacDonald's pioneering work on the relation of Acts to the writings of Homer moved clearly beyond the limitations of historiography into the world of prose epic as a conceptual system for understanding the we-voyages. In a later essay he states openly that "Luke-Acts is thus epic, not history."[88] In addition, he reiterates in response to Marianne Palmer Bonz's stunning contribution to the discussion, discussed below, that many scenes in Acts have a closer imitative relation to scenes in Homer's writings than Vergil's *Aeneid*.[89] This leads him to argue: "To understand Acts we may have to replace historical and form-critical concerns with aesthetic and comparative literary ones, and to do this we must steep ourselves in the literature that formed the cultural competence of Luke's intended readers."[90] In conclusion, then, he asserts: "In other words, the truth of Luke's narrative lies in its imaginative reconstruction of the past to address the ideological needs of the nascent church. If he intended to write a history, he failed, even by the standards of ancient historiography. On the other hand, if he set out to write a prose epic, he succeeded brilliantly."[91]

Marianne Palmer Bonz's Journey with Virgil's *Aeneid*

Marianne Palmer Bonz has made a substantive contribution to the discussion of the we-passages by perceiving that the sea voyages in Acts participate in Mediterranean "epic" tradition. Unfortunately, as we will discover below, there were limitations in her approach that kept her from building on her insights in a fully sociorhetorical manner.[92] Nev-

---

[86] Ibid., 96, 101 n. 71.

[87] Dennis R. MacDonald, Does the New Testament Imitate Homer? Four Cases from the Acts of the Apostles (New Haven/London: Yale University Press, 2003), 9.

[88] Dennis R. MacDonald, "Paul's Farewell to the Ephesian Elders and Hector's Farewell to Andromache: A Strategic Imitation of Homer's *Iliad*," in *Contextualizing Acts: Lukan Narrative and Greco-Roman Discourse* (ed. Todd Penner and Caroline Vander Stichele; Symposium 20; Atlanta: SBL, 2003), 190 [189–203].

[89] Ibid., 191–203.

[90] Ibid., 202.

[91] Ibid., 203.

[92] Cf. the discussion of the strengths and weaknesses of Palmer Bonz's contribution in MacDonald, *Does the New Testament Imitate Homer?*, 7–9; idem, "Paul's Farewell to the Ephesian Elders and Hector's Farewell to Andromache," 189–90.

ertheless, her contribution is central to the current discussion. Palmer Bonz's contribution lies in her focus on the Latin epics that were translated into Greek in the historical, social, literary, and ideological milieu of Luke-Acts, with particular attention to "their famous Augustan prototype, Virgil's *Aeneid*."[93] Her proposal is that Luke-Acts is "a prose adaptation of heroic or historical epic" that provides "a hermeneutical model that is both universal in its theological message and essentially popular in its narrative presentation."[94] In the context of presenting her thesis, she cites C. H. Talbert as "one of the heirs to Cadbury's remarkable literary legacy, which launched an entirely new phase in Lukan research...."[95] She attributes to Talbert "a genuinely creative and comprehensive attempt to rethink the issues of genre and of Luke's literary links with the wider Greco-Roman world...."[96] She observes how Talbert begins with Virgil's *Aeneid* as "the clearest and most clearly executed contemporary example" of a stylistic approach that presents "a carefully worked-out system of parallels and contrasts that extends throughout the entire composition."[97]

After showing great appreciation for the work of Robert C. Tannehill,[98] and some approval of the creative structuralist analysis of Luke-Acts by Robert L. Brawley,[99] she praises Richard I. Pervo more, recounting in some detail the nature of his analysis of Acts in relation to "edifying narrative fiction" in the Greco-Roman world.[100] In particular, she attributes to Pervo the ability "to demonstrate that Acts exhibits in abundance many of the literary characteristics found more often in works of fiction than in works of history."[101] The major criticism of

---

[93] Marianne Palmer Bonz, *The Past as Legacy: Luke-Acts and Ancient Epic* (Minneapolis: Fortress Press, 2000), vii.

[94] Ibid., vii.

[95] Ibid., 7.

[96] Ibid., 7.

[97] Ibid., 7, with a qualification in n. 28 that "many of Talbert's parallelisms are rather forced, and Talbert has been justly criticized on this account"; Charles H. Talbert, *Literary Patterns, Theological Themes and the Genre of Luke-Acts* (SBLMS 20; Missoula, Mont.; Scholars Press, 1974), 5–7, 16–17. In n. 100, p. 26, Bonz appropriately credits Thomas L. Brodie as the first one who "suggested that Luke's appropriation of the Septuagint was analogous to Virgil's appropriation of Homer: "Greco-Roman Imitation of Texts as a Partial Guide to Luke's Use of Sources," in C.H. Talbert (ed.), *Luke-Acts: New Perspectives from the Society of Biblical Literature Seminar* (New York: Crossroads, 1984), 17–46.

[98] Ibid., 9; Robert C. Tannehill, *The Narrative Unity of Luke-Acts: A Literary Interpretation*, 2 vols. (Philadelphia/Minneapolis: Fortress Press, 1986–1994).

[99] Ibid., 9–10; Robert L. Brawley, *Centering on God: Method and Message in Luke-Acts* (Louisville: Westminster John Knox, 1990).

[100] Ibid., 10–12; Richard I. Pervo, *Profit with Delight: The Literary Genre of the Acts of the Apostles* (Philadelphia: Fortress Press, 1987).

[101] Ibid., 11.

Pervo, she asserts, is that he failed "to offer an interpretation that is theologically substantive."[102] In the end, she praises Pervo for showing that Acts "creates an imaginative and schematized historical story in order to provide a memorable and definitive interpretation of the underlying meaning of Christian history."[103]

From the realm of critical literary theory, Bonz uses the work of Meir Sternberg to distinguish between historiography and "history-telling" to set up her argument.[104] Then in her detailed discussion of epic narrative she indicates in a footnote that Mikhail Bakhtin considered "the essence of epic" to be its narration of the transcendent world of "the national epic past ... a world of 'beginnings' and 'peak times' in the national history ... a world of founders ... of 'firsts' and 'bests.'"[105] In addition, referring to the work of Burton L. Mack, she asserts that "inasmuch as Luke-Acts is written as a continuation – albeit a redirection – of the ongoing biblical narrative, Mack suggests that Luke-Acts must also be considered as part of Israel's national epic."[106] After reviewing the role of *Epic of Gilgamesh*, Homer's *Iliad* and *Odyssey*, Virgil's *Aeneid*, and Aristotle's discussion of epic in his *Poetics*,[107] Bonz discusses Luke-Acts as "A Foundational Epic for the Early Christian Church."[108] Underlying this discussion is Bonz's conviction that "the author known to us as 'Luke' was one of those authors upon whom Virgil's epic of Roman origins and divinely guided destiny had a profound influence" (in Greek translation).[109] Her conclusion is that: "Appropriating and adapting the biblical style and traditions characteristic of the Septuagint, while at the same time incorporating as many of the elements of Greco-Roman epic structure and dramatic presentation as were compatible with a prose narrative, Luke has composed a foundational epic for the early Christian communities of the Greco-Roman world."[110]

In the end, Bonz does not see the decisive contribution of the we-voyages to the epic rhetoric of Acts. After praising MacDonald's discovery of the importance of the Homeric sea-voyages in *Odyssey* 9–12

---

[102] Ibid., 13.

[103] Ibid., 13.

[104] Ibid., 15; Meir Sternberg, *The Poetics of Biblical Narrative: Ideological Literature and the Drama of Reading* (Bloomington, Ind.: Indiana University Press, 1987), 10, 12, 25, 77–78.

[105] Bonz, *The Past as Legacy*, 20 n. 86; Mikhail M. Bakhtin, *The Dialogic Imagination* (ed. M. Holquist; trans. C. Emerson and M. Holquist; Austin: University of Texas Press, 1981), 13.

[106] Bonz, *The Past as Legacy*, 16; Burton L. Mack, *Who Wrote the New Testament* (San Francisco: HarperCollins, 1989), 14.

[107] Bonz, The Past as Legacy, 17–25.

[108] Ibid., 25–29.

[109] Ibid., 39.

[110] Ibid., 29.

for understanding the we-voyages in Acts, she emphasizes the importance of Aeneas's sea voyage from Troy/Ilium to Rome but then reaches the simplified conclusion that "the 'we' references serve as rhetorical shorthand for the Pauline Christians – those who are vicariously privy to Paul's example and who, as heirs to his legacy, have been called by him to continue his unfinished mission."[111] At this point, Bonz misses the "epic" rhetoric of the we-voyages, which take the Pauline Christians to whom she refers first from Troy to Macedonia, from which Paul travels to Greece, and second from Troy to Rome via Jerusalem. Since the investigations of Loveday Alexander help to explain how Bonz's conclusion about the rhetorical function of the we-voyages is insufficient, we must now turn to Alexander's work on the cognitive map of Luke-Acts.

Loveday Alexander's Journey with Cognitive Geography: Luke's Paul invades Greek Cultural Territory by Sea

After her creative work on the prologues to Luke and Acts,[112] Loveday Alexander has established the importance of "cognitive geography" in ancient writings[113] and skillfully applied this approach to Acts.[114] One of the dramatic results of her analysis is the observation that there is a shift in cognitive maps as the narrative proceeds. A Jerusalem centered world-map is present in Acts 2:9–11. Following the insights of Richard Bauckham, she observes that the names of the locations are best understood as different directions viewed from Jerusalem: East (Parthians, Medes, Elamites and residents of Mesopotamia); center (Judea); North (Cappadocia, Pontus, Asia, Phrygia, and Pamphylia); South-West (Egypt and Libya); West (Rome and Crete); and South (Arabia).[115] This map is "a reversal of the usual Greek perspective on the world: for

---

[111] Bonz, The Past as Legacy, 173.

[112] Loveday C.A. Alexander, "Luke's Preface in the Context of Greek Preface-Writing," *NovT* 28 (1986): 48–74; idem, *The Preface to Luke's Gospel: Literary Convention and Social Context in Luke 1.1–4 and Acts 1.1* (SNTSMS 78; Cambridge: Cambridge University Press, 1993).

[113] Loveday Alexander, "Narrative Maps: Reflections on the Toponomy of Acts," in M. D. Carroll et al (eds.), *The Bible in Human Society: Essays in Honour of John Rogerson* (JSOTSSup 200; Sheffield Academic Press, 1995), 15 [15–57].

[114] Loveday Alexander, "'In Journeyings Often': Voyaging in the Acts of the Apostles and in Greek Romance," in C.M. Tuckett (ed.), *Luke's Literary Achievement: Collected Essays* (JSNTSup 116; Sheffield: Sheffield Academic Press, 1995), 17–49; idem, "Mapping Early Christianity: Acts and the Shape of Early Church History," *Interpretation* 57 (2001): 163–73.

[115] Alexander, "In Journeyings Often," 30; citing Richard Bauckham, "James at the Centre: A Jerusalem Perspective on New Testament History and Canon" (Inaugural Lecture, University of St. Andrews, 1994).

Luke's hero, Syria and Phoenicia are home ground, while the Aegean is unexplored territory."[116] The barbarians in Acts are "in the West, not in the East (28.2); and it is the Athenians, in the heartland of Greek culture, who are described as 'superstitious' (*deisidaimonesterous*, 17.22). For the Greek reader, this is 'turning the world upside down' (17.6) with a vengeance."[117] The full dimensions of the map from Acts 16 to the end is a result of the we-voyages that begin in Acts 16. In her words, "Paul's sea-voyages ... represent a parallel act of narrative aggression."[118] In contrast to Paul's letters, which may suggest "that Paul simply did not like the sea (his attitude to it in 2 Cor. 11 certainly suggests that),"[119] the narrator of Acts "... (note the association of 'we-narration' with the sea) is perfectly at home on the sea, able to find seagoing connections with east, familiar with the names of winds and harbours, alert to the complexities of shipping traffic in the Aegean and the Mediteranean. The sea is presented as a proper sphere of activity for the emissaries of the gospel."[120] The map after Acts 16, Alexander proposes, indicates "that the narrator is implicitly laying claim to a cultural territory which many readers, both Greek and Judaeo-Christian, would perceive as inherently 'Greek'."[121] In this map, "Jerusalem is no longer the centre of a circle but the eastern edge of a westerly voyage which follows the sea-routes more familiar to the Greek reader than to the Bible."[122]

At this point, Alexander's insights need to be supplemented with insights from the work of MacDonald and Palmer Bonz. The we-voyages contribute the key to Luke's reconfiguration of the cognitive maps of both the Homeric sea-voyaging of Odysseus and the Virgilian sea-voyaging of Aeneas. Alexander observes in a later essay that "The final chapters of the book [Acts] ... combine a strong outward movement [from Jerusalem] with an odd sense of homecoming: outward, towards the periphery of the narrative map, crossing the uncharted and storm-tossed Ionian Sea to landfall on a barbarian island; and homecoming, back to familiar territory, as the party pick up the regular shipping lanes and make their way up the Appian way to be greeted by 'brothers' in Rome."[123] Luke reconfigures the map of the Mediterra-

---

[116] Ibid. 36.
[117] Ibid.
[118] Ibid., 36.
[119] Ibid., 32.
[120] Ibid., 37.
[121] Ibid., 37.
[122] Ibid., 31.
[123] Alexander, "Mapping Early Christianity," 164; idem, "Reading Luke-Acts from Back to Front," in *The Unity of Luke-Acts* (ed. J. Verheyden; BETL 142; Leuven: Peeters, 1999): 426–27 [419–46].

2. The We-Voyages in Acts

nean work through the "epic" rhetography of the we-voyages. Paul's "epic" movement from region to region in the we-voyages is on the Mediterranean Sea. When "a man of Macedonia" appears to Paul in a vision at Troas, Paul and his companions begin an "epic" mode of sea-voyaging first from "Troy" to Macedonia and Greece, with a return to Troas. After this, Paul returns to Jerusalem by sea, and this establishes the "odd sense of homecoming"[124] at Rome for Paul and his companions, where Paul greets "brothers" (28:17) and explains to them how God's plan of salvation had created the context for the we-voyage to Rome. In other words, after the we-voyages in Acts 16:10–18; 20:5–6 reconfigure the Homeric map of the *Odyssey,* the we-voyages in Acts 20:7–15; 21:1–18; 27:1–28:16 reconfigure the Vergilian map of the *Aeneid.*

Freeing the Rhetography of the We-Voyages for 21st Century Exploration of the Christian Journey of Acts throughout the Mediterranean World

The "epic" story of Luke-Acts presents Christian believers traversing the Mediterranean world from Jerusalem to Troy to Rome through perils, prophecies, and promises that reconfigure the epic stories of both Homer and Vergil. The we-voyages provide the "epic" mapping that secures Luke's reconfiguration of the Homeric and Vergilian regions of the Mediterranean world into "Christian" territory. For Luke, it is not Odysseus's return to Ithaca from Troy or Aeneas's long sea voyage from Troy to Rome that tells the important "epic" story of the Mediterranean world. Rather, the we-voyages are the accounts that present Paul's "epic" travel from the Troad to Macedonia, which gives Paul access to Greece, followed by the account of Paul's sea voyaging from the Troad to Rome via Jerusalem. The sociorhetorical effect of the we-voyages is to introduce an "epic" vision that takes Paul's mission to Macedonia and Greece in a manner that reconfigures Odysseus's journey home, followed by a "desire" by Paul to go to Jerusalem, which takes him to Rome, like the migration of Aeneas and his companions to Rome.

To test the epic importance of the we-voyages in Acts, we can look at what the story would be like if these epic sea voyages were omitted. Indeed, without the we-voyages, Bonz's proposal that Luke-Acts is Christian "epic literature" would have great difficulty attracting serious scholarly attention. Suppose, first of all, that Acts omitted the we-voyage in 16:10–17. Instead of sailing on the sea to Philippi, Paul and

[124] Ibid.

his companions would go to Macedonia and Achaia as a result of Paul's resolve, like he does in 19:21: "Now after these things had been accomplished, Paul resolved in the Spirit to go through Macedonia and Achaia, and then to go to Jerusalem." Traveling by land, Paul and Silas would go to Philippi (16:16–40), then by land through Amphipolis and Apollonia to Thessalonica (17:1), and then to Beroea (17:10). This inland travel would then gain Paul access to Athens (17:14–15), Corinth (18:1), Cenchreae (18:18), Ephesus (18:19), and Caesarea (18:22). Then, Paul would go by land from Caesarea back through Antioch (18:22), Galatia, Phrygia (18:23), and Ephesus (19:1) to Macedonia and Greece (20:1–2).

After traveling from Greece back to Macedonia (20:3), suppose that instead of anyone setting sail, which brings forth the second we-voyage in 20:5–15 from Philippi to Troas, Paul and his companions simply traveled by land through Beroea, Apollonia, Amphipolis, and Thessalonica (cf. 17:1, 10) to Miletus, where Paul addressed the Ephesian elders (20:17–38). Then suppose that instead of Paul being brought "to the ship" in Miletus (20:38), Paul and his companions simply traveled by land back through Phrygia and Galatia (cf. 18:23) to Antioch and Caesarea (cf. 18:22) to Jerusalem (21:18). Such inland travel would exclude the "setting sail from Troas" to Philippi, a leading city of Macedonia and a Roman colony, in 16:11; it would exclude the sailing from Philippi back to Troas in 20:5–6; and it would exclude the sailing from Troas in 20:13 to Miletus (20:15), Cos, Rhodes, and Patara (21:1) alongside Cyprus to Tyre (21:3), Ptolemais (21:7), and Caesarea (21:8).

Then let us suppose that instead of the we-voyage from Caesarea to Rome (27:1–28:16), the Centurion took Paul and his companions by land via Roman roads from Caesarea to Rome. The narrative might then read (cf. 27:1–2): "When it was decided that we were to travel to Italy, they transferred Paul and some other prisoners to a centurion of the Augustan Cohort, named Julius. Starting on our long journey, we traveled by land to Antioch, then, following Roman roads, Julius led us day and night toward Rome." Then the story would continue with: "While we were traveling along the road near [...], a band of thieves approached ...." There would, in other words, truly be travel on land in the we passages! This land travel would contain dangerous episodes as they traveled along the roads, which would put Acts clearly in the genre of romance, rather than epic, literature. Instead of presenting Paul's movement from Troy to Macedonia, then from Troy to Rome via Jerusalem on Roman roads, the story of Acts contains we-voyages that depict Paul and companions sailing from Troy (Troas) to the major city in Macedonia named after Philip, the father of Alexander the

Great. Then after the companions sail back to Troy (Troas), Paul sails from Troy with these companions to Rome via Jerusalem.

It has been more than thirty years since I produced the essays on the we-passages in Acts as sea-voyages. As a result of some of the criticisms that emerged in the ensuing decades, I began to wonder if somehow the wording of the text of Acts had changed. I have been pleased to find, upon returning to the we-passages, that in fact every one of them still starts a sea-voyage! I have also been pleased that the insightful and courageous work in particular of Richard Pervo, Dennis MacDonald, Marianne Palmer Bonz, and Loveday Alexander have moved the study of the we-voyages, as well as Luke-Acts itself, decisively beyond a literary-historical paradigm that limits our insights toward a sociorhetorical paradigm that envisions the narration as Mediterranean discourse with dramatic social, cultural, ideological, argumentative, and religious effects on people's perspectives of the Mediterranean world and the place of Christianity within it. I trust that the 21st century will bring even further insights into the way in which the cognitive mapping in Luke-Acts plays a decisive role in leading all the New Testament writings into the world of Mediterranean literature, society, culture, and ideology, and, as a result, into the religious belief systems of the Mediterranean world and through it into the global world of humans on earth.

3

The Social Location of the Implied Author of Luke-Acts

Introduction: Social Location

In the tradition of literary-historical interpretation, the social setting of Luke-Acts is highly debated. Susan Garrett recently asserted:

> Interpreters of biblical texts cannot question their authors. Further, because very little is known about the social setting in which some of the biblical documents were produced, interpreters often do not even know for certain which culture or cultures are relevant to a given text. Was "Luke" a second generation Christian, or third? What was his ethnic origin? Was he an inhabitant of country, town, or city, and in what part of the empire? What was the character of his and his community's relationship to Jews and to pagans in that locale?[1]

Despite debate about such questions, explicit inquiry about the context in which we interpret Luke-Acts contributes to our understanding of it in the milieu of first-century Mediterranean Christianity.

Yet it would not be enough to know the social context in which an author produced Luke-Acts. We often assume that once we know this, it would then be a simple task to trace correlations between that context and an author's thought. For example, if the author of Luke-Acts was urban, we assume that he might think like other urbanites we know about from the first century. If Gentile, he probably shares a way of thinking typical of that world.

Tracing correlations between thought and social context, however, is a notoriously difficult task in the sociology of knowledge. We can never assume that all persons in a given context thought alike. Nor is there any necessary causality linking context and ideas. It is much more likely that a range of ideas will appear as plausible alternatives to people who share a given social location. In a positive sense, therefore, our task is to show that Luke's ideas are within the range that would seem

---

[1] Susan R. Garrett, *The Demise of the Devil: Magic and the Demonic in Luke's Writings* (Minneapolis: Augsburg/Fortress, 1989), 12.

plausible in a particular context. Negatively we can show that the ideas are unlikely in the context we imagine for the author. Identifying such a range of ideas is never an easy task. Hence, our search for the context of Luke-Acts will have to be both indirect and hypothetical.

Defining Social Location
We use the term "social location" because "context" is too broad for our purposes. A "social location" is a position in a social system which reflects a world view, or what Peter Berger calls "a socially constructed province of meaning": a perception of how things work, what is real, where things belong, and how they fit together.[2]

Of course, understanding a social location assumes that there is a relation between thought and the social conditions under which it occurs. There is a so-called social base – what Karl Mannheim first termed an "existential base" – underlying any particular way of thinking, as if a substructure of social conditions were the foundation on which the superstructure of thought can be said to rest.[3] We must also ask of what this social base for knowledge or belief consists and how it is to be identified. What characteristics qualify a group or process as a social location of thought?

Social Base of Knowledge
Marxist theorists see social class as the key social location of thought. Important as class may be, other locations are important as well. R.K. Merton, for example, notes that not only groups, but also social processes, such as social position, class, ethnicity, and mobility, can themselves provide a social base for certain types of thinking.[4]

Obviously some social locations are easier to specify than others. For example, groups designated by gender tend to have clear and identifiable boundaries. Similarly sharp boundaries can be found in distinctions such as citizen/non-citizen, Jew/Gentile, and slave/free.

As New Testament scholars think about additional social groups and social locations, however, particularly those which do not fall as neatly together as do gender or race, how are we to know what counts as a group? How do we handle the complexities created by the overlapping character of group participation? We need criteria to designate a social location of thought in a clear and distinct way. In laying these out, we

---

[2] Peter Berger and Thomas Luckmann, *The Social Construction of Reality* (Garden City, N.Y.: Doubleday, 1966), 24–25; Richard L. Rohrbaugh, "'Social Location of Thought' as a Heuristic Construct in New Testament Study," *JSNT* 30 (1987): 109.

[3] Karl Mannheim, *Ideology and Utopia: An Introduction to the Sociology of Knowledge* (New York: Harcourt & Brace, 1968).

[4] R.K. Merton, *Social Theory and Social Structure* (New York: Free Press, 1968), 514.

recognize what a social location is and what it is not. It is what Peter Berger calls a "plausibility structure," a socially constructed province of meaning.[5] It is not reducible to the material conditions of life because it is itself a mental construct, a socially produced and maintained picture of the world.

This means that the social base is not the cause of other ideas, but the context in which other ideas are interpreted and understood as realistic possibilities. Social locations are heuristic constructs, not explanatory ones.

To begin to say what social locations are, it is necessary to sharpen the way we use the terms "group" and "social location," particularly insofar as the term group is commonly used in a non-technical sense. A generation, for example, may be a social location of thought, but it is not a group. It is not an organization or association. Members of a generation, class, or any other social location may never get to know each other, may have no physical association whatsoever, but nonetheless live, so to speak, at the same location and hence share similar experience. Thus a generation lives through the same historical period. A class shares the same relation to the means of production. Common position or structural location in a social system thus provides the key.

It is not that certain experiences produce certain beliefs, but given certain experiences, a limited range of beliefs should be plausible options for most of those who share the social location.[6] And for our purposes, description of such limited ranges of experience should help us understand the way a set of ideas were taken by those who adopted them.

In sum, then, the common structural position occupied by a number of individuals in relation to a larger social whole entails a social location. Specification of a social location would ideally designate the limited range of experience a position implies (showing how it is distinctive), together with the process by which that position comes to be occupied. If we could reach some agreement about the social location of the thought in Luke-Acts, it might be possible to correlate the ideas with plausible social contexts in the Mediterranean world.

Language and Socio-Rhetorical Criticism

We must now reckon with the nature of language in the documents we are analyzing, and for this we draw on insights from sociolinguistics

---

[5] Berger and Luckmann, *Social Construction*, 24–25.

[6] See N. Abercrombie, *Class, Structure and Knowledge: Problems in the Sociology of Knowledge* (New York: New York University Press, 1980), 38.

discussed by Bruce Malina.⁷ We use them, however, in the context of a method called socio-rhetorical criticism.⁸ Some of its presuppositions are as follows:
  a. Language is constitutive of social communication.
  b. Language signifies social functions.
  c. Statements in a document are intratextual functions that presuppose extratextual systems of social interaction.
  d. Some of the major issues of socio-rhetorical criticism concern the relation of information to patterns of activity in various arenas of the social system presupposed by the intratextual phenomena. For example, what is the relation of the information and functions in the social arena of beliefs and ideologies to information and functions in other social arenas, such as culture, technology, and population structure?

At the beginning, the interpreter must be aware that language signifies social functions. Any understanding of the signs in a document presupposes social arenas that provide meanings for human beings. Since understanding is a present activity, all knowledge is contemporary knowledge, even what we call knowledge of the past. This means that every person, at whatever time, reads a document through envisioned social arenas. What differs considerably are the conceptual frameworks and technologies people develop to investigate documents from the past.

If a reader wishes to interpret ancient Mediterranean literature through techniques that contextualize literature in pre-industrial society during the time of the Roman Empire, then it is necessary to find conceptual frameworks and scenarios designed to position our modern knowledge in pre-industrial social contexts. Malina's essay on reading theory indicates that because language is constitutive of social communication, we use social scenarios to contextualize what we read, and this contextualization produces the meanings we perceive in the text.⁹ If we can identify the arenas of the social system presupposed by various phenomena in the text, and if we can delineate the location, role, and competencies certain phenomena exhibit within different arenas of

---

⁷ Bruce J. Malina, "Reading Theory Perspective: Reading Luke-Acts," in *The Social World of Luke-Acts: Models for Interpretation* (ed. Jerome H. Neyrey; Peabody Mass.: Hendrickson, 1991), 3–23. See Michael A.K. Halliday, *Language as Social Semiotic: The Social Interpretation of Language and Meaning* (Baltimore: University Park Press), 1978; Roger Fowler, *Literature as Social Discourse* (Bloomington, Ind.: Indiana University Press, 1981).

⁸ Vernon K. Robbins, *Jesus the Teacher: A Socio-Rhetorical Interpretation of Mark* (Philadelphia: Fortress, 1984); idem, "The Woman Who Touched Jesus' Garment: Socio-Rhetorical Analysis of the Synoptic Accounts," *NTS* 33 (1987): 502–15.

⁹ Malina, "Reading Theory."

the social system, then we can make some progress toward identifying the social location of the thought within the entire document.

A Model of the Social Location of Narrative Discourse

Previous discussions of the social context of Luke-Acts have lacked a systematic framework for the investigation. One of the contributions from the social sciences is its use of carefully constructed and empirically tested conceptual models to provide a framework which orients modern readers toward arenas within pre-industrial social systems.[10]

Social Science Model of Social Location
The present study uses a conceptual model for analyzing the social location of Luke-Acts. A comprehensive framework for investigating phenomena in Mediterranean society during the time of the Roman Empire is available in the works of T.F. Carney and J.H. Elliott.[11] In Figure 1 the nine basic arenas of a social system are listed in the column on the left of the model: previous events, natural environment and resources, population structure, technology, socialization and personality, culture, foreign affairs, belief systems and ideologies, and the political-military-legal system. Our model can help us to identify the social framework for documents written in Mediterranean society during the Roman Empire. Once we have itemized this social framework, our next challenge is to determine the intratextual phenomena that should be placed in the narrative function column. What can be said about these nine categories from the document Luke-Acts?

Narrative Discourse Model
Since Luke-Acts is narrative discourse, we must develop a second part of our model, namely, a comprehensive list of four intratextual functions from narrative communication. This study uses intratextual categories from Seymour Chatman's narrative-communication model as modified by Jeff Staley.[12] Accordingly, we give special attention to four aspects of intratextual functions in Luke-Acts:
    1.   characters and their audiences
    2.   narrator and narratee
    3.   inscribed author and inscribed reader
    4.   implied author and implied reader

---

[10] Thomas F. Carney, *The Shape of the Past: Models and Antiquity* (Lawrence, Kans.: Coronado Press, 1975), xiii-ix, 1–43.

[11] Ibid., 246; John H. Elliott, "Social Scientific Criticism of the New Testament: More on Models and Methods," *Semeia* 35 (1986): 14.

[12] Jeffery Lloyd Staley, *The Print's First Kiss: A Rhetorical Investigation of the Implied Reader in the Fourth Gospel* (SBLDS 82; Atlanta: Scholars Press, 1988), 21–49.

By analyzing intratextual functions in Luke-Acts in light of the social systems in Mediterranean society during the Roman Empire, we hope to be able to identify aspects of the social location of thought within Luke's two volumes.

Characters and Audiences. A "character" is "a category of existents which inhabit the story world of a narrative and mimic human beings.... These characters ... can ... tell stories, becoming narrators...."[13] Characters have an audience or a sequence of audiences as they speak and act. Because these audiences signify socially perceived contexts for speech and action, consideration of them contributes to our analysis. A full study of the characters in Luke-Acts observes both the presence (and absence) of certain characters and their limited range of knowledge. We select here those characters in Luke-Acts who appear to function prominently in one or another social arena in the Mediterranean world.

Figure 1: The Social Location of Luke-Acts: A Two-part Model

2. NARRATIVE FUNCTIONS

1. ARENAS OF THE SOCIAL SYSTEM

1. Previous Events
2. Natural Environment and Resources
3. Population Structure
4. Technology
5. Socialization and Personality
6. Culture
7. Foreign Affairs
8. Belief Systems and Ideologies
9. Political-Military Legal System

CHARACTERS/ AUDIENCES

NARRATOR/ NARRATEE

INSCRIBED AUTHOR/ INSCRIBED READER

IMPLIED AUTHOR/ IMPLIED READER

---

[13] Ibid., 47.

Narrator. Since Luke-Acts is by internal definition a narrative (Luke 1:1), the discourse has a narrator. The narrator, or "the teller of a story," presents the characters and the situations in which they speak and act.[14] Although it is tempting to think that the narrator speaks directly to us the readers, we must be on our guard. Since we are self-reflective readers, we see both ourselves reading the text and the narrator speaking intratextually to an imagined counterpart. This imagined counterpart is called the narratee, the figure "to whom narrators address comments; and like narrators, they are always intratextual."[15]

Inscribed Author and Inscribed Reader. In Luke-Acts, a narrator speaking in third person presents the characters in their situations. But in the prefaces and sea voyages of Luke-Acts the narrator speaks in a first person mode. We will call this narrator the inscribed author, whose counterpart is the inscribed reader. The narrator in Luke-Acts never gives the inscribed author a name. Since Christian tradition attributes the two volumes to Luke, the associate of Paul, readers regularly perceive this inscribed author to be a male named Luke.

The inscribed author addresses an inscribed reader named Theophilus. From what the inscribed author says to Theophilus, we see that an inscribed reader may have prior knowledge of some of the characters and events in the story. In Luke-Acts the inscribed author wants to give more accurate information concerning the things of which Theophilus has already "been informed" (Luke 1:4). The inscribed author reappears in the sea-voyages in Acts through the medium of first person plural narration, but here the inscribed reader Theophilus is only implied.

Implied Author and Implied Reader. Of all the intratextual functions, the most pervasive and important is that of the implied author, whose counterpart is the implied reader. The implied author is "that singular consciousness which the reader constructs from the words of a text; a consciousness which knows the story backward and forward ...the static, overarching view of a text that a reader might develop from multiple readings."[16] Since "the implied author in the text ...operates within a closed medium (print) whose linguistic signifiers (Koine Greek) open up into the much broader social world of the first century C.E.," our primary goal is to identify the social location of the implied author as constituted the language, ideology, and social relations in the text.[17]

---

[14] Ibid., 37.

[15] Ibid., 43.

[16] Ibid., 29.

[17] Ibid., 30. See Janet Wolff, *The Social Production of Art* (New York: St. Martin's, 1981), 136.

The implied author has the competencies of all the characters plus the competencies of the narrator and inscribed author. Thus the implied author transcends the limitations of any one of the characters or other actants in the text by also possessing the competencies of the forms, styles, strategies, and manipulative ploys of the narrative discourse.[18] Thus, the social location of the implied author lies in all the competencies that signify certain kinds of relations to and activities within processes at work in various arenas of Mediterranean society.

> Implied authors address implied readers. A text's implied reader is the affective quality of a text. It is an entity evoked and continually nurtured by the text ... the "moving toward the gradual revelation," the text's "linearity...." The implied reader only has knowledge of what has been read up to the given moment ...is limited by its temporal status. An implied reader must also gain all its knowledge of the story from the narrative medium itself, even if the general outline of the story is known in a culture.[19]

Let us recall that we, the real readers, provide the meanings that the characters, narrator, inscribed author, and implied author communicate to their intratextual counterparts. We supply these meanings by means of the scenarios we envision for their interaction. If our scenarios are twentieth-century situations and contexts in industrialized society, then we will supply these meanings to their interaction. But if we use scenarios introduced in other chapters in this volume to envision the meanings, we may take some steps toward an interpretation of Luke-Acts in a social location of thought in pre-industrialized Mediterranean society.

The Model Applied to Luke-Acts

We simply cannot explore all aspects of the social location of the implied author of Luke-Acts. Our strategy, then, is to make sorties through the text according to the basic arenas of a social system (see Figure 1).

Previous Events

A common social location may arise from a common relation to previous events. For example, today a generation of people in the United States has a relation to the Vietnam War. People born after it may have a relation to the war through discourse of one kind or another about it. Narrative accounts of previous events are one kind of discourse about

---

[18] See Staley, *Print's First Kiss*, 29.
[19] Ibid., 33–35.

it, and a particular selection and way of telling the stories evokes a common social location.

Luke-Acts is narrative discourse about previous events. Throughout Luke-Acts a particular selection of characters from Israel's heritage and Roman history appears in the narrative. On the one hand, the narrator selects events associated with Abraham, Joseph, Moses, David, Solomon, Elijah, and Elisha from previous biblical history (Acts 7:2–47; Luke 4:25–27). In other words, characters from biblical history come from the "great traditions" of Israel located in the Torah and the Prophets. From the perspective of the narrator, events from the great traditions of Israel lead to Christian events in an environment of Jewish-Roman rule.

On the other hand, we do not find events associated with great moments in Greco-Roman culture and history prior to Caesar Augustus. For example, no reference is made to Homeric literature, Alexander the Great, or the Punic Wars. There is a reference to Zeus and Hermes in Acts 14:12–13, but otherwise Luke-Acts is generally silent about Greco-Roman history.

Beginning with Caesar Augustus and Herod the Great, the events in Luke-Acts occur in an environment of Jewish-Roman history through the reign of Tiberius Caesar (14–37 CE; Luke 3:1), Gaius Caligula (37–41 CE), and Claudius (41–54 CE; Acts 11:28; 18:2), ending during the reign of the emperor Nero (54–68 CE), which overlaps the reign of Herod Agrippa II (53–ca. 100 CE; Acts 25:13–26:32). Luke-Acts contains no reference to Nero by name, but various people refer to him either as Caesar (Acts 25:8, 10–12, 21; 26:32; 27:24; 28:19) or Sebastos [Augustus] (Acts 25:21, 25).

Within this framework, Luke-Acts selects events that begin with Zechariah the priest, of the division of Abijah (1 Chron 24:10), and his wife Elizabeth (Luke 1:5–67); Joseph, of the house of King David, and his wife Mary (Luke 1:26–56; 2:1–51); John the Baptizer (Luke 1:57–66); the righteous and devout Simeon (Luke 2:22–35); the prophetess Anna (Luke 2:36–38); and Jesus of Nazareth (Luke 2:4–52). Then major additional people appear through twelve disciples who become apostles (Luke 6:13–16); seventy (or seventy-two) additional people who go into mission; seven Hellenists who serve their widows (Acts 6:1–6). Saul/Paul, who appears at the death of Stephen (Acts 8:1), becomes a member of the Christian movement after being encountered by the risen Lord (Acts 9:1–19) and begins to preach in the name of Jesus (Acts 9:27). Events surrounding Paul's activities occupy Acts from chapter 13 to the end of the narrative. All of these events occur as previous events in Luke-Acts. As a result, the social location evoked by previous events is complex but limited in striking ways to biblical heritage and to Jewish-Roman history from the time of Caesar Augustus and Herod to Nero and Herod Agrippa II. The special events within this Jewish-Roman environment concern John the Baptizer, Jesus, and their followers.

But the events recounted in Luke-Acts do not simply have the nature of events that lay outside the text. Rather, the implied author has produced previous events in the form of a social product, a product to be read.

As a beginning point, a number of characters in Luke-Acts recall previous events for particular social reasons. Jesus presents events associated with Elijah and Elisha to show healings of Gentiles (Luke 4:25–27), and Stephen recounts actions of Abraham, Joseph, Moses, David, and Solomon to criticize the "temple made with hands" (Acts 7:2–47). The Pharisee Gamaliel, in the presence of the Jerusalem council, refers to earlier revolutionary activity by Theudas and Judas the Galilean to recall their deaths and the scattering of their followers (Acts 5:36–37); and Paul recounts to the inhabitants of Jerusalem (Acts 22:4–21) and to King Agrippa (Acts 26:9–20) previous events in his life to try and change their perceptions and allegiances.

Not only do certain characters recount previous events, but at one point the narrator intrudes to refer to Herod Agrippa I's killing of James the brother of John (Acts 12:2) and to Agrippa I's death shortly thereafter (12:20–22). In Luke-Acts, therefore, both the narrator and the characters produce previous events for audiences in a manner that shows special interest in biblical heritage, healing of Gentiles, criticism of the Jerusalem temple, recruitment into activities and beliefs associated with Jesus, persecution of people whom public authorities consider to be dangerous, and death administered to specific people for various reasons.

Beyond the narrator and the characters, the inscribed author refers to previous events where eyewitnesses and ministers of the account (or "word") have transmitted information, and "many" have compiled a narrative of the things he himself is narrating (Luke 1:1–2). The inscribed author, then, performs a specialized function of finding accounts of previous events from both oral and written discourse and producing previous events as a social product. The inscribed author refers to his own writing of the document (Luke 1:4), then refers to the writing of the first volume as a previous event (Acts 1:1). The "ordered" fashion (Luke 1:3) in which the inscribed author produces the events indicates that special goals and values are at stake. Moreover, the inscribed author's presentation of the previous events to an inscribed reader with the Roman name Theophilus evokes a social location similar to Josephus, who also exhibits a knowledge of events in biblical heritage and post-biblical Jewish history, and addresses an inscribed reader with a Roman name.

Natural Environment and Resources

The arena of natural environment, which concerns geographical space, can take us a step further in defining social location. The resources perceived as really or potentially present within a geographical space depend on the perspective of the person viewing that space.

The implied author of Luke-Acts envisions a geographical space that extends from Ethiopia (Acts 8:26–39) and Cyrenaica (Acts 2:10) at the southern and southwesternmost point around the eastern Mediterranean to Rome at the northwesternmost point. Yet the primary geographical space lies between Jerusalem and Rome. From the point of view of Luke-Acts, this space contains land, the Great Sea, one river called the Jordan, and one lake called Gennesareth (Luke 5:1), which the other Gospel writers call the Sea of Galilee. The implied author of Luke-Acts will not call any inland body of water a sea; this terminology is reserved for the great Mediterranean Sea.[20]

For the implied author, the major resource on land are ports (Acts 27:2), cities, and towns. And the major resource in ports, cities, and towns are houses where people receive hospitality. Alternative social locations of thought could perceive major resources on land to be wild animals to be hunted, gold, copper, or iron to be mined, or pyramids to be plundered; not so in Luke-Acts.

The perception of houses within cities locates the thought within human-made culture rather than undeveloped natural environment. This presupposes, therefore, the amassing of material goods that support the hospitality that occurs in houses. The implied author has in view barns full of grain, flocks of sheep, and vineyards, but these are simply presupposed as sources for the presence of the resources in the ports, cities, and towns. Also, the thought of the implied author is located at points of receiving hospitality rather than giving hospitality. There is never any criticism of a person who accepts hospitality. But the thought in the document criticizes or commends ways in which people offer hospitality to those who, it is presupposed, should receive it. The implied author also has in view houses in which people are kept under guard. In some instances, people who experience this kind of imprisoned hospitality may invite others to visit them in these houses (Acts 28:16–29).

---

[20] Vernon K. Robbins, "By Land and By Sea: The We-Passages and Ancient Sea Voyages," in *Perspectives on Luke-Acts* (ed. Charles H. Talbert; Danville Va.: Association of Baptist Professors of Religion, 1978), 215–42.

Where, then, is the social location of the implied author? The implied author both produces previous events as a social product among persons who live in cities and towns and implies that the natural environment of land and sea is a place of travel, and thus of hospitability to the traveler. Accordingly, one of the highest values of the implied author is hospitality. In the geographical space between Jerusalem and Rome, the implied author evokes a social location seeking hospitality in the midst of a heritage that merges biblical, Jewish, Roman, and Christian events in a particular way.

Population Structure

Population structure opens the issues of age, gender, level of health and resources, and location in country, village, town, or city.[21] Our analysis already points to a social location within cities, and Richard Rohrbaugh, Douglas Oakman, and Halvor Moxnes have analyzed aspects of city/country and poverty/wealth.[22] Therefore, we will not discuss location in country, village, town, or city, or repeat previous materials on poverty and wealth here. In addition, with Pilch's chapter on illness, we need not pursue levels of health.[23] This section, then, will focus on age, gender, and the mixed population in view in Luke-Acts.

With respect to young people in Luke, John the Baptizer and Jesus appear at birth (Luke 1:57; 2:7), then Jesus amazes the teachers in the Jerusalem temple when he is twelve years old. The adult Jesus uses a child to illustrate greatness (Luke 9:47–8) and insists that small children be allowed to come to him (Luke 18:16–17). Jesus heals a demonized boy (Luke 9:38–42) and a girl who is about twelve years old (Luke 8:41–42, 49–56). There are but a few old people in Luke. Zechariah and Elizabeth, the parents of John the Baptizer, are advanced in years (Luke 1:7). The righteous and devout Simeon is approaching death (Luke 1:25–35), and the prophetess Anna is more than eighty-four years old. Beyond this, however, there is little emphasis on advanced age in Luke.

In contrast to Luke, there are no young children in sight in Acts. A slave girl (Acts 16:16–18) and four unmarried daughters (Acts 21:9) appear, but they are engaged in adult, not children's activity. The implied

---

[21] Carney, *Shape of the Past*, 88–89.

[22] Richard L. Rohrbaugh, "The Pre-industrial City in Luke-Acts: Urban Social Relations," in *Social World of Luke-Acts*, 125–49; Douglas E. Oakman, "The Countryside in Luke-Acts," in *The Social World of Luke-Acts*, 151–79; Halvor Moxnes, "Patron-Client Relations and the New Community in Luke-Acts," in *Social World of Luke-Acts*, 241–68.

[23] John J. Pilch, "Sickness and Healing in Luke-Acts," in *Social World of Luke-Acts*, 181–209.

author views the world in which Christianity spreads from Jerusalem to Rome as an adult domain.

We are told of a large number of females in the adult world of Luke-Acts.[24] Elizabeth and Mary have prominent roles in the setting of the birth and infancy of John and Jesus (Luke 1:24–2:35). The prophetess Anna, sees Jesus and praises God for the redemption of Israel (Luke 2:36–38). Then throughout Luke, the narrator either refers to or presents a significant number of named and unnamed women: Herodias (3:19); a widow of Zarephath (4:26); Simon's mother-in-law (4:38); a widow (7:13); a woman of the city (7:37–50); Mary Magdalene, Joanna, and Susanna (8:3); Jesus' mother (8:19–20); Martha and her sister Mary (10:38–42); an unnamed woman (11:27–28); the queen of the South (11:31); a woman with an eighteen-year infirmity (13:11–13); Lot's wife (17:32); a widow (18:1–8); a poor widow (21:1–4); a maid (22:56–57); a great multitude of women (23:27–31); and women from Galilee (23:49, 55; 24:10).

Also throughout Acts the narrator either refers to or presents a significant number of women: Sapphira (5:1–11); widows (6:1); Candace, queen of the Ethiopians (8:27); widows (9:39, 41); Dorcas [Tabitha] (9:36–41); Mary, mother of John Mark (12:12); a maid named Rhoda (12:13); Lydia, a seller of purple goods (16:14, 40); a slave girl with a spirit of divination (16:16–18); leading women (17:4); Greek women of high standing (17:12); Damaris (17:34); Priscilla, a tentmaker (18:2–3, 18, 26); four unmarried daughters who prophesied (21:9); Drusilla, wife of Felix (24:24); and Bernice, wife of King Agrippa (25:13, 23; 26:30).

Perhaps the most remarkable feature of population structure, however, is the ethnic variety the narrator of Acts presents among members of the Christian movement. The variety comes into view in Acts through three related motifs: (1) gathering in cities; (2) scattering as a result of persecution; and (3) traveling. Through these motifs, people with different native languages and identities programmatically join the Christian movement sanctioned by God.

On the one hand, a representative mixture of all peoples and areas join the Christian movement as a result of their presence in cities. In the narrative sequence of Acts, this motif begins with Pentecost. From the narrator's point of view, the people gathered in Jerusalem were "Jews from every nation under heaven" (Acts 2:5). The narrator identifies Galileans (2:7), Parthians, Medes, Elamites (2:9), Cretans, Arabs, and Romans (2:11) in a manner that appears to be based on race, language, or dialect. The narrator identifies others on the basis of geogra-

---

[24] M.I. Finley, "The Silent Women of Rome," in *Aspects of Antiquity: Discoveries and Controversies* (ed. M.I. Finley; New York: Viking, 1969), 129–42.

phy: those who dwell in Mesopotamia, Judea, Cappadocia, Pontus, Asia, Phrygia, Pamphylia, Egypt, and the parts of Libya belonging to Cyrene (2:9). In addition, the narrator identifies both Jews and proselytes among the Romans staying in Jerusalem (2:10–11). From the narrator's perspective, when Peter preached to this mixed population of Jews in Jerusalem, three thousand of them joined the Christian movement, and additional ones joined day by day after this (2:41, 47). At the end of this episode, then, more than three thousand Jews or proselytes representing a wide mixture of native languages and identities joined the Christian movement in its initial stages. A few chapters later, an Ethiopian eunuch who had come to Jerusalem to pray becomes a member of the Christian movement. Thus, the view of the narrator is that "Jews from every nation under heaven" gather in Jerusalem, and since the Christian movement begins with a large number of people from this group, Christianity is constituted by a wide mixture of people with different native languages, locations, and identities.

Through the related motif of scattering, people of still different varieties join Christianity.[25] Among the Christians in Jerusalem were Hellenists and Hebrews (6:1). The stoning of Stephen (7:58), one of the Hellenist deacons, led to the scattering of Christians from Jerusalem (8:1, 4; 11:19). As a result, Samaritans (8:12), a Gentile centurion Cornelius with his kinsmen and close friends (10:1–8, 44–48), Jews from Phoenicia, Cyprus, and Antioch (11:19), and Greeks at Antioch (11:20) joined the Christian movement. The acceptance of Gentiles is a shock to Peter and other leaders from Jewish heritage (Acts 10), but the presence of wide diversity within Judaism itself prepares the implied reader for this move. As a result of the gathering and the scattering that occurs in the first eleven chapters of Acts, Christianity begins as a highly mixed population.

Once the Christian movement has become a highly mixed population, additional varieties of people join the movement as a result of traveling. Programmatically, people respond throughout Cyprus (13:4–12), Asia Minor, Macedonia (Acts 16:9–17:14), and Greece (Acts 17:15–18:17).

In sum, the implied author has in view people from as far south and west as Ethiopia and Cyrenaica, as far east as Arabia, Elam, Media, and Parthia, as far north as the southern coast of the Euxine Sea and the northern coastal region of the Aegean Sea, and as far west as Rome. Every kind of person living in this area, including many women, become fully-constituted members of Christianity. Yet, the implied read-

---

[25] W.C. van Unnik, "Solitude and Community in the New Testament," in *Sparsa Collecta II* (ed. W.C. van Unnik; NovTSup 30; Leiden: Brill, 1980), 242–7.

er observes the implied author's lack of vision west beyond Italy, north above the Euxine Sea, and east into India. Indeed, the social location of thought appears to lie among a cosmopolitan population mixture somewhere between the western coast of Asia Minor and Syria.

Thus, a look at the mixture of population in Luke-Acts suggests a social location of thought among the kind of mixed population found in cosmopolitan cities in the eastern Mediterranean. The limited boundaries of the implied author's vision suggest that the social location of thought in Luke-Acts does not lie in elite groups that have access to Gaul, Spain, and India, nor in ethnic groups that refuse to associate with a mixed population. Rather, the thought is located among networks of people in eastern Mediterranean cities representing a wide variety of native languages and geographical areas.

Technology
Technology is identifiable by the application of knowledge for practical ends. In our experience, a wide variety of technological phenomena signify vigorous activity in the spheres of written, spoken, and visual communication, medicine, agriculture, fabrics, travel, and many other areas. We live in a technological age, and the spheres where technology is present appear through the objects and procedures that come into view as we go from one situation to another.

According to T.F. Carney, "a lack of technological development is one of the most striking characteristics of the traditional societies of antiquity."[26] Since the dominant values of the ruling elite are anti-economic, expertise is built up in the areas of literature, the military, and administration, not in the areas of commerce and industry.[27]

Our search through Luke-Acts reveals technological activity in four spheres: administration, sea travel, writing, and crafts.

In the sphere of administration, we know of census taking, as well as tax collection. Also, geographical space has been divided into districts over which specific people have jurisdiction. In addition, the administrative aspects of the military are in view, though the major technology of warfare like stone-throwing machines or machines for shooting spears or arrows are not in view. The reader sees only whips, swords, and crosses on which people are hung.

There is a surprising amount of technology of sea travel. Not only does the implied author exhibit knowledge of the storms and winds on the Great Sea but harbors, lees, and depths of the water at various places. In addition, the reader encounters data about kinds of anchors and techniques for sailing in rough weather (Acts 27:1–20).

---

[26] Carney, *Shape of the Past*, 106, 132–33.
[27] Ibid., 107.

The technological sphere of writing includes literary skills and rhetoric. Loveday Alexander recently made a breakthrough in analysis of this sphere in Luke-Acts.[28] Her extensive search through Mediterranean literature for comparative analysis of the prefaces to Luke and Acts reveals a social location that is perhaps best described as "technical writer." The Lukan preface, which she identifies as "label + address," exhibits writing practices in a social location of technical or professional prose, which she calls "the scientific tradition." Writing within this social location reveals an appreciation for work of people in the artisan class, in contrast to the disdain elite writers hold for work performed by artisans. Using a detailed scheme for the syntactical structure of the prefaces, Alexander discovers the closest analogy to the Lukan prefaces in "middlebrow," technical literature, and the closest individual analogy to the first-century CE author, Hero the Engineer. Composition at this middlebrow level is "literate but not literary, a written language designed primarily for conveying factual information."[29] She observes, in this regard, that the Lukan prefaces do not contain the "more flowery, 'Alexandrian' vocabulary" of the prefaces found in Hellenistic Jewish literature.[30]

It is important, however, to extend this kind of analysis beyond the prefaces. It is noticeable, as Alexander has observed, that the implied author changes from septuagintal style into other styles throughout the narrative.[31] Moreover, as a recent study of the Beelzebul episode in Luke has shown, the author uses a strategy for developing rhetorical topics by adding sayings, fables, examples, analogies, and exhortations that exhibits a rather advanced level of writing.[32] A similar strategy is at work in the well-known travel narrative in Luke which, through the addition of sayings and apophthegms, creates ten chapters of material as Jesus travels to Jerusalem. Also, the implied author exhibits a signifi-

---

[28] Loveday Alexander, "Luke's Preface in the Context of Greek Preface-Writing," *NovT* 28 (1986): 48–74.
[29] Ibid., 61.
[30] Ibid., 60.
[31] Also E. Plumacher, *Lukas als hellenisticher Schriftsteller: Studien zur Apostelgeschichte* (Göttingen: Vandenhoeck & Ruprecht, 1972); idem, "Lukas als griechischer Historiker," PWSup 14:235–64; idem, "Wirklichkeitserfahrung und Geschichtsschreibung bei Lukas," *ZNW* 68 (1977): 2–22; idem, "Die Apostelgeschichte als historische Monographie," in *Les Actes des Apôtres* (ed. J. Kremer; BETL 48; Louvain: Louvain University Press, 1979), 457–66.
[32] Burton L. Mack and Vernon K. Robbins, *Patterns of Persuasion in the Gospels* (Sonoma, Calif.: Polebridge, 1982), 185–91.

cantly competent rhetorical approach to defense speeches[33] and sea voyages[34] in Acts.

What social location, then, does the implied author exhibit in the arena of technology? The implied author produces written accounts of previous events from a social perspective cordial to the production of tents (Acts 18:1–3), aware of the activities of silversmiths (Acts 19:23–24), and interested in the value of books written by people who practice magical arts (Acts 19:19). There is a lack of interest in the production of the raw materials themselves, like the leather produced through the slaughter and skinning of sheep and goats, though the tanning of skins is in view with the mention of Simon the Tanner (Acts 10:32). The process of mining silver and bringing it to the city is not in view. But the plight of silversmiths significantly occupies the narrator as the narratee is told how certain patterns of buying and not buying influence their livelihood (Acts 19:23–41). As mentioned above, the narrator also refers to the specific value of books produced for magic arts as fifty thousand pieces of silver (Acts 19:19). Moreover, members of the Christian movement make friends with a woman named Lydia, a seller of purple goods, and receive hospitality from her (Acts 16:14). The point is that artisans performing their crafts and sellers of goods produced by artisans are significantly in view as a result of the social location of the thought of the implied author. Though technically skillful with writing and highly aware of administrative technology, the implied author does not locate his thought among the elite, who look with disdain upon the artisan class;[35] neither is his thought located among the daily workers in the mines, fields, vineyards, or hillside grazing sheep and goats. Rather, the thought of the implied author is located near the artisan class, aware of the dynamics of life at this level of society, comfortable with working with one's hands at this level of production, and interested in friendship with sellers of goods and buyers of books that contain information about the practices of groups about which one may have only the most basic information.

---

[33] Fred Veltman, "The Defense Speeches of Paul in Acts," in *Perspectives on Luke-Acts*, 243–56; William R. Long, "The Paulusbild in the Trial of Paul in Acts," *SBL Seminar Papers, 1983* (SBLSP 22; Missoula, Mont.: Scholars Press), 87–105; Jerome H. Neyrey, "The Forensic Defense Speech and Paul's Trial Speeches in Acts 22–26: Form and Function," in *Luke-Acts: New Perspectives from the Society of Biblical Literature Seminar* (ed. C. H. Talbert; New York: Crossroad, 1984), 210–24.

[34] Robbins, "By Land and By Sea."

[35] See Ronald F. Hock, *The Social Context of Paul's Ministry: Tentmaking and Apostleship* (Philadelphia: Fortress, 1980).

Socialization and Personality
If an exploration of technology within the thought of the implied author suggests significant association with artisan workers in cities in the eastern Mediterranean, perhaps analysis of socialization and personality can give us even clearer definition. The inscribed author claims to be an insider to the story and has "followed all things closely for some time past" (Luke 1:3). As an insider, the inscribed author seeks to communicate with a person who has been informed (κατηχήθης) but who, in the inscribed author's terms, needs accurate, secure (ἀσφάλεια) knowledge. It is not clear why the inscribed reader needs this information about the Christian movement. The inscribed author simply says that "inasmuch as" others have compiled a narrative, it "seemed good" for him also to write an orderly account and to make it available to the one whom he addresses as "most excellent Theophilus." The pretense, real or fictive, is that this true information is a gift. The implied reader is left to wonder why. Is the implied reader to suppose that Theophilus already is a patron of this writer, that this patron is wavering in his support or expressing uncertainty because someone has suggested that the movement is politically or otherwise problematic? Or is the implied reader to see in this prologue competition with other Christians who present a theologically or politically different story of Christianity? The social location of the thought of the implied author contains an upward-looking stance but also a competitive stance toward Christians who have produced narratives of some sort about Jesus and/or early Christians. In any case, the social posture of the inscribed author is to evoke a friend or patron who has in the past, is currently, or will be expected in the future to reciprocate in some manner for the honor bestowed by the dedication of this work and the gift of this information.

The lack of certainty concerning whether Theophilus is a genuine patron requires that we interpret the prologues with great caution.[36] But whether the relation to Theophilus is fictive or real, the inscribed author knows the kind of social location experienced by a friend writing for a friend or a client writing for a patron. If writing as a friend to a friend, he evokes a status for himself among those with social rank in Mediterranean society. If writing as a client to a patron, he issues a fictive or real challenge for patronage present or future.

If the inscribed author knows about such social locations and has the resources to adopt the persona of one of these in a written document, then we have uncovered an important aspect of the social location of

---

[36] Vernon K. Robbins, "Prefaces in Greco-Roman Biography and Luke-Acts," *PRSt* 6 (1979): 94–108.

the thought of the implied author. A social location is "a structural term describing a position in a social system."[37] Our inscribed author is in a social location that allows time and materials for writing and for adopting a persona either of a friend of social rank writing to another friend of social rank, or of client to patron. The length of the two documents testifies to this, since, whatever the location is, it has sustained itself long enough to produce two volumes of the work.

The narrator in Luke and Acts addresses Theophilus as "most excellent," analogously to Josephus' address to Epaphroditus (*Life* 430; *AgApion* 1.1). Thus the person producing Luke-Acts does not have the inscribed author adopt a position of equality with the one whom he addresses, as Plutarch does to Socius and Polycrates (see *Theseus* 1.3; *Demosthenes* 1.3; *Dion* 1.3), but a subordinate position, as Josephus does to his patron Epaphroditus. It surely is informative that the inscribed author of Luke-Acts has used the same form of address in the prologues that subordinates use for their Roman superiors in the stories in Acts.

Outside the prologues, a tribune displays the use of the honorific appellation "most excellent" in a letter to the governor (Acts 23:26), a spokesman for the high priest, Tertullus addresses the governor in the same manner (Acts 24:2), and Paul addresses the governor Festus in this manner in a formal trial before the king (Acts 24:24). From the narrator's point of view, subordinates address superiors in the Roman hierarchy as "most excellent," and Paul does not adopt this subordinate position before the governors except in a formal trial setting when the king is present (Acts 26:2, 7, 19; cf. Acts 25:8, 10, 11).

In contrast to all of this, people in Luke-Acts do not use forms of honorific address when they speak to subordinates, and political leaders of high rank do not use honorific appellations when they address each other. Thus, Paul addresses the crewmen on the ship that is taking him to Rome as "men" (ἄνδρες; Acts 27:10, 21), and local Jewish leaders in Rome who come to him as "men, brothers" (ἄνδρες ἀδελφοί; Acts 28:17). In turn, the Jewish leaders use no special form of address when speaking to Paul (Acts 28:21). Also, the governor Felix uses no honorific form of address when he speaks to Paul, whom he perceives to be below him in social and political rank (Acts 23:35; 24:22, 25; 25:5, 9, 12); and neither the governor Festus nor King Agrippa employ honorific appellations when they talk to each other (Acts 25:14–22, 31–32) or to Paul (Acts 26:1, 24, 28).

These data suggest that our inscribed author addresses Theophilus in a mode associated with a person who is willingly or unwillingly in a subordinate position to a person of rank in Roman society. We know this form of address was used for a procurator of the equestrian order

---

[37] Rohrbaugh, "Social Location," 114.

from the time of the emperor Septimius Severus on (after 193 CE). As the equivalent of the Latin *optimus*, it is attested to in first-century documents in reference to any official.[38] It is likely we are getting an important look into the social location of the thought of the implied author when we see this data.

There is a possibility, as mentioned at the outset, that the address to Theophilus is fictive, that there is no real individual person to whom Luke and Acts are addressed. In this case, one or more unseen patrons, matrons, or associates are supporting the production of these documents by providing daily sustenance, shelter, freedom from labor, and the economic ability to acquire materials and time. The prologue to Acts, which refers to the first volume, implies that the support continues for a significant amount of time. But the challenge to Theophilus somehow facilitates the production of the documents. The inclusion of "most excellent" suggests a social location where one or more persons either seek to communicate with people who possess some prestige in Roman society or seek the image of communicating with such people. The inscribed author is adopting a stance subordinate to the one with whom he wishes to communicate. Two possibilities, therefore, already can be excluded--the inscribed author does not evoke a social location which communicates downward to people with lower social ranking, and it is not considered wise to communicate as though there were equality in social rank. The social location of the thought of the implied author suggests it is advantageous to adopt a stance of respect that evokes a social location slightly below but in communication with people who have higher status in the social structure. Thus, although the thought of the implied author is near the artisan class, and holds no disdain for artisan labor, there is a social posture of communicating upwards in the social order rather than downward to artisans or peasants.

Culture
Culture is a humanly constructed arena of artistic, literary, historical, and aesthetic competencies. Since writing itself constitutes a basic cultural product, when we examine the conception of reading and writing in Luke-Acts, we gain a further definition of the location of the thought in the two volumes. Let us begin in the arena of the characters.

In the social location of the Jerusalem temple, a male named Zechariah, a member of the social class of priests, with a defined status in the division of Abijah, was fulfilling his role of burning incense when

---

[38] Joseph A. Fitzmyer, *The Gospel According to Luke: Introduction, Translation, and Notes* (2 vols.; AB 28–28A; Garden City, N.Y.: 1981–1985) 1:300.

an angel of the Lord addressed him about his social role as husband (Luke 1:5–17). In the domain of culture, special interest arises when the angel speaks to him in poetic verse (1:14–17). This is not the poetic verse of Homer, Greek tragedy, or Greek lyric poetry, but poetry in the style of Septuagint Greek. Six months later, when the angel Gabriel speaks to Mary, a virgin betrothed to a man named Joseph, a member of the royal family of David, this angel speaks in a similar septuagintal style of poetic verse (1:32–33, 35). When Mary visits Elizabeth, the now pregnant wife of the priest Zechariah, Mary speaks in even lengthier septuagintal-styled poetic verse (1:46–55). Then, after Elizabeth gives birth to John, Zechariah, the priestly father of John, first writes the name of John on a tablet, then produces extended prophetic speech in the style of septuagintal verse (1:67–79). Zechariah's ability to speak in this manner and to write reminds us that he comes from a priestly family that nurtures at least basic educational skills. After an angel of the Lord speaks in short septuagintal-styled verse to shepherds in the field (2:14), a righteous and devout man named Simeon also speaks in this stylized manner as he blesses God (2:29–32) and speaks to Mary about her son (2:34–35).

A very interesting social location begins to exhibit itself. The implied reader observes that the father of John, the mother of Jesus, the righteous and devout man Simeon, and angels of the Lord, including Gabriel, display a social location within Jewish culture that gives them the competence to produce poetic verse that imitates Septuagint Greek. And the implied reader sees that the father of John can write at least basic information on a tablet.

After the first two chapters the status of poetic verse styled according to the Septuagint verse changes. Prior to chapter 3, the poetic verse is produced either by heavenly beings or humans upon whom the Holy Spirit has come (Mary, 2:35; Zechariah, 1:67; Simeon, 2:27). This speech is characterized as prophetic (1:67; 2:26), and the impression is that it is being composed in the setting of oral performance rather than being quoted from a written document. In the ideology of the implied author, then, the poetic verse is "divine, spirit-inspired, prophetic speech" (which the inscribed author has now written). After Luke 1–2 and throughout Acts, all the poetic speech is said to be from a written document, and this speech occurs in two intratextual arenas. First, the narrator quotes septuagintal verse "written in a book of words of Isaiah the prophet" in Luke 3:4–6 and Acts 8:32–33. The words have the style of septuagintal poetic verse, like the poetic verse that was performed orally in Luke 1–2. With these quotations, the narratee sees that the narrator can find and read passages from Isaiah. Second, a large number of characters quote written poetic verse. After Jesus' response to his mother in the temple at twelve years of age (2:49), he responds to all three temptations by the devil by quoting scripture (4:4, 8, 12). But the devil also can quote from these written materials (4:10–11). In a Jewish cultural environment, Jesus has skillfully defeated the devil, since he quoted each time from the Torah (Deut 9:9; 8:3; 6:16), while the devil quoted only from the Writings (Ps 91:11–12). But the narrator does not tell the narratee this, and we can not know for certain that the implied author is aware of it. At this point, the implied reader knows that Jesus has the ability to recite verses of written scripture orally, but the implied reader cannot be absolutely sure, yet, that Jesus can read these verses from a written document. Perhaps, Jesus simply has heard them so often that he can reproduce them orally.

When Jesus goes to the synagogue at Nazareth on the sabbath, he opens the book of Isaiah, finds a specific passage, and reads the passage with rhetorical grace (4:16–22). The implied reader will notice that this is the same book from which the narrator quoted in 3:4–6, but this reader will not yet know that the narrator will quote again from this book in Acts 8:32–33. Jesus, then, like the narrator, has access to a book of Isaiah's words. We never see Jesus carry this book, but he has access to it in the Nazareth synagogue. Like the narrator and the implied author, Jesus has the competence to find a specific passage in this book. When Jesus continues by telling about the days of Elijah and Elisha (4:24–27), the implied reader probably concludes that Jesus reads about these things in some other book that tells about Elijah and Elisha. But no one indicates where these stories could be found.

Jesus' social location, then, appears to be somewhat different from that of Zechariah, Mary, and Simeon, since he is a reader and oral performer of scripture, while they were oral performers of spirit-inspired poetic verse which no one claims was written before our implied author scripted it. Therefore, Jesus, as presented in Luke-Acts, is located within the social sphere of reading culture. This view of Jesus' social location is further supported by his quotation from the book of Psalms in Luke 20:17, 42–44, his specific reference to the passage in the Torah about the bush (Luke 20:37), and his interpretation of the things concerning himself "beginning with Moses and all the prophets" (Luke 24:27). Jesus, then, occupies a social location of reading literacy within Jewish culture. He has a reading knowledge of the Torah, the prophet Isaiah, and the Psalms.

In Acts, the implied reader sees Peter, John, Stephen, and James orally reciting passages from the Jewish writings, but only the Ethiopian eunuch is portrayed as possessing a book (Isaiah) and reading it. In fact, it surely is instructive about the social location of Luke-Acts that every major character quotes (often lengthy passages) verbatim from the Jewish scriptures very soon after being introduced to the implied reader (Peter, Acts 1:20; 2:16–21, 25–28, 34–35; 3:22–23; 4:11; other apostles, -4:25–26; Stephen, 7:3, 26–28, 32–34, 35, 37, 40, 42–43, 48–50; James, Acts 15:15–18). In his inaugural speech (Acts 13:33, 33–35, 41, 47) and likewise at the end of his career (28:25–27) Paul quotes extensively from the Jewish writings. But for Paul there is more.

In Athens Paul quotes from both Epimenides and Aratus' *Phaenomena* (Acts 17:28). Culturally Paul is thus exhibited in a social location that reaches beyond Jewish writing into Greek poetry. It is possible that Peter and the apostles also have some ability in the sphere of Greek sayings, since Acts 5:29 may be a saying associated with Socrates.[39]

Every competence the characters exhibit to the implied reader reveals an aspect of the competence of the implied author. Thus, the implied author is not limited to septuagintal poetic verse, but also has competence, though perhaps quite limited, with Greek poetry. To these things, however, we must add the implied author's competence in the prologues to Luke and Acts, the defense speeches of Paul in Acts, the sea voyage narratives, and the kind of historical biography and novelistic monograph the implied reader sees in Luke and Acts. Thus, the implied author occupies a social location within Jewish culture which is not limited to knowledge of the Septuagint. There is no attempt, however, to write a dactylic hexameter line of Homer or a poetic line of tragedy and there are no references to these written works alongside written Jewish scripture.

What does this mean in terms of social location? Perhaps we can get a clearer view if we compare Luke-Acts with the *Infancy Gospel of Thomas*. On three different occasions in *Infancy Thomas*, teachers agree to educate Jesus, that is, to teach him "letters." The first two times Jesus resists the presupposition that proper knowledge and behavior comes through learning how to read and write (*Inf. Gos. Thom.* 6:2–6; 14:1–3). The third time (15:1–2) he takes a book lying on the reading desk and, without reading any of the letters in it, opens his mouth and by the Holy Spirit teaches the law to people who are standing by. To understand this we must know that *Infancy Thomas* is rejecting the concept that "all knowledge" can be taught through letters, that is "Greek letters." The teachers try to teach Jesus the Greek alphabet, which is the basis of παιδεία – the education that makes people truly learned. In contrast to the portrayal in Luke, the *Infancy Gospel of Thomas* exhibits a social location that depicts Jesus refusing to learn from people

---

[39] Richard I. Pervo, *Profit with Delight: The Literary Genre of the Acts of the Apostles* (Philadelphia: Fortress, 1987), 169.

who teach reading and writing. Along with this social location, the author of *Infancy Thomas* presents no quotations from scripture in the entire document. For reasons beyond the scope of this study, the social location of the *Infancy Gospel of Thomas* reflects a position against people who teach reading and writing in Greek. In contrast, Luke presents Jesus as a person comfortable with and trained in written scripture, and both the Gospel and Acts exhibit a high facility with scripture written in Greek language.

Also, Paul can quote brief lines from some ancient Greek poets (Acts 17:28) and produce articulate speeches that exhibit knowledge and skill. But in one of the speeches Paul makes it clear that he is an urban Jew who received a proper education under a tutor named Gamaliel (Acts 22:3). Thus, his learning came from Jewish culture, and this learning gives him competence even with some Greek poetry.

With this analysis of reading and writing culture in Luke-Acts, we see an interest in presenting Jesus and his followers as "lettered," but it is a literacy based on Jewish culture. The thought of the implied author, therefore, is emphatically bicultural: grounded in Jewish culture but competent in Greco-Roman culture. This biculturality also produces problems for this kind of Christianity. Festus recognizes Paul's "great learning" (τὰ πολλὰ γράμματα), but fears that his pursuit of truth is turning him mad (Acts 26:24). However, the high priestly family of Jerusalem perceives Peter and John to be uneducated and ungifted men (Acts 4:13). People in the narrative, then, can label the competencies of its characters as "unlettered" or "lettered," and they may describe the people themselves as "ungifted" or "mad."

Foreign Affairs

Once we see the attempt of the implied author to communicate upward from a bicultural location, our investigation of foreign affairs produces interesting results. In truth there are few foreign affairs in view in Luke-Acts. There are references to Roman emperors in two historical synchronisms: Caesar Augustus decreed that the inhabited world should be counted (Luke 2:1); and John began baptizing in the fifteenth year of the reign of Tiberius Caesar (Luke 3:1). In addition, the Emperor Claudius is known to have commanded all Jews to leave Rome (Acts 18:2). Since the reign and decrees of the Caesars are essentially foreign to the history of Syria, Judea, Galilee, Iturea, Trachonitis, and Abilene, the thought of the implied author is located where the decrees of the emperors are perceived to be foreign history.

But what is the meaning of foreign? The first people who appear to be foreign are the Samaritans who will not welcome Jesus (9:52). Yet soon after, Jesus presents a Samaritan as a model neighbor (10:29–37). And later, when Jesus heals ten lepers it is the Samaritan, who is called a foreigner (17:18), who appropriately gives praise to God for his cleansing. Then in Acts 8:1–24, the people of Samaria, at one point called the "nation" of Samaria (8:9), respond positively to the preaching among them.

The people in Acts 2 who are gathered together begin to speak in their own native languages: Parthians, Medes, Elamites; people from Mesopotamia, Judea, Cappadocia, Pontus, Asia, Phrygia, Pamphylia, Egypt, parts of Libya belonging to Cyrene, Rome, and Cretans and Arabians. When these "foreigners" join Christianity, the Christian community begins to be constituted by foreigners. Next, the church is "scattered" throughout many regions. People in Athens call Paul a "babbler" and "preacher of foreign deities" (17:28).

It depends on where a person is located as to whether he or she is a foreigner, and the thought in Luke-Acts appears to exhibit a location of "inverted" foreignness. Christians appear to be the primary foreigners. In other words, the affairs recounted in Luke-Acts are the true foreign affairs. The thought of the implied author is located in a bicultural environment that has brought a self-consciousness of foreignness among people established in cities throughout the eastern Mediterranean. But the implied author has a solution to the anxiety this foreign identity produces. The "foreign" affairs of Christians must be narrated to people above them in the social order. In other words, some kind of advantage is to be obtained by admitting that the affairs of the Christian community are foreign events to established people in Roman society and by arguing that it is important for them to have a well-ordered, detailed account of these foreign affairs. Thus, the implied author is located socially in a position where he wants the foreign affairs that lie within his biculturality to find an accepted place within the affairs of Rome.

Belief Systems and Ideologies

The basic ideology of Luke-Acts appears to be the belief that God has ordained a place for the "foreign affairs" of Christianity within the affairs of the Roman empire. This aspect of Luke-Acts regularly has been pursued under the rubric of an apologia for Christianity that shows that Christians are not guilty of illegal activity under Roman law.[40] The ideology of Luke-Acts, however, moves much beyond this goal. The implied author wishes to show that God has "cleansed" a widely divergent and mixed group of peoples within a movement in-

---

[40] See Peter W. Walaskay, *"And So We Came to Rome": The Political Perspective of St. Luke* (Cambridge: Cambridge University Press, 1983).

augurated by Jesus of Nazareth. The word "cleansed" challenges the purity system of Judaism at its center. As Elliott has shown in this volume, Luke-Acts replaces the centric ideology of the temple with the distribution ideology of the household.[41] One of the major aspects of this change is a transformation of the purity system of Judaism.[42]

Luke-Acts replicates the distributive economic approach within the realm of purity. As food is distributed to people of every social rank, so every social rank and ethnically divergent person may be "cleansed by God" through baptism into the Christian movement. The key verse occurs in Acts 10:15: "What God has cleansed, you must not call common." This ideology is exhibited through the cleansing of lepers, which includes Samaritans and Naaman the Syrian (Luke 4:27; 5:12, 13; 7:22; 17:14, 17). Also it emerges in a discussion with Pharisees, where Jesus tells them that God has made not only the outside but also the inside, and therefore giving for alms those things which are within will cleanse everything for them (Luke 11:40–1). This change of purity systems coheres with the ideology that God has cleansed a wide variety mixed together (Acts 11:9), which includes Gentiles whose hearts God cleanses by faith (Acts 15:9). Purity, then, is to be found within the mixed and diverse social and ethnic groups in the Christian movement. God's cleansing activity is exhibited in the devoutness (Luke 2:25; Acts 2:5; 3:12; 8:2; 10:2, 7; 17:23; 22:12) and righteousness or innocence (Luke 1:6, 17; 2:25; 5:32; 12:57; 14:14; 15:17; 18:9; 20:20; 23:47, 50; Acts 3:14; 4:19; 7:52; 10:22; 22:14; 24:15) of people associated with Christianity. When disagreements arise between Jews and Christians over precise practices, the implied author suggests that these disagreements are simply a matter of inconsistency within some people's thinking about how God has cleansed the diversity that lies within Judaism itself, and now within Christianity, throughout the Roman empire.

Thus, the thought of the implied author is located in a social environment that accepts its foreignness and mixedness as blessed by God. This confidence in God's action reflects a social location in which Christians consider themselves equal to Pharisees and able to challenge them to be hospitable in their homes and generous in almsgiving. In addition, it gives these Christians confidence with the leaders of Roman society, which leads us to our last section.

---

[41] John H. Elliott, "Temple versus Household in Luke-Acts: A Contrast in Social Institutions," in *Social World of Luke-Acts*, 211–40.

[42] Mary Douglas, *Purity and Danger: An Analysis of Concepts of Pollution and Taboo* (London: Routledge & Kegan Paul, 1966); Bruce J. Malina, *The New Testament World: Insights from Cultural Anthropology* (Atlanta: John Knox, 1981), 122–52; Jerome H. Neyrey, "Symbolism in Mark," *Forum* 4/3 (1988): 63–92.

Political-Military-Legal System

According to Carney, during the time of the Roman Empire, the political-military-legal system stood in a close symbiotic relationship with socio-economic affairs, affecting almost everything everywhere in the system.[43] It is widely recognized that a political-military-legal system is extensively in view in Luke-Acts. Some have argued that the primary purpose of Luke-Acts was to show that no Christian had ever been found guilty of a crime against the Roman legal system. More recently, Philip Esler has argued that Luke-Acts legitimatizes Christianity by exhibiting favorable relationships between early Christian leaders and Roman officials.[44]

On the one hand, we must remind ourselves of those parts of the political-military-legal system that are outside the boundaries of what is in view to the implied author. While Luke-Acts contains many references to Roman emperors, only three are referred to by name (Caesar Augustus, Luke 2:1; Tiberius Caesar, Luke 3:1; Claudius, Acts 18:2). Moreover, there is no scene in Luke-Acts where a Roman emperor is present. Paul is taken to Rome so he can appeal directly to Caesar, but such an appeal is never shown to the reader nor referred to as accomplished. In fact, there is such a social separation from the environment of the emperor that references to a specific emperor are absent except in the two synchronisms at the beginning of Luke and the reference to Claudius' edict against Jews in Rome. References to certain decrees and laws imply the presence of the emperor as a symbol of supreme political and legal power.

In contrast to the absence of emperors themselves, a number of upper-level representatives of the emperor's domain appear in Luke-Acts. The narrator depicts a majority of these people as holding a favorable attitude toward Christians.[45] Thus, Lysias, the Roman tribune in Jerusalem, goes to great lengths to protect Paul from the Jews in Acts 21–23; Sergius Paulus, the proconsul of Cyprus, converts to Christian belief (Acts 13:6–12); and Asiarchs in Ephesus, who are priests of the imperial cult, are described as friends of Paul (Acts 19:31). Most of the people at the level of prefect, proconsul, or king will take no legal action against individual Christians, but most exhibit some social distance from Christianity. Thus, Pontius Pilate declares Jesus innocent, but his social location is clearly distant from the activity of Jesus and his followers. Likewise Gallio, the Roman proconsul of Achaea, dismisses

---

[43] Carney, *Shape of the Past*, 235–79; cf. A. Andreski, *Military Organization and Society* (Berkeley, Calif.: University of California Press, 1968).

[44] Philip F. Esler, *Community and Gospel in Luke-Acts* (Cambridge: Cambridge University Press, 1987).

[45] Ibid., 202.

3. Social Location of the Implied Author of Luke-Acts   141

the case of the Corinthian Jews against Paul, and his reason is that this is a matter of dispute over Jewish words and names (Acts 18:12–17). In other words, people at the highest levels of the political-military-legal system are located socially at a distance from the Christian movement.

The number of centurions mentioned in Luke-Acts, and their favorable relation to Jesus and the later apostles, is quite a different matter. It would appear that Luke-Acts is produced in a social location where a number of centurions are members of the Christian community. The centurion of Capernaum has a favorable experience with Jesus (Luke 7:1–10); the centurion at the foot of the cross "glorifies God," probably indicating a personal stance within Christian belief (Luke 23:47);[46] the first gentile convert is the centurion Cornelius, along with his entire household (Acts 10:1–11:18); and Julius, the centurion in charge of Paul during the voyage to Rome, is especially kind to Paul, allowing friends to visit him (Acts 27:3) and saving him from being thrown overboard by the ship's crew (Acts 27:42–43). Luke-Acts is located in an environment where centurions are among the members of the community, not simply outsiders looking in.

What, then, is the social relation of Christianity to the political-military-legal system in the thought of the implied author? It implies that representatives from this arena of the social system are fully constituted members of the Christian movement alongside the other representatives of diversity within it. Likewise the political-military-legal system has an established practice of protecting, or at least attempting to protect, Christians. Thus, in the ideology of the implied author, there is every reason why members of the political-military-legal system can feel at home within Christianity and every reason why Christianity should be considered to have a comfortable place within the Roman political-military-legal system.

Yet there is a deep uneasiness within this "at homeness." Throughout Luke-Acts, the political-military-legal system protects or attempts to protect Christians. But in the end there is a social location of imprisonment within the system. On the one hand, Paul is a Roman citizen (Acts 22:27–28), he is free to move about openly and unhindered (Acts 28:31), and he is able to meet with local Jewish leaders (Acts 28:17–23). Yet, a soldier must guard him (Acts 28:16), much as there are representatives of the political-military-legal system keeping an eye on the affairs of this "foreign people" throughout the narrative. Paul, like the Christian movement, has a rightful home within the Roman Empire; yet his home, and he himself, is continually guarded. The attentive guarding protects the members of the movement, but it also

---

[46] See ibid.

imprisons them socially. Thus, in this social location, the thought of the implied author hovers between being at home, enjoying the hospitality and benefits of Roman society, and being in prison, always guarded by people both inside and outside the movement.

Conclusion

Many interpreters have claimed knowledge either about the author of Luke-Acts or about the community in which he lived. Other interpreters have denied that the interpreter can know anything about either the author or his community. There is, however, another way to ask the question. What can we know about the social location of the thought of the implied author?

The goal of this chapter has been to create a model for exploring systematically the social location of the implied author of a document written in Mediterranean society during the time of the Roman Empire and to make an initial application of the model to the study of Luke-Acts. As a result of our sortie through the arenas of the social system identified by Thomas Carney, a picture has begun to emerge. The implied author produces previous events as a written product, and this production of events is observable in virtually every arena of the narrative functions of the text. Major characters, the narrator, and the inscribed author produce previous events as a social product for their audiences. While most people in Mediterranean culture produced previous events as a social product, only certain people produced them in written form. The inscribed author refers to both written and oral production of previous events as a resource, the raw material if you will, for this production of an ordered account. The implied author produces previous events as a means of establishing and maintaining sets of relationships among various kinds of Christians, Jews, and Romans who encounter one another and exchange values, goods, beliefs, and challenges.

The thought of the previous events that constitute Luke-Acts occurs in a geographical space extending from Ethiopia and Cyrenaica east to Elam and west to Rome. The resources within this space are ships for travel and islands for protection and hospitality on the Great Sea, fish and boats for travel on Lake Gennesareth, and houses for hospitality in ports, cities, and towns on the mainland and on islands. The differentiated people in view in this space are wealthy and powerful Jews, wealthy and powerful Romans, and afflicted men and women. Thus, the thought of the implied author is located in the midst of the activities of adult Jews and Romans who have certain kinds of power in cities and villages throughout the Mediterranean world from Rome to Jerusalem.

Within this space and among these people, the thought of the implied author exhibits technology in four spheres: administration, sea travel, writing, and crafts. The arena of socialization reveals an upward-looking use of technology toward Roman officials with political power. Jewish officials, however, are considered equal in social status and rank. Wealthy Pharisees are singled out as people who regularly offer hospitality to Christians sharing the social location of thought with the implied author, yet those Pharisees are accused of often not fulfilling aspects of social action valued by the Christians who receive hospitality from them. Christians in this social location of thought pride themselves on offering healing to afflicted people[47] and food to beggars, lame, maimed, blind, and those not allowed to stay in the city overnight.[48] In this social location, Christians argue for distribution of wealth to the poor, but they do not argue the case for allowing the poor to become landowners or householders.[49] In other words, the thought is located socially within cities and villages, not out in the countryside.

The primary culture exhibited by the social location is written literature and cultivated speech. The implied author knows substantial portions of Isaiah and the Psalms, as well as other scriptures. In addition, the implied author can produce short lines of Greek poetry, though there is no attempt to produce a hexameter verse from Homer or a poetic line from Greek tragedy. Rather, the implied author produces poetic verse out of the culture of Judaism. In other words, the cultural achievement represented by Luke-Acts reflects a Jewish sphere of society using the Greek language, the lingua franca of the Mediterranean world.

The arena of foreign affairs gives us additional insight into the social location of the thought of the implied author of Luke-Acts. Roman emperors, and thus foreign affairs are in view for the implied author. But the presence of Roman affairs has created a view that the affairs of Israelites, Jews, and Christians are "foreign" to the dominant population in the Mediterranean world. Thus, the thought of the implied author is located socially in a place where it seems advantageous, and perhaps necessary, to tell "these foreign affairs" to people slightly higher in social rank who read Greek and appreciate a people who strive to be devout, righteous, and lettered.

---

[47] See Pilch, "Sickness and Healing."

[48] See Rohrbaugh, "Pre-Industrial City."

[49] See Oakman, "Countryside;" idem, *Jesus and the Economic Questions of His Day* (Lewiston, N.Y.: Edwin Mellen, 1986).

In the arena of belief systems and ideologies, the thought of the implied author appears to challenge the dominant Jewish purity system at its center. The thought in Luke-Acts celebrates diversity and claims that God has "cleansed" it. In this way, the thought of the implied author claims to be an authentic part of the heterogeneous population of the Roman Empire. Part of this diversity includes the presence of political-military-legal personnel within the Christian movement. Thus, it is quite acceptable in this social location to sell one's coat and buy a sword (Luke 22:36). Yet the sword is not to be used carelessly or with undue aggression (22:49–51). Nevertheless, life at this social location is uneasy. Members of the political-military-legal system both protect Christians and imprison them. Accepting a position of subordination, Christians speak with politeness and care upwards to those who dominate the system. Yet, bolstered by God's sanctioning of their diversity and by their ideology of "at homeness" in the Roman Empire, they not only tell their story to those above but engage in vigorous and continued confrontation with those from whom they claim their Jewish heritage and those with whom they enjoy the benefits of Greco-Roman culture.

4

Rhetoric and Culture: Mark 4–11 as a Test Case[1]

Introduction

In an article entitled "Where Is Rhetorical Criticism Taking Us?", published in 1987, Wilhelm Wuellner, quoting Perelman and Olbrechts-Tyteca, proposed that rhetorical criticism "takes us to 'the social aspect of language which is an instrument of communication and influence on others.'"[2] As he developed his argument, he cited Sloan's assertion that in rhetorical criticism "a text must reveal its context," and that "a text's context means for the rhetorical critic the 'attitudinizing conventions, precepts that condition (both the writer's *and* the reader's) stance toward experience, knowledge, tradition, language, and other people.'"[3] Then he asserted that "[c]ontext can also come close to being synonymous with what K. Burke and others call the 'ideology' of, or in, literature."[4] In the middle of the article, he argues that rhetorical criticism must be identical with "practical criticism" rather

---

[1] This essay combines "Rhetoric and Culture: Exploring Types of Cultural Rhetoric in a Text," in *Rhetoric and the New Testament: Essays from the 1992 Heidelberg Conference* (ed. Stanley E. Porter and Thomas H. Olbricht; JSNTSup 90; Sheffield: Sheffield Academic Press, 1993), 443–63 and "Interpreting Miracle Culture and Parable Culture in Mark 4–11," *SEÅ* 59 (1994): 59–81.

[2] Wilhelm Wuellner, "Where is Rhetorical Criticism Taking Us?" *CBQ* 49 (1987): 449; cf. idem, "The Rhetorical Structure of Luke 12 in Its Wider Context," *Neot* 22 (1988): 266; Chaim Perelman and Lucie Olbrechts-Tyteca, *The New Rhetoric: A Treatise on Argumentation* (trans. John Wilkinson and Purcell Weaver; Notre Dame, Ind.: University of Notre Dame, 1969), 513.

[3] Wuellner, "Where?" 450; Thomas O. Sloan, "Rhetoric," in *The New Encyclopedia Britannica* (30 vols.; 15th ed.; Chicago: Encyclopaedia Britannica, 1975), 15:798–99; 802–803.

[4] Wuellner, "Where?" 450 citing Kenneth Burke, "Methodological Repression and/or Strategies of Containment," *Critical Inquiry* 5 (1978): 401–16; Terry Eagleton, *The Function of Criticism* (London: Verso Editions, 1984), 107–24; Peter Hohendahl, *The Institution of Criticism* (Ithaca, N.Y.: Cornell University Press, 1982); E. Bruss, *Beautiful Theories: The Spectacle of Discourse in Contemporary Criticism* (Baltimore: Johns Hopkins University Press, 1982).

than "literary criticism," explaining that literary criticism is "rhetoric restrained."[5] Practical criticism, in contrast to literary criticism, is "rhetoric revalued,"[6] "rhetoric reinvented." This means that

> texts are read and reread, interpreted and reinterpreted, "as forms of *activity* inseparable from the wider social relations between writers and readers."[7] Not only do rhetorical devices of disposition and style get studied as means of creating "certain effects on the reader,"[8] but the very construct of a theory of rhetorical criticism, compared with past and present alternative theorizings, can be, indeed should be, examined "as a practice."[9]

At the end of his article, Wuellner asserts that "rhetorical criticism leads us away from a traditional message- or content-oriented reading of Scripture to a reading which generates and strengthens ever-deepening personal, social, and cultural values."[10] "The divided concerns," he concludes, "are reunited in a new rhetoric which approaches all literature, including inspired or canonical biblical literature, as *social* discourse."[11]

I applaud this view of rhetorical analysis, and I have been trying to work toward a systematic approach that can reach the goals set forth in this article.[12] The approach, which is called socio-rhetorical criticism, explores four arenas of texture in a text: (a) inner texture; (b) intertex-

---

[5] Wuellner, "Where?" 453 citing Brian Vickers, "Introduction," in *Rhetoric Revalued* (ed. Brian Vickers; Medieval & Renaissance Texts and Studies 19; Binghamton, N.Y.: Center for Medieval & Renaissance Studies, 1982).

[6] Vickers, "Introduction."

[7] Citing Terry Eagleton, *Literary Theory: An Introduction* (Minneapolis: University of Minnesota Press, 1983), 205–206; idem, *Function of Criticism*, 119. Cf. George A. Kennedy, *New Testament Interpretation through Rhetorical Criticism* (Chapel Hill, N.C.: University of North Carolina Press, 1984), 158–59.

[8] Citing David Rhodes and Donald Michie, *Mark as Story: An Introduction to the Narrative of a Gospel* (Philadelphia: Fortress, 1982), 35.

[9] Wuellner, "Where?" 453 citing Charles Taylor, *Social Theory as Practice* (Dehli: Oxford University Press, 1983). Cf. W.J.T. Mitchell, ed., *Against Theory: Literary Studies and the New Pragmatism* (Chicago: University of Chicago, 1985).

[10] Wuellner, "Where?" 461.

[11] Ibid., 462.

[12] Vernon K. Robbins, "The Social Location of the Implied Author of Luke-Acts," in *The Social World Of Luke-Acts: Models for Interpretation* (ed. Jerome H. Neyrey; Peabody, Mass.: Hendrickson, 1991), 305–32; idem, *Jesus the Teacher: A Socio-Rhetorical Interpretation of Mark* (paperback ed.; Minneapolis: Fortress, 1992), xix-xliv; idem, "A Socio-Rhetorical Look at the Work of John Knox on Luke-Acts," in *Cadbury, Knox, and Talbert: American Contributions to the Study of Acts* (ed. Mikeal Carl Parsons and Joseph B. Tyson; Atlanta: Scholars Press, 1992), 91–105; "The Reversed Contextualization of Psalm 22 in the Markan Crucifixion: A Socio-Rhetorical Analysis," in *The Four Gospels 1992: Festschrift Frans Neirynck* (ed. Frans van Segbroeck et al.; 3 vols.; BETL 100; Leuven: Leuven University Press, 2:1161–83.

ture; (c) social and cultural texture; and (d) ideological texture. My concern in this paper lies in the third and fourth arenas: social, cultural, and ideological texture. Ideological analysis in literary or cultural study is, in the words of Kavanagh:

> the institutional and/or textual apparatuses that work on the reader's or spectator's imaginary conceptions of self and social order in order to call or *solicit* ...him/her into a specific form of social "reality" and social "subjectivity."[13]

This understanding of ideology is closely related to Kenneth Burke's assertion that:

> Critical and imaginative works are answers to questions posed by the situation in which they arose. They are not merely answers, they are *strategic* answers, *stylized* answers.[14]

The ideology of a text, then, concerns "a specific form of social reality and social subjectivity," and a literary work formulates "strategic, stylized answers" in the context of this specific form of social reality and social subjectivity.

One of the reasons New Testament interpreters have not made more progress in rhetorical analysis and interpretation of social discourse is the priority they have given to sociology over anthropology. It is a mistake for a New Testament interpreter to privilege sociology over anthropology. Sociology is interested first and foremost in social situations, institutions, and structures in which behavior takes place.[15] Sociology regularly has little or no interest in texts. Anthropology, on the other hand, is interested in the interactive relation of body, mind, and culture. As a result, anthropology is highly interested in language, communication, and texts. Anthropology has a close relation to sociolinguistics, and it approaches the data of human thought and activity in a manner highly similar to an interpreter's approach to interpretation of a text.[16] An ability to analyze and interpret social discourse, then,

---

[13] James H. Kavanaugh, "Ideology," in *Critical Terms for Literary Study* (ed. Frank Lentricchia and Thomas McLaughlin; Chicago: University of Chicago Press, 1990), 310.

[14] Kenneth Burke, *The Philosophy of Literary Form: Studies in Symbolic Action* (3d ed.; Berkeley: University of California Press, 1973), 1.

[15] Beth B. Hess, Elizabeth W. Markson, and Peter J. Stein *Sociology* (3d ed.; New York: Macmillan, 1988), 4.

[16] Clifford Geertz, *The Interpretation of Cultures* (New York: Basic Books, 1973); Lee Patterson, "Literary History," in *Critical Terms for Literary Study* (ed. Frank Lentricchia and Thomas McLaughlin; Chicago: University of Chicago Press, 1990), 250–62; James L. Peacock, *The Anthropological Lens: Harsh Light, Soft Focus* (Cambridge: Cambridge University Press, 1986); Hess, *Sociology*, 56–58.

will come from an ability to perform exegesis with anthropological insights that will lead us toward insights from sociology.

Wuellner does not move very far toward "revalued" or "reinvented" rhetoric in his 1987 article that describes where rhetorical criticism is taking us. In the last part of the article, he applies Kennedy's model for analysis of a rhetorical unit to 1 Corinthians 9: (a) defining the rhetorical unit; (b) identifying the rhetorical situation; (c) identifying the rhetorical disposition or arrangement; (d) identifying rhetorical techniques or style; and (e) identifying the synchronic rhetorical function and effect of the whole unit.[17] The discussion is brief, and at some points very suggestive. But there are few observations in these six short pages that move significantly beyond Kennedy's approach.

Wuellner's article on "Paul as Pastor,"[18] which appeared in the previous year, is a different matter. In this article he analyzes the use of codes and shared values in the starting point or premises of arguments and in rhetorical questions.[19] His analysis of modalities, argumentative effect, deductive technique, inductive argumentation, and dissociation-technique, employing insights especially from Perelman and Olbrechts-Tyteca's *The New Rhetoric*, represents a significant step toward revalued or reinvented rhetoric. The progress in this article looks promising indeed, and Steven Kraftchick recently has used insights from it in a creative manner to reassess the debate about the rhetorical nature of Galatians.[20] Wuellner made further progress in "The Rhetorical Structure of Luke 12 in its Wider Context," where he discussed the rhetorical features in: (a) the relationship of the parts of the text; (b) the text's time, place, audience setting; (c) the text's (and reader's) relationship to the real world; and (d) the text's relationship to similar texts.[21] One of the most instructive aspects of this article is its positioning of rhetorical theory in relation to hermeneutical theory. "The triumph of hermeneutical theory," he explains, suppressed the rhetorics of texts with a "theory of extracting 'the' meaning (usually restricted to *theological*, occasionally also *ethical*, but rarely any other meanings)."[22] Rhetorical criticism, in contrast, is designed to explain "the text's 'power,'"[23] and

---

[17] Wuellner, "Where?" 455–56.

[18] Wilhelm Wuellner, "Paul as Pastor: The Function of Rhetorical Questions in First Corinthians," in *L'Apôtre Paul: Personnalité, style et conception du ministère* (ed. Albert Vanhoye; BETL 73; Leuven: Leuven University Press, 1986), 49–77.

[19] Ibid., 63–77.

[20] Steven J. Kraftchick, "Why Do Rhetoricians Rage?" in *Text and Logos: The Humanistic Interpretation of the New Testament* (ed. Theodore W. Jennings and Hendrickus Boers; Atlanta: Scholars, 1990), 56–79.

[21] Wuellner, "Rhetorical Structure."

[22] Ibid., 305.

[23] Ibid., 286.

to explore "possibilities that are manifestly awakened by the language."[24]

The progress Wuellner made in his 1986 and 1988 articles did not reappear, however, in his 1991 essay for the Kennedy Festschrift.[25] In this essay, a remarkably restrained form of rhetorical analysis appears, a form reminiscent of a 1973 article, to which I will turn in a moment. The restraint appears as Wuellner limits the social and cultural context of Luke 12:1–13:9 to Biblical and Jewish traditions, values, and perceived realities. He limits the social and cultural context of the discourse by focusing on "rhetorical genres," arguing, on the one hand, that significant changes occurred in Hellenistic-Roman society, but that, on the other hand, "Jewish 'preconceptual' and later literary rhetoric, with its Near Eastern origin and Hellenistic influences, was controlled by its own, distinctly Jewish social environments, whether in exile and dispersion, or in *Eretz Yisrael*."[26] Here the distinct restraint Wuellner has put on his rhetorical analysis comes from a personal bias toward Christianity's participation in Jewish culture. The salient words are: "controlled by its own, distinctly Jewish social environments." The issue here is whether any culture can fully "control," "limit," and "restrain" the thoughts, values, dispositions, and actions of its people when that culture exists in the context of another culture.

Overcoming Dualistic Social and Cultural Approaches

The restraint Wuellner perceives for early Christian discourse, so that he considers it to be "controlled by its own, distinctly Jewish social envisonments," resonates with the neo-orthodox approach to Christianity and culture during the 1950s and 1960s. In this post-World War II context, H. Richard Niebuhr introduced, in his classic work *Christ and Culture*, an understanding of good Christianity as *against* culture, *above* culture, *paradoxically* related to culture, or as a *transformer* of culture. His approach presupposes that it is bad, in contrast, for Christianity to be *of* culture.[27] Thus, there is a fundamental dualism built into Niebuhr's approach that separates Christianity from culture like oil separates from water. Good Christianity, it proposes, should not "mix" with culture. In Wuellner's approach, "culture" refers to

---

[24] Jonathan Culler, *On Deconstruction: Theory and Criticism after Structuralism* (Ithaca, N.Y.: Cornell University Press, 1982), 247; Wuellner, "Rhetorical Structure," 287.

[25] Wilhelm Wuellner, "The Rhetorical Genre of Jesus' Sermon in Luke 12.1–13.9," in *Persuasive Artistry: Studies in New Testament in Honor of George A. Kennedy* (ed. Duane F. Watson; JSNTSup 50; Sheffield: Sheffield Academic Press), 93–118.

[26] Ibid., 116.

[27] H. Richard Niebuhr, *Christ and Culture* (New York: Harper & Row, 1951).

Hellenistic-Roman society and culture, which cannot be an authentic medium of God's revelation. In contrast, "Jewish social environments" are the contexts in which the revelation of God have occurred throughout history.

We know the context of World War II that crystallized such a separation between Christianity and culture, and many of us have deep convictions that Christianity must always be vigilant about its relation to the ideology and values of the social and political environments in which it exists. Yet the dualism integral to Niebuhr's taxonomy has discouraged theologians and biblical interpreters from engaging in analysis and interpretation that would help us understand just what kind of phenomenon Christianity really is. For this purpose, we need to ask the question: "What kind of culture is Christianity?" "What kinds of subcultures, countercultures, contracultures, liminal cultures, and dominant cultures has Christianity been and is Christianity today?"

Christianity in all of its variations is a "plethora of cultures." The work of an anthropologist like Clifford Geertz helps us to understand that some form of Christianity is "the primary culture" in which many people live.[28] Also, his work helps us to understand the function of "local cultures" and their relation to national and international cultures.[29] Thus, concerning early Christianity we must ask questions like the following:

1. What kinds of local cultures did Christianity create during the first century?
2. What kinds of coalition cultures emerged during first century Christianity?
3. What kind of culture is "New Testament culture," that mixture of subcultures, countercultures, contracultures, liminal cultures, and dominant cultures that are transmitted by canonical New Testament literature? What is it that characterizes "New Testament Christianity" as a culture in the midst of other cultures?

Social and Cultural Analysis of Texts

In order to address this social and cultural issue in rhetorical interpretation, we need a framework for exploring different kinds of social and cultural rhetoric.[30] Fortunately, sociologists and anthropologists have

---

[28] Geertz, *Interpretation of Cultures*.

[29] Clifford Geertz, *Local Knowledge: Further Essays in Interpretive Anthropology* (New York: Basic Books, 1983).

[30] "Culture" is meant in the most neutral way possible in this paper. Culture is not being identified simply with "Greek culture" or "French culture," so that one presumes from the beginning a position of Kulturkampf based on a polarization of "real culture"

been hard at work on these matters, and there is significant current literature to guide us in this pursuit.

A. Religious Types of Social Rhetoric

Bryan Wilson's typology of sects, based on a cross-cultural spectrum of religious groups, is a good beginning place for types of social rhetoric. He organized the data he found in these groups into seven kinds of religious social responses to the world. In the terms of an anthropologist like Clifford Geertz, each kind of response creates a kind of culture that gives meanings, values, traditions, convictions, rituals, beliefs, and actions to people. As an interpreter approaches New Testament literature, each kind of social response appears in a type of social rhetoric. The seven types are as follows:[31]

(1) The *Conversionist* response is characterized by a view that the world is corrupt because people are corrupt. If people can be changed, the world will be changed. Salvation is not considered to be available through objective agencies but only by a profound and supernaturally wrought transformation of the self. The world itself will not change but the presence of a new subjective orientation to it will itself be salvation.

(2) The *Revolutionist* response declares that only the destruction of the world – the natural, but more specifically the social order – will be sufficient to save people. Supernatural powers must perform the destruction, because people lack the power if not to destroy the world then certainly to re-create it. Believers may themselves feel called upon to participate in the process of overturning the world, but they know that they do no more than assist greater powers and give a testimony of faith by their words and deeds.

(3) The *Introversionist* response views the world as irredeemably evil and considers salvation to be attainable only by the fullest possible withdrawal from it. The self may be purified by renouncing the world and leaving it. This response might be an individual response, of course, but as the response of a social movement it leads to the estab-

---

versus "barbarian mentalities." Culture means "interaction of body-mind-culture" that goes back millions of years—that which, in Clifford Geertz's terms, makes humans human (Geertz, *Interpretation of Cultures*; idem, *Local Knowledge*).

[31] Bryan R. Wilson, *Magic and the Millenium: A Sociological Study of Religious Movements of Protest among Tribal and Third-World Peoples* (New York: Harper & Row, 1973), 22–26 and "A Typology of Sects," in *Sociology of Religion* (ed. Roland Robertson; Baltimore: Penguin Books, 1969), 361–83 = "A typology of sects in a dynamic and comparative perspective," *Archives de Sociologie de Religion* 16 (1963): 49–63. Cf. James A. Wilde, "The Social World of Mark's Gospel: A Word about Method," *SBL 1978 Seminar Papers* (2 vols.; SBLSP 16; Missoula: Scholars Press, 1978), 2:47–67.

lishment of a separated community preoccupied with its own holiness and its means of insulation from the wider society.

(4) The *Gnostic-Manipulationist* response seeks only a transformed set of relationships – a transformed method of coping with evil. Whereas the foregoing orientations reject the goals of the culture as well as the institutionalized means of attaining them and the existing facilities by which people might be saved, the gnostic-manipulationist orientation rejects only the means and the facilities. Salvation is possible in the world and evil might be overcome if people learn the right means, improved techniques, to deal with their problems.

(5) The *Thaumaturgic* response focuses on the individual's concern for relief from present and specific ills by special dispensations. The request for supernatural help is personal and local, and its operation is magical. Salvation is immediate but has no general application beyond the given case and others like it. Salvation takes the form of healing, assuagement of grief, restoration after loss, reassurance, the foresight and avoidance of calamity, and the guarantee of external (or at least continuing) life after death.

(6) The *Reformist* response recognizes evil but assumes that it may be dealt with according to supernaturally-given insights about the ways in which social organization should be amended. Amendment of the world is here the essential orientation, and the specific alterations to be made are revealed to people whose hearts and minds are open to supernatural influence.

(7) The *Utopian* response seeks to reconstruct the world according to some divinely given principles, to establish a new social organization that will eliminate evil. This response differs from the demand that the world be overturned (revolutionist), in insisting that people re-make it, even if they do this work strictly in response to a divine calling. It is much more radical than the reformist response in insisting on complete replacement of social organization. It is more active and constructive than the introversionist response of simply withdrawing from the world.

Within literature, these religious types of social rhetoric are found among those kinds of topics rhetoricians call the "specific or material topics." Thaumaturgic social rhetoric talks about "special acts by divine powers" that will remove illness, danger, or death. Revolutionist religious social rhetoric talks about decisive events that will destroy this social order and replace it with another. Gnostic-manipulationist rhetoric talks about secret and mysterious knowledge, wisdom, or teaching that reveals the real story of how a person's life is saved. These specific topics have central place in direct statement and action, in dialogue, and in argumentation.

There are two other kinds of topics: common topics and final topics. Bruce Malina, John H. Elliott, Halvor Moxnes, Jerome Neyrey, Richard Rohrbaugh, and others have worked extensively on common social and cultural topics: kinship, honor and shame, limited good, hospitality, reciprocity, and the like.[32] These are topics social and cultural anthropologists consider to be common to all people in the Mediterranean world, in contrast to the specific topics that distinguish people socially from one another.

B. Types of Culture Rhetoric

Final topics, in rhetorical terms, are those topics that most decisively present one's cultural location. Cultural location, in contrast to social location, concerns the manner in which people present their propositions, reasons, and arguments both to themselves and to other people. These topics separate people in terms of dominant culture, subculture, counterculture, contraculture, and liminal culture. Again, as an interpreter approaches New Testament literature, cultural topics appear in the form of different kinds of culture rhetoric. The recent study of sociology of culture provides our insight on the different kinds of culture, and our analysis brings this information to New Testament interpretation in terms of different kinds of culture rhetoric.

(1) *Dominant Culture Rhetoric* presents a system of attitudes, values, dispositions, and norms that the speaker either presupposes or asserts are supported by social structures vested with power to impose its goals on people in a significantly broad territorial region.

(2) *Subculture Rhetoric* imitates the attitudes, values, dispositions, and norms of dominant culture rhetoric, and it claims to enact them better than members of dominant status. This rhetoric implies that a network of groups and institutions exist for supporting persons throughout their entire life cycle. Both sexes, all ages, and complete family groups are perceived to have a stake in this rhetoric.[33]

Ethnic subculture rhetoric is a particular kind of subculture rhetoric. It has origins in a language different from the languages in the dominant culture, and it attempts to preserve and perpetuate an "old system" in a dominant cultural system in which it now exists, either

---

[32] See, e.g., Bruce J. Malina, *The New Testament World: Insights from Cultural Anthropology* (Atlanta: John Knox Press, 1981); *Semeia* 35 (1986; ed. John H. Elliott, *Social-Scientific Criticism of the New Testament and Its Social World*); Jerome H. Neyrey, ed., *The Social World of Luke-Acts: Models for Interpretation* (Peabody, Mass.: Hendrickson, 1991); John H. Elliott, *Social Science Criticism and the New Testament* (Minneapolis: Fortress Press, 1993).

[33] Keith A. Roberts, "Toward a Generic Concept of Counter-Culture," *Sociological Focus* 11 (1978): 112; Milton M. Gordon, "The Subsociety and the Subculture," in *Subcultures* (ed. D. Arnold; Berkeley: Glendessary Press, 1970), 155.

because a significant number of people from this ethnic culture have moved into a new cultural environment or because a new cultural system is now imposing itself on it. A particular strategy of ethnic rhetoric appears to be the identification of a limited number of aspects of a surrounding culture for persistent attack to establish and maintain boundaries of identification.[34]

(3) *Counterculture Rhetoric* rejects *explicit* and *mutable* characteristics of the dominant or subculture rhetoric to which it responds.[35] The term is best reserved for intra-cultural phenomena; counterculture rhetoric is a culturally heretical rhetoric that evokes "a new future," not an alien rhetoric that evokes the preservation of an "old culture (real or imagined)."[36] Counterculture rhetoric implies "alternative minicultures which make provisions for both sexes and a wide range of age groups, which are capable of influencing people over their entire life span, and which develop appropriate institutions to sustain the group in relative self-sufficiency" (at least twenty-five years).[37] Counterculture rhetoric evokes the creation of "a better society, but not by legislative reform or by violent opposition to the dominant culture." The theory of reform manifest in its rhetoric provides an alternative and hopes "that the dominant society will 'see the light' and adopt a more 'humanistic' way of life." In other words, "social reform is not a preoccupation" of counterculture rhetoric.[38] It evokes a willingness to live one's own life and let the members of dominant society go on with their "madness." Yet, an underlying theme is the *hope* of voluntary reform by the dominant society in accord with the new model of "the good life." Hence, one would expect fully developed counterculture rhetoric to express a *constructive* image of a better way of life. In short, the term counterculture rhetoric might best be reserved for discourse that is not a reaction formation to some form of dominant culture rhetoric, but which builds on a supporting ideology that provides a relatively self-sufficient system of action.[39]

(4) *Contraculture Rhetoric* is a "short-lived, counter-dependent cultural deviance" of dominant culture, subculture, or counterculture rhetor-

---

[34] Fredrik Barth, "Ethnic Groups and Boundaries," in *Process and Form in Social Life* (London: Routledge, 1981), 198–227 = "Introduction," *Ethnic Groups and Boundaries* (ed. F. Barth; Boston: Little Brown, 1969); Uffe Østergård, "What is National and Ethnic Identity" and Koen Goudriaan, "Ethnical Strategies in Graeco-Roman Egypt," in *Ethnicity in Hellenistic Egypt* (ed. P. Bilde et al.; Aarhus: Aarhus University Press, 1992), 16–38, 74–99.

[35] Roberts, "Concept of Counter-Culture," 114.

[36] Ibid., 121.

[37] Ibid., 113.

[38] Ibid., 121.

[39] Ibid.

ic.[40] It is "groupculture" rhetoric rather than "subculture" rhetoric. Contraculture rhetoric implies groups "that do not involve more than one generation, which do not elaborate a set of institutions that allow the group to be relatively autonomous and self-sufficient, and which do not sustain an individual over an entire life span."[41] Contraculture rhetoric is primarily a reaction-formation response to some form of dominant culture, subculture, or counterculture rhetoric. It often is possible to predict the behavior and values evoked by contraculture rhetoric if one knows the values evoked by the rhetoric to which it is reacting, since the values are simply inverted.[42] Contraculture rhetoric, then, asserts "more negative than positive ideas."[43] The positive ideas are simply presupposed and come from the culture to which it is reacting.

(5) *Liminal Culture Rhetoric* is at the outer edge of identity.[44] It exists only in the language it has for the moment. In some instances, liminal culture will appear as people or groups experience transition from one cultural identity to another. In other instances, liminal culture exists among individuals and groups that have never been able to establish a clear social and cultural identity in their setting. The language of a liminal culture is characterized by a "dialectic of culture and identification" that has neither binary nor hierarchical clarity. Its speech is disjunctive and multiaccentual.[45] It starts and stops without obvious consistency or coherence. It features "minimal rationality" as a dialogic process that "attempts to track displacements and realignments that are the effects of cultural antagonisms and articulations – subverting the rationale of the hegemonic moment and relocating alternative, hybrid sites of cultural negotiation."[46]

---

[40] Ibid., 124

[41] Ibid., 113.

[42] Ibid., 123–24; J. Milton Yinger, "Contraculture and Subculture," *American Sociological Review* 25 (1960): 629; Werner Stark, *Sectarian Religion* (New York: Fordham University Press, 1967), 141, 153; G.F.S. Ellens, "The Ranting Ranters: Reflections on a Ranting Counter-Culture," *Church History* 40 (1971): 91–107.

[43] Roberts, "Concept of Counter-Culture," 124, citing Margarite Bouvard, *The Intentional Community Movement: Building a New Moral World* (Port Washington, N.Y.: Kennikat, 1975), 119.

[44] Homi K. Bhabha, "Postcolonial Criticism," in *Redrawing the Boundaries: The Transformation of English and Literary Studies* (ed. Stephen Greenblatt and Giles Gunn; New York: Modern Language Association of America, 1992), 444.

[45] Ibid., 445.

[46] Ibid., 443.

Approaching Dominant Culture Rhetoric and Subculture Rhetoric

To bring into view a socio-rhetorical approach to these multiple social and cultural dimensions of texts, we will focus in particular on Mark 4–11 and start with dominant culture rhetoric and subculture rhetoric together. A dominant culture, as mentioned above, is a system of attitudes, values, dispositions, and norms supported by social structures vested with power to impose itself on people in a significantly bounded territorial region. Subcultures, in turn, are

> wholistic entities which affect all of life over a long span of time. "[The term subculture] stand[s] for the cultural patterns of a subsociety which contains both sexes, all ages, and family groups, and which parallels the larger society in that it provides for a network of groups and institutions extending throughout the individual's entire life cycle."[47]

A major question will be if our texts view Jewish culture as a dominant culture or as a subculture in a dominant Hellenistic-Roman culture. Many current interpreters of New Testament texts proceed as though all of early Christianity were embedded in, and surrounded and protected by, Jewish culture. From this point of view, Christianity had no significant relation to Hellenistic-Roman culture. This approach appears to presuppose that Jewish culture was either a dominant culture in competition with Hellenistic-Roman culture or such a significantly developed subculture that Christianity could live in it so fully that any relation it had to Hellenistic-Roman culture was strictly through features that filtered through Jewish culture and was purified by that filtering process. The presuppositions underlying such a culture-purifying process surely are informed more by a "revelational ideology" than by an adequate analysis of the language, concepts, desires, goals, and content articulated by New Testament texts.

Wuellner's early article on 1 Corinthians 1:26–28 proceeds as though the rhetoric in this text has a significant relation to only one other culture, namely, Jewish culture.[48] He argues that the interrogative style of Paul in the passage has a "striking parallel" in the Babylonian Talmud (*b. Nid.* 69b-70b).[49] Moreover, the language of wisdom, power, and well-born comes from Scripture and is nurtured in post-Biblical Judaism. Only time prevents him from elaborating the data that exists in *b. Sanh.* 101a, *Midrash Rabba Numbers* 22 and its parallels in the *Tanchuma* homilies, and the fourfold pattern in *Pirke Aboth* 41,

---

[47] Roberts, "Concept of Counter-Culture," 112 quoting Milton M. Gordon, "The Subsociety and the Subculture," in *Subcultures* (ed. David O. Arnold; Berkeley: Glendessary Press, 1970), 155.

[48] Wilhelm Wuellner, "The Sociological Implications of I Cor 1 :26–28 Reconsidered," *SE* 6 (= TU 112 [1973]): 666–72.

[49] Ibid, 667–69.

Sayings of R. Nathan 23, and Philo's *de Virtutibus*. "Much more needs to be done by exegetes in the field of post-Biblical Judaism and early Christianity," he says, "in further efforts of identifying the tradition of the three gifts of God to mankind."[50] He does not suggest at any point that additional work should be done in Hellenistic-Roman literature to identify the relation of σόφος, δύνατος and εὐγενής, even though Johannes Munck had found two of the three words together "in traditions concerning sophists and Atticists."[51] Wuellner uses a strategy of dissociation of the language, form, and rhetoric of the passage from Hellenistic-Roman culture to associate it fully with biblical-Jewish culture. The underlying premise is that Paul's language, thought, and action is thoroughly subcultural Jewish rhetoric. Any relation this language and thought has to Hellenistic-Roman culture comes through Jewish culture. In this early article, then, Wuellner interpreted 1 Cor 1:26–28 through a method of "restrained rhetoric" which dissociated Paul's language and thought from Hellenistic-Roman culture.[52]

Thaumaturgic Social Rhetoric in Markan Miracles

Once the spectrum of social and cultural rhetoric is available to us, we have the opportunity to analyze and negotiate social and cultural locations of New Testament literature. To facilitate this exploration of cultural rhetorics, it will be helpful to bring another interpreter into the conversation, namely Burton L. Mack. In *A Myth of Innocence* he describes five different kinds of social and cultural rhetoric in early Christianity, and comparison of some of his discussions with Wuellner's will open new possibilities for us. Markan miracle rhetoric, for example, is a distinctive kind of rhetoric in early Christianity. Miracle rhetoric is especially prominent in Mark 4:35–8:26; it continues in the healing of the demoniac boy in 9:14–29 and the healing of blind Bartimaeus in 10:46–52, and it reaches it fullest form of argumentation in the cursing of the fig tree in Mark 11:12–25.[53]

---

[50] Ibid., 670–72.

[51] Ibid., 671.

[52] Unfortunately, Gail O'Day perpetuates these limitations in a more recent study, "Jeremiah 9:22–23 and 1 Corinthians 1:26–31: A Study in Intertextuality," *JBL* 109 (1990): 259–67.

[53] Previous studies have focused on Markan miracles from the perspective of eschatology, christology, or theology: see Sharyn Echols Dowd, *Prayer, Power, and The Problem of Suffering: Mark 11:22–25 in the Context of Markan Theology* (SBLDS 105; Atlanta: Scholars Press, 1988), 6–24. The present essay is an initial probe into fields of distinctive social and cultural argumentation in Mark. The long range goal is to exhibit the manner in which distinctive fields of argumentation merge in each of the gospels.

Similar to Wuellner's description of subcultural rhetoric in 1 Cor 1:26–28, Mack describes subcultural rhetoric in the miracle chains in Mark 4–8. In these stories:

> Jesus, the founder and leader of the new movement, is like Moses (as leader) and like Elijah (as restorer). Likeness is not identity, however. The difference between Jesus and his prototypes is as great as the difference between the new congregation and the old. The Jesus movement is fully conscious of its novelty. Those without any claim to membership in Israel are nevertheless included. It is not really "Israel" that is being renewed or restored. Jesus does not stand in the office of Moses as a "new Moses." He does not perform a prophetic critique of Jewish institutions from within as a call to repentance or reform. He marches under his own banner without polemic, effecting those changes in people that had to be made if the new congregation was to form. Jesus is the founder of the new society, and the set of stories is its myth of origins.[54]

This is subculture rhetoric and not counterculture rhetoric, which we will consider below, since:

> The stories do not contain a hint of institutional conflict. There is no sense of hostility against representatives of the "old" Israel. The set of stories marks the differences between the new congregation and traditional views of Israel, not as apology or polemic, but merely as definitional. The idea of ritual purity is used, for instance, to make a positive point about the distinctiveness of the new group that is not based on such prerequisite, not to counter charges of illegitimacy or raise the question of conflict between Jesus' authority and the authority of the law. The choice to imagine what was happening on the model of the Exodus story was natural, given the Galilean climate. The model was taken from the epic and haggadic readings of the scriptures, perhaps even at the level of local lore, not from the conceptualized model of Israel as a temple state based on cultic law. The exodus, that is, was not at first understood to be an exodus from Judaism.[55]

With these descriptions Mack, like Wuellner, locates a portion of a New Testament text subculturally in Jewish culture. Also like Wuellner, Mack does not raise the issue of the relation of the miracle chains in Mark 4–8 to Hellenistic-Roman culture, even though Paul Achtemeier's delineation and interpretation of them had an eye on "secular Hellenistic sources" as well as models in the OT and Hellenistic Judaism.[56] In truth, Mack does not seem to suppress the relation of the rhetoric in the mi-

---

[54] Burton L. Mack, *A Myth of Innocence: Mark and Christian Origins* (Philadelphia: Fortress, 1988), 223.

[55] Ibid., 224.

[56] Paul J. Achtemeier, "Toward the Isolation of Pre-Markan Miracle Catenae," *JBL* 89 (1970): 291; idem, "The Origin and Function of Pre-Marcan Miracle Cantenae," *JBL* 91 (1972): 200–202.

racle chains to Hellenistic-Roman culture "intentionally," as Wuellner does in his 1973 article. Rather, Mack's suppression of the relation occurs "by default" – an absence of description – which, even though it is characteristic for a large number of New Testament interpreters, is not customary for Mack.

A. Specific Social Topics in Markan Miracles

To advance beyond Mack's interpretation, it will be helpful to start with specific social topics in Markan miracle discourse and from there to move to a discussion of thaumaturgic argumentation and subculture thaumaturgic rhetoric. Markan miracle stories present thaumaturgic social topics. Underlying this culture rhetoric is a presupposition that God cares whether or not humans perish or are afflicted with disease. This topic is articulated by the disciples when the storm arises on the Sea of Galilee: "Do you not care if we perish?" (οὐ μέλει σοι ὅτι ἀπολλύμεθα: 4:38), they ask Jesus. The father of the demonized boy in chapter 9 also presents this topic: "The dumb spirit seizes my son and dashes him down, and he foams and grinds his teeth and becomes rigid, ...and it has often cast him into the fire and into the water to destroy him" (9:17–18, 22). This culture rhetoric says that Jesus does care; therefore Jesus acts decisively to remove the problems. He stills the storm so the disciples do not perish, and he casts the demon out of the boy.

In the context of the possibility of being destroyed, people plead for divine powers to have mercy on them, to save them. The father of the boy says: "If you can do anything, have pity on us and help us" (9:22). Blind Bartimaeus cries out: "Jesus, Son of David, have mercy on me" (10:47, 48). Jairus pleads with Jesus: "Come and lay your hands on my daughter, so that she may be saved and live" (5:23) and the woman with the flow of blood says: "If I touch even his garments I will be saved" (5:28). After Jesus heals the Gerasene demoniac he tells him: "Go home to your friends, and tell them how much the Lord has done for you, and how he has had mercy on you" (5:19).

In these settings, "fear" and "cowardice" are topics of importance. The disciples are afraid in the boat, both when the storm arises (4:40–41) and when Jesus walks to them on the sea (6:50); the swineherders are afraid when they see the Gerasene demoniac healed (5:15); and the woman with the flow of blood comes to Jesus with fear and trembling (5:33). Jesus tells the father of the twelve year old daughter not to fear (5:36), and he tells the disciples in the boat and blind Bartimaeus to "take heart" (6:50; 10:49).

Faith (or belief) is an important topic in the midst of these other topics. Jesus asks the disciples in the boat: "Have you no faith?" (4:40); he tells the woman with the flow of blood and blind Bartimaeus: "Your faith has made you well" (5:34; 10:52); and he tells the father of the twelve year old daughter: "Only believe" (5:36). Jesus tells the father of the demoniac boy: "All things are possible to him who believes" (9:23), and the father says: "I believe; help my unbelief" (9:24).

These stories present thaumaturgic social rhetoric. People who tell these stories evoke a culture in which divine powers respond to their needs if they approach them in appropriate ways. This rhetoric has been nurtured into an elaborated argumentative culture in Markan discourse: the stories present developed arguments about belief, about what is possible, and about a way of acting that makes these things possible.

B. Thaumaturgic Argumentation in Mark

The first setting of extended thaumaturgic argumentation in Mark is the intermingled stories of the healing of Jairus' daughter and the woman with the flow of blood. In Mark 5:23 Jairus introduces the topics of "death," "touching to restore," "being saved (made well)," and "receiving life."[57] In the sequence of the narrative, the woman with the flow of blood expands these topics argumentatively: "If I touch even his garments, I shall be saved (made well)" (5:28). Her rhetorical logic is proven inductively when she touches Jesus and is healed (5:29). But there was an unstated premise underlying her logical syllogism that the woman herself did not articulate. Jesus presents this premise: The woman's faith has made her well (5:34). Thus:

> *General premise* (Rule): One who has faith can be healed;
> *Specific premise* (Case): The woman's faith caused her to touch Jesus;
> *Conclusion* (Result): The woman was healed because of her faith.[58]

The story about the woman, then, elaborates the topics of touching and being saved (made well), adding the topic of faith to the topics Jairus, the father of the dying daughter, introduced.

Immediately after the story of the woman, people come from Jairus' house and say, "Your daughter is dead" (5:35). Jesus tells him, "Do not fear, only have faith" (5:36). Since the woman with the flow of blood had approached Jesus with fear, and Jesus had identified her faith as the means by which she had been healed (5:33–34), Jesus' statement to

---

[57] I am grateful to Mary Foskett for detailed analysis of this section of Mark in a research paper in a graduate seminar at Emory University.

[58] Vernon K. Robbins, "The Woman who Touched Jesus' Garment: Socio-Rhetorical Analysis of the Synoptic Accounts," *NTS* 33 (1987): 502–15.

Jairus that he should not fear but have faith is a continuation of the thaumaturgic argumentation. The final segment of the story introduces the topic of death into the argument about touching, being saved, fear, and faith. Jesus goes into the house and touches the girl by taking her hand and telling her: "Arise" (5:41). And immediately the girl rises up, comes to life (5:42). At this point the topics of touching, being saved, faith, fear, and death have been expanded into an argument about receiving life in its fullest stage of procreative youthfulness. This twelve year old girl, old enough to give birth to new life in the form of children, has been restored to life as a result of belief by the father and response by Jesus.

The story of the demoniac boy in Mark 9 provides further argumentation for these topics. The father of the boy introduces the topic of "what is possible": "If it is possible, help us" (9:22). Jesus introduces a logical syllogism related to the syllogism in the story of the woman with the flow: "All things are possible to him who believes" (9:23). When Jesus commands the dumb spirit to come out of the boy, the boy becomes like a corpse so that people say: "He is dead" (9:26), like Jairus' daughter was dead. This story, then, elaborates the argumentation the hearer/reader encountered in chapter 5 when the daughter had died and been raised to life. The *quaestio* that must be answered is: "What kinds of things is it possible for divine powers to do?" Belief alone called forth the raising of Jairus' daughter from death to life. Jesus takes the demoniac boy's hand and raises him to life, but to the disciples he says: "This kind can only be cast out by prayer." Thus, at the end of this second elaboration of thaumaturgic argumentation, a new topic, "prayer," appears. The *quaestio* now is: "What is it possible for divine powers to do in the context of prayer?"[59]

The story of the cursing of the fig tree, intermingled with the cleansing of the temple, elaborates thaumaturgic argumentation further. When the disciples see the withered fig tree and call it to Jesus' attention, Jesus responds at first as he responded to Jairus: "Have faith in God," adding "God" as the one to whom faith is to be directed. Jesus elaborates this statement, including an argument from the contrary: "He who requests an incredible thing (like casting Mount Zion into the sea) and does not doubt in his heart, but believes what he says (like the woman with the flow of blood), it will be done for him (as it was for her)." The next verse then integrates the topic "prayer" with the other topics. The reader now is to understand that the statements of Jairus, of the woman with the flow, of the father of the demoniac boy,

---

[59] Dowd, *Prayer, Power, and the Problem of Suffering* investigates this theme throughout Mark and in Greco-Roman literature with excellent result.

and of blind Bartimaeus were "prayers." The logic seems to be this: if a person asks out of belief, that plea is a prayer to God. The final verse then integrates the topic of forgiveness with this well-elaborated thaumaturgic argumentation.

The special social topics of these stories present us, then, with thaumaturgic rhetoric. Wilson's statements fully apply. This rhetoric is concerned with "relief from present and specific ills by special dispensations. The demand for supernatural help is personal and local.... Salvation is immediate but has no general application beyond the given case and others like it. Healing, assuagement of grief, restoration after loss, reassurance, the foresight and avoidance of calamity, and the guarantee of external (or at least continuing) life after death are the elements of the salvation which are sought."[60] For the purposes of the present essay, it is important to notice that these topics do not simply reside as isolated phenomena in Markan discourse. Rather, thickly interwoven networks of argumentation present well-advanced thaumaturgic reasoning. The gospel of Mark exhibits the presence of well-nurtured thaumaturgic social rhetoric within certain early Christian circles. The range of distinctive topics in this thaumaturgic field of argumentation and the complexity of its logic suggests that some early Christians created, developed, and "lived in" a relatively autonomous and comprehensive thaumaturgic culture during the years 30–60 CE.[61] One of the achievements of the Gospel of Mark was to integrate this type of Christian social rhetoric with other types that had been created and nurtured by other early Christian groups.

C. Subculture Thaumaturgic Rhetoric in Mark

But what is the cultural location of this rhetoric? Is it the rhetoric of dominant culture, subculture, counterculture, contraculture, or liminal culture? We must ask the question for two cultures: on the one hand, for Jewish culture and, on the other hand, for Hellenistic-Roman culture. Every New Testament text, written in Greek language during the first century, has some kind of relation to Jewish culture and some kind of relation to Hellenistic-Roman culture. Interpreters need to identify and describe each relation with precision. During the last fifty years, certainly, most interpreters have presupposed that New Testament literature has a relation to Jewish culture, but they have not described that relation with any social and cultural precision. There has been even a greater absence of careful description of the relation of New Testament documents to Hellenistic-Roman culture. Much data is

---

[60] Wilson, *Magic and the Millenium*, 24–25.

[61] For the meaning of "culture" in this statement, see Clifford Geertz, "Religion as a Cultural System," in *Interpretation of Cultures*, 87–125.

4. Rhetoric and Culture: Mark 4–11 as a Test Case

available to describe these cultural relations, but most interpreters have not, for one reason or another, accepted the task.

First let us explore the relation of Markan thaumaturgic rhetoric to Jewish culture. Jewish dominant culture rhetoric contains strong thaumaturgic rhetoric. In relation to this dominant culture rhetoric, Markan thaumaturgic rhetoric functions as Jewish subculture rhetoric. Strong themes and predispositions of the "great traditions" in the Torah and the Deuteronomic History are thaumaturgic. Moses, Elijah, and Elisha figure prominently in these contexts, and dimensions of these stories resonate through the Markan miracle stories. Like Elijah raised the son of the widow of Zarephath, Jesus raises the twelve year old girl from death to life. Like Moses parted the sea and Elisha made an axe head float on water, so Jesus stills the storm and walks on the sea. Like Moses and Elisha fed large numbers of people in the wilderness with small amounts of food, so Jesus feeds 5,000 and 4,000 people with small amounts of bread and fish. The rhetoric in these stories does not disagree with the values of life and salvation espoused by dominant Jewish culture; it simply claims to have special access to divine powers through Jesus. Jesus helps people receive the food, life, and healing about which the Torah and the Deuteronomic History speak. In Markan rhetoric, it simply is necessary that people believe and pray persistently enough. Markan thaumaturgic rhetoric is subculture Jewish rhetoric related to dominant Jewish rhetoric in the Torah and the Deuteronomic History.

The cursing of the fig tree story in the context of the cleansing of the Temple presents the sharpest thaumaturgic encounter with dominant Jewish rhetoric in the gospel of Mark. On the one hand, Jesus' action appears to have a goal of fulfilling a "true value" expressed within the Hebrew Bible when Jesus asserts that the temple should be "a house of prayer for all peoples" (Isa 56:7). On the other hand, his action attacks the chief priests and scribes for making the temple "a den of robbers" (Jer 7:11). The first statement is subculture rhetoric that claims to fulfill the values of dominant culture better than people who follow dominant culture practices, and the second statement is contraculture rhetoric that inverts a behavior in the dominant culture without providing a clear rationale for an alternative system of action and thought. The full passage in Isaiah reads as follows:

> And the foreigners who join themselves to the Lord,
> to minister to him, to love the name of the Lord,
> and to be his servants,
> everyone who keeps the Sabbath,
> and does not profane it,

> and holds fast my covenant –
> these I will bring to my holy mountain,
> and make them joyful in my house of prayer;
> their burnt offerings and their sacrifices
> will be accepted on my altar;
> for my house shall be called a house of prayer
> for all peoples.
> Thus says the Lord God,
> who gathers the outcasts of Israel,
> I will gather yet others to him
> besides those already gathered. (Isa 56:6–8)

Markan rhetoric significantly changes traditional biblical rhetoric by creating a new context for a rationale that supported the acceptance of devout foreigners in the temple, where they would offer burnt offerings and sacrifices. The rhetorical change occurs as special action and additional speech creates a context that changes the rationale into a contracultural assertion characteristic of a Cynic chreia during the Hellenistic period. The Markan Jesus introduces the rationale as a maxim in a context of contracultural action: driving buyers and sellers out of the temple, overturning the tables of the money-changers and sellers of doves, and not allowing anyone to carry a vessel through the temple. Do the action and speech of Jesus nullify all sacrifices and offerings in the temple when they prohibit buying, selling, and carrying of vessels to make it a house of prayer for all peoples? No definite answer is ready at hand. In Mark, Jesus never asserts the famous line from Hosea 6:6: "I desire mercy and not sacrifice." Perhaps it would be acceptable for people to bring their own sacrifices and offerings, and to bring them without using containers. The attack may focus entirely on the manner in which chief priests and scribes have turned rituals of sacrifices and offerings into a monetary activity. The Markan Jesus criticizes the scribes in 12:40 for "devouring the houses of widows," which is quite clearly a reference to indebtedness that occurs in relation to religious practices. In addition, he supplements the statement from Isaiah with a statement from Jeremiah 7:11 that accuses the leaders of making the temple a den of thieves or brigands. In Jeremiah the statement was a question: "Has this house, which is called by my name, become a den of robbers in your eyes?" The Markan Jesus changes the line from a question to an assertion and abbreviates it so that it functions as an epilogue to a maxim: "My house shall be called a house of prayer for all nations, but you have made it a den of thieves."[62]

Subculture rhetoric regularly incorporates contraculture rhetoric in settings of conflict. Contraculture rhetoric is deeply embedded in the

---

[62] See Aristotle, *Rhetoric* II.1394a.

culture to which it is reacting, and it simply inverts, reverses, certain actions and thoughts in that other culture. The Markan Jesus inverts the practices of buying, selling, and using vessels in the temple. Does this mean that all rituals of offering and sacrifice should end? Possibly, but not necessarily. On the one hand, it would appear that a person could go to the temple regularly to pray, and possibly it would be appropriate to bring offerings and sacrifices on those occasions. On the other hand, in the midst of his discourse on prayer in 11:22–25 the Markan Jesus makes an offhand remark about casting "this mountain" into the sea. This is the nature of contraculture rhetoric: it attacks without providing clear guidelines and rationales for alternative behavior. Markan thaumaturgic rhetoric adopts contraculture features when it is brought into contact with traditions about the Jerusalem temple. If a person has faith enough, he or she could say to this mountain, "Be taken up and cast into the sea." But the important thing is that the temple should be a house of prayer for all peoples and not a den of thieves. In this context, subcultural thaumaturgic rhetoric in Mark incorporates a contracultural relation to Jewish dominant culture rhetoric.

Now let us explore the relation of Markan thaumaturgic rhetoric to Hellenistic-Roman culture. Thaumaturgic rhetoric is a pervasive subculture rhetoric in Hellenistic-Roman culture. Dominant Hellenistic-Roman rhetoric does not place thaumaturgic rhetoric as centrally in its great traditions as dominant Jewish rhetoric does. Dominant Hellenistic-Roman rhetoric exhibits significant restraint about individual action by divine powers to remove illness and affliction. Trained physicians following traditions associated with the healing god Asclepius and the physician Hippocrates diagnosed illnesses and prescribed curative powders, liquids, and activities for a patient who was ill. Miraculous healing and portent was widespread, but it functioned in a subculture relation to the rhetoric of dominant Hellenistic-Roman culture. The rhetoric in Mark 4–11 has a subculture relation to this Hellenistic-Roman subculture rhetoric. Thus, most non-Jewish and non-Christian people in Mediterranean society could hear and understand Markan thaumaturgic rhetoric as a particular ethnic form of Hellenistic-Roman subculture rhetoric.

There are two major places where Markan thaumaturgic rhetoric sets itself against Hellenistic-Roman culture. The woman with the flow of blood had gone to physicians, and they had caused her great suffering, taken all her money from her, and had only made her worse (5:26). Also, the name of the demon in the Gerasene demoniac is "legion," a reference to a dominating Roman military force in the region.

Here again Markan rhetoric functions contraculturally: it remains deeply embedded in the values of Hellenistic-Roman thaumaturgic subculture which features healing and restoring people, yet it "inverts" certain behaviors and attitudes. Instead of going to a physician, one should go to a religious healer who works with divine powers. But so do other people in Hellenistic-Roman society. Instead of a legion of the army bringing peace and sanity in a region, it brings the most insane kind of violence and brutality. Some other people in Hellenistic-Roman society cautiously communicate this "inversion" of official rhetoric also. Again, Markan rhetoric does not set forth distinctively alternative behaviors and attitudes supported by well-developed rationales. Rather, certain behaviors and attitudes are inverted in a context where actions and thoughts are deeply embedded in the surrounding culture.

D. Conclusion

To conclude this section, the thaumaturgic rhetoric in Mark 4–11 is subculture rhetoric that engages in contracultural inversion at specific points of encounter. The goal of the rhetoric is to fulfill expressed thaumaturgic values in dominant Jewish culture and Hellenistic-Roman subculture in better ways than these other cultures do. The argumentation in these stories is deeply embedded in Hellenistic-Roman discussions and traditions about what it is possible and impossible for gods to do.[63] Also, it is deeply embedded in the Jewish presentation of God as creator, sustainer, and redeemer.

There is an inversion of certain practices and thoughts at places in this rhetoric, reflecting contraculture features. But the overall thaumaturgic behavior and reasoning exhibits "subculture rhetoric." Markan thaumaturgic rhetoric does not present a system of behavior and action that rejects "explicit and mutable characteristics" of dominant Jewish culture or Hellenistic-Roman thaumaturgic subculture. In other words, Markan thaumaturgic rhetoric is not a fully-formed "counter-culture" rhetoric. It does not present a clearly distinct alternative to values, actions, and beliefs in dominant Jewish culture and Hellenistic-Roman thaumaturgic subculture. The rhetoric is subculture rhetoric; it claims to fulfill the values of dominant Jewish culture and Hellenistic-Roman thaumaturgic subculture in better ways than these dominant cultures do. But there is no fully articulated system of argumentation in Mark that produces a fullfledged alternative to Jewish or Hellenistic-Roman culture.

---

[63] Dowd, *Prayer, Power, and the Problem of Suffering*, 69–122.

4. Rhetoric and Culture: Mark 4–11 as a Test Case

Gnostic-Manipulationist Social Rhetoric in Markan Parables

When the hearer/reader shifts attention from miracle rhetoric to parable rhetoric in Mark, immediately one notices topics one does not see at all in the miracle rhetoric in chapters 4–11. Here there is talk of the "kingdom of God," and this phrase does not appear once in the miracle stories in Mark 4–11. In parable rhetoric Jesus talks about people becoming "fruitful," and this also does not appear in the miracle stories. The goal of Markan thaumaturgic rhetoric is for people to be healed and the major question is "How is this possible?" The goal of the parable rhetoric of Mark 4 is "How can a person receive the Kingdom of God and become fruitful?"

A. Specific Social Topics in Markan Parables

While at first an interpreter may anticipate the presence of conversionist rhetoric in Markan parables, the specific topics enact gnostic-manipulationist social rhetoric in Wilson's terms. The specific topic of speaking "in parables" (ἐν παραβολαῖς: 3:23; 4:2, 10, 11, 13, 30, 33, 34; 7:17; 12:1, 12; 13:28) refers to something significantly puzzling, enigmatic, unclear, and mysterious. Jesus emphasizes that people must "listen" to what he says (ἀκούειν: 4:3, 9, 12, 15, 16, 18, 20, 23, 24, 33; cf. 7:14, 16). People must "see" and "take heed" (βλέπειν: 4:12, 24; 8:15, 18; 12:38; 13:2, 5, 9, 23, 33). The question is whether, once they have heard and seen, they can understand (συνιέναι: 4:9, 12; 7:14; 8:17, 21) and accept what he has said (παραδέχεσθαι: 4:20). On the one hand, true understanding is "hidden" from them (ἀπόκρυφος, κρυτός: 4:22). On the other hand, certain people are given this understanding as a "secret" (μυστήριον: 4:11) which they possess. This is Gnostic-manipulationist rhetoric, then, where only a few can understand. Most people will not be able to hear, understand, and accept what is spoken. This is not conversionist rhetoric, where the emphasis lies on changing people in such a manner that they change the world. Rather, the nature of the world is such that there is no choice but to live in it as it is. Only a few people will attain an ability to cope by attaining special understanding that sustains them in the midst of their problems.

In the context of these specific topics of hearing, seeing, understanding, heeding, and secrecy; "the Kingdom of God" (βασιλεία τοῦ θεοῦ: 4:11, 26, 30; cf. 1:15; 3:24; 9:1) is a major topic. In particular, speech about the kingdom is ὁ λόγος, "word" or "message": (ὁ λόγος: 4:14, 15, 16, 17, 18, 19, 20, 33). This message brings "joy" (χαρά: 4:16), and an ability to be "fruitful" (4:19–20) and to endure. A major goal here is not to be scandalized so that one falls away in times of tribulation and persecution (4:17). The secret knowledge of the Kingdom of God, which one hears and accepts, makes it possible for a person to endure and be fruitful in a context of extreme hardship and suffering.

B. Gnostic-Manipulationist Argumentation in Mark 4

The goal of the gnostic-manipulationist rhetoric in Mark 4 is to seek "a transformed set of relationships – a transformed method of coping with evil." This rhetoric does not necessarily "reject the goals of the culture." It "rejects only the means and the facilities" for attaining the goals.[64] These people have a "revealed understanding" – a "message" about how God works – that makes it possible for them to live in the world and endure the evil, tribulation, and persecution in it.

The most extensive Markan gnostic-manipulationist argumentation appears in Mark 4:1–34. Burton L. Mack has helped us to see how the entire chapter elaborates the parable of the sower according to conventional steps of argumentation in Hellenistic-Roman culture.[65] The initial telling of the parable of the sower rehearses how a sower sowed seed in various conditions of soil. Birds came and devoured some that fell along the path, some sprang up quickly in shallow soil and died, some fell among thorns that choked it out, and some fell into good soil and produced a bountiful harvest (4:1–9). When the twelve ask Jesus about this enigmatic parable, he presents a rationale for teaching in parables. Teaching in parables makes it possible for the twelve to be given the secret of the Kingdom of God while everyone outside sees and hears but does not understand (4:10–12). Then Jesus paraphrases the parable for the twelve in terms of "sowing the word." The sower, he tells them, sows words. Satan takes away some of the words; some receive the word with joy, endure for a while, then fall away under tribulation or persecution; some hear the word but cares of the world and delight in riches and other things makes them unfruitful; but others hear the word, accept it, and bear fruit (4:13–20). Then Jesus presents an argument from the contrary about lamps that asserts that nothing that is secret is meant to be kept secret, but the purpose is for it to become visible at a particular time (4:21–23).[66] After this, Jesus presents a rhetorical judgment that a person receives in relation to the measure one has given (4:24–25). Then an argument from example shows a man scattering seed and waiting with patience until the seed produces a

---

[64] Wilson, *Magic and the Millenium*, 24.

[65] Mack, *Myth of Innocence*, 150–65; Burton L. Mack and Vernon K. Robbins, *Patterns of Persuasion in the Gospels* (Sonoma, Calif.: Polebridge Press, 1989), 143–60.

[66] Vernon K. Robbins, "Rhetorical Argument about Lamps and Light in Early Christian Gospels," in *Context, Festskrift til Peder Johan Borgen* (ed. Peter Wilhelm Böckman and Roald E. Kristiansen; *Relieff* 24; Universitetet i Trondheim: Tapir, 1987), 177–95.

harvest, even though the process is a mystery to him (4:26–29). An argument from analogy shows that the tiny mustard seed grows into the largest of shrubs (4:30–32), then a conclusion says that Jesus told the twelve many such parables and explained to them everything about them (4:33–34).

This parable rhetoric is very different from the miracle rhetoric we analyzed earlier. The primary topics concern the willingness to present a message that is impossible for most people to understand, the selection of a small group to receive special instruction about the enigmatic wisdom in the message, and the success of the truth of the message even though its success itself is a mystery. The Kingdom of God, so the argument goes, is not understandable to most people, nor is it supposed to be. It is a mystery to most people, but everything that is secret will gradually be made visible. Those who understand the message are not only joyful, but are able to endure and be fruitful under the most extreme circumstances of tribulation and persecution.

If this argumentation is not as clear as the miracle argumentation, it is not supposed to be. It is the nature of gnostic-manipulationist rhetoric to remain a puzzlement to people outside a specially defined group. There are supposed to be images in the rhetoric that are suggestive, tantalizing, and inspiring without ever being fully understandable. Only this kind of speech is considered to be the appropriate vehicle for something so impossible to understand as God's ways of working in the world. If there is wisdom specially revealed from God, that will by necessity be difficult to understand. Most people will never understand it; only certain people will receive the gift of its insight.

C. Subculture Gnostic-Manipulationist Rhetoric in Mark 4

If parable rhetoric is, in Wilson's terms, gnostic-manipulationist social rhetoric; what kind of culture rhetoric is it? Is it dominant culture rhetoric, subculture rhetoric, counterculture rhetoric, contraculture rhetoric, or liminal rhetoric? Again we must ask this question individually in relation to Jewish culture and Hellenistic-Roman culture.

Burton Mack's discussion of the parables in Mark 4 represents a distinctive breakthrough in New Testament interpretation as it explicitly describes the relation of the rhetoric in the text both to Jewish culture and to Hellenistic-Roman culture. On the one hand, the topics in this parable rhetoric have an important relation to subculture Jewish rhetoric:

> The imageries of the field, sowing, seeds, miscarriage, and harvest are standard metaphors for God's dealing with Israel in Jewish apocalyptic, wisdom, and prophetic literatures. Depending on the context, the use of such imagery would automatically have suggested a statement of theo-

> logical import about Israel's destiny.... Since the parable [of the sower] only works when the listener is concerned about the fate of the seeds, and since the fate of the seeds is calculated to heighten that concern by imagery of loss through destruction, the most plausible reference is not directly to the history of Israel, but to the early history of the Jesus movements. The parable makes good sense about the kingdom of God Jesus announced, but only in retrospect upon some adverse history of its failed attempts to take root.[67]

For Mack, then, the parable of the sower exhibits subcultural Jewish rhetoric. These images are not prominent in the Torah and the Deuteronomic History – the "great" traditions. Apocalyptic, wisdom, and prophetic literature points to Jewish subculture which invites contraculture rhetoric that asserts critical pressure on dominant Jewish rhetoric. Markan parable rhetoric perpetuates an amalgam of Jewish subculture and contraculture rhetoric that nurtured significant countercultures in Judaism itself. The rhetoric in Mark 4 claims to be in a position to receive special benefits articulated as values within Jewish tradition. This makes the rhetoric subcultural. In the mouth of Jesus in Mark, this subculture rhetoric is energized by eschatological expectations and by traditions that only a remnant of Israel will understand and be saved. The eschatology invites contraculture rhetoric that can, when nurtured by significant networks of reasoning, become fully developed counterculture rhetoric. The rhetoric refers to failure and rejection, but it does not move to a rejection of Jewish tradition. The rhetoric is embedded in Jewish apocalyptic topoi and tradition, and it builds willingly upon it.

Second, one of the astonishing results of recent investigation is the discovery that the topics of Markan parable rhetoric have a close relation to dominant Hellenistic-Roman rhetoric concerning paideia – instruction and education.

> Ears acquainted with Hellenistic culture to any degree at all would immediately have recalled the stock image for offering instruction with a view to the inculcation of Hellenistic culture.[68]

Mack presents four comparative texts from Hellenistic-Roman literature, and I quote them here to show the amazing relation of Mark 4 to them:[69]

> The views of our teachers are as it were the seeds. Learning from childhood is analogous to the seeds falling betimes upon the prepared ground. (Hippocrates, *Law* III)

---

[67] Mack, *Myth of Innocence*, 155.
[68] Ibid., 159.
[69] Ibid., 159–60; Mack and Robbins, *Patterns of Persuasion*, 156.

> As is the seed that is ploughed into the ground, so must one expect the harvest to be, and similarly when good education is ploughed into your persons, its effect lives and burgeons throughout their lives, and neither rain nor drought can destroy it. (Antiphon, frg. 60)[70]

> Words should be scattered like seed; no matter how small the seed may be, if it once has found favorable ground, it unfolds its strength and from an insignificant thing spreads to its greatest growth. (Seneca, *Epistles* 38:2)

> If you wish to argue that the mind requires cultivation, you would use a comparison drawn from the soil, which if neglected produced thorns and thickets, but if cultivated will bear fruit. (Quintilian, *Institutio oratoria* 5.11.24)

Mark 4:1–34, then, presents subculture rhetoric in relation to dominant Hellenistic-Roman rhetoric about nurturing one's mind and action through disciplined attainment of wisdom. Markan parable rhetoric is an ethnic subculture rhetoric related to dominant Hellenistic-Roman rhetoric about education. An ethnic form of reasoning isolates a few discrete items in an overall cultural environment that it attacks vigorously to establish its boundaries and identity.[71] The reasoning, however, leaves a wide range of presuppositions and actions in the overall culture unchallenged. This allows people who live in the worldview of this rhetoric to participate in a wide range of presuppositions and behaviors in the surrounding cultural environment. Markan parable rhetoric claims to fulfill basic values held in dominant culture. People will be productive, they will be able to endure hardships, and they will understand things other people are not able to understand. A rich system of understanding can guide and sustain a life of discipleship to Christ, much like a rich system of understanding guides and sustains a person who follows the teachings of Aristotle, Socrates, Plato, Zeno, Pythagoras, Diogenes, or Epicurus.

No noticeable contraculture features appear in the parable rhetoric of Mark 4 in relation to Hellenistic-Roman rhetoric. But strong contraculture features are present in relation to Jewish rhetoric. Most of the images come from prophetic literature that performs a strong contracultural function in the tradition of Israel. Markan rhetoric sets the gnostic-manipulationist subculture rhetoric of Mark 4:1–34 in a context of strong Jewish contraculture rhetoric in Mark 3:23–30; 7:17–23; 12:1–12. Again subculture rhetoric in the context of Markan rhetoric becomes strong contraculture Jewish rhetoric.

---

[70] Found in Hermann Diels, *Die Fragmente der Vorsokratiker: Griechisch und Deutsch* (3 vols.; 10th ed.; Berlin-Charlottenburg: Weidmann, 1961), 2:365.

[71] Barth, "Ethnic Groups and Boundaries."

In addition, there is no open animosity to either culture. Rather, self-definition emerges in a subcultural posture both to Jewish and Hellenistic-Roman culture. The strategy of analysis Mack uses does not shut off one or the other culture in Mediterranean society but plumbs the resources of both to position the rhetoric in the texts he interprets. Mack proceeds with Mark 4, then, in a manner that exhibits "rhetoric revalued" rather than "rhetoric restrained," a procedure that he did not attain in his interpretation of the miracle chains in Mark 4–8 and that Wuellner did not achieve in his interpretation of 1 Corinthians 1:26–28. Nevertheless, these analyses by Wuellner and Mack bring three kinds of subcultural rhetoric in early Christianity into view. While further description of these subcultural rhetorics would be informative, this will have to be left for another context. For the matter under discussion, it is more important to move to contracultural and countercultural rhetoric. But, first, let us review some of our conclusions thus far.

Miracle and Parable Rhetoric as Subcultural Rhetorics in Mark

Our analysis thus far has investigated thaumaturgic and gnostic-manipulationist subcultural rhetorics in Mark. Further analysis of Mark suggests that there is very little introversionist, utopian, or reformist rhetoric in the Gospel of Mark. Features of conversionist rhetoric appear in Mark 1:14–15 and 7:20–23, but there is surprisingly little conversionist rhetoric in Mark. Markan rhetoric takes the stance that people do not easily change. The primary issue is whether people come to an understanding of the secret of the kingdom which makes it possible for them to endure and be fruitful, and whether they have faith that God will respond to their prayers. Thaumaturgic rhetoric and gnostic-manipulationist rhetoric, both inherently subculture rhetorics, present an ideology that sustains people in a world that produces suffering, affliction, illness, deafness, and blindness.

Beyond thaumaturgic and gnostic-manipulationist rhetorics in Mark, there are three additional fields of argumentation: (a) controversy stories; (b) Markan apocalypse; and (c) passion narrative. The gospel of Mark merges these five fields of argumentation. In socio-rhetorical terms, Markan "culture" negotiates a merger among five "local" or "group" culture rhetorics. Scholars agree that the "revolutionist" rhetoric of Mark 13 plays a significant role, as well as the rhetoric of the passion narrative. But scholars have not explored the nature of Mark as a merger of this variety of culture rhetorics.[72] If we can identify thaumaturgic and gnostic-manipulationist argumentation respectively in miracle stories and the parables in Mark 4, there will be little difficulty in reaching agreement that Mark 13 also contains revolutionist rhetoric. The challenge lies, finally, in negotiating the relation of cultural argumentation in the controversy stories and the passion narrative to the three other kinds of argumentation. On the one hand, both the controversy stories and the passion narrative appear to provide bases for nurturing Christian argumentation into fully developed counterculture rhetoric. On the other hand, neither presents a fully articulated countercultural system of understanding. In Mark, controversy argumentation in 2:1–3:6; 7:1–23; and 12:13–44 introduces an amalgam of rationales that can function as a seedbed for developing a clearly outlined Christian counterculture rhetoric. In their present form, however, the rationales do not present a network of reasoning that supports a comprehensive and distinctive system of alternative behaviors and attitudes. Likewise, the passion narrative contains dimensions of a significantly alternative form of behavior and belief, but this system of thought lacks clear guidelines and rationales for a wide range of actions and convictions.[73]

At this stage of analysis, Markan discourse is emerging as a tensive form of subcultural and contracultural argumentation. On the one hand, the argumentation is deeply embedded both in Jewish and Hellenistic-Roman modes of culture. On the other hand, there are significant contracultural features in the argumentation, features that simply invert behaviors and attitudes in local Jewish and Hellenistic-Roman spheres of culture. The gospel of Mark does not appear to contain fully formed counterculture discourse, in other words, argumentation that expresses a constructive image of a better way of life that provides a relatively self-sufficient system of action.[74] Rather, this form of New Testament discourse is deeply dependent on the surrounding cultures for a wide range of beliefs and actions.

To come full circle, it is often presupposed that Christianity is only "genuine" if it is a fully countercultural phenomenon. Analysis of "New Testament Christianity" may not bear this out. Perhaps the "genuine" nature of Christianity is something more like a plethora of competing local cultures containing a variety of relationships to sur-

---

[72] Major movement in this direction has been achieved in Ched Myers, *Binding the Strong Man: A Political Reading of Mark's Story of Jesus* (Maryknoll: Orbis Press, 1988) and Mack, *Myth of Innocence*.

[73] Robbins, *Jesus the Teacher*; idem, "Reversed Contextualization."

[74] Roberts, "Concept of Counter-Culture," 121.

rounding local and dominant cultures. This may be a context for rethinking both the meaning of the doctrine of incarnation and the relation of Christian belief in salvation to Christian belief in God's creation of a highly complex and unfathomable world. This leads us beyond dominant and subculture rhetorics to contraculture and counterculture rhetorics.

Contraculture Rhetoric

In various places above, we have referred to contraculture rhetoric, which inverts features in a dominant culture or subculture in its context. Let us turn now directly to a discussion of contraculture rhetoric. Burton Mack has raised the issue of the relation of Cynic rhetoric to rhetoric in the early Jesus movement, and with this discussion contraculture in early Christianity comes into view. In its early stages, Cynic tradition appears to have been a contraculture in Hellenistic society. Especially the rhetoric associated with Diogenes exhibits the nature of contraculture rhetoric: it does not articulate an extensive ideology; it specializes in "inverting" whatever remark an interlocutor makes. Mack sees contraculture rhetoric in Jesus' speech in early stages of the gospel tradition and in the earliest stage of the Q tradition. This rhetoric is systematically "domesticated" by early Christian rhetoric, and we will address this in a moment. Contraculture rhetoric does not present a network of rationales to support its alternative behavior; it prefers the shock that deliberate abandonment of conventional attitudes, values, mores, and dispositions produces. First, some of Mack's words about the Cynics; then one of his comments about Jesus:

> The sayings of the Cynics sprang from a frequently unexpressed system of thought that was highly rationalized and firmly in place. They also knew, along with others in the Socratic tradition of popular philosophy, about *nomos* (law), *physis* (nature), wisdom, virtue, *paideia* (culture, education), authority, and especially about the difference between kings on the one hand and tyrants on the other. They stood on the edges of society reminding conventional folk of their foolishness. The only program they had to suggest was to join them in their unconventional way of life. But the wellspring for the entire venture was a preoccupation with the question of society and its foundations.

> Cynics were best known for their pointed remarks and behavior. A game seems to have been played with them by those daring enough to tackle it. Cynics seem to have delighted in the game, seeking occasions to set it up to their advantage. Finding themselves in a tight situation where accommodation to conventional expectations would seem to make sense or be the easiest thing to do, the Cynic would accept the

challenge of exposing the absurdity of the expectations.[75]

With these comments, Mack describes a particular kind of contracultural rhetoric in Mediterranean society. On the one hand, the rhetoric is embedded in dominant Hellenistic culture, fully informed about it, articulate in it, and dependent on it. On the other hand, the goal of the rhetoric was not to argue a particular point of view but to overturn other people's remarks. What Cynics would share in common, then, was the "overturning" of other people's arguments (a negative tactic) rather than a positive system of thought. As it began, then, Cynic tradition was a contraculture, which is a group culture, dependent upon and reactive to dominant Hellenistic culture.

Mack sees dimensions of this kind of rhetoric in speech attributed to Jesus in the earliest stages of the gospel tradition:

> Jesus' use of parables, aphorisms, and clever rejoinders is very similar to the Cynics' way with words. Many of his themes are familiar Cynic themes. And his style of social criticism, diffident and vague, also agrees with the typical Cynic stance.[76]

This kind of rhetoric also exists, according to John Kloppenborg, in a stage of the Q tradition. As he compares it with Cynic traditions, he concludes:

> The idiom of Q is controlled not by a philosophic notion of freedom, but by a historical and soteriological schema of God's constant invitation of Israel to repent, and by the expectation of the imminent manifestation of the kingdom – an event which calls forth a radical response in its adherents, and which produces conflict and polarization in the world.... Q ... does not appear to hold out much hope for the repentance and salvation of "this generation." All that awaits is judgment.[77]

The implication of these statements is a dual cultural relationship both for Jesus and for a sector of the Jesus movement in its earliest stages: a relation not only to Jewish culture but also to Cynic Hellenistic-Roman culture. These comments by Mack and Kloppenborg suggest a contracultural relation of Jesus and a sector of early Christianity to Jewish culture. In turn, the comments imply some kind of relation to Cynic culture. This raises three issues. First, if the rhetoric of Jesus and at least one sector of early Christianity had a contracultural relation to Jewish culture, their thought, speech, and action was deeply embedded in Jewish culture and dependent on it. Their particular relation to Jewish culture would have been an "inversion" of key aspects of pat-

---

[75] Mack, *Myth of Innocence*, 67–68.
[76] Ibid., 68.
[77] John S. Kloppenborg, *The Formation of Q* (Philadelphia: Fortress, 1987), 324.

terns of thought and behavior in Jewish culture. Second, it will be important to describe the kind of Jewish culture in which Jesus and this sector of early Christianity were located. Is the Jewish culture a dominant culture that competes with dominant Hellenistic-Roman culture, a strong Jewish subculture embedded in dominant Hellenistic-Roman culture, or a Jewish subculture in a dominant or subcultural Jewish culture (like Pharisaic Judaism would have been prior to 70 CE). In other words, the kind of Jewish culture in which contracultural thought, speech, and action are generated will be important for understanding and interpreting them. Third, if the rhetoric of Jesus and a sector of early Christianity had a subcultural relation to Cynic culture during the first century, the issue is the particular kind of Cynic culture. While the Cynic rhetoric of Diogenes probably was contraculture rhetoric, Cynic culture by the first century had become a more established "system of thought" and "way of life."[78] To describe this social and cultural phenomenon, we need the term "counterculture" rather than "contraculture." As we turn to a discussion of counterculture rhetoric, then, we entertain the possibility that the Jewish contracultural nature of the rhetoric of Jesus and a sector of the early Jesus movement had a subcultural relation to the rhetoric of Hellenistic-Roman Cynic counterculture. We can describe this relation properly only after we understand the nature of a counterculture and its rhetoric.

Counterculture Rhetoric

As noted above, a counterculture is "interested in creating a better society, but not by legislative reform or by violent opposition to the dominant culture." The theory of reform is to provide an alternative, and to "hope that the dominant society will 'see the light' and adopt a more 'humanistic' way of life." In other words, "social reform is not a preoccupation" of a counterculture.[79] Its constituents

> are quite content to live their lives and let the dominant society go on with their "madness." Yet, an underlying theme is the *hope* of voluntary reform by the dominant society in accord with this new model of "the good life." Hence, one would expect a fully developed counterculture to have a *constructive* image of a better way of life. In short, the term counterculture might best be reserved for groups which are not just a reaction formation to the dominant society, but which have a supporting ideology that allows them to have a relatively self-sufficient system of action.[80]

---

[78] Abraham J. Malherbe, *The Cynic Epistles: A Study Edition* (SBLSBS 12; Missoula, Mont.: Scholars Press, 1977).

[79] Roberts, "Concept of Counter-Culture," 121.

[80] Ibid.

The value conflict of a counterculture with the dominant society "must be one which is central, uncompromising, and wrenching to the fabric of the culture. The concept of counterculture also implies a differentiation *between* the two cultures which is more distinct than the areas of *overlap*."[81] There is, then, a "fundamental difference between a counterculture and a subculture." A subculture "finds ways of affirming the national culture and the fundamental value orientation of the dominant society"; "a counterculture rejects the norms and values which unite the dominant culture."[82] There is also a fundamental difference between a counterculture and a contraculture. A contraculture is a short-lived group culture. If it does not develop into a different kind of culture, it disappears through absorption or discontinuation. A counterculture, in contrast, may continue for generations.

In Wuellner's article entitled "Paul as Pastor,"[83] he describes a significant countercultural dimension in Paul's thought. The key passage reads:

> I disagree with Meeks' formulation, according to which Paul was working for "the transformation of the multiplicity of individuals into a unity."[84] Certainly that was one component. But, in the light of our study of the functions of rhetorical questions in 1 Cor, we must add: Paul works also for the transformation of the multiplicity of different social and ethnic/cultural value systems into a unity. It is a new social order, an *imperium* or βασιλεία whose ideology, though different from the imperial norms of Rome and zealotic Jewish nationalism, was yet compatible with "the hope of Israel," the kingdom of God.[85]

Wuellner's reference to "the transformation of the multiplicity of different social and ethnic/cultural value systems into a unity" and "a new social order [which is] ... different from the imperial norms of Rome" evokes a countercultural relation of the thought, speech, and action in 1 Corinthians to Hellenistic-Roman culture. He elaborates this point of view by agreeing with E.A. Judge's claim that "three cultural systems were profoundly affected by Paul's critical use of rhetorical conventions": (1) the culture of higher education, by promoting a new kind of community education for adults; (2) the social patronage system, by refusing to accept gifts and benefactions; and (3) the system of self-esteem or boasting, by deliberately tearing down the structure of privilege with which his followers wished to surround him."[86] This

---

[81] Ibid.
[82] Ibid., 112–13.
[83] See n. 18 above.
[84] Citing Wayne A. Meeks, *The First Urban Christians: The Social World of the Apostle Paul* (New Haven: Yale University Press, 1983), 159.
[85] Wuellner, "Paul as Pastor," 73.
[86] Ibid., 76–77.

additional analysis by Wuellner represents movement toward "revalued rhetorical analysis" when it does not suppress the presence of Hellenistic-Roman culture like the earlier article on 1 Cor 1:26–28 did.[87] The comment brings Hellenistic-Roman culture into view as a contributor to the cultural environment of early Christianity. This does not mean that Wuellner changes his mind about the subcultural relation to Jewish culture. Rather, in his view 1 Corinthians contains subcultural Jewish rhetoric that functions as countercultural Hellenistic-Roman rhetoric. For him, Paul's view is "compatible with 'the hope of Israel', the kingdom of God" as it "profoundly affects" three Hellenistic-Roman systems. Whether Wuellner's view is right or not, the visibility of the bi-cultural nature of the rhetoric, rather than an implication of thorough embeddedness in Jewish dominant culture or subculture, is a significant advance over the analysis in 1973.

If we return now to Mack's work, we find a discussion of counter-culture rhetoric in his analysis of the pronouncement stories in the gospel of Mark, and his analysis once again explores the bi-cultural nature of the rhetoric. In Mack's words:

> Approximately two-thirds of the pronouncement stories in Mark are set as conflictual situations between Jesus and Jewish leaders. In many of the settings a place has been made both for the disciples and the Pharisees. The questions are sometimes addressed to the disciples about Jesus, sometimes to Jesus about the disciples, but always about issues that divide the synagogue reform movement from the synagogue. One has to assume that the chreiai were elaborated by a group whose social history merged for a time with that of the synagogue and eventually brought it into conflict with proponents of Pharisaic Judaism.[88]
>
> The issues up for debate ... break unevenly into two classes. The larger class pertains to the constitution of the group, its unconventional behavior, and the question of codes by which to judge obligations.... But they all share one thing in common: charge and countercharge about social identity. The Jesus people have not accepted Pharisaic codes of obligation, ritual purity, and halakha. The problem centers in the constitution of the Jesus group as mixed, and the behavior of the Jesus people as unclean (from a Pharisaic point of view).... The members of the Jesus movement rejected the Pharisaic critique, but they did take it seriously because they believed that they had some place in the Jewish scheme of things. Mostly ...the pronouncement stories reveal a posture of adamant affirmation of their own way of doing things in the face of Pharisaic criticism.[89]

---

[87] Wuellner, "Sociological Implications."
[88] Mack, *Myth of Innocence*, 195.
[89] Ibid., 195–96.

In the pronouncement stories, then, there is countercultural Jewish rhetoric, rather than subcultural Jewish rhetoric. In the pronouncement stories, early Christians are emphasizing "their own way of doing things" in a manner that exhibits value conflict that is "central, uncompromising, and wrenching to the fabric of the culture."[90] This counterculture rhetoric has a significant relation to Jewish culture, because "they believed that they had some place in the Jewish scheme of things." But this place, in the end, is like "new wine in new wineskins" (Mark 2:22).

In the spirit of a revalued rather than restrained rhetoric, Mack does not stop his analysis here. There is, he observes, an "exceptionally odd" dimension in the rhetoric:

> Jesus becomes his own authority. Everything is attributed to Jesus: chreia, rationale, supporting arguments, and even the authoritative pronouncements.[91]

His exploration of this kind of rhetoric in Mediterranean society leads him to Hellenistic-Roman Cynic tradition:

> The weird effect for Hellenistic ears would have been the image of a Cynic sage preoccupied with proving his wisdom authoritative. The circle closes. There is no point of leverage outside the sayings of Jesus to qualify or sustain the argumentation and its conclusion. Jesus' authority is absolute, derived from his own Cynic wisdom, and proven by his own pronouncements upon it.[92]

The rhetoric in the pronouncement stories, then, reveals a dual cultural relationship. It is countercultural Jewish rhetoric that stands in some kind of relation to Cynic rhetoric. What is that relation? As indicated above, Cynic rhetoric had moved beyond its initial contracultural stage to a countercultural movement by the first century. This would mean that the rhetoric in the pronouncement stories would have some kind of relation to eastern Mediterranean Cynic counterculture. We should not too quickly consider it to be a subcultural relation. Perhaps this early Christian counterculture itself functions as a counterculture to a well-developed eastern Mediterranean Cynic counterculture. If the account of Jesus' instructions to the twelve in Mark 6:7–13 is part of the cultural environment of the pronouncement stories, the definition of the disciples "over against" practices by Cynics could exhibit a countercultural relation to Cynic counterculture as well as to subcultural Pharisaic Judaism. This would not be surprising for a countercul-

---

[90] Roberts, "Concept of Counter-Culture," 121.
[91] Mack, *Myth of Innocence*, 199.
[92] Ibid.

ture, since a counterculture is grounded in "alternative behavior" for which it has its own rationales.

Before this discussion comes to a conclusion, one issue has been postponed until now: the relation of contraculture rhetoric in the thought, speech, and action of Jesus and an early sector of the Jesus movement to eastern Mediterranean Cynic counterculture. The descriptions by Mack and Kloppenborg imply a deep embeddedness of this early Christian contraculture rhetoric in Jewish culture. This means that this "contraculture" style, experience, and life was dependent on Jewish culture. Its relation to Cynic culture must, of necessity then, be other than contracultural, since it is Jewish culture it inverts in its embedded and dependent location. The short-lived contraculture Mack and Kloppenborg describe could be either subcultural or countercultural to Hellenistic-Roman Cynic counterculture, and the likelihood at the earliest stage would be subcultural. In other words, much like some Jewish culture functioned as a subculture of dominant Hellenistic-Roman culture, so a Cynic contracultural Judaism could function as a subculture in eastern Mediterranean Cynic counterculture. Within time, this subcultural Cynic Judaism became a countercultural Cynic Judaism through the rationales it developed in its interaction with subcultural Pharisaic Judaism. If this seems complex, it is no more complex than cultural relationships that exist today, and it is exactly the kind of complexity we should expect in the syncretistic, eclectic cultural environment of the Hellenistic-Roman world during the first century CE. The implication would be that this early sector of the Jesus movement would use some of the *topoi* and rationales that some of the members of the Cynic counterculture use in their speech and action. These *topoi* and rationales, however, would be adapted in the manner in which a subculture adapts the norms of a dominant culture. This is precisely the kind of data scholars have found in various strata of the synoptic tradition.[93] In the earliest stage, a contracultural figure (Jesus) and a contracultural sector of the Jesus movement would have had a subcultural relation to a Hellenistic-Roman counterculture. As time went on, the subcultural relation provided rhetorical resources to use as they developed countercultural rhetoric over against Pharisaic culture, which itself was a subculture in Jewish culture. As the Jesus contraculture developed countercultural rationales, it distinguished itself not only from the Pharisaic subculture but from the Hellenistic-Roman Cynic counterculture as well. At this point, the concern is not so much that we have the description precisely right, but that we see how a finely-tuned description would proceed.

---

[93] Ibid., 69, n. 11.

Conclusion

In summary, varieties of social and cultural rhetoric appear in the language in New Testament texts. As a result, the possibility of cultural rhetorical analysis and interpretation of early Christian texts stands before us. Only if we use a form of "rhetoric revalued" or "rhetoric reinvented," however, will we meet the task that lies before us. We are poised to make significant advances if we begin to discuss the bicultural nature of rhetoric in New Testament texts using a framework of dominant, subcultural, contracultural, countercultural, and liminal rhetoric. This paper has not attempted to discuss liminal rhetoric. Also, it has not attempted to move through "cultural" categories to more "sociological" categories. But the opportunity lies ready at hand. For the moment, this essay issues an invitation to rhetorical critics to engage in forms of practical criticism that explore the cultural nature of the rhetoric in New Testament texts. This will be a revalued and reinvented rhetoric that will lead us forward into regions of analysis we have not yet undertaken.

5

Social-Scientific Criticism and Literary Studies: Prospects for Cooperation in Biblical Interpretation

During the last two decades both literary and social scientific approaches to biblical texts have developed at an increasing pace, significantly changing the appearance and the substance of biblical interpretation. For some interpreters, these two approaches represent opposite interests: any marriage of the two produces either bastard or stillborn children. For other interpreters, some kind of merger is desirable or even essential.

Disciplinary, Interdisciplinary and Eclectic Methods of Interpretation

The dominant mode of twentieth-century biblical criticism prior to the 1970s was disciplinary, and this was the mode in which literary and social-scientific approaches began their work. Disciplines of study emerged vigorously during the nineteenth century and began to represent the "true nature of things" during the twentieth century. A discipline emerges when a group of people acquire authoritative status to guide research, analysis and interpretation. The major means for establishing a discipline is to identify certain phenomena for investigation and certain strategies for investigating the phenomena. Anyone who investigates the same data with different strategies is "out of the bounds" of the discipline, as well as anyone who investigates different data with the same or similar strategies.

A disciplinary approach, therefore, is a power structure, and its inherent nature is hierarchical. An overarching model or method provides a framework for negotiating the use of subdisciplines and practices. During the first seventy years of the twentieth century, the disciplines of history and theology sparred with one another for ascendancy. Sparring between disciplines, of course, establishes an essentially hidden polarity that excludes a wide range of approaches from the realm of "serious exegesis" of the Bible. Prior to 1970, data in the Bible was either "historical" or "theological," it could represent either historical theology or theological history but not something else. The battles, victories and defeats – drawn in historical versus theological lines – kept other disciplines from entering the battlefield, or playing field if you prefer, with any kind of status. Theologians decided what kind of philosophy they would use as a subdiscipline, if they used any; historians decided on the terms on which they would incorporate insights from anthropology, sociology or literary analysis into their practices and results, if they incorporated any.

The boundaries of a discipline not only create a power structure; they evoke a purity system for interpreters whereby any "mixing" of approaches, practices or methods creates "impurities." The primary way to keep impurities out is to establish an overarching method or model for filtering the impurities when practices or methods are incorporated from other disciplines. In other words, a disciplinary approach only uses the methods of another discipline on the terms of the "home" discipline that uses another discipline. The home discipline "incorporates" methods from other disciplines in a subordinate position – as subdisciplines. I vividly recall a discussion with Martin Hengel at Emory University where he agreed that literary analysis could be informative if it were "kept in control" by theology and history working together as co-partners.

For the most part, a disciplinary mood guided the emergence both of literary and social-scientific approaches during the last two decades. For most literary critics, the discipline of literary criticism – with its primary location either in New Criticism, Russian Formalism or some combination of the two – stood in a polar relation to historical criticism. Literary critics, they said, were interested in issues "intrinsic to texts"; historical critics in issues "extrinsic to texts." Social-scientific critics, on the other hand, appear to be somewhat more divided on their relation to historical criticism. Bruce Malina appears to perceive social-scientific criticism as a discipline on its own terms. For him, social science rather than the discipline of history or literary study offers an overarching model for negotiating a comprehensive range of methods, strategies and subdisciplines.[1] John H. Elliott, on the other hand, has persistently described social-scientific criticism as a subdiscipline of historical criticism. For him, it appears that social-scientific criticism is the subdiscipline that brings historical criticism to it fullest expression. For this reason, Elliott first called his method "sociological exegesis" and incorporated the full range of practices of historical criticism in his

---

[1] Bruce J. Malina, *The New Testament World: Insights from Cultural Anthropology* (rev. ed.; Louisville, Ky.: Westminster/John Knox, 1993).

work.[2] Through the influence of Malina, he has changed the name of his activity to "social-scientific criticism," but he still emphasizes that his method is simply an expansion – a completion, if you will – of historical criticism.[3]

Whether social-scientific critics have considered their activity to be disciplinary on its own terms or part of the discipline of history, until recently most have emphasized the distinct difference between their discipline and the kind of approach that distinguishes between authors, implied authors, narrators, narratees, implied readers and real readers – i.e. literary criticism. Most social-scientific critics have simply considered time and serious intellectual activity to be too precious to lose oneself in such esoteric activity. Bruce Malina has created a reading theory based on "scenarios," in part, it would seem, to show either the insignificance or the misguided nature of "literary" views of reading. For Malina, readers read on the basis of social and cultural scenarios they are able to construct in their minds.[4] Only when readers learn how to construct strange and foreign scenarios in their minds are they able to start to read New Testament texts from the perspective of the first-century Mediterranean contexts in which they were written. In Malina's words:

> adequate scenario building involves the same steps as getting to understand a group of foreigners with whom we are inevitably and necessarily thrown together, for better or worse. On the one hand, we can choose to ignore the foreigners.... In that way we can never find out what those authors said and meant to say. On the other hand ... we can come to understand our strange and alien biblical ancestors in faith ... it is the reading process that both enables and facilitates this task.[5]

Here Malina has articulated a widespread presupposition among social-scientific interpreters: readers understand texts on the basis of social and cultural scenarios they are able to construct in their minds. Most readers, historians included, construct these scenarios on the basis of their own modern social and cultural experiences. Only substantive reconstruction of our social and cultural imaginations, using extensive resources from the

---

[2] John H. Elliott, *A Home for the Homeless: A Sociological Exegesis of 1 Peter, its Situation and Strategy* (Philadelphia: Fortress, 1981); idem, *A Home for the Homeless: A Social-Scientific Criticism of 1 Peter, its Situation and Strategy with a New Introduction* (rev. ed.; Philadelphia: Fortress, 1990).

[3] John H. Elliott, ed., *Social-Scientific Criticism of the New Testament and Its Social World*, Semeia 35 (1986); idem, *A Home for the Homeless* (1990); idem, *What is Social Scientific Criticism?* (Minneapolis: Fortress, 1993).

[4] Bruce J. Malina, "Reading Theory Perspective: Reading Luke-Acts," in *The Social World of Luke-Acts: Models for Interpretation* (ed. Jerome H. Neyrey; Peabody, Mass: Hendrickson, 1991), 3–23.

[5] Ibid., 23.

disciplines of sociology and anthropology and from multiple foreign societies and cultures, can equip us with insights for reading texts from the perspective of their own social and cultural contexts.

When interpreters function in a most highly charged disciplinary mode, they encounter others with statements like the following: "In order for you to make any kind of significant interpretation of this text you need to take into consideration this phenomenon in the text which we have investigated and interpreted in such and such a manner." A significant number of both social-scientific and literary critics have responded either to or about one another in this mode during the last two decades, and one of the major reasons is a "disciplinary" perception of the task of biblical studies, which is the major model of "serious academic studies" that has been communicated to students and colleagues alike in biblical studies during the twentieth century.

Those who consider disciplinary analysis and interpretation to be the only "truly responsible" form of biblical study regularly consider the alternative to be "eclecticism." Eclecticism is a matter of selecting something here and something there to do the job, because this phenomenon is significantly different from that one. The joy of interpreting a wide range of phenomena overrides the exhilaration of interpreting a more limited range of phenomena systematically, precisely and clearly – in other words, definitively. Some people are born eclectics, it would appear; they simply cannot be bothered with all the concerns of precision and control. They will not "sell their lives" to disciplinary investigation. In response to criticism that their approach is not truly "scholarly" or "academic," their response is that at least it is interesting, creative and liberating.

There is, however, another significant alternative: interdisciplinary analysis and interpretation. An interdisciplinary approach invites data into investigation in the context of boundaries that various disciplines have established. The mood is to ask: "What phenomena does this particular discipline investigate, how does it investigate it and what conclusions does it draw from the investigation?" Then, however, the interdisciplinary critic redraws the boundaries and asks the same questions of another discipline. The interpreter then develops strategies to place these multiple activities, insights and conclusions in dialogue with one another. The underlying presupposition is that conceptual frameworks are essential for significant analysis and interpretation, yet phenomena are constituted by a complexity that transcends any conceptual frame humans create. In other words, disciplinary approaches create a context for systematic investigation that yields significantly greater results than "unbounded investigation," yet every disciplinary approach yields a highly insufficient explanation and interpretation of the complex phenomena of the world.

A Model for Interdisciplinary Investigation

You will have perceived that my own mode of choice is an interdisciplinary model, and the diagram (Figure 1) displays a model for interdisciplinary investigation and interpretation that places literary and social-scientific disciplines in dialogue with one another. It is necessary, of course, to have a mode of analysis that guides the interdisciplinary arbitration, and for me it is rhetoric.[6] Rhetoric provides a socially and culturally oriented approach to texts, forming a bridge between the disciplines of social-scientific and literary criticism.

Figure 1: Socio-Rhetorical Model of Textual Communication

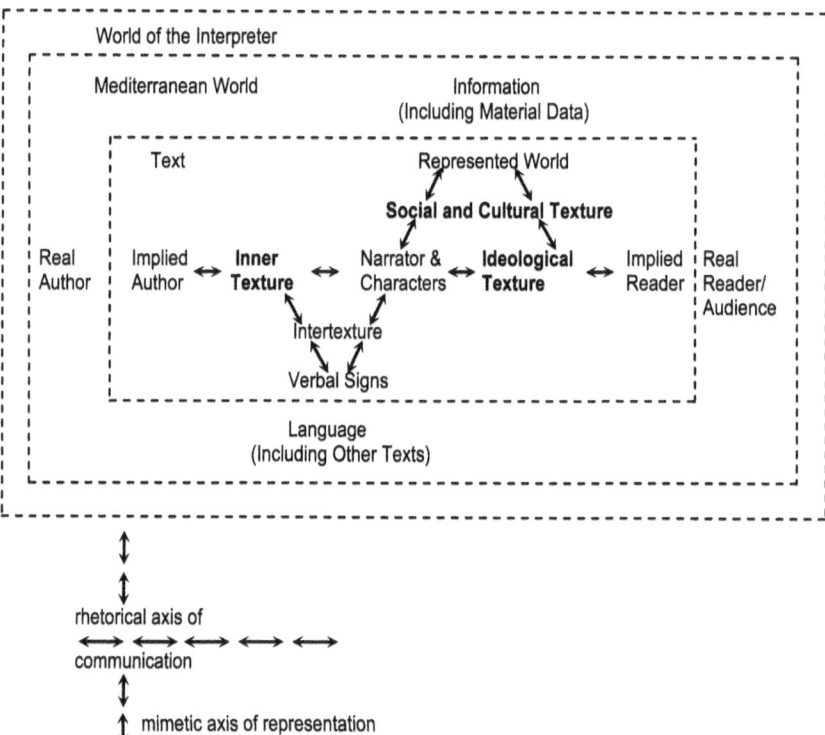

---

[6] Patricia Bizzell and Bruce Herzberg, *The Rhetorical Tradition: Readings form Classical Times to the Present* (Boston: Bedford Books of St. Martin's Press, 1990); Vernon K. Robbins, *Jesus the Teacher: A Socio-Rhetorical Interpretation of Mark* (rev. ed.; Minneapolis: Fortress, 1992); idem, "Socio-Rhetorical Criticism: Mary, Elizabeth, and the Magnificat as a Test Case," in *The New Literary Criticism and the New Testament* (ed. Elizabeth Struthers Malbon and Edger V. McKnight; JSNTSup 109; Sheffield: Sheffield Academic Press, 1994), 164–209.

5. Social-Scientific Criticism and Literary Studies 187

According to this socio-rhetorical model, New Testament interpreters function in the context of their own social, cultural, historical and ideological worlds. Their instinctive social and cultural presuppositions come from their own world rather than the world of the texts they interpret. For the purpose of interpreting texts written in the context of the first-century Mediterranean world, however, they construct a tentative image of the Mediterranean world from a wide range of data. They imbed this image of the Mediterranean world into their own world, and they embed New Testament texts in their image of the Mediterranean world. For this reason, there is a rectangle that separates the world of the interpreter from the ancient Mediterranean world, and there is another rectangle that separates the ancient Mediterranean world from a text produced in that world. The activity of interpretation, then, is an on-going project of reinterpreting the Mediterranean world and our modern world on the basis of interpretation of New Testament and other texts. Interpreters who do not consciously construct an image of the Mediterranean world in which to embed New Testament texts are considered by socio-rhetorical critics, through their indebtedness to social-scientific critics, to be in danger of unexamined ethnocentrism and anachronism. Ethnocentrism arises from the absence of attentiveness to the "foreign, strange" society and culture in which people produced New Testament texts, and the anachronism arises from an absence of attentiveness to the "pre-industrial" social and cultural environment in which people lived during the first century CE.

Ethnocentric and anachronistic interpretations misconstrue the basic social and cultural meanings and meaning effects of words, phrases, thoughts and actions evoked by texts. In additions, socio-rhetorical readers know that the real author and real reader/audience stood outside texts in the Mediterranean world. The real author, language, information in the world and the real reader/audience stand outside the text, which is represented by the innermost rectangle in the socio-rhetorical model above. Real authors are historical persons. The texts they make somehow are extensions of themselves, but the real author and the text are separate social, cultural and historical phenomena. Thus, the real author is not inside the box, but outside it. Likewise, language is a phenomenon outside of texts which authors use to write texts. Again, a text is a particular manifestation of language, but language itself is a phenomenon outside any particular text. In a related manner, information is also outside the text; some kind of manifestation of this outside information stands inside a text, but not the information itself. Also, readers and audiences to whom the text is read stand outside the text.

The boundary around the text is a broken line, because it is a human-made boundary for the purpose of focusing analysis on a text. Likewise, the boundary around the Mediterranean world is a broken line. All kinds of meanings and meaning effects travel through the gaps in these boundaries. They traveled through the boundary between the Mediterranean world and the text when the author wrote the text, and they travel through the boundaries when any person reads the text. Language and other texts travel through the boundaries just as information and material data travel through the boundaries. Interpreters at least temporarily build boundaries to keep various things out of texts, but since texts are located in the world, were created in it and are related to it, there is no way finally to keep either the Mediterranean world or the world of the interpreter out of them. Texts are in the world and of it.

Literary interpreters have concluded that the inner texture of a narrative text contains a narrator who tells the story and characters who think, act, and have their being in the story. The narrator and characters, however, exist in a context of "images" of the real author, language, information and the real reader/audience. In other words, the inside of a text is a combination of "show" and "tell." The narrator tells the story. The narratee hears the narrator and sees the characters, who may themselves speak and "look." Readers cannot see the real authors of texts, because the real authors are hidden behind their work. But readers see an image of authors in what authors have done. The image "implies" an author of a certain kind, so literary interpreters regularly call the image of an author in a text the "implied author." The implied author is the image created by everything the reader sees in the text.[7] Also, readers do not hear language in the text; rather, they "see" verbal signs, printed letters, to which they give "voice." That is, readers turn the signs into sounds that are "language" among people. Thus, the verbal signs in a text are "implied language." In addition, readers cannot hear and see real information and material data in a text but they hear and see "implied" information and material data. Finally, readers of texts create an image of a reader who can read a particular text with understanding. If they themselves cannot understand the text, they create an image of a reader whom the implied author imagined could read and understand the text. Whether or not all of this is clear to the real reader who is now reading this, literary interpreters have drawn these conclusions about the inner texture of texts. These conclusions guide socio-rhetorical criticism as it approaches the inner texture of a text, and the goal is to create activities for an interpreter that

---

[7] Vernon K. Robbins, "The Social Location of the Implied Author of Luke-Acts," in *Social World of Luke-Acts*, 302–32.

will make it possible to investigate these and other inner phenomena in texts.

At the bottom of the diagram are horizontal and vertical arrows. The horizontal arrows represent what literary interpreters call the rhetorical axis. An axis is an imaginary line through the center of something, like the imaginary line through the center of the earth as it spins, as we say, "on its axis." Through the center of a text is an imaginary "rhetorical" line between the author and the reader. The rhetorical axis is the "speaking" or "communicating" line through the center of the text from the author to the reader. In addition to horizontal arrows there are vertical arrows at the bottom of the diagram. The vertical arrows indicate a "mimetic" axis. The word mimetic comes from the Greek word μίμησις, meaning "imitation." The written signs in the text "imitate" the sounds of language, and the narrator, actors and things in the "textual world" imitate information and material data in the world. Thus, the vertical lines represent an axis of "imitation." This axis exists in angles in the diagram, rather than straight up through the center, since the horizontal movement of the communication causes the vertical axis to run up and down at angles. In other words, the diagram is meant to exhibit action. There is dynamic movement from the author to the reader and from the reader to the author. In the context of this movement words, characters, represented world, implied author and implied reader all "imitate" the world.

In the midst of all of these phenomena in the text are four arenas of texture printed in bold print: (1) inner texture; (2) intertexture; (3) social and cultural texture; and (4) ideological texture. One of the special features of socio-rhetorical criticism is its identification of these four arenas in a text. Pointing to these arenas, the method gathers practices of interpretation for each arena to enable a person to investigate each arena both on its own terms and in relation to the other arenas. Each arena is given a name for its own particular "text-ure." The texture of a text is so "thick" that no discipline can satisfactorily approach all the aspects of thought, feeling, sight, sound, touch, smell and desire that its signs evoke. At present socio-rhetorical criticism uses four disciplines. In the future it will add psychological texture, but this is an additional task that very few biblical scholars at present are ready to tackle in a disciplinary manner.

The Beginning Point for the Literary and Social-Scientific Critic

The standard lore suggests that a literary critic begins "inside" the boundaries of a text and a social-scientific critic begins "outside" the boundaries of a text. But let us test this conventional point of view with a comparison of John Dominic Crossan's interpretation of the parable of the Good Samaritan in his book *Raid on the Articulate* with Richard Rohrbaugh's interpretation of the parable of the Great Supper in *The Social World of Luke-Acts*.[8] I will begin with Crossan's interpretation of the parable of the Good Samaritan in Luke 10. Crossan establishes the context for his interpretation with a discussion of language as play and literature as a system. Language is a game. As people play with language, they create reality. Reality, then, is "the interplay of worlds created by human imagination."[9] Language creates tragic world and comic world. It breaks and cracks one kind of world with tremors that bring new worlds into being. Language actually functions in a ritual manner – a "human *interplay* of structure and antistructure ...which reminds us continually that our structures are both absolutely necessary and completely relative."[10] Literature is a particular manifestation of the game of language. Literature functions as a system that makes and breaks genres. For Crossan, this system is closed. Each new example of literature changes the species itself. In other words:

> It is as if all the chairs and all the space in the auditorium were occupied so that one new arrival involves a total reorganization of those already present. It is of course this new arrival which stops the entire proceedings from becoming static, lifeless, and boring since all those in the audience face not the empty stage but rather the closed door. This subversive advent is necessary because without it the established forms and genres of a period's language and style would become absolutes and their frozen immobility would effectively hide the foundations of play on which and in which they operated.[11]

For Crossan, then, literature is a closed system created by the game of language that people play. As a result, some of the most vigorous action in literature occurs as "forms and genres" clash with one another. Here the interpreter sees that literature not only plays with language but, as Crossan says, literature also plays with itself.[12]

From the perspective of the model that is before us, Crossan begins outside any particular text with language as a particular kind of human game, and from this context he approaches literature as a closed system in which forms and genres clash with one another to create new "literary worlds." As Crossan explores the arena of the literary system that

---

[8] John Dominic Crossan, *Raid on the Articulate: Cosmic Eschatology in Jesus and Borges* (New York: Harper & Row, 1976); Richard L. Rohrbaugh, "The Pre-Industrial City in Luke-Acts," in *Social World of Luke-Acts*, 125–49.
[9] Crossan, *Raid on the Articulate*, 28.
[10] Ibid., 36.
[11] Ibid., 61.
[12] Ibid.

will inform his interpretation of the parable of the Good Samaritan, he develops a taxonomy of forms and genres which includes law, proverb, beatitude, novel, myth, parable and allegory. This taxonomy informs the model that guides his interpretation of the parable. His beginning point, then, is the construction of a model of literary forms and genres which he perceives to function in a closed system that people create with the game of language.

Now let us turn to Rohrbaugh's interpretation of the parable of the Great Supper in Luke 14. To set the context for his interpretation, he observes that "fully one half of the references to the 'city' in the New Testament are in the Lukan writings."[13] To understand this phenomenon, Rohrbaugh investigates what he calls "the urban system." This system stands in contrast to Crossan's investigation of "literature as a system." It stands at the opposite end of the mimetic axis of representation, and it also stands outside any particular text. For Rohrbaugh, within the social world there is a phenomenon he calls "the urban system." This system contains "nucleations" including villages, town and cities, which link cities and hinterland, and make the specialties in the nucleations intrinsic parts of a single system.[14] A correct understanding of the urban system, then, does not pit "urban" and "rural" as "polar opposites or closed system" but as phenomena in "a structure of interrelated differentiations."[15]

Within this system there are, however, two opposed systems: the modern urban system and the pre-industrial system of antiquity. In the modern system the labor unit is "the individual person" who as an aggregate "constitute a flexible work-force for employers seeking to adapt to changing market conditions at minimum cost."[16] In modern industrial society, therefore, there is a pattern linking city and hinterlands that

> ensures the flow of capital and labor toward the cities. Marketplace and channels of communication/transportation come to include the hinterlands along with the city.... By contrast, pre-industrial cities existed in a system which required a socially and geographically fixed labor force. Specialists in the city primarily produced the goods and services needed by the urban elite, who were the only existing consumer market. Since that market was small the labor force needed to supply it was correspondingly small and, as Leeds notes, it thus became "a major interest to keep others than these out of the towns, fixed in their own agrarian,

---

[13] Rohrbaugh, "Pre-Industrial City," 125.
[14] Ibid., 130.
[15] Ibid.
[16] Ibid., 131.

mining or extractive areas."[17]

Both Crossan and Rohrbaugh, it will be noticed, begin by constructing a model in their own world that functions as a context for interpretation of texts written in the world of late Mediterranean antiquity. Crossan approaches the text from the bottom of the model with language as a game and literature as a system. Rohrbaugh starts at the top of the model with the social world as a playing field and the urban world as a system. Both interpreters, then, presuppose the value of identifying a system as an overall context for interpreting a text. Crossan uses modern literary theory to define the relation of phenomena in the literary system; Rohrbaugh uses modern social-scientific theory to define the relation of phenomena in the urban system. So far, then, these literary and social-scientific interpreters have a good basis for dialogue. Both presuppose the value of modern theory, of systems within the realm of human activity, of models as contexts for interpretation, of the interrelation and opposition of certain phenomena as articulated in modern theory and of the Mediterranean world as the context in which the text first attained and evoked its meanings and meaning effects. Both start with phenomena outside of texts and create a model as a context for interpretation of a text.

It would be interesting to hear a dialogue between Crossan and Rohrbaugh concerning the nature of human activity in the realm of the literary and the urban system. Crossan emphasizes the activity of "play" in literature which creates new "worlds of reality." Rohrbaugh appears to presuppose that the pre-industrial urban system represents the "social world of reality" for anyone living in Mediterranean antiquity. Yet as Rohrbaugh proceeds, he concludes that the parable presents "a member of the elite, a host, making a break with the 'system' in the most public and radical sort of way."[18] In Rohrbaugh's approach, does this "break" create something new? If so, what "new" phenomenon has been created? Crossan talks about "new worlds of reality," because he perceives human imagination to be the source of "reality" as humans can know it. Rohrbaugh does not analyze what occurs when the host "breaks with the system." Is it possible that Crossan's analysis picks up where Rohrbaugh's stops? In other words, do their approaches to interpretation stand in a continuum? In the model in Figure 1, narrator and characters represent the meeting ground between the place where Crossan starts and the place where Rohrbaugh starts. It looks like these two interpreters ought to be able to dialogue fruitfully with one another. Before moving on it may be

---

[17] Ibid., 131–32, quoting Anthony Leeds, "Forms of Urban Integration: Social Urbanization in Comparative Perspective," *Urban Anthropology* 8 (1979): 238.

[18] Rohrbaugh, "Pre-Industrial City," 145.

worth our time to notice that the beginning place for Crossan's analysis challenges the conventional lore that literary critics work strictly with phenomena intrinsic to texts while social-scientific critics concern themselves with phenomena extrinsic to texts. Both, it would appear, begin with data extrinsic to texts to create a model for reading a text. Literary critics begin with language and literature to gain entrance into the verbal signs in the text; social-scientific critics begin with social and material data in the world to gain entrance into the represented world in the text. Once they have established a system to guide their interpretations, they start their readings of the text.

The Things Literary and Social-Scientific Critics Personify

As literary and social-scientific critics engage in dialogue, they may discover quite soon that one of the greatest sources of irritation is the different things they personify as they talk. As we interpret, the phenomena we personify exhibit our point of view about reality and truth in the world.

Beginning with information and material data in the world, social-scientific critics personify aspects of human activity in the social world outside of texts and transfer this "worldly" mode of personification onto aspects of a text. This means that the social-scientific critic is interested primarily in verbal signs in texts that evoke things related to "persons" and "their social world." Other aspects of verbal signs in the text are of little or no importance. Literary critics, in contrast, personify verbal signs in texts and transfer these personified aspects of "verbal signs" onto texts. I will illustrate by continuing with the interpretations by Crossan and Rohrbaugh.

After constructing a literary context for interpretation, Crossan asks the reader to perform a particular mental act: "I would ask you to forget everything or anything you know about the story's present setting or editorial interpretation within the Gospel of Luke. Here is the story, the whole story, and nothing but the story."[19] At this point, Crossan prints the entire parable for the reader. The purpose is to get the reader to focus entirely on the story itself as a story. He is interested in the nature of story as story, in other words the nature of this particular form or genre within literature as a system. How does this story function? What makes this story different from other stories? Look, he says, at the story itself and nothing but the story.

As Crossan continues he emphasizes that he is concerned with the "implicit narrator" rather than the historical author (Jesus) and with an

[19] Crossan, *Raid on the Articulate*, 101–2.

"implicit hearer or audience."[20] This language keeps him "inside" the boundaries of the text in the socio-rhetorical model printed above. Then he distinguishes between an example story and a parable. At this point Crossan personifies forms of literature. As he says: "The story of Jesus is not an example but a parable. It presents the audience with a paradox involving a double reversal of expectations."[21] Notice how "story" has become the subject of a verb of action: the story "presents the audience with a paradox." This is a matter of personifying "story": this story does things to an audience. At this point, then, the literary critic depersonifies the person who tells the story – this person, be it author, implied author, or narrator, is simply the device that brings the story before us, and there are great difficulties trying to talk about that device as a real person. Rather, we have the story, and it is the story that is doing things to us as readers.

I have both heard Bruce Malina object specifically to this kind of personification and I have read comments he has written to me in this regard. Stories do not do anything, he says, people do. The problem, from the literary critic's point of view, is that the "people" in antiquity who told this story are no longer accessible to us. We have remnants of their language in verbal signs in texts. We activate these signs as we read them. If we are careful with our words, we know we are giving voice and action to verbal signs, not to real people. We cannot give voice and action to the person who told this story; we can only give voice and action to the story itself.

In contrast, Rohrbaugh personifies the author and the audience, both of whom stand outside the text. Rohrbaugh does not talk about an implied author or narrator, or about a narratee or implied hearer of the parable of the Great Supper. He is interested in "Luke's" version of the parable and in Luke's "intended audience." There is nothing "implicit" either about the author or about the audience in Rohrbaugh's interpretation. Luke is the author and he tells it to a particular audience with specific intentions in mind. As Rohrbaugh says: "our thesis is that Luke's version of this parable knowingly uses features of the urban system in order to make its point and that these features would have been readily apparent to Luke's intended audience."[22]

It appears that Rohrbaugh also "personifies" the parable he interprets, but he embeds that personification in "Luke" who told it rather than in the nature of language as it functions in "parable." In other words, for Crossan this is "language's" story; for Rohrbaugh this is "Luke's" story. Crossan is very careful about any talk about anyone's

---

[20] Ibid., 102.
[21] Ibid., 104.
[22] Rohrbaugh, "Pre-Industrial City," 137.

"intentions" with the story, since the discussion of "the intentional fallacy" has been an important part of literary theory.[23] Rohrbaugh has no such concern. For him, people have intentions, Luke had intentions as he told this story, and therefore there are intentions in this story for an intended audience.

What about the different phenomena Crossan and Rohrbaugh personify in their interpretations? My experience has been that this difference is very difficult to overcome in dialogue. What the literary critic personifies in contrast to the social-scientific critic is the tip of an iceberg with deep roots that evoke emotional and cognitive animosity. For literary critics, neither Luke nor any other person from antiquity is available to us. We cannot bring them to life no matter what we do. We bring their verbal and material signs to life as we read and look, and we can investigate how these verbal and material signs function within language and literature as systems. For social-scientific critics, on the other hand, language and verbal signs do not do anything; people do things with language and verbal signs. Social-scientific critics are not concerned, it appears, with literary critics' discussions of "mimetic," "intentional," and "affective" fallacies. Most social-scientific critics presuppose that language and texts are clear windows to social reality. These windows are "transparent": what you see is what you get. Here, then, we seem to have an immovable barrier between literary and social-scientific critics. At least I have not found much willingness on either side to give.

There may be one sign of hope. There is very little difference in what is personified as Crossan and Rohrbaugh talk about the characters in the parables they are interpreting. Both interpreters presuppose that the characters function in realms of social and cultural "realities." Crossan posits all kinds of social and cultural aspects functioning in and through the story he interprets. In turn, Rohrbaugh posits the nature of the story as parable rather than allegory and posits a significant number of literary aspects in and around the story he interprets. But is this enough of a meeting ground to engage in fruitful dialogue? I think the answer to this question is no. The interpretation of the characters in the story is more of a battleground than a congenial playing field. The reason, I suggest, is the unexplored presuppositions on both sides of the discussion. Let us turn, then, to areas in which literary and social-scientific critics have presupposed they did not need any more refined knowledge.

---

[23] W.K. Wimsatt, *The Verbal Icon* (Lexington, Ky.: University of Kentucky Press, 1954), 3–18; Crossan, *Raid on the Articulate*, 90.

Unexamined Presuppositions of Literary and Social-Scientific Critics

Given the different arena of focus for the literary and social-scientific critic, the major arena of attention of the one is the major arena of least attention for the other. By this I mean that the literary critic regularly considers the social dynamics of the Mediterranean world to be "transparent" to any reasonably intelligent historian while the nature of literature is highly complex, requiring extensive investigation. In turn, the social-scientific critic considers literature of any period to be "transparent" to any reasonably intelligent reader while the nature of social interaction is highly complex, requiring extensive investigation. For the literary critic, it does little good to work out all kinds of theories and models about social systems and institutions if the interpreter does not read the text with intricate care, precision and theoretical guidance. For the social-scientific critic, it does little good to work out all kinds of theories and models about language and literature if the interpreter does not understand the social systems, institutions and dynamics in Mediterranean antiquity with care, precision and theoretical guidance. So is there any beginning place, any hope for cooperation?

The basic hope for serious dialogue and cooperation lies, as I see it, in an admission by both sides that the other side has data that is important for the act of interpretation. Such an approach to each other, given the highly developed nature of each field, calls for an interdisciplinary spirit. If interpreters are "disciplinary" in their approach to things, in the spirit of nineteenth- and twentieth-century disciplinary investigation, there will be very little gain by either side – both sides will consider the central insights of the other side to be obsessive, irrelevant or simply wrong.

The question about Crossan is whether he could have a deeper interest in the social nature of the Mediterranean world. His recent books on Jesus suggest that he has such an interest.[24] The question for Rohrbaugh is whether he could have a deeper interest in the literary nature of the parable of the Great Supper. Inasmuch as he distinguishes between parable and allegory, he may also find an interest in more detailed literary aspects of the parable.

But I suggest that this overlap of interest is still not enough. In my view, each side needs to have a much more comprehensive conception of the nature of text. This is where rhetorical criticism comes into the discussion, and here I refer to rhetorical criticism based on the tradition of rhetorical analysis and interpretation from its beginnings in pre-

---

[24] John Dominic Crossan, *The Historical Jesus: The Life of a Mediterranean Jewish Peasant* (Edinburgh: T & T Clark, 1991); idem, *Jesus: A Revolutionary Biography* (San Francisco: Harper San Francisco, 1994).

Socratic times to its presence today in post-modern criticism.[25] In an appendix to *In Defence of Rhetoric*, Brian Vickers lists and defines forty-eight rhetorical tropes and figures.[26] Literary criticism pays significant attention to only four of these: metaphor, metonymy, synecdoche and irony. Thus conventional literary criticism investigates a very limited range of phenomena of signification in a text. Social-scientific criticism explores a different range of signification in texts — namely what Aristotle calls the "common topics." Social-scientific critics have been exploring those topics that span all sectors of society and culture in the Mediterranean world — the knowledge, conceptions and presuppositions present with any person at any level of society. Aristotle's analysis in his *Ars Rhetorica* makes it clear that the common topics are only one aspect of rhetoric both in speech and in texts. In addition to the common topics are the special or material topics and the final topics.[27] Social-scientific criticism has the potential to participate fully in a context of comprehensive interpretation of signification in texts if it attends not only to the common social and cultural topics but also the specific and final topics in texts.

Bryan Wilson's typology of sects is the most successful spectrum I can currently find to explore the specific or material topics in texts that evoke a religious view of the world. Through the specific topics in written discourse, a text evokes a response to the world that is conversionist, reformist, revolutionist, introversionist, manipulationist, thaumaturgical or utopian.[28] James A. Wilde began this kind of analysis with the Gospel of Mark in the 1970s.[29] John H. Elliott included this kind of analysis in *A Home for the Homeless* and has been working hard to refine it in recent years.[30] Philip Esler used it in his investigation of

---

[25] Bizzell and Herzberg, *Rhetorical Tradition*.

[26] Brian Vickers, *In Defence of Rhetoric* (Oxford: Clarendon, 1988), 491–98.

[27] George A. Kennedy, *Aristotle, On Rhetoric: A Theory of Civic Discourse* (New York: Oxford University Press, 1991), 45–47, 50–52, 187–204; Burton L. Mack, "Elaboration of the Chreia in the Hellenistic School," in *Patterns of Persuasion in the Gospels* (Burton L. Mack and Vernon K. Robbins; Sonoma, Calif.; Polebridge, 1989), 38.

[28] Bryan R. Wilson, "A Typology of Sects," in *Sociology of Religion* (ed. Roland Robertson; Baltimore: Penguin Books, 361–83; idem, *Magic and the Millennium: A Sociological Study of Religious Movements of Protest among Tribal and Third-World Peoples* (New York: Harper & Row, 1973); Vernon K. Robbins, "Socio-Rhetorical Criticism," 185–86.

[29] James A. Wilde, "A Social Description of the Community Reflected in the Gospel of Mark" (Ph.D. diss., Drew University, 1974); idem, "The Social World of Mark's Gospel: A Word About Method," *SBL Seminar Papers, 1978* (2 vols.; SBLSP 13; Chico, Calif.; Scholars Press, 1978), 2:47–70.

[30] John H. Elliott, *Home for the Homeless* (1990); idem, *What is Social Scientific Criticism?*; idem, "Phases in the Social Formation of Early Christianity: From Faction to Sect – A Social-Scientific Perspective," in *Recruitment, Conquest, and Conflict: Strategies in Judaism, Early Christianity, and the Greco-Roman World* (ed. Peder Brogen, Vernon K. Robbins and

the Lukan community and has recently applied it to 4 Ezra in a study which also subjects the text to a literary analysis inspired by a central aspect of Russian formalism.[31] Much more analysis of specific or material topics in texts needs to be undertaken to facilitate dialogue between literary and social-scientific critics.

But also social-scientific critics need to attend to the final or strategic topics. The final topics are those which specific cultures use to deliver their most decisive points of persuasion. The final topics of the rabbis often occur in contexts where brief recitation of a text from Torah contains a particular word with special meaning. The final topics in this kind of rhetoric are distinctive from the final topics at work in the speech and writings of people deeply influenced by Homer and the tragedians. For this kind of analysis, the social-scientific critic needs to use the tools of the sociologist of culture. At present, the most suggestive taxonomy I have been able to find to explore the final topics is to correlate insights into elaboration of the χρεία (pithy sayings associated with particular persons) with definitions of dominant culture, subculture, counterculture, contraculture and liminal culture.[32] A beginning place is to explore the cultural nature in which each New Testament text participates both in Jewish culture and in Greco-Roman culture.[33] Burton Mack's work on the Gospel of Mark and Q presents the most advanced data currently available for this kind of analysis, but Mack himself does not use the resources of the sociology of culture to analyze and display what he has found.[34] Extensive investigation of the final topics in New Testament texts with the aid of rhetorical criticism working in tandem with sociology of culture will bring a significant advance to dialogue between literary and social-scientific critics.

David B. Gowler; Emory Studies in Early Christianity 6; Atlanta: Scholars Press, 1998), 273–313.

[31] Philip F. Esler, *Community and Gospel in Luke-Acts: The Social and Political Motivations of Lucan Theology* (SNTMS 57; Cambridge: Cambridge University Press, 1987); idem, *The First Christians in their Social Worlds: Social Scientific Approaches to New Testament Interpretation* (London: Routledge, 1994), 110–30; idem, "The Social Function of 4 Ezra," *JSNT* 53 (1994): 99–123.

[32] Robbins, "Socio-Rhetorical Criticism," 189–90.

[33] Vernon K. Robbins, "Rhetoric and Culture: Exploring Types of Cultural Rhetoric in a Text," in *Rhetoric and the New Testament: Essays from the 1992 Heidelberg Conference* (ed. Stanley E. Porter and Thomas H. Olbright; JSNTSup 90; Sheffield: Sheffield Academic Press, 1993).

[34] Burton L. Mack, *A Myth of Innocence: Mark and Christian Origins* (Philadelphia: Fortress, 1988); idem, *The Lost Gospel: The Book of Q and Christian Origins* (San Francisco: Harper, 1993).

Conclusion

Literary and social-scientific criticism of the Bible emerged in a context where post-modern methods were moving into the humanities and the social sciences. The theoretical consciousness of both approaches is an important part of the new environment. The real antagonists of literary and social-scientific criticism are interpreters who claim to apply tested and proven methods that are free from theory. Approaches that are part of the post-modern era presuppose that every method is not only theoretically grounded but also ideologically driven. Just as no method is free from theory, so no theory is free from the particular interests and view of reality of those who formulate it.

Another characteristic of these approaches is to engage in rigorous, systematic and programmatic investigation, analysis and interpretation in the context of its theoretical and ideological discussions. The contextually limited and subjectively driven nature of its work does not introduce any special concern since that is the nature of all scientific work. Still another characteristic of both literary and social-scientific criticism is that the disciplinary work they do is inherently interdisciplinary. Both literary and social-scientific criticism have been deeply influenced by linguistics and structuralism, which are both richly informed by anthropology, which itself is a rich product of reciprocal exchange between the humanities and the social sciences. This means that the kind of literary and social-scientific criticism that was coming to birth during the last two decades presupposes cross-cultural, pluralistic investigation, analysis and interpretation.

It is natural that both literary and social-scientific approaches began with a disciplinary spirit characteristic of the first half of the twentieth century, since the spirit of historical criticism – the context out of which they emerged – is disciplinary. There is also another reason. Any approach must attain a "disciplinary" rigor before colleagues in the field of biblical interpretation consider it to be a "significant" practice in "serious exegesis." In other words, there should be no surprise that literary critics started with types of new-critical, structuralist and Russian formalist modes of interpretation that looked as thoroughly scientific as the most rigorous historical practices of interpretation. Social-scientific critics, in turn, could claim to be the practitioners who brought historical criticism to its fullest expression. In other words, while literary critics were imitating the rigor of historical method, social-scientific critics were aspiring to fulfil the grandest dreams of historical method.

The result has not only been the practice of new historicism[35] in biblical interpretation but also new rhetoricism.[36] Socio-rhetorical criticism merges new rhetoricism with new historicism.[37] The boundaries established by earlier literary critics have openings through which social, cultural, historical and ideological data freely traffic. The insights of the social-scientific critic are more and more influenced by the textuality of society, culture and reality itself. Language is understood as a social phenomenon and texts are perceived in relation to voices in spoken language. In this new context, both fields become aware of the rhetoric not only of the discourse of the texts they analyze but also of their own discourse. Is there a potential for cooperation? Dialogue and cooperation are already beginning. The only question is who and how various critics undertake the task.

---

[35] Aram H. Vesser, ed., *The New Historicism* (London: Routledge, 1989); Brook Thomas, *The New Historicism and Other Old-Fashioned Topics* (Princeton: Princeton University Press, 1991).

[36] Bizzell and Herzberg, *Rhetorical Tradition*, 899–1266; Burton L. Mack, *Myth of Innocence*; idem, *Rhetoric and the New Testament* (Minneapolis: Fortress, 1990); idem, *The Lost Gospel*.

[37] Robbins, "Socio-Rhetorical Criticism."

6

Picking up the Fragments:
From Crossan's Analysis to Rhetorical Analysis

> It is a clever deceit, when talking about something, to talk about it in such a manner that it becomes isolated from all other things. Things, whether ideas, artifacts, or attitudes, exist in relation to one another. Therefore, we must find ways to talk about things in their relationships.
> — Anonymous

This year Robert W. Funk started a national research seminar for the purpose of displaying to a wider audience the results of past and present scholarly activity on ancient materials that depict speech and activity by Jesus of Nazareth. A major question for the members of the seminar is what kind of investigation of the ancient stories and sayings this will be. The nineteenth century saw "the quest of the historical Jesus,"[1] now regularly called the "Old Quest," and the middle of the twentieth century saw the "New Quest of the Historical Jesus."[2] What could make this quest different from other quests?

The primary answer lies in the unprecedented access to ancient documents purporting to present the speech and action of Jesus, and the unprecedented development of methods for understanding these documents in their own cultural environment. Both the access and the methodological developments result from discoveries that began near the end of the nineteenth century, editing and translation projects that continue to occupy numerous scholars, and investigations of sayings, stories, and legends in a wide variety of cultural arenas that allow us to see aspects of society we have not seen before.

---

[1] Recounted in Albert Schweitzer, *The Quest of the Historical Jesus: A Critical Study of Its Progress from Reimarus to Wrede* (trans. W. Montgomery; New York: Macmillian, 1968).

[2] This phrase became standard in American scholarship with James M. Robinson's book, *A New Quest of the Historical Jesus* (SBT 25; London: SCM Press, 1959).

This essay concerns a "socio-rhetorical" method for analyzing and interpreting aspects of action and speech attributed to Jesus.[3] Its purpose is to probe the inner reasoning and modes of argumentation in the data. On the one hand, the method is new, because it uses rhetorical and social analysis in a manner not applied previously to sayings of Jesus. Yet the method began before Jesus lived, since it was first nurtured into being when philosophers, orators, and teachers in Mediterranean antiquity used their skills to analyze, refine, and instruct others in the use of language in public life. Since then the method has been refined, especially by researchers in folklore and the Hebrew Bible. The use of an approach which is simultaneously new and old uncovers a bias of the writer of this essay, since an underlying presupposition is that new advances regularly occur when resources from older data (in this instance approximately 2,000 years older) are used to critique that which is recent. Another bias in the approach derives from a belief that an understanding of the dynamics of communication and transmission in Mediterranean culture at the time of the beginning of Christianity will facilitate our understanding of the transmission of traditions about Jesus.

This essay introduces a socio-rhetorical method through a critique of John Dominic Crossan's 1983 book entitled *In Fragments*, which is one of the most valuable studies of the sayings of Jesus to appear in recent years. Crossan tells us in the introduction to the book that he deliberately chose the title to evoke his earlier book *In Parables*.[4] In his own terms, the earlier book contained an analysis of the narrative metaphors or short stories attributed to Jesus. In his 1983 book, he uses the term aphorism for sayings attributed to the personal speech and wisdom of Jesus. The parables are easier to analyze comprehensively, he says, because they are restricted to Matthew, Mark, Luke, and the Gospel of Thomas. The aphorisms, in contrast, "extend like hermeneutical tentacles throughout both intracanonical and extracanonical sources and throughout both first and second centuries."[5] He lists 133 aphorisms in parallel columns in appendix I and says in his first chapter that he counts approximately "102 sayings in the synoptics which could be considered wisdom sayings."[6]

---

[3] The author first introduced the method in Vernon K. Robbins, *Jesus the Teacher: A Socio-Rhetorical Interpretation of Mark* (Philadelphia: Fortress, 1984; repr., Minneapolis, Fortress, 1992).

[4] John Dominic Crossan, *In Parables: The Challenge of the Historical Jesus* (New York: Harper & Row, 1973).

[5] John Dominic Crossan, *In Fragments: The Aphorisms of Jesus* (New York: Harper & Row, 1983), x.

[6] Ibid., 28.

The lasting contribution of *In Fragments* will not only be Crossan's collection and numbering of sayings of Jesus for systematic analysis but also his inclusion of papyrus fragments and extracanonical sayings alongside the canonical sayings. The book is an invaluable fund of information for further work on the teaching of Jesus, the Q material, and the sayings of Jesus in canonical and extracanonical literature. Moreover, Crossan's display of data is excellent. In the midst of detailed analysis, the reader is given tables, section headings, and clarifying sentences which position the reader throughout the book. In this way, Crossan makes the tradition of Jesus' sayings accessible in a hitherto unparalleled manner, and he invites us through his clear approach to engage in conversation with him. In my view, Crossan's *In Fragments* is an excellent vehicle for a transition to a new era of investigation of the aphorisms of Jesus. Therefore, I will set forth a socio-rhetorical approach in a framework that probes his analysis under three headings: How we begin influences where we go; What we look for influences what we see; and How we relate an aphorism to settings and other aphorisms influences how we understand the tradition.

How we begin influences where we go

Crossan's beginning point is an extremely important aspect of his book, and we will use discussions from rhetorical treatises in Mediterranean antiquity, modern analysis of proverbs in the Hebrew Bible, and rhetorical analysis of folklore in various cultures to reflect upon it. Crossan's beginning point is a discussion of the nature of aphorisms, which establishes a framework for detailed analysis of 40 of the approximately 102 synoptic sayings which could be considered wisdom sayings. In form, he says, an aphorism is like a proverb. The real difference lies in purpose and function. A proverb presents collective wisdom; an aphorism presents a personal vision through a personal voice. An aphorism receives its initial authority from the person to whom it is attributed. Then it earns its authoritative status by offering a new solution to an old problem or an old solution in a new form.[7] When articulated in an aphorism, the new solution, the new form, or the new combination of solution and form has the quality of originality. Thus, according to Crossan, an aphorism presents newly formed content which an auditor hears as an original pronouncement by a person with a creative, personal vision.

From the perspective of rhetorical discussions contemporary with Jesus and the Gospels, Crossan's distinction between proverb and

---

[7] Ibid., 4.

aphorism is an appropriate beginning point for a study of sayings attributed to Jesus. The common Greek term for proverb is γνώμη. Theon of Alexandria, who is one of our most important sources since he writes in Greek toward the end of the first century CE and reflects a point of view based on first century activity,[8] says that a γνώμη has four basic qualities. First, it is not attributed to a specific person; second, it makes a general statement; third, it is concerned with matters useful in life; and fourth, it is a saying and not an action.[9] To this list, William McKane's analysis of proverbs in the Ancient Near Eastern, Egyptian, and Israelite literature suggests the importance of adding that a proverb may be either concrete or abstract.[10]

It may be well to reflect briefly on these attributes of a proverb. First, a proverb's lack of attribution to a specific person allows any person to apply it without implication that some other person's application was especially informative or authoritative. The saying is restricted or enabled, in the terms of the folklorist Roger Abrahams, by its own "combination of elements of description" and "felicity of phrasing."[11] Second, the "general" nature of a proverb means that its articulation of wisdom is not limited by reference to a "specific" person or group or to a "specific" occasion or event. In this context, "specific" means "precisely specified," like "Socrates," "Pythagoreans," or "the Trojan War." Third, the attribute of "useful in life" means that the proverb is neither simply a joke or retort, nor is it a logical theorem like "all sides of an isosceles triangle are equal." In Aristotle's

---

[8] Welhelm von Christ and Wilhelm Schmid, *Geschichte der griechische Literatur, nachklassische Periode* (2 vols.; 6th ed; Munich: C.H. Beck'sche Verlagsbuchhandlung,1912–1924), 2:460–61; Stanley F. Bonner, *Education in Ancient Rome: From the Elder Cato to the Younger Pliny* (Berkeley: University of California Press, 1977), 251.

[9] T. Christian Walz, *Rhetores Graeci* (9 vols.; Stuttgart: J.G. Cotta, 1832–1836), 1:202, 2–10. Aristotle's definition represents the basis for understanding the γνώμη in antiquity: "A *gnome* is a statement, not however concerning particulars, as, for instance, what sort of a man Iphicrates was, but general; it does not even deal with all general things, as for instance that the straight is the opposite of the crooked, but with the objects of human actions, and with what should be chosen or avoided with reference to them" (*The "Art" of Rhetoric*, 2.21.2). Since Aristotle did not attempt to distinguish between unattributed proverbs and attributed aphorisms (χρείαι), he intermingled proverbs and aphorisms in his analysis. Crossan's work perpetuates this pre-chreia approach without many of the benefits of Aristotle's insights.

[10] William McKane, *Proverbs: A New Approach* (Philadelphia: Westminster, 1970). I am deeply grateful to Professor David M. Gunn, now at Columbia Theological Seminary, Decatur, Georgia, not only for making McKane's study available to me when it was difficult to find another copy, but also for calling to my attention Carole R. Fontaine's *Traditional Sayings in the Old Testament: A Contextual Study* (Bible and Literature Series 5; Sheffield: Almond Press, 1982), which contains an excellent survey of Old Testament and folklore research as well as her own contextual analysis of proverbs.

[11] Roger Abrahams, "Introductory Remarks to a Rhetorical Theory of Folklore," *Journal of American Folklore* 81 (1968): 151.

terms, a proverb deals with "objects of human actions, and with what should be chosen or avoided with reference to them."[12] For this reason, a proverb may be applied by any individual to circumstances that confront daily living. Fourth, a proverb is a saying rather than an action. In other words, it is speech action which combines elements of description with felicity of phrasing rather than speech which rehearses someone else's speech or action. Fifth, while a proverb is not "specific," it may be "concrete" rather than abstract. Something which is tangible, like a shirt, is concrete; something which is intangible, like hope, is abstract. When these become objects of human action in the form of making a shirt or making a wish, both are concrete. Yet a concrete situation need not be "specific." Proverbs do not speak in terms of specific persons or specific occasions. Accordingly, "weaving a garment" is concrete; "Penelope weaving a garment" is specific. William McKane has observed that:

> The paradox of the "proverb" is that it acquires immortality because of its particularity [concreteness]; that because of its lack of explicitness [specificity], its allusiveness or even opaqueness, it does not become an antique, but awaits continually the situation to illumine for which it was coined.[13]

It is important, in other words, to distinguish "specificity" or "explicitness" from "concreteness." A proverb may be either concrete or abstract, but it is not limited by reference to an explicitly specified person or occasion.

Crossan's use of "a stitch in time saves nine" is an excellent example of what the ancients meant by a γνώμη. It circulates without attribution to a specific person; it is general, not specific like "If George makes a stitch in time, he will save nine"; it can be and has been applied to various situations in daily life; it is a saying rather than an action, and it is concrete rather than abstract.

While Crossan's use of the term and approach to the proverb is akin to the rhetorician's use of the term and approach to the γνώμη, his understanding of aphorism is part of their understanding of χρεία. As Theon says:

> every concise γνώμη, if it is attributed to a person, makes a χρεία.[14]

---

[12] *The "Art" of Rhetoric*, 2.21.2.
[13] McKane, *Proverbs*, 414. Square brackets added.
[14] Quoted in Walz, *Rhetores Graeci*, 1:202, 1.

It is understandable that Crossan does not want to use the term χρεία, since a χρεία may be constituted by either a saying or an action. In the words of Theon:

> A χρεία is a concise statement (ἀπόφασις) or action attributed with aptness to some specific (ὡρισμένον) person or something analogous to a person.[15]

The term "aphorism" is an appropriate term to use for a saying attributed to a specific person, since the term captures the ἀπο- of ἀπόφασις (a statement "from") and the ὡρισμ- of ὡρισμένον (specific) in the definition of a χρεία. The specificity of an aphorism derives, as we shall see more clearly below, both from its attribution to a specific (ὡρισμένον) person and from the implication that it speaks from within the horizons (ὥρισμα) of a specific person's thought and action. Thus, an aphorism is appropriately "a saying attributed to a specific person and perceived within the horizons of that person's wisdom and action."

Crossan's next step is to distinguish an aphorism from a proverb on the basis of "personal" in contrast to "collective" wisdom. Again his terminology is appropriate, but here we get a lack of clarification that haunts the remaining analysis. Theon observed three attributes of personal wisdom in the aphorism, and analysis shows that these observations obtain for the aphorisms of Jesus. First, the personal aspect emerges in the attribution of the saying to a specific person. This means that an aphorism must not be isolated from the person to whom it is attributed. Second, personal wisdom as expressed in an aphorism may or may not be concerned with daily living, while a proverb always has this concern. Third, personal wisdom in an aphorism may be "general" or "specific," while it is always "general" in a proverb.[16] To this we add a fourth observation that either a proverb or an aphorism may be abstract or concrete. Analysis of these aspects of personal wisdom in aphorisms can lead us into the inner workings of the sayings attributed to Jesus in early Christian tradition. In contrast, Crossan's analysis does not engage the inner workings of Jesus' aphorisms, because it does not enter the inner world of the aphorism as an attributed saying which is general or specific, which may or may not concern daily living, and which may be either concrete or abstract.

A good way to begin to see the lack of clarification in Crossan's analysis is to observe what he does *not* probe in his discussion of the proverb "a stitch in time saves nine." His major interest, as mentioned

---

[15] Quoted in ibid., 201, 27–29. See the Greek text and discussion in Vernon K. Robbins, "Pronouncement Stories and Jesus' Blessing of the Children a Rhetorical Approach," *Semeia* 29 (1983): 45–51.

[16] Theon in Walz, *Rhetores Graeci*, 1:202, 5–7.

above, is to make the appropriate observation that the proverb and the aphorism may have the same form, but the proverb presents "collective" wisdom while the aphorism presents "personal" wisdom. For this reason, he gives special attention to the form and felicity of phrasing of "a stitch in time saves nine" to show why it is such an excellent proverb.[17] The weakness of this analysis lies in the failure to ask us to notice that the "Stitch" proverb is "general" rather than specific, "concrete" rather than abstract, and concerned with something useful for living. The "general" quality of the proverb is present in two aspects: (a) an absence of personal pronouns allows anyone to be included in it, and (b) its wisdom is grounded in general knowledge. Let us take the absence of personal pronouns first. The proverb may potentially include anyone, even the speaker and the auditor, without explicitly including or excluding anyone, because no personal pronouns limit its direction. To say this another way, any speaker or auditor may add a first, second, or third person pronoun mentally to this proverb as follows:

> a stitch in time (made by him, her, you, or me) saves nine (stitches by him, her, you, or me).

The general, inclusive nature of this proverb is supported by general knowledge about a tear or hole in a garment. Anyone who has stitched a garment, seen a person stitch a garment, or seen the results of someone's stitching or not stitching can readily understand the proverb. The general nature of this proverb is strengthened by its concreteness. The concrete image of making a stitch in a garment grounds the saying in experienced reality that gives rise to the general wisdom that "it is good to stitch a tear or hole in a garment." The proverb does not, however, simply present the general wisdom as a thesis. It activates the thesis in the form of general advice -- the form of rhetoric the ancients called συμβουλετικός (advisory) and which we translate as "deliberative."[18] The "general" advice based on concrete data concerns daily life. It can be, and has been, applied by many people to a variety of daily circumstances. The ancients saw this concern for daily life in proverbs, and by this means distinguished a proverb such as this from a saying attributed to a specific person.

The approach we are using to distinguish a proverb from an aphorism means, of course, that a proverb can be made into an aphorism simply by attributing it to a specific person. Crossan himself observes that:

---

[17] Crossan, *In Fragments*, 12–13.
[18] George A. Kennedy, *New Testament Interpretation through Rhetorical Criticism* (Chapel Hill: University of North Carolina Press, 1984), 19–20.

> Put crudely but accurately: "A stitch in time saves nine" is a *Gnome,* but "Jesus said: a stitch in time saves nine" is a *Chreia.*[19]

This is a very important point. When "a stitch in time" exists as a proverb, it is available for any person to apply to a situation as that person considers it appropriate. In contrast, when it is asserted that "Jesus said it," the auditor searches for, infers, or implies Jesus' application of it. In other words, a proverb like this is applied by means of analogy. When it exists as a proverb, the initiative lies with any person to apply it to a situation or topic he/she considers to be analogous to stitching a garment in time. When, however, it exists as an attributed aphorism, the issue becomes, "To what did that person apply the proverb?" If attributed to Jesus, the auditor of the aphorism would search for a characteristic emphasis or occasion in Jesus' action or speech for which it would serve as an analogy. For example, a person might wonder if Jesus said "a stitch in time saves nine" to present an analogy for preparation for or participation in the kingdom. But if we consider the proverb to be inappropriate as an aphorism of Jesus, and I think we should, we should ask why we readily accept it as a proverb but resist it within the perceived horizons of Jesus' speech and action. And if we would accept it as an aphorism of Benjamin Franklin, we should probe why we would consider it appropriate for him but not appropriate for Jesus.

There is, in fact, an aphorism attributed to Jesus which has an interesting relation to the "Stitch" proverb. It exists in an aphoristic compound (combination of two similar aphorisms) which Crossan entitles "Patches and Wineskins":

> And Jesus said to them ...
>
> "No one sews a piece of unshrunk cloth on an old garment; if he/she does, the patch tears away from it, the new from the old, and a worse tear is made. And no one puts new wine into old wineskins; if he/she does, the wine will burst the skins, and the wine is lost, and so are the skins; but new wine is for fresh skins" (Mark 2:21–22).[20]

The formed content in this saying presents concrete wisdom similar to "a stitch in time saves nine." There are, however, a number of differences. First, the "Stitch" proverb focuses entirely on a concrete action and its results. Advice emerges directly from deliberation on an action. In contrast, "no one sews a piece of unshrunk cloth on an old garment," or "no one puts new wine into old wineskins" gives prominence to a personal actor in a setting of negative deliberation. To be precise, deliberation occurs through a person who has acted improper-

---

[19] Crossan, *In Fragments,* 229.
[20] Ibid., 122.

ly. From the perspective of classical rhetoric, the personalization of the issue takes a significant step toward either judicial or epideictic rhetoric. Judicial rhetoric accuses or defends a person in a setting where auditors will present a verdict of guilty or innocent. Epideictic rhetoric praises or censures a person in a setting which confirms the values of the auditors.[21] The emphatic position of the personalized negative ("no one") at the beginning of the "Patches and Wineskins" compound focuses the attention on a person engaged in an inappropriate form of activity. This posture could serve a deliberative purpose, that is, its goal could be to advise a person to do the opposite. In a deliberative setting, however, it would be natural to indicate the kind of person who would *not* do this (e.g., no one *who is wise* sews ... or puts ...). The omission of a qualifier intensifies the personal engagement. In other words, "no one does it this way" implies that the speaker is either censuring someone who is unthinkingly combining the new with the old or defending someone who has engaged appropriately in activity which varies from the conventional (old) pattern. This leads to the next observation.

Each aphorism in the "Patches and Wineskins" compound contains a rationale clause which gives argumentative support to the initial assertion. In the terminology of classical rhetoric, these aphorisms are rhetorical syllogisms called enthymemes.[22] The discussion of enthymemes arose in the setting of the two basic forms of argument rhetoricians perceived to be available to anyone -- inductive and deductive argumentation. Inductive argumentation produces a series of examples or analogies to support a proposition. The existence of a saying about a garment and a saying about wine in this compound functions inductively, since two examples support an underlying proposition through a gathering of additional, similar evidence. Deductive argumentation, in contrast, produces a logical syllogism. The most famous logical syllogism, undoubtedly, is:

> *General premise*: All men are mortal.
> *Specific premise*: Socrates is a man.
> *Conclusion*: Therefore, Socrates is mortal.

This syllogism argues from the general to the specific, from all men to Socrates. The nature of the general premise is to ground the syllogism in general knowledge. The nature of the specific premise is to relate the general knowledge to a specific case. The conclusion, then, applies the remaining term in the general premise to the specific case.

---

[21] Kennedy, *New Testament Interpretation*, 19–20.
[22] Ibid., 7, 16–17, 49–51, 56–61.

In a setting of rhetorical discourse the speaker will usually omit either the general or specific premise, since he/she presupposes the auditors will provide it. Thus, in the form of an enthymeme (a rhetorical syllogism), the statement could be either "Socrates is mortal, because all men are mortal" or "Socrates is mortal, because he is a man."[23] The syllogism in the "Patches and Wineskins" compound is:

> *Hypothetical Concrete Premise*: If someone puts an unshrunk cloth on a new garment or new wine into old wineskins, he/she tears the garment, bursts the wineskins, and loses the wine.
>
> *Conclusion*: Therefore, no one sews an unshrunk cloth on a new garment or puts new wine into old wineskins.

This compound aphorism gains its power not only from inductive argumentation which produces two examples (patches and wineskins) but deductive argumentation which uses a concrete premise to support a conclusion. The point is that the aphoristic compound does not simply "combine elements of description with felicity of phrasing." Rather, it combines initial negative assertions with hypothetical concrete cases either to censure or to defend someone's action. This is the stuff of which aphorisms are made, and they reflect the "personal" wisdom to which Crossan refers. In other words, this aphoristic compound is an argumentative package which reflects the aphoristic tradition of Jesus rather than general proverbial tradition. In fact, this compound probably provided the setting for the formulation of the general proverb, "New wine is for new wineskins" (Mark 2:22c; cf. Matt 9:17c/Luke 9:38) and for reflection on the known proverb "The old is good" (Luke 9:39).[24]

If an aphorism has an enthymematic form, analysis of its rhetorical logic is a beginning point for displaying both its internal and external aspects as a unit of communication. Among other things, the rhetorical posturing in the aphorism is important to consider. Instead of simply presenting deliberative exhortation in the form of "new wine for new wineskins," the compound presents a personalized argument postured against an alternative form of action. In other words, while a proverb like "a stitch in time saves nine" is designed to move a person from inaction (not stitching) to action (stitching), the "Patches and Wineskins" compound is designed to censure or defend a particular form of action. The "personal" nature of the aphorisms shows an investment in a situation where an action has been questioned in relation to an established (old) practice. In these aphorisms, then, there is a special "post-

---

[23] For a very important recent discussion of the enthymeme, see Thomas Conley, "The Enthymeme in Perspective," *Quarterly Journal of Speech* 70 (1984): 168–87.

[24] Cf. Sir 9:10; Pirke Aboth 4:20; b.Ber. 51a; Plautus, *Cas.*, 5.

uring": if one has a new garment or new wine, then one will not mix it with the old in a manner that does not work properly. The posturing of the aphorism resides partly in its assertion that "a new thing is available." But beyond this, it cites concrete "negative examples" which can be used whenever anyone questions an action which could be interpreted as "new." It is, then, an argumentative compound arising out of a situation of conflict and designed for argumentation in a setting of conflict. In the synoptic tradition, it is linked specifically to fasting (Mark 2:18–22; Matt 9:14–17; Luke 5:33–39). While a person might think that "not fasting" is "an old thing," regularly encountered in a setting where fasting has been established as a way to show one's faithfulness to a covenant relationship to God, "not fasting" should be understood as part of "a new approach." This aphorism establishes its leverage by presupposing that a particular action is "new" and applying concrete knowledge concerning how to deal with "the new" in appropriate ways.

But there is one additional matter before leaving the "Patches and Wineskins" compound. The inner reasoning in the aphorisms is grounded in basic knowledge about life. Its concrete premises concerning patches and wineskins would be shared by almost anyone anywhere. We should also notice that its concrete premises suggest an underlying general premise like: "No one damages or destroys a thing useful for life." The entire syllogism underlying the compound, therefore, seems to be:

General Premise: No one damages or destroys a thing useful for life.

Hypothetical Concrete Premise: If someone puts an unshrunk cloth on a new garment or new wine into old wineskins, he/she tears the garment, bursts the wineskins, and loses the wine.

Conclusion: Therefore, no one sews an unshrunk cloth on a new garment or new wine into old wineskins.

The recovery of the general premise raises some interesting questions. Was it characteristic of Jesus to support actions which violated established conventions with images from conventional daily living? How does this underlying premise cohere with premises presupposed by other aphorisms attributed to Jesus? A new attempt to reconstruct the teaching of Jesus surely must attempt to uncover the network of presuppositions at work in the action and speech attributed to Jesus. This network can be uncovered and displayed if interpreters will analyze the constituents of argumentation in the speech and action attributed to Jesus.

While the "Patches and Wineskins" compound may be general, concerned with daily living, and concrete, an aphorism may be specific, not concerned with daily living, and abstract. The aphorism Crossan entitles "On Hindering Others" is a good example of the latter, since it is specific, referring to and addressing scribes and Pharisees (or lawyers), it is only useful in daily living if you are a special kind of person, and it is abstract. The aphorism is as follows:

> Then Jesus said to the crowds and to his disciples.... "But woe to you, scribes and Pharisees, hypocrites! because you shut the kingdom of heaven against men; for you neither enter yourselves, nor allow those who would enter to go in" (Matt 23:1, 13).[25]

This aphorism, like the "Patches and Wineskins" compound, is attributed to Jesus. But the "Hindering" aphorism is specific rather than general, since it not only refers to but explicitly addresses scribes and Pharisees (Luke 11:52: lawyers). Also, this aphorism is not based on general knowledge like repairing a garment or making wine, but on a special form of belief, namely: "It is good to enter the kingdom of God." Within the arena of this special belief, the aphorism concerns the habits of the scribes and Pharisees rather than basic daily living. This aphorism, therefore, not only differs from a proverb, but differs from the "Patches and Wineskins" compound by its specificity of reference and address, its grounding in a special form of belief, and its concern with the special habits of the scribes and Pharisees.

It is informative first to compare the "Hindering" aphorism with the proverb "a stitch in time saves nine." In order for the "Stitch" proverb to contain the qualities of the "Hindering" aphorism, it would have to be formulated something like the following:

> Woe to you, seamstresses and garmentmakers, because you prevent people from having sound garments; for you neither stitch them yourselves, nor allow others to stitch.

The process of transforming the "Stitch" proverb through imitation makes a person aware of three constituents in the "Hindering" aphorism. First, there is a harangue against the Pharisees in the form of a statement of woe. Second, a rationale statement presents a general basis for the harangue. Third, an additional statement divides the rationale into two parts (neither entering themselves nor allowing others to enter). The saying, therefore, contains an initial statement, a rationale, and a division of the rationale.

---

[25] Crossan, *In Fragments*, 30.

When we analyze the "Hindering" aphorism as an enthymeme, we gain a clearer understanding of its attributes. In syllogistic form, it looks as follows:

Specific Premise: You [scribes and Pharisees] shut the kingdom from men.

Division of the Specific Premise: You [scribes and Pharisees] neither enter yourselves nor allow others who would enter to go in.

Conclusion: Woe [is] to you, scribes and Pharisees, hypocrites.

In this instance, as well as in the "Patches and Wineskins" compound, the general premise is not articulated. Rather, (1) a specific premise applies a presupposed general premise to a specific case, (2) a division of the specific premise partitions the "shutting" activity into "neither entering yourselves nor allowing others to enter," and (3) a conclusion announces that scribes and Pharisees are cursed as a result of their activity. The general premise, which is presupposed but not stated, appears to be: "Cursed be [woe to] anyone who keeps men from entering the kingdom." This presupposed premise is two steps away from a general premise about "daily living" in general culture. The first step away results from a lack of "general" wisdom about "the kingdom" in general culture. Most people in most societies would have no knowledge about whatever "kingdom" is referred to in this aphorism. The second step away concerns general wisdom in a cultural milieu like first century Judaism. Probably most first century Jewish people either presupposed for themselves or knew the meaning of the presupposition: "It is good to enter the kingdom." One wonders how widespread the presupposition might have been that "it is good to help others enter the kingdom." The "Hindering" aphorism presupposes an activation of this latter presupposition in a negative form reminiscent of curses that accompany the violation of a covenant: "Cursed be anyone who keeps men from entering the kingdom." This means that the "Hindering" aphorism presupposes a negative aphorism which is assumed by a particular Jewish group to be one of the curses that accompanies their special covenant with God. This curse would likely be one step away from a more general Jewish presupposition that it is good to enter the kingdom. Therefore, the aphorism as we have it is two steps away from "general" wisdom, since it not only presupposes a premise within Jewish culture but a premise within a special group within that cultural arena. At this second remove, you and I are asked to contemplate our own actions only via the actions of two specific kinds of Jews who are censured, namely scribes and Pharisees (or lawyers).

We may draw together our observations thus far by noting that the "Hindering" aphorism contains intense epideictic censure (commonly called "invective") in a setting of role opposition.[26] The intensity of the censuring distinguishes it not only from the "deliberative" quality of the "Stitch" proverb but also from the milder judicial or epideictic tone of the "Patches and Wineskins" compound. As mentioned above, the epideictic mode achieves its goals through people as the subject matter. By this means, general virtues and vices are identified and targeted for emulation or avoidance. In contrast to proverbs, and to aphorisms like those in the "Patches and Wineskins" compound, the "Hindering" aphorism is "specific" internally, referring explicitly to the scribes and Pharisees. Yet the premise for censuring them is abstract. One is interested in knowing how the Pharisees shut the kingdom off from others. There is no demonstration of "concrete" knowledge about the Pharisees either in the premise or the division of the premise. The basis for the accusation is "abstract," without tangible substance. In other words, the aphorism censures a specific group by means of a negative caricature which has no concrete substance. In form and substance, the rationale for the censure is simply a logical reversal of a goal presupposed among Christians who believe they are blessed if they help others enter the kingdom. But, according to Aristotle, we can expect this kind of creation of the opposite in both judicial and epideictic material, since both kinds of rhetoric rely heavily on enthymemes which introduce contraries in a framework of deductive logic about the past. As he says:

> Enthymemes are most suitable for judicial speakers, because the past, by reason of its obscurity, above all lends itself to the investigation of causes and to demonstrative proof. Such are nearly all the materials of praise or blame [epideictic rhetoric], the things which those who praise or blame should keep in view, and the sources of encomia and invective; for when these are known their contraries are obvious, since blame is derived from the contrary things.[27]

Invective, therefore, may derive simply from contrary deduction without concern for specific grounding. The "Hindering" aphorism appears to be such an instance. It confirms the attitude of a group which feels threatened by "scribes and Pharisees," and it confirms the attitude through an epideictic enthymeme containing no "concrete" subject matter within its premise or conclusion. This kind of aphorism is not only different in nature from the "Stitch" proverb, but it is different from the "Patches and Wineskins" aphorisms as well. It will be

---

[26] See Robbins, *Jesus the Teacher*, 110–13.
[27] Aristotle, *The "Art" of Rhetoric*, 1.9.40–41.

necessary not only to negotiate the relation of this aphorism to proverbs, but it will be necessary to analyze its relation to other aphorisms attributed to Jesus in the tradition. It would be good, therefore, to gather together aphorisms like this one and analyze the relation of their presuppositions and assertions to one another.

The interpretive challenge with the "Patches and Wineskins" compound and the "Hindering" aphorism differ, therefore. With the "Patches and Wineskins" compound, we need to know what the unshrunk cloth and the new wine are meant to represent. In other words, while the aphorism has an enthymematic form, its inner content works inductively through analogy. Are there other analogies in the tradition which, alongside this one, help to explain some aspect of that to which the "unshrunk cloth" and the "new wine" are analogous? Are the majority of these analogies based on conventional values in daily life? Aphorisms which communicate inductively through analogy should be gathered and their presuppositions and assertions should be analyzed systematically. In contrast, the "Hindering" aphorism works deductively. Supposedly, no analogy is necessary for "scribes and Pharisees." The speaker has identified a group and censured them with deductive logic based on the premise that anyone is cursed who hinders others from entering the kingdom. Much of the power of the "Hindering" aphorism, therefore, lies in its deductive logic. Its weakness, however, lies in its lack of grounding in general knowledge. It not only presupposes a special belief that it is possible to help people into or keep them out of the kingdom, and a person is blessed or cursed accordingly, but it presupposes that we will accept the invective against the scribes and Pharisees without concrete evidence.

It would appear, then, that Crossan's discussion needs precision based on analysis of the reasoning and argumentation in aphorisms. This kind of analysis will seek to clarify presuppositions underlying the assertions and exhibit the deductive and inductive reasoning which give the aphorisms their persuasive power. Also, this approach will start the interpreter on a program of establishing the network of communication which exists within presuppositions and arguments in the aphoristic tradition. Such a program will begin to exhibit the relation of "radical rhetoric" (grounded only in authoritative statement) to "reasoned argument" (grounded in general knowledge) in early Christian tradition[28] and establish a basis for a new humanistic and theological appraisal of the speech and action attributed to Jesus.

---

[28] Kennedy, *New Testament Interpretation*, 7–8, 93, 96, 104–106.

What we look for influences what we see

The next step in Crossan's agenda is to discuss how aphorisms are transmitted in oral tradition.[29] Aphorisms exist in oral memory, according to Crossan, as *ipsissima structura*, not *ipsissima verba*. Basic to an aphorism, then, is a "structure" which he calls an "aphoristic core."

Beginning with this premise, he draws a boundary between performancial variations and hermeneutical variations. Performancial variations occur within the basic core or structure in the form of contraction, expansion, conversion (from negative to positive, or vice versa), substitution (of one synonymous term for another), or transposition (of first for second part, or vice versa). These variations, he suggests, do not change the meaning substantially. In the midst of performancial variations, hermeneutical variations (by which he means "interpretational" variations) occur by adding commentary or reconfiguring the saying.

Crossan's approach makes a significant advance in the discussion of aphorisms in early Christian tradition. Yet, the actual application of the approach has severe limitations. In my opinion, "what we look for" in aphorisms is the initial issue. Crossan's approach leads him to find "structures," and by this means he "generalizes" aphorisms into proverbial forms. To put it another way, Crossan begins with a "semiotic" analysis, and this approach restricts the semantic dimensions which make the sayings aphorisms rather than proverbs. The performancial variations Crossan sees in aphorisms represent the alternative selections and substitutions Jakobson assigns to the metaphoric aspect of language.[30] These variations occur in proverbs as well as aphorisms. Crossan's discussion lacks analysis of "meaning through contiguity," the aspect Jakobson terms metonymic. The first element of contiguity must be the association of the aphorism with the person to whom it is attributed. The remaining elements of contiguity lie within the aphorism itself and the perceived horizons in which that aphorism functioned during the life of the person to whom it is attributed.[31] I think the best way to confront this problem is to continue with the "other way of seeing" with which this essay began.

---

[29] Crossan, *In Fragments*, 37–42.

[30] Roman Jakobson and Morris Halle, *Fundamentals of Language* (The Hague: Mouton, 1971), 68–96

[31] Exceptionally helpful analyses are available in the works by Eleanor A. Forster, "The Proverb and the Superstition Defined" (Ph.D. diss., University of Pennsylvania, 1968); Heda Jason, "A Multidimensional Approach to Oral Literature," *Current Anthropology* 10 (1969): 413–26; Barbara Kirschenblatt-Gimblett, "Toward a Theory of Proverb Meaning," *Proverbium* 22 (1973): 821–27; Carolyn Ann Parker, "Aspects of a Theory of Proverbs: Contexts and Messages in Swahili" (Ph.D. diss., University of Washington, 1973); and Fontaine, *Traditional Sayings*.

Instead of seeing "structures" in aphorisms, I see "postured meaning effects." A postured meaning effect contains basic rhetorical effect in a tensive framework.[32] A good way to see the difference is again to see what is lacking in Crossan's analysis. The "For and Against" aphorism[33] is a good place to start, though I will call it the "Against or Not Against" aphorism. In Mark and Q the aphorism reads as follows:

> But Jesus said, "... For he that is not against us (Luke: you) is for us (Luke: you)" (Mark 9:39, 40; cf. Luke 9:50).

> Knowing their thoughts, he said to them, "... He who is not with me is against me, and he who does not gather with me scatters" (Matt 12:25, 30/Luke 11:17, 23).

This aphorism, in contrast to the aphorisms on "Hindering" or "Patches and Wineskins," is constituted solely by an aphoristic premise. In other words, instead of functioning as an argumentative unit with a premise and a conclusion, it functions either as a rationale in an enthymeme or as a thesis which contains an aura of proverbial grounding. Internally, the images lack concreteness. Instead of "he who does not *speak* against you" or "he who does not *hit* you," it refers simply to "he who is not *against* or with...." In other words, its subject matter is more concerned with "the qualities of people" than "the objects of human actions." The "personalized" concern of the aphorism is present not only in the "he who is not ... is," but also in the "us," "you," or "me" which are present in the different performances of the aphorism. The aphorism adopts personal pronouns which orient it toward specific people in specific situations. With these attributes, the aphorism functions intrinsically in the arena of judicial or epideictic rhetoric with a concern for evaluating or locating people, rather than the arena of deliberative rhetoric which concerns future action. If the aphorism used concrete terms like "friend" or "enemy" instead of "for" or "against," its appeal in the realm of general knowledge would be strengthened. In the absence of these concrete terms, its strength lies in the potential of the phrases to evoke such concrete images.

Surely the most interesting challenge of the "Against or Not Against" aphorism lies in the variation between "he who is *not against* is for ..." and "he who is *not with* ... is against ..." in the different performances in the tradition. How shall we explain the potential of the aphorism for this variation, and how shall we understand the significance of the variation?

---

[32] For a discussion of "tensive," see Robert C. Tannehill, *The Sword of His Mouth*, (Semeia Supplements 1; Philadelphia: Fortress, 1975), 12 14, 51–56, 152–6.

[33] Crossan, *In Fragments*, 47–50.

The basic item Crossan observes in the five available performances of this aphorism is the "substitution of 'for' and 'against' for one another within the same chiastic framework."[34]

> In all cases, in Greek, the construction is chiastic: is/us//us/is. This formal unity underlines the fact that the inclusive (not against, for) and the exclusive (not for, against) versions are simple performancial variations stressing in both cases the impossibility of *neutrality*.[35]

Through a "structural" analysis, then, Crossan locates a common idea, namely "the impossibility of neutrality," among all the variations. The basic problem with such an approach is that it reduces the aphorism to an "independent, general principle." In other words, the approach bypasses the specificity of the aphorism, wherever that specificity lies, and treats the aphorism as though it had the general nature of a proverb.

In my perspective and terminology, an interpreter may locate the particular qualities of an aphorism by looking for the "postured meaning effect" rather than simply a structure. A postured meaning effect has two essential qualities: (a) tensive pattern and (b) rhetorical effect. A tensive pattern is a semantic structure rather than a semiotic structure. A semantic structure has some aspect of specificity, and this specificity signals a meaning potential within the horizons of activity and thought associated with the person to whom the aphorism is attributed.[36] In addition, the aphorism contains rhetorical effect, that is, an ordering of words and thoughts that postures the saying in relation to alternatives that may exist in the culture. An aphorism has a close relation to one or more social situations associated with the person to whom it is attributed. When it is applied to different social situations, it adapts internally unless it has sufficient attributes of a proverb to maintain its internal details. The adaptation of an aphorism occurs in special ways, since the tensive pattern and rhetorical effect interact with the situation.

Crossan's structural analysis misrepresents the common features of the "Against or Not Against" aphorism when it reduces them to "for and against" and the chiastic arrangement "is/us//us/is." The postured meaning effect common to all the performances is rather: "location may or may not imply opposition, depending on the situation." This meaning effect is present in a sequence where a negated "universal particular" clause introducing personal relationship vis-à-vis spatial

---

[34] Ibid., 47–50.

[35] Ibid., 49.

[36] Cf. Paul Ricoeur, *The Rule of Metaphor: Multi-disciplinary Studies of the Creation and the Meaning of Language* (Toronto: University of Toronto Press, 1977), 129–33.

location serves as the subject of a positive predication which contains a contrary constituent with the same personal pronoun (either included or elided). The negation creates a framework for contraries (not with/against; not against/for), the combination of personal relationship and spatial location creates a framework for substitution of terms (for/with), and the ordering of words and thoughts requires that the transposition (against/ -; -/against) be accompanied by the conversion (not against/-; not -/against). The result is a "postured meaning effect" which adapts to particular situations in particular ways.

The postured meaning effect is present in the Mark/Q tradition in the form:

> He who is not (in a particular relation or location to a person) is (in a particular relation to that person).

The rhetorical posture of the aphorism lies in the tensive pattern and rhetorical effect of "he who is not ... is ..." The special bias of this structured, rhetorical pattern is its focus on opposition (being against) rather than alliance (being for). The issue of opposition (either opposing or being opposed) lies within the postured meaning effect in such a manner that its positive form (being against) or its negative form (not being against) is central to the aphorism. Around either a positive or negative expression of opposition lies the theme of alliance (being for), location (being not with, far, or near), or a combination of opposition and location (scattering or not gathering with). The postured meaning effect, then, does not allow a conversion from "not against" to "for," but from "not against" to "against."

The special nature of the tensive pattern keeps the topic of "opposition" central and "alliance" subordinate. This is a result of the negative posturing in the tensive pattern. This aphorism differs, for example, from "he who receives you, receives me, and he who receives me receives him who sent me" (Matt 10:40).[37] The absence of any negative components in this aphorism allows it to be converted into its opposite: "He who rejects you rejects me, and he who rejects me rejects him who sent me" (Luke 10:16).[38] In contrast to the "Against or Not Against" aphorism, the "Receiving the Sender" aphorism is based on general knowledge about sending and receiving, and it has a structure which can easily be converted. It is also closely related to proverbs like "he who does not honor the son does not honor the father who sent him" (John 5:23) and "every one whom the master of the house sends to do his business ought to be received as him who sent him"

---

[37] Crossan, *In Fragments*, 106.
[38] Ibid.

(Ignatius, Eph. 6:1). But the "Against or Not Against" aphorism does not maintain contact with "presupposed general knowledge" in the manner of the "Receiving the Sender" aphorism.

The special nature of the "Against or Not Against" aphorism is exhibited in the manner in which it moves closer or further away from "general proverbial" articulation. When the performance of the aphorism speaks about being "with," the leader is speaking personally from the perspective of being "with me" (Matt 12:30/Luke 11:23 [twice]). When it speaks of being "for," the group is the matter of concern in either "for us" or "for you" (Mark 9:40/Luke 9:50b/POxy 1224). Only "against" or "not against" are found in connection with both the leader and the group. If a person reads "he who is not against us is for us" as though it were the general proverb "he who is not an enemy is a friend," he/she will miss the aphoristic nature of the saying. The saying is not meant to fit general situations in life like "a friend in need is a friend indeed," "birds of a feather flock together," or "one man's friend is another man's enemy." Rather, it reflects the specific situation of a group which identifies with a leader, and the issue is whether people who identify with this leader should reject people who do not join the group, since there are people who reject the leader. The aphoristic tradition, attributing authoritative speech to the leader, presents a perspective about the leader and a perspective about the group in variant performances of the same aphorism.

Luke moves the aphorism toward a proverb when he has "he who is not against you is for you." In this form, the aphorism approaches "he who is not your enemy is your friend." Crossan's analysis "proverbializes" the tradition further by reducing all the aphoristic performances to "he who is not for you (your friend) is against you (your enemy)" and "he who is not against you (your enemy) is for you (your friend)." Once he has done this, he calls it the "For or Against Aphorism" and proposes that it argues for the "impossibility of neutrality" (a person is either a friend or an enemy). Indeed, aphorisms may be nurtured into proverbs. In fact, most, if not all, proverbs undoubtedly began as aphorisms. As we saw with the "Patches and Wineskins" compound, early Christian tradition exhibits the process in which aphorisms were "generalized" or "proverbialized" as they were used as vehicles of communication and argumentation in Mediterranean society and culture. Unfortunately, New Testament scholarship often has gravitated toward the proverbialized form which could be more easily applied to "modern situations" than to the aphoristic forms which transmit the specific situations from which they arose and in which they functioned.

This analysis means that an aphorism's specificity expresses itself in terms of specific situations pertaining to "this" person and "this" group. "He who is not against us/you is for us/you" represents a specific stance by a specific group. It does not appear, for example, that the Dead Sea Community held the view that one who was not against them was for them, and one wonders how broadly such a view might have been held by other groups during the first century. On the other hand, "he who is not with me is against me" could be expressed by any number of individuals who desired to be understood or selected as a leader. Therefore, both aphorisms may reflect a postured meaning effect arising from Jesus' speech. It is informative that "he who is not against us/you is for us/you" is linked with a specific situation in which a man was performing exorcisms in the name of Jesus but did not identify himself with the group. This performance of the aphorism, therefore, is likely to reflect a special view held by Jesus. The form of the aphorism with "me" in it could well have been said by Jesus, since it could have been said by almost any person wishing to be viewed as a leader.

The import of this analysis is to assert that performances of aphorisms presuppose specific situations. In other words, specific social situations are an integral part of their content. Crossan's analysis misses this crucial aspect of aphorisms when it collapses them into a common structure. The performance, "He that is not against ( ) is for ( )," presupposes a situation in which one or more people who are not located in the group which identifies with Jesus use some of the group's tactics but do not do anything to oppose or harm the group. In contrast, the performance, "He that is not with ( ) is against ( )," presupposes a situation in which one or more people actively oppose, malign, or attempt to hinder the leader. In other words, if a person is a certain kind of "non-enemy" of the group, he/she should not be rejected. On the other hand, if a person is a certain kind of "non-friend" of the leader, he/she will reject the leader. Within these two forms of the aphorism, therefore, lie the specific dynamics of a specific group rather than "general knowledge" about life.

In summary, aphorisms regularly presuppose and arise from specific situations. To say that situations are secondary to them, or to say that an aphorism "circulates" freely, is to misunderstand the function of aphorisms within a tradition and to misconstrue the process of transmission. Proverbs circulate freely, ready for application to situations without internal modification because of their concrete, general nature. Aphorisms, in contrast, arise from specific situations and adapt when applied to other situations. An aphorism may adapt enough to become a proverb. In this case, it has acquired a general quality which allows it to function in various situations without modification.

For Crossan, the variations we have just explored are "performancial" rather than "hermeneutical" variations. A person may wonder why Crossan draws the boundary line between performancial and hermeneutical variations in the manner in which he does. The answer lies partially within the unfortunate heritage of "oral" versus "scribal" culture which has haunted New Testament criticism for many years. The approach exhibits a misunderstanding of communication through speech and writing in Mediterranean culture. Writers, speakers, and teachers in first century Mediterranean culture presupposed a close relation between speaking and writing. As a result, Hellenistic education interwove four activities: (1) oral replication, (2) oral composition, (3) scribal replication, and (4) scribal composition.[39] New Testament interpreters regularly introduce a lack of precision by collapsing these four activities into only oral or scribal activity as though oral activity were of one basic kind and scribal activity were of another kind. Both oral and scribal activity, however, interwove replication and composition. Crossan's "hermeneutical variations" are based primarily on the establishment of a written source behind another written form.[40] By this means, he gets artificial leverage on the analysis of a performance he considers to have occurred in the presence of a written source. Most writers and speakers, including the Gospel writers, followed a principle of replication or composition as they chose.[41] Crossan's positing of a "written source behind another written form," therefore, regularly is superfluous and often is misleading. Whether written or oral, or whether written or oral in the presence of a written or oral form, the test lies in the wording of the aphorism and its function in its setting. In fact, even oral or scribal replication may entail some kind of hermeneutical variation, because the performance may relate the postured meaning effect to different data.[42]

A basic implication of the discussion above is to call attention to the artificial nature of source analysis, that is, the artificing which comes from the analyst who posits that one saying is one source of another. Because of the artificial nature of source analysis (which Crossan considers to be one aspect of "transmissional analysis"), it should not be allowed to obstruct analysis which exhibits both the inner and the relational nature of the data in its present form and setting. Instead of engaging in source analysis, the analyst should examine the available

---

[39] See the stages of teaching during primary education (oral and scribal replication) and the preliminary exercises in grammar school (oral and scribal composition) in Bonner, *Education in Ancient Rome*, 165–80, 25–76.

[40] Crossan, *In Fragments*, 54–56.

[41] See Robbins, "Pronouncement Stories," 48–70.

[42] For changes in a proverb's meaning when it is placed in different contexts, see Fontaine, *Traditional Saying*, 28–71.

performances of an aphorism in the tradition. If a postured meaning effect maintains itself throughout three, four, or more performances which relate the aphorism to different situations, the tenacity of the meaning effect makes it necessary to consider whether that meaning effect is an early datum in the Jesus tradition. Analysis of the inner nature and relation of the postured meaning effect to presuppositions and arguments in the overall network of communication in sayings and actions attributed to Jesus will serve as the testing ground for distinguishing early from late tradition.

Crossan proposes that instances of transposition, conversion, and substitution are performancial variations which do not make significant changes in an aphorism. What he should propose is that performances which contain variations in the form of transposition, conversion, and substitution bear a particular kind of similarity to one another, namely, they reveal a postured meaning effect which possessed a certain kind of tenacity in the tradition. The tenacity of these postured meaning effects is extremely important, and they surely are a basic means for talking about the teaching of Jesus himself. But most performancial variations are hermeneutical variations, because the variation represents part of a different configuration among speech, action, and reference within the horizons of the person to whom the aphorism is attributed. The interpreter must pursue the meaning of the variations that exist in an individual performance by finding the relation of the variations to a situation presupposed in the tradition.

How we relate an aphorism to settings and other aphorisms influences how we understand the tradition

Since Crossan envisioned his task as gathering variations of aphorisms together, he did not attempt to uncover the relation of presuppositions and arguments in various aphorisms. I have no desire to criticize the task he undertook. In fact, more work must be done to gather all the variations of aphorisms together, since Crossan only displays the variations in 40 aphorisms in the tradition. A basic problem arises, however, when the initial task of gathering all variations of aphorisms generates the model for interpretation, and this is what has happened in Crossan's book. Beginning with variations of single aphorisms, he develops an "aphoristic model" through a principle of addition and agglomeration, instead of attempting to relate the presuppositions and arguments to one another and to settings and actions in the tradition.

Before attempting to show how the interpreter should attempt to uncover the network of relationships among aphorisms, settings, and actions, let us look at the model generated by Crossan. Beginning with single aphorisms, Crossan organizes the aphoristic tradition according to six basic forms it acquires in transmission:

 aphoristic saying
 aphoristic compound
 aphoristic cluster
 aphoristic conclusion
 aphoristic dialogue
 aphoristic story

Three of the forms are distinct from one another primarily on the basis of the number of sayings that comprise the unit. First, the tradition may have the form of an individual saying with as many as four *stichoi*.[43] The essential dimension in these sayings is interaction. The interaction includes parallelism, repetition, and antithesis, but it also includes more subtle dynamics between protagonists, actions and thoughts in verbs, and positive and negative statements set in relation to one another. Second, the tradition may have the form of an aphoristic compound comprised of two sayings integrally linked as a unit.[44] The sayings concerning a new patch on an old garment and new wine in old wineskins (Mark 2:21–22/Matt 9:16–17/Luke 5:36–37/*Gos. Thom.* 47b) existed, suggests Crossan, as an aphoristic compound unified by the theme of impossible combinations.[45] Third are aphoristic clusters.[46] These, Crossan suggests, contain more than two sayings and are unified by common verbs, common forms, common themes, or external unifying structures. Three of the forms are therefore constituted by the content of one, two, or more aphorisms in a transmissional unit. The remaining forms are units which contain narration, conversation, or other discourse as a setting for one or more aphorisms. Unlike the first three forms, therefore, these forms are not constituted entirely by aphorisms. Rather, they present one or more aphorisms in a framework established by some other kind of discourse. In this vein, the fourth form is the aphoristic conclusion.[47] Here, an aphorism occurs at the end of a miracle, a prayer, a parable, a dialogue, or a story. Fifth, the aphoristic tradition may take the form of a dialogue where aphorisms emerge in a series of statements and responses.[48] Sixth and last is the aphoristic story.[49] This kind of story is characterized by "no interaction, dynamics or dialectic between situation and/or address and

---

[43] Crossan, *In Fragments*, 67–119.
[44] Ibid., 120–52.
[45] Ibid,, 121–27.
[46] Ibid., 153–82.
[47] Ibid., 183–226.
[48] Ibid., 227–76.
[49] Ibid., 277–312.

the climactic saying."[50] The story part is simply a "set up" or convenient framework for an independent aphorism. The preceding part often includes a question or statement that could be articulated in the first part of an aphorism, and there is no discrepancy between the question and the statement. Crossan devotes an entire chapter to each form of the aphoristic tradition. This approach gives him an opportunity to present a detailed history of the transmission of traditions in the form of sayings, compounds, clusters, conclusions, dialogues, and stories.

The model Crossan has generated exhibits an interpretational approach based on a principle of "isolation." An aphorism contains "external isolation of formed content," according to Crossan.[51] Therefore, the issue is "whether or not" an aphorism has interacted with any other phenomenon in the tradition, since it may have "circulated freely." This underlying principle leads him to a distinction between "aphoristic" and "dialectic." I would like to pursue issues raised earlier in this essay by addressing this distinction, which Crossan introduces at the beginning of his discussion of aphoristic dialogues.[52] In his words:

There are certain sayings whose only force or whose total force occurs in dialectic with their preceding situation and/or address, be it question, comment, or request. That is the dialectical tradition. And there are other sayings, certainly in the Jesus tradition at least, which appear quite separately as aphoristic sayings and also elsewhere as aphoristic dialogues and stories. As such they are best interpreted within the aphoristic tradition.

In this manner, Crossan isolates aphorisms he considers to be "aphoristic" from aphorisms which depend on "dialectic" for their understanding. This "isolating" approach means the saying has no significant relation to settings, actions, or other aphorisms in the tradition unless there is an exhibited dependence. I consider this approach to be a basic weakness of the book. It is a weakness inherited from form criticism in its New Testament mode and intensified by a semiotic deconstructionism. The issue, I suggest, is whether "an interpreter" maintains the dialectic which is present in the aphoristic tradition or, alternatively, isolates the aphorisms and reduces them to structures which do not exhibit the dialectic which they contain internally.

Before returning to the aphorisms we have already investigated and looking at an additional example, let us explore Crossan's distinction between "aphoristic" and "dialectic" for a moment to ask where he got the distinction and what it means to him. The origin of the distinc-

---

[50] Ibid., 236–37.
[51] Ibid., 17.
[52] Ibid., 227–37.

tion appears to lie in Stanley Fish's contrast between "rhetoric" and "dialectic,"[53] which Crossan quotes in *Finding is the First Act*.[54] Fish's distinction, quoted by Crossan, is as follows:

> A presentation is rhetorical if it satisfies the needs of its readers. The word "satisfies" is meant literally here; for it is characteristic of a rhetorical form to mirror and present for approval the opinions its readers already hold. It follows then that the experience of such a form will be flattering, for it tells the reader that what he has always thought about the world is true and that the *ways* of his thinking are sufficient. This is not to say that in the course of a rhetorical experience one is never told anything unpleasant, but that whatever one is told can be placed and contained within the categories and assumptions of received systems of knowledge.
>
> A dialectical presentation, on the other hand, is disturbing, for it requires of its readers a searching and rigorous scrutiny of everything they believe in and live by. It is didactic in a special sense; it does not preach the truth, but asks that its readers discover the truth for themselves, and this discovery is often made at the expense not only of a reader's opinions and values, but of his self-esteem. If the experience of a rhetorical form is flattering, the experience of a dialectical form is humiliating.

In the book *In Fragments,* Crossan has replaced "rhetorical" with "aphoristic." With this dichotomy, Crossan (following Fish) collapses "deliberative, judicial, and epideictic" rhetoric into "epideictic rhetoric," the branch which confirms the values of its auditors. This is a common bias of interpreters since the modern claim of philosophy on epistemology. The reduction suggests that no "critical" faculty functions in the realm of rhetoric.

Such a position subverts the fact that both deliberative and judicial rhetoric function critically, requiring the auditor to make a decision (κρίσις) about persons and actions. Regularly, deliberative, judicial, and epideictic rhetoric interact with one another, disturbing, overturning, and satisfying in different configurations. In fact, disturbing and overturning rhetoric, which Fish and Crossan value so highly, is often extraordinarily "satisfying" in particular social and cultural environments which are, in modern terms, "deconstructionist." To miss the manner in which this "overturning dialectic" plays into the hands of a particular group with a particular epistemology, and "satifies" the requirements of the group, is to miss the presuppositions on one side

---

[53] Stanley E. Fish, *Self-Consuming Artifacts* (Berkeley: University of California Press, 1972), 1–2.
[54] John Dominic Crossan, *Finding is the First Act: Trove Folktales and Jesus' Treasure Parable* (Philadelphia: Fortress, 1979), 118–19.

while exposing them on the other. To dichotomize the three basic realms of communication into "rhetoric which satisfies" and "dialectic which humiliates" is to fall prey to binary thinking which parodies the arena of communication as a place either of "uncritical propagandization and loyalty" or "critical subversion and rebellion." Such a polarization of the arena of communication does little justice to the interplay of critical and affirming rhetoric which is the warp and woof of communication even in a deconstructionist mode.

A good way to see the problem is to look at Crossan's analysis of the units concerning Jesus and the Children,[55] which were the subject of a joint session of the Pronouncement Stories Group and the Structuralism and Exegesis Seminar at the 1982 SBL meetings.[56] Crossan's analysis perpetuates Bultmann's emphasis on "independently circulating sayings." This leads him to reassert that Mark 10:15, "Truly I say to you, whoever does not receive the kingdom of God like a child shall not enter it," was "an independent aphoristic saying."[57] Mark "created the entire *dialectical story* in 10:13, 14, 16 and imbedded the pre-Markan redactionally rephrased 10:15 within it."[58] The difficulty with this approach is its persistently isolating approach to interpretation. In contrast to such an approach, I would suggest that we must begin to investigate the nature of the "dialectic" within the entire aphoristic tradition attributed to Jesus.

In this instance, the dialectic could begin with the postured meaning effect in Mark 10:15. This saying, like other aphorisms we have investigated earlier in this essay, has a negative posturing which is externally dialectical since, in Robert Tannehill's terms, "it first negates a position assumed by some in the milieu of the speaker."[59] In addition, the negative formulation advances a dialectical strategy within the mind and will of the auditor, challenging the auditor to formulate the proper will by transforming the negative into its active form.[60] In other words, a "dialectic" is at work at two levels. The reference to "not receiving the kingdom like a child" establishes a pragmatic dialectic with a situation which calls for a decision against improper action, and negative formulation of the aphorism establishes a cognitive dialectic within the mind

---

[55] Crossan, *In Fragments*, 314–20.
[56] *Semeia* 29 (1983): *Kingdom and Culture: Aphorism, Chreia, Structure*.
[57] Crossan, *In Fragments*, 317.
[58] Ibid., 318.
[59] Robert C. Tannehill, "Response to John Dominic Crossan and Vernon K. Robbins," *Semeia* 29 (1983): 107.
[60] Daniel Patte, "Jesus' Pronouncement about Entering the Kingdom like a Child: A Structural Exegesis," *Semeia* 29 (1983): 11; cf. Bernard Brandon Scott, "The Rules of the Game: A Response to Daniel Patte," *Semeia* 29 (1983): 119.

which compels the reader to reformulate the statement positively to carry it out. This means that the saying establishes semantic tension both externally in the realm of action and internally in the realm of thought.[61]

A rhetorical approach will seek both the dialectic with situations and the dialectic with attitude, reason, and will in the aphorisms. The dialectic will be pursued through a networking of presuppositions and arguments about situations, actions, attitudes, and beliefs in life. Tannehill observes that although Mark 10:15 is not introduced by γάρ or ὅτι, it "provides an important reason why the kingdom is closely associated with children and why the disciples must accept the children, ..."[62] This means that the sayings in Mark 10:13–16 make a syllogism:

> *Concrete Premise*: Whoever does not receive the kingdom like a child shall not enter it.
>
> *Conclusion*: Let the children come to me,
>
> *(opposite)*: Do not hinder them.
>
> *(rationale)*: For to such is the kingdom of God.

Once again, then, we see an enthymematic formulation with a concrete premise and a conclusion. Where, however, is the general premise? Lou Silberman's discussion helps us to locate it when he asserts that "In Mark 10:13–16 the acceptance of social marginality is a prerequisite for entering the kingdom."[63] Silberman's statement "generalizes" the meaning of the story, arguing that the child is the sign of "least-ness." Such an approach suggests that the general premise of the syllogism is something like "whoever embodies leastness (like a child) shall enter the kingdom of God." This means, then, that the rationale, "For to such is the kingdom of God" (Mark 10:16), is an aphoristic paraphrasing of the general premise, "The least shall enter the kingdom of God."

With this approach, the interpreter begins to uncover the network of communication among these aphorisms. The general premise, "The least shall enter the kingdom of God," is closely related to "the first shall be last and the last first." Also closely related is "if anyone would be first, he must be last of all and servant of all" (Mark 9:35). The difference between the aphorisms often is rhetorical mode. The first two stand in the form of a thesis. The form in Mark 9:35 is motivational,

---

[61] See Fontaine, *Traditional Sayings*, 43–62.

[62] Tannehill, "Response," 105.

[63] Lou Silberman, "Schoolboys and Storytellers: Some Comments on Aphorisms and Chreia," *Semeia* 29 (1983): 113.

talking about the will. These sayings are all "general" aphorisms, functioning at the level of general premises in the tradition. It would be informative to gather all such "general" aphorisms together to analyze their presuppositions and uncover the range of rhetorical modes used to clarify them, posture them, and motivate people to adopt them.

After finding the aphorisms which express general premises or theses, it is informative to work with conclusions. In the "Children" aphorism, the conclusion is stated both in a positive and negative form: "Let the children come to me. Do not hinder them." This conclusion stands in an imperative form which activates its premises in exhortations. With the conclusion, we can see the dialectical relation of the aphorism to aphorisms we analyzed earlier. The division of the concrete premise in the "Hindering" aphorism asserted that the scribes and Pharisees "neither enter themselves nor let the enterers enter." We recall that the "Hindering" aphorism lacks concreteness, while the "Children" aphorism stands in dialectic with a situation where disciples are not letting children come to Jesus. The lack of concreteness in the "Hindering" aphorism signals a creation of the aphorism out of contraries from aphoristic traditions which presuppose concrete situations. Thus, "you do not let the enterers enter" is a transformation of the deliberative imperative, "Let the children come to me, do not hinder them, for to such belongs the kingdom of God," into epideictic invective without a concrete basis. The invective against the scribes and Pharisees is projected out of aphoristic traditions which stand in both internal and external dialectic with concrete situations. The invective itself, however, lacks the concrete dialectic.

Next it will be informative to see the dialectic at work in the aphorisms which apply general premises to concrete situations. We notice immediately the negative posturing in:

> Whoever does not receive the kingdom like a child shall not enter it (Mark 10:17).

The negative posturing calls to mind:

> No one sews an unshrunk cloth on a new garment.

> No one puts new wine into old wineskins.

We notice also the negative posturing in the following aphorisms:

> He who is not with me is against me.

> He who is not against us (you) is for you.

To these a person can add:

> No one who does a mighty work in my name will be able soon after to speak evil of me.

The presence of "me" in the aphorisms calls attention to the negative feature in the positive formulation:

> Whoever receives one such child in my name receives me, and whoever receives me *receives not me* but him who sent me.

The tenacity of negative posturing in concrete premises, and its presence in a significant number of "me" sayings, must be the subject of investigation and discussion. Many interpreters have emphasized the importance of parables (which Crossan calls "narrative metaphors" or "short stories") for reconstructing the teaching of Jesus, and these have been studied in detail. If a person uses socio-rhetorical analysis, the opportunity arises for rigorous investigation of aphorisms on the basis of the logic, appeal, and attitude not only of their images but also their premises, arguments, and conclusions. Crossan's initial collection of the aphorisms provides a new resource for this analysis. If we entertain the possibility that contraction, expansion, conversion, substitution, and transposition are not simply performancial variations but are hermeneutical variations showing us the dialectic within the aphoristic tradition, we may begin to reconstruct the network of communication within the aphorisms which instructed, argued, supported, and motivated people through theses, reasoning, premises, exhortation, praise, and blame.

Crossan's analysis concentrates so completely on aphorisms as isolated phenomena that it does not account for the dialectic of aphorisms with one another and with specific settings and actions. Crossan has inherited this approach with integrity from the discipline of New Testament criticism. The basic problem arises from the role of the New Testament interpreter as a literary analyst. Beginning with literary documents, interpreters have developed a model of transmission which begins with the literary forms and projects back into the social setting. The irony is that the analysis reverses the process of transmission, and New Testament interpreters have not been able to liberate themselves from the shackles of that model. Stories and sayings emerge from the social situations of a person's action and speech in this manner:

1. First come actions, attitudes, and speech intermingled in social situations;
2. second comes perpetuation of actions, attitudes, and speech through "interpretive speech";
3. third comes distilled speech which purports to give "the essence" of the person.

Starting with aphorisms, Crossan begins with the most thorough distillations of speech from the tradition. When Crossan isolates these distillations from settings and actions, and analyzes them as "fragments," he traps the interpreter into the model which arose before social history had significantly influenced New Testament scholarship. New Testament interpreters must turn this model around by looking at the actions and attitudes upon which the speech was dependent before speech dominated through interpretation and distillation. In other words, the analyst must not be lured first into the "expressions of essence" in the aphorisms. Rather, the analyst must seek the intermingled actions, attitudes, and speech which provide the base for the interpretive and distilled speech.

Crossan's concept of "dialectic" places the burden of proof on narrative and situations and presupposes that a saying will be independent unless it is proven to be dependent. The burden of proof must lie the other way. Every saying emerges from a situation. Therefore, every saying is initially related to some kind of situation and dependent upon that situation for the framework in which it communicated successfully enough to be transmitted. Only nurturing from the language of traditional scholarship "freed" the saying and began to give it "independence." Therefore, we should look at every saying from the perspective of its dialectic with other aphorisms and with situations and actions in the tradition.

Conclusion

Crossan's collection and indexing of aphorisms provides an opportunity for interpreters to investigate the aphoristic tradition in new ways. Within Crossan's creative approach to the aphorisms, he does not try to uncover the network of relationships that exists among the aphorisms. Rather, he talks about aphorisms as isolated units. In addition, he uses a heuristic approach that collapses tensive patterns into semiotic structures which bypass the semantic particularities of aphorisms. A closer look at the analysis might suggest that the model emphasizes a particular kind of cognition (λόγος) at the expense of other features in the sayings. This conflicts, I would suggest, with Crossan's use of the term aphorism to signify a personal vision. A model for personal aphorisms should not isolate cognitive structures. It should find the interrelation among presuppositions, reasons, and arguments (λόγος); actions, interactions, and attributes (ἦθος); and attitudes, desires, and responses (πάθος). A socio-rhetorical approach will seek the logical and affective dimensions in aphorisms, uncover the network of presuppositions, arguments, and conclusions among them, and seek their grounding in concrete knowledge and understanding. Such an approach could present a picture of Jesus' teaching and action based on a more thorough dialectic among situations, actions, attitudes, arguments, and beliefs than any previous quest. We are grateful to Crossan for a good beginning. We should build on his work with a model that emerges from the context of transmission itself rather than a model that emerges from the context of the interpretation of texts.

7

Writing as a Rhetorical Act in Plutarch and the Gospels

Introduction

This paper addresses an issue that is pertinent especially for interpretation of literature from antiquity which contains biographical dimensions. The phrase "biographical dimensions" refers broadly to portrayal of a human being during the span of time from conception to afterlife. Much biblical literature falls within the purview of this discussion, as well as much non-biblical literature. Stories about individuals and sayings attributed to them played an important role in the transmission of culture in antiquity. These stories and sayings have come to us in written form, and here a major challenge arises. How shall we understand the act of writing which produced the story or saying as it comes to us? Or, more importantly, what kinds of acts of writing do we consider possible, and what kind dominates our attention?

From Textual Criticism to Rhetorical Criticism

When interpreters began to develop literary-historical methods of analysis during the 17th, 18th, and 19th centuries, settings in which scribes copied and recopied manuscripts guided the analysis. Scribal copying produced "errors" and "corruptions" through accidental omissions or additions, or through intentional revisions to improve the text.[1] The major goal for this analysis was to construct the earliest version of the text available to us on the basis of extant manuscripts. By the beginning of the 20th century, a significant number of "critical texts," that is,

---

[1] Bruce M. Metzger, *The Text of the New Testament: Its Transmission, Corruption, and Restoration* (New York: Oxford University Press, 1964); Jack Finegan, *Encountering New Testament Manuscripts: A Working Introduction to Textual Criticism* (Grand Rapids: Eerdmans, 1974), 54–177; Eldon J. Epp and Gordon D. Fee, eds., *New Testament Textual Criticism: Its Significance for Exegesis* (New York: Oxford University Press, 1981).

texts constructed out of critically established early readings, were available to the scholarly community.

Once textual criticism had shown its worth and produced "better," in the sense of "earlier" texts, the same literary-historical skills that were attained and refined through textual criticism were applied to reconstruct written sources used by the writers of the earliest texts. This step invited greater creativity than textual criticism, but the literary-historical procedures of textual criticism provided the basic tools for the analysis. Much as textual criticism negotiated different readings in manuscripts to reconstruct the earliest text, so source criticism negotiated different readings to reconstruct written sources used by one or more authors. In other words, the literary-historical skills that had been learned to reconstruct "early texts" simply were extended to reconstruct "early sources."

Analysis especially of stories and sayings in the gospels invited the extension of the literary-historical skills associated with text and source criticism yet one more step, namely to the reconstruction of "oral sources." One might think that biblical scholars used significantly different methods of analysis during the era of form criticism, but perusal of form-critical investigations reveals that no significant break with the literary-historical procedures of text and source criticism occurred. The major shift was to concentrate on the "life" of individual pericopae. The methods for reconstructing the life-stages of these stories and sayings were the same literary-historical methods used for text and source criticism. In other words, the analytical steps in form criticism proceeded as though oral transmission and variation occurred in a manner analogous to "scribal" transmission and variation.[2]

Redaction criticism, in contrast to form criticism, has opened the door for interpretive skills significantly different from the literary-historical skills that were formulated to reconstruct written and oral sources of a text on the basis of intertextual similarities and differences. To be sure, most interpreters in Europe stay within the boundaries of the literary-historical skills of text, source, and form criticism as they use redaction criticism to envision the theological and historical situation of the gospels.[3] Yet through the influence of interpreters like Norman Perrin redaction criticism in the United States has from the beginning emphasized the "whole range of creative activities" in a

---

[2] Cf. Werner H. Kelber, *The Oral and Written Gospel: The Hermeneutics of Speaking and Writing in the Synoptic Tradition, Mark, Paul, and Q* (Philadelphia: Fortress, 1983), 1–43.

[3] Cf. Edgar V. McKnight, "Form and Redaction Criticism," in *The New Testament and Its Modern Interpreters* (ed. Eldon J. Epp and George W. MacRae; The Bible and Its Modern Interpreters 3; Philadelphia: Fortress, 1989), 153–60.

gospel.[4] This emphasis has given redaction criticism an open-ended agenda that invites interaction with various kinds of structural, literary, and rhetorical modes of analysis.

One of the renewed interests during the transitional period provided by redaction criticism has been the relation of oral to written speech, and in the midst of the discussion a new problem has arisen. The problem is that a discussion of "print culture" appropriate for our time has been imposed onto the first centuries of the common era in such a manner that the relation between oral and written culture during early Christian times is badly misconstrued. Werner Kelber's discussion not only typifies the problem but contributes a major voice to the confusion. The confusion arises through a failure to recognize the pervasiveness of rhetorical culture throughout Mediterranean society during the Hellenistic period.[5] Kelber distinguishes between "oral culture," "scribal culture," and "print culture," placing an improper mystique on scribal culture using Elizabeth Eisenstein's statement:

> There is nothing analogous in our experience or in that of any living creature within the Western world at present. The conditions of scribal culture thus have to be artificially reconstructed by recourse to history books and reference guides. Yet for the most part, these works are more likely to conceal than to reveal the object of such a search. Scribal themes are carried forward, post-print trends are traced backward in a manner that makes it difficult to envisage the existence of a distinct literary culture based on hand-copying. There is not even an agreed-upon term in common use which designates the system of written communications that prevailed before print.[6]

A major problem with this manner of stating the issue is the lack of reference to rhetorical culture in Mediterranean antiquity. The system of communication that prevailed before print, and during the first phase of print, was called "rhetoric." For this reason it would be more helpful for us to distinguish between:

(1) oral culture;
(2) scribal culture;
(3) rhetorical culture;
(4) print culture.

---

[4] Norman Perrin, *What is Redaction Criticism?* (Philadelphia: Fortress, 1969), 66.

[5] See Mary Ann Tolbert, *Sowing the Gospel: Mark's World in Literary-Historical Perspective* (Minneapolis: Fortress, 1989), 44–45, n. 36.

[6] Elizabeth L. Eisenstein, *The Printing Press as an Agent of Change: Communications and Cultural Transformations in Early Modern Europe* (Cambridge: Cambridge University Press, 1979), 19; quoted by Werner H. Kelber, "From Aphorism to Sayings Gospel and from Parable to Narrative Gospel," *Foundations & Facets Forum* 1/1 (1985): 26–27.

New Testament documents were produced in a culture characterized by interaction among oral, scribal, and rhetorical environments. The phrase "oral culture" should be used for those environments where written literature is not in view.[7] The phrase "rhetorical culture," in contrast, should refer to environments where oral and written speech interact closely with one another.[8] It would be best to limit "scribal culture" to those environments where a primary goal is to "copy" either oral statements or written texts. Hand-copying in Mediterranean antiquity produced a distinct literary culture in an advanced rhetorical culture where written and spoken composition were closely related to one another.

If we are to be true to writing activity in antiquity, we must be aware of a spectrum of various kinds of writing.[9] This paper focuses on scribal reproduction and progymnastic composition. "Scribal reproduction" consisted of making copies of extant texts, transcribing messages and letters from dictation, and reproducing stock documents like receipts. A person received training in these skills during the elementary and grammatical phases of education.[10] "Progymnastic composition," in contrast to scribal reproduction, consisted of writing traditional materials clearly and persuasively rather than in the oral or written form it came to the writer. The full spectrum of progymnastic composition is outlined and discussed in documents entitled *Progymnasmata* (Elementary Exercises),[11] and we recommend the phrase "progymnastic rhetoric" to refer to the phenomenon and the phrase "progymnastic composition" to refer to the writing activities associated with it. Progymnastic composition was intended for the end of grammatical training in preparation for rhetorical training, but there were disagreements during the early centuries of the common era concerning how much grammatical

---

[7] Albert Bates Lord, *Singer of Tales* (Harvard Studies in Comparative Literature 24; Cambridge, Mass.: Harvard University Press, 1960); Walter J. Ong, *The Technologization of the Word* (London: Methuen, 1982).

[8] Tony M. Lenz, *Orality and Literacy in Hellenic Culture* (Carbondale, Ill.: Southern Illinois University Press, 1989).

[9] The primary spectrum of writing in Mediterranean antiquity, in our view, consists of five kinds of writing: (1) scribal reproduction; (2) progymnastic composition; (3) narrative composition; (4) discursive composition; and (5) poetic composition.

[10] Stanley F. Bonner, *Education in Ancient Rome: From the Elder Cato to the Younger Pliny* (Berkeley: University of California Press, 1977), 165–211.

[11] See Ronald F. Hock and Edward N. O'Neil, *The Chreia in Ancient Rhetoric: The Progymnasmata* (Atlanta: Scholars Press, 1986), 9–22; Burton L. Mack and Vernon K. Robbins, *Patterns of Persuasion in the Gospels* (Sonoma, Calif.: Polebridge, 1989), 33–35; James R. Butts, "The 'Progymnasmata' of Theon: A New Text with Translation and Commentary" (Ph.D. diss., Claremont Graduate University, 1987); Bonner, *Education in Ancient Rome*, 250–76.

training a student needed to complete before beginning to compose at the progymnastic level.¹² A major thesis of this paper is that progymnastic composition is the activity that bridges the gap between the kind of rhetorical analysis performed by people like George A. Kennedy and text, source, form, and redaction analysis.

In order to display the nature of progymnastic composition and to distinguish it from scribal reproduction, this paper exhibits multiple versions of Lysander's use of his sword to discuss territorial boundaries, Jesus' healing of Peter's mother-in-law, Jesus' calling of two sets of brothers, Alexander's refusal to run in the Olympic footrace, and the woman who touched Jesus' garment. The documents entitled *Progymnasmata* which were written by Aelius Theon of Alexandria (ca. 50–100 CE) and Hermogenes (2d cent. CE) will serve as guides for analysis of these short units in Plutarch and the synoptic gospels.¹³

Recitation Composition in Traditional Rhetorical Culture

In traditional rhetorical culture, repetition of words and phrases in a written document regularly is the result of "recitation composition" rather than "copying." Aelius Theon explains recitation composition in the following manner:

> and so 1) "Recitation" (ἀπαγγελία) is obvious. For we try to the best of our ability to report (ἑρμηνεῦσαι) the assigned chreia very clearly in the same words or in others as well.¹⁴

When Theon refers to "reporting" chreia (a statement or action attributed to a specific person), he is talking about writing it. A traditional rhetorical culture is based on stories and sayings that people are able to use in different ways for different purposes. Recitation composition in Hellenistic education built on this insight and, as a result, marked the transition from scribal copying to rhetorical writing. The dynamics and presuppositions surrounding recitation composition emerged as a teacher recited a traditional fable, anecdote, event, or saying in his own words to one or more students and the students wrote the brief unit in their own words, using as much or as little of the teacher's wording as worked well for them. It is not accidental that the recitation exercise marked the transition from scribal copying to rhetorical writing, since

---

[12] Quintilian, in *Institutio Oratorica*, especially book 1, refers to some of these discussions and clarifies his position in the midst of them.

[13] See Butts, "The 'Progymnasmata' of Theon"; Hock and O'Neil, *The Chreia in Ancient Rhetoric*.

[14] Hock and O'Neil, *The Chreia in Ancient Rhetoric*, 95.

once a student moves away from verbatim reproduction of an oral or written text, the dynamics of rhetorical culture invade the act of writing itself. John Dominic Crossan has seen the variations that result from recitation composition in his study of early Christian aphorisms, and he refers to them as "performancial variations."[15] Unfortunately, as an heir of literary-historical criticism, he does not use insights from rhetorical criticism or information about different kinds of writing during the Hellenistic period to inform the analysis.

Since recitation composition stands at the entrance to rhetorical culture as it functioned in Mediterranean society, writing and speaking are closely intertwined in much Mediterranean literature. The customary introductory phrase "it is said" (λέγεται), "they say" or "they were saying" (λέγουσιν or ἔλεγον), or some such variation, exhibits the pervasive nature of recitation in the culture. When people transferred material from one written document to another, they regularly performed the material anew. The new performance contained as much or as little verbatim reproduction as was congenial to the writer. An author attributed specific words to specific authors, and this act produced arguments from ancient authorities or witness. The result appears in references to specific people like Xenophon, Homer, Isaiah, or David; and authors regularly refer to these citations through "according to" (κατά with accusative) or some form of reference to something "written" (γέγραπται, ἐστίν γεγραμμένον, etc.). As a result of recitation composition, even specific citations often exhibit variation rather than verbatim transmission.

The dynamic relation between oral speech and written literature is evident from the opening discussion in the *Progymnasmata* of the first-century rhetorician and sophist Aelius Theon. Theon tells his reader that the only way to become a skillful orator is to "write every day":

> For those who are going to be orators, not the words of the older writers, not their wealth of thoughts, not the purity of their style, not their well-proportioned arrangement, not their elegant oral presentation, in a word, not any of the good elements in rhetoric, are at all useful unless each one practices writing every day for himself.[16]

For Theon, a primary dimension in practicing writing every day is learning to present something well in varying ways. As Theon says:

> For thinking is stirred by one subject in not just one way (so that the sense impression falling upon it is conveyed the same way), but rather in several ways. And since we sometimes make statements,

---

[15] John Dominic Crossan, *In Fragments: The Aphorisms of Jesus* (San Francisco: Harper & Row, 1983), 37–66.

[16] Theon I, 88–92 in Butts, "The 'Progymnasmata' of Theon." 105-107.

sometimes ask questions, sometimes make inquiry, sometimes express a wish, and sometimes express our thought in some other way, nothing prevents our expressing the same impression equally well in all these ways.[17]

Writing in a rhetorical culture builds on speaking and writing from the past, and the goal is to learn to present the thoughts and actions of the past equally well in varying ways.

The issue is, then, where is the line to be drawn between scribal reproduction, which includes "corrections and improvements," and recitation composition? Many gospel units that have been discussed from the perspective of scribal revision are more appropriately described as different recitation performances. Since the person thinks the sounds, and perhaps says them during the writing, written speech remains closely related to oral speech. The person hears the words, and the sounds influence the written form. If we wonder why the synoptic gospels contain so much variation in settings of so much verbatim agreement, the answer surely lies here. These authors are working in close relation to one another or to common sources, yet they continually recast the material by adding to it, subtracting from it, rearranging it, and rewording it. To posit an "oral source" for these variations is wrong, because it merges the literary-historical approach associated with text and source criticism directly with oral transmission without bringing into view the kind of culture in which oral and written speech interact closely with one another. In other words, those who posit oral sources for the variation are presupposing a "copying culture" linked directly to an "oral culture." The evidence we have in the *Progymnasmata* and other documents suggests that this approach bypasses a pervasive culture in Mediterranean society in which oral and written speech interacted closely with one another.[18]

A reader of texts from antiquity can see the kind of variation that results from recitation composition in Plutarch's three versions of Lysander's use of his sword in a discussion of territorial boundaries.[19] The texts are as follows:

---

[17] Theon I, 96–102 in ibid., 107.
[18] Mack and Robbins, *Patterns of Persuasion*.
[19] More versions of this story are displayed in Vernon K. Robbins, *Ancient Quotes & Anecdotes: From Crib to Crypt* (FF; Sonoma, Calif.: Polebridge, 1989), 23–24.

240   Sea Voyages and Beyond

Plutarch, *Lysander* 22.1	Plutarch, *Moralia* 190E	Plutarch, *Moralia* 229C
Ἀργείοις μὲν γὰρ ἀμφιλογουμένοις	Πρὸς δὲ Ἀργείους δικαιότερα τῶν Λακεδαιμονίων λέγειν περὶ τῆς	Πρὸς Ἀργείους δὲ περὶ γῆς ὅρων
περὶ γῆς ὅρων καὶ	ἀμφισβητουμένης χώρας	ἀμφισβητοῦντας
δικαιότερα τῶν Λακεδαιμονίων οἰομένοις λέγειν	δοκοῦντας,	πρὸς Λακεδαιμονίους καὶ δικαιότερα λέγειν αὐτῶν φάσκοντας,
δείξας τὴν μάχαιραν, "ὁ ταύτης," ἔφη, "κρατῶν βέλτιστα περὶ γῆς ὅρων διαλέγεται."	σπασάμενος τὴν μάχαιραν, "ὁ ταύτης," ἔφη, "κρατῶν βέλτιστα περὶ γῆς ὅρων διαλέγεται."	σπασάμενος τὴν μάχαιραν, "ὁ ταύτης," ἔφη, "κρατῶν βέλτιστα περὶ γῆς ὅρων διαλέγεται."
For instance, when the Argives were arguing about boundaries of land, and thought they stated a better case than the Spartans, he pointed to his sword, and said, "He who is master of this discourses best about boundaries of land."	To the Argives when they seemed to state a better case than the Spartans about the disputed territory, he drew his sword, and said, "He who is master of this discourses best about boundaries of land."	To the Argives, who were disputing with the Spartans about boundaries and said they stated the better case than them, he drew his sword and said, "He who is master of this discourses best about boundaries of land."

The variations among these three accounts look very much like variations among synoptic gospel versions. All three versions share verbatim reference to the Spartans' stating (λέγειν) of a better case (δικαιότερα) concerning (περί) the boundaries, to the sword (τὴν μάχαιραν), and reference to the saying, "He who is master of this discourses best about boundaries of land." In the midst of this verbatim reproduction, however, significant variation exists. The second and third accounts have "to the Argives" (with variation in the placement of δέ, and agree on "drawing" rather than "pointing to" the sword, the first and second have "a better case than the Spartans"' (but in inverted order in the clause), and the first and third have "about boundaries of land." Beyond these agreements, each account contains slightly variant wording.

These phenomena display well the results of recitation composition. It is obvious from the verbatim reproduction that one or more of the accounts functioned as a reference text when one of the other accounts was written. Yet the variation among the accounts indicates that there was no concern to copy another text word for word. If the guiding principle had been to copy another text verbatim, the variations among the accounts would have taken the form of different separations of words that create different punctuations of the text, minor variations in spelling and/or wording that correct or improve the text, or absence or presence of clauses through omission, attempts at restoration, and/or conflations of corrected texts.[20] Instead, the three versions of the Lysander account contain multiple variations of wording and rearrangements of phrases prior to the saying. Only the reference to the sword and the saying which follows it stand in verbatim agreement in the three accounts, and this is one kind of verbatim overlap that is natural, though not mandatory, in an environment of recitation composition. Here, then, the interpreter sees a good example of the kind of verbatim repetition that may exist in the midst of significant variation in a text produced within the guidelines of recitation composition. There has been no attempt to copy an entire text verbatim, nor has there been complete modification of everything in another text. Rather, the performance of the traditional story combines significant variation with significant verbatim overlap.

There is dispute among interpreters whether the materials in one or both of the accounts in the *Moralia* were notes Plutarch made and subsequently used when he wrote his *Lysander*, or the materials were excerpted from the *Lysander* by himself or some other person for the two accounts in the *Moralia*.[21] Thus, similar disputes exist in scholarship about the source relationships of the accounts in Plutarch and the synoptic gospels. The important thing is for us to see that the same kind of recitation reproduction and variation among multiple accounts exists among documents attributed to Plutarch as among the gospels. This phenomenon displays, in our opinion, the widespread activity of recitation composition of stories and sayings attributed to specific persons in Mediterranean literature during the early centuries of the common era.

A generally analogous relation of texts exists among the three versions of Jesus' healing of Peter's mother-in-law in the synoptic gospels. The texts are as follows:

---

[20] For an excellent example, see the analysis of Jn 1:1–18 in Finegan, *Encountering New Testament Manuscripts*, 111–77.

[21] *Plutarch's Moralia* III (trans. F.C. Babbitt; Cambridge, Mass.: Harvard University Press, 1968), 3–7.

Matthew 8:14–15	Mark 1:29–31	Luke 4:38–39
Καὶ	Καὶ εὐθὺς ἐκ τῆς συναγωγῆς ἐξελθόντες ἦλθον	Ἀναστὰς δὲ ἀπὸ τῆς συναγωγῆς εἰσῆλθεν
ἐλθὼν ὁ Ἰησοῦς, εἰς τὴν οἰκίαν Πέτρου	εἰς τὴν οἰκίαν Σίμωνος καὶ Ἀνδρέου μετὰ Ἰακώβου καὶ Ἰωάννου.	εἰς τὴν οἰκίαν Σίμωνος.
εἶδεν τὴν πενθερὰν αὐτοῦ βεβλημένην καὶ πυρέσσουσαν·	ἡ δὲ πενθερὰ Σίμωνος κατέκειτο πυρέσσουσα, καὶ εὐθὺς λέγουσιν αὐτῷ περὶ αὐτῆς.	πενθερὰ δὲ τοῦ Σίμωνος ἦν συνεχομένη πυρετῷ μεγάλῳ, καὶ ἠρώτησαν αὐτὸν περὶ αὐτῆς.
καὶ	καὶ προσελθὼν ἤγειρεν αὐτὴν	καὶ ἐπιστὰς ἐπάνω αὐτῆς
ἥψατο τῆς χειρὸς αὐτῆς, καὶ ἀφῆκεν αὐτὴν ὁ πυρετός·	κρατήσας τῆς χειρός· καὶ ἀφῆκεν αὐτὴν ὁ πυρετός,	ἐπετίμησεν τῷ πυ- ρετῷ, καὶ ἀφῆκεν αὐτήν·
καὶ ἠγέρθη, καὶ διηκόνει αὐτῷ.	καὶ διηκόνει αὐτοῖς.	παραχρῆμα δὲ ἀναστᾶσα διηκόνει αὐτοις.
And when Jesus entered the house of Peter,	And immediately he left the synagogue, and entered the house of Simon and Andrew, with James and John.	And he arose from the synagogue, and entered the house of Simon.
he saw his mother-in-law lying sick with a fever;	Now the mother-in-law of Simon lay sick with a fever, and immediately they told him of her.	Now Simon's mother- in-law was ill with a high fever, and they besought him for her.
and he touched her hand,	And he came and took her by the hand and lifted her up,	And he stood over her and rebuked the fever,
and the fever left her,	and the fever left her;	and it left her; and immediately
and she rose and she served him.	and she served them.	she got up and served them.

Among these three versions the dynamics of recitation composition are fully evident. All three versions share verbatim reference to going "into the house" of Simon, to the "mother-in-law," to the fever "leaving her," and to her "serving." Some agreements, however, exist only among two versions. The second and third accounts have Jesus come from "the synagogue," use the name "Simon" rather than "Peter," have the disciples tell or ask Jesus "about her," and have the mother-in-law serve "them" rather than "him." The first and second accounts agree in wording as they refer to being "sick with a fever," to touching or grasping "the hand" of the woman, and to "the fever" leaving her. In the midst of this kind of agreement, each account varies slightly from the other in wording and arrangement of phrases.

Whether Matthew and/or Luke used Mark as a source or Mark used Matthew and/or Luke is less significant than the fact that whoever used whom as a source has exercised freedom in varying the wording. In other words, each writer has proceeded according to the guidelines of recitation composition rather than copying.

Once we become aware of the phenomena common to recitation composition in texts in Hellenistic culture, we may acquire new eyes for understanding synoptic texts that we usually perceive to stand in a relation of "scribal revision." The Matthean and Markan versions of the calling of two sets of brothers present a good example of the kind of variation that usually would be considered to be the product of scribal revision, because of the nature and extent of the verbatim agreement. The texts look as follows:

Matthew 4:18–22	Mark 1:16–20
περιπατῶν δὲ	καὶ παράγων
παρὰ τὴν θάλασσαν τῆς	παρὰ τὴν θάλασσαν τῆς
Γαλιλαίας εἶδεν δυο ἀδελφούς,	Γαλιλαίας εἶδεν
Σίμωνα	Σίμωνα
τὸν λεγόμενον Πέτρον	
καὶ 'Ανδρέαν τὸν ἀδελφὸν αὐτοῦ,	καὶ 'Ανδρέαν τὸν ἀδελφὸν Σίμωνος
βάλλοντας ἀμφίβληστρον	ἀμφιβάλλοντας
εἰς τὴν θάλασσαν· ἦσαν γὰρ ἁ-	ἐν τῇ θαλάσσῃ· ἦσαν γὰρ ἁλεεῖς.
λεεῖς.	
Καὶ λέγει αὐτοῖς·	Καὶ εἶπεν αὐτοῖς ὁ 'Ιησους
δεῦτε ὀπίσω μου, καὶ ποιήσω	δεῦτε ὀπίσω μου, καὶ ποιήσω
ὑμᾶς	ὑμᾶς
	γενέσθαι
ἁλεεῖς ἀνθρώπων.	ἁλεεῖς ἀνθρώπων.
οἱ δὲ εὐθέως ἀφέντες τὰ δίκτυα	καὶ εὐθὺς ἀφέντες τὰ δίκτυα
ἠκολούθησαν αὐτῷ.	ἠκολούθησαν αὐτῷ.
Καὶ προβὰς ἐκεῖθεν	Καὶ προβὰς ὀλίγον
εἶδεν	εἶδεν
ἄλλους δύο ἀδελφούς,	
'Ιάκωβον τὸν τοῦ Ζεβεδαίου καὶ	'Ιάκωβον τὸν τοῦ Ζεβεδαίου καὶ
'Ιωάννην τὸν ἀδελφόν αὐτοῦ,	'Ιωάννην τὸν ἀδελφὸν αὐτοῦ,

<table>
<tr><td>

ἐν τῷ πλοίῳ
μετὰ Ζεβεδαίου τοῦ πατρὸς αὐτῶν
καταρτίζοντας τὰ δίκτυα αὐτῶν·
καὶ ἐκάλεσεν αὐτούς·
οἱ δὲ εὐθέω ἀφέντες

τὸ πλοῖον
καὶ τὸν πατέρα αὐτῶν

ἠκολούθησαν αὐτῷ.

As he walked
by the Sea of Galilee, he saw
two brothers,
Simon
who is called Peter
and Andrew his brother,
casting a net
into the sea; for they were fishermen.
And he says to them,
"Follow me, and I will make you

fishers of men."
Immediately they left their nets
and followed him.
And going on from there
he saw
two other brothers,
James the son of Zebedee and
John his brother,
in the boat
with Zebedee their father,
mending their nets,
and he called them.
Immediately they left

the boat
and their father,

and followed him.

</td><td>

καὶ αὐτοὺς
ἐν τῷ πλοίῳ

καταρτίζοντας τὰ δίκτυα,
καὶ εὐθὺς ἐκάλεσεν αὐτούς.
καὶ ἀφέντες
τὸν πατέρα αὐτῶν Ζεβεδαῖον
ἐν τῷ πλοίῳ

μετὰ τῶν μισθωτῶν
ἀπῆλθον ὀπίσω αὐτῷ.

And passing along
by the Sea of Galilee, he saw

Simon

and Andrew the brother of Simon
casting
in the sea; for they were fishermen.
And Jesus said to them,
"Follow me and I will make you
become
fishers of men."
And immediately they left their nets
and followed him.
And going on a little farther,
he saw

James the son of Zebedee and
John his brother,
who were in their boat

mending the nets.
And immediately he called them;
and they left
their father Zebedee
in the boat

with the hired servants,
and went away behind him.

</td></tr>
</table>

The verbatim overlap in these two accounts is extensive, and most of the variations have the nature of addition or omission from the other account. Thus, the phrases "two brothers," "who is called Peter," "become," "two other brothers," "with Zebedee their father", and "with the hired servants" have been added or subtracted by one of the writers. Yet there also is variation in wording, and this rewording combines with rearrangement of the order of phrases near the end of the account. Thus,

Matthew has "as he walked" for Mark's "and passing along," Matthew has "casting a net" for Mark's "casting," Matthew has "says" for Mark's "Jesus said," and Matthew has "they followed him" for Mark's "they went away behind him." The overall impression is that each composition contains more and more freedom from the wording of the other as the unit progresses, for the end of the accounts have the most variation in wording and arrangement of phrases. When all is said and done in the investigation of these accounts, what we must consider most remarkable in the setting of this much overlap are the variations. There is no embarrassment with extensive verbatim reproduction, yet there is no commitment to verbatim copying. This, I submit, reveals the presence of "recitation composition" as a guiding principle.

Argumentation in Progymnastic Composition

A major reason for insisting that variations among gospel texts are the result of "recitation composition" is the range of progymnastic composition throughout the gospels. The nature of the relationship of texts when there is a greater degree of variation than we have analyzed in the preceding section is explained well in the *Progymnasmata* of Aelius Theon, and initial interpretations have been offered in *Patterns of Persuasion in the Gospels*.[22] In Hellenistic education, after the student became proficient in recitation composition, the teacher continued with exercises in inflexion, positive comment, negative comment, expansion, abbreviation, refutation, and confirmation.[23] More often than we might suppose, these variations create different kinds of argumentation, something of great importance in a rhetorical culture. In order to see how variations in rhetorical argument accompany small variations in wording, we will examine multiple accounts in Plutarch of Alexander's refusal to compete in the footrace at Olympia and multiple accounts in the synoptic gospels of the woman who touched Jesus' garment.

In three extant accounts of the young Alexander's refusal to run in the footrace at Olympia he responds that he would compete if he had kings as competitors. The agreement and variation look as follows:

---

[22] Mack and Robbins, *Patterns of Persuasion*.
[23] Hock and O'Neil, *The Chreia in Ancient Rhetoric*, 95–106; Mack and Robbins, *Patterns of Persuasion*, 35–41; Bonner, *Education in Ancient Rome*, 25–76.

246   Sea Voyages and Beyond

Moralia 179D	Alexander 4.10	Moralia 331B
Ἐλαφρὸς δὲ ὢν καὶ ποδώκης καὶ παρακαλούμενος ὑπὸ τοῦ πατρὸς	ἀλλὰ καὶ τῶν περὶ αὐτὸν ἀποπειρωμένων εἰ βούλοιτ' ἂν	ποδωκέστατος γὰρ τῶν ἐφ' ἡλικίας νέων γενόμενος καὶ τῶν ἑταίρων αὐτὸν
Ὀλύμπια δραμεῖν στάδιον,	Ὀλυμπίασιν ἀγωνίσασθαι στάδιον, ἦν γὰρ ποδώκης,	ἐπ''Ολύμπια παρορμώντων, ἠρώτησεν, εἰ
"εἴγε", ἔφη, "βασιλεῖς ἕξειν ἔμελλον ἀνταγωνιστάς."	"εἴγε", ἔφη, "βασιλεῖς ἔμελλον ἕξειν ἀνταγωνιστάς."	βασιλεῖς ἀγωνίζονται· τῶν δ' οὐ φαμένων, ἄδικον εἶναι τὴν ἅμιλλαν, ἐν ᾗ νικήσει μὲν ἰδιώτας, νικηθήσεται δὲ βασιλεύς.
Being nimble and swiftfooted, when he was appealed to by his father to run at the Olympic footrace, he said: "Indeed, if I were to have kings as competitors."	In contrast, when those around him inquired whether he would be willing to compete in the Olympic footrace, for he was swiftfooted, he said: "Indeed, if I were to have kings as competitors."	Since he was the swiftest of foot of the young men of his age, and his comrades urged him to enter at Olympia, he asked if kings were competing. And when they replied in the negative, he said that the contest was unfair in which victory would be over commoners, but a defeat would be the defeat of a king.

In the version in the first column, Alexander's father is the person who raises the issue with Alexander, and Alexander responds with a conditional affirmative, namely, only on the condition that his competitors be kings. This story stands in a collection of apophthegms of kings and commanders, and it is preceded by this story:

While Alexander was still a boy and Philip was winning many successes, he was not glad, but said to his playmates, "My father will leave nothing for me to do." "But," said the boys, "he is acquiring all this for you." "But what good is it," said Alexander, "if I possess much and accomplish nothing?" (*Moralia* 179D)

In this context it appears to be important that Alexander's father Philip is the one who apppeals to Alexander to compete. The effect of Alexander's response is to suggest that he will no be distracted by activities that are less prestigious than the exploits of his father. The unstated premises with the conclusion, therefore, appear to be something like this:

> *Major premise*: Alexander will do nothing less prestigious than his father Philip.
> *Minor premise*: Philip wins many successes competing with kings.
> *Conclusion*: Alexander will compete at the Olympic footrace only if kings are competitors.

The presence of Alexander's playmates in the preceding story may play a role, since they imply that they would simply enjoy the successes their fathers won. Alexander, in contrast to his playmates, displays the true spirit of the son of Philip by remaining unhappy until he competes with kings themselves – which, of course includes his father. Thus, another implication may be that Alexander would run at Olympia if his own father were willing to run against him.

The version in *Alexander* 4.10 shares nine Greek words in common with *Moralia* 179D: ποδώκης (swiftfooted); Ὀλύμπια ... στάδιον (Olympian footrace); "εἴγε," ἔφη, "βασιλεῖς ἔμελλον ἕξειν ἀνταγωνιστάς" ("Indeed," he said, "if I were to have kings as competitors"). The saying of Alexander contains exactly the same words, but the order of ἔμελλον and ἕξειν is reversed in the two versions. Despite the verbatim agreement, those around Alexander, rather than his father, ask if he will compete. The issue in this instance appears to be whether Alexander will seize the opportunity to display his swiftness of foot. In the narrative context, the story is an illustration that

> it was neither every kind of fame nor fame from every source that he [Alexander] courted, as Philip did, who plumed himself like a sophist on the power of his oratory, and took care to have the victories of his chariots at Olympia engraved upon his coins. (*Alexander* 4.9)

In this instance, therefore, the story does not concern competition with Philip's successes but self-restraint and maturity of purpose greater than Philip, who seeks and flaunts his successes. The change of interlocutors from Philip himself to Alexander's playmates appears to contribute to the broader goal. Instead of responding sharply to his father,

Alexander responds to the inquiry of his playmates with restraint and maturity by showing an unwillingness to flaunt his swiftness before his peers. He will use his skills only for his major task at hand – competition with kings. Thus, the premises and conclusion of this version appear to be something like this:

> *Major premise*: Alexander possessed self-restraint and maturity of purpose in contrast to his father who sought and displayed every kind of fame.
> *Minor premise*: If Alexander ran in the Olympic footrace without the most rigorous competition, he simply would be seeking and displaying childhood fame, since he was swiftfooted.
> *Conclusion*: Alexander will compete at the Olympic footrace only if kings are his competitors.

This version of the story evokes a fully epideictic situation as it praises Alexander at Philip's expense. Through the technique of comparison (σύγκρισις), Alexander emerges as a personage of restraint and maturity of purpose while Philip lives on as a personage who sought prizes and flaunted them when he attained them.

Why would a transmitter of this story feel free to substitute Alexander's playmates for his father Philip as the ones who ask if he will compete in the Olympic footrace? The answer lies in the dynamics of recitation in rhetorical culture. A person feels free to vary the story to bring clarity and persuasiveness to the argument at hand. One may be concerned to establish if the first version of the story is earlier, later, or more authentic than the other, or if it was composed by someone other than Plutarch. But these concerns, which focus on "copying" and "sources," may have no certain answer, while an interpreter may uncover and explore the different strategies of argumentation in the two versions with considerable precision.

A third version in *Moralia* 331B also features Alexander in conversation with his playmates. In this instance, the performance expands the dialogue by having Alexander respond with a question that seeks information before he gives his final response. The result is a dialogue that creates an occasion for Alexander to explain why he would not compete unless kings were his competitors. The reasoning appeals to that which is just and unjust:

> *Major premise*: The principle of justice requires that people of equal status compete with one another.
> *Minor premise*: If Alexander competes in the Olympic footrace, his defeat would be the defeat of a king but his victory would be over commoners.
> *Conclusion*: Alexander will not compete in the footrace at Olympia.

There are two dynamics within this reasoning that make the account especially interesting. First, Alexander's statement implies that he himself is a king. Neither of the other versions takes this step: the only assertion was that Alexander would not compete unless kings were his competitors (or at least were among his competitors). Second, while the saying of Alexander articulates a principle of justice as the reason for the refusal to run, the overall saying intermingles a dynamic of honor with a concern about justice. If a king defeats commoners, the primary issue would appear to be justice; but if commoners defeat a king, the primary issue would appear to be the king's honor. So here the reasoning becomes subtle and witty. Once Alexander calls himself a king, he need not compete with commoners. Since he is a king's son but not yet actually a king, however, one might think he would display his royal abilities like he does in other boyhood stories.[24] According to the narrator, this should have been no problem for Alexander, since he was the "swiftest" of the young men of his age (an assertion only this version makes). But the issue appears to concern the ambiguous nature of athletic victories. As the narrator says:

> Alexander appears to have been averse to the whole race of athletes; at any rate, though he instituted very many contests, not only for tragic poets and players on the flute and players on the lyre, but also for the rhapsodists, as well as for hunting of every sort and for fighting with staves, he took no interest in offering prizes either for boxing or for the pancratium. (*Alexander* 4.11)

Kings, then, cannot display their true character competing at Olympia; those abilities must emerge in the unexpected situations that confront a person who pursues "a king's business."

But there appears to be yet one more attribute of character to be valued in a king when this attribute intermingles with a sense of justice, namely cleverness (μῆτις) – the wit and candor that give a person the ability to handle difficult situations skillfully, quickly, and definitively.[25] To the extent that the story seriously raises the issue of "fairness" among different ranks of people, it contributes well to Plutarch's presentation of Alexander as "a philosopher in his purpose not to win for himself luxury and extravagant living, but to win for all people concord and peace and community of interests" (*Moralia* 330E). Alexander's suggestion that commoners might defeat a king, however, reveals a moment of candor about himself as well as an ability to get out of a

---

[24] Cf. Plutarch, *Alexander* 5–7.

[25] Marcel Detienne and Jean-Pierre Vernant, *Cunning Intelligence in Greek Culture and Society* (Atlantic Highlands, N.J.: Humanities Press, 1978).

potentially embarrassing situation with skill. In each version, then, the act of composition has produced a significantly different rhetorical argument. It is not necessary to posit the existence of an oral source for each new form of the story. Rather, the dynamics of progymnastic composition have created an environment for writing as a rhetorical act.

A similar relation exists among the synoptic versions of the woman who touched Jesus' garment:

Matthew 9:20–22	Mark 5:24b-34	Luke 8:43–48
Καὶ ἰδοὺ γυνὴ αἱμορροοῦσα δώδεκα ἔτη	Καὶ γυνὴ οὖσα ἐν ῥύσει αἵματος δώδεκα ἔτη, καὶ πολλὰ παθοῦσα ὑπὸ πολλῶν ἰατρῶν καὶ δαπανήσασα τὰ παρ' ἑαυτῆς πάντα, καὶ μηδὲν ὠφεληθεῖσα ἀλλὰ μᾶλλον εἰς τὸ χεῖρον ἐλθοῦσα, ἀκούσασα τὰ περὶ τοῦ Ἰησοῦ,	Καὶ γυνὴ οὖσα ἐν ῥύσει αἵματος ἀπὸ ἐτῶν δώδεκα, ἥτις οὐκ ἴσχυσεν ἀπ' οὐδενὸς θεραπευθῆναι
προσελθοῦσα ὄπισθεν ἥψατο τοῦ κρασπέδου τοῦ ἱματίου αὐτοῦ· ἔλεγεν γὰρ ἐν ἑαυτῇ ἐὰν μόνον ἅψωμαι τοῦ ἱματίου αὐτοῦ, σωθήσομαι.	ἐλθοῦσα ἐν τῷ ὄχλῳ ὄπισθεν ἥψατο τοῦ ἱματίου αὐτοῦ· ἔλεγεν γὰρ ὅτι ἐὰν ἅψωμαι κἂν τῶν ἱματίων αὐτοῦ, σωθήσομαι. καὶ εὐθὺς ἐξηράνθη ἡ πηγὴ τοῦ αἵματος αὐτῆς, καὶ ἔγνω τῷ σώματι ὅτι ἴαται ἀπὸ τῆς μάστιγος. καὶ ἐθὺς ὁ Ἰησοῦς ἐπιγνοὺς ἐν ἑαυτῷ τὴν ἐξ αὐτοῦ δύναμιν ἐξελθοῦσαν, ἐπιστραφεὶς ἐν τῷ ὄχλῳ ἔλεγεν· τίς μου ἥψατο τῶν ἱματίων;	προσελθοῦσα ὄπισθεν ἥψατο τοῦ κρασπέδου τοῦ ἱματίου αὐτοῦ, καὶ παραχρῆμα ἔστη ἡ ῥύσις τοῦ αἵματος αὐτῆς. καὶ εἶπεν ὁ Ἰησοῦς, Τίς ὁ ἁψάμενός μου; ἀρνουμένων δὲ πάντων εἶπεν ὁ Πέτρος, Ἐπιστάτα, οἱ ὄχλοι συνέχουσίν σε καὶ ἀποθλίβουσιν. ὁ δὲ Ἰησοῦς εἶπεν, Ἥψατό μού τις, ἐγὼ γὰρ ἔγνων δύναμιν ἐξεληλυθυῖαν ἀπ' ἐμοῦ.
ὁ δὲ Ἰησοῦς στραφεὶς	καὶ ἔλεγον αὐτῷ οἱ	

7. Writing as a Rhetorical Act in Plutarch and the Gospels 251

	μαθηταὶ αὐτοῦ· βλέπεις τὸν ὄχλον συνθλίβοντά σε, καὶ λέγεις· τίς μου ἥψατο; καὶ περιεβλέπετο ἰδεῖν	ἰδοῦσα δὲ ἡ γυνὴ ὅτι οὐκ
καὶ ἰδὼν αὐτὴν	τὴν τοῦτο ποιήσασαν. ἡ δὲ γυνὴ φοβηθεῖσα καὶ τρέμουσα,	ἔλαθεν τρέμουσα ἦλθεν καὶ προσπεσοῦσα αὐτῷ δι᾽
εἰδυῖα ὃ	γέγονεν αὐτῇ, ἦλθεν καὶ προσέπεσεν αὐτῷ καὶ	ἣν αἰτίαν ἥψατο αὐτοῦ ἀπήγγειλεν ἐνώπιον παντὸς τοῦ λαοῦ καὶ ὡς
	εἶπεν αὐτῷ πᾶσαν τὴν ἀλήθειαν.	ἰάθη παραχρῆμα.
εἶπεν· θάρσει, θύγατερ· ἡ πίστις σου σέσωκέν σε. καὶ ἐσώθη ἡ γυνὴ ἀπὸ τῆς ὥρας ἐκείνης	ὁ δὲ᾽εἶπεν αὐτῇ θυγάτηρ, ἡ πίστις σου σέσωκέν σε· ὕπαγε εἰς εἰρνήν, καὶ ἴσθι ὑγιὴς ἀπὸ τῆς μάστιγός σου.	ὁ δὲ εἶπεν αὐτῇ, θυγάτηρ, ἡ πίστις σου σέσωκέν σε· πορεύου εἰς εἰρήνην.

And behold, a woman who had suffered from a hemorrhage for twelve years	And there was a woman who had had a flow of blood for twelve years, and who had suffered much under many physicians, and had spent all that she had, and was no better but rather grew worse. She had heard the reports about Jesus,	And a woman who had a flow of blood for twelve years and could not be healed by any one,
came up behind him	and came up behind him in the crowd	came up behind him,
and touched the fringe of his garment; for she said to herself, "If I only touch his garment, I shall be made well."	and touched his garment. For she said, "If I touch even his garments I shall be made well." And immediately the hemorrhage ceased; and she felt in her body that she was healed of her disease. And Jesus, perceiving in himself that	and touched the fringe of his garment; and immediately her flow of blood ceased. And Jesus said, "Who was it that touched me?" When all denied it, Peter said, "Master, the

Jesus turned,	power had gone forth from him, immediately turned about in the crowd, and said, "Who touched my garments?" And his disciples said to him, "You see the crowd pressing around you, and yet you say, 'Who touched me?'" And he looked around to	multitudes surround you and press upon you!" But Jesus said, "Some one touched me; for I perceive that power has gone forth from me."
and seeing her	see who had done it. But the woman, knowing what had been done to her, came in fear and trembling and fell down before him, and told him the whole truth.	And when the woman saw that she was not hidden, she came trembling, and falling down before him declared in the presence of all the people why she had touched him, and how she had been immediately healed.
he said, "Take heart, daughter, your faith has made you well." And instantly the woman was made well.	And he said to her, "Daughter, your faith has made you well; go in peace and be healed of your disease."	And he said to her, "Daughter, your faith has made you well; go in peace."

As with the two accounts in Plutarch, there is enough verbatim language to suggest some kind of dependence among the three versions. Yet the final form of each account is the result of a compositional act that produces a significantly different version. This kind of relationship should, in our view, be seen as the result of composition at the level of progymnastic rhetoric.

The Matthean version of the woman who touched Jesus' garment (9:20–22) contains abbreviated narrative,[26] a saying by the woman, and a saying by Jesus. This story, like the first two versions of the account of Alexander's refusal to compete in the Olympic footrace, contains only one exchange of conversation among the featured characters. In this instance, however, the display of the logic behind the woman's act creates a setting in which Jesus' speech turns the woman's logic into an actualized syllogism containing a dimension the woman did not articu-

---

[26] Hock and O'Neil, *The Chreia in Ancient Rhetoric*, 101; Vernon K. Robbins, "Pronouncement Stories and Jesus' Blessing of the Children: A Rhetorical Approach," *Semeia* 29 (1983): 49; idem, "The Chreia," in *Greco-Roman Literature and the New Testament: Selected Forms and Genres* (ed. David E. Aune; Atlanta: Scholars Press, 1988), 17; idem, "Pronouncement Stories from a Rhetorical Perspective," *Foundations & Facets Forum* 4, no. 2 (1988): 10; Mack and Robbins, *Patterns of Persuasion*, 17–18.

late and the auditor probably would not supply. In other words, the woman's statement evokes the following conditional syllogism:

Unstated premise: Touching any part of Jesus can make a person well.
Conditional premise: If I touch only his garment,
Conditional conclusion: I will be made well.

When Jesus says, "Your faith has made you well," he has introduced a premise that changes the initial premise of the woman's conditional logic, and therefore changes the syllogism. The resultant syllogism is:

Major premise: An act of faith can make a person well.
Minor premise: The woman's act of touching was an act of faith.
Conclusion: Therefore, the woman was made well.[27]

The logic has moved the term "Jesus" out of the unstated premise and introduced a general principle that could be made concrete in various ways. The faith simply could be confidence that healing would occur, or it could be confidence that Jesus or God could make it happen. The logical progression has transformed the initial premise, and therefore the entire logic, into a multi-valent form of reasoning which perpetuates Jewish heritage, attributes distinctive power and understanding to Jesus, and engages cultural beliefs in Asklepios' ability to heal.[28] The special dynamic of the story, however, is that Jesus' interpretation of the woman's logic enacts the healing. With this version, then, appropriate logic and healing occur simultaneously.

Mark 5:25–34 presents the story in the mode of an expanded chreia.[29] The writer presents extended narration, verbal exchange between Jesus and his disciples, and a saying of Jesus that not only announces that the woman's faith has made her well but gives a blessing of peace and health at the end. First, this version narrates the plight, actions, and inner thoughts of the woman that is in the Matthean version (vv. 25–28). Then, inner perception of healing by the woman occurs simultaneously with inner perception by Jesus that power has gone forth from him (v. 30b). Next, Jesus' speech in the form of a question calls forth a response from his disciples. This response repeats Jesus' question in a manner that intensifies emotions between Jesus and

---

[27] Vernon K. Robbins, "The Woman who Touched Jesus' Garment: Socio-Rhetorical Analysis of the Synoptic Accounts," *NTS* 33 (1987): 507.

[28] Gerd Theissen, *The Miracle Stories of the Early Christian Tradition* (ed. John Riches; trans. Francis McDonagh; Edinburgh: T. & T. Clark, 1983), 130–33.

[29] Hock and O'Neil, *The Chreia in Ancient Rhetoric*, 100–103; Robbins, "Pronouncement Stories and Jesus' Blessing of the Children," 50; idem, "The Chreia," 18; idem, "Pronouncement Stories from a Rhetorical Perspectives," 15–16; idem, "The Woman who Touched Jesus' Garment," 508; Mack and Robbins, *Patterns of Persuasion*, 17–18.

his disciples as Jesus looks around to see who touched him (v. 32). This sequence is based on Jesus' statement of a conclusion that is based on an unstated major premise and a narrated minor premise:

> *Major premise*: Touching causes healing power to go forth from Jesus.
> *Minor premise*: Jesus felt power go forth from him.
> *Conclusion*: Someone touched Jesus.

While the major premise that touching causes healing power to go forth from Jesus lies implicitly in the Matthean version, that version of the story does not develop either the minor premise or the conclusion that is present in the Markan version. In the next step in the Markan version, Jesus' search for the person produces emotions in the woman which cause her to come forth and tell him the whole truth (v. 33). At the end of the story, Jesus responds to the woman's truth-telling with an interpretation of her act as faith and a double blessing to "go in peace," and "be healthy." Since the healing already occurred earlier in the story, Jesus' saying does not enact the healing, as it does in Matthew, but registers approval of the woman's act. Jesus' saying in the Markan version, therefore, functions as the positive comment (ἐπιφωνεῖν) that students were taught to add to a brief unit as they were learning the techniques of progymnastic composition.[30]

Thus, the Markan version contains interaction between the main character and his associates as well as between the main character and his primary counter character. Also, it presents argumentative logic about healing power flowing from Jesus' body that the Matthean version does not explore. This way of writing the episode enriches the display of *ethos* and broadens and intensifies the range of emotions (*pathos*). The longer version of Jesus' saying that contains a double blessing of peace and health also is part of this way of writing the episode. The act of writing this story using the technique of amplification, one of the approaches in progymnastic composition, then, changes the function of the saying and introduces a range of rhetorical features not in the Matthean version. Whether Matthew abbreviated Mark's version or Mark expanded Matthew's version can remain a matter for debate, but the rhetorical differences the two accounts are amazingly clear and should not be missed in interpretation of either story.

The Lukan version (Luke 8:42–48) is different yet from the other two versions, featuring no speech by the woman but attributing speech to Peter (v. 45) and containing more speech by Jesus than the other two versions (v. 46). The opening part simply presents the woman touching the fringe of Jesus' garment and being healed (vv. 43–44). Then, in the next two verses (vv. 45–46) Jesus explicitly articulates the

---

[30] Hock and O'Neil, *The Chreia in Ancient Rhetoric*, 69–70, 98–101.

syllogism that lies partly in narrative comment and partly in Jesus' speech in Mark:

> *Major premise*: Touching causes healing power to go forth from Jesus.
> *Minor premise*: Jesus felt power go forth from him.
> *Conclusion*: Someone touched Jesus.

After this, the woman not only reveals to everyone the inner logic present in Matthew and Mark about touching and being healed, but she also tells them how she touched Jesus and immediately was healed. When Jesus responds in the final part of the story, then, he is not responding simply to the woman's act, but responding to her public announcement of the logic and success of her act. Since the woman's statement makes Jesus the object of praise in this public setting, Jesus' final saying now guards against offensive self-praise by calling attention to the woman's faith rather than the power that went forth from him. Thus it functions like Epameinodas' saying when he told the men of Thebes:

> But it is *your doing*, men of Thebes; with *your help alone* I overthrew the Spartan empire in a day. (Plutarch, *Moralia* 542C)[31]

In essence, Jesus is telling the woman:

> But it is *your doing*, daughter, with *your faith alone* the power in me caused your flow of blood to cease.

In this instance, then, the saying of Jesus deflects praise the woman has bestowed dramatically upon him in a public setting where he has just insisted that he felt power go forth from him. If he accepts her praise without demurral, he emerges as a person who loves to flaunt his powers and make women recount them in public. His quick response, giving the woman the credit rather than taking the credit himself, escapes this danger and establishes his status as the gracious patron of a needy client.[32]

In all of the instances cited from Plutarch and the synoptic gospels, then, different argumentation accompanies internal variations in the stories. The variations are part of writing in a rhetorical culture. While recitation composition begins the process, techniques like abbreviation, expansion, and commentary create different kinds of argumentation using the same story. These kinds of variations, which are typical in the synoptic gospels, exhibit composition as influenced by rhetorical culture rather than scribal culture focused on copying previous documents.

---

[31] Robbins, "The Woman who Touched Jesus' Garment," 513.

[32] John H. Elliott, "Patronage and Clientism in Early Christian Society: A Short Reading Guide," *Foundations and Facets Forum* 3/4 (1987): 39–48.

Conclusion

In previous research, verbal similarities among written versions of stories and sayings regularly have been discussed in terms of "dependence" on written or oral sources. This terminology emerges from a presupposition that written performance of the material was guided by copying an oral or written antecedent. This language and this perception impose goals and procedures on the writers which are inaccurate, since, even if the writer recently had heard or was looking at a version of the story, the version existed in the eye, ear, and mind of the writer as a "recitation" that should be performed anew rather than a verbal text that should be copied verbatim. Within a rhetorical culture, then, similarity in wording exhibits "recitation composition." A writer in rhetorical culture perceives an antecedent oral or written version of a story or saying as a performance, and a new performance can perpetuate as much or as little verbatim wording as is congenial to the writer. The similarities and variations in wording in both Plutarch and the NT synoptic writers should make it obvious to us that the guiding principle behind their transmission of stories and sayings is recitation composition.

In this paper we tried to introduce some markers for identifying progymnastic composition. Also, we have explored some argumentative features that accompany variations among versions of stories produced by progymnastic composition. In addition, we have proposed that recitation composition – writing that presupposes that sources and new compositions are performances in particular contexts – marks the boundary between scribal reproduction and progymnastic composition. We have not explored the boundaries between progymnastic composition and other kinds of writing, because this is a topic too large for this paper. As implied earlier in this paper, the documents entitled *Progymnasmata* in antiquity show the outer parameters. The book *Patterns of Persuasion in the Gospels* displays a broader range of progymnastic composition in the synoptic gospels than has been displayed here, and it explores more complex rhetorical strategies. A discussion of the ways in which composition in Plutarch's writings goes beyond the progymnastic level of composition in the synoptic gospels also must await another context. It has seemed fitting, however, to discuss the place where progymnastic composition begins, since the art of rhetorical interpretation itself is in a new stage of beginnings. With the help of such people as George A. Kennedy, interpreters are challenging the view that writers come into view in biblical texts as copiers of oral and written sources. In fact, most of the writers who produced biblical texts probably were trying to persuade readers to think, feel, and act in particular ways for particular reasons. From our perspective, this means that their placing of writing instrument upon writing material was a rhetorical act.[33]

---

[33] I am grateful to David B. Gowler and Mark Ledbetter for their insightful responses to earlier versions of this paper.

8

The Reversed Contextualization of Psalm 22 in the Markan Crucifixion: A Socio-Rhetorical Analysis

Introduction

This paper is an intertextual study of the Markan account of Jesus' crucifixion.[1] Such a study calls attention to language as a social possession. Mikhail Bakhtin has helped us to understand that many voices from many socio-ideological locations speak through any individual person's use of language: "[L]anguage ... lies on the borderline between oneself and the other. The word in language is half someone else's.... Prior to [the speaker's] moment of appropriation, the word ... exists in other people's mouths, in other people's contexts, serving other people's intentions."[2] Consonant with this observation, Roland Barthes and Julia Kristeva have helped us to understand that all texts are a re-writing of previous texts and a reaction to present texts.[3] Moreover, every text is a product of various cultural discourses – "a tissue of quotations drawn from innumerable centers of culture."[4] Intertextuality, then, "refers to the whole complex of relationships between texts within the general 'text of culture.' Seen in this way, intertextuality is closely connected with the cultural codes and conventions of thought of a particular period and even with the rules of logic in accordance

---

[1] Sipke Draisma, ed., *Intertextuality in Biblical Writings: Essays in Honour of Bas van Iersel*, (Kampen: Kok, 1989) is a foundational collection of essays on intertextual analysis in New Testament literature.

[2] M.M. Bakhtin, *The Dialogic Imagination*, (ed. Michael Holquist; trans. Caryl Emerson and Michael Holquist; Austin: University of Texas Press, 1981), 293–94.

[3] Julia Kristeva, Σημειωτική: *Recherches pour une sémanalyse* (Paris: Editions du Seuil, 1969), 52, 85; Roland Barthes, *S/Z* (Paris: Editions du Seuil, 1970); see Willem Vorster, "Intertextuality and Redaktionsgeschichte," in *Intertextuality in Biblical Writings*, 20–21.

[4] Roland Barthes, *Image, Music, Text* (New York: Hill & Wang, 1977), 146; see James Voelz, "Multiple Signs and Double Texts: Elements of Intertextuality," in *Intertextuality in Biblical Writings*, 27.

with which people can or must reason."[5] Intertextual study challenges the limited range of language usage New Testament interpreters traditionally bring into conversation with the text in the foreground. Willem Vorster and Jean Delorme observe that intertextual analysis is not restricted to canonical writings.[6] In addition, it is not limited to causative influence. As Ellen van Wolde has explained:

> The writers of the synoptic gospels, like all writers, chose their own ordering arrangements from the total of the possibilities their time and their codes offered them, and this selection and arrangement cannot be reduced to one or two causal influences.... The exegete or textual analyst is the reader who informs other readers about the possible worlds of a text, or the person who, on the basis of intertextual study, actualizes the possible textual relationships so that the "universe of discourse" becomes visible.[7]

Intertextual study does not limit itself, therefore, to similar and different phenomena considered to be directly influenced by each other, causally or diachronically. This means that primary differences among interpretations arise as a result of the boundaries an interpreter draws for finding texts that contain the conversation in which the foregrounded text is engaged in the culture.[8]

This essay is an exploration in broadening the horizons of the universe of discourse for the Markan account of the crucifixion. In 1980, George W.E. Nickelsburg widened the horizons of intertextual study of the Markan Passion narrative with an analysis of literature in the Hebrew Bible and extra-canonical Jewish literature antecedent to and contemporary with early Christianity.[9] New Testament interpreters have responded favorably to the study, because it explores accepted canonical and near-canonical literature in an informed, creative manner.[10] More recently, John Dominic Crossan has widened the horizons

---

[5] Ellen van Wolde, "Trendy Intertextuality?" in *Intertextuality in Biblical Writings*, 45, based on Michel Foucault, *Les mots et les choses: une archéologie des sciences humaines* (Paris: Gallimard, 1966).

[6] Vorster, "Intertextuality," 22; Jean Delorme, "Intertextualities about Mark," in *Intertextuality in Biblical Writings*, 36.

[7] Van Wolde, "Trendy Intertextuality?," 47–48.

[8] Cf. the following, which limit intertextuality to the Hebrew Bible: Richard B. Hays, *Echoes of Scripture in the Letters of Paul* (New Haven: Yale University Press, 1989); Gail R. O'Day, "Jeremiah 9:22–23 and 1 Corinthians 1:26–31: A Study in Intertextuality," *JBL* 109 (1990): 259–67.

[9] George W.E. Nickelsburg, "The Genre and Function of the Markan Passion Narrative," *HTR* 73 (1980): 153–84.

[10] For the concept of "near-canonical," see William H. Myers, "The Hermeneutical Dilemma of the African American Biblical Student," in *Stony the Road We Trod: African American Biblical Interpretation* (ed. Cain Hope Felder; Minneapolis: Fortress, 1991), 53–54.

of intertextual analysis of the canonical Passion narratives by integrating the extracanonical (usually called "apocryphal") Gospel of Peter into the history of the tradition of the crucifixion and resurrection of Jesus.[11] This study, in contrast to Nickelsburg's study, is controversial, because it challenges traditional boundaries for intertextual study of New Testament literature.

This essay explores the possibility that the intertextual boundaries for interpretation of the Markan account of the crucifixion and resurrection should be expanded beyond Jewish and Christian literature. In other words, it accepts the dictum that intertextual analysis is not restricted to canonical writings. A failure to widen the boundaries of interpretation runs the risk of presupposing that all sectors of early Christianity created a "unique" culture separate from Mediterranean society and culture in which it grew and, finally, flourished. In the end, such a procedure imposes a "ghetto religion" ideology on all sectors of early Christianity.[12] It would be advantageous, in our opinion, to distinguish different sectors of early Christianity on the basis of their language usage and to explore the particular kind of subcultural or countercultural dynamics present in each sector.[13]

In pursuit of this broader goal, this paper introduces a text that has, in recent years, not appeared in an extended analysis of the Markan account of the crucifixion. This text exists in Dio Chrysostom's *Oration 4* and describes the ritual mocking and abuse of a prisoner at an annual festival in eastern Mediterranean society and culture.[14] Once this text

---

[11] John Dominic Crossan, *The Cross that Spoke: The Origins of the Passion Narrative* (San Francisco, Harper & Row, 1988). The initial challenge to reassess the relationship of the passion account in the Gospel of Peter to the NT gospels came from Helmut Koester, "Apocryphal and Canonical Gospels," *HTR* (1980): 126–30; idem, *Introduction to the New Testament. Vol. 2: History and Literature of Early Christianity* (Philadelphia: Fortress, 1982), 49, 162–63.

[12] See Jonathan Z. Smith, *Drudgery Divine: On the Comparison of Early Christianities and the Religions of Late Antiquity* (Chicago: University of Chicago Press, 1990), esp. 70–71. Arthur Darby Nock used the language "ghetto religion" to describe early Christianity in *Arthur Darby Nock: Essays on Religion and the Ancient World* (ed. Zeph Stewart; 2 vols.; Cambridge, Mass.: 1972), 1:344. Wilhelm Wuellner recently has articulated a similar position in "The Rhetorical Genre of Jesus' Sermon in Luke 12.1–13.9," in *Persuasive Artistry: Studies in New Testament Rhetoric in Honor of George A. Kennedy* (ed. Duane F. Watson; JSNTSup 50; Sheffield: JSOT Press, 1991), 93–118, esp. 112–14.

[13] See Burton L. Mack, *A Myth of Innocence: Mark and Christian Origins*, (Philadelphia: Fortress Press, 1989).

[14] Hans A. Vollmer, *Jesus und Sacäenopfer* (Giessen: Töpelmann, 1905); idem, "Der König mit der Dronenkrone," *ZNW* 6 (1905): 194–98 credits Wettstein with the honor of discovering its affinity with Matthew and Mark. Erich Klostermann, *Das Markusevangelium* (HNT 3; Tübingen: Mohr Siebeck, 1950), 161 includes a reference to the passage. Rudolf Pesch, *Das Markusevangelium* (2 vols.; HTKNT 2; Freiburg: Herder, 1976–1977), 2:470 refers to it, but gives it no serious attention.

brings to light a possible cultural network of significations in the Markan account, the essay exhibits aspects of the conversation among this network, Ps 22, and the narratorial voice of the Markan text. Voices from other contexts also speak through the Markan text,[15] since this Gospel is an excellent example of a text that lived "a real life ... in an environment of social heteroglossia."[16] The limits of space inherent in an essay like this, however, make it necessary to attend only to the cultural discourse evoked by the Dio text, Ps 22, and the Markan narratorial voice.

Since a major challenge for intertextual study is to place texts in relation to one another in such a way that the dialogue respects the autonomy of each text,[17] the essay begins with a programmatic analysis of the inner texture of the Markan account before it moves to intertextual analysis.[18] Thus, the initial section of the essay displays the scenes that emerge as a result of repetitive speech in the Markan narration. This approach, which takes duality and three-step progression seriously in the text of Mark,[19] yields five scenes in the account of the crucifixion. After an exploration of the inner texture of the account with this strategy of reading, a second section investigates the presence in the Markan account of discourse similar to the ritual abuse of a prisoner during the Persian Sacian festival in eastern Mediterranean society. The third section explores the occurrence of language from Ps 22 in the Markan account of the crucifixion. The context of mockery and death into which Markan discourse places Psalm 22 reverses the sequence of scenes in the psalm and subverts the rhetoric of confidence expressed in it. This observation contributes to a reading of the account of Jesus' death as "son of God" that hears the many voices in Mediterranean culture that are engaged in dialogue about the nature of kingship and sonship. The overall purpose of the paper is to explore the tension between rhetorical progression in the Markan account and rhetorical progression in Ps 22. A second purpose is to exhibit the importance of

---

[15] E.g., Ps 69:21 in Mark 15:35–36; possibly Prov 31:6–7 in Mark 15:23; possibly Ps 38:11 in Mark 15:40.

[16] Bakhtin, *Dialogic*, 292, see n. 2.

[17] Delorme, "Intertextualities," 42, see n. 6.

[18] For a discussion of the relation of the inner texture of a text to intertextual analysis, see the introduction to the paperback edition of Vernon K. Robbins, *Jesus the Teacher: A Socio-Rhetorical Interpretation of Mark* (Minneapolis: Fortress, 1992), xix-xlix.

[19] F. Neirynck, *Duality in Mark: Contributions to the Study of Markan Redaction* (rev. ed.; BETL 31; Leuven: Leuven University Press, 1988), esp. 187–90, 222–27, 242–43. Vernon K. Robbins, "Summons and Outline in Mark: The Three-Step Progression," *NovT* 23 (1981): 97–114; idem, *Jesus the Teacher*, 20–47.

including data from outside Jewish and Christian literature in our intertextual analyses of New Testament literature.

Repetitive and Progressive Form in the Crucifixion of Jesus in Mark

Since it is necessary for this paper to establish boundaries that produce a manageable unit in the Markan text, the analysis begins with Mark 15:1 and ends with 15:46. Pilate's function as the overseer of the selection and deliverance of Jesus to the soldiers (15:15) and the one who grants Jesus' corpse to Joseph of Arimathea (15:45) establishes the opening and closure of this unit.[20] These boundaries exclude Peter's denial and the trial before the Sanhedrin. Also, the focus on Pilate's role does not provide the framework for significant commentary on the role of the women who observe Jesus' death and burial at a distance (15:40–41, 47) and find an empty tomb when they go to anoint his body on the day after the sabbath (16:1, 5).[21] The strength of this approach to the Markan account of the crucifixion lies in its focus on the mockery of Jesus and its analysis of the language from Ps 22 in the inner scenes of the account.

Duality and three-step progression reveal five basic scenes in Mark 15:1–46.[22] Pilate's role as the political figure in charge establishes (1) 15:1–15 as the opening scene. In it, the crowd selects Jesus, who has been bound as a prisoner for torture and crucifixion, rather than Barabbas, who was taken prisoner earlier. The crucifixion of Jesus occurs in three stages: (2) the mockery of Jesus as royalty: 15:6–24; (3) the ridicule of Jesus while he hangs on the cross: 15:25–32; and (4) Jesus' crying out and death: 15:33–39. The final scene in this unit features: (5) the permission for and burial of Jesus' corpse: 15:40–46. The scenes depict abuse which leads to Jesus' experience of complete abandonment before he dies. At his death, only a centurion recognizes the implications of the ordeal. Women, who had followed Jesus and ministered to him, watch from afar as Joseph of Arimathea places his body in a tomb. During all of this, no one speaks a kind word to Jesus, nor he to them, as he experiences humiliation and brutality which leads to his death and burial.

---

[20] See George A. Kennedy, *New Testament Interpretation through Rhetorical Criticism* (Chapel Hill: University of North Carolina Press, 1984), 33–34 for the establishment of a rhetorical unit.

[21] See Robbins, *Jesus the Teacher*, 191–93.

[22] See n. 19 for duality and three-step progression. Cf. Frank J. Matera, *Passion Narratives and Gospel Theologies. Interpreting the Synoptics Through Their Passion Stories* (New York: Paulist Press, 1986), 34–48 for a close reading of the unit containing many similar observations about the text.

1. Selection of Prisoner to be Humiliated and Crucified: Mark 15:1–15

The first scene features Pilate's direct action with Jesus (Mark 15:1–15). In fifteen verses, Pilate's name occurs eight times, and he is the subject of fifteen verbs and the antecedent of five participles.[23] The scene opens with the handing of Jesus over to Pilate and closes with Pilate's handing of Jesus over to be crucified. Near the middle of the scene, the narrator tells us in a digression in pluperfect tense that Pilate "knew that out of envy the chief priests had handed him over." Thus, the overall theme of the action is the handing over of Jesus, and the scene depicts the final stage of the process which started when Judas Iscariot went to the chief priests and reached an agreement with them (Mark 14:10–11). Much as the scene with Judas contains an opening and closure governed by παραδοῖ (14:10, 11), so 15:1–15 contains an opening, middle and closure which features the handing over of Jesus as the central action:

15:1 ... δήσαντες τὸν Ἰησοῦν ἀπήνεγκαν
 καὶ παρέδωκαν Πιλάτῳ.
15:10 ἐγίνωσκεν γὰρ ὅτι διὰ φθόνον
 παραδεδώκεισαν αὐτὸν οἱ ἀρχιερεῖς.
15:15 ... παρέδωκεν τὸν Ἰησοῦν
 φραγελλώσας ἵνα σταυρωθῇ.

Within the framework of the handing over of Jesus, Pilate releases Barabbas. This action highlights the entrapment of Jesus in a process which is driven so forcefully by internal and external forces that there is no escape. The enactment of the release emerges subtly from its opposite – being bound: δέω. In the opening sentence of the scene, the chief priests, with the elders, scribes, and entire council, "bind" (δήσαντες) Jesus, lead him away, and hand him over to Pilate (Mark 15:1). Then in 15:6, the narrator tells us that "one prisoner" (ἕνα δέσμιον) regularly was released during the feast and that Barabbas is imprisoned (δεδεμένος) among the rebels who had committed murder during the insurrection. The persistent use of δέ- root-words associates the containment of Jesus with the containment of Barabbas. Then the release of Barabbas, who committed murder in consort with other insurrectionists, creates bitter contrast with the containment of Jesus. After the narrator introduces the custom of releasing a prisoner during

---

[23] Verbs: ἐπηρώτα/ησεν (15:2, 4); θαυμάζειν (15:5); ἀπέλυεν (15:6); ἐποίει (15:8); ἀπεκρίθη (15:9); ἀπολύσω (15:9); ἐγίνωσκεν (15:10); ἀπολύσῃ (15:11); ἔλεγεν (15:12, 14); ποιήσω (15:12); ποιῆσαι (15:15); ἀπέλυσεν (15:15); παρέδωκεν (15:15). Participles: λέγων (15:4, 9); ἀποκριθείς (15:12); βουλόμενος (15:15); φραγελλώσας (15:15).

the feast (15:6), Pilate steps forward to perform the action. First, Pilate asks the people if he should release the King of the Jews to them (15:9); secondly, the chief priests stir up the crowd to have Pilate release Barabbas (15:11); and thirdly, he releases Barabbas to them (15:15). With this sequence, the contrast between binding and releasing accentuates the plight of Jesus. The progressive form emerges as follows:

15:1 ... <u>δήσαντες</u> τὸν Ἰησοῦν ... <u>παρέδωκαν</u> Πιλάτῳ.
15:6 ... <u>ἀπέλυεν</u> αὐτοῖς ἕνα <u>δέσμιον</u> ὃν παρῃτοῦντο.
15:7 ἦν δὲ ὁ λεγόμενος Βαραββᾶς ... <u>δεδεμένος</u> ...
15:9 ὁ δὲ Πιλᾶτος ἀπεκρίθη αὐτοῖς λέγων,
θέλετε <u>ἀπολύσω</u> ὑμῖν τὸν βασιλέα τῶν Ἰουδαίων;
15:11 ... μᾶλλον τὸν Βαραββᾶν <u>ἀπολύσῃ</u> αὐτοῖς.
15:15 ὁ δὲ Πιλᾶτος ... <u>ἀπέλυσεν</u> αὐτοῖς τὸν Βαραββᾶν,
καὶ <u>παρέδωκεν</u> τὸν Ἰησοῦν ... ἵνα σταυρωθῇ.

With this progression, Jesus, who was bound and handed over to Pilate (15:1), is now handed over to be crucified, while Barabbas, who was imprisoned for insurrection and murder, is released (15:15).

The dynamics of the interaction among Pilate, the Jewish leaders, and the crowd prepare the stage for Jesus' death by crucifixion. The selection of this mode of death emerges only toward the end of the scene. When Pilate asks the people what he should do with the King of the Jews, they cry out, "Crucify him" (15:13). When Pilate asks them what evil Jesus has done, they cry out all the more, "Crucify him" (15:14). This response leads to the final item in the closing sentence where he hands him over "to be crucified" (15:15). The scene closes, then, with two completed actions, Pilate's release of Barabbas and Pilate's handing over of Jesus. In the midst of threefold or fourfold references to the handing over of Jesus (15:1, 10, 15), to being bound or imprisoned (15:1, 6, 7), to the release of a prisoner (15:6, 9, 11, 15), to Barabbas (15:7, 11, 15), and to crucifixion (15:13, 14, 15), Pilate identifies Jesus near the beginning, middle, and end as "the King of the Jews" (15:2, 9, 12). In the Markan narrative, no one has used this title for Jesus prior to this scene, but once it occurs on the lips of Pilate, it plays a major role in the Markan version of Jesus' death.

2. Mockery of Jesus as Royalty: Mark 15:16–24

The next phase features soldiers who gather the entire battalion to mock, abuse, and torture Jesus, then take Jesus out and crucify him. Language of crucifixion and address of Jesus as "King of the Jews" unites this scene with the previous scene. The opening, middle, and closure of the scene occur through a progression which links "leading away" and "leading out" with "crucifying":

15:16 οἱ δὲ στρατιῶται ἀπήγαγον αὐτόν...
15:20 καὶ ἐξάγουσιν αὐτὸν ἵνα σταυρώσουσιν αὐτόν.
15:24 καὶ σταυροῦσιν αὐτόν.

First, the soldiers lead Jesus away and call the entire cohort together; secondly, they lead Jesus out to crucify him; and thirdly, they crucify him. In the context of the spatial movement, the dressing and undressing of Jesus establishes a progression which gives the scene dramatic closure:

15:17 καὶ ἐνδιδύσκουσιν αὐτόν πορφύραν ...
15:20 ἐξέδυσαν αὐτὸν τὴν πορφύσαν
       καὶ ἐνέδυσαν αὐτὸν τὰ ἱμάτια τὰ ἴδια.
15:24 καὶ διαμερίζονται τὰ ἱμάτια αὐτοῦ ...

First, they dress him in purple garb; then, they remove the purple garb and put his own clothes on him; and finally, they divide his own clothes among themselves. The changing of clothes reaches its conclusion in the absence of clothes on Jesus while he is on the cross. This feature underscores the brutality and humiliation of Jesus' crucifixion. The mocking of Jesus dramatizes Pilate's designation of Jesus as "King of the Jews." In addition to clothing Jesus in purple, the soldiers place a woven crown of thorns on his head, hail him as "King of the Jews," strike his head with a reed, spit on him, and kneel down in homage to him (15:17–19). This is a kingship ritual which the narrator tells us is a mockery (15:20: ἐνέπαιξαν αὐτῷ). When the changing of clothes (15:17, 20) leads to the distribution of Jesus' own clothes (15:24), the reader has seen a sequence in which Jesus was taken prisoner, condemned to death, mocked as a king, and hung naked on a cross.

3. Ridicule of Jesus while He Hangs on the Cross: Mark 15:25–32

The narrator continues the account with a comment that it was the third hour of the day (15:25). The comment introduces information on which the account will build, much like the narrator's earlier comment that a prisoner customarily was released at the feast (15:6). Unlike the earlier comment, 15:24 introduces a time sequence rather than an action. Also, instead of beginning with flashback information (15:6: in the past he regularly released someone) and moving into contemporary background information (15:7: Barabbas was among the rebels in prison), the narrator begins with contemporary background information (15:25: "It was the third hour") and continues with contemporary foreground information: "and they crucified him, and the inscription of the charge against him read 'the King of the Jews,' and they crucify two thieves with him, one on the right and one on his left" (15:26–

27). With this digression, the narrator introduces a new scene: responses to Jesus while he is on the cross between two thieves. The transition is smooth and skillful, since it continues the language of crucifixion and the designation of Jesus as "King of the Jews":

15:25 ἦν δὲ ὥρα τρίτη
       καὶ ἐσταύρωσαν αὐτόν.
15:26 καὶ ἦν ἡ ἐπιγραφὴ τῆς αἰτίας αὐτοῦ ἐπιγεγραμμένη,
       ὁ βασιλεὺς τῶν Ἰουδαίων.
15:27 καὶ σὺν αὐτῷ σταυροῦσιν δύο λῃστάς ...

In the center of the digression stands the second reference to Jesus as "the King of the Jews"[24] after the three references in the scene with Pilate. Thus, the narrator maintains the presence of this designation for Jesus in the setting where the soldiers crucify Jesus. With this action, the attention shifts to Jesus on a cross between two thieves.

The shift from the torture and abuse of Jesus to responses as Jesus hangs on the cross is exhibited by the opening and closure of this stage of the crucifixion:

15:27 καὶ σὺν αὐτῷ σταυροῦσιν δύο λῃστάς ...
15:32 καὶ οἱ συνεσταυρωμένοι σὺν αὐτῷ ...

The two thieves are the last people who speak to Jesus before his death, and their response to him is startling. One might expect them to exhibit respect for Jesus or expect Jesus to say something gracious to them. Instead, Jesus becomes as isolated from the two thieves as he does from everyone else. The progressive isolation occurs as follows:

15:29 καὶ οἱ παραπορευόμενοι
       ἐβλασφήμουν αὐτόν ...
15:31 ὁμοίως καὶ οἱ ἀρχιερεῖς
       ἐμπαίζοντες πρὸς ἀλλήλους μετὰ τῶν γραμματέων
       ἔλεγον ...
15:32 καὶ οἱ συνεσταυρωμένοι σὺν αὐτῷ
       ὠνείδιζον αὐτόν.

The scene depicts three groups who react to Jesus: (1) people who pass by; (2) the chief priests with the scribes; and (3) those crucified with him. The first people speak blasphemy against him. Earlier in the narrative scribes had claimed that Jesus blasphemed (evidently against God) when he forgave the paralytic's sins (2:7), and later Jesus implies that scribes from Jerusalem blasphemed against the holy spirit when they said he possessed an unclean spirit (3:29–30). When Jesus is tried before the Sanhedrin, the high priest asserts that Jesus' response is blasphemy (14:64). Now, people who pass by are said to blaspheme against

---

[24] The first reference after the opening scene occurs in 15:18.

8. The Reversed Contextualization of Ps 22 in the Markan Crucifixion 267

Jesus by wagging their heads, claiming that he would destroy the temple and build it in three days, and taunting him to save himself by coming down from the cross (15:30). After this, the chief priests with the scribes are said to "mock to one another" (15:31). Earlier in the narrative, Jesus predicted that Gentiles would mock him (10:34), and this prediction was fulfilled by the soldiers (15:20), as discussed above. Now, the chief priests and scribes add to the mockery with remarks about "saving" and "coming down from the cross" which reverberate with Jesus' earlier remarks about "losing one's life to save it" and "taking up one's cross and following" (8:34–35). The response of the chief priests and the scribes creates the setting for the third reference to Jesus as "King" since the scene with Pilate. The presence of this designation may have made it natural for the Markan narrator to refer to the statements of the chief priests and scribes as mockery, since they are referring in jest to Jesus much as the soldiers did in their ritual (15:18). Markan narration adapts the wording of the title to fit the language of Jewish leaders: they call Jesus "the Messiah, the King of Israel" (15:32) while Pilate called him "the King of the Jews." This is the last reference to Jesus as king in the Markan narrative. In the next scene, a Roman centurion who has seen the proceedings refers to Jesus as "son of God." The significance of this change in language is one of the major interests in this paper. For now, we notice that the title "King" occurs systematically throughout the selection process, the mockery, and the crucifixion. In this context, even those who hang on the crosses beside Jesus "revile" him. In the end, everyone mentioned in the scene, including those crucified with him, reacts negatively to Jesus as he hangs on the cross.

4. Jesus' Crying Out and Death: Mark 15:33–39
The final stage of the crucifixion (15:33–39) depicts the death of Jesus. During this stage, there is no reference to the cross, the two thieves alongside Jesus, or the chief priests and scribes. There are many bystanders, and one runs and fills a sponge with vinegar while another is a centurion standing in front who speaks out after Jesus dies. All the foreground and background information directs the reader's attention to Jesus as he dies.

The scene opens with reference to a three hour span of time (from the sixth to the ninth hour) when there was darkness over the whole earth (15:34). Then at the ninth hour Jesus cries with a loud voice: Ελωι ελωι λεμα σαβαχθανι (Ps 22:1 in Aramaic). This cry of Jesus introduces a new pattern of irony in the Markan version. The pattern unfolds as follows:

15:34 ἐβόησεν ὁ Ἰησοῦς φωνῇ μεγάλῃ,
       Ελωι ελωι λεμα σαβαχθανι;
15:35 καί τινες τῶν παρεστηκότων ἀκούσαντες ἔλεγον,
       ἴδε Ἠλίαν φωνεῖ.
15:36 ἄφετε ἴδωμεν εἰ ἔρχεται Ἠλίας καθελεῖν αὐτόν.
15:37 ὁ δὲ Ἰησοῦς ἀφεὶς φωνὴν μεγάλην ἐξέπνευσεν.

When Jesus cries out, Ελωι ελωι, bystanders say, "Look, he is calling Elijah." Then someone runs and gets vinegar for him to drink and says, "Let us see if Elijah comes to take him down." Then Jesus lets out a loud cry and breathes his last breath. The alliteration and repetition in this sequence underscores the irony. Jesus has cried out the first verse of a psalm which contains a graphic depiction of agony suffered by someone who is encircled, entrapped, and tortured. God does not answer, and the people mock the cry by understanding it as a call to Elijah rather than to God. Jesus' cry exhibits his experience of complete abandonment: in this hour he is abandoned not only by all the people around him but also by God. Jesus is a victim with whom people play for entertainment – to see what happens – and whom God allows to die.

The centurion standing in front of Jesus responds when he sees and hears Jesus die. The relation of the centurion's response to the scene is apparent from the verbal relationship:

15:35 τινες τῶν παρεστηκότων ... ἔλεγον, ἴδε ...
15:36 ... ἴδωμεν ...
15:37 ... ἐξέπνευσεν.
15:39 ἰδὼν δὲ ὁ κεντυρίων ὁ παρεστηκὼς ἐξ ἐναντίας αὐτοῦ
       ὅτι οὕτως ἐξέπνευσεν εἶπεν,
       Ἀληθῶς οὗτος ὁ ἄνθρωπος υἱὸς θεοῦ ἦν.

The centurion who was placed in front of Jesus represents those to whom Jesus was delivered for crucifixion and those who have mocked him as "King of the Jews." When this representative sees the manner of Jesus' death, he infers that Jesus was "son of God." The construction of the response connects the manner of the death with "this" man:

15:39 ἰδὼν ... ὅτι οὕτως ἐξέπνευσεν εἶπεν,
       Ἀληθῶς οὗτος ὁ ἄνθρωπος υἱὸς θεοῦ ἦν.

We must seek to find out why, from the narrator's perspective, the centurion would call this particular man son of God.

5. Permission for and Burial of Jesus' Corpse: Mark 15:40–46

The narrator begins the next scene with a digression much as he began the scene with Jesus and the two thieves. First, he gives us contemporary background information (15:40: there also were women watching from afar, among whom were Mary Magdalene, and Mary the mother of James the younger and of Joses, and Salome); then he gives us flashback information (15:41a: who, when he was in Galilee, regularly followed him and ministered to him), and this leads to additional background information (15:41b: and many others who had come up with him to Jerusalem). Then he continues with foreground information (15:42–43: and when evening already had come ... Joseph of Arimathea came ... and requested the body of Jesus). At this point Pilate marvels if Jesus is already dead (15:44). This establishes a point of contact with the opening scene when Pilate marvelled when Jesus no longer answered anything (15:5). Pilate's uncertainty leads him to summon the centurion, and this feature brings the centurion from the foot of the cross into the center of the scene which leads to the burial of Jesus. Then, in the mode of the opening scene where Pilate had asked Jesus if he was the King of the Jews (15:2) and again if he was not going to answer anything (15:4), Pilate asks the centurion if Jesus has already died (15:45). When the centurion informs Pilate that Jesus is dead, Pilate grants the corpse to Joseph who buys a linen cloth, takes Jesus down, wraps him in the cloth, and puts him in a tomb.

The Markan version of these episodes, then, emphasizes the role of the centurion who sees Jesus expire, comes to Pilate when summoned, and informs Pilate of his death. This sequence forms a three-step progression:

(1) ἰδὼν δὲ ὁ <u>κεντυρίων</u> ὁ παρεστηκὼς ἐξ ἐναντίας αὐτοῦ
  ὅτι οὕτως ἐξέπνευσεν εἶπεν ... (15:39).
(2) ὁ δὲ Πιλᾶτος ἐθαύμασεν εἰ ἤδη τέθνηκεν,
  καὶ προσκαλεσάμενος τὸν <u>κεντυρίωνα</u> ... (15:44).
(3) καὶ γνοὺς ἀπὸ τοῦ <u>κεντυρίωνος</u> ἐδωρήσατο
  τὸ πτῶμα τῷ Ἰωσήφ (15:45).

The closing scene of the crucifixion is concerned to verify the death and burial of Jesus. It is succeeded by a scene in which the women who saw the death and burial also see the tomb standing empty and are told that Jesus, who was crucified, has risen.

Conclusion

The Markan version of Jesus' crucifixion has five scenes. The opening and closing scenes feature Pilate, who hands Jesus over to soldiers for crucifixion and grants Jesus' body to Joseph of Arimathea for burial. The three scenes in the middle feature mockery and torture of Jesus. First, Jesus is mocked and abused as he is dressed in royal clothes, reclothed in his own garments, then undressed as he is hung on the cross.

Second, Jesus is mocked by people who pass by, by chief priests and scribes, and by those who are crucified with him. Third, Jesus is mocked by people who mistake his cry to God (Ελωι) as a cry to Elijah. These episodes enact Jesus' experience of programmatic abandonment by everyone at his death. When Jesus dies in the context of the ritual mockery of him as a king, a centurion refers to him as "son of God," and Joseph of Arimathea buries Jesus in a tomb. Women who watch the crucifixion from afar see where Joseph puts the corpse and come after the sabbath to an empty tomb.

The Markan Crucifixion and a Persian Ritual at the Sacian Feast

Now that we have before us an initial reading of the Markan text from the perspective of repetition within its progression, let us begin to ask what meanings may accompany the complex network of significations in it. It is clear that Ps 22 (LXX: 21) plays a generative role in the Markan formulation of the account, but there appears to be additional "cultural discourse" involved in the repetitive reference to Jesus as king and the extension of the mockery beyond the ritual by the soldiers (Mark 15:17–20) into the scene where Jesus is hanging on the cross (cf. ἐμπαίζω in 15:20, 31) and the scene of Jesus' death cry where they make a mockery of his reference to Ελωι (15:34–36).

An intertextual search for the broader cultural discourse brings one to a fascinating discussion in the Fourth Oration of Dio Chrysostom (ca. 40–after 112 CE).[25] In this text, Dio speaks about activities of the Persians at the Sacian feast that present a sequence of activities that contain many similarities with the Markan account of the crucifixion:

1. "They take one of their prisoners who has been condemned to death" (Dio 4.67).

> Jesus, who has been condemned to death by the Sanhedrin, is taken by Pilate and his soldiers (Mark 15:15–16).

2. "[They] set him on the king's throne, give him the royal apparel, and permit him to give orders, to drink and carouse, and to dally with the royal concubines during those days, and no one prevents his doing anything he pleases" (Dio 4.67).

> Jesus is clothed in a purple cloak; a crown of thorns is placed on his head; he is hailed as "King of the Jews"; and they kneel down in homage to him (Mark 15:17–19).

---

[25] A helpful analysis of this discourse is present in Ragnar Höistad, *Cynic Hero and Cynic King: Studies in the Cynic Conception of Man* (Lund: Bloms, 1948), 150–222. Also, see n. 18.

3. "After that they strip and scourge him and then hang him" (Dio 4.67).

   Jesus is stripped (Mark 15:20), and since he has already been scourged (15:15), he is led out and hung on a cross (15:25).

4. "If [the prisoner] understands [the meaning of the action], he probably breaks out into wailing and refuses to go along without protesting ..." (Dio 4.69).

   Jesus cries out, "My God, my God, why have you forsaken me?" (Mark 15:34).

When compared with the Dio account of the Sacian festival, the Markan account contains: (a) embellishment of the process by which a prisoner who has been condemned to death is handed over for the festival; (b) embellishment of the mockery of the prisoner as king but omission of activities which allow Jesus to function for a time as king; (c) embellishment of mockery of Jesus while he hangs in public humiliation on the cross; and (d) addition of an account of burial of the condemned prisoner after his death.

The presence of the tradition of the Sacian festival in Mediterranean society suggests an alternative to traditional interpretation of the scenes. The purpose for releasing a condemned prisoner would have been to allow the people to mock, abuse, and humiliate the prisoner during the days of the festival celebration. In other words, if Pilate were functioning culturally "in character," he would release a condemned prisoner to the people with the understanding that they would put him through an ordeal of royal mockery during the festival. Whether the prisoner would be killed or not would be a matter of circumstance, or consensus, among the people. The first ironic dimension, then, is a process of selection whereby a prisoner guilty of murder is released without the conditions of an ordeal, while an unjustly condemned prisoner is turned over, according to the people's wishes, to the brutality of soldiers. When this happens, the "real" king of the Jews (from the point of view of the narrator) undergoes the ordeal intended for a "real" condemned prisoner. This would be a "Christian" transformation of the broader cultural discourse.

The second ironic dimension emerges as Jesus is not allowed to live as a king during the festival. Athenaeus presents Berosus' account of the five-day Sacian festival in his *Babylonian History* (5th–4th cent. BCE) as follows: "it was customary for the masters to be ruled by their slaves, and one of them, as leader of the household, was clothed in a robe similar to the king's" (Athenaeus, *Deipnosophistae* 14.639). This reversal of roles brings Mark 10:42–45 into special prominence:

   And Jesus called them to him and said to them, "You know that those who are supposed to rule over the Gentiles lord it over them, and their great men exercise authority over them. But it shall not be so among you; but whoever would be great among you must be your servant, and whoever would be first among you must be slave of all. For the Son of man also came not to be served but to serve, and to give his life as a ransom for many.

If an interpreter supposes that the Gospel of Mark presents Jesus' enactment of the principles he has taught earlier in the narrative,[26] then these verses reveal the reason why there is no depiction of an interval of time when Jesus gives orders and lives the traditional life of a king. According to Markan discourse, Jesus will not exercise traditional kingly authority over others or live for a period of time in luxury and abundance. Rather, his role is as a servant who loses his life for his own sake and the gospel's sake.

Third, the events in the Markan sequence appear to result from Jesus' choice of "the ways of God" rather than "the ways of men" (8:33). Jesus is doing what he understands to be necessary as a result of the will of God.[27] Dio emphasizes that a king who is a son of Zeus (Διὸ παῖς/υἱός: 4.21, 27, 31) will choose the way[28] that divine instruction rather than human instruction has taught him (4.29). He will know the foolishness of attempting to gain (κερδαίνειν) money and possessions (Dio 4.6; cf. Mark 8:36) and to clamor after wealth (πλοῦτος: Dio 4.10; cf. Mark 4:19; 10:25; 12:41). Rather, he will be a shepherd of peoples (Dio 3.41; 4.43; cf. Mark 6:34; 14:27), considering himself to be doing his duty only when he helps people: "having been appointed to this work by the greatest god, whom it is not right for him to disobey..." (Dio 3.55). The king depends on the loyalty (πίστις) of his friends, whom he needs as co-workers (Dio 3.86), and his greatest sufferings arise when he is wronged by friends whom he did not know to be his enemies (Dio 3.114).

This means that the Roman centurion could be functioning culturally "in character" when he calls Jesus son of God/Zeus. If so, his language may speak out of a much wider horizon of cultural discourse than traditional interpretations of this scene entertain. First, the high priest's understanding of Jesus as Messiah, Son of the Blessed (14:61–62), intermingles with Pilate's and the soldiers' understanding of Jesus as King of the Jews (15:2, 9, 12, 18). When the title "son of God" emerges from the lips of the centurion, the concept of kingship from Hellenistic-Roman circles may be entering the conversations about kingship in Jewish and Christian circles. It is a well-known tradition in

---

[26] See Robbins, *Jesus the Teacher*, esp. 184–94, 209–13.
[27] See Mark 3:35; 8:31; 9:11; 13:10; 14:36.
[28] ἡ ὁδός: Dio 4.33; cf. Mark 1:2–3; 8:27; 9:33–34; 10:17, 32, 52; 12:14.

the first century Mediterranean world that a king can benefit his people by dying for them. The well-known verse of Horace (65–68 BCE), *dulce et decorum est pro patria mori* ("sweet and fitting it is to die for one's fatherland"),[29] included kings by the first century. One of the most widely known traditions of a king's voluntary sacrifice exists in the "example of Codrus, the legendary last king of Athens, who on the basis of an oracle went out to meet the enemy alone in slave's clothing; unrecognized, he was killed by them and in so doing saved Athens."[30] Direct evidence for the interest of Christians in the tradition of kings dying for their subjects is known from Clement of Rome: "Many kings and rulers, when a time of pestilence has set in, have followed the counsel of oracles, and given themselves up to death, that they might rescue their subjects through their own blood" (1 Clement 55:1–5).[31] These is evidence that suggests the possibility, therefore, that the Markan account of Jesus' death intermingles broader cultural discourse with widespread discursive traditions in Jewish and Christian sectors of Mediterranean society and culture.[32]

Psalm 22 (LXX: 21) and the Markan Crucifixion

As noted above, embellishment of the crucifixion account in Mark occurs not only in the scene of selection of the condemned prisoner but also in the changing of Jesus' clothes, the public humiliation of Jesus as he hangs on the cross, and the mockery when Jesus cries out his death cry to God. This section of the essay focuses on the presence of language from Ps 22 (LXX: 21) in the three inner scenes of the account, and it uses modes of "progymnastic composition" to describe the rhetorical practice by which the Markan text incorporates the language from the psalm.[33]

---

[29] Horace, *Odes* 3.2.13; see Martin Hengel, *The Atonement: The Origins of the Doctrine in the New Testament* (Philadelphia: Fortress, 1981), 13, 82, n. 47.

[30] Hengel, *Atonement*, 14, 82, n. 48. Cf. David Seeley, *The Noble Death: Graeco-Roman Martyrology and Paul's Concept of Salvation* (JSNTSup 28; Sheffield: JSOT Press, 1990), 113–41; Sam K. Williams, *Jesus' Death as Saving Event: The Background and Origin of a Concept* (HDR 2; Missoula: Scholars Press, 1975), esp. 137–63.

[31] Hengel, *Atonement*, 14.

[32] See Dio 4.39–45; contra Martin Hengel, *The Son of God: The Origin of Christology and the History of Jewish-Hellenistic Religion* (Philadelphia: Fortress, 1976), 30, n. 57, who argues that "Son of Zeus" is fundamentally distinct from "Son of God."

[33] The term "progymnastic rhetoric" refers to the rhetorical practices presented in treatises in antiquity entitled ΠΡΟΓΥΜΝΑΣΜΑΤΑ. For the concept and range of progymnastic rhetoric see Vernon K. Robbins, "Writing as a Rhetorical Act in Plutarch and the Gospels," in *Persuasive Artistry: Studies in New Testament Rhetoric in Honor of George A. Kennedy* (ed. Duane F. Watson; Sheffield: JSOT Press, 1991), 157–86. Also see idem, "The Crucifixion and the Speech of Jesus," in *Foundations & Facets Forum* 4/1 (1988): 33–46.

The first use of language from Ps 22 occurs in Mark 15:24. As noted above, the Markan account presents the dividing of Jesus' garments at the point where they crucify him. This is the final act in a sequence where Jesus first is clothed in royal garments, then reclothed in his own garments, and then reduced to nakedness (15:17, 20, 24). Wording from Ps 22 emerges as the soldiers divide Jesus' garments among themselves by casting lots, but the exact wording of Ps 22:19 (LXX 21:19) is not simply recontextualized in the Markan text. Rather, 15:24 contains a "recitation" of the psalm verse in typical Markan style.[34] The LXX text reads as follows:

διεμερίσαντο τὰ ἱμάτια μου ἑαυτοῖς
καὶ ἐπὶ τὸν ἱματισμόν μου ἔβαλον κλῆρον.

Markan composition has transformed the verse into a climactic statement that ends the initial mocking scene:

καὶ σταυροῦσιν αὐτόν,
καὶ διαμερίζονται τὰ ἱμάτια αὐτοῦ,
βάλλοντες κλῆρον ἐπ' αὐτὰ τίς τί ἄρῃ.

First, the Markan text has transformed the *parallelismus membrorum* construction of the psalm verse into a three-clause statement by adding σταυροῦσιν αὐτόν and introducing καί-paratactic plus present participle:

(a) *and* they crucify him,
(b) *and* they divide his garments,
(c) casting lots for them who takes what.

The initial clause about crucifying Jesus is a narratorial continuation of 15:20c, and the participial clause ends with an ironic turn on "carrying" as the soldiers carry a piece of Jesus' garment away, in contrast to Simon who carried Jesus' cross (15:21). Second, the Markan text sustains historic present tense throughout the clause, in contrast to aorist tense in the LXX text. Third, the Markan text presents a third person narrative voice, "they divide *his* garments," rather than the first person narrative voice, "they divided *my* garments."[35] These features exhibit standard Markan style as language has been rephrased from Ps 22:19 to formulate the dramatic conclusion to a scene in which Jesus, mocked as "King of the Jews," is dressed in royal garments, reclothed in his own garments, then left without clothing as he hangs in public humiliation on the cross.

---

[34] Ronald F. Hock and Edward N. O'Neil, *The Chreia in Ancient Rhetoric: The Progymnasmata* (Atlanta: Scholars Press, 1986), 94–95; Robbins, "Writing," 146–55. Also Bakhtin, *Dialogic*, 341–42, see n. 2.

[35] Cf. Mark 1:2, where third person voicing is changed to first person.

The next scene (Mark 15:25–32) exhibits "expansion composition"[36] as it incorporates language from Ps 22 to describe the people's mocking of Jesus while he hangs on the cross. Ps 21:8–9 (LXX) reads:

πάντες οἱ θεωροῦντες με ἐξεμυκτήρισάν με,
ἐλάλησαν ἐν χείλεσιν, ἐκίνησαν κεφαλήν
ἤλπισεν ἐπὶ κύριον, ῥυσάσθω αὐτόν·
σωσάτω αὐτόν, ὅτι θέλει αὐτόν.

All who have observed me sneered at me,
they spoke with their lips, they wagged their head,
"He hoped in the Lord, let him rescue him;
let him save him, because he wants him."

First, the Markan text divides "all who have observed me" into three groups: (a) the ones passing by (v. 29); (b) the chief priests with the scribes (v. 31); (c) the ones crucified with him (v. 32). This provides a three-step structure in which the text embellishes language from Ps 21:8–9 with Markan discourse. Mark 15:27 builds on the final step in the previous scene (15:24) by repeating "and they crucify." Now, however, the language shifts the scene to Jesus' crucifixion between two thieves, "one on his right and one on his left." In Mark 10:37, James and John had envisioned being seated on the right and left hand of Jesus in his glory. Markan narration stands this hope on its head, inverting the disciples' expectation as it presents Jesus' right and left hand men as thieves crucified along with him. Using καί-paratactic plus present participle, Mark 15:28–29 transforms the first *parallelismus membrorum* of the psalm verses into:

καὶ οἱ παραπορευόμενοι ἐβλασφήμουν αὐτόν
κινοῦντες τὰς κεφαλὰς αὐτῶν
καὶ λέγοντες·

Then, integrating preceding Markan discourse about destroying the temple (14:58), Mark 15:29–32 expands σωσάτω αὐτόν from Ps 21:9 to:

And those who passed by derided him, wagging their heads, and saying:
(a) "Aha, he who destroys the temple and builds it in three days;
(b) save yourself (σῶσον σεαυτόν),
(c) come down from the cross."
So also the chief priests mocked him to one another with the scribes, saying:

---

[36] Hock and O'Neil, *The Chreia*, 100–103. Vernon K. Robbins, "Pronouncement Stories and Jesus' Blessing of the Children: A Rhetorical Approach," *Semeia* 29 (1984): 43–74, esp. 48–51.

(a) "Others he saved (ἄλλους ἔσωσεν);
(b) himself he cannot save (ἑαυτὸν οὐ δύναται σῶσαι);
(c) let the Messiah the King of Israel come down now from the cross;
(d) that we may see and believe."

Then, the third step provides dramatic closure with a brief statement that reiterates language in Mark 15:27:

(15:32c) καὶ οἱ συνεσταυρωμένοι σὺν αὐτῷ ὠνείδιζον αὐτόν.

This final statement incorporates language from Ps 21:7, which refers to the sufferer as "reviled of men" (ὄνειδος ἀνθρώπου) just before verses 8–9 discussed above. We will return to this use of language from the preceding verse in the psalm. Suffice it to say at this point that the Markan text has expanded aspects of Ps 21:7–9 into a three-step display of mockery and humiliation of Jesus while he hangs on the cross.

The scene that presents the death of Jesus (Mark 15:33–39) begins with a recontextualization of the opening verse of Ps 22 (LXX: 21).[37] The new context, however, turns the verse into a chreia attributed to Jesus.[38] The chreia, which contains transliterated Aramaic words, provides a context for mockery as Ελωι is heard as Elijah. Between the Aramaic version and the mockery stands a rephrasing in Greek translation. The translation is very interesting in relation to the LXX version available to us:

ὁ θεὸς ὁ θεός μου, πρόσχες μοι·
ἵνα τί ἐγκατέλιπές με;
μακρὰν ἀπο τῆς σωτηρίας μου οἱ λόγοι τῶν παραπτωμάτων μου
ὁ θεός μου, κεκράξομαι ἡμέρας, καὶ οὐκ εἰσακούσῃ,
καὶ νυκτός, καὶ οὐκ εἰς ἄνοιαν ἐμοί.

The Markan text reformulates "I shall cry out day ... and night ..." (LXX: 21:3) into "when it became dark ... Jesus cried out with a loud voice ..." (Mark 15:33–34). Then the Markan text strengthens the call "God, my God," by doubling the ὁ θεός μου in the manner of its

---

[37] For "reciting by heart," see Bakhtin, *Dialogic*, 341.

[38] See Vernon K. Robbins, "The Chreia," in *Greco-Roman Literature and The New Testament: Selected Forms and Genres* (ed. David E. Aune; SBLSBS 21; Atlanta: Scholars Press, 1988), 1–23, esp. 2–4. For the placement of quotations from authoritative literature on the lips of personages in Mediterranean literature contemporary with the gospels, see, e.g., Plutarch, *Alexander* 28.3: "At a later time, however, when Alexander had been hit by an arrow and was suffering great pain, he said: 'This, my friends, that flows here, is blood, and not "Ichor, such as flows from the veins of the blessed gods"'" (Homer, *Iliad* 5.340). For this and other examples, see Vernon K. Robbins, *Ancient Quotes & Anecdotes: From Crib to Crypt* (Sonoma, Calif.: Polebridge Press, 1989), see 96–97 for variant versions of this chreia.

double occurrence in 21:2, 3 and by the absence of "give heed to me." This creates a poignant three-step cry: (a) my God, (b) my God, (c) why have you forsaken me?

Interpreters who have tried to turn this cry into a positive statement have imposed the rhetoric of Psalm 22 on the rhetoric of Markan discourse.[39] Interpreters are right that Psalm 22 contains a rhetoric of confidence, trust, and hope. It is improper, however, to let this rhetoric silence the rhetoric of abandonment displayed in Mark. Interpreters have overlooked the Markan context and selection of language from the Psalm. The Markan scene occurs when all hope of rescue has disappeared. Mark 15:37 tells the reader that when Jesus let out his loud cry, his breath went out of him. In other words, this was Jesus' last cry, his death sound.

This brings this essay to an observation that, to my knowledge, has not been made in prior interpretation of the Markan account. The Markan sequence uses scenes from Ps 22 (21) in the reverse order in which they occur in the Psalm. In the Psalm, the sufferer's cry is a cry for help; in Mark, Jesus' cry is his final death cry. In the Psalm, the sufferer says many things after this initial cry, and in the end he tells God how he will praise his name in the midst of the congregation (22:22), how all the proud of the earth will bow down to him (22:29), and how the Lord's deliverance will be proclaimed to the coming generation (22:30–31). In Mark, in strong contrast, Jesus' final utterance is, "My God, my God, why have you forsaken me."

To put this another way, the sequence of Mark 15 inverts the sequence of Ps 22, and with this inversion comes a subversion of its rhetoric. The sufferer in the psalm expresses hope to the end; Jesus on the cross expresses the agony of abandonment by everyone including God. An interpreter needs only to look at Ps 38:21–22 (LXX: 37:22–23) to see how Jesus' cry would read if he were expressing hope:

μὴ ἐγκαταλίπῃς με, κύριε·
ὁ θεός μου, μὴ ἀποστῇς ἀπ' ἐμοῦ·
πρόσχες εἰς τὴν βοήθειάν μου,
κύριε τῆς σωτηρίας μου.

Do not abandon me, Lord;
my God, do not desert me.
Give heed to my help,
Lord of my salvation.

---

[39] E.g., see this tradition of interpretation in Frank J. Matera, *The Kingship of Jesus: Composition and Theology in Mark 15* (SBLDS 66; Chico, Calif.: Scholars Press, 1982), 127–35, 194–96. For the use of Psalm 22 in Jewish tradition, see Mark G.V. Hoffman, "Psalm 22 (LXX 21) and the Crucifixion of Jesus" (Ph.D. diss., Yale University, 1996).

The final words of Ps 38 are a plea for God to help, and the plea is punctuated with reference to God as "Lord of my salvation." The Markan account of the crucifixion, in contrast, presents a Jesus who no longer holds any hope for rescue from the agony of death. This is the reality of human suffering Jesus enacts on the cross in Mark.

The Markan approach, which emphasizes the agony and reality of Jesus' death, produces a backwards reading of Ps 22. The reading begins with verse 19, the place in the middle of the psalm were the sufferer refers to the dividing of his garments by the casting of lots. The reading continues by proceeding backwards to verses 7–8, where the sufferer refers to the wagging of heads and the mocking speech, "let him save him." Then the Markan text moves back to verse 6 of the psalm as the narratorial voice says that those crucified with Jesus "reviled" him, just as the sufferer in the psalm refers to himself as "reviled" of men. Last of all, the reading proceeds backwards to the first two verses of the psalm. The Markan reading ends with the death cry of Jesus, "My God, my God, why have you forsaken me?"

The mockery of Jesus, then, creates the framework for the selection of the scenes from Ps 22, and broader cultural discourse contributes to the ironic understanding of the mockery. Narratorial emphasis on the death and burial of Jesus works in consort with the broader cultural discourse to create a reverse reading of Ps 22. Only accounts containing the ritual mockery of Jesus as king (Mark, Matthew, *Gos. Pet.*) place the first verse of Ps 22 on Jesus' lips at or near his death. In other words, the presence of the use of scenes from Ps 22 in reverse order occurs only in those accounts that exhibit the kingship ritual from the broader cultural discourse. The Lukan version, which does not have a sustained use of scenes in reverse order from Ps 22, also does not have the initial ritual mockery of Jesus as king of the Jews.

During the last decade, a fascinating debate has occurred concerning the juxtaposition of Jesus' death cry, the centurion's assertion that Jesus is "son of God," and the splitting of the temple curtain from top to bottom.[40] This debate has made it clear that the expulsion of Jesus' spirit and the splitting of the temple curtain has an important relation to the baptism of Jesus, where the heavens split apart and the spirit descends into Jesus. The entrance and departure of the spirit signifies

---

[40] Harry L. Chronis, "The Torn Veil: Cultus and Christology in Mark 15:37–39," *JBL* 101 (1982): 97–114; Howard M. Jackson, "The Death of Jesus in Mark and the Miracle from the Cross," *NTS* 33 (1987): 16–37; Stephen Motyer, "The Rending of the Veil: A Markan Pentecost?" *NTS* 33 (1987): 155–57; David Ulansey, "The Heavenly Veil Torn: Mark's Cosmic *Inclusio*," *JBL* 110 (1991): 123–25.

the beginning and end of Jesus' public career in Mark.[41] Moreover, the curtain to which the Markan text refers is likely to be the outer curtain, not the inner curtain around the Holy of Holies in the Temple.[42] This outer curtain, which was 80 feet high, contained "a panorama of the entire heavens."[43] When the spirit comes out of Jesus, the heavens on the outer veil of the temple split open, giving the centurion a view into the outer court, to which all nations are supposed to have access (Mark 11:17). The centurion recognizes that Jesus was a king who accepted the will of his God that he should die to benefit the people over whom this God rules. In the speech of the Roman centurion, widespread cultural discourse speaks through Christian discourse. Language of sonship that was in the mouth of God, on the lips of demons, and in the speech of the High Priest now emerges from the tongue of a Roman centurion. When the centurion hears the cry of abandonment on Jesus' lips, this cry evokes an awareness that Jesus understood the nature of true kingship (Dio 4.69). Jesus possessed the divine instruction that informed him of the necessity to be willing to die for his people if the greatest God willed it. Also, the centurion sees the simultaneous expulsion of spirit from Jesus and splitting of the veil of the heavens on the outer court of the temple. A cosmic sign like this, which gives him and others sight into the house of prayer for all nations, convinces him that Jesus was "son of God," a true king informed by and supported by divine knowledge and power.

Conclusion

Whose speech, then, is on the lips of the Roman centurion? Is it Jewish speech? Is it Christian speech that appropriates only Jewish speech? Or is it speech that contains many cultural voices? Whose concepts of kingship, sonship, and benefit interweave in and through the voices in his language? The contention in this essay is that the language of the Roman centurion is borderline language in Mediterranean culture. This language belongs to many people. As a result, it is always "half someone else's language." When the centurion comes to speech, he

---

[41] Matera, *The Kingship of Jesus*, 139; Jackson, "Death," 21–22; Motyer, "Veil"; Ulansey, "Heavenly Veil." It is important to observe that Mark refers to the spirit descending "into" (εἰς) Jesus, not "upon" (ἐπί) him. At the end, then, the spirit goes out of Jesus (Mark 15:37, 38: ἐξέπνευσεν).

[42] Donald Juel, *Messiah and Temple: The Trial of Jesus in the Gospel of Mark* (SBLDS 31; Missoula: Scholars Press, 1977), 140–41; Jackson, "Death," 24; Ulansey, "Heavenly Veil," 124–25.

[43] Based on Josephus, *War* 5.5.4 (212–14). See André Pelletier, "La tradition synoptique du 'voile déchiré' à la lumière des réalités archéologiques," *RSR* 46 (1958): 168–79.

evokes the many voices throughout Mediterranean culture who care deeply about the nature of true kingship, because their lives depend on it. They care deeply about those people through whom God, or the gods, work, because these are the people who nurture and support them, or abuse and destroy them. In other words, these discussions concern life and death. They concern the manner in which people either live together in mutual support or dominate and destroy one another when the opportunity arises.

The centurion stands opposite Jesus. But, in truth, he stands on a borderline between various groups who are interested in the benefits of heaven. The narrator says that boundary lines split open when Jesus dies. The veil between the people and the temple splits open, and the true nature of kingship becomes visible to all – Jewish, Christian, and Gentile. Finally, the voices may engage in dialogue with one another, because someone, namely a centurion, has discovered the common language among them – language that is always half someone else's language.

The sustained mockery in the Markan account of the crucifixion becomes deeply ironic when the narrator uses Ps 22 in an inverted order. The inversion places the initial expression of an experience of abandonment by God on Jesus' lips as he dies, rather than placing one of the final verses of the psalm that would express a plea that contains hope and confidence in God's activity. And why not, we ask, express that confidence, since the narrator gives every reason for it in the account of the empty tomb? Our analysis suggests that the key lies in the ironic play on kingship which results from Pilate's use of the title "King of the Jews," from the chief priests' and scribes' mocking of Jesus as "Messiah King of Israel," and from Joseph of Arimathea's expectation of the "Kingdom of God." According to the Markan version, the kingdom of God occurs in and through the sequence of the ironic death of Jesus as "King of the Jews" followed by the empty tomb which points to his appearance in the future. We must look, therefore, for clues to this kind of ideology through intertextual analysis.

The Gospel of Mark places patterns of understanding and action at home in first-century Mediterranean literature outside of Jewish and Christian circles in conversation with patterns, traditions, and titles from biblical and Jewish literature. The centurion's ability to see Jesus as a "real" Son of God occurs when he dies with a cry of abandonment on his lips. Through the thought and action of Jesus as a true king, the kingdom of God has drawn near. In the future this true king will come as the "Son of man" and gather the elect together from the four corners of the earth (Mark 13:27).

8. The Reversed Contextualization of Ps 22 in the Markan Crucifixion 281

This portrayal raises a question whether there may be additional traditions about kings that could call forth the centurion's recognition of Jesus as a "Son of God" at his death. One of the most ironic portrayals of kingship outside of Mark resides in the cultural tradition of the Persian ritual during the Sacian feast. The context of Dio's discussion of the Persian ritual raises the possibility that the centurion in Mark associates Jesus' death as a mocked king with "a son of God" as a result of traditions about the true suffering king who is perceived to be a son of Zeus in Hellenistic-Roman society and culture. If this interpretation is correct, the title Son of God on the lips of the centurion strikes the ear of the Hellenistic-Roman reader with special force in the context of the splitting of the temple curtain from top to bottom. The Roman general Titus would burn the temple to the ground, but it was the messianic king of Israel, who died as a true suffering king, who removed the outer curtain and opened the benefits of God's activity beyond the boundaries of Israel to all people in the Roman Mediterranean world. But these benefits would come only to those who refuse to inflict suffering and death on others (Mark 10:42–45) and who are willing to lose their lives as a means of saving them (Mark 8:34–37).

9

Socio-Rhetorical Criticism: Mary, Elizabeth, and the Magnificat as a Test Case

The Emergence of Socio-Rhetorical Criticism

Socio-rhetorical criticism is a textually based method that uses programmatic strategies to invite social, cultural, historical, psychological, aesthetic, ideological and theological information into a context of minute exegetical activity. In a context where historical criticism has been opening its boundaries to social and cultural data, and literary criticism has been opening boundaries to ideology, socio-rhetorical criticism practices interdisciplinary exegesis that reinvents the traditional steps of analysis and redraws the traditional boundaries of interpretation. Socio-rhetorical criticism, then, is an exegetically-oriented approach that gathers current practices of interpretation together in an interdisciplinary paradigm.

Both the textual base for the strategies and the interdisciplinary mode of analysis distinguish socio-rhetorical criticism from historical criticism, social scientific criticism, sociological exegesis, social-historical criticism and the study of social realia and social organization – all of which are historical methods based on data external to texts. Historians and sociologists regularly focus on signs in texts that ostensibly refer to data outside of texts, and they criticize interpreters who appear to have an "obsession" with the nature of texts themselves rather than the "data" within texts. Socio-rhetorical critics are interested in the nature of texts as social, cultural, historical, theological and ideological discourse. They approach a text much like an anthropologist "reads" a village and its culture.[1] The interpreter perceives the dwellings and their arrangement; the interaction of the people and their rituals; and the sounds of the speech, the songs, the drums and the

---

[1] James L. Peacock, *The Anthropological Lens: Harsh Light, Soft Focus* (New York: Cambridge University Press, 1986).

barking as signs that invite research, analysis and interpretation.[2] Within this approach, historical, social and cultural data stand in an intertextual relation to the signs in the texts. Socio-rhetorical interpretation, then, invites the data of the historical and social-scientific critic into exegesis at the stage where it explores the intertexture of a text.

Socio-rhetorical criticism differs from most types of literary criticism by a practice of "revaluing" and "reinventing" rhetoric rather than practicing one or more forms of "restrained rhetoric."[3] Socio-rhetorical critics, perceiving texts to be "thickly textured" with simultaneously interacting networks of signification, reinvent rhetoric by reading, interpreting and reinterpreting texts "as forms of *activity* inseparable from the wider social relations between writers and readers, orators and audiences."[4] Socio-rhetorical criticism reinvents the stages of interpretation by replacing George A. Kennedy's five stages of analysis – unit, situation, disposition of arrangement, techniques or style and rhetorical criticism as a synchronic whole[5] – with programmatic analysis of inner texture, intertexture, social and cultural texture and ideological texture.[6] Through this process, socio-rhetorical critics explore the full range of rhetorical figures and tropes in texts. Most modern literary critics, in contrast, reduce rhetoric to four master tropes – metaphor, metonymy, synecdoche and irony – and explore

---

[2] Clifford Geertz, *The Interpretation of Cultures* (New York: Basic Books, 1973); idem, *Local Knowledge: Further Essays in Interpretive Anthropology* (New York: Basic Books, 1983).

[3] Brian Vickers, "Introduction," in *Rhetoric Revalued* (ed. Brian Vickers; Medieval and Renaissance Texts and Studies 19; Binghamton, N.Y.: Center for Medieval and Renaissance Studies, 1982), 13–39.

[4] Terry Eagleton, *Literary Theory: An Introduction* (Minneapolis: University of Minnesota Press, 1983), 206. Cf. Wilhelm H. Wuellner, "Where is Rhetorical Criticism Taking Us?" *CBQ* 49: 453; Vernon K. Robbins, "Rhetoric and Culture: Exploring Types of Cultural Rhetoric in a Text," in *Rhetoric and the New Testament: Essays from the 1992 Heidelberg Conference* (ed. Stanley E. Porter and Thomas H. Olbricht; JSNTSup 90; Sheffield: JSOT Press, 1993), 443–44.

[5] George A. Kennedy, *New Testament Interpretation through Rhetorical Criticism* (Chapel Hill: University of North Carolina Press, 1984), 33–38; Wuellner, "Where?" 455–60.

[6] Vernon K. Robbins, "Introduction to the Paperback Edition," in *Jesus the Teacher: A Socio-Rhetorical Interpretation of Mark* (repr., Minneapolis: Fortress, 1992), xix–xliv; idem, "Using a Socio-Rhetorical Poetics to Develop a Unified Method: The Woman Who Anointed Jesus as a Test Case," in *SBLSP* (1992): 302–19; idem, "The Reversed Contextualization of Psalm 22 in the Markan Crucifixion: A Socio-Rhetorical Analysis," in *The Four Gospels* (eds. F. van Segbroeck et al.; 3 vols.; BETL 100; Leuven: Leuven University Press, 1992), 2:1161–83; idem, "A Male Reads a Feminist Reading: The Dialogical Nature of Pippin's Power: A Response to Tina Pippin, 'Eros and the End,'" *Semeia* 59: 211–17; idem, "Rhetoric and Culture," 111–49.

texts in the context of this "restrained" rhetoric.[7] Socio-rhetorical critics differ from formalist and structuralist literary critics by exploring the rhetorical nature of the discourse both in the text and in traditional and nontraditional interpretations of the text. They differ from literary critics who invest primarily in anti-scientific and deconstructionist efforts by programmatically analyzing and interpreting texts within changing sets of boundaries. Socio-rhetorical criticism, then, is a form of literary analysis that invites programmatic, self-critical analysis and interpretation of the full range of rhetorical figures and tropes in texts. The goal is to nurture disciplined exploration, analysis and interpretation characteristic of *wissenschaftliche* research, but to do so in a manner that maintains a self-critical perspective on the data and strategies the interpreter uses to bring referents, meanings, beliefs, values, emotions, and intentions to the signs in the text.

The beginnings of socio-rhetorical criticism lie in the goals for biblical interpretation Amos N. Wilder set forth in his presidential address to the Society of Biblical Literature in 1955 entitled "Scholars, Theologians, and Ancient Rhetoric."[8] Wilder began by raising "the basic question of the nature of religious symbol and of symbolic discourse."[9] Referring to New Testament eschatology as "a tremendous expression of the religious imagination, an extraordinary rhetoric of faith,"[10] he quoted Theodor Gaster's statement that "our task must be to get behind the words to what semanticists call their 'referents'; and this is the domain of Cultural Anthropology and Folklore rather than of Philology."[11] Asserting that we have much to learn "from what is now known of the 'mythic mentality' or 'mythic ideation' as explored by the anthropologists and by students of the origins of language and myth,"[12] Wilder turned to an analysis of the strengths and weaknesses of Bultmann's demythologization of myth, Dodd's "Platonizing tendency," and Cullmann's conforming of disparate expressions in biblical texts to a pattern in a selected body of material.[13] In the end, Wilder's focus on biblical texts as literature causes him to limit the source for new insights into myth and symbol to aesthetic criticism, because "workers in

---

[7] For a comprehensive discussion of the reduction of rhetoric in various centuries, see Brian Vickers, *In Defense of Rhetoric* (Oxford: Clarendon Press, 1988), 435–79, and for the reduction of tropes, 439–42. For his definition of rhetorical figures and tropes, see 491–98.

[8] Amos N. Wilder, "Scholars, Theologians, and Ancient Rhetoric," *JBL* 75 (1956): 1–11.

[9] Ibid., 1.

[10] Ibid., 2.

[11] Ibid., 3 quoting Theodor H. Gaster, *Thespis: Ritual, Myth and Drama in the Ancient Near East* (New York: Henry Schuman, 1950), 112.

[12] Wilder, "Scholars," 5.

[13] Ibid., 6–8.

aesthetics ... have learned much from anthropology and psychology."[14] As a result, it has taken New Testament interpreters a quarter of a century to begin to integrate analysis of the inner imaginative and argumentative aspects of early Christian texts with analysis of the social aspects of their discourse. Most New Testament interpreters who responded to Wilder's call to use new forms of literary criticism have resisted the insights of social scientists into myth, the social construction of reality, and the ideological nature of culture.

In 1972, Wayne A. Meeks moved Wilder's vision of interpretation decisively forward in an article entitled "The Man from Heaven in Johannine Sectarianism."[15] Meeks analyzed both "the special patterns of language" in the Gospel of John and the special logic of the myth of the descending and ascending redeemer, integrating a close, rhetorical reading of the text with anthropological and sociological insights into the formation and maintenance of sectarian communities.[16] His interpretation demonstrates the profound relationship in Johannine discourse between the redeemer who belongs to the "world of the Father" yet comes into the "world which does not know or comprehend" him, and those who are "in the world" yet are drawn to the redeemer by "believing" in him. In the end, the reader sees that the redeemer's foreignness to the world is directly related to the sect's perception of itself as foreign to the world – "in it but not of it." In Meeks' words:

> The Fourth Gospel not only describes, in etiological fashion, the birth of that community; it also provides reinforcement of the community's isolation. The language patterns we have been describing have the effect, for the insider who accepts them, of demolishing the logic of the world, particularly the world of Judaism, and progressively emphasizing the sectarian consciousness. If one "believes" what is said in this book, he is quite literally taken out of the ordinary world of social reality.[17]

This article, in my view, is a superb initial step toward socio-rhetorical criticism, since it attends equally to exegesis and to social and cultural dimensions of early Christian discourse. In the intervening years Meeks has written a number of important articles that advanced this kind of analysis yet further.[18] His books, however, have featured

---

[14] Ibid., 8–9.

[15] Wayne Meeks, "The Man from Heaven in Johannine Sectarianism," *JBL* 91 (1972): 44–72.

[16] Ibid., 44.

[17] Ibid., 71.

[18] See bibliography in Wayne A. Meeks, *The Origins of Christian Morality: The First Two Centuries* (New Haven: Yale University Press, 1993).

rather conventional exegetical practices to exhibit social and moral aspects of early Christianity rather than developed new practices to exhibit the social, cultural and ideological dimensions of Christian discourse in its Mediterranean context.[19]

The year after the appearance of Meeks's article, Jonathan Z. Smith presented a paper on "The Social Description of Early Christianity" that called for the incorporation of highly developed anthropological theory in analysis and interpretation of early Christian data.[20] In his article, Smith referred to an "almost total lack of persuasive models," a seduction "into a description of a *Sitz im Leben* that lacks a concrete (i.e., non-theological) seat and offers only the most abstract understanding of 'life,'" the writing of social histories of early Christianity "in a theoretical vacuum in which outdated 'laws' are appealed to and applied ... which no longer represent a consensus outside the New

---

[19] See Wayne A. Meeks, *The First Urban Christians: The Social World of the Apostle Paul* (New Haven: Yale University Press, 1983); idem, *The Moral World of the First Christians* (Philadelphia: Westminster, 1986); idem, *The Origins of Christian Morality*. Three explanations, I suggest, are ready at hand. First, Meeks began his work when the traditional exegetical tools of historical criticism completely dominated New Testament interpretation. Second, the overwhelming majority of Meeks' colleagues were, and still are, historians who emphasize data they perceive to be referred to by texts rather than methods that explore the nature of texts themselves. Third, it has taken much diligent work to develop rhetorical and social analysis to a level advanced enough to guide analysis of texts that do not evoke the same kind of countercultural, sectarian ideology as the discourse in the Fourth Gospel.

[20] Jonathan Z. Smith, "The Social Description of Early Christianity," *RelSRev* 1 (1975): 19–25. Despite his four books since that time, New Testament interpreters have been slow to adopt the critical insights of cultural anthropology: Jonathan Z. Smith, *Map Is Not Territory: Studies in the History of Religions* (Leiden: Brill, 1978); idem, *Imagining Religion: From Babylon to Jonestown* (Chicago: University of Chicago Press, 1982); idem, *To Take Place: Toward Theory in Ritual* (Chicago: University of Chicago Press, 1987); idem, *Drudgery Divine: On the Comparison of Early Christianities and the Religions of Late Antiquity* (Chicago: University of Chicago Press, 1990). There are numerous reasons. First, a full picture of Smith's agenda emerges only through a careful reading of the complete corpus of his work, much of which first appeared in articles that were later gathered into book form. Second, Smith has published books with an obviously unified agenda only since 1987. Prior to this, his books contained articles that revealed only part of his agenda at a time. Third, Smith works at the "critical" end of interpretive discourse, the high end that calls for a deeply informed self-consciousness about one's own work. Most New Testament interpreters who devote time to theory have preferred to generate formal theories about deep linguistic structures and self-referential features of narrative than to generate self-critical theories about interpretive practices. Fourth, Smith's work challenges the innermost nature of the discipline itself, including the "myth of origins" in which biblical interpreters embed their interpretive practices. Since one of the characteristics of scientific (*wissenschaftliche*) analysis is to hide its ideological foundations, it is natural that New Testament interpreters have been reluctant to evaluate their deepest commitments programmatically and submit them to public scrutiny. Socio-rhetorical criticism calls for interpretive practices that include minute attention to the ideologies that guide interpreters' selection, analysis, and interpretation of data.

Testament or church history fields," and "unquestioned apologetic presuppositions and naive theories."[21] He suggested, however, that there were many resources available to move ahead, including a few "major syntheses, lacking only the infusion of new theoretical perspectives."[22] Calling for "careful attention to the inner history of the various religious traditions and cults" and analysis and interpretation that are "both richly comparative and quite consciously situated within contemporary anthropological and sociological theory," he pointed to Meeks' article on the Johannine Man from heaven as a "happy combination of exegetical and sociological sophistication."[23] Smith's critical agenda introduces theoretical practices that move socio-rhetorical interpretation beyond aesthetic criticism toward a comprehensive, critical method for constructing a new picture of the social and religious nature of early Christianity.

In the midst of these beginnings, Helmut Koester and James M. Robinson proposed a dynamic, pluralistic model for investigating early Christian groups, communities, and cultures that interacted with one another in a context that, after two to three centuries, produced a Christianity with its own sacred scriptures, theological systems, ecclesiastical offices, and institutional structures.[24] Hans Dieter Betz contributed to this endeavor by bringing widespread rhetorical practices of Mediterranean speakers and writers into interpretation of New Testament texts, and Wilhelm H. Wuellner began to apply insights from "the new rhetoric" to argumentation in New Testament literature.[25]

---

[21] Smith, "Social Description," 19–20.

[22] Ibid., 20.

[23] Ibid., 20–21.

[24] James M. Robinson and Helmut Koester, *Trajectories through Early Christianity* (Philadelphia: Fortress, 1971).

[25] Hans Dieter Betz, *Der Apostel Paulus und die sokratische Tradition: Eine exegetische Untersuchung zu seiner "Apologie" 2 Kor 10–13* (BHT 45; Tübingen: Mohr-Siebeck, 1972); idem, "The Literary Composition and Function of Paul's Letter to the Galatians," *NTS* 21 (1975): 353–79; idem, *Galatians: A Commentary on Paul's Letter to the Churches in Galatia*, (Hermeneia; Philadelphia: Fortress, 1979); idem, *2 Corinthians 8 and 9* (Hermeneia; Philadelphia: Fortress, 1985); idem, *Essays on the Sermon on the Mount* (trans. L. L. Welborn; Philadelphia: Fortress, 1985); idem, "The Problem of Rhetoric and Theology According to the Apostle Paul," in *L'Apôtre Paul: Personnalité, style et conception du ministère* (ed. A. Vanhoye; BETL 73; Leuven: Leuven University Press, 1986), 16–48; Wilhelm H. Wuellner, "Paul's Rhetoric of Argumentation in Romans: An Alternative to the Donfried-Karris Debate over Romans," *CBQ* 38 (1976): 330–351; repr. in *The Romans Debate* (ed. K.P. Donfried; Minneapolis: Augsburg, 1977), 152–74; idem, "Methodological Considerations Concerning the Rhetorical Genre of First Corinthians," (paper presented at the SBL Pacific Coast Regional Paul Seminar, 26 March 1976); idem, "Der Jakobusbrief im Licht der Rhetorik und Textpragmatik," *LB* 43 (1978): 5–66; idem, "Greek Rhetoric and Pauline Argumentation," in *Early Christian Literature and the Classic-*

Meanwhile, Robert C. Tannehill produced an aesthetic, rhetorical analysis and interpretation of sayings of Jesus with unusual sensitivity to the forcefulness of their vivid images and tensive patterns.[26]

The same year as the appearance of Smith's initial paper,[27] Betz's first rhetorical analysis of Paul's letter to the Galatians[28] and Tannehill's aesthetic, rhetorical analysis of sayings of Jesus,[29] John G. Gager's *Kingdom and Community: The Social World of Early Christianity* introduced models from twentieth-century sociology and anthropology for the study of early Christianity.[30] Gager's analysis was part of the same intellectual world as Smith's; but this was a world distant from the work of Betz, Wuellner, and Tannehill. Many interpreters knew that these intellectual worlds should come together, but they also knew that the road would be steep and rocky. Gager broached the issue with a well-placed quotation from Peter Brown: "The need to link disciplines is frequently expressed among us. Discussion of this need takes place in an atmosphere, however, that suggests the observation of an African chieftain on a neighboring tribe: 'They are our enemies. We marry them.'"[31]

Gager himself used social anthropological studies of millennialist cargo cults in Melanesia, social psychological studies of cognitive dissonance and a merger of cultural anthropological and "history of religion" interpretations of myth to approach "the end of time and the rise of community" in first century Christianity.[32] Then he discussed the transition from charisma to canon and orthodoxy,[33] the social class or status of early Christians,[34] and the challenge of the success of Christianity for interpreters of early Christianity.[35] Rich with sociological and anthropological insight as well as information about the first four centuries of

---

al Intellectual Tradition (ed. W.R Schoedel and R.L. Wilken; Paris: Beauchesne, 1979), 177–88; idem, "Paul as Pastor: The Function of Rhetorical Questions in First Corinthians," in *L'Apôtre Paul: Personnalité, style et conception du ministère* (ed. A. Vanhoye; BETL 73; Leuven: Leuven University Press, 1986), 49–77.

[26] Robert C. Tannehill, *The Sword of His Mouth* (Philadelphia: Fortress, 1975).

[27] Smith, "Social Description."

[28] Betz, "Literary Composition."

[29] Tannehill, *Sword*.

[30] John G. Gager, *Kingdom and Community: The Social World of Early Christianity* (Englewood Cliffs, N.J.: Prentice-Hall, 1975).

[31] Peter Brown, "Sorcery, Demons and the Rise of Christianity from Late Antiquity into the Middle Ages," in *Witchcraft Accusations and Confessions* (ed. Mary Douglas; London: Tavistock, 1970), 17. Quoted in Gager, *Kingdom and Community*, xii; cf. John G. Gager, "Shall We Marry Our Enemies? Sociology and the New Testament," *Int* 36 (1982): 256–65.

[32] Gager, *Kingdom and Community*, 19–65.

[33] Ibid., 66–92.

[34] Ibid., 93–113.

[35] Ibid., 114–58.

early Christianity, this book established an agenda for a new paradigm of investigation and interpretation. While a number of its agendas have been pursued in one way or another, the task of incorporating the insights of this paradigm programmatically into exegesis of New Testament texts still lies in the future. Socio-rhetorical criticism sets forth a programmatic set of strategies to pursue, test, enrich, and revise the provisional conclusions Gager advances in his book.

At the beginning of the 1980s, then, various approaches and analyses had advanced a program of investigation and interpretation of the social, cultural, religious and theological dimensions of early Christian discourse. It would take another decade, however, for these activities to come together in a programmatic, critical method. As the 1980s began, John H. Elliott developed "sociological exegesis,"[36] and Bruce J. Malina introduced widespread topics of Mediterranean social and cultural life into New Testament studies under the name of cultural anthropology.[37] A few years later, a *Semeia* volume appeared on *Social Science Criticism*,[38] and soon after Philip Esler's study of the social and political motivations of Lukan theology became available.[39] Recently, an edited volume on *The Social World of Luke-Acts*,[40] and a volume on *Social Science Criticism and the New Testament*[41] have displayed the results of more than a decade of work by Malina, Neyrey, Elliott, Rohrbaugh, and others on honor-shame, dyadic personality, limited good, kinship, purity, and other widespread features of Mediterranean society and culture. Meanwhile, Norman R. Petersen has produced studies of Paul and the Gospel of John that merge formalist literary criticism and sociology.[42] Both the formalist approach to the text and the use of sociology without the rich resources of social and cultural anthropology

---

[36] John H. Elliot, *A Home for the Homeless: A Sociological Exegesis of 1 Peter, Its Situation and Strategy* (Philadelphia: Fortress, 1981; repr. with new introduction, Minneapolis: Fortress, 1990). Reprint edition contains the new subtitle *A Social Scientific Criticism of I Peter, Its Situation and Strategy*.

[37] Bruce J. Malina, *The New Testament World: Insights from Cultural Anthropology* (rev. ed., Atlanta: John Knox, 1993). First edition published 1981.

[38] John H. Elliot, ed., *Semeia* 35 (1986): *Social-Scientific Criticism of the New Testament and Its Social World*.

[39] Philip Francis Esler, *Community and Gospel in Luke-Acts: The Social and Political Motivations of Lucan Theology* (SNTSMS 57; Cambridge: Cambridge University Press, 1987).

[40] Jerome H. Neyrey, ed., *The Social World of Luke-Acts: Models for Interpretation* (Peabody, Mass.: Hendrickson, 1991).

[41] John H. Elliot, *Social Science Criticism and the New Testament* (Minneapolis: Fortress, 1993).

[42] Norman R. Petersen, *Rediscovering Paul: Philemon and the Sociology of Paul's Narrative World* (Philadelphia: Fortress, 1985); idem, *The Gospel of John and the Sociology of Light: Language and Characterization in the Fourth Gospel* (Valley Forge, Pa.: Trinity, 1993).

limit the studies to a conventional view of the historical and social nature of early Christianity.

In 1984 and 1987, I used the term "socio-rhetorical" in the title of a book and in an article that merged rhetorical analysis with insights from anthropologists, sociologists, and social psychologists to interpret early Christian texts. Works by Kenneth Burke provided an initial rhetorical framework[43] and first century BCE and CE rhetorical treatises provided insights from the Mediterranean social environment of early Christianity.[44] Writings by Clifford Geertz, in turn, provided an initial anthropological framework for comparative analysis and interpretation,[45] and folklore studies and social psychological role theory guided the interpretation of the relation of the teacher to his disciples.[46] Then, in 1987, Wilhelm H. Wuellner introduced the terms "reinvented" or "revalued" rhetoric for rhetorical analysis that interprets biblical texts as "social discourse" and biblical hermeneutics as "political discourse."[47] Elizabeth Schüssler Fiorenza's presidential address to the Society of Biblical Literature at the end of that same year and her article on "The Rhetorical Situation in I Corinthians" placed the issue of ideology in the text and in the interpreter's strategies directly before biblical scholars.[48] Burton L. Mack's *A Myth of Innocence*, *Rhetoric in the New Testament*, and *The Lost Gospel* have advanced rhetorical, textual practices informed by insights about myth and ritual from cultural anthropology and about social discourse and ideology from modern and postmodern criticism.[49]

I presented the framework for developing socio-rhetorical criticism as a programmatic, comprehensive method within biblical studies in the introduction to the 1992 paperback edition of *Jesus the Teacher* and in an article for the Society of Biblical Literature later that year.[50] These essays introduced a "four-texture" approach to socio-rhetorical criti-

---

[43] Vernon K. Robbins, *Jesus the Teacher: A Socio-Rhetorical Interpretation of Mark* (Philadelphia: Fortress, 1984; repr. Minneapolis: Fortress, 1992 with new introduction and additional indexes), 5–14, 20–48; idem, "The Woman Who Touched Jesus' Garment: Socio-Rhetorical Analysis of the Synoptic Accounts," *NTS* 33 (1987): 502, 505, 508–509.

[44] Robbins, *Teacher*, 29, 64; "Woman," 503, 506–509, 512.

[45] Robbins, *Teacher*, 5–6.

[46] Ibid., 7–8, 39, 83, 110, 112–14, 158, 162, 165.

[47] Wuellner, "Where?" 435, 456, 462–63.

[48] Elisabeth Schüssler Fiorenza, "The Ethics of Interpretation: De-Centering Biblical Scholarship," *JBL* 107 (1988): 3–17; idem, "Rhetorical Situation and Historical Reconstruction in I Corinthians," *NTS* 33 (1987): 386–403.

[49] Burton L. Mack, *A Myth of Innocence: Mark and Christian Origins* (Philadelphia: Fortress, 1988); idem, *Rhetoric and the New Testament* (Minneapolis: Fortress, 1990); idem, *The Lost Gospel: The Book of Q and Christian Origins* (San Francisco: Harper San Francisco, 1993).

[50] Vernon K. Robbins, "Using a Socio-Rhetorical Poetics," 302–19.

cism: (a) inner texture, (b) intertexture, (c) social and cultural texture and (d) ideological texture. A four-texture approach was utilized in Clarice J. Martin's interpretation of the Ethiopian eunuch in Acts 8 and in Bernard Brandon Scott's comprehensive interpretation of the parables of Jesus.[51] Other socio-rhetorical studies have appeared during the last few years, usually with some reference to the socio-rhetorical nature of their investigation and interpretation.[52] The remaining part of this essay exhibits practices associated with socio-rhetorical criticism utilizing the four-texture approach. The goal is both to explain strategies and to illustrate them in actual exegesis. The text under consideration is the account of Mary's encounter with the angel Gabriel and Elizabeth in the Gospel of Luke.

Inner Texture: Every Reading has a Subtext

The overall goal of "inner" textual analysis and interpretation in a socio-rhetorical mode is to attain initial insight into the argumentation in

---

[51] Clarice J. Martin, "A Chamberlain's Journey and the Challenge of Interpretation for Liberation," *Semeia* 47 (1989): 105–35; repr. in *The Bible and Liberation: Political and Social Hermeneutics* (rev. ed.; ed. Norman K. Gottward and Richard A. Horsley; Maryknoll, N.Y.: Orbis Books, 1993); Bernard Brandon Scott, *Hear Then the Parable: A Commentary on the Parables of Jesus* (Minneapolis: Fortress, 1989).

[52] See the works of: James E. Altenbaumer, "The Salvation Myth in the Hymns in Revelation" (Ph.D. diss., Emory University, 1992); Willi Braun, "The Use of Mediterranean Banquet Traditions in Luke 14:1–24" (Ph.D. diss., University of Toronto, 1993); Mary R. Huie-Jolly, "The Son Enthroned in Conflict: A Socio-Rhetorical Analysis of John 5:17–23" (Ph.D. diss., University of Otago, New Zealand, 1994); John S. Kloppenborg, "The Dishonoured Master (Luke 16,1–8a)," *Bib* 70 (1989): 474–95; idem, "Alms, Debt and Divorce: Jesus' Ethics in Their Mediterranean Context," *TJT* 6/2 (1990): 182–200; idem, "Literary Convention, Self-Evidence and the Social History of the Q People," *Semeia* 55 (1991): 77–102; idem, "The Sayings Gospel Q: Recent Opinion on the People Behind the Document," *Currents in Research: Biblical Studies* 1 (1993): 9–34; Vernon K. Robbins, "The Social Location of the Implied Author of Luke-Acts," in *Social World of Luke-Acts*, 305–32; idem, "Using a Socio-Rhetorical Poetics," 302–319; idem, "The Reversed Contextualization of Psalm 22," 2:1161–83; idem, "A Male Reads a Feminist Reading," 211–17; idem, "A Socio-Rhetorical Look at the Work of John Knox on Luke-Acts," in *Cadbury, Knox, and Talbert: American Contributions to the Study of Acts* (ed. M.C. Parsons and J.B. Tyson; Atlanta: Scholars Press, 1992), 91–105; idem, "Rhetoric and Culture," 443–63. Russell B. Sisson, "The Apostle as Athlete: A Socio-Rhetorical Interpretation of 1 Corinthians 9" (Ph.D. diss., Emory University, 1994); Wesley Wachob, "The Rich in Faith and the Poor in Spirit: The Socio-Rhetorical Function of a Saying of Jesus in the Epistle of James" (Ph.D. diss., Emory University, 1993); Randall C. Webber, "'Why Were the Heathen So Arrogant?' The Socio-Rhetorical Strategy of Acts 3–4," *BTB* 22 (1992): 19–25; John O. York, *The Last Shall Be First: The Rhetoric of Reversal in Luke* (JSNTSup 46; Sheffield: JSOT Press, 1991).

the text.⁵³ Any strategies of analysis and interpretation, from the most simple repetition of signs to the most subtle argumentative strategies, may contribute to readings of the inner nature of a text. Every reading of the "inner" text, even a reading that an interpreter calls "intrinsic" to the text itself, is guided by "extrinsic" interests, perspectives and meanings. These extrinsic dimensions may derive from disciplinary codes or "subtexts" for the reading. A disciplinary code is a master discourse like history, anthropology or theology, which is guided, sanctioned and nurtured by authorized institutional structures, groups, and organizations.⁵⁴ A subtext, by contrast, is a theory, approach or other text that somehow helps to illumine an aspect of the text a person is interpreting.⁵⁵ Socio-rhetorical criticism calls for critical consciousness about codes and subtexts an interpreter brings to "intrinsic" readings. It also investigates the boundaries interpreters set that limit subtexts to "Jewish" modes of thinking rather than opening them to "Hellenistic-Roman" modes of thinking; theological modes rather than social, cultural, psychological and religious modes; formal literary modes rather than argumentative, interactive, rhetorical modes; and modes of the mind alone rather than modes that include both body and mind.

One important subtext is the basic rhetorical nature of language as explained by Kenneth Burke: language has repetitive, progressive, conventional, and minor rhetorical form.⁵⁶ The basic question related to this subtext is: On the basis of sign repetition and patterns of progression, where are the beginning, middle, and end of a significant span of text? A strategy in answering this question is the giving of "basic lexical sense" to signs signifying "narrative agents" in Luke 1:26–56.

In terms of sign repetition and progression, the priest Zechariah and his wife Elizabeth, who live in the region of Judea, are the first characters to appear in the Gospel of Luke (1:5), and they are the center of attention through Luke 1:25. In a sentence that constitutes Luke 1:26–27, the name Mary occurs for the first time in the text, and twice in this verse the text refers to this woman as a παρθένος, which is regularly translated "virgin" in English. The occurrence of these signs signals

---

⁵³ Chaim Perelman and L. Olbrechts-Tyteca, *The New Rhetoric: A Treatise on Argumentation* (trans. John Wilkinson and Purcell Weaver; Notre Dame: University of Notre Dame Press, 1969); Chaim Perelman, *The Realm of Rhetoric* (trans. William Kluback; Notre Dame: University of Notre Dame Press, 1982).

⁵⁴ Mieke Bal, *Murder and Difference: Gender, Genre, and Scholarship on Sisera's Death* (Bloomington, Ind.: Indiana University Press, 1988), 2–13.

⁵⁵ Mieke Bal, *Death and Dissymmetry: The Politics of Coherence in the Book of Judges* (Chicago: University of Chicago Press, 1988), 42, 51–65.

⁵⁶ Kenneth Burke, *Counter-Statement* (Berkeley: University of California Press, 1931), 123–83.

the potential beginning of a span of text with special focus on "a παρ-θένος named Mary."

It is noticeable that the name Zechariah, which appears six times (1:5, 12, 13, 18, 21) prior to the occurrence of the name Mary (1:27), reappears only once in the phrase "house of Zechariah" (1:40) until it recurs twice in Luke 1:59, 67. This means that a significant span of text occurs in which two women interact with one another in the absence of the husband Zechariah or any other man. A programmatic display of narrative agents reveals repetition of four words or phrases that refer to deity and two that refer to two women named Mary and Elizabeth.

Narrative Agents in Luke 1:26–56

26: God	angel				
27:				Mary	
28:		the Lord			
30: God	angel			Mary	
32: God		the Lord			
34:	angel			Mary	
35: God	angel		Holy Spirit		
36:					Elizabeth
37: God					
38:	angel	the Lord		Mary	
39:				Mary	
40:					Elizabeth
41:			Holy Spirit	Mary	Elizabeth
					Elizabeth
43:		my Lord			
45:		the Lord			
46:				Mary	
47: God		the Lord			
56:				Mary	

As this display shows, there is reference to God and the angel Gabriel in Luke 1:26 before there is reference to Mary in Luke 1:27. This signifies that something with reference to God and the angel Gabriel establishes the context of utterance for the circumstances in which Mary functions.[57] In addition to God and an angel, the discourse refers to "the Lord" and "the Holy Spirit." While references to God, the Lord and Mary span the entire unit (1:26–56), a basic "beginning" pairs Mary with the angel Gabriel through 1:38. A basic "middle" for this span of text appears in the double occurrence of the phrase "the Holy Spirit" (1:35, 41) and four occurrences of the name Elizabeth (1:36–41); and a basic "end" appears with references to Mary, my/the

---

[57] Roger Fowler, *Linguistic Criticism* (New York: Oxford University Press, 1986), 86–88, 93–96.

Lord, and God in the absence of reference to the angel, Elizabeth and the Holy Spirit (1:42–56). Basic repetition of names of narrative agents, therefore, exhibits a span of text with a basic beginning, middle, and end.

In the first step of analysis "voice" has not yet been given to the sign patterns in the text. In order to locate the narratorial boundaries of the beginning, middle, and end of this unit, it is necessary for the interpreter to give "voice" to the signs in the text.[58] Narratorial voice in Luke 1:26–56 differentiates narration from attributed speech. There are two and one half verses of narration (1:26–28a) that open the beginning of the unit. In the context where the language refers to Elizabeth, there is a span of three and one half verses of narration (1:39–42a) that open the middle of the unit. A short "And Mary said" in 1:46a opens the final unit, which contains nine and one half verses of attributed speech before a final verse of narration (1:56). This reveals the narratorial boundaries of the beginning (1:26–38), middle (1:39–45), and end (1:46–56); and the voicing leads the interpreter to strategies of argumentation that occur throughout the unit.

The voice of the narrator, the first level of narration,[59] introduces Mary to the reader/hearer within a narrative pattern that features an angel Gabriel sent from God. This pattern begins when the narrator asserts that an angel of the Lord appeared to Zechariah while he was praying inside the Temple at the hour of incense (Luke 1:10–12), and it recycles with the assertion that the angel Gabriel appeared to Mary at Nazareth in the sixth month of Elizabeth's pregnancy. At the second level of narration, the level of the voices of characters that are embedded in the voice of the narrator (first level), the angel Gabriel tells Mary that she is God's "favored one" and that the Lord is with her (1:26–28). The narrator tells the reader/hearer that Mary was troubled at the statement and debated in her mind concerning what it might mean (1:29), much as the narrator's voice says that Zechariah was troubled and afraid when he first saw the angel of the Lord (1:12). The implied reader begins to detect, then, a dialogue between the voice of the narrator and the voices of characters in the story. In the context

---

[58] "Narrative critics" give "voice" to signs in the text by generating a subtext of an "implied" author and reader whom they perceive to be "presupposed by the narrative" itself (Mark Alan Powell, *What is Narrative Criticism?* [Minneapolis: Fortress, 1990], 19–21). It is important to be attentive to the "meanings" narrative critics embed in the voices they give to the signs. It is customary for narrative critics to embed twenty-first century, post-industrial values, meanings, convictions, and perspectives in the voices while insisting that these meanings are "in the text." Socio-rhetorical criticism attends programmatically to this issue in the intertextual, social and cultural, and ideological arenas of analysis.

[59] Mary Ann Tolbert, *Sowing the Gospel: Mark's World in Literary-Historical Perspective* (Minneapolis: Fortress, 1989), 90–106.

where the narrator focuses on Mary's puzzlement, the angel tells her she has found favor with God, she will conceive and bear a son, and the son

    (a) will be called Jesus;
    (b) will be great;
    (c) will be called Son of the Most High;
    (d) will be given the throne of his father David by God;
    (e) will reign over the house of Jacob forever; and
    (f) will have a kingdom that has no end. (Luke 1:30–33)

The narrator tells the reader that Mary is "a virgin betrothed" to "Joseph, of the house of David" (1:27). The angel tells Mary the Holy Spirit will come upon her, the Most High will overshadow her, and therefore the child will be called holy, the Son of God. In addition, the angel tells Mary that her kinswoman Elizabeth is six months pregnant after being barren, because with God no word will be impossible.[60]

When Mary speaks, she presents a different perspective from the narrator and the angel. The first time she speaks, she tells the angel she has no man (1:34). The second time, she refers to herself as a maidservant of the Lord and says, "Let it be according to your word" (1:38). Mary has believed and consented, then, in a context of concern that she has no man. From the point of view of the angel, Mary is a fortunate young woman with everything she could hope for on her side. She has been specially favored by God, and the child within her is specially blessed. The narrator, however, says Mary is troubled, and when Mary tells her story in song, the reader gets a somewhat new insight into things.

Mary's voice in the Magnificat uses and reconfigures other characters' voices in the text. First, Mary repeats language the angel speaks to Zechariah about joy and gladness (1:14, 47). Second, Mary reconfigures language Elizabeth uses when Elizabeth says that the Lord has shown regard for her and taken away her reproach among men (1:25, 48a). Third, Mary reconfigures language Elizabeth uses when she tells Mary that she, Mary, is blessed because she has believed in the fulfillment of the things spoken to her (1:45, 48b). Fourth, Mary uses, reconfigures and embellishes language the angel Gabriel spoke to her about the power of the Most High (1:35, 49). Fifth, Mary reconfigures the angel's statements about her son's "father David" and about his reigning "over the house of Jacob forever" (1:32–33, 54). Mary asserts that God "puts down the mighty from their thrones," and "exalts those who live in humiliation" (1:52). Thus, Mary's voice not only intro-

---

[60] See Arie Troost, "Using the Word in Luke 1–2" (Short Paper, Colloquium Biblicum Lovaniese, 1992), for the importance of "word" throughout Luke 1–2.

duces a dialogue with the narrator's voice but with the voices of the angel that appeared to Zechariah, of the angel Gabriel who appeared to her, and of her kinswoman Elizabeth. Is Mary simply perpetuating the views of these other narrative agents, or does she have a somewhat different perspective? This will be a point at issue as we proceed to other arenas of interpretation. From the narratorial perspective, Mary's Magnificat engages in dialogue with other voices in the discourse.

Robert Tannehill has produced a compelling reading of the inner texture of the Magnificat by using Hebrew poetry as a subtext to give meaning to Mary's voice.[61] Tannehill emphasizes parallelism, repetition and the natural rhythm of reading, and his analysis yields two stanzas or strophes: (a) 1:46–50 and (b) 1:51–55. The division is marked, he says, by two concluding lines for each strophe (1:49b–50; 1:54b–55), which resemble each other in thought and form. For Tannehill, then, the inner texture of the poem yields a traditional hymn, which opens with a statement of praise and follows with a series of reasons for this praise. To reiterate, the subtext for this compelling reading of the inner texture of the hymn comes from presuppositions about Hebrew poetry. Tannehill observed that the opening statement of the hymn is a statement of praise and the following statements provide reasons for the praise, but he did not analyze the nature of the reasons. Lucy Rose, in an unpublished paper written at Emory University, approached the Magnificat with a very different subtext, namely argumentation in Hellenistic-Roman rhetoric.[62] The argumentative texture of the Magnificat comes into view if one follows guidelines from the *Rhetorica ad Herennium*, which was written in the 80s BCE.

Theme or *Topic*:
> My soul magnifies the Lord,
> And my spirit has gladness in God my Savior. (Luke 1:46b–47)

Rationale:
> because he has shown regard for the humiliation of his maidservant. (Luke 1:48a)

Confirmation of the rationale:
> For behold, henceforth all generations will call me blessed. (Luke 1:48b)

Embellishment:
> (1) For he who is mighty has done great things for me,
> and holy is his name,
> and his mercy is on those who fear him from generation to generation.

---

[61] Robert C. Tannehill, "The Magnificat as Poem," *JBL* 93 (1974): 263–75; idem, *The Narrative Unity of Luke-Acts: A Literary Interpretation* (2 vols.; Philadelphia: Fortress, 1986–1989), 1:26–32.

[62] Lucy A. Rose, "A Rhetorical Analysis of the Magnificat" (Ph.D. seminar paper, Emory University, 1989).

(2) He has shown great strength with his arm,
he has scattered the proud in the imagination of their hearts,
(3) he has put down the mighty from their thrones,
and exalted those of low degree;
(4) he has filled the hungry with good things,
and the rich he has sent empty away. (Luke 1:49–53)

Conclusion:
He has helped his servant Israel,
in remembrance of his mercy,
as he spoke to our fathers,
to Abraham and to his posterity for ever. (Luke 1:54–55)

After Mary's announcement of her topic of magnifying of the Lord (1:46b–47), she provides an initial rationale for her speech-action: (because) "God has shown regard for the humiliation of his maidservant" (1:48a). These two steps set the stage for "the most complete and perfect argument," to use the words of *Rhetorica ad Herennium* 2.18.28–19.30.[63] With this announcement, Mary has started her hymn with an enthymeme – a rhetorical syllogism that provides a minor premise for her topic and leaves the major premise unstated. The unstated major premise appears to be embedded in ritual logic that suggests that when the Lord God focuses special attention on the humiliation of a woman, such a woman responds naturally with hymnic speech from her glad heart. This produces the following underlying syllogism:

Implied major premise:
When the Lord God shows regard for the humiliation of the soul and spirit of one of his maidservants, the favored woman praises the Lord God as her savior.
Minor premise:
God has shown regard for the humiliation of the soul and spirit of his maidservant Mary.
Conclusion:
Mary's soul magnifies the Lord and her spirit rejoices in God her savior.

From a rhetorical perspective, the hymn begins syllogistically rather than paradigmatically. In other words, the beginning of the speech introduces the deductive logic of a rhetorical syllogism rather than the inductive logic of a rhetorical example. This raises the fascinating issue of whether there was a specific instance of "humiliation" that Mary

---

[63] Vernon K. Robbins, "Progymnastic Rhetorical Composition and Pre-Gospel Traditions: A New Approach," in *The Synoptic Gospels: Source Criticism and the New Literary Criticism* (ed. Camille Focant; BETL 110; Leuven: Leuven University Press), 123–25.

could narrate if asked, or whether Mary's "humiliation" was some general state common to most, if not all, women.

After the opening enthymematic argument in 1:46–48a, verse 48b voices a confirmation of the rationale. This is a natural next step for a "most complete and perfect argument." The confirmation that "God has given regard to my humiliation" lies in the future: "From now on, all generations will bless me" (or, "will call me blessed"). In 1:48b, then, Mary buttresses her initial rationale with a *rationis confirmatio*, a confirmation of the initial rationale.

After stating the theme, rationale and confirmation to open her argument (1:46–48), Mary embellishes the opening statements (1:49–53). This move fulfills the next step in a most complete and perfect argument. The embellishment contains two stanzas (1:49–50, 51–53), each beginning with what the mighty one "has done" (ἐποίησεν). The first stanza links what God has done for Mary with what God does for "those who fear him"; the second stanza presents a series of basic actions by God:

    (a) God has scattered the proud in the imagination of their hearts;
    (b) God has put down the mighty from their thrones and exalted the humiliated;
    (c) God has filled the hungry with good things and sent the rich away empty. (Luke 1:51–53).

These statements assert that God watches over all generations (1:48b, 50) and that God has been especially attentive to those who live in humiliation (1:48a, 52); and they imply that God welcomes those with a rejoicing, praising spirit, since he "scatters" those who are "proud in the imaginations of their hearts" (1:46b–47, 51). These statements amplify and more deeply ground the opening assertions of the speech. Mary concludes with a recapitulation that refers to the help God gave to Israel in the past, to Abraham and his seed forever (1:54–55). Thus Mary, standing in the line of "Abraham's posterity forever," praises God with reasoning that fulfills Hellenistic-Roman guidelines for "the most complete and perfect argument."

The final part of the inner-textual reading has proposed the presence of argumentative features that did not appear when Hebrew poetry provided the only subtext for the reading. This suggests a bi-cultural nature for the discourse that will be important to pursue in additional interpretive steps. The unit ends with an argument by Mary that God's benevolence to her has a relation to God's benevolence in the past and God's plans for the future. Yet Mary has come to this point only through a troubling encounter with the angel Gabriel and a supportive encounter with Elizabeth. It will be necessary to investigate additional dimensions of meaning in the context of other textures of the language in this unit.

The present discussion of the inner texture of Luke 1:26–56 has introduced a limited number of subtexts for its reading. Socio-rhetorical criticism invites any number of subtexts to approach the unit, with the goal of enriching the understanding of the topics, voices and arguments in it. Readings from yet other angles can explore the interchange between male and female voices and the reverberation of topics about different classes and statuses of people. Analysis of inner texture has introduced an initial set of strategies to identify topics and get a glimpse of the argumentative interaction in the unit.

Intertexture: Every Comparison has Boundaries

A second arena of rhetorical criticism is intertextual comparison, analysis and interpretation. Here the strategies emerge from the following questions: From where has this passage adopted its language? With what texts does this text stand in dialogue? Comparison takes us into canonical issues, understood in the broad terms introduced by postmodern criticism.[64] All interpretations can be characterized in terms of the data with which they allow a particular text to be compared. These issues appear in an interpreter's observation, analysis, and interpretation of reference, recitation, recontextualization, reconfiguration and echo in a text.

An initial dimension of intertexture is reference. Reference to proper names in Luke 1:26–56 indicates explicit dialogue with people and places in Israelite tradition. There is reference to the angel Gabriel, God, a city of Galilee, the house of David, the Most High, the Lord God, the throne of David, the house of Jacob, the Holy Spirit, the Son of God, a city of Judah, his servant Israel, and our fathers, Abraham and his posterity. There also is reference to a virgin betrothed to a man (1:27), a woman called barren (1:36) and a maidservant of the Lord (1:37,48). With what texts and textual traditions are these phrases in dialogue? We will see that this is a highly contested issue in interpretation.

A second dimension of intertexture is recitation, which includes rehearsal of attributed speech in exact, modified or different words from other accounts of the attributed speech, and rehearsal of an episode or series of episodes, with or without using some words from another account of the story. Recitation appears in the form of generalized

---

[64] Terry Eagleton, *Literary Theory: An Introduction* (Minneapolis: University of Minnesota Press, 1983), 1–53.

summary in 1:51–55: in the past God has shown strength with his arm, scattered the proud, put down the mighty from their thrones, exalted those in humiliation, filled the hungry with good things, sent the rich empty away, helped his servant Israel, and spoke to our fathers, to Abraham and to his posterity. It is not clear exactly what events are being rehearsed; this is recitation of past events in a generalized, summary form. Such recitation allows an interpreter freedom to draw boundaries in various ways around episodes recounting God's interaction with Israel; an interpreter may include or exclude stories according to the interpreter's inclination.

A third dimension of intertexture is recontextualization, which is the placing of attributed narration or speech in a new context without announcing its previous attribution. There is a long list of recontextualized speech from the Septuagint in this unit, which we will discuss below.[65]

A fourth dimension of intertexture is reconfiguration. Certainly the Lukan unit is reconfiguring the long tradition of barren Israelite women who have conceived in their old age and born a son. Exactly which stories are the strongest intertexts is an important issue. But what of accounts of virgins? Does this account of the virgin Mary reconfigure any accounts of virgins in the Septuagint? Are there any Mediterranean accounts of virgins that this account of Mary may be reconfiguring? We will see below that the established boundaries for discussion of reconfiguration in traditional New Testament interpretation not only suppress discussion of the stories of virgins in the Septuagint but completely exclude well-known stories about virgins impregnated by gods in Mediterranean society. Here a purity system has been functioning with the intensity of all purity systems, keeping stories about the immoral Hellenistic gods raping virgins on earth out of "scientific" exegesis. The result is the absence of biblical monographs that programmatically compare the Lukan account of the conception of the virgin Mary, when the Holy Spirit comes upon her and the power of the Most High overshadows her (Luke 1:34), and accounts of the conception of virgins in Mediterranean literature, when gods come upon them in different forms and circumstances. It is highly likely that the account of Mary is multi-cultural, reconfiguring Mediterranean stories about virgins as well as Israelite stories about virgins and barren women. We will return to this below in the discussion of the social and cultural texture of the account.

---

[65] Raymond E. Brown, *The Birth of the Messiah: A Commentary on the Infancy Narratives in Matthew and Luke* (Garden City, N.Y.: Doubleday, 1977), 357–62. Joseph A. Fitzmyer, *The Gospel According to Luke: Introduction, Translation, and Notes* (2 vols.; AB 28–28A; Garden City, N.Y.: Doubleday 1981–85), 1:356–57.

A fifth dimension is intertextual echo. Beyond specific configuration of traditions and episodes lies echoes.[66] When the Lukan account of Mary and Elizabeth is recounted in Greek toward the end of the first century CE, the echoes in its intertexture are manifold. Again, the traditional boundaries in New Testament exegesis have been drawn in such a way that interpreters saturate the discussion with echoes from Israelite and Jewish tradition but suppress echoes from broader Mediterranean tradition, society and culture.

The spectrum of intertexture, from reference to echo, intensely raises the issue of canon in interpretation.[67] For most interpreters, canonical boundaries for interpretation of the Lukan account of Mary and Elizabeth have been drawn in a manner that intentionally excludes comparison of the Magnificat with hymns of praise in Hellenistic-Roman culture and the conception of Mary with accounts of the conception of other virgins in Mediterranean literature. The strategy that keeps such data out is a "canonical strategy," and the elements of this strategy are basic canon, canon within the canon (or "inner canon") and near canon.[68] The basic canon for New Testament interpretation of this unit is comprised by the Old and New Testaments. Central to any canonical strategy, however, is the establishment of a canon within the canon, an "inner" canon. The canon within the canon for interpretation of this unit comprises the Israelite tradition of barren women and the account of Hannah and her hymn of praise in 1 Sam 1:1–2:10. This strategy produces an interpretive near canon comprised of material from Psalms (35:9; 111:9; 103:17; 89:11; 107:9; 98:3) and other passages in the Old Testament, Apocrypha, and Pseudepigrapha.[69] It is noticeable that this inner canon and near canon exclude any stories about virgins in Israelite tradition. Beginning with the tradition of barren Israelite women, it opens its boundaries to hymns of praise within the book of Psalms and within prophetic, apocalyptic, pseudepigraphic, and Qumran literature. If interpreters open the boundaries of near canon further they may bring in information from rabbinic literature and from the church fathers, monastics, and mystics in Christian tradition. But all of this opening of the boundaries carefully avoids stories about virgins who are forced to conceive, either by gods or by men

---

[66] John Hollander, *The Figure of Echo: A Mode of Allusion in Milton and After* (Berkeley: University of California Press, 1981); Richard B. Hays, *Echoes of Scripture in the Letters of Paul* (New Haven: Yale University Press, 1989).

[67] Eagleton, *Literary Theory*, 1–53.

[68] William H. Myers, "The Hermeneutical Dilemma of the African American Biblical Student," in *Stony the Road We Trod: African American Biblical Interpretation* (ed. Cain Hope Felder; Minneapolis: Fortress, 1991), 53–54.

[69] Raymond Brown, *Birth of the Messiah*, 358–60; Fitzmyer, *Luke*, 1:356–69.

fulfilling the will of a god. The absence of significant comparative work on Hellenistic-Roman hymns to gods and goddesses and on accounts of virgins who are overpowered and made pregnant by gods makes it impossible to redraw those boundaries here. Instead, the discussion will focus on the one major, recent attempt to open these boundaries in New Testament interpretation.

The Lukan account is susceptible to non-conventional boundaries. In Luke, the angel appears to the husband Zechariah concerning the conception and birth of the son John the Baptist to the barren wife Elizabeth (Luke 1:11–20); but the angel appears to the betrothed virgin Mary, and to her alone, concerning the conception and birth of Jesus (Luke 1:26–38). In the Matthean account, in contrast, the angel appears to the man Joseph rather than to the virgin Mary (Matt 1:20; 2:13, 19). In Luke, no male is part of Mary's scene unless the reader genders Gabriel as male.[70] The Lukan account is closer to the account of the birth and conception of Samson in Judges 13:2–25 than to any other account of conception by a barren woman, since the messenger of God appears to the future mother in the account and tells her that she will conceive and bear a son. In Luke, a kinswoman Elizabeth, whose barrenness has been removed by God, in effect replaces the role that the husband Manoah plays in the story of the conception and birth of Samson. The function of Elizabeth raises another issue, namely the relation of one blessed woman to another blessed woman in Israelite tradition. This essay will turn to that issue in the section on ideology; for now the discussion turns to the Lukan reconfiguration of a "dishonorable" Israelite tradition about the overpowering of virgins by embedding it in the honorable tradition of the perpetuation of Israel's patriarchal line through barren women.

The special dynamics of a "canon within the canon" are at work in Mary's reference to her "humiliation" in the rationale she provides for her joyful soul and spirit (Luke 1:48b). Her humiliation is different from the humiliation of a barren woman: Mary is pregnant before marriage, and conventional social logic presupposes that a male causes a female to become pregnant. When a male causes a female to become pregnant outside of marriage, he is said to have "humiliated (ταπεινόω) her." Interpreters suppress the difference between the humiliation of a married, barren woman and an unmarried, pregnant woman in the Lukan account by establishing boundaries of intertexture that keep the accounts

---

[70] Athalya Brenner and Fokkelien van Dijk-Hemmes, *On Gendering Texts: Male and Female Voices in the Hebrew Bible* (Biblical Interpretation Series 1; Leiden: Brill, 1993); Arie Troost, "Reading for the Author's Signature: Genesis 21:1–21 and Luke 15:11–32 as Intertexts," in *Feminist Companion to Genesis* (ed. Athalya Brenner; FCB 2; Sheffield: Sheffield Academic Press, 1993).

of Israel's dishonored virgin women outside the interpretive "canon within the canon" and, indeed, outside the interpretive near canon. In essence, the interpretive strategy erases the accounts of dishonored virgins from Israelite, Jewish and Mediterranean literature. It erases the accounts by displacing them with accounts of honorable barren women. This may, of course, be a natural effect of the Lukan narration on readers. But interpreters should exhibit the nature of Lukan discourse in exegetical practice rather than simply replicating its discursive strategies.

Jean Schaberg has challenged the traditional inner canon of intertexture for the Lukan account of Mary by calling attention to legislation about and accounts of sexually dishonored women in Israelite tradition. Deuteronomy 22:23–24 (cf. 22:29) presents specific legislation about betrothed virgins who are dishonored:

> And if there be a young virgin betrothed (παῖς παρθένος μεμνηστευμένη) to a man (ἀνδρί), and a man (ἄνθρωπος) has found her in the city and lain (κοιμηθῇ) with her, you shall take them both out to the gate of their city and they shall be stoned with stones, and they shall die; the young woman because she did not cry out in the city, and the man because he humiliated (ἐταπείνωσεν) his neighbor's woman (γυναῖκα). (Deut 22:23–24 LXX)

The language of virgin, betrothal, and humiliation in this legislation is precisely the same as in the Lukan account. Mary is a virgin betrothed to a man (Luke 1:27: παρθένον ἐμνηστευμένην ἀνδρί), and when she becomes pregnant she refers to that pregnancy as humiliation (Luke 1:48: τὴν ταπείνωσιν). From her perspective, her pregnancy has humiliated her.

As stated above, this humiliation of Mary perpetuates a "dishonorable" tradition of important women in Israel's history. In Genesis 34:2, Dinah, the daughter of Leah and Jacob, was "humiliated" (ἐταπείνωσεν) by "Shechem the son of Hamor the Hivite, the prince of the land," when he seized her and lay with her. In Judges 19:24 and 20:5 the father of the Levite's concubine offers both "my virgin daughter" (ἡ θυγάτηρ μου ἡ παρθένος) and the Levite's concubine to the men of the city that "you might humiliate" (ταπεινώσατε) them. In 2 Samuel 13:12, 14, 22, 32 David's daughter Tamar pleads with Amnon not to humiliate her, but he overpowers her and lies with her, and his death was considered to be a punishment for this act. Deuteronomy 21:14 is an additional, instructive form of legislation. When Israel goes forth to war, and an Israelite captures a beautiful woman and desires her and takes her for a wife,

> "Then, if you have no delight in her, you shall send her out free, and you shall not sell her for money; you shall not treat her with contempt,

since you have humiliated (ἐταπείνωσας) her."

An Israelite is given the right to humiliate a foreign woman whom he has taken captive, but certain regulations govern his activity, including the recognition that he has humiliated her. Lamentations 5:11 offers a cry of anguish over the "dishonorable" tradition of humiliated women:

> They humiliated (ἐταπείνωσαν) women in Zion,
>
> Virgins (παρθένους) in the cities of Judah.

In Ezekiel 22:10–11 the prophet indicts the princes of Israel themselves:

> In you men uncover their fathers' nakedness; in you they humiliate (ἐταπείνουν) women who are unclean in their menstruation. One deals unlawfully with his neighbor's wife; another has defiled his daughter-in-law in ungodliness; and another in you has humiliated (ἐταπείνουν) his sister, the daughter of his father.

The humiliation to which Mary refers in Luke 1:48a refers to this "dishonorable" tradition. In Jean Schaberg's words, "The virgin betrothed to a man (Luke 1:27) was sexually humiliated. But her humiliation was 'looked upon' and reversed by God."[71] This information suggests the importance of including Deut 22:24; Gen 34:2; Judges 19:24; 20:5; 2 Kings 13:12–32; and Lam 5:11 as inner canonical intertexts for interpretation of Luke 1:26–56. Yet these texts are never mentioned by Raymond Brown and Joseph Fitzmyer, to mention two interpreters who have worked in detail with the intertexture of the Lukan account.

If the inner canon included all the information in the Bible about virgins who were overpowered by males, then new data would emerge from the near canon of the apocrypha, pseudepigrapha and other Mediterranean literature. The beginning point for the strategy that keeps this information out is the suppression of a dimension of the "inner texture" of the Lukan account itself. Namely, the virgin Mary refers to "her" humiliation in Luke 1:48a, not Elizabeth's. Mary's "low estate," as it is often translated, results from conception outside of marriage, not absence of conception within marriage. Mary's rationale for praising God is that God has shown special regard for the pregnancy that was forced upon her. Unfortunately, there is no space to develop this fur-

---

[71] Jean Schaberg, *The Illegitimacy of Jesus: A Feminist Theological Interpretation of the Infancy Narratives* (New York: Crossroad, 1987), 100; idem, "Luke," in *The Women's Bible Commentary* (eds. Carol A. Newsom and Sharon H. Ringe; Louisville, Ky.: Westminster/John Knox, 1992), 284–85.

ther here; it is necessary to summarize and move on to social and cultural texture.

Socio-rhetorical criticism calls for a detailed assessment of the manner in which inner canonical boundaries have been established for interpretation in relation to the inner texture of a unit itself. In the instance of the Magnificat, New Testament interpreters have suppressed the intertexture of Mary's speech with virgins overpowered by men or male gods by changing the reference of her speech to barrenness instead of pregnancy outside of marriage. Once an "inner canon" for interpretation has excluded all discussion of overpowered virgins in the Bible, it can easily push back any comparison with accounts of virgins in extracanonical Jewish texts and other Mediterranean literature.

Social and Cultural Texture: Every Meaning has a Context

The social and cultural texture of a text raises questions about the response to the world, the social and cultural systems and institutions, and the cultural alliances and conflicts evoked by the text.[72] These social and cultural phenomena are primary topics in rhetorical theory.[73] Particular social data regularly are the "material" topics in discourse, specific "subject matter." Social and cultural systems and institutions are common topics, those that span all subject matter in society and culture. Cultural alliances and conflicts are "final" topics are those that function specially to make one's own case to other people. These topics functioning together evoke the social and cultural nature of a particular discourse.[74]

Bryan Wilson's analysis of types of religious sects can assist an interpreter initially in ascertaining the social response to the world in the discourse of a particular New Testament text. James A. Wilde introduced Bryan Wilson's sociological typology of sects into New Testament study in his dissertation and an article, and in 1981 John H. Elliott incorporated Wilson's insights into the method he called socio-

---

[72] Fowler, *Linguistic Criticism*, 85–101.

[73] Aristotle, *Ars Rhetorica* 1.2.21–22; 2.22.1–23.30; 3.15.1–4. See *On Rhetoric: A Theory of Civic Discourse* (trans. George A. Kennedy; New York: Oxford University Press, 1991), 46–7, 186–204, 265–8.

[74] Robbins, "Rhetoric and Culture"; Wilhelm H. Wuellner, "Rhetorical Criticism and its Theory in Culture-Critical Perspective: The Narrative Rhetoric of John 11," in *Text and Interpretation: New Approaches in the Criticism of the New Testament* (eds. P.J. Martin and J.H. Petzer; NTTS 15; Leiden: Brill, 1991), 171–85; John H. Elliot, *Social Scientific Criticism*, 36–51.

logical exegesis.[75] Later, Philip Esler used them for an initial test of Lukan discourse, and his lead can be helpful to our analysis. Since this essay is designed to introduce the reader to socio-rhetorical criticism, it seems good to describe all seven of Wilson's types briefly, each of which, from our perspective, is evoked by the specific topics which occupy the discourse.

1. The *conversionist* response views the world as corrupt because all people are corrupt: if people can be changed then the world will be changed.
2. The *revolutionist* response assumes that only the destruction of the world, of the natural but more specifically of the social order, will suffice to save people.
3. The *introversionist* response sees the world as irredeemably evil and presupposes that salvation can be attained only by the fullest possible withdrawal from it.
4. The *gnostic (manipulationist)* response seeks only a transformed set of relationships – a transformed method of coping with evil – since salvation is possible in the world if people learn the right means, improved techniques, to deal with their problems.
5. The *thaumaturgical* response focuses on the concern of individual people for relief from present and specific ills by special dispensations.
6. The *reformist* response assumes that people may create an environment of salvation in the world by using supernaturally-given insights to change the present social organization into a system that functions toward good ends.
7. The *utopian* response presupposes that people must take an active and constructive role in replacing the entire present social system with a new social organization in which evil is absent.[76]

---

[75] James A. Wilde, "A Social Description of the Community Reflected in the Gospel of Mark" (Ph.D. diss., Drew University, 1974); idem, "The Social World of Mark's Gospel: A Word about Method," *SBL Seminar Papers, 1978* (2 vols.; SBLSP 15; Missoula, Mont.: Scholars Press, 1978), 2:47–67; Elliott, *Home for the Homeless*, 75–77, 96, 102–6, 122; cf. John H. Elliott "Phases in the Social Formation of Early Christianity: From Faction to Sect – A Social-Scientific Perspective," in *Recruitment, Conflict, and Conquest: Strategies in Judaism, Early Christianity, and the Greco-Roman World* (eds. Peder Borgen, Vernon K. Robbins, and David B. Gowler; Emory Studies in Early Christianity 6; Atlanta: Scholars Press, 1998), 273–313.

[76] Bryan Wilson, "A Typology of Sects," in *Sociology of Religion* (ed. R. Robertson; Baltimore: Penguin Books, 1969), 361–83; idem., *Magic and the Millenium: A Sociological Study of Religious Movements of Protest among Tribal and Third-World Peoples* (New York: Harper & Row, 1973), 22–36.

Most historical manifestations of religious communities exhibit a tensive relation among two, three or four of these responses to the world. A strong focus on only one often signals the manifestation of a cult – a group organized around a new idea or an imported alien religion – rather than a sect.[77] Esler concludes that the thaumaturgic, conversionist and revolutionist types of response are relevant for Luke-Acts.[78] Let us test his conclusion in the context of an analysis of Luke 1:26–56.

First, the miraculous intervention of God upon both Elizabeth and Mary signals thaumaturgic rhetoric. This essay will explore a few of the details below, but perhaps it is sufficient at this point to cite the statement of the angel: "For with God no word will be impossible" (1:37). Secondly, the change of Mary from being "greatly troubled" (1:29) to her agreement to "let it be to me according to your word" (1:38) exhibits conversionist rhetoric. Mary changes from a young woman who does not believe she can conceive a son apart from a man to a young woman who accepts the promise of the angel, and this seems to introduce a model for people's response to God's miraculous intervention in the affairs of the world. Other stories, like Zaccheus's change of heart, distribution of half of his wealth to the poor, and fourfold restoration of all he has defrauded (Luke 19:1–10), exhibit fully this kind of rhetoric in Luke and Acts. The view is that changes of heart produce salvation. Thirdly, "reversal rhetoric" is prominent in Mary's speech.[79] In the past, God "has put down the mighty from their thrones, and exalted those who have been humiliated; he has filled the hungry with good things, and the rich he has sent empty away" (Luke 1:52–53). God is overturning, and promises further to overturn, the world, and specifically the social order. Esler condisers this to be revolutionist rhetoric, but we will need to return to this below. The "reversal" rhetoric may be utopian or reformist rather than revolutionist in the context of Lukan thaumaturgic and conversionist rhetoric that brings salvation to people in the world (1:69, 71, 77).

Let us deepen this initial perception of the social response to the work in the text with analysis of common social and cultural topics in the text – kinship, honor and shame, limited good, purity codes, patron-client relations and hospitality codes – what David B. Gowler calls "cultural scripts."[80] These common topics have been the special do-

---

[77] Werner Stark, "The Class Basis of Early Christianity: Inferences from a Sociological Model," *Sociological Analysis* 47 (1986): 216–25.

[78] Esler, *Community and Gospel*, 59.

[79] York, *Last Shall be First*.

[80] David B. Gowler, *Host, Guest, Enemy, and Friend: Portraits of the Pharisees in Luke and Acts* (Emory Studies in Early Christianity 1; New York: Peter Lang, 1991).

main of New Testament social science critics for more than a decade and they can help us to make the analysis more precise.[81]

The concern about "humiliation" (ταπείνωσις) in Luke 1:26–56 especially concerns kinship, honor and shame. The narrative leaves the ascribed family status of Mary unstated, in contrast to that of Elizabeth, who was "of the daughters of Aaron" (Luke 1:5). Mary's honor is embedded in her betrothal to a man "of the house of David" (Luke 1:27). Her humiliation derives from pregnancy before marriage has occurred (Luke 1:34, 48a). But God has removed this humiliation by communicating honor through the angel Gabriel beforehand and through the responses of the honored Elizabeth to her pregnancy. When the angel Gabriel comes to Mary in her private chambers, however, the speech on the lips of the angel attributes fear to Mary. Malina and Rohrbaugh, gendering both God and Gabriel as male in their reading of this text, evoke a social situation in which a man encounters a young woman and threatens her virginity. In their view, the male angel has persuaded her to consent to be overpowered by the Holy Spirit, the Most High. They comment as follows:

> Notice how readily Mary gives in when "cornered" by the angel. While obviously no lust is involved in this case, the scenario still points to traditional Mediterranean urgency to keep women duly encompassed. And Mary's answer in this difficult situation is: "Let it be with me according to your word" (v. 38). What this means in typical Mediterranean fashion is: "As you like!"[82]

Serious questions are being raised in current interpretation about this kind of male gendering of biblical texts.[83] Both traditional and nontraditional readers have implicitly, if not explicitly, gendered God as male in relation to Mary. Malina and Rohrbaugh's reading is highly similar to Schaberg's reading in gendering Gabriel as well as God as male. This is, without a doubt, one of the most explosive issues of our time. The gendering of both God and Gabriel as male takes us to the heart of ideology. Would it be possible for us to read this text in such a manner that neither God nor Gabriel are gendered as male in relation to Mary? The work of Brenner, van Dijk-Hemmes and Troost promises to give us such a reading in the near future. Let us look more closely at the text itself to see the nature of the social and cultural topics in it.

When the angel Gabriel first told Mary that his visit meant that she was being favored by God with conception and birth of a special son,

---

[81] Malina, *New Testament World*; Elliott, *Semeia* 35; idem, *Social Scientific Criticism*; Neyrey, *Social World*.

[82] Bruce Malina and Richard J. Rohrbaugh, *Social Science Commentary on the Synoptic Gospels* (Minneapolis: Fortress, 1992), 289.

[83] Brenner and van Dijk-Hemmes, *On Gendering Texts*.

she protested that she had no man (1:34). Here, then, the text explicitly evokes the traditional perception that a woman becomes pregnant only as the result of the presence of a man. When the angel draws an analogy between the honorable conception of her barren kinswoman Elizabeth and her own impending conception, Mary believes the angel's word of promise to her (1:36–38). We lack comparison of the argumentation the angel uses to persuade Mary with argumentation by gods who visit virgins in Mediterranean antiquity. But we should not be surprised to find similar strategies of persuasion. The angel has confronted Mary with powerful words and she has been persuaded by them. The "central" concern for a woman in this situation in Mediterranean antiquity is honor, and the powers have provided for her honor. This appears to be the primary reason for her praise of God: God has shown regard for the humiliation of this maidservant; from now on, all generations will call her blessed – instead of a dishonorable woman (1:48).

The result of this analysis suggests an inner relation between thaumaturgy and conversion: Mary will encounter a miracle just like Elizabeth has experienced a miracle; acceptance of this miracle requires a deep change of heart on behalf of Mary. Mary's first response to Gabriel was that she had no man, therefore she could not imagine how she could have a son (1:34). The answer of the angel persuades her to change her mind and accept the possibility (1:25–27), and Elizabeth's statements affirm her new point of view (1:42–45). Thus, argumentation that features honor and kinship confirms and deepens our understanding of the centrality of thaumaturgy and conversion in the discourse. But what about the reversal of the powerful and the lowly in Mary's Magnificat? Let us turn to cultural alliances and conflicts to deepen our understanding of this discourse.

A beginning context for investigating cultural argumentation in a text emerges in the distinction sociologists of culture make between dominant culture, subculture, contraculture, counterculture, and liminal culture. On the one hand, a cultural system has its own set of premises and rationales.[84] On the other hand, every cultural system is comprised of multiple "local cultures."[85] Local cultures interact with other local cultures, either by dominating or embedding themselves in another culture. Each culture develops its own premises and rationales within this context of domination and/or embedding.

The rhetorics of dominant culture, subculture, counterculture, contraculture, and liminal culture are a factor in producing these cultures,

---

[84] Peacock, *Anthropological Lens*, 35.
[85] Geertz, *Local Knowledge*.

and in turn these cultures generate these kinds of rhetoric. The relation of rhetoric to culture and culture to rhetoric, then, is reciprocal. What kind of culture rhetoric is at work in Luke 1:26–56? To pursue this issue it is necessary to have definitions of these types of culture rhetoric.[86]

1. *Dominant culture rhetoric* adopts a point of view according to which its own system of attitudes, values, dispositions and norms are supported by social structures vested with power to impose its goals on people in a significantly broad territorial region.
2. *Subculture rhetoric* imitates the attitudes, values, dispositions and norms of dominant culture rhetoric, and it claims to enact them better than members of dominant status.
3. *Ethnic subculture rhetoric* is a particular kind of subculture rhetoric. It has origins in a language different from the languages in the dominant culture, and it attempts to preserve and perpetuate an "old system" in a dominant cultural system in which it now exists, either because a significant number of people from this ethnic culture have moved into a new cultural environment or because a new cultural system is now imposing itself on it.[87]
4. *Counterculture rhetoric* is a "heretical" intra-cultural phenomena that articulates a *constructive* image of a better way of life in a context of "rejection of *explicit* and *mutable* characteristics" of the dominant or subculture rhetoric to which it is responding.[88] It is not simply a reaction formation to another form of culture, but it builds on a supporting ideology that provides a relatively self-sufficient system of action.[89]
5. *Contraculture rhetoric* is "groupculture" rhetoric that is deeply embedded in another form of culture to which it is a reaction formation. It asserts "more negative than positive ideas"[90] in a context where its positive ideas are simply presupposed and come from the culture to which it is reacting. It often is possible to predict the behavior and values evoked by contra-

---

[86] Robbins, "Rhetoric and Culture."

[87] Keith A. Roberts, "Toward a Generic Concept of Counter-Culture," *Sociological Focus* 11 (1978): 111–26. Milton M. Gordon, "The Subsociety and the Subculture," in *Subcultures* (ed. D. Arnold; Berkeley: Glendessary Press, 1970), 150–63.

[88] Roberts, "Generic Concept," 114.

[89] Ibid., 121; idem, *Religion and the Counter-Culture Phenomenon: Sociological and Religious Elements in the Formation of an Intentional Counter-Culture Community* (Ph.D. diss., Boston University, 1976); J. Milton Yinger, *Countercultures: The Promise and Peril of a World Turned Upside Down* (New York: Free Press, 1960).

[90] Roberts, "Generic Concept," 124, citing Margarite Bouvard, *The Intentional Community Movement: Building a New Moral World* (Port Washington, N.Y.: Kennicat Press, 1975), 119.

culture rhetoric if one knows the values evoked by the culture to which it is reacting, since the values are simply inverted.[91]

6. *Liminal culture rhetoric* is "disjunctive and multiaccentual" speech that evokes a cultural space "outside the sentence." It uses cacophonic, syncopated sounds and articulations in "heterogeneous and messy array" to evoke a possibility of "enunciation" and "identity." It is a liberating strategy "articulated at the liminal edge of identity" to create the possibility for an emergent cultural identity.[92]

If we analyze the text that features Mary and Elizabeth from the perspective of culture rhetoric, we begin to test the dynamics of revolutionist rhetoric in relation to reformist and utopian rhetoric. The angel Gabriel represents the power of God, and the speech of the angel represents a form of dominant culture rhetoric. After Mary accepts Gabriel's promise to her she speaks about the nature of God's power in terms of making the mighty low and the low mighty. Is Mary simply amplifying the dominant culture rhetoric Gabriel has introduced to her, or is this a different kind of culture rhetoric? Let us remain in touch with the topics that concern the social response to the world in the discourse as we pursue this issue. Does Mary's discourse introduce a revolutionist vision in which God's power "destroys" the present evil world, a utopian vision in which God's power "replaces" the present social structures and powerful people with a new kind of structure and role for leaders, or a reformist vision in which God's power "changes" something within the present system to make it function benevolently?

The answer to this question must come from the overall rhetoric of Luke and Acts. For this reason, it is important to embed Luke 1:26–56 in the discourse of both volumes. In a recent study of the social location of the implied author of this two volume work, I drew the conclusion that

> the thought of the implied author is located in the midst of the activities of adult Jews and Romans who have certain kinds of power in cities and villages throughout the Mediterranean world from Rome to Jerusalem.... The arena of socialization reveals an upwardlooking use of technology toward Roman officials with political power. Jewish offi-

---

[91] Roberts, "Generic Concept," 123–24; J. Milton Yinger, "Contraculture and Subculture," *American Sociological Review* 25 (1960): 629; Werner Stark, *Sectarian Religion* (New York: Fordham University Press, 1967), 141, 153; G.F.S. Ellens, "The Ranting Ranters: Reflections on a Ranting Counter-Culture," *CH* 40 (1971): 91–107.

[92] Homi K. Bhabha, "Postcolonial Criticism," in *Redrawing the Boundaries: The Transformation of English and American Literary Studies* (eds. S. Greenblatt and G. Gunn; New York: MLA, 1992), 443–45.

cials, however are considered equal in social status and rank... . Thus, the thought of the implied author is located socially in a place where it seems advantageous, and perhaps necessary, to tell "these foreign affairs" to people slightly higher in social rank who read Greek and appreciate a people who strive to be devout, righteous, and lettered... . Accepting a position of subordination, Christians speak with politeness and care upwards to those who dominate the system. Yet, bolstered by God's sanctioning of their diversity and by their ideology of "at homeness" in the Roman empire, they not only tell their story to those above but engage in vigorous and continued confrontation with those from whom they claim their Jewish heritage and those with whom they enjoy the benefits of Greco-Roman culture.[93]

The exchanges among the angel Gabriel, Mary and Elizabeth exhibit a subset of these dynamics. The angel Gabriel represents the power and will of God in much the same way that King Agrippa represents the power and will of the emperor (Acts 25:13–26:32), thus they both use dominant culture rhetoric. When the angel Gabriel speaks to Mary, he speaks uses command and "name dropping" characteristic of representatives of hierarchical structures. He is fully authorized by dominant power and he fills his discourse with the authorities that stand behind him as he works.

Since both Gabriel who represents God and King Agrippa who represents the emperor use dominant culture rhetoric, there is an inner tension in the accounts in the discourse of Luke-Acts. Do two dominant cultures stand in unmitigated opposition in Luke-Acts, or does the dominant rhetoric of one of the cultures accept a subordinate position in relation to the other? It seems clear from the relation of the discourse in the prefaces to the discourse in the speeches of Paul in Acts that representatives of Christianity accept a subordinate role to the emperor and his representatives.[94] The discourse in Luke-Acts adopts a position according to which people like Theophilus and King Agrippa are likely to view the story of Christianity as a matter of "foreign affairs," but it challenges such a view by embedding the affairs of Christianity within the affairs of the emperor and his representatives. When a decree of the emperor creates a movement of people whereby Jesus of Nazareth is born in the City of David (Luke 2:1–5), the stage is set for a cooperative relation between the power of the emperor and the power of God throughout the story. As the story progresses, events among early followers of Jesus work symbiotically with power structures within the Roman empire to create a story in which power that travels from Rome to Jerusalem creates an environment for Christiani-

---

[93] Robbins, "Social Location," 331–2.
[94] Vernon K. Robbins, "Prefaces in Greco-Roman Biography and Luke-Acts," *PRSt* 6 (1979): 94–108.

ty to travel from Jerusalem to Rome.⁹⁵ In this context, representatives of Christianity adopt subcultural rhetoric as they converse with representatives of empire.

The dominant culture rhetoric Gabriel uses with Mary, then, stands in an ethnic subculture relation to the dominant culture rhetoric King Agrippa uses with Paul. After Mary's encounter, she takes the initiative to go alone to the honored, no longer barren, woman Elizabeth, much like Paul goes to the synagogues of cities in Asia Minor, Macedonia and Greece. When Mary speaks in the presence of Elizabeth, she speaks a high form of Jewish rhetoric, a form containing the poetic qualities of royal Davidic and classical prophetic speech. At the highpoint of Mary's speech, however, she speaks a rhetoric of reversal: those who are powerful will be made low, and those who live in humiliation will be exalted (Luke 1:52). In other words, speaking the highest level of this ethnic subculture rhetoric, Mary introduces a contraculture phenomenon in her rhetoric – a phenomenon that "inverts" some aspect of another cultural system. Whose culture is Mary's speech inverting, and what is she inverting in that culture? Is Mary's rhetoric countercultural rather than contracultural? In other words, are the inversions part of an overall positive vision, or does her speech emphasize more negative than positive things?

The strategy of the narrative is to present a form of dominant Jewish culture rhetoric primarily on the lips of Pharisees.⁹⁶ In these contexts, Lukan discourse regularly presents itself as Jewish contraculture rhetoric. This rhetoric claims to represent Jewish tradition authentically by inverting certain behaviors in dominant Jewish culture. From the perspective of dominant Jewish culture rhetoric as Lukan discourse presents it, Christian discourse is a "dishonorable" tradition. But Lukan discourse also presents sources of power within Jewish tradition investing this "dishonorable" tradition with honor. In other words, Lukan discourse claims that Christianity does not reject the central values of Jewish tradition; it simply inverts objectional dominant Jewish culture thought and behavior. The Gospel of Luke, then, embeds Mary's rhetoric in a narrative context that inverts hierarchies within its own presentation of dominant Jewish culture rhetoric, and Mary herself

---

⁹⁵ Vernon K. Robbins, "Luke-Acts: A Mixed Population Seeks a Home in the Roman Empire," in *Images of Empire* (ed. Loveday Alexander; JSOTSup122; Sheffield: JSOT Press, 1991), 218–21.

⁹⁶ Halvor Moxnes, *The Economy of the Kingdom: Social Conflict and Economic Relations in Luke's Gospel* (Philadelphia: Fortress Press, 1988); David B. Gowler, "Chracterization in Luke: A Socio-Narratological Approach, " *BTB* 19 (1989): 54–62; idem, *Host, Guest, Enemy, and Friend*; idem, "Hospitality and Characterization in Luke 11:37–54: A Socio-Narratological Approach," *Semeia* 64 (1993): 213–51.

embodies an inversion of "dishonored" and "honored" traditions in dominant Jewish tradition. She asserts that God authorizes the honoring of her dishonor, and in other parts of the narrative God authorizes the honor of Jesus, Stephen and Paul, who also represent "dishonorable" traditions within dominant Jewish culture rhetoric as Lukan discourse presents it.

But now let us pursue the relation of Mary's rhetoric to Roman culture. When the angel speaks in Greek to Mary, the language is Greek, and Mary responds in Greek. Even the greeting of the angel is Greek, χαῖρε (1:28), rather than Hebrew, *shalōm*. Mary's rhetoric, then, uses the *lingua franca* of the dominant culture and is emboldened by it. Moreover, when Mary praises God, she uses high level Jewish hymnic verse that incorporates a form of reasoning and confirmation of its reasoning that reaches upward toward a subcultural form of Hellenistic-Roman argumentation. Mary's rhetoric reaches up in social status, like the narratorial voice reaches up toward Theophilus in the preface (Luke 1:1–4).[97] The hierarchical structure of the social order seems not to be in contention, but only the benevolence of those who hold positions of power in that structure. This rhetoric, then, seems not to reject "explicit and mutable characteristics" of Roman culture, which claims peace, salvation and benevolence as central values. Rather, Mary's rhetoric has a subcultural relation to Roman culture – her discourse claims that God fulfils central values of Roman culture better than the kingdom of the emperor does. In the end, the discourse of Luke and Acts perpetuates a contracultural rhetoric as an ethnic subcultural form of Roman culture. How close is Mary's speech to dishonored virgins who bore the heroes, gods and goddesses of Mediterranean culture? Only future investigation, analysis, and interpretation can tell us. New Testament interpreters have not yet confronted the issue and explored it.

Returning to the social response in the discourse, then, the issue is whether the discourse perceives evil to be present in the people or in the structures that run society. Mary's rhetoric evokes an image of changing the people in power: God will remove those who now have power and put the lowly in those positions. Mary does not assert that the structures of power themselves should be changed but only the people who have the power. Nor does Mary claim that God will destroy the people who have the power – God will depose and scatter them. This means that her discourse probably is not appropriately described as revolutionist, which would imply destruction of both the structures of the social order and the powerful people who run it. Nor does the discourse appear to be utopian, where an entirely new social

---

[97] Robbins, "Prefaces," 94–108; idem, "Social Location," 321–23.

9. Mary, Elizabeth, and the Magnificat as a Test Case 315

system will replace the present one. Rather, Mary's discourse is reformist, with an emphasis on changing the people in power. When Lukan discourse embeds this reformist vision in thaumaturgical, conversionist discourse, the vision is significant reform indeed. As God's thaumaturgic powers raise the lowly to positions of power, the vision is that God's conversionist powers change the hearts of the honored ones to goals of benevolence and mercy. The changes in the social order, then, will occur as leaders use power structures to "show mercy" and to "fill the hungry with good things." Mary's discourse, then, shows no desire that the hierarchical power structures be taken away. She simply has her own view of how those who hold the positions of power should embody the thaumaturgical and conversionist powers of God.

Ideological Texture: Every Theology has a Politics

Exploration of the ideological texture of a text focuses on self-interests. What and whose self-interests are being negotiated in this text? If the dominant voices in the text persuade people to act according to their premises, who will gain and who will lose? What will be gained and what will be lost?[98]

These questions move into ideology, point of view, and theology. And here the motto is that every theology has a politics. Ideology is "an integrated system of beliefs, assumptions and values, not necessarily true or false, which reflects the needs and interests of a group or class at a particular time in history."[99] This integrated system proceeds from the need to understand, to interpret to self and others, to justify, and to control one's place in the world. Ideologies are shaped by specific views of reality shared by groups – specific perspectives on the world, society and people, and on the limitations and potentialities of human existence. Inasmuch as all religious groupings and movements have specific collective needs, interests and objectives that they seek to relate to ultimate sacred norms and principles – in Christianity, to the will and action of God as revealed in Jesus Christ – all religious movements, including early Christianity, develop ideological positions and perspectives.[100]

---

[98] Elliott, *Social Scientific Criticism*, 119–21; Terry Eagleton, *Ideology: An Introduction* (New York: Verso, 1991); John McGowan, *Postmodernism and Its Critics* Ithica, N.Y.: Cornell University Press).

[99] David B. Davis, *The Problem of Slavery in the Age of Revolution 1770–1823* (Ithaca, N.Y.: Cornell University Press, 1975), 14.

[100] Elliott, *Home for the Homeless*, 268; idem, *Social Scientific Criticism*, 51–53; Elisabeth Schüssler Fiorenza, *In Memory of Her: A Feminist Theological Reconstruction of Christian*

Who, we must ask, is benefitting by having Mary, a virgin, speak as she does in the Magnificat? Who is benefitting by having Mary speak out about raising the lowly up to power and driving the powerful away empty-handed? Whose ideology is being advanced, for whose benefit, by Mary's dialogue with the angel and Elizabeth, and by the argumentation in the Magnificat? Let us approach the issue from three angles: (a) the voices of the narrator and the angel, (b) the dialogue between Mary and Elizabeth and (c) the monologue by Mary to God.

The narratorial voice throughout Luke and Acts presents a case for Christianity as a healing, peace-loving group of people who encounter conflict when Jewish leaders attempt to run them out, imprison, or kill them. This narratorial voice presents a case for certain Christian leaders throughout the Mediterranean world from Ethiopia throughout Syria-Palestine, Asia Minor, Macedonia, Greece, and Rome. The rhetoric of Luke and Acts offers a certain group of Christian leaders the benefit of a bi-cultural founder and leader. Simultaneously, Jesus functions as a messiah, who launches high level contraculture rhetoric against established Jewish leaders, and a Hellenistic-Roman benefactor-savior who engages in high artisan, low elite subculture rhetoric that challenges all leaders. Social identity is at stake for Christians. From a social perspective, Christians look to an outsider like subversive troublemakers. The narratorial voice, with the voices of characters embedded in it, argues the case that all the troubles Christians have arise with Jewish leaders who are proud, greedy, and lovers of money. Jesus and his followers, in contrast, enact humility and benevolence.

Social and political benefits are at stake in Luke and Acts, and wherever its narratorial rhetoric is successful Christians will attain positive social identity and will receive accompanying political benefits. Material benefits also are at stake. Of key importance are the resources in cities throughout the Mediterranean world, the location of storing and distributing grain supplies and the like.[101] If Christians can be Roman citizens, as the converted Pharisee Paul is, then Christians have the right to receive a portion of the grain dole and other services of the cities. Individual benefits also are at stake. Christian leaders, both individually and in pairs, receive the right to travel freely throughout the empire, entering regions, villages, and cities at will.

This is the overall context in which the voice of the narrator and the voice of the angel function in Luke 1. According to the narratorial voice, the God of the Jews, whom the angel calls "Most High" and

---

Origins (New York: Crossroad, 1983); idem, *Bread Not Stone: The Challenge of Feminist Biblical Interpretation* (Boston: Beacon, 1985); idem, *But She Said: Feminist Practices in Biblical Interpretation* (Boston: Beacon, 1992).

[101] Robbins, "Social Location."

"Lord God," initiates Mary's pregnancy through the agency of the power of God and the "Holy Spirit" (1:32, 35). When it is made clear to Mary that this pregnancy outside of marriage will bring her honor through her prestigious son, she accepts the action in the obedient mode of a client responding to a powerful patron. Mary cannot refuse God's offer; she accepts the role of an obedient servant/client and expresses gratitude that she will be held in honor by all people. The rhetorical effect is to claim that Christians are specially favored with the benefits of the patron God of the Jews. This God works contraculturally within Jewish tradition, at times creating human situations that are traditionally dishonorable in order to bring honor to certain dishonored people. God's activity presupposes and advances hierarchical structures within a patriarchical ideology, yet it inverts certain dishonored conditions within the context of those structures. In Luke 1, God advances the ideology of patrilineal honor in the form of prestigious sons who have political power (1:32–33) and holy status (1:35). But God also offers an inversion of weak and powerful, hungry, and well-fed (1:51–53). Patrilineal hierarchy remains in place, but there is reform within it.

This ideology among first-century Christians proved to be highly successful. On the one hand, this kind of rhetoric presents a willingness to accept the patronage system within Hellenistic-Roman culture and work within it. Luke and Acts, therefore, share much of the ideology of a document like Plutarch's *Alexander*, which challenges patrons to be generous. Yet, Luke and Acts are reformist within that system. They activate reformist activities by means of contraculture rhetoric against Jewish leaders. In other words, through aggressive criticism of Jewish leaders, Lukan discourse calls for reform within the established political system of patronage and the centralized economic system of distribution.[102] This Christian discourse, then, calls for selected reform at the expense of established Jewish leaders. The people who will benefit present themselves as leaders of an ethnic subculture that fulfills the highest claims of dominant Roman government, namely salvation (σωτηρία) and peace.

The dialogue between Mary and Elizabeth features the mothers of the founders of the Christian movement supporting one another in a manner that overturns the usual competition that accompanies the

---

[102] Richard Rohrbaugh, "Methodological Considerations in the Debate over the Social Class Status of Early Christians," *JAAR* 52 (1984): 519–46; idem, "'Social Location of Thought' as a Heuristic Construct in New Testament Study," *JSNT* 30 (1987): 103–19; idem, "The Pre-Industrial City in Luke-Acts: Urban Social Relations," *Social World of Luke-Acts*, 125–49. Halvor Moxnes, *The Economy of the Kingdom*; Esler, *Community and Gospel*; Braun, "Banquet Traditions."

births of specially endowed sons who are potential rivals over power and leadership. The "honorable" tradition of barren women characteristically contains rivalry between kinwomen. The dialogue between Mary and Elizabeth engages this rivalry and reconfigures it. When Elizabeth became pregnant, she said the Lord had looked upon her to take away her reproach "among men" (Luke 1:25). She tells Mary, in contrast, that she, Mary, is blessed "among women" (Luke 1:42). Mary rephrases Elizabeth's statement to claim: "all generations will call me blessed" (Luke 1:48b).

This exchange reverberates with Israelite traditions of rivalry among women in a context where they are trying to win the special place of favor from their husbands. Leah speaks of "being called blessed" in a context of desperation after she has been unsuccessful in getting her husband Jacob to love her. Leah had hoped that her bearing of Reuben for Jacob would cause him to love her (Gen. 29:32). But this did not happen. Leah's rivalry with Rachel over Jacob's love continued as Rachel gave her maidservant Bilhah to Jacob and she had two sons, Dan and Naphtali (Gen. 20:3–8). Leah in turn gave her maidservant Zilpah to Jacob, and she bore Jacob two sons, Gad and Asher (Gen. 30:9–13). The name Asher means "happy, blessed." Leah called him Asher, because, as she said, "the women will call me *asher*" (in Greek, μακαρία: Gen. 30:13). With this statement Leah gave up on removing the reproach from "her man." Instead, she looked to women, who would look at her and "call her μακαρία happy, blessed." Mary's rationale for her joy in the Magnificat captures the dynamics of this tradition and reconfigures them. When she asserts that "all generations will call me blessed" (Luke 1:48b), she is embodying the rivalries of the past and the hopes for the future. If men and women can honor each other as God takes away their reproach and manifests powers of mercy and benevolence, then both the people and the social order may receive God's promises from the past

What does this mean for interpretation in this paper? It means, on the one hand, that Mary's assertion holds the potential for evoking a sense of rivalry between herself and Elizabeth. Rivalry between "knowing only the baptism of John" and "knowing the way of God" as taught by Jesus is well known in the Lukan narrative (Acts 18:24–26), and readers could expect rivalry between the mothers of John and Jesus. The narrator implies, on the other hand, that there is no rivalry; in the context of the narration, Mary appears to be trying to overcome a division between receiving honor among men and among women. The narrator may also be trying to overcome this division by featuring Simeon's blessing of both Mary and Joseph (Luke 2:34) followed by

Anna's thanks to God and interpretation of the redemption Jesus brings to Jerusalem (Luke 2:38).

The overall rhetoric of the interchange between Mary and Elizabeth, then, suggests an attempt to remove all rivalry between the mothers of the specially honored sons who stand at the beginning of the story of Christianity. In contrast to the rivalry between Sarah and Hagar, Rachel and Leah, Hannah and Penninah, Mary takes her body to Elizabeth, and together they celebrate and honor their pregnant bodies. The rhetoric of Lukan discourse is to claim that Christians perpetuate a culture of the body, impregnated by Holy Spirit, that overcomes rivalry, division, and hatred. Christians confront other people with their bodies for the purpose of overcoming hatred, healing illness, enacting forgiveness, and calling for generosity without expectation of return.

Mary's monologue to God in the presence of Elizabeth offers additional social and self benefits to Christian women. When Elizabeth says that "all women" will call Mary blessed and Mary asserts that she herself will be called blessed by "all generations," there is a special claim of honor for women both among Christian men and among Christian women. This is ambiguous honor, to be sure, since the primary base of it is honor from men. Mary's hymnlike speech emulates the tongue of David; which, of course, befits a woman betrothed to a man "of the House of David." Her body is forced to perpetuate dominant Jewish tradition in a dishonorable manner that is declared honorable by a God who maintains patrilineal tradition. Mary upholds the male line of tradition, and through her appropriate consent and expression of gratitude she receives honor. In other words, Mary receives honor in the great tradition in which men protect the reputation of "their women."

But does Mary's voice say something more? Does anyone hear, or notice, her initial cry that she will become pregnant without a man? She has no real choice in the matter. From the perspective of patriarchal tradition, this is God's doing and Mary is fortunate, blessed, the mother of the messiah. What about Mary's perspective? She says she has been afflicted, dishonored. Why? Not because she is barren and wants a child, but because she is with child outside a marriage contract. If someone, benevolent or otherwise, decides she is to have a son, is that to be her station in life?

We need an ethnography of virgins in Mediterranean culture in order to explore the further nuances of Mary's speech to God. So far we do not have a comprehensive study of virgins in Mediterranean society and their speech to gods. What would the implications be for a virgin to speak like Mary speaks? Through the help of Mieke Bal, we are coming closer to an understanding of virgins in Israelite tradition.[103] In her study, Bal distinguishes between *na'arah* (young girl), *'almah* (mostly already married woman before her first pregnancy), and *bethulah* (a woman confronted with the passage from young girl to almost already married woman). What does it mean for a woman who is going through this transitional phase of insecurity and danger in a patriarchal society to speak of being humiliated, of having God show regard for her humiliation, and of having a conviction that from now on all generations will call her blessed? New Testament interpreters have yet to gather the data and programmatically address this issue.

Male interpreters regularly celebrate Mary's speech as liberating for her and for all who are poor in social, political or economic status. Victor Turner, however, shows that rituals of announcement and enactment of reversal by those of lower status support and reaffirm the hierarchical system that is in place. People of higher status, if they are wise, permit, indeed encourage, those of lower status to speak out and enact their frustrations in a context of reversal. The key is to establish boundaries, either spatially or temporally, for these announcements and enactments. In other words, those in power establish a clear definition of these people as a subculture or counterculture with an important but limited function in society *or* they designate a period of time during the year when the lower classes celebrate a reversal whereby they experience power and humiliate those of higher status.

The enactment of reversal, either within a subculture or within a designated time period, strengthens the ideology of hierarchy, of the necessity of having powerful people over weak people. The weak have their momentary experience of being powerful, or they have their limited social domain in which to perform their powerful acts. Either strategy allows and encourages the weak to turn their energy toward the work of service, and perhaps reconciliation, which is welcomed by the established hierarchy.

Conclusion

Socio-rhetorical criticism suggests that we need to look carefully outside many of the boundaries within which we customarily interpret the Magnificat. I am aware that I, like others, speak from within a bounded context. My approach to this text is socially located, as is anyone else's approach. I consider it important, however, to establish clear boundaries for the purpose of programmatic analysis. But then I consider it essential to subject those boundaries to analysis and criticism, and to look through and beyond those boundaries for additional

---

[103] Bal, *Death and Dissymmetry*, 41–93.

9. Mary, Elizabeth, and the Magnificat as a Test Case

insight, even if those insights explode and reconfigure insights I had within that other context of analysis and interpretation. This, for me, is the nature of language, whether it is oral or written. Since different sets of boundaries establish different contexts for meanings, language signifies complexly interwoven textures of signification that appear only when analysis explores language from the perspective of multiple contexts. Socio-rhetorical criticism invites the interpreter to establish more than one set of boundaries for interpretation because multiple interpretations will bring into sight, sound, and feeling aspects of oral and written discourse that otherwise will remain hidden.

Mikhail Bakhtin has observed that speech is a social possession, and for this reason much, in fact most, of our speech comes from other people. He speaks, then, of many voices in our speech, *heteroglossia*. Exploration of Luke 1:26–56 from the perspective of multiple contexts reveals that "each word (text) is an intersection of words (texts) where at least one other word (text) can be read."[104] "Intertextuality" is the current term for this observation that "any text is constructed as a mosaic of quotations; any text is the absorption and transformation of another"[105] Intertextuality is not, therefore, limited to explicit presentation of other texts as second or third level narration (as Acts 2:26). Speaking, writing, and reading are social acts. This means that social meanings surround the words at all times. A speaker, writer, and reader play with boundaries they themselves establish and transgress for their own purposes. The interplay between boundaries and transgressions of boundaries, then, is the very nature of communication. If one person tries to keep someone's voice out, another is likely to let it in.

When Mary refers to her "humiliation," she uses a word that can connote a wide range of meanings, and the question is what range of meanings any reader entertains for the signs in the text. At this point, the text is extremely vulnerable; an interpreter must remember that every sign should be viewed "as an active component of speech, or text, or sign, modified and transformed in meaning by variable social tones, valuations, and connotations it condenses within itself in specific social conditions."[106] Since the community that uses language is a heterogeneous society, Mary's "humiliation" is "a focus of struggle and contradiction. It

---

[104] Julia Kristeva, *The Kristeva Reader* (ed. Toril Moi; New York: Columbia University Press, 1986), 37.

[105] Ibid.; Julia Kristeva, *La Révolution du langage poétique* (Paris: Seuil, 1974); M. M. Bakhtin, *The Dialogic Imagination* (ed. M. Holquist; trans. C. Emerson and M. Holquist; Austin, Tex.: University of Texas Press, 1981); S. Draisma (ed.), *Intertextuality in Biblical Writings: Essays in Honor of Bas van Iersel* (Kampen: Kok, 1989); Robbins, "Reversed Contextualization."

[106] Wilhelm H. Wuellner, "Is There an Encoded Reader Fallacy?" *Semeia* 48 (1989): 43.

is not simply a matter of asking 'what [this] sign means,' ... but of investigating its varied history," since "conflicting groups, classes, individuals, and discourses" contend with each other for its meaning.[107]

John York has analyzed the manner in which Jesus picks up and embellishes the language of reversal Mary introduces in the Magnificat.[108] This means that Mary does not have the last word in Luke. Her male son, Jesus, picks up and reconfigures Mary's language in the beatitudes, parables, and sayings. When, in Luke 11:27–28, a woman in the crowd tries to restore the importance of Mary by saying to Jesus, "Blessed is the womb that bore you, and the breasts that you sucked!", Jesus replies, "Blessed rather are those who hear the word of God and keep it!" Mary does not have the last word with the language she uses in the Magnificat. In Lukan discourse, her male son takes over her language and determines much of her future by his use of it. Who is the narrator who speaks in this way, and what is the narratorial voice trying to achieve by this refiguring of Mary's language in the narrative? The reader is asked to believe that Mary speaks in the Gospel of Luke, but does she? She tries to speak, and it may be possible to recover a voice that has been trying desperately to speak but cannot because it is continually drowned out by men's voices, my own included. In Lukan discourse, Mary seeks solace from another woman, going to Elizabeth who is an honored, no longer barren, woman. In this context, she finally directs her speech to God. As she argues her case, she expresses her gratitude to God for declaring her pregnancy outside of marriage to be honorable and continues with an embellishment that appeals to the God who reforms traditions of patronage so that particular forms of dishonor are removed within them. In this manner, Mary becomes the mother of a Christian discourse that envisions the possibility of winning its way in the Roman empire through aggressive speech against established Jewish leaders that contains implications for reform within actual practices of patrons, patronesses, leaders and members of all ranks within Christianity – be they Jewish, Roman, Phrygian or Lycaonian.

---

[107] Ibid.
[108] York, *Last Shall Be First*.

10

The Present and Future of Rhetorical Analysis

Proemium: We are participants in an exciting time that calls for responsible action

As Thomas Olbricht remarks in an informative autobiographical paper,[1] the international interest in rhetorical analysis and interpretation is remarkable. A number of diligent, creative people have created a context of opportunity for us. It is my view that contexts of opportunity are also contexts of responsibility. At a time when people who embody multiple rhetorics come into our lives through our ears, our eyes, the printed materials we hold in our hands and the airplanes, trains, buses and cars that come into our cities and countryside, it is appropriate for rhetorical analysis and interpretation to become a major player in religious studies, the humanities, the social sciences, and even the practical and hard sciences.

In other words, people are becoming more and more aware that the use of language is as important as the use of science for the lives of millions of people on this planet. We possess the scientific knowledge and the productive abilities to bring health and well-being to an overwhelming majority of people who inhabit the earth. People's use of words plays a central role in who benefits from our knowledge and abilities, who is put at a disadvantage, who is put to flight, and who is destroyed from the face of the earth. In short, the ability to use language across this entire planet and throughout a growing part of our solar system makes us substantive co-creators of life and death. Those who have been privileged to be at the right places at the right time, to use again the words of Thomas Olbricht, should look carefully at the opportunities we have to take positions of leadership toward constructive action in cooperation with highly different kinds of people.

---

[1] Thomas Olbricht, "The Flowering of Rhetorical Criticism in America," in *The Rhetorical Analysis of Scripture: Essays from the 1995 London Conference* (ed. Stanley E. Porter and Thomas H. Olbricht; JSNTSup 146; Sheffield: Sheffield Academic Press, 1997), 79–102.

The question is how we can use the resources, skills and insights that a host of hardworking people have made available to us to move toward these ends. I will formulate my answer first in terms of a general agenda, then I will divide this agenda into parts so each of us may identify the places where we have already been contributing individually to it and we may assess where we may join with others to participate even more vigorously in it.

Statement of the Case: Rhetorical interpreters should reinvent rhetorical method and theory into an interpretive analytics

Since its reintroduction into the field of secular and biblical literature during the last half of the twentieth century, rhetorical criticism has functioned both as interpretive method and interpretive theory. As a method, rhetorical criticism has brought new light to the argumentative nature of biblical literature. As a theory, rhetorical criticism challenges every method to break open its boundaries, to reassess its powers of reduction and to reconfigure its programs and goals. In my view, to meet the tasks that lie before it now, rhetorical criticism needs to move beyond the traditional interplay of method and theory into the mode of a comprehensive interpretive analytics.

This is a demanding task for those who wish to perform it with scholarly competence. In short, it requires three steps. First, one must acquire substantive facility with the skills, knowledge and insights in the range of ancient literature synthesized by Josef Martin's *Antike Rhetorik* and Heinrich Lausberg's *Handbuch der Literarischen Rhetorik*.[2] Second, one must absorb the lesson from Patricia Bizzell and Bruce Herzberg's *The Rhetorical Tradition* and Thomas M. Conley's *Rhetoric in the European Tradition* that the tradition of Greco-Roman rhetoric adapts, reforms, and revisions itself in the new social and cultural contexts that confront humans century by century.[3] Third, one must apply the knowledge, insights and skill of the rhetorical tradition as an interpretive analytics both to "primary" texts and to texts we identify as "commentary" and "criticism." To gain a basic understanding of what it can mean for rhetorical criticism to become an interpretive analytics during the twenty-first century, let us look at the role rhetorical criti-

---

[2] Josef Martin, *Antike und Rhetorik: Technik und Methode* (Munich: Beck, 1974); Heinrich Lausberg, *Handbuch der Literarischen Rhetorik: Eine Grundlegung der Literaturwissenschaft* (3d ed.; Stuttgart: Franz Steiner, 1990); ET: *Handbook of Literary Rhetoric: A Foundation for Literary Study* (ed. David E. Orton and R. Dean Anderson; Leiden: Brill, 1998).

[3] Patricia Bizzel and Bruce Herzberg, *The Rhetorical Tradition: Readings form Classical Times to the Present* (Boston: Bedford Books of St. Martin's Press, 1990); Thomas M. Conley, *Rhetoric in the European Tradition* (New York: Longman, 1990).

cism plays both as method and as theory, then let us explore how it could function as an interpretive analytics.

Wilhelm Wuellner has helped us to see rhetorical criticism as both a method and a theory. In his words,

> As method, rhetorical criticism comes into focus primarily on *one* issue: The text's potential to persuade, to encourage the imagination and will, or the text's symbolic inducement.[4]

In the commonly known rhetorical environment of speaker-author, speech-text, and audience-reader, this means that rhetorical interpreters have focused primarily on the speech-text rather than the speaker-author or the audience-reader. Rhetorical criticism as method in biblical interpretation has a recent history that is known well. After initial beginnings with James Muilenburg and his students (Jackson et al.), a series of studies by Wilhelm Wuellner and Hans Dieter Betz decisively moved New Testament studies toward a traditional mode of rhetorical criticism.[5] The special focus was on epistles as speeches. When George A. Kennedy, professor of classical studies, assisted with this kind of analysis and interpretation, a number of interpreters began to acquire the skills of rhetorical criticism and apply them to biblical texts.[6]

As Wuellner's statement indicates, interpreters who use the traditional method of rhetorical criticism limit the resources of rhetorical theory and practice to analysis and interpretation of a text as a speech or argument. Limiting the focus in this manner, practitioners of this

---

[4] Wilhelm Wuellner, "Rhetorical Criticism and its theory in Culture-Critical Perspective: The Narrative Rhetoric of John 11," in *Text and Interpretation: New Approaches in the Criticism of the New Testament* (ed. P. J. Martin and J. H. Petzer; NTTS 15; Leiden: Brill, 1991), 178.

[5] James Muilenberg, "Form Criticism and Beyond," *JBL* 88 (1969): 1–18; Jared J. Jackson and Martin Kessler, eds., *Rhetorical Criticism: Essays in Honor of James Muilenburg* (PTMS 1; Pittsburgh: Pickwick, 1974); Wilhem Wuellner, "Paul's Rhetoric of Argumentation in Romans: An Alternative to the Donfried-Karris Debate over Romans," *CBQ* 38 (1976): 330–51; repr. in *The Romans Debate* (ed. Karl P. Donfried; Minneapolis: Augsburg, 1977): 152–74; idem, "Der Jakobusbrief im Licht der Rhetorik und Textpragmatik," *LB* 43 (1978): 5–66; idem, "Greek Rhetoric and Pauline Argumentation," in *Early Christian Literature and the Classical Intellectual Tradition: In Honorem Robert M. Grant* (ed. William R. Schoedel and Robert L. Wilken; Paris: Beauchesne, 1979): 177–88; Hans Dieter Betz, *Galatians: A Commentary on Paul's Letter to the Churches in Galatia* (Hermeneia; Philadelphia: Fortress Press, 1979).

[6] George A. Kennedy, *New Testament Interpretation through Rhetorical Criticism* (Chapel Hill: University of North Carolina Press, 1984); Duane F. Watson, ed., *Persuasive Artistry: Studies in New Testament Rhetoric in Honor of George A. Kennedy* (JSNTSup 50; Sheffield: JSOT Press, 1991); cf. Duane F. Watson and Alan J. Hauser, eds., *Rhetorical Criticism of the Bible: A Comprehensive Bibliography with Notes on History and Method* (Leiden: Brill, 1994).

form of rhetorical criticism have been able to give rhetorical analysis and interpretation a status near to twentieth-century scientific discourse. Its procedures are precise, its resources are explicit and its results are testable. Many have experienced this as a decisive gain. Rhetorical criticism in this form can go head to head with every other scientific form of analysis and interpretation in the field of biblical studies and hold its own. During the twentieth century, forms of analysis and interpretation that have acquired the nature of scientific precision and power have taken center stage in authoritative biblical commentary. If they lacked scientific stature, they needed philosophical stature. Bultmannian form criticism acquired both scientific and philosophical stature. Traditional rhetorical criticism has enjoyed philosophical support primarily from Aristotle's *Ars Rhetorica*, but it has staked its reputation on its use of authoritative terms and precise analytical practices more than on the philosophical soundness of its observations.

As traditional rhetorical interpreters have focused on the text as speech, they have approached the context of both the speaker-author and the audience-reader in the mode of historical rather than rhetorical critics. They have added a few new insights into social situations from classical rhetorical theory, but they have not revalued or reinvented our approach to the wily ways of speaker-authors or the selective ways of audience-readers. Traditional rhetorical interpreters enact a form of interpretation that, for the most part, reduces contexts in life to environments either of acceptance or rejection, of approval or opposition. In other words, the interpreter either submits to or rejects the author-narrator – taking a traditional position of submission or of suspicion. Likewise, the interpreter projects a polarized audience containing some people who respond favorably (the good, authentic people) and others who resist the argument (the bad, inauthentic people). This approach re-enacts the polarizing categories in which modern western thought perpetuates authority and tradition, rather than analyzing and interpreting author, audience, and interpreter with revalued and reinvented categories currently available to rhetorical criticism from modern communication theory, the social sciences and postmodern theory and interpretation.

As Wuellner has pointed out, traditional rhetorical interpretation not only limits its focus to texts as speeches; it limits the resources of rhetorical analysis and interpretation to a particular kind of time in relation to text – namely, the time of reading. To use Wuellner's words: "Traditionally rhetorical criticism as method is almost exclusively concerned with the textual constraints *while* reading."[7] The interpreter does not programmatically investigate time before reading or after reading. Ra-

---

[7] Wuellner, "Rhetorical Criticism," 178.

ther, the interpreter analyzes the persuasive nature of the text during the time of reading and re-enacts the categories of authority and tradition in either a positive or negative manner during this time. The traditional mode of rhetorical analysis and interpretation, then, is another form of "restrained rhetoric" on the scene of literary interpretation.[8] It restrains the resources of rhetorical criticism by focusing its energies and resources on the text itself to interpret its potential to persuade during a time of hearing or reading.

Alongside rhetorical interpreters who have been focusing on the text as speech, some interpreters have been attempting to tap resources that lie beyond the boundaries of traditional rhetorical criticism. The resources of twentieth-century rhetorical theory have been most prominent in their approaches, and the resources lie in so many areas – argumentation theory, communication theory, linguistic theory, speech-act theory, and so on – that it is not feasible to describe them here. In Wuellner's view, the incorporation of rhetorical theory during the twentieth century has worked in two ways. First, odern theory has widened the scope, beyond the temporal limits *while* reading, by emphasising the inescapable constraints imposed both *before* and *after* reading.[9]

This moves the rhetorical study of literature into the realm of political and ethical life both in the past and in the present.[10] We engage the past, present and future of antecedent speaker-authors, speech-texts and hearer-readers for the purpose of reconstruing the political and ethical issues that lie in our own past, present and future.

> This leads to the second issue, where postmodern theory invites reflection on the rhetoric of scholarship. The *rhetoric* of shared critical inquiry is perceived as different from the logic of shared scholarly work .. this extended level rhetorical criticism is reconceived as rhetorico-political activity.[11]

---

[8] Wilhelm Wuellner, "Where is Rhetorical Criticism Taking Us?" *CBQ* 49 (1987): 453; Brian Vickers, "Introduction," in *Rhetoric Revalued* (ed. Brian Vickers; Medieval and Renaissance Texts and Studies 19; Binghamton, N.Y.: Center for Medieval and Renaissance Studies), 13–39.

[9] Wuellner, "Rhetorical Criticism," 179.

[10] J. Hillis Miller, "Is There an Ethics of Reading?" in *Reading Narrative: Form, Ethics, Ideology* (ed. James Phelan; Columbus, OH: Ohio State University Press), 84; Wayne C. Booth, *The Company We Keep: An Ethics of Fiction* (Berkeley: University of California Press, 1988).

[11] Wuellner, "Rhetorical Criticism," 179, citing Frank Lentricchia, *Criticism and Social Change* (Chicago: University of Chicago Press, 1983), 145–63.

Moving beyond a reflective political and ethical life, postmodernism takes us to commentary as rhetorico-political activity. This means that we need to include rhetorical analysis and interpretation of antecedent and current commentary discourse in the context of our rhetorical analysis and interpretation of ancient texts. In other words, rather than simply accepting or rejecting the commentary of our past and present colleagues – simply re-enacting the dominating modes of authority and tradition in western culture – interpreters should analyze and interpret commentary discourse with the same resources they use to analyze ancient texts.

Practitioners of rhetorical theory have grown in number during the last few decades alongside practitioners of rhetorical method. What their discourse lacks in scientific stature, it regularly overcomes in philosophical stature. By achieving a mode of philosophical facility, rhetorical theorists have attained significant power and authority both in secular and biblical literary interpretation. A primary limitation of theoretical discourse is the limited range of its textual practices. Theoretical practitioners reinscribe only very limited dimensions of the texts they interpret, for very good philosophical reasons, of course. They limit their focus to dimensions of discourse under vigorous discussion in the intellectual company they keep. The result is that in the process of contributing substantively to the reconfiguration of meanings and meaning effects in texts for a new time and place, rhetorical theory regularly adopts an authoritative, philosophical mode that excludes multiple aspects of the discourse in texts from analysis and interpretation.

This brings us to the issue of an interpretive analytics. Neither rhetorical method nor rhetorical theory, either separately or in a position of jousting with one another, will fulfill the tasks that need to be undertaken during the twenty-first century. We need a mode of rhetorical criticism that programmatically revalues and reinvents rhetorical criticism into a new *modus operandi*. Wuellner has given us glimpses into how we might proceed toward a "revalued"[12] or "reinvented"[13] rhetorical criticism.[14] But he has not programmatically created and put such a mode of rhetorical criticism into practice. My proposal is to reinvent rhetorical criticism as an interpretive analytics, and the re-

---

[12] Vickers, "Introduction."

[13] Terry Eagleton *Literary Theory: An Introduction* (Minneapolis: University of Minnesota Press, 1983), 105–106.

[14] Wuellner, "Where is Rhetorical Criticism Taking Us?" 453; cf. idem, "Rhetorical Criticism"; idem, "Biblical Exegesis in the Light of the History and Historicity of Rhetoric and the Nature of the Rhetoric of Religion," in *Rhetoric and the New Testament: Essays from the 1992 Heidelberg Conference* (ed. Stanley E. Porter and Thomas H. Olbricht; Sheffield: JSOT Press): 492–513.

mainder of this paper will describe and delineate basic attributes of such an approach.

I first encountered the phrase "interpretive analytics" in Dreyfus and Rabinow's description of the interpretive practices of Michel Foucault.[15] As I understand it, an interpretive analytics uses the strategies and insights of both theory and method, but it uses these strategies and insights in a manner that perpetually deconstructs its own boundaries and generates new ones in the ongoing process of interpretation. The stance of the interpreter is to "tak[e] seriously the problems and conceptual tools of the past, but not the solutions and conclusions based on them."[16] The goal is to replace "ontology with a special kind of history that focuses on the cultural practices that have made us what we are."[17] The task of investigation is "to find the rules which determined or controlled the discourse that there was."[18] The role of the interpreter is to adopt a form of commentary discourse that presents

> a pragmatically guided reading of the coherence of the practices of the society. It does not claim to correspond either to the everyday meanings shared by the actors or, in any simple sense, to reveal the intrinsic meaning of the practices.... . [It goes] beyond theory and hermeneutics and yet [takes] problems seriously. The practitioner of interpretive analytics realizes that he himself [or she herself] is produced by what he [or she] is studying; consequently he [or she] can never stand outside it. [He or she sees] sees that cultural practices are more basic than discursive formations (or any theory) and that the seriousness of these discourses can only be understood as part of a society's ongoing history.[19]

In this mode, rhetorical criticism uses its resources to explore texts in their social, cultural, aesthetic, historical, political, ideological and psychological contexts. As an interpretive analytics, rhetorical criticism moves beyond method and theory, beyond the role of a subdiscipline of historical or literary criticism and beyond the role of a discipline that performs restrained rhetorical analysis and interpretation into a revalued and reinvented rhetorical criticism that brings resources from multiple disciplines of study into dialogue with one another on their own terms. The remaining task, then, is to display an overall program for rhetorical criticism as an interpretive analytics.

---

[15] Hubert L. Dreyfus and Paul Rabinow, *Michel Foucault: Beyond Structuralism and Hermeneutics* (2d ed.; Chicago: University of Chicago Press, 1983).
[16] Ibid., 122.
[17] Ibid.
[18] Ibid., 123.
[19] Ibid., 124–25.

Reconstructing the Texture of Discourse

An initial task for rhetorical criticism as an interpretive analytics is to reinvent the terminology we use to describe the multiple dimensions of discourse within texts. Literary interpreters regularly reduce the rhetoricity of a text to four "master tropes": metaphor, metonymy, synecdoche, and irony; while linguistic interpreters regularly reduce it to two: metonymy and metaphor.[20] Brian Vickers, in contrast, lists forty-eight figures and tropes in discourse as the domain of traditional rhetorical criticism. Rhetorical criticism as an interpretive analytics for our time and place needs to reinvent and revalue these categories in the context of the strategies and insights of modern and postmodern methods and theories.[21] I have used the term "texture" as a means to reconfigure our approach to the rhetoricity of texts, and I have started by grouping and describing the textures of texts I see both my colleagues and myself interpreting. I have started by analyzing the multiple rhetorical dimensions of texts that secular and biblical interpreters currently interpret with some success. This analysis appears under the titles *The Tapestry of Early Christian Discourse* and *Exploring the Texture of Texts*, but aspects of it have been appearing since the 1980s.[22]

---

[20] Brian Vickers, *In Defence of Rhetoric* (Oxford: Clarendon, 1988), 439–53.

[21] Ibid., 491–98.

[22] Vernon K. Robbins, *The Tapestry of Early Christian Discourse: Rhetoric, Society, and Ideology* (London: Routledge, 1996); idem, *Exploring the Texture of Texts: A Guide to Socio-Rhetorical Interpretation* (Valley Forge, Pa.: Trinity, 1996). See also idem, "Pragmatic Relations as a Criterion for Authentic Sayings," *Forum* 1, no. 3 (1985): 35–63; idem, "The Woman who Touched Jesus' Garment: Socio-Rhetorical Analysis of the Synoptic Accounts," *NTS* 33 (1987): 502–15; repr. in *New Boundaries in Old Territory: Forms and Social Rhetoric in Mark* (Emory Studies in Early Christianity 3; New York: Peter Lang, 1994), 185–200; idem, "The Social Location of the Implied Author of Luke-Acts," in *The Social World of Luke-Acts: Models for Interpretation* (ed. Jerome H. Neyrey; Peabody, Mass.: Hendrickson, 1991), 305–32 [Chapter 3 in this volume]; idem, *Jesus the Teacher: A Socio-Rhetorical Interpretation of Mark* (Philadelphia: Fortress, 1984; repr. Minneapolis: Fortress, 1992); idem, "The Reversed Contextualization of Psalm 22 in the Markan Crucifixion: A Socio-Rhetorical Analysis," in *The Four Gospels 1992: Festschrift Frans Neirynck* (ed. F. van Segbroeck; 3 vols; BETL 100; Leuven: Leuven University Press, 1992), 2:1161–83 [Chapter 8 in this volume]; idem, "Using a Socio-Rhetorical Poetics to Develop a Unified Method: The Woman who Anointed Jesus as a Test Case," *SBLSP* 16 (1992): 302–19; idem, "Progymnastic Rhetorical Composition and Pre-Gospel Traditions: A New Approach," in *The Synoptic Gospels: Source Criticism and the New Literary Criticism* (ed. Camille Focant; BETL 110; Leuven, Leuven University Press, 1993), 111–47; idem, "Rhetoric and Culture: Exploring Types of Cultural Rhetoric in a Text," in *Rhetoric and the New Testament: Essays from the 1992 Heidelberg Conference* (ed. Stanley E. Porter and Thomas H. Olbricht; JSNTSup 90; Sheffield: JSOT Press,1993), 447–67 [Revised as Chapter 4 in this volume]; idem, *New Boundaries in Old Territory: Forms and Social Rhetoric in Mark* (Emory Studies in Early Christianity 3; New York: Peter Lang, 1994); idem, "Socio-Rhetorical Criticism: Mary, Elizabeth, and the Magnificat as a Test Case," in *The*

The metaphor of texture guides the generation of new terminology. Five major arenas of texture regularly appear in analysis and interpretation of texts in our books, journals and speech: (1) inner texture (intratexture); (2) intertexture; (3) social and cultural texture; (4) ideological texture; (5) sacred texture.[23] I accepted the challenge to describe a basic spectrum of each arena of texture both as I saw it in the work of various colleagues and as I myself have been developing it. Thus, in each arena I have described and displayed a spectrum of textures in a text:

1. In the arena of inner texture, interpreters regularly work with aspects of repetitive, progressive, opening-middle-closing, narrational, argumentative, and/or sensory-aesthetic texture.
2. In the arena of intertexture, interpreters regularly work with aspects of oral-scribal, historical, social or cultural intertexture.
3. In the arena of social and cultural texture, there are specific social topics, common social and cultural topics, and final cultural categories. Social-scientific critics have worked primarily with common social and cultural topics like honor and shame, limited good, hospitality, household, etc. A few social scientific critics have worked with specific social topics, using Bryan Wilson's religious types of response to the world: conversionist, revolutionist, reformist, thaumaturgic, introversionist, utopian, and gnostic-manipulationist. Analysis of final cultural categories is in its infancy. E.A. Judge, Wilhelm Wuellner and Burton L. Mack have produced data for this kind of analysis and I will say more about it when I discuss Jewish and Greco-Roman modes of argumentation.
4. In the arena of ideological texture, there are ideological dimensions in biblical texts, in authoritative commentary, in individuals and groups, and in intellectual discourse. Biblical interpreters regularly deal with aspects of ideological texture in all of these except ideology in intellectual discourse. Stephen

---

New Literary Criticism and the New Testament (ed. Elizabeth Struthers Malbon and Edgar V. McKnight; JSNTSup 109; Sheffield: Sheffield Academic Press, 1994), 164–209 [Chapter 9 in this volume]; idem, "The Ritual of Reading and Reading a Text as a Ritual: Observations on Mieke Bal's *Death and Dissymmetry*," in *In Good Company: Essays in Honor of Robert Detweiler* (ed. David Jasper and Mark Ledbetter; Atlanta: Scholars Press, 1994), 385–401; idem, "Interpreting Miracle Culture and Parable Culture in Mark 4–11," *SEÅ* 59 (1994): 59–81; idem, "Oral, Rhetorical, and Literary Cultures: A Response," *Semeia* 65 (1994): 75–91; idem, "Social-Scientific Criticism and Literary Studies: Prospects for Cooperation in Biblical Interpretation," in *Modelling Early Christianity: Social-Scientific Studies of the New Testament in its Context* (ed. Philip F. Esler London: Routledge, 1995), 274–89 [Chapter 5 in this volume]; idem, "The Dialectical Nature of Early Christian Discourse," *Scriptura* 59: 353–62.

[23] Robbins, *Exploring*.

Moore is one of the few who has undertaken careful analysis and interpretation of the mode of intellectual discourse biblical interpreters use.[24] I will say more about this at the end when I discuss the nature of commentary in rhetorical criticism as an interpretive analytics.

5. In the arena of sacred texture, interpreters explore aspects of deity, holy person, spirit being, divine history, human redemption, human commitment, religious community, and ethics.

Whether or not your categories would be the same as mine is not the issue I would like to raise here. I hope, however, that the task is somewhat clear. As an interpretive analytics, rhetorical criticism needs to reinvent our vocabulary for referring comprehensively to dimensions of rhetoricity in texts by incorporating twenty-first century practices of interpretation into it. So far as I am concerned, this has been a natural initial step in the process of reinventing rhetorical criticism as an interpretive analytics for the twenty-first century.

Revaluing the Modes of Biblical Discourse

Once rhetorical criticism has a new vocabulary to describe the multiple textures of rhetoricity in discourse, it is in a position to revalue the modes of biblical discourse. Here I have to apologize to our colleagues who specialize in the Hebrew Bible. While I may make a few comments that indicate to you some of the revaluing rhetorical criticism can undertake in Hebrew Bible studies, I will focus on New Testament literature, which is the area in which I have performed specific rhetorical analysis and interpretation.

A major problem in New Testament studies is the separation between rhetorical interpreters of epistolary and narrative discourse. Another way to say this is that few rhetorical interpreters of New Testament literature have moved beyond analysis of epistolary discourse or speeches to analysis and interpretation of narrative and apocalyptic discourse. Since the appearance of *Patterns of Persuasion in the Gospels* in 1989, a growing number of interpreters have been working with rhetorical interpretation of narrative discourse.[25] Only when rhetorical interpreters are able to approach narrative and apocalyptic discourse with similar facility with which they approach epistolary and speech discourse will rhetorical criticism become an equal player with histori-

---

[24] Stephen D. Moore, "Deconstructive Criticism: The Gospel of Mark," in *Mark and Method: New Approaches in Biblical Studies* (ed. Janice Capel Anderson and Stephen D. Moore; Minneapolis: Fortress, 1992), 84–102.

[25] Burton L. Mack and Vernon K. Robbins, *Patterns of Persuasion in the Gospels* (Sonoma. Calif.: Polebridge, 1989). Cf. Willi Braun, *Feasting and Social Rhetoric in Luke 14* (SNTSMS 85; Cambridge: Cambridge University Press, 1995).

cal, literary, and social-scientific criticism in biblical studies. Again, the issue is the reinvention of rhetorical criticism as an interpretive analytics to enable rhetorical interpreters to find common ground with one another in all forms of discourse. My survey of the field suggests that the following steps may be a way to build on present achievements toward a comprehensive interpretive analytical approach to New Testament literature.

a. Assertions and Rationales

The first place I see us working together is with assertions and rationales – the components of the rhetorical enthymeme. A number of interpreters have been at work on the enthymeme during the last few years, and enthymemes exist throughout New Testament literature – in epistolary, narrative and apocalyptic discourse. David Hellholm has identified and discussed the enthymemes he sees in Romans 6 and Richard Vinson has listed the enthymemes he sees in the synoptic Gospels.[26] To activate rhetorical criticism as an interpretive analytics, we need to know all of the assertions that are supported by rationales in the New Testament. These appear in narration, in speech of characters, and in combinations of narration and the speech of characters.

The reason we need to gather all the assertions and rationales in the New Testament is as follows. Culture is a logico-meaningful human construct, and the most immediate aspect of human activity to which language gives access is culture. To understand this, we need to begin to distinguish between the social and cultural aspects of human activity. The anthropologist James L. Peacock is an important guide for us at this point:

> Culture does not float in a vacuum; it is sustained by persons who are members of society. The understandings that constitute culture exist only when they are shared by persons whose relationships constitute some kind of organized system.[27]

The way that culture is organized has been characterized as logico-meaningful, in contrast to the "causal-functional" organization of society:

> By logico-meaningful integration, characteristic of culture, is meant the "sort of" integration one finds in a Bach fugue, in Catholic dogma, or in the general theory of relativity: it is a unity of style, of logical implica-

---

[26] David Hellholm, "Enthymematic Argumentation in Paul: The Case of Romans 6," in *Paul in his Hellenistic Context* (ed. Troels Engberg-Pedersen; Minneapolis. Fortress, 1995), 119–79; Richard Vinson, "A Comparative Study of the Use of Enthymemes," in *Persuasive Artistry*, 119–41.

[27] James L. Peacock, *The Anthropological Lens: Harsh Light, Soft Focus* (Cambridge: Cambridge University Press, 1986), 34.

> tion, of meaning and value. By causal- functional integration, characteristic of the social system, is meant the kind of integration one finds in an organism, where all the parts are united in a single causal web: each part is an element in a reverberating causal ring which "keeps the system going."[28]
>
> A cultural system can be envisioned as a set of major premises – similar to a philosophical, theological, or legal system – from which its more specific minor premises can be derived. Thus, from the notion that "there is one God and He is all powerful," as in Islam, Judaism, or Christianity, derive more particular points, such as mistrust of animism (which locates spiritual power not in a single being but in many), or dilemmas (such as how a God could create evil, if He is both good and all powerful). Such elements are connected in a more or less logical way and could be diagrammed as a chart showing the major premises at the top and minor ones fanning out toward the bottom. Less formal cultural patterns, such as views of time and classifications of nature and culture, show something like this logical structure too, though less neatly.[29]

Once we have an exhibit of all the assertions (theses) and premises throughout the New Testament, we are on the doorstep of serious cultural analysis of early Christianity as it reveals itself to us through these early texts. The important thing will be that we not reduce the analysis to propositional logic, but analyze the abductive, cultural logic operative within the juxtaposition of the assertions and the rationales.[30] I will use an illustration from Revelation, since this is a book on which I have seen almost no rhetorical analysis and interpretation. A governing enthymeme for the discourse appears in Rev 1:3: "Blessed is the one who reads aloud the words of the prophecy, and blessed are those who hear and who keep what is written in it; for the time is near."

This is a "literary" or "text" enthymeme. It exhibits one example of early Christian reasoning about writing, reading the written text to others, and expectations that members of the community will do what they hear. Luke 1:1–4 and John 20:30–31 are two other examples, and there are many in the writings of Paul. "The time is near" is the specific premise for the conclusion. The unstated general premise is that when the events of the endtime occur, it is only those who read aloud the words of the prophecy in this book and those who hear and keep what is written in it who will not be destroyed but will be taken into

---

[28] Clifford Geertz, "Ritual and Social Change: A Javanese Example," *American Anthropologist* 59 (1957): 32–54.

[29] Peacock, *Anthropological Lens*, 35.

[30] Cf. R.L. Lanigan, "From Enthymeme to Abduction: The Classical Law of Logic and the Postmodern Rule of Rhetoric," in *Recovering Pragmatism's Voice: The Classical Tradition, Rorty, and the Philosophy of Communication* (ed. Lenore Langsdorf and Andrew R. Smith; Albany, N.Y.: State University of New York Press), 49–70.

the world of the new creation. The reasoning in Luke 1 and John 20 represents significantly different cultural environments in first-century Christianity where writers were reasoning about the texts they were writing.

After the governing enthymeme in Revelation 1, Rev 6:15–17 presents another richly textured enthymeme:

> 15 Then the kings of the earth and the magnates and the generals and the rich and the powerful, and everyone, slave and free, hid in the caves and among the rocks of the mountains, 16 calling to the mountains and rocks, "Fall on us and hide us from the face of the one seated on the throne and from the wrath of the Lamb; 17 for the great day of their wrath has come, and who is able to stand?"

A fascinating thing about the reasoning in this enthymeme is that not only kings, magnates, generals, the rich, and the powerful will experience the wrath of God and his Messiah but also slaves and free people. One can see that this enthymeme is supplementing the earlier enthymeme with narration of events that exhibit how this endtime situation will play out on various people.

Common ground for rhetorical analysis throughout all the literature in the New Testament exists in the places where a text presents a reason or rationale for an assertion or thesis. This reasoning is an opening to the logico-meaningful aspect of early Christianity which is properly called culture. It is also the ground on which rhetorical analysts with specialties in different areas can begin to work seriously with one another.

b. Social and Cultural Analysis of Assertions and Rationales

Once we have gathered all the assertions with their rationales, we need to reconstruct their unexpressed premises[31] and analyze their social and cultural location[32] and import.[33] The unexpressed premise in Rev 1:3 is that those who hear the revealed word of God and do it will be taken into God's new creation rather than destroyed when God annihilates all the wickedness on this earth and creates a new world for the righteous. This reasoning is, in the sociological terms of Bryan Wilson, revolutionist, rather than conversionist, introversionist, gnostic-manipulationist, thaumaturgic, reformist, or utopian.[34] Here we see

---

[31] Cf. Robbins "Pragmatic Relations"; idem, "Woman"; Mack and Robbins, *Patterns*.
[32] Robbins, "Social Location."
[33] Robbins, "Rhetoric and Culture"; idem, "Interpreting Miracle Culture."
[34] Bryan Wilson, "A Typology of Sects in a Dynamic and Comparative Perspective," *Archives de Sociologie de Religion* 16 (1963): 49–63; idem, "A Typology of Sects," in *Sociology of Religion* (ed. Roland Robertson; Baltimore: Penguin Books, 1969): 361–

the presuppositions of a significant countercultural sector of early Christianity. This movement is, on the one hand, significantly different from the countercultural sector exhibited in the Gospel of John.[35] It also is different from sectors of early Christianity that are subcultural, contracultural, and liminal cultural in nature.[36]

The social and cultural nature of the reasoning in assertions and rationales, then, is a gateway into early Christianity as a social and cultural movement during the first century. Rhetorical analysis, moving from rhetorical data in all the texts in the New Testament toward the data that has been gathered by historical, social-scientific, and literary interpreters of the New Testament, can begin to fill out the social and cultural nature of early Christianity in a manner that interpretation has not yet exhibited.

c. Chreia Analysis of Assertions and Rationales

The next step must be to identify the personage to whom each juxtaposed assertion and rationale is attributed. The attribution of speech or action to a particular individual occurs throughout all New Testament literature. Where assertions and rationales exist in New Testament literature without specific attribution in the text, interpreters regularly attribute them to the writer of the text. In other words, many assertions with rationales exist in narration in the Gospels, Acts, letters, and Revelation. Interpreters customarily attribute the reasoning in this narration to the writer of the text using terminology like "Mark says" or "Hebrews says." This means that the category of "personage" is a dynamic medium through which the reasoning of early Christianity is transmitted to modern and postmodern interpreters and readers.

This is a substantive matter for rhetorical analysis and interpretation. First, rationales juxtaposed with assertions regularly break the bounds of any easily reconstructable logic. Assertions that appear to be syllogistic often do not proceed logically either from generally accepted premises or from premises explicitly stated in the discourse. The reason is that personal assertions are grounded in cultural views of the world. A sequence of assertions may be a "logical" sequence only within a particular cultural view of the world. The logic of the assertion is not the logic of a widespread spectrum of society but the logic of a particular cultural group. The logic will not be clearly deductive, even though

---

83; idem, *Magic and the Millenium: A Sociological Study of Religious Movements of Protest among Tribal and Third-World Peoples* (New York: Harper & Row, 1973), 22–26. James A. Wilde, "The Social World of Mark's Gospel: A Word about Method," *SBLSP* 2 (1978): 47–67.

[35] Wayne A. Meeks, "The Man from Heaven in Johannine Sectarianism," *JBL* 91: 44–72.

[36] Robbins, "Rhetoric and Culture"; idem, "Interpreting Miracle Culture."

the discourse may imitate deduction. Even more important, the logic may not be clearly inductive, even though again it may imitate induction. Rather, imitative deduction and imitative induction provide a context for authoritative, cultural assertions about humans, the divine, and the world.

In accord with the cultural location of early Christian discourse, narrative functioning either as example or as analogy provides both theses and premises (rationales) for cultural reasoning in New Testament literature. This means that inductive and deductive reasoning continually interact in decisive ways throughout New Testament literature. Wherever this happens in literature, deeply hidden social and cultural premises are at work in such complex and decisive ways that the task of exhibiting them is almost unending. Another interpreter will almost always be able to find another manner in which social and cultural presuppositions relate to one another in the context.

Rev 1:3 occurs in narration in the opening of the book. Thus, the social and cultural reasoning of this enthymeme is embedded in the writer of this account. This is evident in the words of David E. Aune, for example: "By calling his composition a prophetic book (1:3; 22:7, 10, 18, 19), he clearly implies that he is a prophet."[37] In contrast, the enthymeme in Rev 6:15–17 is attributed to kings, magnates, generals, the rich, the powerful, slaves, and free people. This means that the text suggests that all of these people in addition to the writer of this text share the presupposition that "the great day of wrath has come, and who is able to stand?" In fact, it is an interesting issue whether the rationale ("for the great day...") in this enthymeme should be attributed to the narrator or to all the people described in the verse. The NRSV attributes it to all the people while the NEB (perhaps accurately) attributes it to the narrator.

Comprehensively grouping and exhibiting all the premises (stated and unstated) throughout New Testament literature, with careful attention to whom they are attributed would be a decisive contribution to New Testament studies. Presumably this has not been an interest among New Testament scholars during the rise and dominance of historical criticism, because historical interests emphasize the individual nature and contribution of each book rather than the overall relation of reasoning in each social and cultural sector of early Christianity as we can see them through the New Testament writings.

---

[37] David E. Aune, "The Revelation to John (Apocalypse)," in *The HarperCollins Study Bible* (ed. Wayne A. Meeks et al.; New York: HarperCollins, 1993), 2307.

d. Rhetorical Elaboration

Early Christian discourse achieves its rhetorical power not only by enthymematic or chreiic assertion, but by elaboration and amplification. From the perspective of Greco-Roman rhetoric, the amplification may "elaborate" in a manner that is implicitly or explicitly "complete." Any perception of completeness is cultural, that is, the discourse evokes images, values, emotions, or reasons deemed to be "sufficient" for a particular time and place. Greco-Roman rhetoricians at the time of the emergence of Christianity considered a complete argument to be present in a sequentially arranged presentation of a thesis accompanied by a rationale, a confirmation of the rationale, embellishment, and a conclusion (*Rhet. Her.* 2.18.28).[38] New Testament discourse participates in this mode of "complete argumentation" to an extent that is remarkable for a movement that explicitly grounds its images of authority in biblical and Jewish traditions rather than Greco-Roman traditions.[39]

Once rhetorical interpreters have an organized display of the juxtapositions of rationales and assertions throughout New Testament literature, an initial challenge is to analyze and interpret the presence of constituents of "complete argumentation" in those assertions and rationales. What I mean is this. Juxtaposed rationales and assertions contain most of the rhetorical features a person uses to elaborate assertions and rationales. An assertion or a rationale, or both, may be an analogy, an example, an ancient written testimony, a contrary, or an exhortation. Since these are basic media people use to elaborate assertions and rationales, it will be informative to set a clear picture of the rhetorical "media," that is, the major figures and tropes that exist in the assertions and rationales themselves. After analysis and interpretation of the assertions and rationales, then, the task will be to analyze the kinds of elaboration that exist throughout the discourse. At least three basic kinds of elaboration are beginning to appear.[40]

The first is "expansion," where the composition is periodic.[41] This means that the discourse amplifies narrative, speech, and/or dialogue to a point where it presents a statement that evokes the image of a "conclusive" or "final" assertion. The final statement may be a rationale, an

---

[38] Mack and Robbins, *Patterns*, 56–57.

[39] Mack and Robbins, *Patterns*; Burton L. Mack, *Rhetoric and the New Testament* (Minneapolis: Fortress, 1990).

[40] Vernon K. Robbins, "Introduction: Using Rhetorical Discussions of Chreia to Interpret Pronouncement Stories," *Semiea* 64 (1993): ix.

[41] Ronald F. Hock and Edward N. O'Neil, *The Chreia in Ancient Rhetoric volume I: The Progymnasmata* (Atlanta: Scholars Press, 1986), 100–103; Mack and Robbins, *Patterns*, 17–19; Robbins, "Introduction," xiii–xiv.

analogy, a contrary, and so on – the tropes, figures and dynamics that chreiai contain in Mediterranean discourse.

The second is Theonian elaboration "of the parts" – named on the basis of Aelius Theon of Alexandria's discussion of an exercise that elaborated "the parts" of a chreia.[42] This mode presents a sequence of arguments that amplifies the discourse on the basis of specific or common topics. Sets of opposites that characterize the dynamics of praise or blame in epideictic discourse underlie this form of elaboration.

The third is Hermogenian elaboration – named on the basis of the elaboration of the chreia in the *Progymnasmata* of Hermogenes of Tarsus.[43] This kind of elaboration gives priority of value in argumentation to certain discursive "media": introductory encomium, chreia, rationale, contrary, analogy, example, authoritative testimony, and exhortation. This mode of elaboration embeds the dynamics of epideictic discourse in the reasoning environment of judicial and deliberative argumentation.

The degree to which different kinds of discourse elaborate their assertions and rationales and the means by which they elaborate them are central issues for New Testament interpretation. This takes us into significantly different cultures of discourse in early Christianity and into initial analysis and interpretation of final categories in different kinds of discourse.[44]

Contracultural people and groups, for example, give very few reasons for their views and behaviors. They presuppose the resources of a dominant culture, subculture, or counterculture and invert certain views and behaviors to distinguish themselves in their setting. They need not elaborate, since their thoughts and actions simply are reactive to the culture in which they are embedded. They simply presuppose or invert the values of the culture in which they are "inner negative participants." A contraculture is, then, a group culture within a larger culture, and its membership is limited to a certain age group in a particular generation of people. In other words, contraculture is not a form of culture that spans more than one generation of people. This form of discourse will become part of a counterculture, subculture, or dominant culture, or else it will become a liminal, marginal, or extinct culture.

If a large enough group of people begin to elaborate contracultural discourse but are not in a position to be a dominant culture, their discourse becomes either counterculture or subculture discourse. Coun-

---

[42] Hock and O'Neil, *Chreia*, 72–73, 106–107; Robbins, "Introduction," xiv.
[43] Hock and O'Neil, *Chreia*, 176–77; Mack and Robbins, *Patterns*, 51–52, 57–63.
[44] Robbins, "Dialectical Nature."

terculture discourse features rejection of one or more "central" and "explicit" values in a major alternative culture and provides reasons in support of its alternative thought and action. Counterculture discourse, therefore, contains rhetorical elaboration. Where the actions of countercultural people look like the actions of other people in the setting, their discourse regularly provides distinctive reasons for the actions ("Yes, we offer healing to people, but not because Asclepius makes his powers of healing available but because belief in Jesus of Nazareth can bring healing"). To support actions that are different from other people in the setting, the discourse may recite a rather well-known proverb ("We anticipate that people will persecute us, because 'a servant is not greater than his master'": John 15:20).

In certain settings, contraculture discourse can become subculture discourse. Subcultural people share the values of the dominant culture in the setting, but they claim to fulfill these values better than the dominant culture. Subculture discourse, then, also contains elaboration. "Better than" or "perfectly" may appear in this discourse to distinguish the thought and activity of members of this culture from others in the setting.

The presence or absence of rhetorical elaboration, and the inner dynamics of the elaboration, exhibit aspects of definition, distinction, and social and cultural location in the discourse. Rhetorical analysis and interpretation of elaboration throughout New Testament discourse, then, would contribute in yet one more way to the program of rhetorical criticism as an interpretive analytics.

e. Jewish and Greco-Roman Modes of Argumentation

As mentioned above, an overarching issue in assertions, rationales, and elaboration is the "final categories" in the discourse.[45] Different cultures of discourse not only feature different topics and discursive media (like story, proverb, parable, or miracle story) but "final categories" regularly emerge as a distinguishing feature between one discursive culture and another. The *Rhetoric of Alexander* 1.1421b.21–1422b.12 gives the following list of final categories: right (δίκαιον), lawful (νόμικον), beneficial (συμφέρον), honorable (καλόν), pleasant (ἡδύς), easy (ῥᾴδιον) possible (δυνατόν) and necessary (ἀναγκαῖον).[46] Using rhetorical criticism as an interpretive analytics, interpreters should ascertain the final categories operative in New Testament discourse. On the face of it, New Testament discourse appears to value the categories of right, lawful, beneficial, honorable, possible, and necessary. In the place of pleasant and easy, it may feature categories like pure, holy, and glorious. Uncovering the overlap, the differences and the priorities among various discursive cul-

---

[45] Mack and Robbins, *Patterns*, 38, 58.
[46] Mack and Robbins, *Patterns*, 38.

tures in New Testament discourse itself and among Jewish, Greco-Roman, and early Christian discourse could contribute yet further to a program of rhetorical criticism as an interpretive analytics.

This raises the possibility for inviting specialists in Hebrew Bible, apocrypha, pseudepigrapha, and rabbinic literature to join with analysts trained in the skills of Greco-Roman rhetoric for the purpose of delineating and displaying the interplay of dominant, subcultural, countercultural, contracultural, and liminal cultural Jewish and Greco-Roman argumentation in New Testament discourse. Jack N. Lightstone's recent rhetorical work in the Babylonian Talmud augures well for the willingness of specialists to engage in cooperative work with us.[47] My first experiment with this occurred at the SBL meeting in Chicago in 1994, where a series of interpreters analyzed Mark 7:1–23 in a context where they were aware of the patterns of elaboration in dominant Greco-Roman cultural discourse. It was a promising session, attracting excellent attention and attendance on the final morning of the meeting. In addition, George Kennedy is currently working on a book on comparative rhetorical analysis.[*] It is possible that this book will provide helpful resources for this task. If we begin to get some good comparative ways to talk about the manner in which Jewish, Greco-Roman and early Christian discourse use final categories to configure topics and figures in argumentation, we will contribute in yet another way toward the program of rhetorical criticism as an interpretive analytics of New Testament culture.

f. Reinventing the Decades of First-Century Christianity

Another topic under rhetorical criticism as an interpretive analytics is the possibility and benefit of constructing a new account of first-century Christianity decade by decade on the basis of discourse in New Testament texts. At present the Acts of the Apostles, which is a highly ideologically driven narrative that appeared near the end of the first century, regularly establishes a basic, overall framework for scholarly conception of the emergence of Christianity. During the twentieth century, most New Testament interpreters presented only the authentic epistles of Paul as a major challenge to the ideologically formulated picture the Acts of the Apostles gives of the first three decades of early Christianity. During the twenty-first century, all of New Tes-

---

[47] Jack N. Lightstone, *The Rhetoric of the Babylonian Talmud: Its Social Meaning and Context*(Studies in Christianity and Judaism/Etudes sur le christianisme et le judaïsme 6; Waterloo: Wilfrid Laurier Press, 2002).

[*] Editor's note: Later published as George A. Kennedy, *Comparative Rhetoric: An Historical and Cross-cultural Introduction* (New York: Oxford University Press, 1998).

tament literature plus contemporary Christian literature outside the New Testament should be included in the analysis.

Rhetorical criticism as an interpretive analytics holds the potential for providing resources to substantively reconstruct our picture of earliest Christianity. It is obvious from the work of Burton Mack that the first three decades of early Christianity contained at least five significantly distinctive cultures of discourse.[48] If a person does serious rhetorical analysis and interpretation in these different cultures of discourse, one finds significantly different topoi with significantly different modes of argumentation to support the theses they formulate in the context of these topoi.[49]

As interpreters use rhetorical criticism as an interpretive analytics, they can give equal voice to the multiple modes of discourse in New Testament literature as they reconstruct the emergence of Christian speech and identity during the first century. This can overcome the problem that traditional rhetorical criticism regularly re-enacts the hierarchies and subordinations that authority and tradition established during the first century or some subsequent century. The means by which biblical discourse creates authority and tradition must become a primary focus of attention rather than simply the end result of the discursive activity of early Christians. One of the means by which the discursive practices created authority and tradition was to interrupt, exclude, and/or subordinate other forms of discourse. Rhetorical interpreters should display the means by which various modes of early Christian discourse won out, rather than simply perpetuate the victories this discourse achieved.

Rhetorical interpreters could work together toward a vision of the overall interplay of discursive practices during each of the seven decades of the first century after the death of Jesus.[50] We might fight most vigorously about the discursive practices of these Messianites during the first two decades from 30–50 CE. But very large issues also are at stake for the discursive practices from 50–60, 60–70, 70–80, 80–90 and 90–100. We have sufficient resources at our disposal to begin such investigations. Few rhetorical interpreters glimpse the prospects, though some do. If we use rhetorical criticism as an interpretive analytics to assist in this endeavor, we will contribute important new insights to the field of New Testament studies.

---

[48] Burton L. Mack, *A Myth of Innocence: Mark and Christian Origins* (Philadelphia: Fortress, 1988).

[49] Robbins, "Interpreting Miracle Culture"; idem, "Dialectical Nature."

[50] Robbins, *Tapestry*, 240–43.

Reconfiguring the Discourse of Commentary

The last issue I will discuss is ideology in rhetorical interpretation. One of the most important issues the discussion of ideology raises is the kind of commentary discourse we generate to interpret New Testament texts.[51] An interpreter's ability to choose one rather than another intellectual mode of commentary discourse was at least implicitly recognizable during the 1970s, and it became more and more obvious during the 1980s and 1990s. It was obvious that there were distinctively different modes of discourse at work in the analyses of Robert Tannehill and Hans Dieter Betz during the 1970s, even though both used the term "rhetorical" to describe their analysis and interpretation. A rhetorical analysis of the different discourses they and other commentators use reveals two major ideological aspects of commentary discourse.

First, it is important to observe the mode of twentieth-century intellectual discourse commentators enact in their commentary discourse. Secondly, it is important to analyze the rhetorical aspects of the biblical text their mode of commentary re-enacts. I will explain. Every commentator performs some configuration of modern and postmodern modes of intellectual discourse as they perform their commentary. Every intellectual mode of discourse makes its own range of ideological interests available to a commentator. The particular goals of the commentator along with the mode of intellectual discourse he or she performs invite certain aspects of a text rather than others to comprehend or grasp their commentary.[52] Commentators, then, reinscribe select aspects of a text as they perform a twentieth-century mode of intellectual discourse in their own particular way.

Tannehill and Betz were both engaged in a project of rhetorical analysis of biblical texts, but the discursive mode they used in their commentary was noticeably different. Here is a sample of Tannehill's commentary on Matt 5:39b-42 in the Sermon on the Mount:

> These commands are an attack on our natural tendency to put self-protection first. Because they do not fit together topically but refer to different sorts of situations (a blow, a lawsuit, forced labor), the similarity in meaning, for which the similar form sets us seeking is found not at a superficial level of topic but at the deeper level of a surprising rejection of our tendency to put self-protection first.[53]

This commentary enacts a twentieth-century mode of aesthetic-literary discourse. This is a well-established form of discourse going

---

[51] Robbins, *Exploring*, 105–10.
[52] Cf. Moore, "Deconstructive Criticism," 93.
[53] Robert C. Tannehill, *The Sword of his Mouth* (Philadelphia: Fortress, 1975), 71.

back to T.S. Eliot, I.A. Richards, and others. Tannehill adopts this mode in a form that re-enacts dimensions of the inner texture of biblical text that can be called its psychological-moral texture. Tannehill's discourse concerns "us" – how we regularly live our daily lives and how the words in the biblical text attack our everyday assumptions and engage us in a reassessment of our regular patterns of behavior. Tannehill's performance of an aesthetic-literary mode of interpretation, then, invites the psychological-moral texture of the text to grasp his interpretive thoughts, words and actions.

Here, in contrast, is an excerpt from Hans Dieter Betz's commentary on the Sermon on the Mount:

> The SM is an expressly polemical text and reflects conflicts in a number of directions. Alongside the inner-Jewish controversy with Pharisaism and conventional Judaism, there is an inner-Christian polemic against Gentile Christianity. Of great importance, finally, is the deep-seated debate with the Greco-Roman world. This aspect of the SM's polemic is difficult to grasp, because it is presented to a large extent in veiled form. Here belong the subtle debates with the concepts of Greek philosophy in a wider sense, as well as the attitude that the SM takes toward the political situation. The characteristically veiled nature of the political attitude indicates that the community regards itself as a threatened minority. Of course the Romans represent a threat, but there is also a threat from the Jewish authorities.[54]

This commentary enacts a modern mode of historical-philosophical discourse. This is a well-established mode made famous by Rudolf Bultmann in the twentieth century. Betz adopts this mode in a form that re-enacts aspects of historical, social, and philosophical intertexture in the biblical text. Betz's commentary concerns "them" – how the people who used and wrote this discourse lived with their loved ones, their friends, their neighbors, their superiors, and their enemies. Betz's enactment of historical-philosophical discourse, then, only implicitly concerns the relation of the twentieth-century reader to the aesthetic, psychological, and moral texture of the discourse that energizes Tannehill's commentary. Rather, Betz's mode of discourse enacts aspects of the text's "intertexture" – the discourse's historical, social and cultural world – rather than its inner textual aesthetic, psychological, and moral world.

Additional ideological issues come into view with Elisabeth Schüssler Fiorenza's published work in 1987–88. Her commentary discourse on 1 Corinthians enacts a form of twentieth-century feminist discourse. Here is a sample of it:

> The rhetorical situation to which 1 Corinthians can be understood as a

---

[54] Betz, *Galatians*, 92–93.

"fitting" response might then be conceived as follows: The Corinthians had debates and discussions as to how their new self-understanding expressed in the pre-Pauline baptismal formula in Gal 3:28 could and should be realized in the midst of a society rooted in the patriarchal status divisions between Greeks and Jews, slave and free, men and women, rich and poor, wise and uneducated....

In this situation of competing interpretations and practices of what it meant to realize the "new life" in Christ the Corinthian community decided to write to different missionaries for their advice since some of their differing interpretations most likely originated in different theological emphases of these missionaries....

Paul ... presents himself not only as the father of the community who in analogy to God, the Father, has begotten or brought forth the community in Christ through the gospel, but also as the one who has the power to command and to punish.... His rhetoric does not aim at fostering independence, freedom, and consensus, but stresses dependence on his model, order and decency, as well as subordination and silence. His theological reasoning and skillful rhetorical argument demonstrate, however, that the rhetorical situation required persuasion but did not admit of explicitly coercive authority. Whom did Paul seek to persuade to accept his interpretation as authoritative?... If my assessment of 1 Corinthians as deliberative discourse is correct, then Paul appeals to those who, like himself, were of higher social and educational status. They should make the ecclesial decisions which are, in his opinion, necessary in Corinth.... His "veiled hostility" and appeal to authority in the so-called women's passages indicates ... that he does not include women of high social and educational status in this appeal.[55]

Fiorenza enacts a historical-ideological mode of commentary that has an interesting relation to Betz's commentary. She, like Betz, discusses "them" rather than "us." Her focus is on the historical, social, and cultural intertexture of the biblical text, namely the relation of the text to the historical, social, and cultural context of the Corinthians. She merges this historical mode of commentary with an ideological mode of discourse that focuses on Paul and on women in the context of varying social and educational status in the Corinthian community. Paul does not foster "independence, freedom, and consensus" but "subordination and silence."

---

[55] Elizabeth Schüssler Fiorenza, "Rhetorical Situation and Historical reconstruction in 1 Corinthians," NTS 33 (1987): 397–99.

Elizabeth Castelli builds on Schüssler Fiorenza's work, using Michel Foucault's proposal for analysis of power relations in a text.[56] She focuses her analysis and interpretation initially on modern commentary on 1 Corinthians. Most interpreters, she posits, either spiritualize the text – removing it from any historical or social context that implies complex dynamics of conflict and competition – or they presuppose or assert continuity, authority, and unity in tradition.[57] Castelli's commentary, then, includes the ideological texture of modern commentary discourse on 1 Corinthians. After this, she turns to careful analysis of the inner texture of 1 Cor 1:10–4:21 which I will not attempt to describe here. In her commentary, she concludes that Paul describes his role simply as "mediation" of the gospel, so that his nature is "contentless"; "he is simply the conduit through which the gospel passes" (1 Cor 1:17).[58] In this way Paul constructs a privileged status for himself: he has special authority to speak and he has "an emptiness which removes him from the fray."[59]

Characteristic of both Schüssler Fiorenza's and Castelli's commentary discourse, then, is a focus on Paul and how he constructs his authority within the discourse. Interestingly, both commentators re-enact this aspect of Pauline discourse themselves, adopting a powerful, authoritative rhetorical mode of discourse filled with rich inner textual images and intertextual recitation. In many ways, then, their own discourse is imitative of the powerful and richly textured discourse the New Testament writings attribute to Paul.

It is informative to place David Jasper's commentary on 1 Thessalonians in this context as yet another alternative. Jasper re-enacts a configuration of modern and postmodern Nietzschean philosophical discourse in his commentary. Like Castelli, he starts with the ideological texture of modern commentary. He, however, focuses on modern rhetorical interpretation of New Testament literature. In this context, he describes his own commentary in terms of sharp opposition to the approach of George Kennedy and Wilhelm Wuellner. In his words,

> These laudable proposals in the face of the generality of traditional scholarship rapidly begin to evaporate, however, as one realises time and again that what is presented by Paul as argument invariably gives a misleading impression.... The power of the writing ... lies not in any logical development of thought, but actually from the excitement of a series of

---

[56] Elizabeth A. Castelli, *Imitating Paul: A Discourse of Power* (Louisville: Westminster/John Knox, 1991).
[57] Ibid., 24–32.
[58] Ibid., 99.
[59] Ibid.

10. The Present and Future of Rhetorical Analysis 347

bold contrasts vigorously stated."[60]

This discourse re-enacts, in a Nietzschean philosophical mode of intellectual discourse, an important aspect of the inner texture of Pauline discourse. The interesting thing is the manner in which, in one fell swoop, it attempts to exclude from serious consideration the range of textures in Pauline discourse that both Kennedy and Wuellner re-enact in their commentary. Jasper's commentary itself focuses on a much more limited spectrum of rhetoricity in Pauline discourse than either Kennedy or Wuellner. It is informative to see how the "bold contrasts vigorously stated" in Pauline discourse "grasp" or "comprehend" the commentary discourse of Jasper. Jasper describes himself as "in the exercise of no little Socratic suspicion of rhetoric."[61] He must vigorously state a bold contrast between his approach and the approach of Kennedy and Wuellner. And he fulfills his rhetorical goal. In contrast to the "self-evident spiritual truth" he perceives Kennedy and Wuellner to present in the context of their analyses and interpretations of argumentation in Pauline discourse, Jasper recommends a second naïveté that can

> rescue religious experience and the experience of the church in formation through an indirect, reflective, reflexive, creative adoption of a rhetorical consciousness which is deeply aware that in text we acknowledge our metaphorical perspectives, our fictions and our interpretations.[62]

An interesting aspect of this is the deep roots of Jasper's commentary discourse in romanticism. It is quite natural that he contrasts his approach to a pragmatically-based approach both to texts and to life. His discourse has no significant engagement with the interaction of body and mind characteristic of twentieth-century pragmatic discourse. Rather, it focuses on the reflective, reflexive, creative, and self-aware mind that romanticism so beautifully features in its discourse. The texture of Jasper's discourse is, on the one hand, closer to Tannehill's aesthetic-literary commentary than to Betz's historical-philosophical discourse. Yet, on the other hand, the ideological interests of his discourse have an interesting relation to the commentary of Schüssler Fiorenza and Castelli. In the end, Jasper's commentary excludes a much wider range of rhetoricity in Pauline discourse than either Schüssler Fiorenza's or Castelli's, since they use multiple strategies and insights from rhetorical method and rhetorical

---

[60] David Jasper, *Rhetoric, Power and Community: An Exercise in Reserve* (London: Macmillan, 1993), 40.
[61] Ibid., 39.
[62] Ibid., 68–69.

theory to enrich their analysis and interpretation of the ideological texture of Pauline discourse.

Where, then, does this discussion of ideology and rhetorical criticism leave us? The major implication I want to evoke is that none of us has the final say on ideology. Ancient texts are richly textured environments of analysis and interpretation. Twentieth-century commentaries on these texts adopt various locations in various twentieth-century modes of intellectual discourse. From these locations, twentieth-century commentary discourse re-enacts highly different aspects of ancient texts.

The name of the game here needs to be perspicuity and humility. Rhetorical criticism offers resources to analyze a comprehensive range of textures in a text, and modern and postmodern modes of intellectual discourse invite commentators into rich environments of analysis and interpretation. This means that rhetorical critics need to analyze commentary discourse with the same range of resources with which they analyze and interpret ancient texts or texts of any era. The commentator who claims to deliver "the" most decisive insight into the discourse of an ancient biblical text is adopting a mode that was highly fashionable in the modern era of "hermeneutics."[63] The word is out that there is no "one" insight that holds "the" key to any text. Rather, every text invites commentators to re-enact multiple meanings and meaning effects in their new context. We have been entering a postmodern era of interpretive "self-awareness" for some time now, and my recommendation is to build upon traditional, modern, and postmodern rhetorical method and theory by reinventing it into an interpretive analytics both of biblical discourse itself and of past and present commentary on biblical discourse.

---

[63] Wuellner, "Rhetorical Criticism," 172–75.

11

From Enthymeme to Theology in Luke 11:1-13*

Luke 11:1–13 presents an abbreviated version of the Lord's Prayer followed by nine verses that elaborate parts of the prayer.[1] Among the notable rhetorical features in this text is a series of rationales (beginning with "for," "because," or "since"), including one in the Lord's Prayer itself. These rationales invite a special way to analyze this passage.[2] Rationales in discourse create enthymemes. An enthymeme is an asser-

---

* I am grateful to H.J. Bernard Combrink, David Armstrong-Reiner, Lynn R. Lutes, and Thomas D. Stegman for their probing rhetorical exegeses of this sequence in Luke for my Ph.D. seminar on rhetorical criticism in the New Testament at Emory University during the spring of 1997. In addition, I am highly indebted to Gordon D. Newby, Laurie L. Patton, R. Alan Culpepper, and Margaret E. Dean for their supportive, critical reviews of this ongoing work.

[1] Matt 6:9–13 contains an expanded version of the Lord's prayer. See Vernon K. Robbins, "Divine Dialogue and the Lord's Prayer: Sociorhetorical Interpretation of Sacred Texts," *Dialogue* 28 (1995): 117–46, for a sociorhetorical analysis of the abbreviated and expanded versions of the Lord's Prayer in Matt, Luke, Did., and the *Book of Mormon*.

[2] Cf. Burton L. Mack and Vernon K. Robbins, *Patterns of Persuasion in the Gospels* (Sonoma, Calif.: Polebridge, 1989); Richard B. Vinson, "A Comparative Study of the Use of Enthymemes in the Synoptic Gospels," in *Persuasive Artistry: Studies in New Testament in Honor of George A. Kennedy* (ed. Duane F. Watson; JSNTSup 50; Sheffield; JSOT Press, 1991), 119–41; Wesley H. Wachob, "The Rich in Faith and the Poor in Spirit: The Socio-Rhetorical Function of a Saying of Jesus in the Epistle of James" (Ph.D. diss., Emory University, 1993); Vernon K. Robbins, *The Tapestry of Early Christian Discourse: Rhetoric, Society, and Ideology* (London: Routledge, 1996); idem, *Exploring the Texture of Texts: A Guide to Socio-Rhetorical Interpretation* (Philadelphia: Trinity Press International, 1996); idem, "The Dialectical Nature of Early Christian Discourse," *Scriptura* 59 (1996): 353–62; and idem, "The Present and Future of Rhetorical Analysis," in *The Rhetorical Analysis of Scripture: Essays from the 1995 London Conference* (ed. Stanley E. Porter and Thomas H. Olbricht; JSNTSup 146; Sheffield: Sheffield Academic Press, 1997), 32–41 [Chapter 10 in this volume]; Anders Eriksson, *Traditions as Rhetorical Proof: Pauline Argumentation in 1 Corinthians* (ConBNT 29; Stockholm: Almquist & Wiksell International, 1998); and L. Gregory Bloomquist, "The Place of Enthymemes in Argumentative Texture," forthcoming.

tion that is expressible as a syllogism.[3] A special characteristic of an enthymeme is to leave a premise or conclusion unexpressed, with a presumption that the premise or conclusion is obvious from the overall context. Enthymemic discourse, then, is discourse that presumes a context to fill out its meanings. The question then becomes the context a particular enthymeme evokes. Every text somehow enacts the social, cultural, and ideological context in which it was written. A reader who stands outside that context uses that enacted context as a medium for another context. Readers, from their own contexts, may be preoccupied with looking back on the context in which the work was written, may intentionally intertwine looking back with looking forward to another context, or may simply use the context embedded in the discourse as a medium for a new context.

Literary works vary in the manner in which they present enthymemes in their discourse. A literary work may articulate premises somewhere in the work that are exactly or approximately equivalent to the unexpressed premises evoked by enthymemes in another location. This kind of work creates an enthymemic network in the text that may invite readers to turn most of their attention toward negotiating the reasoning in the work's inner content rather than negotiating the reasoning in relation to social, cultural, and ideological contexts outside the work. In contrast, a literary work may not articulate unexpressed premises or conclusions for its enthymemes. This kind of text invites the reader into a process of evoking contexts of various kinds outside the work to understand these enthymemes.

A major thesis in this essay is that the Gospel of Luke interweaves enthymemic networks in the text with social, cultural, ideological, and theological enthymemes that evoke contexts outside the work. In some instances, unexpressed premises or conclusions for enthymemes are expressed elsewhere in the work and create an explicit enthymemic network in the text. In the same portion of text, however, the premises or conclusions missing from the enthymemes may reside in social, cultural, ideological, and theological environments outside the text. These enthymemes create a conventional context that provides a matrix for depicting conventional, ideological, and/or idiosyncratic thought and behavior. Conventional behavior enacts the inductive and deductive logic of generally accepted social, cultural, ideological, and theological reasoning. Ideological behavior participates in presuppositions, dispositions, and values that reflect "the needs and interests of a

---

[3] George A. Kennedy, *Aristotle, On Rhetoric: A Theory of Civic Discourse* (New York: Oxford University Press, 1991), 297–98; and Patrick J. Hurley, *A Concise Introduction to Logic* (2d ed.; Belmont Calif.: Wadsworth, 1985), 230–35.

group or class at a particular time in history."[4] Idiosyncratic behavior counters conventional actions and thought, creating an especially dynamic context for new meanings and meaning effects.

In the context of social, cultural, ideological, and theological enthymemes, abductive reasoning may redirect and reconfigure inductive and deductive reasoning. Abductive reasoning is a procedure of discovery that works off of suggestion rather than formal logic.[5] Early Christians used generally presupposed premises as a fertile environment for flashes of insight – "suggestions" or "hypotheses" for life – that introduce new social, cultural, ideological, and theological reasoning. Commitment to this reasoning provided a distinctive identity for early Christians. Sometimes they intertwined conventional premises and conclusions in an unconditional manner to explain their way of life; they placed special value on this reasoning which they shared in common with one another. At other times they intertwined new insights with conventional premises or conclusions. Both procedures were a matter of bottling and aging new wine while still enjoying the old, as well as creating a new wardrobe without destroying all of the old garments. The Gospel of Luke exhibits both kinds of interweaving in the "kingdom wisdom" presented in 11:1–13. Unusual interweaving of conventional premises and conclusions as well as new insights in the presence of conventional insights create new social, cultural, ideological, and theological patterns. This essay describes both processes at work in the discursive progression in Luke 11:1–13.

Chreia and Enthymeme in Luke 11:1–4

Luke 11:1 presents a span of time in which Jesus prays, then a disciple, speaking for all the disciples, asks Jesus to teach them how to pray. When Jesus responds by speaking to all the disciples (11:2–4), the beginning of this unit exhibits conventional features of a "responsive" (ἀποκριτικόν) chreia.[6] An intriguing part of the disciple's statement is

---

[4] David B. Davis, *The Problem of Slavery in the Age of Revolution 1770–1823* (Ithaca NY: Cornell University Press, 1975), 14; John H. Elliott, *A Home for the Homeless: A Social-Scientific Criticism of 1 Peter, Its Situation and Strategy* (Philadelphia: Fortress, 1981; repr., Philadelphia: Fortress, 1990), 268; Robbins, *Tapestry*, 193; and Robbins, *Exploring*, 96.

[5] See Bruce J. Malina, "Interpretation: Reading, Abduction, Metaphor," in *The Bible and the Politics of Exegesis: Essays in Honor of Norman K. Gottwald on His Sixty-fifth Birthday* (ed. David Jobling et al.; Cleveland: Pilgrim, 1991), 253–66; and John H. Elliot, *What is Social-Scientific Criticism?* (Minneapolis: Fortress, 1993), 48–49; cf. Rebecca S. Chopp, *The Power to Speak: Feminism, Language, God* (New York: Crossroad, 1989).

[6] Ronald F. Hock and Edward N. O'Neil, *The Chreia in Ancient Rhetoric, vol 1, The Progymnasmata* (Atlanta: Scholars Press, 1986), 87.

his comparison of Jesus with John the Baptist who, according to this disciple, taught his disciples to pray (Luke 11:1; cf. 5:33). However, no extant text reveals any prayer attributed to John the Baptist.[7] Comparison is a standard rhetorical feature of biographical literature in antiquity,[8] and one feature of Lukan discourse is to highlight the character of Jesus through comparison with John the Baptist.[9] An additional feature in the opening sentence is the unnamed disciple's address of Jesus as κύριε (lord or master). This mode of address is an implicit act of praising Jesus, which also occurs in the preceding episode, both in the narration (10:39, 41) and in the speech of Martha (10:40) as she provides hospitality for him in her home. Thus, Luke 11:1 communicates such a high esteem for Jesus that it exhibits an intriguing relation to the first step in the elaboration of a chreia. Hermogenes asserts that an elaboration should begin with "encomium in a few words for the one who spoke or acted."[10] Luke 11:1–13 begins with honorific address to Jesus and comparison that evokes a tone of authority for Jesus' speech.

Jesus responds to the disciple by reciting the Lord's Prayer in abbreviated form. An ability to expand and abbreviate traditional stories and sayings with respectable grammatical and syntactical skill is fundamental to progymnastic rhetorical composition, which is the mode of writing the Gospel of Luke exhibits.[11] Luke may have found this abbreviated version in "Q,"[12] but if he did not, he has abbreviated the prayer for this context.[13] In its abbreviated form, the Lord's Prayer contains an

---

[7] See Joseph A. Fitzmyer, *The Gospel according to Luke: Introduction, Translation and Notes* (2 vols.; AB 28–28A; New York: Doubleday, 1981–1985), 2:902, for references to Essene forms of prayer some scholars have thought might be relevant to a discussion of prayer-forms that John the Baptist might have used.

[8] Comparison (σύγκρισις) is a primary dynamic underlying Plutarch's *Parallel Lives*. Most of the fifty lives highlight the characteristics of either a Greek or Roman leader through comparison with one or more other leaders with whom they are compared.

[9] Cf. Luke 3:18–20; 5:33; 7:18–35; 9:7–9, 18–19; 16:16; 20:1–8; see Ron Cameron "'What Have You Come Out To See?' Characterizations of John and Jesus in the Gospels," *Semeia* 49 (1990): 35–69. See Philip L. Shuler, "The Rhetorical Character of Luke 1–2," in *Literary Studies in Luke-Acts: Essays in Honor of Joseph B. Tyson* (Macon, Ga.: Mercer University Press, 1998), 173–89.

[10] Hock and O'Neil, *The Progymnasmata*, 177.

[11] For the meaning of "progymnastic" rather than fully developed "oratorical" rhetorical skills, see Vernon K. Robbins, "Progymnastic Rhetorical Composition and Pre-Gospel Traditions: A New Approach," in *The Synoptic Gospels: Source Criticism and the New Literary Criticism* (ed. Camille Focant; BETL 110; Leuven: Leuven University Press, 1993), 111–47.

[12] John S. Kloppenborg, *Q Parallels: Synopsis, Critical Notes and Concordance* (Sonoma Calif.: Polebridge, 1988), 82–85; and Shawn Carruth and Albrecht Garsky, *Document Q 11:1b-4* (Leuven: Peeters, 1996).

[13] An expanded chreia features amplification within the chreia itself, while a chreia elaboration regularly features recitation of the chreia in an abbreviated form; see Vernon

address ("Father"), two petitions of praise, and three petitions for communal benefaction.[14]

    Address: Father
    Petitions of praise:
        (1) Hallowed be thy name.
        (2) Thy Kingdom come.
    Petitions for communal benefaction:
        (3) Give us each day our daily bread.[15]
        (4) Forgive us our sins, for we ourselves forgive every one indebted to us.
        (5) Lead us not into temptation.

The opening address introduces the image of God as Father, the two petitions of praise request that God manifest his holiness and enact his power with his rule, and the three petitions for communal benefaction ask God to provide daily bread and forgiveness, and not to lead people into testing.

The second petition for communal benefaction in Lord's Prayer differs from the other two petitions by containing a rationale. In its current discursive context in Luke, this petition is a cultural enthymeme, that is, the enthymeme expresses a point of view held by people who were born or educated into this particular tradition, rather than by people who accepted the belief and practice that shaped society generally. The enthymeme is a petition by a specific community of people for a benefit from God. Only in this instance does a petition in the prayer give a reason why God should grant the request,[16] and the reason is because the people who pray the prayer also forgive everyone indebted to them. This petition participates in an enthymemic network of reasoning related to "Forgive, and you will be forgiven" (6:37–38):

K. Robbins, "Introduction: Using Rhetorical Discussions of the Chreia to Interpret Pronouncement Stories," *Semeia* 64 (1994): xii–xvi.

[14] Cf. Fitzmyer, *The Gospel according to Luke*, 2:898; Fred B. Craddock, *Luke* (Louisville Ky.: Westminster/John Knox, 1990), 153–4; Luke T. Johnson, *The Gospel of Luke* (Sacra Pagina 3; Collegeville Minn.: Liturgical, 1991), 179; and Sharon H. Ringe, *Luke* (Louisville Ky.: Westmister/John Knox, 1995), 162–5.

[15] For variations in the translation, and the reasons for the variations, see Fitzmyer, *The Gospel according to Luke*, 2:904–6.

[16] The version of the Lord's Prayer commonly recited by Protestant Christians concludes with the supporting premise: "For thine is the Kingdom and the power and the glory forever." In other words, the reason it is presupposed that God the Father can grant the petitions in the prayer is the Father's possession of kingdom, power, and glory.

Luke 6:37–38	Luke 11:4
Rule. The measure you give will be the measure you get back.	
[*Case.* Judging, condemning, forgiving, and giving are measures given.]	
Result. Judge not, and you will not be judged; condemn not, and you will not be condemned; **forgive, and you will be forgiven**; give, and it will be given to you; good measure, pressed down, shaken together, running over, will be put into your lap.	[*Rule.* **Forgive, and you will be forgiven.**]
	Case. We forgive every one indebted to us.
	Result. Forgive us our sins.

One result in the enthymemic reasoning in 6:37–38 is that forgiving is an action related to judging, condemning, and giving. In the context of early Christian discourse, the passive voice in the second part presupposes that God is the one who forgives the person who has forgiven someone else.[17] The manner in which a person judges, condemns, forgives, and gives relates directly to the manner in which God judges, condemns, forgives, and gives to this person. In other words, these actions are part of the text's "sacred texture,"[18] in which human actions are intricately interconnected with divine actions. There is not space here to pursue all the topics in this network. Let us notice, however, that the statement about giving bridges back to the statement in the Lord's Prayer where petitioners pray, "Give us this day our daily bread." As the statement bridges back, it would be natural for an implication to be evoked concerning giving that would replicate the reasoning concerning forgiving.[19] In other words, it would be natural to reason: "Give us this day our daily bread, because we give bread to others who need it." We will see some of the implications of this in the section below.

When Luke 11:4 is placed in the enthymemic network that includes Luke 6:37–38, there is a problem in the syllogistic logic. If the reason-

---

[17] God is the presupposed agent of the forgiveness in the second part, not the person who has been forgiven; see Ernst Käsemann, *New Testament Questions of Today* (trans. W.J. Montague; London: SCM, 1969), 66–107.

[18] Robbins, *Exploring*, 120–31.

[19] For replication, see Bruce J. Malina, *The New Testament World: Insights from Cultural Anthropology* (rev. ed.; Louisville Ky.: Westminster/John Knox, 1993), 39–40, passim.

ing in relation to the rule "Forgive, and you will be forgiven" were strictly inductive-deductive, it would be as follows.[20]

Deductive	Inductive
	Case. We forgive everyone indebted to us.
Rule. Forgive, and God will forgive you (Luke 6:37).	[Result. God will forgive us.]
	Rule. Forgive, and God will forgive you (Luke 6:37).
Case. We forgive everyone indebted to us (Luke 11:4).	
[Result. God will forgive us.]	

The statement in the Lord's Prayer is "Forgive us our sins," not "God will forgive us." Therefore, something has changed. According to modern analysis, this change is a result of abduction. Despite the rule, "Forgive, and you will be forgiven," the formulator of the enthymeme in Luke 11:4 experienced God as a being who does not grant forgiveness simply on the basis of forgiving the indebtedness of another person. The experience of the speaker overrides the inductive-deductive reasoning and produces an alternative result. Richard L. Lanigan describes reasoning like this as rhetorical rather than descriptive or dialectic.[21] Its logic concerns particular individuals and groups of people and is characteristic of the "cultural psychology of a rhetor."[22] Rather than staying within an inductive-deductive cycle, "particular" reasoning uses abductive reasoning as an assistant to imagine transcendent realities that can never be seen or deduced. The reasoning in the petition in 11:4 reaches beyond the inductive-deductive reasoning to grasp the transcendent reality of God and God's forgiveness. When this happens, the reasoning adds the necessity to "ask" God, and it inverts the "case" and the "result" in the deductive reasoning:[23]

---

[20] For display of an inductive-deductive cycle of reasoning, see Richard L. Lanigan, "From Enythymeme to Abduction: The Classical Law of Logic and the Postmodern Rule of Rhetoric," in *Recovering Pragmatism's Voice: The Classical Tradition, Rorty, and the Philosophy of Communication* (ed. Lenore Langsdorf and Andrew R. Smith; Albany N.Y.: SUNY Press, 1995), 58.

[21] Ibid., 52–53.

[22] Ibid., 62; cf. Vernon K. Robbins, "Pragmatic Relations as a Criterion for Authentic saying," *Forum* 1/3 (1985): 35–63; and Shawn Carruth, "Strategies of Authority: A Rhetorical Study of the Character of the Speaker in Q 6:20–49," in *Conflict and Invention: Literary, Rhetorical, and Social Studies on the Sayings Gospel Q* (ed. John S. Kloppenborg; Philadelphia: Trinity Press International, 1995), 107–10.

[23] For a display of the enthymeme argument cycle, see Lanigan, "From Enthymeme to Abduction," 62.

Abductive	Deductive	Inductive
		Case. We forgive everyone indebted to us.
[*Rule.* Forgive, and God will forgive you (**if you ask God to forgive your sins**) (6:37).]	[*Rule.* Forgive, and God will forgive you (**if you ask God to forgive your sins**).]	*Result.* **Forgive us our sins!**
Result. **Forgive us our sins** (11:4a)!	*Case.* We forgive every one indebted to us.	[*Rule.* Forgive, and God will forgive you (**if you ask God to forgive your sins**).]
Case. We forgive everyone indebted to us (11:4b)	*Result.* **Forgive us our sins!**	

The statement "Forgive, and you will be forgiven" could function as a statement about human relationships, where one person forgives another, if there were no language about God in the context. The presence of language about God, however, creates a consciousness of the nature of God and God's forgiveness. In turn, this creates an awareness that our ability to forgive is in fact defective in relation to God's ability. This "discovery" produces an inversion of the deductive reasoning so that our asking God to forgive us creates the "case" whereby we "forgive others." In technical terms, in abductive reasoning the result of the deductive reasoning (a petition to God to forgive us our sins) becomes the because-motive (abductive "result") that produces the case (we forgive everyone indebted to us).[24]

An underlying reason why people must ask God for forgiveness probably is that Father God (11:2) is a patron whom one must approach in "lowliness" if one is to receive from him. Thus, the abductive reasoning is related to well-known cultural reasoning. Bruce J. Malina, John H. Elliot, and others propose that the meanings of God the Father emerge primarily from the social system of patronage and clientage in Mediterranean society.[25] It is God's natural role to enter into patron-client contracts whereby he provides benefactions for various kinds of services his clients render to him. But a client must approach this patron in "lowliness" in order to receive the benefactions. A major stimulus for reconfiguring "God will forgive us our sins" into the petition "Forgive us our sins," then, appears to be the presence of the principle, "those who lower themselves will be exalted." This reasoning occurs inductively in Luke 18:13–14.

---

[24] Ibid., 63.

[25] Bruce J. Malina, "Patron and Client," *Forum* 4/1 (1988): 2–32; and John H. Elliot, "Patronage and Clientage," in *The Social Sciences and New Testament Interpretation* (ed. Richard L. Rohrbaugh; Peabody Mass.: Hendrickson, 1996), 144–56.

Case. A tax collector lowers himself by standing afar, not lifting up his eyes to heaven, beating his breast and saying, "God, be merciful to me a sinner" (18:13).
Result. The tax collector is justified (exalted) (18:14).
Rule. All who exalt themselves will be lowered, and those who lower themselves will be exalted (18:14).

Inductive reasoning that the tax collector's action brings forgiveness (justification) evokes the principle that God exalts those who lower themselves. The principle that "those who lower themselves are exalted" has widespread currency in Mediterranean culture.[26] Thus, deductive application of this principle is readily available for use by any group within its environs. In Lukan reasoning, the principle by which the tax collector received the benefit of forgiveness can be expressed in these terms: Do not expect forgiveness on the basis of anything good you might have done, but "lower yourself," asking God for forgiveness simply on the basis of his mercy.

Once we have seen the enthymemic network concerning forgiveness that interconnects Luke 11:4, 6:37–38, and 18:13–14, we are in a position to go to another location in the Lukan text. Luke 23:24 depicts Jesus as saying, "Father, forgive them, for they know not what they are doing."[27] This statement itself is enthymemic, evoking a premise about God forgiving people who do not know what they are doing:

[*Rule.* The Father forgives people who do not know what they are doing.]
Case. They do not know what they are doing.
Result. Father, forgive them.

For our purposes here, it is instructive to observe that Jesus' statement has a relation to the "case" in the cycle of enthymemic reasoning established by 11:4 ("We forgive every one indebted to us ..."). Since Jesus' action in 23:34 exhibits an enactment (an example or paradigm) of a generalized form of the principle, it can be helpful to display the

---

[26] See Vernon K. Robbins, *Ancient Quotes and Anecdotes: From Crib to Crypt* (Sonoma Calif.: Polebridge, 1989), 37–38.

[27] Possibly 23:34 was added by a later scribe. Luke 23:34 is absent from P^{75}, $\aleph^1$, B, D*, W, Θ, etc. but present in $\aleph^{*2}$, (A), C, D^2, L, Ψ, etc. Whether originally in the text of Luke, or added later, it is fully consonant with the principle that is taught by Luke 11:4; cf. Charles H. Talbert, *Reading Luke: A Literary and Theological Commentary on the Third Gospel* (New York: Crossroad, 1982), 219–20; and Vernon K. Robbins, "The Crucifixion and the Speech of Jesus," *Forum* 4/1 (1988): 40.

reasoning in an inductive (case + result = rule) rather than deductive syllogism.[28]

Deductive	Inductive Enthymemic Enactment		Deductive
		[Rule. People should imitate the actions of God.]	
		Case. The Most High is kind to the grateful and the selfish (6:35).	
		[Result/Rule. People should be kind to the grateful and selfish.]	
[Rule. Forgive, and you will be forgiven (Luke 6:37).]	Case. They do not know what they are doing.	[Case. Praying for someone who engages in negative actions (e.g., abuses you) is a form of kindness.]	[Case. Loving one's enemies is a form of kindness.]
Case. **We forgive every one** who is indebted to us.	Result. Father, forgive them (23:24).	Result. Pray for those who abuse you (6:28).	Result. **Love your enemies** (6:35).
Result. Forgive us our sins (Luke 11:4).	[Rule. A person should pray to Father God to ask him to forgive people who do not know what they are doing.]		

Jesus' statement in 23:24 appears to be an act of forgiving those who have beaten, humiliated, and crucified him.[29] What Jesus actually does, however, is petition God to forgive them. Adopting the mode he instructs his followers to adopt in 11:2–4, he addresses God as Father and petitions God to forgive those who have wronged him. In other words, Jesus does not personally forgive them and then petition God to forgive him because he has forgiven them. The presupposition is that those who have abused and crucified Jesus need God's forgiveness, not

---

[28] See Lanigan, "From Enthymeme to Abduction," 53, 58, 62.
[29] Robbins, "The Crucifixion and the Speech of Jesus," 40.

simply Jesus' forgiveness.[30] Indeed, the formulators of this discourse may presuppose that Jesus does not need forgiveness, either because he never committed a sin or because, if he did, he petitioned God for forgiveness and God granted it. Jesus' petition to God to forgive those who have wronged him moves beyond the principle he articulates in the Lord's Prayer to the principle of "praying for those who abuse you" (6:28), which in turn is an enactment of "loving your enemies" (6:35). Both praying for those who abuse you and loving your enemies occur in an enthymemic context that grounds the actions in belief that God "is kind to the ungrateful and to the selfish" (6:35).

The enthymeme about forgiveness in the Lord's Prayer, then, is part of a Lukan enthymemic network of reasoning about forgiving others and about petitioning God to forgive oneself and others. These topics are important enough in the social, cultural, and ideological environment of the Gospel of Luke to be expressed in enthymemic form. Assertions about these topics rarely stand unsupported. Rather, rationales accompany the assertions. The rationales create enthymemic reasoning, and this reasoning both interconnects statements in different locations in the work and introduces new topics that branch out to other related topics of importance.

Ideological Subversion of a Social Enthymeme in Luke 11:5–8

After Jesus recites the Lord's Prayer to his disciples, he asks the disciples a lengthy and complex rhetorical question beginning with "which one of you ...?" and anticipating the answer "no one" (Luke 11:5–7).[31] A rhetorical question makes an assertion, and this question asserts that no one has a friend who will refuse to get up and give three loaves to him when he needs bread for another friend who has come on a journey – even if the request for bread is made at midnight when the person being requested is sleeping comfortably in bed with his family.

These assertions evoke two syllogisms, one in which conventions of hospitality and friendship intertwine, and another that focuses more directly on friendship.

---

[30] When Jesus forgives sins in Luke, either there is criticism that God alone forgives sin (5:21) or there is an expression of consternation (7:49).

[31] Bernard Brandon Scott, *Hear Then the Parable: A Commentary on the Parables of Jesus* (Minneapolis: Fortress Press, 1989), 87; and Robert C. Tannehill, *Luke* (Nashville: Abingdon, 1996), 189.

Hospitality and Friendship	Friendship
[*Rule*. Social conventions of both hospitality and friendship require a host-friend to feed bread to a hungry guest-friend.]	[*Rule*. A friend willingly gives of his possessions to another friend.]
Case. A guest-friend arrives at midnight and the host-friend does not have any bread.	
Result/Case. At midnight the host-friend asks his sleeping-friend for bread for his hungry guest-friend.	
	Result. At midnight the sleeping-friend will give the host-friend bread for his hungry guest-friend.

These syllogisms exhibit social reasoning: principles that all people in the Mediterranean world, whatever their specific cultural tradition, know. The reasoning concerns both hospitality and friendship. On the one hand, the arrival of the traveling friend enacts conventions of hospitality that overlap with friendship. There are many nuances to hospitality conventions,[32] including the nuance that a host invites a guest into his home and attends to the needs of that guest for food and rest, even if the guest arrives at an inconvenient time. In addition, friends offer hospitality to one another. These conventions explain why, according to Plutarch, having too many friends can be a problem (Plutarch, *On Having Many Friends* 95C).[33] Both as a friend and as one who knows the conventions of hospitality, the host-friend welcomes the traveling-friend into his home and does what is necessary to meet his needs. On the other hand, the host-friend's need to give bread to his guest-friend enacts additional conventions of friendship. It was a cultural assumption in Mediterranean antiquity that "friends own everything in common."[34] When the host-friend goes to his sleeping-friend, the sleeping-friend is obligated to give the host-friend the bread he needs for his guest-friend. At this point, the result of the reasoning about hospitality becomes the case in the reasoning about friendship.

---

[32] Bruce J. Malina, "Hospitality," in *The HarperCollins Study Bible Dictionary* (ed. Paul J. Achtemeier; rev. ed.; San Francisco: HarperSanFrancisco, 1996), 440–41.

[33] Friends also offer hospitality to the friends of one's friends (Bruce J. Malina, *Windows on the World of Jesus: Time Travel to Ancient Judea* [Louisville Ky.: Westminster/JohnKnox, 1993], 48–49), but the sleeping-friend is not asked to offer this act of kindness in Luke 11:5–7.

[34] Κοινὰ γὰρ τὰ τῶν φίλων: Aeschylus, *Oresteia* 735; Plutarch, *How to Tell a Flatterer* 65A. See Scott, *Hear Then the Parable*, 90–91, for more examples.

The intersection of the reasoning creates a double-column of reasoning in the story that intersects where the host-friend asks his sleeping-friend for bread.

The argument in Luke 11:5–7 introduces an analogy between the acts of hospitality within friendship and the acts of Father God to humans. The argument is similar to Hermogenes' introduction of farmers' toil over the land and its crops as an analogy for teachers' education of their students. These verses, then, have an intriguing relation to the fifth step in Hermogenean elaboration: argument from analogy.[35] Their basic function is the assertion that just as no one has a friend who will refuse to give something needed, even under extreme circumstances, so also no one has a heavenly Father who will refuse one's requests, even under extreme circumstances. Thus, verses 5–7 present what host-friends do as an analogy to what God the Father does.[36]

Luke 11:8 appends a rationale in the form of an objection[37] to the argument from analogy in Luke 11:5–7. Since verse 7 uses the verb δίδωμι (give) once, verse 8 uses it twice, and the subject is asking, giving, and receiving bread, the argument from analogy and the objection clearly elaborate the first petition for communal benefaction in the Lord's Prayer (11:3: "Give us this day our daily bread."). The analogy intertwines hospitality with friendship, but the objection delimits the focus to an issue of friendship: "Why does one friend, when asked, give bread to another friend, even when it is a severe imposition?" Social convention would suggest the rationale: "Because the one asked is a friend of the one who asks." Jesus' statement subverts customary social reasoning by emphatically replacing this rationale with: "Because of his shamelessness" (ἀναίδεια). Thus Jesus' statement presents an ideological reconfiguration of conventional social reasoning. The emphatic manner in which the objection is introduced ("I tell you") evokes an authority for the saying that approximates the phenomenon Hermogenes describes as an authoritative judgment (κρίσις).[38] In addition, the strong objection in the saying produces an argument from the contrary, the fourth step in Hermogenean elaboration:[39] One friend

---

[35] Hock and O'Neil, *The Progymnasmata*, 177.

[36] Some interpreters (e.g., Talbert, *Reading Luke*, 132–33) consider vv. 5–7 to be an argument from lesser (friend) to greater (heavenly Father), but this imposes 11:13 and 18:1–8 on these verses.

[37] ἀντιλέγειν: Hock and O'Neil, *The Progymnasmata*, 100–101.

[38] For discussion of the authoritative judgment in rhetorical elaboration, see the page references in the index to Mack and Robbins, *Patterns of Persuasion in the Gospels*, 228.

[39] It was conventional practice to include rationales in the argument from the contrary (see *Rhetorica ad Herennium* 4.43.57). The reason appears to be twofold. First, both the contrary and the rationale serve the function of clarifying the nature and scope of the

gives bread to another friend when it is a severe imposition not because he is a friend but because of his shamelessness (ἀναίδεια).

A problem arises, however, because one can dispute whether the shamelessness is an attribute of the sleeping-friend or the host-friend. The "his" (αὐτοῦ) may refer to either person.[40] One aspect of the problem has been the mistranslation of ἀναίδεια as "importunity" or "persistence." This mistranslation results from imposing the persistence of the widow in Luke 18:1-8 onto the analogy and objection in 11:5-8. Recent investigations have shown that the meaning of ἀναίδεια is "shamelessness,"[41] but whether the αὐτοῦ in verse 8 refers to the sleeping friend's or the host-friend's shamelessness is still disputed. Bernard Brandon Scott, in a context of interpretation well-informed about the meaning of shamelessness, concludes that the shamelessness is an attribute of the sleeping-friend. This conclusion is the result of a misconstrual of verses 5-7 as a "how much more" argument,[42] a rhetorical misunderstanding of these verses that is widespread among interpreters. While the common topic of "the more and the less" (Aristotle, *Rhetoric* 2.23.4) emerges in the conclusion in (v. 13), this common topic is not present in the earlier stages of the elaboration (vv. 5-8). Rather, as stated above, verses 5-7 present an argument from analogy and verse 8 replaces the conventional social rationale for the action with an ideological rationale by using the common topic of the contrary or opposite (Aristotle, *Rhetoric* 2.23.1). The sleeping-friend gives bread "not" because of friendship but because of the petitioner's shamelessness. The rhetorical question asserts that a person should address God with a feeling of assurance that Father God, like a friend, will respond to a person's petitions. The objection replaces the conventional social rationale for the action with an ideological rationale based on the shamelessness of the one who asks.

Social conventions are known by all, but idiosyncratic ways of understanding may generate a particular ideology. When looked at from a social perspective, the important thing is that one friend be willing to provide for another friend's needs. If one does not, the person is not a friend. But one's understanding of the reasons why one person gives to

---

chreia or theme. Second, articulating a series of rationales in both positive and negative formulations points to wider horizons of the chreia or theme available from the arguments from analogy, example, and authoritative judgment.

[40] Cf. Talbert, *Reading Luke*, 132-3; and Scott, *Hear Then the Parable*, 89-90.

[41] Kenneth E. Bailey, *Poet and Peasant: A Literary-Cultural Approach to the Parables in Luke* (Grand Rapids Mich.: Eerdmans, 1976), 125-7; David Catchpole, "Q and 'The Friend at Midnight,'" *JTS* 34 (1983): 407-24; Scott, *Hear Then the Parable*, 88-89; and Bruce J. Malina and Richard L. Rohrbaugh, *Social-Science Commentary on the Synoptic Gospels* (Minneapolis: Fortress, 1992), 350-1.

[42] Scott, *Hear Then the Parable*, 90.

another can be ideological – grounded in a point of view held only by a particular group of people. The understanding in this objection does not appear to be basic social or cultural knowledge in the ancient Mediterranean world. In other words, no clear statement in Jewish or Greco-Roman literature declares that friends give to other friends because they shamelessly ask each other for things. Friends unhesitatingly ask each other for things, but people do not perceive this request as a shameless activity. Since friends return favors, their requests are not shameless; beggars, in contrast, are shameless because they look on another's table and beg with no plan or ability to return the favor (Sir 40:28–30). Thus, verse 8 articulates a particular deductive ideology about petitioning.

> [*Rule.* A sleeping-friend will give bread at midnight to a host-friend who is willing to petition shamelessly for a hungry guest-friend.]
> *Case.* A host-friend petitions his sleeping-friend shamelessly at midnight for bread for a hungry guest-friend.
> *Result.* At midnight the sleeping-friend will give the host-friend bread for his hungry guest-friend.

The key to the ideological reasoning appears to be the willingness of the host-friend to adopt a social role of being shameless on behalf of another person's need. As we have seen above, the petition in the Lord's Prayer for one's own forgiveness raises the issue of the petitioner's relation to other people who also need forgiveness. The enthymemic network about forgiveness not only includes directives to forgive others and to pray for those who abuse you, but it also includes a portrayal of Jesus' petition for God to forgive people who are abusing him. One sees, then, an ideological texture in the discourse whereby one's relation to God is implicated in one's relation to the needs of other people. The objection in verse 8 extends this ideological texture through an interruption of conventional social reasoning. The host-friend receives the bread from his sleeping-friend because he has been willing to be shameless by his request on behalf of his guest-friend's needs. On the one hand, this shamelessness is akin to the boldness (παρρησία) of a cynic. On the other hand, there is an ideological shift of conventional cynic reasoning as well as conventional social reasoning when the person acts boldly on behalf of another person rather than simply for oneself. The host-friend is, indeed, maintaining his honor as he petitions his friend for the bread. But the ideological twist is that he maintains his honor in the context of an unconventional understanding of why the bread was given.

It will be important in future studies to pursue the ideological texture of shamelessness throughout Luke. While the word itself occurs nowhere else in the New Testament, the social mode of shamelessness certainly appears in the parable of the dishonest steward and its subsequent commentary (Luke 16:1–9) and may be an aspect of the woman's action in Luke 7:36–50. Several other sayings and episodes appear to participate in an ideology of shamelessness in this gospel.

Thus, Luke 11:5–8 embodies a combination of argument from analogy and from the contrary (objection). The argument from analogy (vv. 5–7) plus the objection (v. 8) address the topic of petitioning bread for others who need it, elaborating the first petition for communal benefaction, which on its own simply asks for daily bread for oneself. The first step in the elaboration introduces conventional social reasoning about hospitality and friendship as an analogy for the relation of petitioners to God the Father. The second step introduces ideological social reasoning that emphasizes the need for petitioners to ask shamelessly on behalf of the needs of others.

A Cultural Enthymeme as a Rationale for the Lord's Prayer in Luke 11:9–10

The argument from analogy and the objection in Luke 11:5–8 set up the enthymemic sentence[43] in verses 9–10. These verses provide a rationale (Hermogenean step 3) for all the petitions in the Lord's Prayer. It is notable that Lukan discourse here presents both the objection (v. 8) and the rationale (vv. 9–10) as authoritative judgments. There is no appeal to Scripture for authoritative judgment, precedent, or example throughout this elaboration. Rather, this portion of Luke, like a number of other portions of kingdom wisdom in the New Testament, uses only other sayings of Jesus as authoritative judgments to elaborate the pronouncement that stands at the beginning of the elaboration. Verses 9–10 expand the vocabulary of giving with the topics of asking and giving and receiving, of seeking and finding, and of knocking and opening as they provide a rationale for praying in the manner that Jesus instructs in the opening verses. One of the most noticeable results of this configuration of topics is the association of asking, giving, and receiving with seeking. The presence of the seeking reveals an enthymemic network of reasoning that interrelates Luke 11:1–13 with Luke 12:30–32:

Luke 11	Luke 12
Rule. Everyone who asks receives; **everyone who seeks finds**; to everyone who knocks, it will be opened (11:10).	[*Rule.* The Father's kingdom gives food, drink, and clothes, as well as other things.]

[43] For a definition and discussion of the enthymemic sentence, see Kennedy, *Aristotle*, 297–98.

11. From Enthymeme to Theology in Luke 11:1–13

[*Case.* **It is your Father's good pleasure to give you the kingdom** (12:32).]

Result. Ask and [the Father's kingdom] will be given you; **seek, and you will find [the Father's kingdom]**; knock, and [the Father's kingdom] will be opened to you (11:9).

Case. **It is your Father's good pleasure to give you the kingdom** (12:32).

Result. **Seek the Father's kingdom** and food, drink, and clothes shall be yours as well (12:31).

The enthymemic sentence in Luke 11:9–10 contains the rule and result of its reasoning. The unexpressed case of the reasoning is located in Luke 12:32. That which a person asks for, seeks, and knocks upon to have opened is "the Father's kingdom." Thus, the unexpressed phrase throughout 11:9 is "the Father's Kingdom," which people receive, find, and have opened to them. The enthymemic construction in Luke 12:31–32 contains the case, rather than the rule and the result of its reasoning. The result clarifies that one aspect of the benefactions of the kingdom is the needs of the body – food, drink, and clothes. The case expressed in 12:32 clarifies why simply asking, seeking, and knocking will be successful: "It is the Father's good pleasure to give you the kingdom" [if one only asks for it, seeks it, and knocks for it to be opened].

The case (minor premise) in the reasoning in these enthymemes is a Christian reconfiguration of widespread wisdom in Hellenistic culture. It is widely recognized that gods like to give benefits to humans. Thus it not only exists as an assertion but as a premise for enthymemic reasoning. The following enthymeme appears in Plutarch, *How to Tell a Flatterer* (63F).

> *Rule.* It is in the nature of the gods to take pleasure in being gracious and doing good.
> [*Case.* Something that is in a being's nature to do is done regularly without display that creates public knowledge of the action.]
> *Result.* The gods confer their benefits, for the most part, without our knowledge.

In this instance, the topic is the secrecy of the work of the gods. Christian discourse configures the rule in terms of God as Father giving his kingdom to people. Luke 11:9–10 reasons from this rule to a conclusion that people must engage in earnest and extended action to receive the Father's kingdom. Luke 12:31–32, in contrast, clarifies that one aspect of the benefits of God's gracious activity is the needs of the body – food, drink, and clothing.

The reasoning in Luke 11:9–10 presents a rationale for the entire act of praying the Lord's Prayer. One addresses God as Father, because one hopes to receive the Father's kingdom. One addresses the Father's name as holy, because as a divine being he is able to confer extraordinary benefits on humans. One petitions God's kingdom to come, because asking God for his kingdom is one condition for receiving it. One petitions for daily bread, because one benefit God's kingdom brings is food, drink, and clothing for the body. One petitions for forgiveness, because the benefits of God's kingdom reach beyond bodily needs to the removal of one's sins. One petitions not to be led into testing where one may seek the kingdom and authority of the devil rather than the kingdom and authority of God (cf. Luke 4:1–13). The rationale in Luke 11:9–10 explains that a condition for receiving these benefits is to ask, seek, and knock for God's kingdom and its benefits. These two verses, then, present the rationale for a Lord's Prayer dominated by petitions.

The enthymemic rationale in Luke 11:9–10, then, is built on deductive reasoning related to widespread cultural reasoning about gods in ancient Mediterranean culture. The gods take pleasure in being gracious and giving benefits. The gods have the power to do beneficial things, and they delight in using this power. Lukan discourse configures this Mediterranean reasoning in terms of God as king whose kingdom brings basic benefits of bodily needs as well as forgiveness and protection from testing. Lukan discourse asserts that people must actively seek and petition God for the benefits of his kingdom. The implication is that God's people cannot be inactive and receive all the benefits. Rather, they must ask, seek, and knock to have the benefits come to them. When a person undertakes these actions, however, it is God's pleasure to give the benefits of God's kingdom.

While this passage of Luke 11:5–8 elaborates the petition for the Father to give daily bread (v. 3) through an argument from analogy, verses 9–10 provide the rationale for praying the entire prayer. The unexpressed premise in the enthymemic sentence in 11:9–10 exists in 12:32, clarifying that the petitioner is asking, seeking, and knocking for the Father's kingdom. The enthymemic network of reasoning that links 12:31–32 with 11:9–10 confirms that one benefit of the Father's kingdom is basic provisions for the body. There are, however, other benefits as well; an explanation of these leads us into the next steps in the elaboration.

A Social-Cultural Enthymeme as a Theological Conclusion in Luke 11:13

After the rationale, two arguments from comparison emerge in the form of rhetorical questions in Luke 11:11–12. The verses begin like verses 5–7 and, like them, also expect the answer "no one." The difference is that the subject of the questions in verses 11–12 is "fathers" rather than "friends." Verse 8 suggests that friends sometimes do not act out of friendship but out of shamelessness. Therefore, relationships of friends to one another function as an analogy but not a direct comparison to the relationship between God and humans. Verses 11–12 appeal to earthly fathers in comparison with a heavenly Father.

Luke 11:13 is a conclusion to the unit in the form of an if-(then) statement that uses the common topic of "the more and the less" (Aristotle, *Rhetoric* 2.23.4). Perpetuating the address to "you," which plays a prominent role throughout the elaboration, this verse gathers together the topics of asking and giving in a context where it refers to God as "heavenly Father" and compares God's giving with that of earthly fathers. This comparison produces the following syllogism.

> [*Rule.* Your heavenly Father is greater than earthly fathers.]
> *Case.* All fathers, even if they are evil, know how to give good gifts to their children.
> *Result.* How much more will the heavenly Father give **the Holy Spirit** to those who ask him.

The result in this syllogism leaps beyond the reasoning in the premises. If the reasoning remained within the boundaries of an inductive-deductive cycle, the conclusion would be that the heavenly Father gives "better gifts" to those who ask him. Instead, the enthymeme uses abductive reasoning which makes constructions that "sometimes succeed in binding us to the underlying reality they imagine by giving us an intellectual tool – a metaphor, a premise, an analogy, a category – with which to live, to arrange our experience, and to interpret our experiences so arranged."[44] As humans use abductive reasoning to create intellectual tools, they create openings that reach out beyond inductive-deductive circles of reasoning. In other words, humans remain inventive and creative as they organize and interpret their experiences. Abductive reasoning is

> the faculty of imagination, which comes to the rescue of sensation and logic by providing them with the intellectual means to see through experience and leap beyond empty syllogisms and tautologies to some creative representation of an underlying reality that might be grasped and reacted to, even if that imagined reality cannot be found, proved, or disproved by inductive or deductive rule-following.[45]

---

[44] Richard A. Schweder, *Thinking through Cultures: Expeditions in Cultural Psychology* (Cambridge Mass.: Harvard University Press, 1991), 361; in Lanigan, "From Enthymeme to Abduction," 55.

[45] Schweder, ibid.

368   *Sea Voyages and Beyond*

The reasoning in the conclusion in Luke 11:13, then, reveals another use of "abductive" reasoning to assist inductive-deductive reasoning. As the abductive reasoning leaps beyond inductive-deductive reasoning, it invites elaborative reasoning. We can see this reasoning if we display in three columns how the reasoning reaches out into a Lukan enthymemic network about giving.

Deductive	**Abductive**	**Elaborative**
[*Rule*. Your heavenly Father is greater than earthly fathers.]	[*Rule*. Your heavenly Father is greater than earthly fathers.]	A: Setting: 14:1–2 B: Challenge/Question: 14:3 C: Response:
Case. All fathers, even if they are evil, know how to give good gifts to their children.		(1) Introduction: 14:4a (2) Chreia: 14:4bc (3) Rationale: 14:5 Amplification: 14:6, 7b (5) Analogy: 14:7a,c-10
Result. How much more will the heavenly Father give **better gifts** to those who ask him.	*Result*. How much more will the heavenly Father give **the Holy Spirit** to those who ask him (11:13)!	(7,4) Judgment and Contrary: All who exalt themselves will be lowered, and those who lower themselves will be exalted (14:11).
	Case. All fathers, even if they are evil, know how to give good gifts to their children (11:13).	
	[*Inference*. Fathers, if they have the Holy Spirit, will give greater gifts than earthly fathers regularly do.]	
	[*Rule*. Give, and it will be given to you; good measure, pressed down, shaken together, running over, will be put into your lap (6:38).]	
	Analogy. When you give a dinner or a banquet, do not invite your friends or your brothers or your kinsmen or your rich neighbors, lest they also invite you in return, and you be repaid. But when you give a feast, invite the poor, the maimed, the lame, the blind, and you will be blessed, because they cannot repay you. You will be repaid at the resurrection of the just (14:12–14).[46]	
	Example. A man gave a great dinner and invited many. When those who were invited declined, he invited the poor, the crippled, the blind, and the lame, then sent his slave into the roads and lanes to compel others to come in until his house was filled (14:16–24).[47]	
	Another example in Luke. Zacchaeus, possessing the gift	

---

[46] See Willi Braun, *Feasting and Social Rhetoric in Luke 14* (SNTSMS 85; Cambridge: Cambridge University Press, 1995), 164, 171–73.

[47] See ibid., 164, 174–75.

of salvation, gives half of his goods to the poor and fourfold to anyone he has defrauded (19:8–9).

The result of deductive reasoning simply would be that God gives "better gifts" than earthly fathers, but once again in this rhetorical reasoning the rhetor invites abductive reasoning (the faculty of imagination) as an "assistant" to deductive reasoning. As the rhetor uses abductive reasoning to reflect on the transcendent realities of God's giving, interaction occurs once again between deductive and inductive reasoning that produces an inversion between the minor premise and the result in the deductive reasoning. Through abductive reasoning, "by shock, question, puzzlement, surprise, and the like, the rhetor or inquirer *discovers similarity* between" the giving of earthly fathers (deductive case) and the giving of God the father (first part of deductive rule) "because of the *experience of consciousness* constituted in" the greatness of God the Father (last part of deductive rule).[48] In other words, the statement, "all fathers know how to give good gifts," functions as a statement about human relationships, where fathers give to their children. The presence of language about God evokes a sudden experience of the consciousness of God's giving, which leads to an awareness that our ability to give is decisively inferior to God's ability to give. This "discovery" produces an inversion of the deductive reasoning so that the premise "All fathers give good gifts" calls forth the insight that "the heavenly Father gives the Holy Spirit"! Once this result emerges in the abductive reasoning, an inference is nearby that the presence of the Holy Spirit within earthly fathers will enable them to give greater gifts than they usually do. Similar to the reasoning about forgiving, the result of the deductive reasoning about giving (How much more does God give good gifts) becomes a newly discovered because-motive that extends beyond inductive and deductive reasoning (abductive result: God gives the Holy Spirit!). The emergence of this new insight generates a new result that also extends beyond inductive-deductive reasoning (fathers, if they have the Holy Spirit, will give greater gifts than earthly fathers regularly do).[49]

In a context where a rhetor has generated the result that extends beyond inductive-deductive reasoning, the new insight reduces the importance of the result of the deductive reasoning and creates a major inference that invites elaboration. One may naturally find other places in the Gospel of Luke that elaborate various results of the abductive reasoning (that is, "greater" behaviors in humans produced by the Holy

---

[48] Cf. Lanigan, "From Enthymeme to Abduction," 59.
[49] Cf. Ibid., 63.

Spirit in them). Willi Braun's analysis of Luke 14 exhibits people (including Jesus) distributing benefactions in a manner "greater" than conventional human action. This elaboration of the abductive reasoning emphasizes that the presence of Holy Spirit in humans can produce "greater" giving than most earthly persons enact. Luke 14:11 characterizes this mode of giving beyond conventional social practice as "lowering oneself and being exalted." Thus, one lowers oneself to give, much as one lowers oneself to be forgiven. Once again, giving and forgiving intertwine in the enthymemic texture of Luke. Luke 14:12–24 elaborates the lowering by giving boldly to the poor, maimed, lame, and blind; the story of Zacchaeus (19:1–10) shows how "giving" brings "salvation"; and Luke 18:13–14 displays how asking forgiveness in a position of lowering oneself (rather than asking in a position one may consider to bolster one's request, that is, having forgiven the debt of another; 11:4) puts one in a position to receive forgiveness from God. Lowering oneself either to give or to ask for forgiveness brings exaltation in the enthymemic texture of the Gospel of Luke.

Conclusion

Luke 11:1–13, then, contains both intriguing similarities with and intriguing differences from Hermogenes' elaboration of the chreia. After an introduction that evokes an image of Jesus as an authoritative speaker, Jesus recites an abbreviated form of the Lord's Prayer to his disciples. Immediately after this recitation, Jesus presents an argument from analogy that depicts relationships among friends. Jesus then appends this analogy with an authoritative objection that asserts that a friend gives bread to his friend at midnight not because of friendship but because of the petitioner's willingness to ask shamelessly for another person's needs. After this parable, Jesus presents an enthymemic rationale for praying to God in the petitionary manner manifest in the Lord's Prayer. After the rationale, Jesus presents two arguments from comparison with earthly fathers and a conclusion that summarizes how much more their heavenly Father is able to give than earthly fathers.

There can be no doubt, then, that the units in Luke 11:5–13 elaborate aspects of the Lord's Prayer. But this elaboration differs in significant respects from Hermogenean elaboration. In Hermogenean elaboration, a well-articulated rationale occurs immediately after the chreia or maxim, then the argumentation moves on to the contrary, to analogy, to example, to authoritative judgment, and finally, to an exhortative conclusion. In Luke 11:1–13, the rationale occurs only after an initial argument from analogy with an objection. Then, after two arguments from comparison, the conclusion ends with an if-(then) statement that is enthymemic in nature. In Luke, enthymemic discourse occurs already in the recitation of the Lord's Prayer, and it continues into the conclusion. In the Hermogenean elaboration, in contrast, enthymemic discourse has its primary function immediately after the recitation of the chreia or maxim. In addition, Luke 11:1–13 is part of a longer text, namely the entire Gospel of Luke. The enthymemes throughout the unit create an enthymemic network that extends into various portions of the Gospel. An enthymeme in the prayer itself creates a dynamic interaction between forgiving and giving. Then a surprise emerges in the conclusion of the elaboration when Jesus says the heavenly Father gives the Holy Spirit. At this point, the elaboration moves decisively beyond inductive-deductive reasoning characteristic of conventional social, cultural, and ideological reasoning into a mode of abductive reasoning that generates special ways of thinking and acting.

Does the conclusion to the elaboration in Luke 11:13 imply that people should petition God to send the Holy Spirit upon them? The answer probably is no. The Father gives the Holy Spirit as an addition when people petition for those things itemized in the Lord's Prayer, but with this conclusion the topics for debate become fully theological. The issue is not what ordinary friends or fathers do, but what God does when people petition God in the manner Jesus teaches in the Lord's Prayer. Enthymemic social, cultural, and ideological reasoning moves into theological reasoning as the elaboration reaches its conclusion. The topic is the heavenly Father's giving of the Holy Spirit in contexts where people pray the prayer Jesus taught his disciples. The authoritative placing of the recitation of the prayer on Jesus' lips at the beginning of the elaboration produces a context in which theological discussion will inevitably move into Christological discussion. God not only gives the Holy Spirit; God's son (10:21–22) has revealed special wisdom about the Father's kingdom. Through rhetorical elaboration, enthymemic reasoning configures social, cultural, and ideological topics into topics that inhabit the sacred texture of the text.[50] These topics interweave theology and Christology in a manner that creates not only a new social, cultural, and ideological world, but also a new theological and Christological world for the reader.

---

[50] Robbins, *Exploring*, 120–31.

12

The Socio-Rhetorical Role of Old Testament Scripture in Luke 4-19

It is a special pleasure to write an essay in honor of Professor Doctor Zdenek Sazava. We first met in 1986, when he came to the Studiorum Novi Testamenti Societas meetings at Emory University in Atlanta, Georgia, U.S.A. He stayed in our home after the meetings, and my wife Deanna and I remember fondly his visit with us. We have seen each other at yearly meetings since then, and on one occasion Prof. Sazava was a gracious host to my wife and me in Prague. Prof. Sazava has shown great interest in my work, and he has reviewed some of my books for journals in the Czech Republic. One of his special interests is the Gospel of Luke, and I will focus on this Gospel in Prof. Sazava's honor.

It is widely known that Isaiah 61:1-2 plays a programmatic role in the Gospel of Luke as a result of Jesus' public reading of it at the beginning of his adult ministry in his home synagogue at Nazareth (Luke 4:18-19).[1] It is also widely recognized that the author of Luke and Acts exhibits extensive knowledge of the Septuagint Greek Old Testament (LXX).[2] Few interpreters, however, have a clear view of the manner in which significant portions of the OT function as socio-rhetorical resources for the configuration of major scenes and major shifts in emphasis as the Lukan story unfolds.

This essay investigates the intertextural relation of the Lukan story to portions of the Old Testament with guidelines set forth in *The Tapestry of Early Christian Discourse* and *Exploring the Texture of Texts*,[3] as well as

---

[1] L.C. Crockett, "The Old Testament in the Gospel of Luke: With Emphasis on the Interpretation of Isaiah 61.1-2" (Ph.D. diss., Brown University, 1966).

[2] Joseph A. Fitzmeyer, *The Gospel According to Luke: Introduction, Translation, and Notes* (2 vols.; AB 28-28A; Garden City, N.Y.: Doubleday, 1981-1985), 1:114-6; cf. Vernon K. Robbins, "The Social Location of the Implied Author of Luke and Acts," in *The Social World of Luke-Acts: Models for Interpretation* (ed. Jerome H. Neyrey; Peabody, Mass.: Hendrickson, 1991), 323-6.

[3] Vernon K. Robbins, *The Tapestry of Early Christian Discourse: Rhetoric, Society and Ideology* (London: Routledge, 1996), 96-115, 121-24, 129-43; idem, *Exploring the Texture of*

a series of essays the author has published alongside these two books.[4] The essay focuses only on Luke 4:1–19:27, the section of the story from the beginning of Jesus' adult ministry to the point where he goes into Jerusalem. In Jerusalem, Jesus' death provides a means for the renewal of the story of God's people through the coming of the spirit into a multitude gathered together from wide regions of the Mediterranean world after Jesus' ascension into heaven (Acts 2).

The thesis of the essay is that Luke 4:1–13 introduces major topics from Deuteronomy 6 and 8, which concern possessions and devotion to God. Then Luke 4:14–30 reconfigures those topics through recitation or reference to passages from Isaiah and 1–2 Kings.[5] After Luke 7:11–35 summarizes the results of the attempts of John the Baptist and Jesus to bring the renewal program of Deuteronomy, 1–2 Kings, and Isaiah to the people of Israel, Jesus is a dinner guest in the home of prominent Pharisees on three occasions (7:36–50; 11:36–54; 14:1–24). These dinners provide a beginning, middle, and end to Luke 7:36–14:35, and at these dinners major *topoi*[6] from Deuteronomy, 1–2 Kings, and Isaiah are contextualized in households owned by wealthy people.[7] Jesus' interaction with Pharisees at these dinner parties establishes as the

---

Texts: A Guide to Socio-Rhetorical Interpretation (Valley Forge, Pa.: Trinity Press International, 1996), 40–62. See the online *Dictionary of Socio-Rhetorical Terms*: http://www.religion.emory.edu/faculty/robbins/SRI/defns/index

[4] Vernon K. Robbins, "From Enthymeme to Theology in Luke 11:1–13," in *Literary Studies in Luke-Acts: A Collection of Essays in Honor of Joseph B. Tyson* (ed. Richard P. Thompson and Thomas E. Phillips; Macon, Ga.: Mercer University Press, 1998), 191–214 [Chapter 11 in this volume]; idem, "Socio-Rhetorical Hermeneutics and Commentary," in *EPI TO AYTO. Essays in honour of Petr Pokorny* (ed. J. Mrazek, R. Dvorakova, and S. Brodsky; Praha-Trebenice, Czech Republic: Mlyn, 1998), 284–97. Online: http://www.religion.emory.edu/faculty/robbins/commentary/commentary284.html; idem, "The Present and Future of Rhetorical Analysis," in *The Rhetorical Analysis of Scripture: Essays from the 1995 London Conference* (ed. Stanley E. Porter and Thomas H. Olbricht; JSNTSup 146; Sheffield: Sheffield Academic Press, 1997), 24–52. Online: http://www.religion.emory.edu/faculty/robbins/future/future24.html; cf. David B. Gowler, "The Development of Socio-Rhetorical Criticism," in Vernon K. Robbins, *New Boundaries in Old Territory: Form and Social Rhetoric in Mark* (ed. David B. Gowler; Emory Studies in Early Christianity 3; New York: Peter Lang, 1994), 1–36. Online: http://userwww.service.emory.edu/~dgowler/chapter.htm.

[5] For recitation, reference, and reconfiguration, see Robbins, *Tapestry*, 96–115, 120–24; idem, *Exploring*, 40–50.

[6] For the meaning of *topos* and its plural *topoi* as used in this paper, see Wilhelm H. Wuellner, "Toposforschung und Torahinterpretation bei Paulus und Jesus," *NTS* 24 (1978): 463–83. A *topos* is a "social, cultural, or ideological location of thought" that has a twofold function: an argumentative-enthymematic and an amplificatory-descriptive function (467).

[7] For opening-middle-closing texture, see Robbins, *Tapestry*, 50–53, 70–72; idem, *Exploring*, 19–21.

dynamics for a major shift in the story at Luke 15 to the *topos* of "seeking and saving the lost." This *topos* exhibits a reconfiguration of Ezekiel 34 by the author of Luke for the purpose of moving the renewal program to the specific issue of gathering God's faithful people in a context where early Christians are gathering in households around the Mediterranean world during the decades after the destruction of Jerusalem and its Temple by the Roman army in 66–70 CE.

In contrast to some essays that simply refer to OT passages, this essay will recite the verses that are important for understanding the broader context in the OT. The purpose is to argue that the Gospel of Luke, like many other books in the NT, exhibits knowledge by the author of major *topoi* in the context of many OT texts and uses these *topoi* as resources to configure scenes and introduce argumentation into them.

Luke 4:1–13: The Testing of Jesus

In the Lukan version of the testing of Jesus in the wilderness, Jesus responds to the devil with recitations of Deut 8:3; 6:13; and 6:16. The Matthean and Lukan versions both present the first temptation as a setting where the devil tells Jesus to turn stone to bread (Matt 4:3; Luke 4:3). In Luke 4:4, Jesus responds with, "One does not live by bread alone," while Matt 4:4 includes an additional clause of the verse, "but by every word that proceeds out of the mouth of God." While the Lukan Jesus does not recite the clause about living by every word that proceeds from the mouth of God, it becomes obvious that Jesus is enacting this principle with his speech and action.[8] People who hold verses in memory regularly will recite only the first part, the last part, or a favorite clause in the middle of a verse as the key to the entire verse. Because of its context in Luke 4:1–4, all of Deut 8:2–3 is important:

> 2: And you shall remember all the way which the LORD your God has led you these forty years in the wilderness, that he might humble you, testing you to know what was in your heart, whether you would keep his commandments, or not. 3: And he humbled you and let you hunger and fed you with manna, which you did not know, nor did your fathers know; that he might make you know that one does not live by bread alone, but that one lives by everything that proceeds out of the mouth of the LORD.

The Lukan story of the testing of Jesus reconfigures the *topos* of forty years of being tested in the wilderness (Deut 8:2) into forty days in which "he ate nothing" (Luke 4:2).[9] The specific reference to "testing"

---

[8] Actually, his unwillingness to act in the way the devil wants him to.
[9] Cf. Moses in Exod 34:28; Deut 9:9, 18; Elijah in 1 Kgs 19:8.

in Luke 4:2 exhibits the recontextualization[10] of an Israelite cultural *topos* of "God's testing of Israel" in Deut 6–8.[11] In addition, the *topos* of "knowing in one's heart, remembering, and keeping" in Deut 6–8[12] sets the stage for Jesus' "knowing by heart" the verses from Deut 6 and 8 so that he can recite them to the devil and enact them (by resisting the devil's challenges)[13] when he is tested. The Lukan story reconfigures the "let you hunger" in Deut 8:3 into "And he ate nothing in those days; and when they were ended, he was hungry" (Luke 4:2).[14] In addition, it is noticeable that "knowing" is part of the repetitive texture[15] of Deut 8:2–3 in the context of "remembering":

1. you shall remember;
2. testing you to know;
3. which you did not know, nor did your fathers know;
4. that he might make you know.

In the Lukan story, Jesus enacts the attributes of knowing by heart, remembering, and keeping the commands God gave to Israel in the context of their testing in the wilderness. There are other *topoi* in Deut 6–8 that also are important for the Lukan story. Deut 8:5 presents the analogy that as a father disciplines his son, so "the Lord your God disciplines you." The devil refers to Jesus as "the Son of God" in this first test and also the last test (Luke 4:3, 9), evoking the concept of God the Father disciplining his Son. Deut 8:11–14 emphasizes the problem that "forgetting" rather than "remembering" causes a person's heart to be "exalted" rather than "humbled" (8:14). Later in the Lukan story, while Jesus is dining in the house of a ruling Pharisee, he discusses the importance of humbling oneself rather than exalting oneself (Luke 14:7–11). On a later occasion, this time as a direct challenge to Pharisees, Jesus says: "You are those who justify yourselves in the sight of others; but God knows your hearts; for what is exalted by human beings is an abomination in the sight of God" (Luke 16:15). On a still later occasion, Jesus tells a parable about a Pharisee and a tax collector to people "who trusted in themselves that they were righteous and

---

[10] For recontextualization, see Robbins, *Tapestry*, 107; idem, *Exploring*, 48–50.

[11] Deut 6:16; 8:2, 16.

[12] Deut 6:1–3, 6, 17, 24–25; 7:9, 11–12; 8:1–2, 6, 11, 18.

[13] To understand the dynamic of these tests as challenges and *ripostes*, see Bruce J. Malina, *The New Testament World: Insights from Cultural Anthropology* (rev. ed.; Atlanta: John Knox, 1993), 42–45; Bruce J. Malina and Richard L. Rohrbaugh, *Social-Science Commentary on the Synoptic Gospels* (Minneapolis: Fortress, 1992), 307–308; Robbins, *Exploring*, 80–82.

[14] Matt 4:2 changes it into: He fasted forty days and forty nights, and afterwards he was famished.

[15] For repetitive texture, see Robbins, *Tapestry*, 46–50, 66–69; idem, *Exploring*, 8–9.

regarded others with contempt" (18:9–14). The parable ends with the premise that all who exalt themselves will be humbled, but all who humble themselves will be exalted" (18:14). In the Lukan understanding, when the hearts of Pharisees, the elect leaders of Israel, are "exalted," they have "forgotten" the commandments of the Lord (Deut 8:2–3, 6). Deut 8:17–18 refers specifically to the problem that when the people of Israel become rich, they may forget that God gave them the power to get their wealth, rather than that they got their wealth through their own power and the power of their hand. When this happens, according to Luke, it is necessary for God to "exalt the humble" (1:52).

In the second and third tests, Jesus responds from the chapter in Deuteronomy that features the famous Jewish Shema: "Hear, O Israel: The LORD our God is one LORD; and you shall love the LORD your God with all your heart, and with all your soul, and with all your might" (Deut 6:4–5). The Lukan order of the second and third tests follows the order of the elaboration of the Shema in Deut 6. In response to the devil's challenge that if Jesus will worship him, he will give him all the kingdoms of the world (Luke 4:6–7), Jesus recites a portion of a verse (Deut 6:13) that elaborates the second *topos*[16] in the Shema, "The LORD our God is one LORD" (6:4). In response to the devil's challenge that he should throw himself down from the Temple, Jesus recites a portion of the verse (6:16) that begins the elaboration of "You shall love LORD your God with all your heart, soul, and might" (6:5).[17] This verse reformulates "loving God" in terms of "not putting the LORD your God to the test." This means that the final two tests of Jesus represent a reconfigured framework of testing into which Jesus introduces *topoi* conventionally associated in the biblical story with interpretation of the Shema.

Immediately after the Shema, Deut 6:6 elaborates the meaning of the first *topos*, "Hear," with: "Keep these words I am commanding you today in your heart...." In the account of the tests by the devil, Jesus exhibits that he has these commands in his heart, and thus he can quote them from memory. Luke 10:27 features the Shema in the response of the lawyer to Jesus before Jesus tells the Parable of the Good Samaritan (10:30–37). At the end of his recitation of the Shema, the lawyer adds Lev 19:18: "and [you shall love] your neighbor as yourself" (Luke 10:27). This means that the lawyer not only knows the Shema "by heart," but he also "knows" the meaning of the Shema in the broader context of the Torah as a result of knowing other places in which the

---

[16] The first *topos* is "Hear," which the discourse elaborates in Deut 6:6–9.

[17] Matt 4:5–8 has the last two tests in reverse order, with the result that Jesus recites the final verse of the paragraph before the first verse.

topos "love" occurs in it. Knowing the meaning of the Shema in the broader context of the Torah enables the lawyer to answer correctly to Jesus that "the one who showed mercy" (10:37) is the neighbor. Jesus then enjoins the lawyer to enact what he has been able to recite and understand (10:37). Here Jesus recontextualizes what it means in Deut 6:3 to "observe the commands diligently" (Deut 6:1, 3). Indeed, they are not to "put the LORD your God to the test" (Deut 6:16), but they are to "diligently keep the commandments of the Lord your God, and his decrees, and his statutes that he has commanded you" (Deut 6:17).

The story of the devil's testing of Jesus, therefore, begins with a response by Jesus that evokes the necessity not to exalt oneself but to humble oneself before God who gives food, progeny, and wealth to God's people. As the middle and ending of the story unfold, Jesus' responses evoke a new context for the challenge of the Shema. Since Jesus "loves the LORD his God with all his heart, soul, and mind," he refuses to bow down and worship the devil, and he refuses to test God by throwing himself off of the Temple. The Lukan story, then, reconfigures the story of Israel into the story of Jesus, and this story becomes an environment for recontextualization of the Shema within the story of the beginnings of Christianity.

Luke 4:14–7:35: The Poor, the Blind, the Leprous, the Dead, and the Deaf

When Jesus comes to his home synagogue in Nazareth, his recitation of Old Testament scripture shifts the *topoi* from remembering God's commandments in a context where one has become rich (Deut 6–8) to confronting God's people with special responsibilities for the poor, the captive, the blind, and the oppressed (Isa 61:1–2; 58:6). This is a shift from special *topoi* in the Deuteronomic history to special *topoi* in the prophets. By the end of Jesus' challenges to the people of Nazareth, he recites an abbreviated account of Elijah's beneficial visit to the widow of Zarephath in Sidon (Luke 4:25–26; cf. 1 Kgs 17:1–16) and Elisha's cleansing of the leprosy of Naaman the Syrian (Luke 4:27; cf. 2 Kgs 5:1–14).

The Lukan story amplifies some, but not all, of the *topoi* in 4:16–30 either in Luke or Acts. The Sermon on the Plain begins with a contrast between the blessed poor and the unfortunate rich (6:20–25) that sets the stage for special teaching about lending without expecting anything in return (6:34–35) and about giving that brings abundance (6:38). Later, Jesus presents highly developed argumentation about wealth, possessions, and unfailing treasure in heaven (12:13–34).[18] Still later, Jesus tells a parable and presents an argument about managing wealth (16:1–13), followed by a statement about the Pharisees' love of money (16:14) and a parable about a rich man who refuses to respond to the hunger and misery of a poor man covered with sores (16:19–31). After the parable of the rich ruler who comes to Jesus (18:18–25), Jesus discusses possessions and "following" with his disciples (18:26–30). This *topos* is developed further in the story of Zacchaeus (19:1–10), the parable of the ten pounds (19:11–27), a discussion of taxes (20:20–26), and the widow's offering (21:1–4). Thus, as is widely known, the Gospel of Luke develops the *topos* of poverty and wealth both with narrative description and with argumentative discourse.

The Greek Septuagint adds "regaining of sight to the blind" to the Hebrew of Isa 61:1, and Luke 4:18 and 7:22 include this *topos*.[19] The narrator gives a summary that includes Jesus' giving of sight to the blind in 7:21, a blind person receives his sight in a narrative account in 18:35–41, and there is an emphasis on Paul's being healed of blindness in Acts 9:17–18; 22:11–13. Thus, among the *topoi* in Luke 4:18–19, only "bringing good news to the poor" is full developed both in narrative and in argumentation, with some development of the giving of sight to blind people, which is present in the Greek Septuagint of Isa 61:1, as well as in Isa 35:5.

It is not clear who all the "oppressed" may be who are "set free" (Luke 4:18) in the Lukan story. Surprisingly, the Gospel of Luke shows no development of the *topos* of release of captives, except Barabbas who is released rather than Jesus (22:18–25). However in Acts, the second volume of the Lukan account, release from prison becomes a prominent feature in the narrative (Acts 12:6–10, 17, 16:23–27).

Jesus' reference to Elijah in Luke 4:25–26 implicitly evokes Elijah's bringing of unlimited food to the widow's household, and this *topos* may be enacted in Jesus' feeding of 5,000 in 9:10–17.[20] Elijah's raising of the son of the widow from death to life in 1 Kgs 17:17–24 is not only enacted in the narrative of the raising of a twelve year old girl (8:40–42, 49–56),[21] but more explicitly in the raising of the son of the widow of Nain earlier in the story (7:11–16). Jesus' reference to Elisha's cleansing of a leper in Luke 4:27 is embellished in Luke not only

---

[18] Abraham J. Malherbe, "The Christianization of a *Topos* (Luke 12:13–34)," *NovT* 38 (1996): 123–35.

[19] Both the Hebrew and the Greek Septuagint of Isa 35:5 refer to "the eyes of the blind" being opened in a context of healing the deaf, lame, and dumb.

[20] Notice Jesus' healing of people also in the context (Luke 9:11), similar to the range of benefits Elijah brought to the widow.

[21] Present also in Mark 5:21–24, 35–43//Matt 9:18–19, 23–26.

with the cleansing of the leper in 5:12–14, but also with the cleansing of ten lepers, one of whom is a Samaritan, in 17:11–19.

In Luke 7:22, Jesus restates the program of activity that Luke 4:16–30 introduced to the story. Jesus' restatement places the receiving of sight by the blind in a place of emphasis at the beginning and the poor having the good news preached to them at a place of emphasis at the end of the list.[22] In between, the Lukan Jesus lists: (a) the lame walk; (b) the lepers are cleansed; (c) the deaf hear; and (d) the dead are raised (7:22). Throughout both Luke and Acts there is no narrative of a deaf person receiving hearing. In turn, there is no story in Luke about a lame man being healed so he can walk, but Acts contains two such stories (3:1–10; 14:8–10) and a summary referring to many lame who were cured (8:7).

It is clear, then, that the Lukan story develops many of the *topoi* of Luke 4:16–30 both in narrative enactment and in argumentative discourse. Preaching good news to the poor, giving sight to the blind, healing lepers, and raising the dead become a programmatic part of Jesus' activity as the story unfolds. Release from prison and healing the lame are developed in Acts rather than the Gospel of Luke. Healing the deaf so they may hear is not enacted explicitly in a story or in an argument in Luke or Acts. Rather, at the end of Acts Paul asserts that "this people" "will never understand", because "their ears are hard of hearing" (Acts 28:27).

Luke 7:36–14:24: Eating with Pharisees

After Jesus' restatement of his activity in Luke 7:22, he dines three times in a house of a Pharisee (7:36–50; 11:35–54; 14:1–24). At these dinners, Jesus introduces *topoi* either from Deuteronomy or from Isaiah in a manner that transforms traditional "religious" issues into issues that concern social responsibility. Jesus' activity in these settings reconfigure emphases at the beginning of the prophetic book of Isaiah. In Isa 1:16–17, the prophet summarizes what the LORD says to the people with an emphasis on social responsibility:

> 1:16 Wash yourselves; make yourselves clean, 17 learn to do good; seek justice, rescue the oppressed, defend the orphan, plead for the widow.

Especially at the three dinners in a house of a Pharisee in Luke 7:36–14:35, Jesus confronts people in a manner similar to Isaiah's confrontation of the people of Israel. In each instance, Jesus criticizes a focus on

---

[22] Regularly, the emphatic positions are at the beginning and the end.

traditional "religious" issues that bypasses "social responsibilities." In the house of Simon the Pharisee, Simon raises a traditional religious issue concerning the association of a holy prophet with a sinner. In 7:41–43, Jesus transforms the "religious" issue into an issue of "forgiving a financial debt" (7:41). Forgiveness, then, concerns wealth, which is an issue that goes back to Deut 6, which Jesus recited to the devil in response to two of the tests (Luke 4:5–12). When Jesus asks Simon which debtor loves the creditor more (Luke 7:42), he has evoked the *topos* of "love" that is central to Deut 6–7. The *topos* of love is not only present in Deut 6:5 (the Shema) but continues into Deut 7, where the assertion is made that the Lord brought Israel out of Egypt, "because the Lord loved you" (7:8) and the Lord is "the faithful God who maintains covenant loyalty with those who love him" (7:9). In Deut 7:13, the assertion is made that if you heed the Lord's ordinances, "he will love you, bless you, and multiply you." He will bless the fruit of your womb, ground, grain, wine, oil, cattle, and flock. Indeed, "you shall be the most blessed of people" (7:14), including the removal of illness and disease (7:15). When Jesus responds to Simon, he is developing a *topos* that the testing of Jesus by the devil implicitly introduced into Lukan discourse. When Jesus' response to Simon turns Simon's concerns about "sinfulness" into the topic of "love," which concerns God's giving of abundant wealth, the woman's willingness to anoint Jesus' feet with expensive ointment (Luke 7:37–38, 46) emerges as a paradigmatic instance of "love" (7:47). The woman, Jesus asserts, knows how to enact love by multiple acts of generosity with oil, an item which is actually mentioned as one of God's "blessings" in abundance to Israel in Deut 7:13. Forgiveness of debts and generosity with one's possessions must have priority as one begins to discuss sinfulness and forgiveness.

At the second dinner, where the Pharisee is concerned that Jesus did not wash his hands before he ate (another "traditional religious issue"), Jesus addresses the following topics:
1. give for alms those things which are within (11:41);
2. do not neglect justice and the love of God (11:42);
3. do not load people with burdens hard to bear (11:46);
4. do not kill and build tombs for prophets [who hold the people of Israel responsible for social and economic expressions of love] (11:47–48);
5. do not take away the key of knowledge (11:52).

This list embellishes the central *topos* of "love of God" in Deut 6:5 with the *topos* of "justice" from Isa 1:17. In the final assertion by Jesus about "the key of knowledge," we recognize the *topos* of "knowing, remembering, and doing" that lies in Deut 8:2–5. Jesus' list, then, builds upon and expands *topoi* central to Deut 6–8 and Isaiah.

At Jesus' last dinner in the house of a ruling Pharisee, his actions begin with healing (14:2–4) in a manner that reconfigures Deut 7:15: The LORD will turn away from you every illness. In Luke 14, the illness of dropsy is a symbol of greed, which is based on the insatiable thirst and hunger of a man with this disease.[23] When Jesus heals the dropsy, he is symbolically healing the illness of greed in the presence of people of wealth. As Jesus interprets the significance of what he has done, he addresses the *topos* of "honor," which is a widespread Mediterranean value, with the argumentative *topos*: "All who exalt themselves will be humbled, and those who humble themselves will be exalted" (Luke 14:11). As we recall, the *topos* of humbling oneself and being exalted is central to Deut 8:3, 14–19. Once the people of Israel receive all their wealth, they must not "exalt themselves" but "humble themselves" before God. This leads into the specific *topoi* of Isaiah concerning "the poor, the maimed, the lame, the blind" (Luke 14:13), which is a Lukan reconfiguration of Isa 61 and 35. Then Jesus asserts that "you will be blessed" (Luke 14:14), which is a reconfiguration of the assertions about being blessed both in Deut 7:13–14 and Isa 61:9. In response to a man who said, "Blessed is he who shall eat bread in the kingdom of God!", Jesus responded with a parable that emphasizes once more the Lukan reconfiguration of Isaiah with a command to "bring in the poor and maimed and blind and lame" (14:21). Luke 14:1–24 presents the highpoint of Jesus' encounter of the Pharisees with the Deuteronomic-Isaiah program of redemption. Jesus' statements at the third and final dinner in a Pharisee's house make it clear that "household" activity is "public" activity that must meet the test of justice and love, which combines emphases in Deuteronomy with emphases in Isaiah, rather than a test of friendship among the wealthy.

Luke 15: Seeking and Saving the Lost

When the Lukan story reaches Luke 15, another *topos* moves into the center: seeking and saving the lost. The socio-rhetorical resource for this *topos* is Ezek 34, where God's word comes to the prophet in a context after the destruction of Jerusalem and its Temple. After Jerusalem and the Temple were destroyed, God's people were scattered throughout the world. In this context, one must not only heal, but one must seek, find, and save the lost who are scattered hither and yon

---

[23] Willi Braun, *Feasting and Social Rhetoric in Luke 14* (SNTSMS 85; Cambridge: Cambridge University Press, 1995).

across the face of the earth. The words of Ezek 34:11–12, 16, responding to the abuse of the people by the leaders of Israel (Ezek 34:3–10), present a challenge to Israel that moves one step beyond the program of Isaiah:

> 11: For thus says the LORD God: I myself will search for my sheep, and will seek them out. 12: As shepherds seek out their flocks when they are among their scattered sheep, so I will seek out my sheep. I will rescue them, from all the places to which they have been scattered on a day of clouds and thick darkness.... 16: I will seek the lost, and I will bring back the strayed, and I will bind up the injured, and I will strengthen the weak, but the fat and the strong I will destroy. I will feed them with justice.

Rather than reciting some portion of Ezek 34 to the Pharisees and scribes who were "grumbling" at Jesus' welcoming and eating with tax collectors and sinners (Luke 15:1–2), Jesus recites a parable that enacts the central *topoi* of Ezek 34. In a context where even one sheep is lost, a shepherd will leave the flock and seek it until he finds it (Luke 15:4). When he finds it, he will rejoice, because he has found the one who was lost (Luke 15:6). The setting for the parable (Luke 15:2) and the ending statement by Jesus (15:7) renew the *topos* of "sinfulness" in Jesus' first dinner in the house of a Pharisee (7:37, 39, 47–49). Still concerned with "sinfulness," the Pharisees and scribes grumble at Jesus' activity, this time at his acceptance of tax collectors and sinners rather than with one specific sinful woman. Occurring immediately after Luke 14, Jesus' description of the "one sinner who repents" evokes an image of a person who is "humble" rather than "exalted" (14:11). With the image of the "shepherd" seeking the lost one, a new *topos* emerges in the midst of the Deuteronomy-Isaiah program, and the primary socio-rhetorical resource for this *topos* is Ezek 34.

After telling the parable of the shepherd with a hundred sheep, Jesus turns to a woman with only ten silver coins. Losing one of them, she lights a lamp, sweeps the house, and searches carefully until she finds it (15:8). At this point, she calls her friends and neighbors together to rejoice, since she has found the coin that was lost. Once again, then, Jesus introduces wealth, or the meagerness of wealth, as a *topos*. The woman exemplifies a person to whom wealth is not abundant. As she rejoices with others over the coin that was lost, she moves the *topos* of sinfulness (15:10) one step toward the issue of wealth, or the lack of it.

Luke 15:1–32 begins with the *topos* of property and the dividing of property among sons. In a context where the younger son "sins against heaven and his earthly father" (15:18, 21) by wasting all his possessions (15:13–14), he returns to his father. The result of the repentant return is the bestowal of gifts of wealth and celebration by the father. This story reconfigures the commands to Israel in Deut 6–8 through the *topos* of seeking and saving the lost in Ezek 34. The father embodies the attributes of a shepherd who will "rescue" (Ezek 34:12) and "feed" (34:13–14) the lost, "bring back the strayed and bind up the injured" (34:16) rather than simply "clothe himself" (34:3), while failing to "bring back the strayed" (34:4). The parable of the prodigal son, then, exhibits a father who embodies the attributes of the shepherd God asks people to be in Ezek 34, rather than the attributes of the shepherds who abuse their people and fail to seek them out when they are lost.

Luke 16–18 elaborate, amplify, and integrate the *topoi* of Deuteronomy 6–8 and Isaiah in a context oriented toward the seeking and saving of the lost. Luke 16:1–8 focuses on a manager of money and follows with an elaboration that ends with the assertion that one cannot serve God and wealth (16:13). The *topos* of "serving God," we recall, is central to Deut 6 (cf. 6:13). The chapter continues with a description of the Pharisees as "lovers of money" (16:14), and when Jesus tells them that "God knows their hearts" (16:15), the story is developing *topoi* central to Deut 6–8 in this new context. The parable of the Rich man and Lazarus (16:19–31) ends with an appeal to "listen to Moses and the prophets" (16:31), the parable of the Widow and the Unjust judge features a God who will "grant justice to his chosen ones who cry out" (cf. Isa 1:17), and the parable of the Pharisee and the Tax Collector paradigmatically exhibits, as mentioned above, the principle from Deut 8:2–3 about the necessity to humble oneself (Luke 18:14). The story of the Rich ruler who came to Jesus, knowing the commandments (Luke 18:20; cf. Deut 6, 8), yet being unwilling to sell his possessions and give the money to the poor (Luke 18:22), sets the stage for a discussion of the relation of Jesus' followers to possessions (18:28–30). Throughout all of this, the Lukan story explores how "those who are lost may be found" and "those who have wealth" may learn to "seek and save the lost."

Luke 19:1–10 presents the climax of the section on seeking and saving the lost (15:1–19:10). Zacchaeus, who is both rich (blessed by the standards of Israel) and a chief tax collector (lost to the house of Israel), welcomes Jesus into his house and explains that he gives half of his possessions to the poor and, if he defrauds anyone, he pays it back fourfold (19:8). When Jesus sees how this person, who is "lost" in the eyes of the Pharisees, embodies the attributes of a rich man who gives generously to the poor and corrects any injustice that occurs, Jesus pronounces him "a son of Abraham." In Jewish tradition, Abraham is the model of a wealthy man who remained generous all his life.[24] The

---

[24] See, for instance, the *Testament of Abraham*.

story ends with Jesus' assertion that "the Son of man came to seek out and to save the lost" (19:10), recalling the *topos* he had introduced in the parable of the shepherd who, having lost one sheep, sought it until he found it (15:4). At this point in the story, the *topos* of seeking, finding, and saving the lost from Ezek 34 reaches its highpoint and conclusion before the transitional parable of the ten pounds that introduces the violent dynamics of the passion narrative in Luke 19:28–23:56.

Conclusion

It is well known that the Gospel of Luke features Isa 61:1–2 at the beginning of Jesus' ministry, by having him recite it in his hometown synagogue in Nazareth. This essay has shown that the socio-rhetorical program of Luke really begins with Jesus' responses to the devil in the context of being tested in the wilderness. The recontextualization of verses from Deut 6 and 8 in this context is an initial step in a program where Jesus will challenge the leaders of Israel in his day to fulfill not only the commandments of God in Deuteronomy but the reconfiguration of those commandments in the prophetic words of Isaiah and the healing actions of Elijah and Elisha. But even this is not enough. In Luke 15, Jesus' discourse introduces central *topoi* from Ezek 34 that move the program into the controversial action of "seeking and saving the lost." In Luke, then, social reform is not only a matter of seeking justice for the poor and downtrodden, it is also a matter of reworking one's stereotypes so that sinners, outcasts, and unacceptable people of all kinds are "sought out" for the purpose of finding them, welcoming them, and bringing them into the "houses" where God offers healing, inclusion, and salvation.

The Major Writings of Vernon K. Robbins
Winship Distinguished Research Professor of Religion in the Humanities, Emory University

Books

Jesus the Teacher: A Socio-Rhetorical Interpretation of Mark. Philadelphia: Fortress, 1984.
Patterns of Persuasion in the Gospels, with Burton L. Mack. Sonoma, Calif.: Polebridge, 1989; Eugene, Ore.: Wipf & Stock, 2008.
Ancient Quotes and Anecdotes: From Crib to Crypt. Sonoma, Calif.: Polebridge, 1989.
Jesus the Teacher: A Socio-Rhetorical Interpretation of Mark. Paperback edition with new introduction and additional indexes. Minneapolis: Fortress, 1992; Fortress ex libris, 2009.
The Rhetoric of Pronouncement. Edited by Vernon K. Robbins. Semeia 64. Atlanta: Scholars, 1993.
New Boundaries in Old Territory: Form and Social Rhetoric in Mark. Edited and introduced by David B. Gowler. New York: Peter Lang, 1994.
The Tapestry of Early Christian Discourse: Rhetoric, Society and Ideology. London: Routledge, 1996.
Exploring the Texture of Texts: A Guide to Socio-Rhetorical Interpretation. Valley Forge, Pa.: Trinity Press International, 1996.
The Invention of Christian Discourse. Volume 1. Rhetoric of Religious Antiquity 1; Blandford Forum, UK: Deo Publishing, 2009.
Sea Voyages and Beyond: Emerging Strategies in Socio-Rhetorical Interpretation. Emory Studies in Early Christianity 14. Blandford Forum, UK: Deo Publishing, 2010.

Edited Volumes

Books Edited as Editor of Emory Studies in Early Christianity

Peter Lang volumes:

Gowler, David B. *Host, Guest, Enemy, and Friend: Portraits of the Pharisees in Luke and Acts*. Emory Studies in Early Christianity 1. New York: Peter Lang, 1991. Repr. Eugene, Ore.: Wipf & Stock, 2007.

Merritt, H. Wayne. *In Word and Deed: Moral Integrity in Paul.* Emory Studies in Early Christianity 2. New York: Peter Lang, 1993.

Scholars Press volumes:

Botha, Jan. *Subject to Whose Authority? Multiple Readings of Romans 13.* Emory Studies in Early Christianity 4. Atlanta: Scholars, 1994.

Morland, Kjell Arne. *The Rhetoric of Curse in Galatians: Paul Confronts a Different Gospel.* Emory Studies in Early Christianity 5. Atlanta: Scholars, 1995.

Borgen, Peder, Vernon K. Robbins, and David B. Gowler, eds. *Recruitment, Conquest, and Conflict: Strategies in Judaism, Early Christianity, and the Greco-Roman World.* Emory Studies in Early Christianity 6. Atlanta: Scholars, 1998.

Trinity Press volumes:

Given, Mark. *Paul's True Rhetoric: Ambiguity, Cunning, and Deception in Greece and Rome.* Emory Studies in Early Christianity 7. Harrisburg, Pa.: Trinity Press International, 2000.

Eriksson, Anders, Thomas H. Olbrich, and Walter Übelacker, eds. *Rhetorical Argumentation in Biblical Texts.* Emory Studies in Early Christianity 8. Harrisburg, Pa.: Trinity Press International, 2002.

James D. Hester and J. David Hester (Amador), eds. *Rhetorics and Hermeneutics: Wilhelm Wuellner and His Influence.* Emory Studies in Early Christianity 9. New York/London: T & T Clark, 2004.

Todd Penner. *In Praise of Christian Origins: Stephen and the Hellenists in Lukan Apologetic Historiography.* Emory Studies in Early Christianity 10. New York/London: T & T Clark, 2004.

Thomas H. Olbricht and Anders Eriksson, eds. *Rhetoric, Ethic, and Moral Persuasion in Biblical Discourse.* Emory Studies in Early Christianity 11. New York/London: T & T Clark, 2005.

Lynn R. Huber. *Like a Bride Adorned: Reading Metaphor in John's Apocalypse.* Emory Studies in Early Christianity 12. New York/London: T & T Clark, 2007.

Articles and Chapters in Books

★ "*Dynameis* and *Semeia* in Mark." *Biblical Research* 18 (1973): 1–16.
★ "The Healing of Blind Bartimaeus (Mark 10:46–52) in the Markan Theology." *Journal of Biblical Literature* 92 (1973): 224–43.
"The We-Passages in Acts and Ancient Sea Voyages." *Biblical Research* 20 (1975): 5–18.
★ "Last Meal – Preparation, Betrayal, and Absence – Mark 14:12–25." Pages 21–40 in *The Passion in Mark*, ed. W. Kelber. Philadelphia: Fortress, 1976.
★★ "By Land and By Sea: The We-Passages and Ancient Sea Voyages.," Pages 215–242 in *Perspectives on Luke-Acts*. Ed. C.H. Talbert. Perspectives in Religious Studies, Special Studies Series, no. 5. Macon, Ga.: Mercer University Press and Edinburgh: T.& T. Clark, 1978.
"Pronouncement Stories in Plutarch's Lives of *Alexander* and *Julius Caesar*." Pages 21–38 in *Society of Biblical Literature Seminar Papers* 17. Vol. 2. Edited by. P.J. Achtemeier. Missoula, Mont.: Scholars, 1978.
"Structuralism in Biblical Interpretation and Theology." *The Thomist* 42 (1978): 349–72.
"Prefaces in Greco-Roman Biography and Luke-Acts." *Perspectives in Religious Studies* 6 (1979): 94–108.
★ "Mark as Genre." Pages 371–99 in *Society of Biblical Literature Seminar Papers* 19. Edited by P.J. Achtemeier. Chico, Calif.: Scholars, 1980.
"Rhetoric and Biblical Criticism." With John H. Patton. *Quarterly Journal of Speech* 66 (1980): 327–37.
★ "Summons and Outline in Mark: The Three-Step Progression." *Novum Testamentum* 23 (1981): 97–114. Reprinted as pages 103–20 in *The Composition of Mark's Gospel: Selected Studies from Novum Testamentum*. Leiden: Brill, 1999.
"Laudation Stories in the Gospel of Luke and Plutarch's *Alexander*." Pages 293–308 in *Society of Biblical Literature Seminar Papers* 20. Edited by K.H. Richards. Chico, Calif.: Scholars, 1981.
"Classifying Pronouncement Stories in Plutarch's *Parallel Lives*." *Semeia* 20 (1981): 29–52.
★ "Mark I.14–20: An Interpretation at the Intersection of Jewish and Graeco-Roman Traditions." *New Testament Studies* 28 (1982): 220–36.
"Pronouncement Stories and Jesus' Blessing of the Children: A Rhetorical Approach." Pages 407–30 in *Society of Biblical Literature Seminar Papers* 21. Edited by K.H. Richards. Chico, Calif.: Scholars, 1982.
★ "Pronouncement Stories and Jesus' Blessing of the Children: A Rhetorical Approach." *Semeia* 29 (1983): 43–74.
"A Rhetorical Typology for Classifying and Analyzing Pronouncement Stories." Pages 93–122 in *Society of Biblical Literature Seminar Papers* 23. Edited by K.H. Richards. Chico, Calif.: Scholars, 1984.
★★ "Picking Up the Fragments: From Crossan's Analysis to Rhetorical Analysis." *Forum* 1.2 (1985): 31–64.
"Pragmatic Relations as a Criterion for Authentic Sayings." *Forum* 1.3 (1985): 35–63.

★ "The Woman who Touched Jesus' Garment: Socio-Rhetorical Analysis of the Synoptic Accounts." *New Testament Studies* 33 (1987): 502–15.
★ "Rhetorical Argument about Lamps and Light in Early Christian Gospels." Pages 177–95 in *Context, Festskrift til Peder Johan Borgen*. Edited by Peter Wilhelm Böckman and Roald E. Kristiansen. *Relieff* 24. Universitetet i Trondheim: Tapir, 1987.
"The Chreia." Pages 1–23 in *Greco-Roman Literature and the New Testament*. Edited by David E. Aune. Atlanta: Scholars, 1988.
"The Crucifixion and the Speech of Jesus." *Forum* 4.1 (1988): 33–46.
"Pronouncement Stories from a Rhetorical Perspective." *Forum* 4.2 (1988): 3–32.
★ "Interpreting the Gospel of Mark as a Jewish Document in a Graeco-Roman World." Pages 47–72 in *New Perspectives on Ancient Judaism*. Edited by Paul V.M. Flesher. Lanham, Md.: University Press of America, 1990.
"A Socio-Rhetorical Response: Contexts of Interaction and Forms of Exhortation." Pages 261–71 in *Paraenesis: Act and Form*. *Semeia* 50. Atlanta: Scholars, 1990.
"Text and Context in Recent Studies of the Gospel of Mark." *Religious Studies Review* 17 (1991): 16–23.
★★ "The Social Location of the Implied Author of Luke-Acts." Pages 305–32 in *The Social World of Luke-Acts: Models for Interpretation*. Edited by Jerome H. Neyrey. Peabody, Mass.: Hendrickson, 1991.
★★ "Writing as a Rhetorical Act in Plutarch and the Gospels." Pages 157–86 in *Persuasive Artistry: Studies in New Testament Rhetoric in Honor of George A. Kennedy*. Edited by Duane F. Watson. Sheffield: JSOT, 1991.
"From New Criticism and the New Hermeneutic to Poststructuralism: Twentieth Century Hermeneutics." Pages 225–80 in *Reading The Text: Biblical Criticism and Literary Theory*. With Robert Detweiler. Edited by Stephen Prickett. Oxford: Basil Blackwell, 1991.
"Luke-Acts: A Mixed Population Seeks a Home in the Roman Empire." Pages 202–21 in *Images of Empire*. Edited by Loveday Alexander. Sheffield: JSOT, 1991.
"Beelzebul Controversy in Mark and Luke: Rhetorical and Social Analysis." *Forum* 7.3–4 (1991): 261–77.
"Introduction to the Paperback Edition." Pages xix-xliv in *Jesus the Teacher: A Socio-Rhetorical Interpretation of Mark*. Minneapolis: Fortress, 1992.
"A Socio-Rhetorical Look at the Work of John Knox on Luke-Acts." Pages 91–105 in *Cadbury, Knox, and Talbert: American Contributions to the Study of Acts*. Edited by Mikeal C. Parsons and Joseph B. Tyson. Atlanta: Scholars, 1992.
★★ "The Reversed Contextualization of Psalm 22 in the Markan Crucifixion: A Socio-Rhetorical Analysis." Pages 1161–83 in *The Four Gospels 1992. Festschrift Frans Neirynck*. Edited by F. van Segbroeck, C.M. Tuckett, G. Van Belle, J. Verheyden. Vol. 2. BETL 100. Leuven: Leuven University Press, 1992.
"Apophthegm." Pages 307–9 in *The Anchor Bible Dictionary*. Edited by David Noel Freedman. Vol. 1. New York: Doubleday, 1992.

"Form Criticism: New Testament." Pages 841–4 in *The Anchor Bible Dictionary*. Edited by David Noel Freedman. Vol. 2. New York: Doubleday, 1992.

"Using a Socio-Rhetorical Poetics to Develop a Unified Method: The Woman who Anointed Jesus as a Test Case." Pages 302–19 in *1992 SBL Seminar Papers*. Edited by Eugene H. Lovering, Jr. Atlanta: Scholars, 1992.

"A Male Reads a Feminist Reading: The Dialogical Nature of Pippin's Power." Pages 211–17 in *Semeia* 59. Edited by David Jobling. Atlanta: Scholars, 1992.

"Progymnastic Rhetorical Composition and Pre-Gospel Traditions: A New Approach." Pages 111–47 in *The Synoptic Gospels: Source Criticism and the New Literary Criticism*. Edited by Camille Focant. BETL 110. Leuven: Leuven University Press, 1993.

*** "Rhetoric and Culture: Exploring Types of Cultural Rhetoric in a Text." Pages 443–63 in *Rhetoric and the New Testament: Essays from the 1992 Heidelberg Conference*. Edited by Stanley E. Porter and Thomas H. Olbricht. Sheffield: JSOT, 1993.

"Introduction: Using Rhetorical Discussions of the Chreia to Interpret Pronouncement Stories." Pages vii–xvii in *The Rhetoric of Pronouncement*. Semeia 64. Atlanta: Scholars, 1993.

"Paradigms in Homer, Pindar, the Tragedians, and the New Testament." With Øvind Andersen. Pages 3–31 in *The Rhetoric of Pronouncement*. Semeia 64. Atlanta: Scholars Press, 1993.

"Biblical Sources for Pronouncement Stories in the Gospels." With Miriam Dean-Otting. Pages 95–115 in *The Rhetoric of Pronouncement*. Semeia 64. Atlanta: Scholars, 1993.

"The Ritual of Reading and Reading a Text as a Ritual: Observations on Mieke Bal's *Death & Dissymmetry*." Pages 385–401 in *In Good Company: Essays in Honor of Robert Detweiler*. Edited by David Jasper and Mark Ledbetter. Atlanta: Scholars, 1994.

** "Socio-Rhetorical Criticism: Mary, Elizabeth, and the Magnificat as a Test Case." Pages 164–209 in *The New Literary Criticism and the New Testament*. Edited by Elizabeth Struthers Malbon and Edgar V. McKnight. Sheffield: Sheffield Academic, 1994.

*** "Interpreting Miracle Culture and Parable Culture in Mark 4–11." *Svensk Exegetisk Årsbok* 59 (1994): 59–81.

"Oral, Rhetorical, and Literary Cultures: A Response." *Semeia* 65 (1994): 75–91.

** "Social-Scientific Criticism and Literary Studies: Prospects for Cooperation in Biblical Interpretation." Pages 274–89 in *Modelling Early Christianity: Social-Scientific Studies of the New Testament in Its Context*. Edited by Philip F. Esler. London: Routledge, 1995.

"Divine Dialogue and the Lord's Prayer: Socio-Rhetorical Interpretation of Sacred Texts." *Dialogue* 28 (1995): 117–46.

"Foreword." Pages xiii–xvii in *The Structure and Persuasive Power of Mark: A Linguistic Approach*, by John G, Cook. Atlanta: Scholars, 1995.

"Narrative in Ancient Rhetoric and Rhetoric in Ancient Narrative." Pages 368–84 in *Society of Biblical Literature Seminar Papers* 35. Atlanta: Scholars, 1996.

"The Dialectical Nature of Early Christian Discourse." *Scriptura* 59 (1996): 353–62.

"Making Christian Culture in the Epistle of James." *Scriptura* 59 (1996): 341–51.

** "The Present and Future of Rhetorical Analysis." Pages 24–52 in *The Rhetorical Analysis of Scripture: Essays from the 1995 London Conference*. Edited by Stanley E. Porter and Thomas H. Olbricht. Journal for the Study of the New Testament Supplement Series 146. Sheffield: Sheffield Academic Press, 1997.

"Rhetorical Composition and Sources in the Gospel of Thomas." Pages 86–114 in *Society of Biblical Literature 1997 Seminar Papers* 36. Atlanta: Scholars, 1997.

"Socio-Rhetorical Hermeneutics and Commentary." Pages 284–97 in *EPI TO AYTO. Essays in Honour of Petr Pokorny on his Sixty-Fifth Birthday*. Edited by J. Mrazek, S. Brodsky, and R. Dvorakova. Praha-Trebenice: Mlyn, 1998.

"Historical, Literary, Linguistic, Cultural, and Artistic Intertextuality – A Response." *Semeia* 80 (1997): 291–303.

** "From Enthymeme to Theology in Luke 11:1–13." Pages 191–214 in *Literary Studies in Luke-Acts: A Collection of Essays in Honor of Joseph B. Tyson*. Edited by Richard P. Thompson and Thomas E. Phillips. Macon, Ga.: Mercer University Press, 1998.

"Enthymemic Texture in the Gospel of Thomas." Pages 343–88 in *Society of Biblical Literature 1998 Seminar Papers* 37. Atlanta: Scholars, 1998.

"Response" and "Dialogue between Vernon Robbins and Reviews." *Journal for the Study of the New Testament* 70 (1998): 101–15.

"The Claims of the Prologues and Greco-Roman Rhetoric: The Prefaces to Luke and Acts in Light of Greco-Roman Rhetorical Strategies." Pages 63–83 in *Jesus and the Heritage of Israel: Luke's Narrative Claim upon Israel's Legacy*. Edited by David P. Moessner. Harrisburg, Penn.: Trinity Press International, 1999.

"Rhetorical Ritual: Apocalyptic Discourse in Mark 13." Pages 95–121 in *Vision and Persuasion: Rhetorical Dimensions of Apocalyptic Discourse*. Edited by Gregory Carey and L. Gregory Bloomquist. St. Louis: Chalice, 1999.

** "The Socio-Rhetorical Role of Old Testament Scripture in Luke 4–19." Pages 81–93 in *Z Noveho Zakona /From the New Testament: Sbornik k narozeninam Prof. ThDr. Zdenka Sazavy*. Edited by Hana Tonzarova and Petr Melmuk. Praha: Vydala Cirkev ceskoslovenska husitska, 2001.

"Why Participate in African Biblical Interpretation?" Pages 275-91 in *Interpreting the New Testament in Africa*. Edited by Mary N. Getui, Tinyiko S. Maluleke, and Justin Ukpong. Nairobi, Kenya: Acton Publishers, 2001.

"The Rhetorical Full-Turn in Biblical Interpretation: Reconfiguring Rhetorical-Political Analysis." Pages 48–60 in *Rhetorical Criticism and the Bible: Essays from the 1998 Florence Conference*. Edited by Stanley E. Porter and Thomas H. Olbricht. Journal for the Study of the New Testament Supplement Series 195. Sheffield: Sheffield Academic Press, 2002.

"Argumentative Textures in Socio-Rhetorical Interpretation." Pages 27–65 in *Rhetorical Argumentation in Biblical Texts: Essays from the Lund 2000 Conference*. Edited by Anders Eriksson, Thomas H. Olbricht, and Walter Übelacker. Emory Studies in Early Christianity. Harrisburg: Trinity Press International, 2002.

"A Comparison of Mishnah Gittin 1:1–2:2 and James 2:1–13 from a Perspective of Greco-Roman Rhetorical Elaboration." Pages 201–16 in *Mishnah and the Social Formation of the Early Rabbinic Guild: A Socio-Rhetorical Approach*, by Jack N. Lightstone. Studies in Christianity and Judaism/Études sur le christianisme et le judaïsme 11. Waterloo: Wilfrid Laurier University Press for the Canadian Corporation for Studies in Religion/Corporation Canadienne des Sciences Religieuses, 2002.

"The Intertexture of Apocalyptic Discourse in the Gospel of Mark." Pages 11–44 in *The Intertexture of Apocalyptic Discourse in the New Testament*. Edited by Duane F. Watson. Atlanta: Scholars/Leiden: E. J. Brill, 2002.

"The Legacy of 2 Corinthians 12:2–4 in the *Apocalypse of Paul*." Pages 327–39 in *Paul and the Corinthians*. Edited by J. K. Elliott and Trevor J. Burke. Leiden: Brill, 2003.

"A Prolegomenon to the Relation of the Qur'an and the Bible." With Gordon D. Newby. Pages 23–42 in *Bible and Qur'an: Essays in Scriptural Intertextuality*. Edited by John C. Reeves. Atlanta, Society of Biblical Literature, 2003.

"The Sensory-Aesthetic Texture of the Compassionate Samaritan Parable in Luke 10," Pages 247-64 in *Literary Encounters with the Reign of God*. Edited by Sharon H. Ringe and H. C. Paul Kim. New York/London: T & T Clark, 2004.

"Where is Wuellner's Anti-Hermeneutical Hermeneutic Taking Us? From Scheiermacher to Thistleton and Beyond." Pages 105-25 in *Rhetorics and Hermeneutics: Wilhelm Wuellner and His Influence*. Edited by James D. Hester and J. David Hester (Amador). Emory Studies in Early Christianity 9. New York/London: T & T Clark, 2004.

"The Rhetorical Full-Turn in Biblical Interpretation and Its Relevance for Feminist Hermeneutics." Pages 109-27 in *Her Master's Tools?* Edited by Caroline Vander Stichele and Todd Penner. Global Perspectives on Biblical Scholarship 9; Atlanta: SBL and Leiden: Brill, 2005.

"From Heidelberg to Heidelberg: Rhetorical Interpretation of the Bible at the Seven 'Pepperdine' Conferences from 1992-2003." Pages 335-77 in *Rhetoric, Ethics, and Moral Persuasion in Biblical Discourse*. Edited by T.H. Olbricht and Anders Eriksson. New York/London: T & T Clark, 2005.

"Lukan and Johannine Tradition in the Qur'an: A Story of *Auslegungsgeschichte* and *Wirkungsgeschichte*." Pages 336-48 in *Moving Beyond New Testament Theology? Essays in Conversation with Heikki Räisänen*. Edited by Todd Penner and Caroline Vander Stichele. Publications of the Finnish Exegetical Society 88; Helsinki: Finnish Exegetical Society and Göttingen: Vandenhoeck & Ruprecht, 2005.

"Bodies and Politics in Luke 1-2 and Sirach 44-50: Men, Women, and Boys." *Scriptura* 90 (2005): 724-838.

"Enthymeme and Picture in the Gospel of Thomas," Pages 175-207 in *Thomasine Traditions in Antiquity: The Social and Cultural World of the Gospel of Thomas*. Edited by Jon Ma. Asgeirsson, April D. DeConick, and Risto Uro. Nag Hammadi and Manichaean Studies 59; Leiden: Brill, 2006.

"Interfaces of Orality and Literature in the Gospel of Mark." Pages 125-46 in *Performing the Gospel: Orality, Memory, and Mark*. Edited by Richard A. Horsley, Jonathan A. Draper, John Miles Foley. Minneapolis: Fortress Press, 2006.

"Oral Performance in Q: Epistemology, Political Conflict, and Contextual Register." Pages 109-22 in *Oral Performance, Popular Tradition, and Hidden Transcript in Q*. Edited by Richard A. Horsley. Semeia Studies 60; Atlanta: SBL, 2006.

"Conceptual Blending and Early Christian Imagination." Pages 161-95 in *Explaining Christian Origins and Early Judaism: Contributions from Cognitive and Social Science*. Edited by Petri Luomanen, Ilkka Pyysiäinen, and Risto Uro. Biblical Interpretation Series 89; Leiden/Boston: Brill, 2007.

"Response – Using Bakhtin's *Lexicon Dialogicae* to Interpret Canon, Apocalyptic, New Testament, and Toni Morrison." Pages 187-203 in *Bakhtin and Genre Theory in Biblical Studies*. Edited by Roland Boer. Semeia Studies 63; Atlanta: SBL, 2007.

"Rhetography: A New Way of Seeing the Familiar Text." Pages 81-106 in *Words Well Spoken: George Kennedy's Rhetoric of the New Testament*. Edited by C. Clifton Black and Duane F. Watson. Studies in Rhetoric and Religion 8; Waco: Baylor University Press, 2008.

"Comparative Sacred Texts and Interactive Reading: Another Alternative to the 'World Religions' Class." With Laurie L. Patton and Gordon D. Newby. *Teaching Theology and Religion* 12.1 (Jan. 2009): 37-49.

"Socio-Rhetorical Interpretation," in *Blackwell Companion to the New Testament*. Edited by David E. Aune. London: Blackwell, 2009.

"Socio-Rhetorical Interpretation of Miracle Discourse in the Synoptic Gospels," in *The Role of Miracle Discourse in the Argumentation of the New Testament*. Edited by Duane F. Watson. Symposium; Atlanta: SBL, 2010.

* The items marked with one asterisk denote essays found in *New Boundaries in Old Territory*.

** The items marked with two asterisks denote essays found in this volume.

*** The items marked with three asterisks denote the two essays that were revised and combined into the version now found in Chapter 4 of this volume.

Index of Names

Abercrombie, N. 116
Abrahams, Roger 204
Achtemeier, Paul J. 158
Alexander, Loveday 104, *109-111*, 113, *129*
Altenbaumer, James E. 291
Aly, W. 60
Andreski, A. 140
Armstrong-Reiner, David 349
Aune, David E. 41, 337

Bailey, Kenneth E. 362
Bakhtin, Mikhail M. 3, 8, 12, *23*, 24, 28, 30-31, 34, 36-37, 42-43, 108, 258, 261, 274, 276, 321
Bal, Mieke 292, 319-320
Barrett, C.K. 84
Barth, Fredrik 154, 171
Barthes, Roland 258
Bascom, Willard 64
Bauckham, Richard 109-110
Berger, Peter 8, 115-116
Betz, Hans Dieter 36, 287-288, 325, *343-345*, 347
Beucheler, F. 53
Bhabha, Homi K. 155, 311
Billerbeck, P. 28
Bizzell, Patricia 186, 197, 200, 324
Bloomquist, L. Gregory 12, 349
Bonner, Stanley F. 25, 204, 222, 236, 245

Bonz, Marianne Palmer 87, 104, *106-109*, 110-111, 113
Booth, Wayne C. 327
Borg, Marcus 18
Boring, Eugene 22
Bornkamm, Günther 25
Bouvard, Margarite 155, 310
Braun, Willi 43, 291, 317, 368, 370, 381
Brawley, Robert L. 107
Brenner, Athalya 302, 308
Brodie, Thomas L. 107
Brown, Dan 99
Brown, Peter 288
Brown, Raymond E. 28-29, 31, 300-301, 304
Brown, Schuyler 83
Bruss, E. 145
Bultmann, Rudolf 25, 284, 344
Bundy, Walter E. 78
Burke, Kenneth 21, 32, 145, 147, 290, 292
Butts, James R. 236-237

Cadbury, Henry J. 64, 87, 107
Cameron, Howard D. 52
Cameron, Ron 352
Campbell, David A. 52
Campbell, William Sanger 97-100
Caputo, John D. 88
Carney, Thomas F. 9, 118, 125, 128, 140
Carruth, Shawn 352, 355
Carter, Warren 34
Casson, Lionel 64

Castelli, Elizabeth 36, 38, 346-347
Catchpole, David 362
Chatman, Seymour 118
Chopp, Rebecca S. 351
Chotard, Henry 59
Chronis, Harry L. 278
Clark, Katerina 37
Combrink, H. J. Bernard 12, 39, 349
Conley, Thomas 210, 324
Conzelmann, Hans 25, 71, 87
Coulter, Cornelia C. 64
Craddock, Fred B. 353
Crockett, L.C. 372
Crossan, John Dominic 16-22, *190-196, 202-203, 205-208*, 210, 212, *216-227, 230-232*, 238, 259-260
Cullmann, O. 284
Culpepper, R. Alan 349

Davis, David B. 315, 351
de Cervantes, Miguel 1
Dean, Margaret E. 349
Delbrueck, Richard 64
Delorme, Jean 259, 261
Derrida, Jacques 99
Detienne, Marcel 249
Dewey, Joanna 72
Dibelius, Martin 25, 87
Diels, Hermann 171
Dodd, C. H. 284
Douglas, Mary 139
Dowd, Sharyn Echols 157, 161, 166
Draisma, Sipke 258, 321
Dreyfus, Hubert L. 88, 329

Eagleton, Terry 145-146, 283, 299, 301, 315, 328
Edwards, Richard A. 64
Eisenstein, Elizabeth L. 235
Ellens, G.F.S. 155, 311
Eliot, T.S. 344
Elliott, John H. 32, 118, 139, 153, 183-184, 197-198, 255, 289, 305-306, 315, 351, 356
Engemann, Joseph 64
Epp, Eldon J. 233
Eriksson, Anders 349
Esler, Philip Francis 32, 140-141, 198, 289, 306-307

Fee, Gordon D. 233
Finegan, Jack 233, 241
Finley, Moses I. 126
Fish, Stanley E. 226
Fitzmyer, Joseph A. 84, *94-95*, 133, 300, 304, 352-353, 372
Fontaine, Carole R. 204, 222, 228
Forster, Eleanor A. 216
Foskett, Mary 160
Foucault, Michel 259, 329, 346
Fowler, Robert 26
Fowler, Roger 117, 293, 305
Funk, Robert W. 201

Gager, John G. 32, 288-289
Garrett, Susan R. 114
Garsky, Albrecht 352
Gasque, Ward 64
Gaster, Theodor H. 284
Geertz, Clifford 32, 147, *150-151*, 162, 283, 290, 309, 334
Germain, G. 60
Gibson, Arthur 41
Gordon, Milton M. 153, 310
Goudriaan, Koen 154
Gowler, David B. 2, 3, 6, 11, 12, 15-16, 24, 26, 28, 43-44, 87, 257, 307, 313, 373
Gunn, David M. 204
Gutman, J. 102

Haenchen, Ernst 64, 71, 87, 98
Halle, Morris 216
Halliday, Michael A.K. 117
Hauser, Alan J. 325
Hays, Richard B. 259, 301
Hellholm, David 333

Index of Names

Hemer, Colin J.   5, 83, *90-94*
Hengel, Martin   30, 183, 273
Herzberg, Bruce   186, 197, 200, 324
Hess, Beth B.   147
Hock, Ronald F.   26, 130, 236-237, 245, 252-254, 274-275, 338-339, 351-352, 361
Hoffman, Mark G. V.   277
Hohendahl, Peter   145
Höistad, Ragnar   270
Hollander, John   301
Holquist, Michael   36-37
Huie-Jolly, Mary R.   291
Hurley, Patrick J.   350
Hyde, Walter W.   57

Jackson, Howard M.   278-279
Jackson, Jared J.   325
Jakobson, Roman   216
Jason, Heda   216
Jasper, David   36, *346-347*
Johnson, Luke Timothy   353
Judge, E.A.   177, 331

Kavanaugh, James H.   147
Kelber, Werner H.   26, 234-235
Kennedy, George A.   24, 197, 207, 209, 215, 237, 256, 260, 262, 283, 325, 341, 346-347, 350, 364
Kessler, Martin   325
Kirschenblatt-Gimblett, Barbara   216
Kloppenborg, John S.   12, 14, 45, 175, 180, 291, 352
Klostermann, Erich   260
Koch, Dietrich-Alex   97
Koester, Helmut   14, 32, 260, 287
Kraftchick, Steven J.   148
Kristeva, Julia   258, 321
Kuhn, Thomas S.   87
Käsemann, Ernst   354

Lanigan, Richard L.   40-41, 334, 355-356, 358, 367, 369

Lausberg, Heinrich   324
Ledbetter, Mark   257
Leeds, Anthony   192
Lefkowitz, Mary R.   52
Lenz, Tony M.   26, 236
Levinskaya, I.   102
Lieberg, Gogo   52
Lightfoot, J.B.   61
Lightstone, Jack N.   341
Long, William R.   130
Lord, Albert Bates   236
Luckmann, Thomas   8, 115-116
Lutes, Lynn R.   349

MacDonald, Dennis R.   83-84, 97, *104-106*, 110, 113
Mack, Burton L.   14, 25, 32, 108, 129, *157-159*, 168-170, 172-175, 178-180, *183-184*, 197-199, 236, 245, 252, 260, 290, 331-332, 338-340, 342, 349, 361
MacRae, George W.   62, 234
Mahaffy, John P.   60
Malherbe, Abraham J.   176, 378
Malina, Bruce J.   32, 117, 139, 153, 289, 308, 351, 354, 356, 360, 362, 375
Mannheim, Karl   115
Markson, Elizabeth W.   147
Martin, Clarice J.   291
Martin, Josef   324
Marxsen, Willi   25
Matera, Frank J.   262, 277, 279
McGowan, John   315
McKane, William   204-205
McKnight, Edgar V.   234
McLaughlin, Thomas   18
Meeks, Wayne A.   32, 177, 285-286, 334
Merton, R.K.   115
Metzger, Bruce M.   74, 233
Michie, Donald   146
Miller, J. Hillis   327
Mitchell, W. J. T.   146
Mitteis, L.   60
Moessner, David P.   42

Moore, Stephen D.   331-332
Motyer, Stephen   278-279
Moxnes, Halvor   125, 153, 313, 317
Muilenburg, James   325
Müller, Karl   57-59
Myers, Ched   173
Myers, William H.   259, 301

Neirynck, F.   261
Newby, Gordon D.   38, 349
Neyrey, Jerome H.   16, 130, 139, 153, 289
Nickelsburg, George W. E.   259-260
Niebuhr, Richard H.   149
Nock, Darby   260
Norden, Eduard   53, 64, 87

O'Day, Gail   157, 259
O'Neil, Edward N.   26, 236-237, 245, 252-254, 274-275, 338-339, 351-352, 361
Oakman, Douglas E.   125, 143
Olbrechts-Tyteca, Lucie   145, 148, 292
Olbricht, Thomas H.   323
Ong, Walter J.   236
Østergård, Uffe   154
Otis, Brooks   51

Page, Denys L.   51-52
Parker, Carolyn Ann   216
Parrott, Douglas M.   62-63
Parsons, Mikeal C.   6, 96
Patte, Daniel   227
Patterson, Lee   147
Patton, Laurie L.   349
Peacock, James L.   147, 282, 309, 333-334
Pearson, Lionel   58
Peron, Jacques   52
Perelman, Chaim   145, 148, 292
Perrin, Norman   234-235
Perry, Ben E.   63
Pervo, Richard I.   6, 83, 87, 104, 107-108, 113, 136

Pesch, Rudolf   260
Petersen, Norman R.   7, 289
Pilch, John J.   44, 125, 143
Pilhofer, P.   102
Pitt-Rivers, Julian   43
Plumacher, E.   129
Polhill, John B.   84
Porter, Stanley E.   84, *100-104*
Powell, Mark Alan   294
Praeder, Susan M.   83, *95-96*
Price, Christopher   83
Pritchard, James B.   49

Rabinow, Paul   88, 329
Reed, Jonathan L.   18
Rhodes, David   146
Richards, I.A.   344
Ricoeur, Paul   43, 218
Ringe, Sharon H.   353
Robbins, Vernon K.   1, 2, 4, 7-8, 10-15, 17, 19-22, 24-35, 37-43, 81-82, 87-89, 96, 117, 129-131, 145-146, 160, 168, 170, 173, 186, 188, 197-198, 200, 202, 206, 214, 222, 236, 245, 252-253, 255, 261-262, 272-273, 275-276, 283, 290-291, 297, 305, 310, 312, 313-314, 316, 321, 330-332, 335-336, 338-340, 342-343, 349, 351-355, 357-358, 361, 371-373, 375
Roberts, Keith A.   153-156, 173, 176-177, 179, 310-311
Robinson, James M.   14, 32, 201, 287
Rohrbaugh, Richard L.   16, 115, 125, 132, 143, 153, *190-196*, 289, 308, 317, 362, 375
Rose, Lucy A.   296

Sandmel, Samuel   28
Sazava, Zdenek   372
Schaberg, Jean   303-304

Schmid, Wilhelm 204
Schoff, Wilfred H. 58, 60
Schweder, Richard A. 367
Schweitzer, Albert 201
Schüssler-Fiorenza, Elisabeth 32, 36, 38-39, 290, 315-316, *344-347*
Scott, Bernard Brandon 41, 227, 291, 359-360, 362
Seeley, David 273
Shiner, Whitney 26
Shuler, Philip L. 352
Silberman, Lou 228
Sisson, Russell B. 12, 291
Sloan, Thomas O. 145
Smith, Jonathan Z. 32, 260, 286-288
Staley, Jeffery Lloyd 7, 118-121
Stark, Werner 155, 307, 311
Stegman, Thomas D. 349
Stein, Peter J. 147
Sternberg, Meir 108
Strack, H. 28
Suerbaum, Werner 50

Tannehill, Robert C. 32, 36, 40, 107, 217, 227-228, 288, 296, *343-344*, 347, 359
Talbert, Charles H. 6, 71-72, 87, 104, 107, 357, 362
Tate, W. Randolph 3
Taylor, Charles 146
Taylor, Vincent 25
Theissen, Gerd 253
Thompson, B.P. 84
Todorov, Tzvetan 37
Tolbert, Mary Ann 235, 294
Troost, Arie 295, 302, 308
Turner, Victor 34, 320
Tyson, Joseph B. 10, 87

Ulansey, David 278-279

van Dijk-Hemmes, Fokkelien 302, 308
van Unnik, W.C. 127
van Wolde, Ellen 259

Varronis, M. Terenti 53
Vattimo, Gianni 88
Veltman, Fred 130
Vesser, Aram H. 200
Vernant, Jean-Pierre 249
Vickers, Brian 32, 146, 197, 283-284, 327-328, 330
Vinson, Richard B. 333, 349
Voelz, James 258
Vollmer, Hans A. 260
Voloshinov, V.N. 37
Von Christ, Welhelm 204
Vorster, Willem 258-259

Wachob, Wesley H. 291, 349
Walaskay, Peter W. 138
Walz, T. Christian 204-206
Wanamaker, Charles A. 12
Watson, Duane F. 39, 325
Webber, Randall C. 291
Wedderburn, A.J.M. *96-98*
Wehnert, Jürgen 97
Wettstein, Ludwig 260
Wilcken, U. 60
Wilde, James A. 151, 197, 305-306, 336
Wilder, Amos N. 32, 284-285
Williams, Sam K. 273
Wilson, Bryan R. 13, 17, 33, 151, 162, 168-169, 197, 305-306, 331, 335-336
Wilson, R. McL. 62-63
Wimsatt, W.K. 195
Witherington, Ben 84
Wolff, Janet 120
Woodhouse, W. J. 50
Wuellner, Wilhelm H. 12, 32, *145-146, 148-149*, 156-159, 172, 177-178, 260, 283, 287-288, 290, 305, 321-322, 325-328, 331, 346-348, 373

Yinger, Milton J. 155, 310-311
York, John 307, 322

Index of Biblical and Other References

Hebrew Bible

Genesis
20:3-8   318
21:1-21   302
29:32   318
34:2   303-304
30:9-13   318

Exodus
34:28   374

Leviticus
19:18   376

Deuteronomy   43, 373
6   43, 373, 375, 380, 383-384
6–8   375, 377, 380-381, 383
6:1-3   375, 377
6:4-5   376, 380
6:6-9   375-376
6:13   374, 376, 383
6:16   374-377
6:17   375, 377
6:24-25   375
7   380
7:8   380
7:9   375, 380
7:11-12   375
7:13-15   380-381

8   43, 373, 375, 383-384
8:1-5   374-376, 381, 383
8:6   375-376
8:11-14   375
8:14-19   381
8:16   375
8:17-18   375-376
9:9   374
9:18   374
21:14   303
22:23-24   33, 303-304
22:29   303

Judges
13:2-25   302
19:24   303-304
20:5   303-304

1 Samuel
1:1–2:10   301

2 Samuel
13:12, 14, 22, 32   303

1 Kings   43, 373
17:1-16   377
17:17-24   378
19:8   374

2 Kings   43, 373
5:1-14   377
13:12-32   304

Psalms
22 (LXX: 21)   26-30, 146, 261-262, 270, 273-278, 280, 283, 291
22:1   267
22:2, 3 (LXX: 21:2, 3)   277
22:6 (LXX: 21:6)   278
22:7-9 (LXX: 21:7-9)   276, 278
22:8-9 (LXX: 21:8-9)   275-276
22:19 (LXX: 1:19)   274, 277
22:22 (LXX: 21:22)   277
22:29 (LXX: 21:29)   277
22:30-31 (LXX: 21:30-31)   277
35:9   301
38   278
38:11   261
38:21-22 (LXX: 37:22-23)   277
69:21   261
89:11   301
98:3   301
107:9   301
103:17   301
111:9   301

Proverbs
31:6-7   261

Isaiah 43, 238, 373
1:16-17   379-380, 383
35   381
35:5   378
56:6-8   163-164
58:6   377
61   381
61:1-2   372, 377, 378, 384
61:9   381

Jeremiah
7:11   163-164

Lamentations
5:11   304

Ezekiel
22:10-11   304
34   43, 373, *381-384*
34:3-4   383
34:11-12   382-283
34:13-14   383
34:16   382-383

Hosea
6:6   164

Apocrypha and Septuagint

4 Maccabees   29

Sirach (Ben Sira or Ecclesiasticus)
9:10   210
40:28-30   363

Old Testament Pseudepigrapha

4 Ezra (2 Esdras)
   198

Testament of Abraham
   384

New Testament

Q Source   35, 174-175, 198, 203, 217, 219, 352, 355

Matthew   47
4:2   375
4:3-4   374
4:5-8   376
4:18-22   243
6:9-13   349
8:14-15   26, 242
9:14-17   211
9:16-17   20, 210, 224
9:18-19   378
9:20-22   26, 250, 252
9:23-26   378
10:40   219
12:25   217
12:30   217, 220
15:21–21:10   85
23   12
23:1, 13   212

Mark   1, 47
1-6:44   78-79
1:2-3   272, 274
1:14-15   172
1:14-20   5
1:15   167
1:16-20   79, 243
1:20   302
1:29-31   26, 242
2:1-3:6   72, 173
2:7   266
2:13   302
2:18-22   211
2:19   302
2:21-22   20, 208, 224
2:22   179, 210

3:23   167
3:23-30   171
3:24   167
3:29-30   266
3:35   272
4-8   158, 172
4-11   13, 156, 165-167
4:1-9   168
4:1-34   168, 171
4:2-3   167
4:9-10   167
4:10-12   168
4:11-13   167
4:13-20   168
4:14-16   167
4:17   168
4:18   167
4:19   167, 272
4:20   167
4:21-23   168
4:23-24   167
4:24-25   168
4:26   167
4:26-29   169
4:30   167
4:30-32   169
4:33-34   167, 169
4:35-41   79
4:35–8:26   157
4:38   159
4:40-41   78, 159, 160
5   161
5:1-20   79
5:15, 19   159
5:21-24   378
5:23   159-160
5:24b-34   27, 250
5:25-34   253
5:26   165
5:28-29   159-160
5:30b   253
5:32   254
5:33-36   159-160
5:35-43   378

5:39b-42   343
5:41-42   161
6:7-13   179
6:34   272
6:45-52   78-79
6:45-8:26   78
6:50   159
6:53-56   79
7:1-23   79, 173, 341
7:14, 16, 17   167
7:17-23   171
7:20-23   172
7:24-37   79
7:24–11:11   85
8:15, 17, 18, 21   167
8:26   78
8:27   272
8:27-33   79
8:31, 33   272
8:34-37   267, 281
8:26   272
9:1   167
9:11   272
9:14-29   157
9:17-18   159
9:22   159, 161
9:23-24, 26   160-161
9:33-34   272
9:35   228
9:39   217
9:40   217, 220
10:13-16   227-228
10:17   229, 272
10:25, 32   272
10:34   267
10:37   275
10:42-45   271, 281
10:46-52   157
10:47, 48-49   159
10:52   160, 272
11:12-25   157, 165
11:17   279
12:1, 12   167
12:1-12   171
12:13-44   173

12:14   272
12:38   167
12:40   164
12:41   272
13   172-173
13:2, 5, 9   167
13:10   272
13:23   167
13:27   280
13:28   167
13:33   167
14:10-11   263
14:27, 36   272
14:58   275
14:61-62   272
14:62   78
14:64   266
15   30, 277
15:1-15   262-264
15:1-46   262
15:2   263-264, 269, 272
15:4-5   263, 269
15:6   263-265
15:6-24   262
15:7   264-265
15:8   263
15:9   263-264, 272
15:10-11   263-264
15:12   263-264, 272
15:13   264
15:14   263-264
15:15-16   262-265, 270-271
15:16-24   264
15:17-20   265-267, 270-272, 274
15:21   274
15:23   261
15:24   30, 265, 274-275
15:25-32   29-30, 262, 265-267, 270-271, 275-276

15:33-39   29-30, 261-262, 267-269, 270-271, 276-277
15:40-41   261-262, 268
15:40-46   262, 268-269
15:47   262
16:1, 5   262

Luke   6-11, 47, 291, 350
1   316, 335
1–2   134, 295
1:1-2   79, 123
1:1-4   109, 314, 334
1:3-4   79, 123, 131
1:5   292-293, 308
1:5-17   134
1:5-67   122
1:5-80   79
1:6   139
1:7   125
1:10-12   294
1:11-20   302
1:12-13   293-294
1:14   295
1:14-17   134
1:17   139
1:18, 21   293
1:24–2:35   126
1:25   292, 295, 318
1:25-27   309
1:25-35   125
1:26-28   292-294
1:26-38   294, 302
1:26-56   122, *292-294*, 299, 304, 307-308, 310-311, 321
1:27   293, 295, 299, 303-304, 308
1:28   314
1:29   294, 307

Index of Biblical and Other References

1:32   317
1:32-33   134, 295, 317
1:34   295, 300, 308-309
1:35   134, 293, 295, 317
1:36   299
1:36-38   309
1:36-41   293
1:37   299, 307
1:38   293, 295, 307-308
1:39-45   294
1:40-41   293
1:42   318
1:42-45   309
1:42-56   294
1:45-46   294-295
1:45-50   295-298
1:46-56   134, 294
1:48   295-299, 302-304, 308-309, 318
1:49-53   295-298, 317
1:51-55   296, 300
1:52   295, 298, 313, 376
1:52-53   307
1:54   295
1:54-55   296-298
1:56   294
1:57-66   122, 125
1:59   293
1:67   134, 293
1:67-79   134
1:69, 71, 77   307
2:1   137, 140
2:1-5   312
2:1-52   122
2:7   125
2:14   134
2:22-35   122
2:25   139
2:26-32   134
2:34   318

2:34-35   134
2:36-38   122, 126
2:38   319
2:49   135
3   134
3:1   122, 137, 140
3:4-6   134-135
3:18-20   352
3:19   126
4–11   11
4–19   11, 42, 372
4:1–19:27   373
4:1-4   374-375
4:1-13   43, 366, 373-374
4:4   135, 374
4:5-12   380
4:6-7   376
4:8   135
4:9   375
4:10-12   135
4:14-30   43, 373
4:14–7:35   377
4:14–9:50   44
4:16-22   9, 135
4:16-30   44, 377, 379
4:18-22   44, 372, 378
4:24-27   135
4:25-26   377-378
4:25-27   122-123
4:26   126
4:27   139, 377-378
4:31-41   44
4:38   126
4:38-39   26, 242
5:1   124
5:1-2   47, 76, 78
5:1-11   76-77
5:12-13   139
5:12-14   379
5:12-26   44
5:32   139
5:33   352
5:33-39   211
5:36-37   20, 224

6:6-11   44
6:13-16   122
6:20-21   44
6:20-25   377
6:28   358-359
6:34-35   358-359, 377
6:37-38   *353-356*, 357-358
6:38   368, 377
7:1-10   10, 12, 44, 141
7:11-16   378
7:11-17   44
7:11-35   43, 373
7:13   126
7:18-35   352
7:21   378
7:22   139, 378-379
7:36-50   43-44, 364, 373, 379
7:36–14:24   *379*
7:36–14:35   43, 373, 379
7:37   382
7:37-38   380
7:37-50   126
7:39   382
7:41-43, 46-47   380
7:47-49   382
8:3, 19-20   126
8:22-23   47, 76, 77
8:22-39   77
8:25   78
8:26   47
8:26-33   44
8:33   47, 76
8:40-56   44
8:40-42   378
8:41-42   125
8:42-48   254
8:43-48   27, 250
8:45-46   254
8:49-56   125, 378
9:7-9   352
9:10-17   378
9:18-19   352

9:37-43   44
9:38-39   44, 210
9:38-42   125
9:47-48   125
9:50   217, 220
9:51–19:46   76
9:52   137
10   190
10:1-24   71
10:16   219
10:21-22   371
10:27   376
10:29-37   138
10:30-37   376
10:37   377
10:38-42   126
10:39-41   352
11:1   351-352
11:1-4   40, 351
11:1-13   39, 349, 351-352, 364, 370-371, 373
11:2   356
11:2-4   351, 358
11:3   361, 366
11:4   354-355, 356-358, 370
11:5-7   41, *359-362*, 364, 366
11:5-8   359, 364, 366
11:5-13   370
11:7   361
11:8   361-364, 367
11:9   365
11:9-10   *364-366*
11:11-12   366-367
11:13   361-362, *366-368*, 371
11:17   217
11:23   217, 220
11:27-28   126, 322
11:31   126
11:31-32   365
11:35-54   379
11:36-54   43, 373
11:40-41   139
11:41, 42, 46-48   380
11:52   212, 380
12   148
12:1–13:9   148, 260
12:13-34   378
12:30-32   364-366
12:57   139
13:11-13   126
13:22–19:46   71
14   191, 370, 381-382
14:1-2   368
14:1-14   43
14:1-24   373, 379, 381
14:2-4   381
14:3-10   368
14:7-11   375
14:11   368, 370, 381-382
14:12-14   368
14:12-24   370
14:13   381
14:14   139, 381
14:16-24   368
14:21   381
15   43, 373, *381*, 384
15:1-2   382
15:1–19:10   383
15:1   382
15:1-32   382
15:4   382, 384
15:6-8, 10   382
15:11-32   302
15:13-14   382
15:17   139
15:18, 21   382
16–18   383
16:1-8   383
16:1-9   364
16:1-13   378
16:13   383
16:14   378, 383
16:15   375, 383
16:19-31   378, 383
16:31   383
17:2, 6   47, 78
17:11-19   379
17:14, 17   139
17:18   138
17:32   126
18:1-8   126, 361-362
18:9   139
18:9-14   376
18:13   357
18:13-14   357, 370
18:14   357, 375, 383
18:16-17   125
18:18-25   378
18:20, 22   383
18:26-30   378
18:28-30   383
18:35-41   378
19:1-10   307, 370, 378, 383
19:8   383
19:8-9   369
19:10   384
19:11-27   378
19:28–23:56   384
20:1-8   352
20:17   135
20:20   139
20:20-26   378
20:37, 42-44   135
21:1-4   128, 378
21:25   47, 78
22:18-25   378
22:36, 49-51   144
22:56-57   126
22:69   78
23:24   357-358
23:26-49   71
23:27-31   126
23:34   357-358
23:47   10, 139, 141
23:49, 55   126
23:50   139
24:10   126
24:27   135

Index of Biblical and Other References 403

John 285, 289, 336
1:1-18   241
5:23   219
11   305
15:20   340
20   335
20:30-31   334

Acts   4-11, 38, *59-61*, 63
1-12   47, 78
1:1   109, 123
1:8   71
1:20   136
2   138, 373
2:5   126, 139
2:7   126
2:9   126-127
2:9-11   109
2:10   124
2:10-11   127
2:11   126
2:16-21, 25-28   136
2:26   321
2:34-35   136
2:41, 47   127
3-4   291
3:1-10   379
3:12, 14   139
3:22-23   136
4:11   136
4:13   137
4:19   139
4:24   78
4:25-26   136
5:1-11   126
5:29   136
5:36-37   123
6:1   126-127
6:1-6   122
7:2-47   122-123
7:3, 26-28, 32-35, 37, 40, 42-43, 48-50   136
7:52   139

7:56   78
7:58   127
8   291
8:1   47, 122, 127
8:1-24   138
8:2   139
8:4   127
8:7   379
8:9   138
8:12   127
8:26-39   124
8:27   126
8:32-33   134-135
9:1-9   47
9:1-19   122
9:17-18   378
9:17-19, 20-30   47
9:27   122
9:27–15:39   98
9:32–11:18   85
9:36-41   126
10   127
10:1-8   127
10:1–11:18   10, 141
10:2   139
10:6   78
10:7   139
10:15, 22   139
10:32   78, 130
10:44-48   127
11:9   139
11:19-20   127
11:25-26   47
11:28   122
11:29-30   47
12:2   123
12:6-10   378
12:12-13   126
12:17   378
12:20-22   123
12:25   47
13   47-48, 122
13-28   72, 75, 76
13:1–14:28   73, 75, 77
13:1–19:20   71, 73, 76

13:1–28:16   71, 76
13:2   77
13:2-3   73
13:4   48, 73-74, 77
13:4-12   127
13:6-12   140
13:9   73
13:13   48, 73-74, 77
13:33, 33-35, 41   136
13:47   71, 136
14:8-10   379
14:12-13   122
14:15   78
14:26   48, 73-74, 77
15   73
15:1–21:26   76
15:1-34   72
15:1-35   73
15:1–19:20   72
15:9   139
15:15-18   136
15:23-29   77
15:36   73
15:36–17:15   72
15:39   48
16   93, 110
16:4   73
16:6-7   74
16:9   66, 74, 77, 101
16:9-10   83
16:9–17:14   127
16:10   66-67, 98
16:10-12   84
16:10-17   48, 66, 69, 71, 74, 77, 90, 93, 101, 105, 111
16:10-18   111
16:10-40   74
16:11   69, 77
16:11-12   66, 104
16:12   83, 102
16:12-13   101-102
16:13-15   66
16:13-18   84

16:14-15   83, 103, 126, 130
16:16   83, 101-102
16:16-18   66, 125-126
16:16-40   112
16:17   64, 66, 68
16:19–17:13   74
16:23-27   378
16:40   126
17:1   67, 112
17:1–20:4   84
17:4   126
17:6   110
17:10   112
17:12   126
17:14-15   74, 112
17:15–18:17   127
17:16-24   72
17:22   110
17:23   139
17:28   136-138
17:34   126
18:1   112
18:1-3   130
18:1-23   72
18:2   122, 137, 140
18:2-3, 18   126
18:12-17   141
18:18-19   112
18:21   77
18:22-23   112
18:24-26   318
18:24–19:20   72
18:26   126
19:1   112
19:10   72
19:11-20   75
19:19   130
19:21   67-68, 112
19:21–21:26   71-72, 76
19:23-41   130
19:31   140
20–21   93
20:1-2   112

20:2   74
20:3, 13   77
20:4   67
20:5   85
20:5-6   67, 84, 104, 111, 112
20:5-15   48, 67, 69, 90, 105, 112
20:7   67, 103
20:7-12   67, 69, 83, 102
20:7-15   111
20:13, 15, 17-38   112
20:9-12   83
20:13-15   85
20:13-16   68
20:13–21:18   86
20:15   104
20:16   68
20:17   83
20:17-38   68-69, 72, 85
20:38   112
21–23   140
21:1   77, 112
21:1-4   68, 85
21:1-14   72, 74
21:1-18   48, 69, 90, 111
21:2   77
21:3   77, 112
21:5   85
21:5-6   68-69
21:7-8   68, 83, 85, 104, 112
21:8-14   68-69
21:9   83, 125-126
21:10-11   83
21:13   68, 75
21:13-20   69
21:15-17   85-86
21:15-18   68
21:15-26   72
21:18   64, 67-68, 86, 112

22:1-21   75
22:3   137
22:4-21   123
22:11-13   378
22:12, 14   139
22:27-28   141
23:1-10   75
23:26   132
23:31-33   86
23:35   132
24:2   132
24:10-21   75
24:15   139
24:22   132
24:24   126, 132
24:25   132
25:5   132
25:8, 10, 11   122, 132
25:9, 12   132
25:13   104, 126
25:13–26:32   122, 312
25:14-22   132
25:21   122
25:23   126
25:25   122
25:31-32   132
26:1   132
26:1-29   75
26:2, 7   132
26:9-20   123
26:19   132
26:24   132, 137
26:28   132
26:30   126
26:32   86, 122
27   102
27–28   83, 90, 92-93
27:1   69, 104
27:1-2   86, 112
27:1-20   127
27:1-8   69
27:1–28:16   48, 69, 86, 71-72, 75-76, 86, 90, 111-112
27:1-44   64, 83

Index of Biblical and Other References 405

27:2   77, 83, 104-105, 124
27:3   10, 141
27:4   69, 77
27:6   77, 90, 102, 104
27:6–28:11   90
27:9-12   69
27:10   75, 132
27:12   77
27:21   77, 132
27:21-26   69, 75
27:24   77, 122
27:27-44   69
27:30   70
27:35   70, 75
27:35-36   103
27:36   75
27:42   70
27:42-43   10, 141
28:1   104
28:2   110
28:1-6   70, 83
28:3-7   75
28:6   70, 83
28:7-10   70, 75
28:8-10   83
28:10, 11   77
28:11   83, 90, 102, 104
28:11-16   70
28:13-14   85-86, 104
28:15   70
28:16   67, 141
28:16-29   124
28:17   111, 132
28:17-23   141
28:18   70
28:19   122
28:21   132
28:25-27   136
28:27   379
28:31   141

Romans
6   333

1 Corinthians   38, 177-178, 287, 290, 344-345, 349
1:10–4:21   346
1:17   346
1:26-28   156-158, 172, 178
9   148

2 Corinthians
8–9   287
10–13   12
11   110

Galatians   148
3:28   345

Ephesians
6:1   220

1 Thessalonians
346

Revelation
1   335
1:3   334-335, 337
6:15-17   335, 337
22:7, 10, 18, 19   337

Early Christian Literature

1 Clement   273

Gospel of Thomas   35, 41, 202
47b   20, 224

Infancy Gospel of Thomas
6:2-6   136
14:1-3   136
15:1-2   136

Other Ancient Texts

Achilles Tatius   5
Adventures of Leucippe and Clitophon   55
2.31.6   55
2.32.2   65
2.33   65
3.1.1   55
3.1.1-3.5.6   66
3.5.1-4   65
3.10.1-6   65
4.9.6   55

The Acts of Peter and the Twelve Apostles   61-63
Nag Hammadi codex
    VI.1   61
    VI.1.1-29   62
    VI.1.20-2.10   62
    VI.5.2-19   62
    VI.10.14-12.22   62

Aelius Theon of Alexandria   339
Progymnasmata   237-239, 245, 256

Aeschines   31

Aeschylus
Libation Bearers   5
Oresteia 735   360
Seven Against Thebes   5, 52

Alcaeus   5, 51-52

Alexamenos   31

Antiochene Acts of the Martyrdom of Ignatius   6, 61

Antiphon
frg. 60   171

Antisthenes   31

Apollonius of Rhodes
Argonautica   58

Aratus
Phaenomena   136

Aristotle   24, 171, 204
Poetics   108

Rhetorica   197, 326
1.2.21-22   305
1.4-8   13
1.9.40-41   214
2.21.2   205
2.22.1-23.30   305
2.23.1   362
2.23.4   362, 367
2.1394a   164
3.15.1-4   305

Arrian
Anabasis of Alexander   58
Indica 8.20.1-8.36.9   58
Periplus of the Euxine Sea   59

Athenaeus
Deipnosophistae
14.639   271

Berosus
Babylonian History   271

Caesar
Gallic Wars 5.11   59

Cicero   24

Crito   31

Dio Chrysostom   5, 53, 55, 281
3.41, 55, 86, 114   272
4   260-261, 270
4.6, 10, 21, 27, 29, 31   272
4.39-45   273
4.43   272
4.67   270-271
4.69   271, 279
7.2   54, 66
7.3-5   65
7.10   54

Diogenes   171, 174-175

Epic of Gilgamesh   49, 108

Epicurus   171

Epimenides   136

Episodes from the Third Syrian War   6, 60
1.1-2.11   60
2.6-25   60

Euclid   31

Glaucon   31

Hanno the Carthaginian
Periplus   6, 59, 87
1   65
1-3   60
2-6   65
4   65
6   65-66
8-17   65

Heliodorus   5
Ethiopian Story
5.17   56
5.18   65
5.27   66

Hermogenes
Progymnasmata   237, 339, 364, 370

Hippocrates
Law III   170

Homer   104, 106-107, 110, 134, 198, 238
Iliad   105, 108
5.340   276

Odyssey   5, 49-50, 55, 66-69, 98, 105, 108, 111
9–12   49, 87, 108
9.39-41   49
9.43-61   65
9.62-63   50
9.67-73   66
9.85, 105, 149-151, 169   50
9.195-470   65
9.546-547, 565-566   50
10.28, 56, 77, 80, 133-134   50
11.20   50
11.90-137   69
12.5-7   50
12.35-126   69

Horace   273

Irenaeus   63

Josephus   5, 8, 55, 100, 124

Index of Biblical and Other References

AgApion 1.1 132
Life
(3) 14-16 54
(76) 430 132

War 5.5.4 279

The Journey of Wen-Amon to Phoenicia
10 49

Lucian 5
A True Story 55
1.5 65
1.5-6 55
1.33 65
2.27, 34 65
2.40 66
2.47 65-66

Midrash Rabba Numbers
22 156

Mishnah
Sayings of the Fathers (Pirke Aboth)
4:20 210
41 156

Ovid 5
Tristia 1.2.31-34 54

Papyri
POxy
1224 220

Periplous Book 2, fr. 418 53

Periplus of the Erythraean Sea 58

Petronius 5
Ch. 114 54

Phaedo 31

Philo
De Virtutibus 157

Pindar
Nemea 4.36-8 52

Plato 31, 171

Plautus
Cas. 5 210

Plutarch 245, 256
Alexander 317
4.9 247
4.10 26, 246-247
4.11 249
5-7 249
14.1-5 26
28.3 276

Demosthenes
1.3 132

Dion
1.3 132

Lysander 241
22.1 26, 239

Moralia 241
63F 365
65A 360
95C 360
179D 26, 246-247
190E 26, 239
229C 26, 239
330E 249
331B 26, 246, 248
542C 255
782A 26

Parallel Lives 352

Theseus
1.3 132

Polybius 100

Pythagoras 171

Quintilian 24
Institutio oratoria
5.11.24 171

Quran
sura 37:139-141 64

Rhetoric of Alexander
1.1421b.21-1422b.12 340

Rhetorica ad Herennium 296
2.18.28 338
2.18.28-19.30 297
4.43.57 361

Sayings of R. Nathan
23 157

Scylax the Younger
Periplus of the Mediterranean Sea 57

Seneca
Epistles 38:2 171

Simias 31

Socrates 171

The Story of Sinuhe 49

Suetonius
Lives of the Caesars
1.79 105

Talmud, Babylonian
Ber. 51a   210
Nid. 69b-70b   156
Sanh. 101a   156

Tanchuma   156

Theognis   52

Theon
Progymnasmata   21, 24-25, 236

Thucydides   5, 100
History of the Peloponnesian War
1.1.1-2   57
4   56
4.104.4ff   57

Varro
Menippean Satires   5, 53
276, 473   53

Virgil   107, 110
Aeneid   5, 55, 66-67, 87, 105-108, 111
2–3   *50-51*
3.1-9   50
3.4-5, 19-21, 26-48, 80-83, 84-120, 124-127, 147-178   65
3.192-208   66
3.358-460, 306-355, 373-376, 463-505, 528-529, 692-708   65

Xenophon   5, 31, 59, 238
Anabasis
3.1.8   57
7.8.25-26   80

Hellenica
3.1.2   57

Zeno   171

www.ingramcontent.com/pod-product-compliance
Lightning Source LLC
Chambersburg PA
CBHW032143010526
44111CB00035B/1042